Finding Birds Around the World

Finding Birds Around the World

Peter Alden and John Gooders

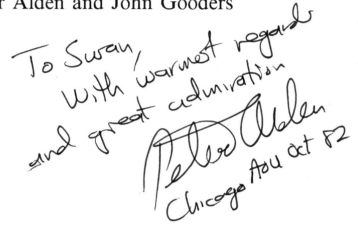

To Swan,
With warmest regards
and great admiration
Peter Alden
Chicago Aou Oct 82

Houghton Mifflin Company Boston 1981

Library of Congress Cataloging in Publication Data
Alden, Peter.
    Finding birds around the world.
    Bibliography: p.
    Includes index.
    1.Bird watching — Guide-books. 2.Birds.
I.Gooders, John, joint author. II.Title.
QL677.5.A39   598'.07'234   80-16375
ISBN 0-395-29114-3

Printed in the United States of America

P 10 9 8 7 6 5 4 3 2 1

Acknowledgments

In our mad wanderings around and over the world the authors have managed to visit, between them, nearly all these localities, some of them many times over. Much of the text and many of the bird lists and the maps have been compiled from firsthand observations. Nevertheless, we have had to seek help from our friends and associates around the world. This help has come in many forms. In some instances, the initial text was prepared by others. In other cases, revised bird lists, tips on localities, and additional input have been received. Our companions on these trips have often aided tremendously in matters of identification and intensive local knowledge. We are proud to have been associated with such a fine fraternity of talented men and women from diverse backgrounds.

Jeremy Brock has been a constant source of information on birding in Europe. His assistance on John Gooders's book on bird finding in Europe has helped with the foundation of those chapters in this work.

Murray Bruce, of Sydney, Australia, is rapidly becoming an expert in birds of remote Pacific islands and eastern Asia (among other areas). Murray contributed the Taiwan chapter and provided valuable information on the Philippines, New Caledonia, Fiji, and Hong Kong.

Thomas Butler, of Durham, New Hampshire, is the author of the new Ecuador checklist. Tom contributed the initial chapters on Quito and the Galápagos.

Thomas Davis, of Woodhaven, New York, and past president of the Linnaean Society of New York, co-wrote the Surinam and Yucatan chapters. Tom has been of great assistance in introducing Peter Alden to Trinidad, Jamaica, New York, and Santa Marta birding.

Paul Donahue, a fine young bird artist, co-wrote the Santa Marta chapter and helped refine the Puerto Maldonado chapter during his Peruvian sojourn.

Robert Fleming, Jr., of Kathmandu, Nepal, has been a valued field companion of both authors in Asia and Africa. Co-author of the new Nepal guide, Bob contributed initial drafts of the Srinigar, Kathmandu, Mt. Everest, and Chitwan chapters, and was helpful in producing the New Delhi–Agra and Nairobi chapters.

Richard Forster, a tour leader for the Massachusetts Audubon Society, wrote the Churchill chapter and was helpful with the Panama, Venezuela, Lapland, Australia, and Texas chapters.

J. Lindsay Gressitt, director of the Wau Ecology Institute in Papua New Guinea, has been of great value in helping with the Wau chapter by mail and as a personal guide.

Steven Hilty, of the University of Arizona, Tucson, is co-author of the upcoming Colombia guide. Steve contributed the initial Buenaventura section and has shared his expertise in the field with Peter Alden while they led birding tours together.

Margaret Hundley, of Stonington, Maine, has retired from her fine work as a birding tour guide for the Florida Audubon Society. Margaret's help on Haiti, Antigua, and Guadeloupe was instrumental in producing the two West Indies chapters.

Robert S. Kennedy, recently of Louisiana State University and Films and Research for an Endangered Environment, has been heavily involved with saving the Monkey-eating Eagle of the Philippines. Bob contributed much of the Philippine information and helped with the Peruvian sections.

Michel Kleinbaum, a bird illustrator based in New York, contributed much of the Senegal chapter and was a matchless companion to Peter Alden in Colombia and Venezuela.

James Lane, author of the fine series of local bird-finding guides to the western United States, is another full-time Massachusetts Audubon Society birding tour leader. Jim contributed much of the information on the Texas, Yellowstone, and Los Angeles chapters.

Christopher Leahy, a birding tour leader associate of Peter Alden with the Massachusetts Audubon Society in Lincoln, has birded extensively on six continents. Chris contributed the initial chapters on Buenos Aires, Bariloche and Trelew, Iguassu Falls, and Merida, Yucatan, in addition to revising sections on Bathurst Inlet, Churchill, Tikal, Istanbul, New Delhi, and Kathmandu.

John O'Neill, of Louisiana State University, is an outstanding bird artist, and has discovered a number of new species in his many years in Peru. John was instrumental in developing all of the Peruvian chapters.

Ron Orenstein, of the University of Michigan, provided the initial chapter on the Canary Islands, and provided much information on Sri Lanka and Sydney.

Ted Parker, of Lancaster, Pennsylvania, and Louisiana State University and formerly the University of Arizona, has a superb knowledge of neotropical birds. Ted has been invaluable in detecting little-known species present in our chapters on Peru, Buenos Aires, Iguassu, and Itatiaia.

Mark Peters, of Cambridge, Massachusetts, spent several years in Malawi and contributed the chapter on Blantyre.

Robert Ridgely, author of the fine new Panama guide, and Peter Alden's birding companion since their early teens, has contributed much of the information on San Jose, the Chiriqui, Panama City, and Belem. He has also been instrumental in the production of the Puerto Maldonado, Asuncion, Iguassu, and Itatiaia chapters.

Ken Scriven and Louis Ratnam, both with Malaysian Tours and Safaris of Kuala Lumpur, provided initial sections on our Malaysian localities.

Guy Tudor, one of the best bird illustrators of the day, co-wrote the Surinam section and provided early information on localities in much of South America.

Donald Turner, of East African Ornithological Safaris, has led countless birders, including the authors, through East Africa and the islands of the Indian Ocean. Don's help was essential in the production of the Kenyan, Madagascar, Mauritius and Reunion, and Seychelles chapters.

Alan Vittery of the British Diplomatic Service, formerly based in Addis Ababa, was instrumental in helping with sections on Africa, Turkey, and Pakistan.

Dora Weyer, past president of the Belize Audubon Society, contributed the initial chapters on Belize.

Peter Willmann, of Livermore, California, was instrumental in aiding Peter Alden's first explorations of such diverse areas as the Bahamas, Brazil, Venezuela, Spain, Australia, New Guinea, New Zealand, Panama, and Costa Rica.

The following have most kindly volunteered their local expertise and specialized knowledge of these areas and their birds. In many cases we have gained valuable insight from these fine workers during memorable days afield in their own areas:

John and Anna Alden (Boston), Allen and Karin Altman (Venezuela), M/M Eric Anders (Asuncion), and Robert Arbib, editor of *American Birds* (Venezuela, Senegal).

Pic and the late Don Bailey (Cali), Wallace and Priscilla Bailey (Cape Cod and Kenya), James Baird of the Massachusetts Audubon Society (valuable advice all along, Andalucia, Australia), Michael Baker (Rio de Janeiro), Ian Beames (Africa), Beatrice Berger of Panorama Tours of Lima (Peru), Hans and Judy Beste (eastern Australia), Tomas Blohm of Hato Masaguaral (Calabozo), Alexander Bock of Bock Travel Service of Boston (world travel arrangements for Peter Alden), David Brewer (Ontario), Laurence Brown (Santiago), Piers Brudenell-Bruce (Andalucia, Bahamas, Valle de Bravo), and Jens Byskov (Denmark).

The late Rudd Campbell (Wyperfeld, Victoria), Jack and Marion Cassels (Cairns), Javier Castroviejo, director of the Coto Donana (Andalucia), Edward Chalif (Mexico), Graeme Chapman (western Australia), S. A. Chavan (India), Jim Clements (Cuba), Lin Cornwallis (Iran), Davis Crompton (Iguassu), and the late Orville Crowder (pioneering many destinations).

Severyn Dana (Boston), Marcia Davis (Camargue), Lisa Decker (Morocco), Liscum Diven (Santiago), Lee Donnell (Asuncion), and Phil Dumont, formerly of the U.S. Fish and Wildlife Service (refuge checklists in the United States, Madagascar).

Ernest Edwards (pioneering many Mexican destinations), Eugene Eisenmann (neotropical advice), Clare Ellinwood (Tucson), Sir Hugh Elliott (general), Victor Emanuel (Texas), Ruth Emery (Andalucia, Boston), and the late M. D. England (India).

John Fitzpatrick (Leticia, Peru), Alec Forbes-Watson (Kenya), Patricia Fox (Hawaii), Warwick Fraser (South Africa), and Jane Frost (Puerto Rico and Virgin Islands).

Martin Gauntlett (India), Clarence Gervais (San Francisco), Paul Gervis (Medillen), Jacolyn Gibb (India), Patrick Gilbert-Hopkins (Kenya), Harvey Gilston (Eilat), Michael Gochfeld (Dominican Republic, Peru, Venezuela, Colombia), Helio Gouveia (Itatiaia), Joe Greenburg (San Francisco), and Edward Gruson (Lapland).

Don Hadden (New Zealand), Winthrop Harrington (Jamaica), D.G.E. Harris (Point Pelee), Michael Harris (Galápagos), Bill Harrison (Tucson), Ken Harte (Sri Lanka, Guatemala City), Martha Hayes (Cayman Islands), Al Hawkes (Block Island), Les Henderson (New Zealand), Toby Hodd (India), Ray Hodgkins of Town and Gown Travel of Oxford (world travel arrangements for John Gooders), Lawrence Holloway of Ornitholidays (Ethiopia), Natalie Houghton (Trinidad and Tobago), and Ned Hudson (Texas).

Ron Johns (Africa) and Terry Johnson (Santa Marta).

Stuart Keith (Kenya, Peru, Colombia), Katherine Ketchum (Point Pelee), Ben King (southern Asia), and R. W. Krebs (Guianas).

Bill Lane (Sydney), Vernon Laux (Mazatlan and Barbados), Lynn Leakey (Kenya), J. Lever (Algonquin), Manuel Lomeli (San Blas), Dorothy S. Long (Alaska), and Tom Lovejay (Belem).

Roy MacKay (Port Moresby), Jacqueline Manley (Venezuela), Lou Marsh (Peru), Carl Marvel (Tucson), Russ Mason of Flying Carpet Tours (pioneering many destinations), Arnold McGill (Sydney), Ross McKenzie (New Zealand), Satish Menon (India), Paul Miliotis (Middle America), Grace Miller (San Francisco), Barry Morgan (Brisbane), Lee Morgan (Itatiaia, Colombia), and Bert Mull (Indonesia, Venezuela).

Ephraim Negeri (Africa), Catherine Noble (Mexico), David Norman (Europe), and Rosemary North-Lewis (Kenya, Seychelles). John Orrell (Cairns) and Fernando Ortiz-Crespo (Quito).

Armando Palomino (Cusco), Ken Parkes (Canary Islands), David Pearson (Rio Napo, Peru, Indonesia), David Pearson (Africa), Roger Tory Peterson (inspiration and advice), Olin Pettingill, Jr. (Falkland Islands), Susan Parker (Peru, Brazil), Chris Parrish (Venezuela), Richard and Moira Pough (Andalucia), and Doug Pratt (Hawaii).

Will Russell (Pribilofs) and Len Robinson (Melbourne, Mallee, Alice Springs, Darwin, Cairns, Sydney, Brisbane, Port Moresby, Wau).

Brian Sage (Alaska), John Schaefer (Tucson, Rio de Janeiro), the late Paul Schwartz (Rancho Grande, Calabozo), Helmut Sick (Rio de Janeiro, Itatiaia), Robert and Kate Sides (Papua New Guinea), Jim Silliman (Colombia), Ricardo Silva (Belem), Arnold Small (Los Angeles, Peru), Fred Smith (Melbourne), J. Stewart-Smith (Persian Gulf), Peter Steyn (Africa), and David Stirling (Vancouver Island).

Dan and Erika Tallmann (Rio Napo, Peru), Joe Taylor (Mexico City), Maya Tirler (Rio de Janeiro), Betsy Trent Thomas (Venezuela, Ecuador), and Jim Tucker of the American Birding Association (Texas).

Peter Vickery (Mexico).

Robert Wallace (Australia), Richard Waller (India), Michael Webster (Europe), Tom and Inez Weston (Port Moresby), Roy Wheeler (Australia), Ed Willis (Brazil), Mrs. Brooke Wright (Montreal), and Charles Wood (Tikal, Guatemala City, Mexico City).

D. W. Yalden (Europe).

Space precludes mentioning the thousands of fine people who have joined both authors on birding tours around the world. Without their confidence and support much of the original information herein gathered would have been impossibly delayed. They have made it all possible.

Finally we must single out our talented typists who surely never wish to see any bird list again. Charlotte Smith, of Weston, and Dorothy Long, of Wayland, both connected with the Massachusetts Audubon Society, both spent hundreds of hours putting this project into final form. Hazel Cooper faithfully carried out the same task in Croydon. Special thanks are due to the many people at Houghton Mifflin who helped bring this work together in its final form, particularly James Thompson, Lois Randall, Austin Olney, Terry Baker, Chris Giriunas, and Helena Bentz. We also wish to thank Piers Burnett of André Deutsch Ltd., London.

Foreword by
Roger Tory Peterson

One of the most extraordinary developments in the birding world in recent years has been the rise of bird tourism; going to out-of-the-way places—literally to the ends of the earth—to see new birds. Organized tours of other sorts have long been in vogue, especially to Europe—garden tours, tours of old castles, museums, and restaurants—but just when the bird tours started I am not certain. In the United States they seem to have had their origin about forty years ago when John Baker, then President of the National Audubon Society, became concerned about the precarious plight of the Everglade (or Snail) Kites around Lake Okeechobee and the Sandhill Cranes and Crested Caracaras on the Kissimmee Prairie. It was hard to stir up enthusiasm locally for the protection of these birds because the duck-shooting fraternity and other hunters brought in money to the local hotels whereas bird watchers did not. It was felt that if the Audubon Society could lure bird watchers to see these unusual birds, it would make a difference. The idea worked. The hotels around Lake Okeechobee in Florida were soon filled with birders who signed up for tours led by Alexander Sprunt, Marvin Chandler, and other Audubon wardens to observe the kites close up in the reed beds of the lake and to see the cranes and caracaras on the palmetto-dotted prairie.

Although a few museum men and professional ornithologists had ventured south of the United States into the tropics, provincialism kept most birders north of the Rio Grande and Gulf Stream. For birds in Britain, any trip south of the English Channel constituted an expedition. All that changed in the fifties with "Major" Bowes and his wife, Ann LaBastille Bowes, taking groups to the Caribbean; Russ Mason of the Massachusetts (and later Florida) Audubon Society organizing tours to Central America and the Antilles; and Orville Crowder pioneering trips all over the globe. In the sixties Peter Alden led dozens of trips to all corners of Mexico. On a more luxurious and adventuresome level, Lars-Eric Lindblad, a Swedish-American, became the first to take penguin watchers and other nature-oriented people to the Antarctic on his ship the *Explorer*.

Today, in the eighties, dozens of individuals, nonprofit conservation organizations, and commercial travel agencies in the United States, Canada, Great Britain, Germany, Scandinavia, and Japan are offering services far and near. Jet planes along with the many good field guides and handbooks available on overseas destinations have aided this boom. One has only to scan the advertisements in *British Birds, American Birds, Birds (RSPB), Audubon* (NAS), *Birding* (ABA), and any number of other nature publications, to be struck by the extraordinary number of outfits now specializing in bird tours. These range from relatively relaxed forays mixing fine birding with local culture and tastes of hedonistic pursuits, to hard-core marathons where only the list matters. Participants rise from their beds while the owls are still calling on most days. On the tougher trips you might be out in the field birding the entire day and turn in only after the thrushes have sung their evensong.

However, a great many birders prefer to do their birding alone, or with children, spouse, or friends. It is for this broader audience that this Baedeker has been planned. Peter Alden and John Gooders, with all the vigor and enthusiasm of their youth, have led many tours themselves, some to parts of the world virtually unexplored by birders. Their book, extensive as it is, may not be the last word about every region, but it is the first word we have seen in print about birding in many tropical countries.

A friend of mine, the late James Fisher, once commented that the observation of birds may be many things; it may be an art, a science, a recreation, a tradition, a sport, or even a bore, depending on the observer. Some birders are abroad strictly for the list, and this book, of course, offers them a gold mine of information. Others simply wish to expand their world knowledge of birds while taking in the sights and the countryside, or attending business meetings. Philosophically they may compare one region or country to another, noting the interactions between people and wildlife and putting into their computer bits of information about the environment. To the person who is aesthetically inclined, the tropics, with their gaudy parrots, toucans, barbets, tanagers, and hornbills, offer a visual feast. The veteran birder, in a new land where nearly every sound he hears in the forest is something that he cannot put a name to, recaptures the sense of wonder and mystery that he experienced as a neophyte.

There are somewhere between 8600 and 9000 species of birds in the world, depending on which taxonomist you listen to. Although a few years ago one eminent ornithologist stated that practically all of the birds of the world had already been discovered and described, new species are still being found at a rate of at least one a year, notably in the Andean forests and tropics of Peru. Although no birder is likely to discover a new species during his travels, he may well make range extensions, take the first photographs or sound recordings, locate the first nest, or add a first record for some province or country. My own astonishing find was a Bridled Tern well south of Cape Horn in the Antarctic Ocean, 6000 miles from its normal habitat in tropical seas. When the tired bird came to rest on a lifeboat on the upper deck of our ship I was able to take it in my hand.

My own personal hope is to see, during my lifetime, half of the birds of the world—4500 species. I am still well short of that goal, though Peter Alden has reached it, and Stuart Keith and several others have seen over 5000 species!

Some globe-trotting ornithophiles may visit all of these spots, others will have the wherewithal and time to visit a dozen or so of the hot (and cold) spots described in this book. But even if your birding sojourns are of the armchair variety, I am sure you will enjoy hours of vicarious fun reading about faraway places that are literally swarming with enticing birds.

Contents

Acknowledgments   v
Foreword by Roger Tory Peterson   xi
Introduction   xix

1. St. Paul, Pribilof Islands, Alaska   1
2. Mt. McKinley National Park, Alaska   5
3. Vancouver Island, British Columbia   8
4. Bathurst Inlet, Northwest Territories   13
5. Churchill, Manitoba   16
6. Pt. Pelee National Park, Ontario   20
7. Boston—New York—Washington, D.C.   24
8. Miami, Florida   31
9. Texas Coast   36
10. Yellowstone National Park, Wyoming   43
11. Bear River Refuge, Utah   47
12. Tucson, Arizona   50
13. Los Angeles, California   56
14. San Francisco, California   61
15. Hawaii   66
16. Mazatlán and San Blas, Mexico   70
17. Mexico City and Valle de Bravo, Mexico   77
18. Mérida, Yucatan, Mexico   82
19. Belize City—Belmopan, Belize   86
20. Tikal National Park, Guatemala   92
21. Guatemala City—Lake Atitlan, Guatemala   96
22. San Jose, Costa Rica   100
23. Chiriqui Highlands, Panama   105
24. Panama City, Panama   109
25. Greater Antilles (West Indies)   116
26. Lesser Antilles (West Indies)   125
27. Trinidad and Tobago   130

28. Henri Pittier (Rancho Grande) National Park, Venezuela   136
29. Calabozo, Venezuela   142
30. Santa Marta, Colombia   147
31. Cali—Buenaventura, Colombia   155
32. Quito, Ecuador   163
33. Rio Napo, Ecuador   168
34. Galápagos, Ecuador   174
35. Lima, Peru   177
36. Cuzco, Peru   181
37. Puerto Maldonado, Peru   186
38. Puno and Arequipa, Peru   192
39. Santiago, Chile   196
40. Falkland Islands   201
41. Trelew and Bariloche, Argentina   204
42. Buenos Aires—Pampas, Argentina   209
43. Asuncion, Paraguay   213
44. Iguassu Falls, Argentina, and Brazil   218
45. Itatiaia National Park, Brazil   223
46. Rio de Janeiro, Brazil   228
47. Belem, Brazil   232
48. Paramaribo, Suriname   239
49. Iceland   247
50. Shetland Islands, United Kingdom   250
51. London, England   254
52. Amsterdam, Holland   259
53. Denmark, and Southern Sweden   264
54. Lapland, Norway, Sweden, and Finland   269
55. Istanbul, Turkey   274
56. Danube Delta, Romania   280
57. Vienna, Austria   284
58. Camargue, France   289
59. Andalucia, Spain   294
60. Morocco   300
61. Canary Islands, Spain   306
62. Senegal and Gambia   310
63. Lagos—Ibadan, Nigeria   318
64. Virunga National Park, Zaïre   323
65. Kakamega Forest, Kenya   329
66. Nairobi, Kenya   335

67. Mombasa, Kenya   347
68. Blantyre, Malawi   351
69. Luangwa Valley National Parks, Zambia   359
70. Victoria Falls, Zimbabwe (Rhodesia) and Zambia   365
71. Cape Town, Cape Province   370
72. Zululand Reserves, Natal   375
73. Kruger National Park, Transvaal   381
74. Madagascar   386
75. Mauritius and Reunion   391
76. Seychelles   395
77. Azraq, Jordan   398
78. Bahrain   402
79. Lahore, Pakistan   405
80. Islamabad, Pakistan   410
81. Srinagar, Kashmir, India   412
82. New Delhi—Agra, India   416
83. Kathmandu, Nepal   422
84. Mt. Everest, Nepal   427
85. Royal Chitwan National Park, Nepal   430
86. Sri Lanka (Ceylon)   434
87. Hokkaido, Japan   440
88. Honshu and Kyushu, Japan   445
89. Beijing (Peking), China   451
90. Shanghai, China   455
91. Taiwan   459
92. Hong Kong   463
93. Khao Yai National Park, Thailand   467
94. Taman Negara National Park, Malaysia   471
95. Singapore   475
96. Kinabalu National Park, (Borneo) Malaysia   479
97. Philippines   483
98. Bali, Indonesia   491
99. Wau, Papua New Guinea   495
100. Port Moresby, Papua New Guinea   500
101. Darwin, Northern Territory   505
102. Alice Springs, Northern Territory   510
103. Perth—Albany, Western Australia   514
104. National Parks of the "Mallee," Victoria   519
105. Melbourne, Victoria   524

Contents

106. Sydney, New South Wales   529
107. Brisbane, Queensland   534
108. Cairns, Queensland   540
109. New Caledonia   546
110. Fiji   550
111. New Zealand   554

Bibliography   561
Taxonomic Index   577
Alphabetical Key to the Taxonomic Index   677

Introduction

Finding Birds Around the World is the first book attempting to bring together in one volume detailed information about many of the top bird localities around the world. Within the space allowed, our aim has been to provide traveling birders with the essential information to get started in a place that is new to them.

Our choice of localities is a blend of frequently visited cities, the most interesting national parks, exciting resorts, and a number of unprotected areas. It will probably be argued that we have neglected some favorite spots. Our field experience, the literature, and current political trends have forced us to favor some areas and miss others.

In describing such diverse areas, we have inevitably had to keep things brief. Some areas have been visited often and recently by the authors or their friends, some have excellent literature references, while other unique areas are hardly known at all. Many birding localities are described for the first time. Several expeditions were organized to gather information for this work. Some material was extracted from old scientific journals, often in foreign languages.

Our text for each area varies greatly in coverage due to local conditions and experience. We have tried to give a mountaintop view of the layout, vegetation, transportation, lodgings, and climate, as well as specific tips on a few of the most visited and/or most productive spots. A map of each area is included so the visitor can orient himself and make decisions on how best to use his time. Most guides have few maps, and our experience has been that acquiring good local maps is essential.

The species list for each area should, on the average, cover 99 percent of all individual birds to be seen in a visit and between 80 and 90 percent of the known avifauna, omitting most rarities and accidentals. Please note that birding intensity and the availability of identification manuals varies greatly around the world.

Although scientific names are traceable, new information and techniques are causing reassignment of many species, genera, and families, forcing common-name changes.

English name problems occupy many minds in our quickly shrinking world. This subject is also messy. Several thousand birds have two, three, or more common names, and the same name is often applied to two different birds. Prefixes are omitted by local custom, while such names as oriole, warbler, catbird, chat, flycatcher, vulture, etc., are in widespread use for species belonging to quite unrelated families of birds. To provide a unique, helpful, nonerroneous name in English for each bird, we have attempted to standardize usage worldwide. Some British names have been used in the New World, and some American names in the Old World, while a few newly proposed names are used when all previous names were deemed inadequate. Consult the taxonomic index (p. 575) for pseudonyms.

Most bird-finding guides provide a short list of birds that the author thinks will interest potential visitors. We have concluded that a relatively complete list of birds is most useful due to the fact that our coverage and readership are worldwide. Birds of interest to one observer will differ from those interesting to another. Such a list is in itself an aid to identification, eliminating similar species that do not occur or occur only rarely. As a further aid in helping decide which areas to visit, we have attempted to specify broad categories of abundance, seasonality, and elevation.

SYMBOLS

Abundance: c = common; r = rare.
Wherever possible we have attempted to distinguish those species of regularly occurring birds that are most likely, and least likely to be seen. If a bird's status fluctuates widely or it is only locally common in the area, we have used no abundance symbol. At the right season visitors should be able to find most of those species listed as common. Obviously one may have to visit most or all of the habitats found in the area discussed.

Seasonal: S = Summer; M = Migration; W = Winter.
"Summer" indicates a breeding species (or assumption of breeding). That species may be present for only a month or up to nine months. The symbol for "migration" is used for birds that habitually do not breed, or winter, in the area in question. In many cases a species is much more common in one migration period than another. The symbol for "winter" is used for birds that spend much time during the cooler months in an area. Some of them may be absent for only a few months.

The foregoing information applies primarily to the Northern Hemisphere. Seasons are reversed in the Southern Hemisphere. *Summer* is used for species that breed in an area, wintering farther north. *Winter* is used for species that come in from farther south for the southern winter. *Migration* is used for species that come from the north and spend the southern summer away from the Northern Hemisphere winter. These do not breed in the south.

While there are hundreds of species that breed in the Northern Hemisphere and winter in the subtropical and temperate areas of the Southern Hemisphere, there are very few Southern Hemisphere breeders that winter north of the tropics in the Northern Hemisphere.

Elevational: L = Lowlands; H = Highlands.

Areas with distinctly different avifaunas at different elevations are identified. The dividing line is rather flexible in most areas. A bird found in both low and high areas will have no annotation. In some lists only those restricted to the highlands are indicated, with all lowland forms left blank.

For readers wishing to find the best place to see or study a given species (such as Satin Bowerbird), the following quick steps are needed:

1. Turn to the alphabetical index on p. 678 and note that bowerbirds are found on p. 638 of the taxonomic index.

2. Turn to p. 638 and locate *Satin Bowerbird,* noting the three localities where it is found.

3. Check for abundance on each area's checklist, and scan the text. You will soon note that the Brisbane area is best and that you can feed the birds out of your hand at O'Reilly's.

Comments, suggestions, and photocopies of your field notes from exotic areas are eagerly solicited by the authors, who can be reached as follows:

Peter Alden   John Gooders
c/o Massachusetts Audubon Society   c/o André Deutsch
Lincoln, Massachusetts 01773 USA   105 Great Russell Street
                                             London WC1, England

HOTELS

The best places in the world for birds are uninhabited pockets of Amazonia, remote stretches of tundra, and unreachable swamps in Africa. However, we have described places that are more easily accessible.

Specific hotels are listed only in areas with little publicity and no choice. In other areas you should rely on travel agents and general travel guides with up-to-the-minute information.

The travel industry today is geared to providing data on rates, presence of pools, TVs, and restaurants, and how convenient each hotel is to airport and city center. Birders, on the other hand, are usually more interested in hotels near natural areas or gardens, and those with 24-hour coffee shops.

Noise is rarely mentioned in hotel listings. Avoid rooms near, under, or over entertainment, near elevators or with views of noisy avenues (inside rooms are cheaper). Consider bringing ear plugs and learn to sleep with a pillow over your ear.

Because of the need to be in the field early, breakfasts are a nuisance in tropical areas. Birding tours can usually bribe the staff into opening early and pay for a special-order breakfast requested the previous day. Travelers should consider taking along a Thermos and organizing their morning the day before. Bring a corkscrew, bottle and can openers, bathplug, and cups from home.

TOURS AND BOOKINGS

There are many ways, means, and reasons for vagabonding around the world occasionally or often to see birds. Such an avocation is no longer restricted to the very rich and privileged. Much overseas birding is done on the side during business trips, scientific conventions, or other visits. There are also legions for whom birding is the primary or only reason to travel, and most decisions revolve around the pursuit of novel species and avifaunas. This book is designed to aid both persons on organized tours and those traveling alone.

Single travelers (and couples) with resourcefulness and stamina will attempt to reach many of these places on their own. Traveling on your own has its advantages — such as going at your own speed, getting up at your hour, learning the birds and the "ropes" the hard way at firsthand, choosing your own exact itinerary, and the freedom to alter your plans. You may also take a general-interest cruise or tour for part or all of your excursion, noting birds as you can alongside cathedrals, museums, statues, beaches, and casinos.

Group birding tours have been featured for only the last thirty years, with more offerings each year. There are hundreds of people who take one or more tours every year, and thousands more who join a birding tour every few years. The advantages of going on a tour with a seasoned leader include more efficient use of time, someone who knows most or all birds (and other things) quickly, freedom from logistics hassles, and the contagious enthusiasm of fellow birders. Ask other birders about reputations and differences among the many societies and individuals offering tours.

Travel agents are very helpful in setting up air-travel packages, securing hotel space in major towns, and sometimes in finding local transportation. They are not so useful in arranging rooms in some of the remote areas birders have to stay in. Since most good birding tours are small-time, privately run, and offer no commission structure, an agent, if asked, will know of and recommend only a few large ticket tours (watered down ones, usually) from big commercial operators.

TRANSPORTATION PROBLEMS

Please be understanding in realizing that rented cars, as well as local public transport, break down at times. Things rarely go smoothly overseas despite all precautions.

Airlines are, in general, quite good but there is little you can do about overbooking, delays, and cancellations, which sometimes occur. Try to avoid going to or from anywhere during local holidays, festivals, and special events. Don't go near Rio on Carnival, stay away from Christmas–New Year's periods, and avoid high-traffic periods. You will lessen problems of being bumped off planes (as well as of disappearing hotel rooms and rental cars) by avoiding such holidays. There is a wide difference among airlines in the number of rows (and widths) of seats, but, alas, these statistics are hard to come by. Book, confirm, and reconfirm as often and as far in advance as you can. It is best to take binoculars, valuable notes and field guides, toiletries, and one change of clothes with you in a bag to store under your seat.

The simplest way to avoid most logistic problems is to join an organized birding tour. Otherwise you will usually have to work with drive-yourself vehicles (hire cars or rental cars). The quality, prices, and availability worldwide are diverse. No matter where you come from, you have to drive on the wrong side of the road in half the world. In most of Africa, Asia, Australia, New Zealand, and most islands of the world (including Britain and Ireland) one drives on the left. It is chiefly in continental Europe and the Americas that one drives on the right.

Try to rent only from companies that offer unlimited mileage. Booking a car overseas in advance and showing up with a fistful of confirmations is no guarantee of obtaining a car, but it is better than nothing. In some tropical countries it is sometimes cheaper and safer to negotiate with a taxi driver for day trips.

Road signs are a lost (if ever discovered) art in much of the world. They rarely mention your destination. Assume that many forks will have no signposts. Always seek detailed local road maps.

Do not leave visible valuables in your vehicle, and remember that break-ins are possible almost anywhere. While violence toward birders is almost unknown, and most rural folk are delightfully friendly, do not invite a loss. It is wise to carry several separate lists of all your important numbers, along with Xerox copies of your passport and driver's license.

Travelers should get used to both metric and English forms of measuring distance and elevation.

Public transportation may be utilized in some rural areas, and frequency of service is often rather good and fares cheap; it also provides a fine way to learn about local customs and attitudes.

Boats must be rented in a number of areas, and these can be dreadfully expensive to single travelers. Whether you are doing the Estero San Cristobal in Mexico or going out to Michaelmas Cay in Australia, it is best to go with a group or be flexible enough to join the odd group of nonbirders going that way.

Sea cruises to the Galápagos and the worldwide adventures of such ships as the *Lindblad Explorer* and the *World Discoverer* appeal to many. Few of these journeys are efficiently or exclusively tailored for birders; yet birders can often do quite well, particularly in Antarctica.

HEALTH

Sanitary conditions vary considerably worldwide. In general there are few problems with food or water in Europe, Australia, New Zealand, and North America north of the Rio Grande. Elsewhere most major hotels and private inns (run with care) are perfectly safe.

Water is often suspect. In most tropical areas it is best to buy bottled water. Do bring a canteen or plastic bottle with a screw-on top for use on stretches between safe sources, and consider taking along some of the various pills and iodine crystals. Local inquiry is needed on each town's drinking water in taps; some hotels have their own filtration systems, and some will tell tourists that good water is bad, to sell more bottled water.

Most tourists are nervous about lettuce and fresh vegetables anywhere overseas. There are hundreds of places in dozens of countries that serve perfectly safe salads. Intuition and local inquiry of natives and frequent visitors are useful. Most tourists avoid all water and salads unnecessarily, and still indiscriminately devour tons of seafood, milk, meat, and butter without a thought, all of which should be discreetly smelled before it is eaten. If it smells strange or old, do not eat it.

There are numerous preparations to aid such problems. We recommend liquid Pepto-Bismol for mild cases and Lomotil only when stomach problems are severe. Few cases require more potent cures.

Although we have selected many localities that provide better access and comfort than others, know your limits and avoid taking foolish chances. Exposure to excessive heat, cold, wind, and altitude is possible in almost any area at one time or another.

Insects occur in all these areas. Flying, blood-sucking insects (curiously enough) are commoner in the Arctic and wetter areas of North America and Eurasia than they are in the tropics. There are local exceptions, but in general the rain forests of the tropics often seem "bug-free." In the Western Hemisphere there are problems with chiggers and ticks in many roadside and grassy areas at lower elevations. You can see hundreds of birds without crossing fields by birding from wide trails, dirt roads, and boats. If you must enter risky areas, spray yourself from the waist down before dressing, and then douse your clothes every few hours. Despite claims, there is no fully effective insect repellent for all things in all places.

In the monsoon forests from Kathmandu to Sydney beware of walking in damp leaf litter. In such places lurk tiny inchwormlike things called leeches. They are very thin and can go through socks. It is best to keep checking and flicking them off before they attach and blow themselves up on your blood. They roll off eventually, but you may bleed for a while owing to an anticoagulant they exude. They are clean otherwise, but just a nuisance.

Owing to the normally retiring and nocturnal habits of poisonous snakes, birders rarely encounter them. Most of us rather wish to see more snakes and are amazed at their seeming scarcity. Nevertheless, caution and alertness are advised.

Large cats are potentially dangerous to your health, but are very scarce except in Africa where most park rules do not allow you a fighting chance to die.

WHAT TO TAKE WITH YOU

Clothing is always a problem. Many national airlines try to balance their country's debt with antiquated 44-pound (20-kilo) baggage limits. Laundry service is fast and cheap in Third World countries, but you can only use it with two-night stands or more. Key words to remember in packing are comfort, wash-and-wear, cold-water detergent, bathtub drying line, lightweight, tough, and conservative. Most travelers take one casual suit/dress for city hotels, a waterproof jacket, one sweater (it can be cold at night even in the Amazon), and 3 to 6 changes of tops, bottoms, and underwear. Footwear involves one pair of city shoes, 2 pairs of birding shoes (one for dust, one for mud). Few birders wade in water up to their waists, but those doing wet tropical areas in the rainy season, or the tundra, should consider waterproof rubber boots with non-slip soles. Larger sizes of boots (and hats) are often unavailable in foreign countries.

Binoculars are the most important item; criteria for choosing them are described well elsewhere. Buy binoculars that allow close focus, and do not let them get rained on excessively. Consider bringing a second pair. Instant focusing can be learned by all of our readers: When your eye catches something flying overhead while you're studying a bird in a nearby bush, your finger should be turning the focusing knob in the right direction, roughly the right distance, so that when you zero in on your new bird it is already in focus.

Telescopes on tripods are a field mark of North American birders and yet are strangely rare among Old World birders. Since one is constantly putting legs up and down, try to find one that can be compacted quickly and is lightweight. Telescopes are most useful with shore and savanna birds and are a great way to show others in your party a new find. A telescope is surprisingly useful in heavy forests, since a number of distant hornbills, toucans, barbets, hawks, trogons, flycatchers, etc., do perch quietly for periods. It is far better to have your party sneak a view in the scope than to repeat confusing directions in a maze of look-alike branches. Do not allow your telescope to get rained on as you will risk fogging; always carry ample plastic bags for storms and spray.

Cameras with telephoto lenses are a passion for some travelers. As with other hardware, try it out, learn its quirks, and feel its weight long before taking it overseas — do not tie another albatross around your neck. Generally, photography is good on coasts, savannas, migration traps, feeders, near lodges, in the tundra, marshes, and along rivers. In forests, whether tropical or temperate, photography is exceedingly difficult and unrewarding. Forest birds are most active at dawn and dusk, and during misty, rainy days, all situations with little light. When the light meter rises the birds retreat. Remote-control, close-range flash arrangements at nests are effective, but they require time and care in order not to disrupt nesting.

It is usually helpful to have bills of sale or customs registration of all hardware with you when crossing borders.

If you're traveling to another country you generally need a passport, onward transportation, and a visa. Some countries still require all visitors to obtain a visa in advance (with photos and a service charge at times). Rules for these can be obtained at any travel agency, and it is usually done through the mail. Other countries require only that you fill in your umpteenth form upon arrival. If you should lose a passport, go to your own country's nearest consulate, after reporting the loss to the police (get a copy of the report), present several photos (it is best to have extras along with you — it takes days overseas), and if your accent is right, no problem.

Someday there will be a world currency, but until that happens you will have to deal with many brands of money. It is always best to have some cash (including small bills) in one of the world's top currencies. Traveler's checks are well respected, but it is best to change them chiefly in major cities, hotels, and airports. It pays to compare rates between banks, exchange houses, and hotels if you have got time. In smaller towns, traveler's checks are often suspect; delays of hours can occur as the bank calls the capital and types up endless forms in triplicate and shuttles you from window to window. Credit cards are most useful in avoiding down payments for rental cars, and can pay for hotel bills (in large cities) and air tickets (which cards will be accepted in which establishments in which country is decided by some bizarre lottery in Macau for all we can gather). Take care with wallets (best carried in the front pocket) and purses (a metal-reinforced strap is recommended) in busy cities, and do not take expensive watches and jewelry overseas.

BIRDING IN THE FIELD

When pointing out a distant bird do not say "look where I'm looking," "straight-out," or "up in the green tree that points toward the sky." Instead, one should employ the clock system in a given tree (halfway out toward ten o'clock) or boat (the bow is always going to 12 o'clock). Under such difficult situations as forests, learn how to describe grayer, yellower, darker, larger, thinner, and dead leaves; smooth, flaky, huge, black, pale, angled, double, and dead limbs and trunks. On mudflats check for nonbird items like boats, buoys, grassy islands, different colors of sand, etc.

None of us wants birders to be given a bad name or to have the next visitors turned away because of our actions. Close gates, ask permission, inform locals about your actions, tip properly, and do not harass the birds. Tell local farmers, hotel owners, and people with authority why you have come, and how many more may follow in your footsteps. Support local conservation projects directly or through the World Wildlife Fund.

RECORD KEEPING AND PUBLISHING

There are scores of methods favored to keep track of sightings on your journeys. There are several considerations in choosing your format. Some do not ever keep track of what they see — fine. Most people do keep records for their own interest. How easy will it be for you to draw on that information five years from now? More thought should be given to area lists in which you can combine your sightings over several days. These should be able to be photocopied (for your safety and peace of mind) and made available to travelers. The best form is a sketch-map of what you did, with dates and estimated numbers, and a handwritten list with columns from which one can extract information. Daily lists covering diverse habitats over a wide area are nearly useless to anyone else.

Most people travel to see birds they have only dreamed of seeing, and some few find dreams interrupting their vision. You will find many exciting birds wherever you go. If you run into unfamiliar birds, do consider subspecies and individual variation. No avifaunal list is complete, and no field guide is perfect. Genuine rarities will occasionally be found, particularly in areas that are rarely visited. Organize your notes, sketches, and photographs, extralimital records and distributional finds for eventual publication.

St.Paul
1

Mt.McKinley
2

Bathurst Inlet
4

Churchill
5

Vancouver Island
3

NORTH AMERICA

Yellowstone
10

Bear River
11

San Francisco
14

Los Angeles
13

Tucson
12

Texas Coast

Pt.Pelee
6

Boston
New York
Washington
7

Atlantic
Ocean

Hawaii
15

Pacific
Ocean

Mazatlán
San Blas
16

Mexico City
Valle de Bravo
20

Guatemala City-Atitlan
21

Chiriqui
23

Panama City
24

17

19

18

Yucatan

Miami
8

Tikal

Belize

San Jose
22

Greater
Antilles
25

Lesser
Antilles
26

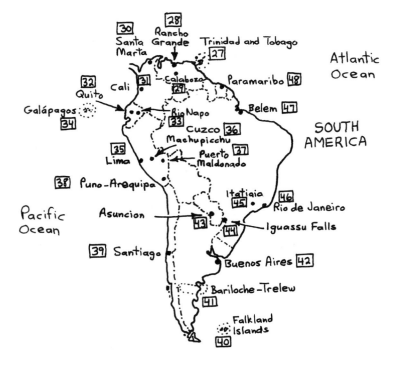

Santa Marta 30
Rancho Grande 28
Trinidad and Tobago 27
Atlantic Ocean
Quito 32
Cali
Calaboza 29
Paramaribo 48
Galápagos 34
Rio Napo 33
Belem 47
Cuzco 36
SOUTH AMERICA
Machupicchu
Lima 35
Puerto Maldonado 27
Puno-Arequipa 38
Itatiaia 45
Rio de Janeiro 46
Pacific Ocean
Asuncion 43
Iguassu Falls 44
Santiago 39
Buenos Aires 42
Bariloche-Trelew 41
Falkland Islands 40

Iceland
49

50
Shetlands

Lapland
54

Amsterdam

EUROPE

53

London, England
51

52

Denmark, South Sweden

Neusiedler See, Vienna
57

Camargue

58

Danube Delta

56

Andalucia
S. Portugal

59

Istanbul
55

60 Morocco

Canary Isles
61

AFRICA

Senegal
and
Gambia
62

Kakamega Forest
65

Lagos-
Ibadan
63

Virunga
64

Nairobi - Serengeti
66

Mombasa
67

Atlantic
Ocean

Seychelles
76

69

Luangwa
Valley

Blantyre

68

Victoria Falls
70

74

Mauritius
and
75 Reunion

Kruger

73

Madagascar

Indian
Ocean

Cape Town
71

72

Zululand

ASIA

Islamabad 80
Srinagar 81
Beijing 89
Hokkaido 87
Honshu – Kyushu 88
Kathmandu 83
Shanghai 90
Mt. Everest 84
Lahore 79
Delhi–Agra
Azraq 77
Bahrain
78
Chitwan 85
Hong Kong 92
Formosa (Taiwan) 91

Pacific Ocean

Khao Yai 93
Taman Negara 94
Philippines 97
Mt. Kinabalu 76
Ceylon (Sri Lanka) 86
Singapore 95

Indian Ocean

Bali 98

Wau 99
Port Moresby 100

Darwin 101
Cairns 108
Fiji 110
New Caledonia 109
Alice Springs 102
AUSTRALIA
Brisbane 107
Perth–Albany 103
Mallee 104
Sydney 106
Melbourne 105
111
New Zealand

*Finding Birds
Around the World*

1

St. Paul, Pribilof Islands, Alaska

THE PRIBILOF ISLANDS are located 285 miles (456 km) off the west coast of Alaska and 800 miles (1280 km) west of Anchorage. St. Paul Island has few tourist facilities: one hotel (the Aleut Community Hotel), one general store, one market, one bar, two cinemas, a small hospital, and two churches. The weather is cold, wet, and windy, with fog, sleet, and snow common even in summer.

Transportation on this 13-mile (21 km) long – 7-mile (11 km) wide island can be difficult because of rough roads. No rental cars are available, although cars with drivers can sometimes be arranged. Reeve Aleutian Airways (343 West Sixth Avenue, Anchorage, Alaska 99501) flies to St. Paul several times a week from Anchorage. The airline also operates, mainly during June, July, and August, package tours that include air fares, hotel accommodations, and some sight-seeing.

The Pribilofs have over a million breeding birds. On St. Paul the best bird colonies are on cliffs at Southwest Point, a ten-minute walk from the hotel. The breeding season is May through August. The major species on the islands include Tufted and Horned Puffins, Para-keet, Crested and Least Auklets, Common and Thick-billed Murres, Black-legged and Red-legged Kittiwakes, Red-legged and Pelagic Cormorants, and Northern Fulmar. Other birds often seen in summer are Harlequin Duck, eiders, Glaucous, Glaucous-winged, and Slaty-backed Gulls, Gray-crowned Rosy-Finch, Lapland Longspur, and Snow Bunting.

The scene changes radically during migration and winter seasons. Most of the alcids disappear into the seas, and sea ducks and geese replace them. Emperor Geese are seen only in migration; Gyrfalcon sometimes winter on the islands. The real highlight is the rare oppor-tunity to observe Asian stragglers, which show up with surprising frequency, often staying for some time at these isolated islands. May and September are the most likely months to observe these rarities.

St. George Island, 40 miles (64 km) southwest of St. Paul, has even

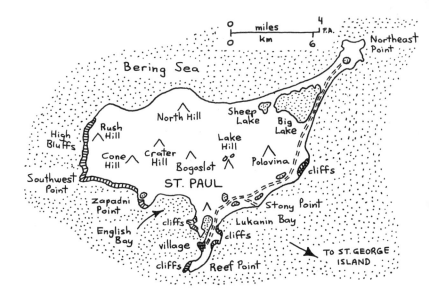

larger bird colonies, with more Red-legged Kittiwake. There are no facilities for tourists there.

Although the following list of birds is long, do not expect to see more than fifty species in a week. The list includes most of the island's rare and sporadic visitors. Many are so unpredictable in frequency and season that the seasonal symbols have been omitted.

CHECKLIST

Yellow-billed Loon r
Black-throated Loon
Red-throated Loon r
Red-necked Grebe r
Horned Grebe
Northern Fulmar c
Short-tailed Shearwater r
Scaled Petrel r
Fork-tailed Storm-Petrel
Pelagic Cormorant
Red-faced Cormorant c
Whooper Swan r
Whistling Swan r
Canada Goose
Brent Goose
Emperor Goose

Mallard c
Gadwall r
Northern Pintail
Falcated Teal r
Green-winged Teal
Baikal Teal
Eurasian Wigeon
American Wigeon
Northern Shoveler r
Redhead r
Northern Pochard
Greater Scaup r
Tufted Duck r
Common Goldeneye r
Barrow's Goldeneye r
Bufflehead r

Long-tailed Duck   c
Harlequin Duck   c
Steller's Eider   c
Common Eider   c
King Eider   c
White-winged Scoter   c
Black Scoter
Smew   r
Goosander
Red-breasted Merganser   r
Bald Sea-Eagle   r
Steller's Sea-Eagle   r
Rough-legged Buzzard   r
Gyrfalcon   r
Peregrine Falcon   r
Sandhill Crane   r
Semipalmated Plover   r
Mongolian Plover   r
Lesser Golden Plover
Black-bellied Plover   r
Ruddy Turnstone
Common Snipe
Bar-tailed Godwit
Whimbrel   r
Bristle-thighed Curlew   r
Common Sandpiper   r
Wood Sandpiper
Wandering Tattler
Polynesian Tattler   r
Spotted Redshank   r
Common Greenshank   r
Lesser Yellowlegs
Greater Yellowlegs   r
Red Knot   r
Rock Sandpiper   c
Dunlin   r
Ruff
Sharp-tailed Sandpiper   r
Pectoral Sandpiper   r
Baird's Sandpiper   r
Least Sandpiper
Long-toed Stint   r
Red-necked Stint   r
Temminck's Stint   r
Semipalmated Sandpiper
Western Sandpiper
Sanderling

Short-billed Dowitcher   r
Long-billed Dowitcher
Stilt Sandpiper   r
Buff-breasted Sandpiper   r
Red Phalarope
Little Phalarope   c
Pomarine Jaeger
Parasitic Jaeger
Long-tailed Jaeger
Glaucous Gull   c
Glaucous-winged Gull
Slaty-backed Gull
Black-headed Gull   r
Ivory Gull   r
Black-legged Kittiwake   c
Red-legged Kittiwake   c
Ross's Gull   r
Sabine's Gull   r
Common Tern   c
Arctic Tern
Common Murre   c
Thick-billed Murre   c
Pigeon Guillemot   c
Marbled Murrelet
Ancient Murrelet   r
Parakeet Auklet   c
Crested Auklet   c
Least Auklet   c
Horned Puffin   c
Tufted Puffin   c
Snowy Owl
Short-eared Owl
Fork-tailed Swift   r
Common Swift   r
Northern Skylark   r
Violet-green Swallow   r
Tree Swallow   r
Sand Martin   r
Cliff Martin   r
Northern Raven   r
Northern Wren
American Robin   r
Eye-browed Thrush   r
Northern Wheatear
Siberian Rubythroat   r
Water Pipit
White Wagtail   r

1 : *St. Paul, Pribilof Islands, Alaska*

Gray Wagtail r
Yellow Wagtail r
Bohemian Waxwing r
Wilson's Warbler r
Rusty Blackbird r
Brambling r
Gray-crowned Rosy-Finch c
Hoary Redpoll r

Common Redpoll
Savannah Sparrow r
White-crowned Sparrow r
Golden-crowned Sparrow r
Fox Sparrow r
Lapland Longspur c
Snow Bunting c

2

Mount McKinley National Park, Alaska

BENEATH THE 20,320-foot (6195 m) peak of Mount McKinley (Denali), a number of fine arctic birds and mammals can easily be seen. The altitude and cold of the peak hardly affect the bird watcher since the valley is at 1000 feet (305 m) and the Denali highway goes only to 4000 feet (1219 m).

The Alaska Railroad connects the park with both Fairbanks and Anchorage. Within the park, a shuttle bus runs on the park road, for private cars now are restricted to the area east of the Savage River. Tour parties can charter their own buses; most buses leave by 6 A.M. The McKinley Park Hotel is located near the park headquarters and the railroad station. Camping sites along the park road are also available.

In the spruce forests that cover much of the park below 3000 feet (915 m) look for Varied Thrush and Bohemian Waxwing, and such rarities as Spruce Grouse, Northern Hawk-Owl, Northern Three-toed Woodpecker, and Boreal Chickadee. Alder, birch, and willow thickets such as those along Savage River, are inhabited by Willow Ptarmigan and Arctic Warbler, and the river itself has Barrow's Goldeneye, Harlequin Duck, and North American Dipper.

The main park road passes through some tundra at Polychrome and Sable Passes. Searching the wet tundra may produce sights of Golden Eagle, Lesser Golden Plover, and Long-tailed Jaeger. In the higher dry tundra, particularly over rocky ground, are Rock and White-tailed Ptarmigan, the rare Surf bird, Northern Wheatear, and Gray-crowned Rosy-Finch. Beware of grizzly bears if walking in the high country; walking is prohibited in some areas.

Camp Denali — a wilderness camp near Wonder Lake, 88 miles (141 km) from the entrance — is great for bird watchers. Besides having a good variety of ducks, Wonder Lake is the best spot for Bald Sea-Eagle, Bonaparte's Gull, and Arctic Tern. The view of Mount McKinley is excellent on the rare clear days.

The park is normally open from June 1 to September 10.

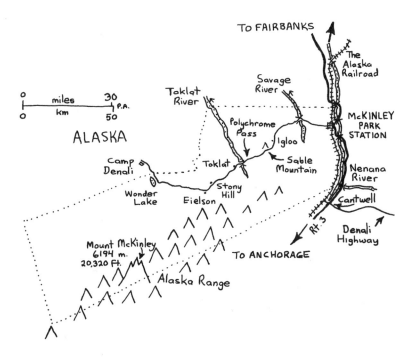

Further information on campground reservations and the park transportation system can be obtained by writing to: Superintendent, Mount McKinley National Park, PO Box 9, McKinley Park, AK 99755.

The bird list is chiefly of summer species, with a few migrants listed.

CHECKLIST

Red-necked Grebe   r M
Horned Grebe
Mallard
American Wigeon
Northern Pintail   c
Green-winged Teal
Greater Scaup   M
Lesser Scaup   M
Barrow's Goldeneye
Bufflehead   M
Long-tailed Duck   c
Harlequin Duck
Surf Scoter
Bald Sea-Eagle   r

Northern Goshawk   r
Sharp-shinned Sparrowhawk
Red-tailed Hawk
Swainson's Hawk   r
Rough-legged Buzzard   r
Golden Eagle   c
Northern Harrier
Gyrfalcon
Merlin
American Kestrel
Spruce Grouse
Ruffed Grouse   r
Willow Ptarmigan   c
White-tailed Ptarmigan   r

Rock Ptarmigan
Sandhill Crane   M
Semipalmated Plover   c
Lesser Golden Plover
Surfbird
Common Snipe
Whimbrel   c
Upland Sandpiper
Spotted Sandpiper
Solitary Sandpiper   r
Wandering Tattler
Lesser Yellowlegs
Baird's Sandpiper   r
Little Phalarope
Long-tailed Jaeger   c
Herring Gull
Mew Gull   c
Bonaparte's Gull
Arctic Tern
Great Horned Owl   r
Snowy Owl   r
Northern Hawk-Owl
Short-eared Owl
Tengmalm's Owl   r
Great Gray Owl   r
Belted Kingfisher   r
Northern (Yellow-shafted) Flicker
Hairy Woodpecker
Downy Woodpecker
Black-backed Three-toed
   Woodpecker   r
Northern Three-toed Woodpecker
Say's Phoebe
Willow Flycatcher
Olive-sided Pewee
Horned Lark
Violet-green Swallow
Sand Martin   r
Barn Swallow   r

Gray Jay   c
Black-billed Magpie   c
Northern Raven   r
Black-capped Chickadee
Boreal Chickadee   c
North American Dipper   r
American Robin   c
Varied Thrush   c
Hermit Thrush
Swainson's Thrush
Gray-cheeked Thrush
Northern Wheatear   c
Townsend's Solitaire   r
Arctic Warbler
Ruby-crowned Kinglet   r
Water Pipit
Bohemian Waxwing
Great Gray Shrike
Orange-crowned Warbler   r
Yellow Warbler   r
Yellow-rumped Warbler   c
Blackpoll Warbler
Northern Waterthrush
Wilson's Warbler
Rusty Blackbird
Pine Grosbeak
Gray-crowned Rosy-Finch
Common Redpoll   c
White-winged Crossbill
Savannah Sparrow
Northern Junco   c
Winter Sparrow   c
White-crowned Sparrow   c
Golden-crowned Sparrow   r
Fox Sparrow
Lincoln's Sparrow   r
Lapland Longspur   c
Snow Bunting

3
Vancouver Island, British Columbia

THIS HUGE ISLAND, 290 miles (464 km) long, with magnificent scenery, offers some of the best birding in Canada. The climate is especially favorable; although winters are rainy, the weather is generally moderate.

Victoria, the provincial capital, is smaller than the nearby cities of Vancouver and Seattle, with which it is connected by frequent ferries. At Beacon Hill Park, a ten-minute walk from the city center, resident birds include California Quail, Chestnut-backed Chickadee, Bushtit, and Northern and Bewick's Wrens, and, in the summer, thrushes, warblers, and Western Tanager. Fresh-water ducks winter in the park's Goodacre Lake. Clover Point, a five-minute walk, is another popular birding place, with its loons, grebes, sea ducks (including Harlequin), Black Oystercatcher, Surfbird, Black Turnstone, Wandering Tattler, Rock Sandpiper, Heermann's Gull, Common Murre, Pigeon Guillemot, and Marbled Murrelet. Portage Inlet and Esquimalt Lagoon on the west side of the city are excellent for grebes, ducks, and Bald Eagle.

Bird watching is also good outside the capital. Twelve miles (19 km) west of Victoria, on Highway 1, Goldstream Park, which has a stream and campsites, often provides a view of North American Dipper, Varied Thrush, Townsend's and MacGillivray's Warblers.

The introduced Northern Skylark is common in the fields along Route 17 about halfway between Victoria and Swartz Bay, the major terminal for ferries connecting the island with the city of Vancouver. A few pairs of Tufted Puffin, as well as numerous gulls, cormorants, and Pigeon Guillemot, breed on Mandarte Island, which is accessible by boats rented in Sidney. At Swartz Bay Northwestern Crows are common. In addition, the Swartz Bay–Vancouver ferry offers excellent pelagic birding, particularly near Active Pass, a narrow passage between Mayne and Galiano Islands. The most interesting birds are the migrant and wintering seabirds seen from September through May: loons, cormorants, Bald Sea-Eagle, jaegers, gulls (including

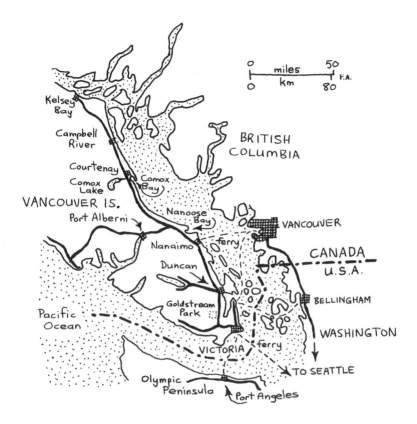

Heermann's and Sabine's), Common Murre, Marbled and Ancient Murrelets.

Along the island's main road that follows the east coast 180 miles (288 km) north to Kelsey Bay, there are hotels in Duncan, Nanaimo, Courtenay, Campbell River, and Kelsey Bay itself. Often a good location for spotting birds, Comox Lake west of Courtenay has Trumpeter Swan in winter. American Black Swift can be seen at Miracle Beach Park. In March and April herring spawn in Nanoose Bay (north of Nanaimo), and Comox Bay attracts thousands of loons, grebes, sea ducks, mergansers, cormorants, and gulls.

CHECKLIST

Common Loon c	Red-necked Grebe c W
Yellow-billed Loon r W	Horned Grebe c W
Black-throated Loon c W	Black-necked Grebe W
Red-throated Loon c W	Western Grebe c W

9

Pied-billed Grebe   c
Black-footed Albatross   M
Northern Fulmar   W
Pink-footed Shearwater   r M
Buller's Shearwater   r M
Sooty Shearwater   c M
Short-tailed Shearwater   c M
Fork-tailed Storm-Petrel
Leach's Storm-Petrel   r
Double-crested Cormorant   c
Brandt's Cormorant   c
Pelagic Cormorant   c
Great Blue Heron   c
Green Heron   r S
Mute Swan
Whistling Swan   r W
Trumpeter Swan   r W
Canada Goose   c
Brent Goose   M
White-fronted Goose   W
Snow Goose   r W
Mallard   c
Gadwall   r W
Northern Pintail   c W
Green-winged Teal   c W
Blue-winged Teal   S
Cinnamon Teal   r S
Eurasian Wigeon   r W
American Wigeon   c W
Northern Shoveler   c W
Wood Duck   r
Redhead   r W
Ring-necked Duck   W
Canvasback   W
Greater Scaup   c W
Lesser Scaup   W
Common Goldeneye   c W
Barrow's Goldeneye   W
Bufflehead   c W
Long-tailed Duck   c W
Harlequin Duck   c W
White-winged Scoter   c
Surf Scoter   c
Black Scoter   W
Ruddy Duck   c W
Hooded Merganser
Goosander

Red-breasted Merganser   c W
Turkey Vulture   M
Bald Sea-Eagle
Northern Goshawk   r W
Sharp-shinned Sparrowhawk
Cooper's Sparrowhawk
Red-tailed Hawk
Rough-legged Buzzard   r W
Golden Eagle   r
Osprey   S
Merlin   W
American Kestrel   r
Blue Grouse
Ruffed Grouse
California Quail   c
Mountain Quail   r
Common Pheasant
Virginia Rail   r
Sora Crake   r S
American Coot   c
Black Oystercatcher
Semipalmated Plover   c M
Killdeer
Lesser Golden Plover   r M
Gray Plover   M
Surfbird   W
Ruddy Turnstone   M
Black Turnstone   c W
Common Snipe   c W
Whimbrel   M
Spotted Sandpiper
Wandering Tattler   c M
Greater Yellowlegs   M
Lesser Yellowlegs   M
Rock Sandpiper   c W
Least Sandpiper   c M
Dunlin   c W
Short-billed Dowitcher   M
Long-billed Dowitcher   r M
Western Sandpiper   c M
Sanderling   c W
Red Phalarope   M
Little Phalarope   M
Parasitic Jaeger   M
Glaucous-winged Gull   c
Western Gull   r W
Herring Gull   c W

Thayer's Gull   W
California Gull   c S
Mew Gull   c
Bonaparte's Gull   c M
Heermann's Gull   M
Black-legged Kittiwake   M
Sabine's Gull   r M
Common Tern   M
Arctic Tern   r M
Caspian Tern   r S
Common Murre   c
Pigeon Guillemot   c
Marbled Murrelet   c
Ancient Murrelet   W
Cassin's Auklet
Tufted Puffin
Band-tailed Pigeon   c
Rock Pigeon   c
Mourning Dove   r
Northern Screech-Owl
Northern Pygmy-Owl   r
Common Nighthawk   c S
American Black Swift   S
Vaux's Swift   S
Rufous Hummingbird   c S
Belted Kingfisher   c
Northern (Red-shafted) Flicker   c
Pileated Woodpecker
Yellow-bellied (Red-breasted)
  Sapsucker
Hairy Woodpecker   r
Downy Woodpecker   c
NorthernThree-toedWoodpecker   r
Eastern Kingbird   r S
Traill's Flycatcher   S
Western Flycatcher   c S
Western Pewee   r S
Olive-sided Pewee   S
Northern Skylark
Horned Lark   r
Violet-green Swallow   c S
Tree Swallow   S
Rough-winged Swallow   r S
Barn Swallow   c S
Cliff Martin   c S
Purple Martin   S
Gray Jay

Steller's Jay   c
Northern Raven   c
Northwestern Crow   c
Clark's Nutcracker   r
Chestnut-backed Chickadee   c
Bushtit
Red-breasted Nuthatch
Northern Treecreeper
North American Dipper
House Wren   S
Northern Wren
Bewick's Wren
Long-billed Marsh Wren
American Robin   c
Varied Thrush
Hermit Thrush
Swainson's Thrush
Western Bluebird   r
Townsend's Solitaire   r W
Golden-crowned Kinglet   c
Ruby-crowned Kinglet   r
Water Pipit   c M
Cedar Waxwing   c
Great Gray Shrike   r W
European Starling   c
Crested Myna   r
Hutton's Vireo   r
Solitary Vireo   r S
Red-eyed Vireo   S
Warbling Vireo   S
Orange-crowned Warbler   c S
Yellow Warbler   c S
Yellow-rumped (Audubon's)
  Warbler   c S
Townsend's Warbler   c S
MacGillivray's Warbler   S
Northern Yellowthroat   S
Wilson's Warbler   c S
House Sparrow
Western Meadowlark
Red-winged Blackbird   c
Brewer's Blackbird   c
Brown-headed Cowbird   c S
Western Tanager   S
Black-headed Grosbeak   r S
Evening Grosbeak
Purple Finch   c

House Finch
Pine Siskin   c
American Goldfinch   c S
Red Crossbill
Rufous-sided Towhee   c
Savannah Sparrow   S

Northern Junco   c
Chipping Sparrow   S
White-crowned Sparrow   c
Golden-crowned Sparrow
Fox Sparrow
Song Sparrow   c

4

Bathurst Inlet,
Northwest Territories

FORMERLY A HUDSON'S BAY TRADING POST, this remote Arctic outpost is now a comfortable lodge, with hot and cold running water, showers, electricity, comfortable beds, a bar, and a restaurant. The inlet itself is 340 air miles (544 km) north of Yellowknife, Northwest Territories, and is 40 miles (64 km) north of the Arctic Circle. The area around the lodge is less swampy than Churchill, having more upland habitat — and thus fewer shorebirds. Well worth visiting (summer only), it is, as you might expect, a bit expensive. Visitors should note that with continual summer sun, sunburn lotions are useful. Although mosquitoes are scarce on breezy days, repellent is necessary for still days. The mushy walking conditions on the tundra make waterproof footwear requisite.

The magnificent Gyrfalcon usually has a nest in the vicinity and is seen regularly. Raptors, arctic mammals, and flowers are the high points of Bathurst. Barren ground caribou, barren ground grizzly bear, musk ox, arctic fox, arctic wolf, and ringed seal are the chief resident mammals. Glaucous Gull, Little Phalarope, Hoary Redpoll, Harris's Sparrow, and Lapland Longspur nest around the lodge. Loons, eiders, Long-tailed Duck and other seabirds are often seen in the bay, with Yellow-billed Loon a specialty.

Bathurst Inlet Lodge (Box 820, Yellowknife, Northwest Territories, Canada) offers package tours that include a round-trip charter flight from Yellowknife, rooms, all meals, boats, and services. Group birding tour packages are also available from both American and Canadian operators.

Yellowknife itself is served by aircraft from Calgary, Churchill, Edmonton, and Winnipeg. Tourists with time to stay a night or two at a hotel in Yellowknife can explore boreal forest and find some of the following subarctic birds: Red-necked and Horned Grebes, Black-throated Loon, Bald Sea-Eagle, Merlin, Lesser Yellowlegs, Mew Gull, Arctic and Caspian Terns, Tengmalm's Owl, Northern Hawk-Owl, Boreal Chickadee, Gray Jay, Bohemian Waxwing, and Lincoln's Sparrow.

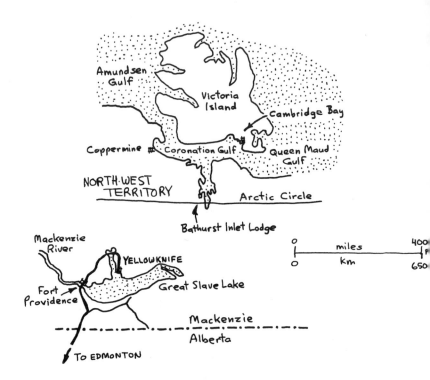

It is worth noting that Cambridge Bay, on Victoria Island (120 miles north of Bathurst Inlet), is now becoming a realistic destination, with a modest hotel and occasional scheduled flights from Yellowknife. This High Arctic site offers fine opportunities to see and photograph Buff-breasted Sandpiper, Red Phalarope, Sabine's Gull, and all three jaegers. It can sometimes be arranged in conjunction with a visit to Bathurst Inlet. Even a half-day stopover there is worthwhile.

CHECKLIST

Summer Birds of Bathurst Inlet

Common Loon r	Snow Goose r
Yellow-billed Loon c	Northern Pintail
Black-throated Loon c	American Wigeon r
Whistling Swan c	Green-winged Teal
Canada Goose	Greater Scaup r
Brent Goose r	Lesser Scaup r
White-fronted Goose r	Long-tailed Duck c

Common Eider
King Eider
White-winged Scoter
Black Scoter　r
Surf Scoter　r
Red-breasted Merganser　c
Rough-legged Buzzard
Red-tailed Hawk
Golden Eagle　c
Gyrfalcon
Peregrine Falcon　c
Rock Ptarmigan　r
Willow Ptarmigan
Sandhill Crane
Semipalmated Plover　c
Lesser Golden Plover　c
Gray Plover
Ruddy Turnstone　r
Common Snipe
Pectoral Sandpiper　r
White-rumped Sandpiper　r
Baird's Sandpiper　r
Spotted Sandpiper
Lesser Yellowlegs　r
Stilt Sandpiper
Least Sandpiper　c
Semipalmated Sandpiper　c
Sanderling　r
Little Phalarope　c

Pomarine Jaeger　r
Parasitic Jaeger
Long-tailed Jaeger　r
Glaucous Gull　c
Herring Gull　c
Thayer's Gull　c
Sabine's Gull　r
Arctic Tern　r
Snowy Owl　r
Short-eared Owl　r
Horned Lark　c
Cliff Martin
Tree Swallow
Sand Martin
Northern Raven　c
American Robin
Gray-cheeked Thrush
Water Pipit　c
Yellow Warbler
Blackpoll Warbler　r
Common Redpoll
Hoary Redpoll　c
Savannah Sparrow　c
Winter Sparrow　c
Harris's Sparrow　c
White-crowned Sparrow　c
Lapland Longspur　c
Snow Bunting

5
Churchill, Manitoba

THE CHURCHILL AREA on the shores of Hudson's Bay is well-known to Canadian and American ornithologists as the closest and cheapest outpost to witness the tundra in all its glory. Transportation includes regular air service from Winnipeg and a 550-mile (880 km) train service from The Pas, but no through highway. Churchill, a deep-water maritime port for grain bound for Europe, has two hotels — the Polar (10 rooms) and the Hudson Hotel and Motel (34 rooms with dining room). Reservations for hotel space and for the few rental cars available should be made early.

Most birders visit Churchill in June and July. Snowstorms can continue into mid-June in bad years. Insects, particularly mosquitoes, get worse in July and August. There is a limited system of roads in the Churchill area. Waterproof footgear for walking across the soggy tundra is essential.

Cape Merry is a high ridge at the mouth of the Churchill River overlooking Churchill and Hudson's Bay. Seals and Beluga whales, as well as Black- and Red-throated Loons, Whistling Swan, sea ducks, jaegers, Arctic Tern, Common Redpoll, and Harris's Sparrow are often seen here. Rarities there may include Long-tailed Jaeger, Sabine's and Ross's Gulls. Several shallow ponds near the grain elevators are good for ducks, small gulls, and shorebirds, notably Stilt Sandpiper and Hudsonian Godwit. Goose Creek Road extends seven miles (11 km) south from the Eskimo village of Akudlik through dense larch and spruce woods, second-growth willows, and muskeg. The woods here are the best places to look for Spruce Grouse, Willow Ptarmigan, owls, Gray Jay, Boreal Chickadee, Gray-cheeked Thrush, warblers, and sparrows.

Landing Lake, three miles (5 km) south of the Trans-Air hangar, is a superb area of broken tundra with pools, spruce thickets, and moss tundra next to the lake. Whimbrel are abundant and the Bonaparte's Gull nests in the trees. Other birds here include Black-throated Loon, American Bittern, many ducks, shorebirds, and Rusty Blackbird.

The town dump, a mile (1.6 km) east of Fort Churchill, is the best place for larger gulls, particularly Thayer's and Glaucous. Short-eared Owl, Northern Harrier, and phalaropes are often found. Bird Cove and the start of the rocket range, about 10 miles (16 km) east, are characterized by barren ground tundra, where Lesser Golden Plover, Great Gray Shrike, and Smith's Longspur may be seen.

Twin Lakes, at the end of the road, located where tundra meets the stunted edge of the boreal forest, provide the best Hudsonian Godwit breeding area. Other specialties here are Merlin, Spruce Grouse, ptarmigan, Bohemian Waxwing, Orange-crowned Warbler, and Pine Grosbeak.

CHECKLIST

(May–September only; M = Migrant only, S = Summer status if different from migrant status)

Common Loon	Horned Grebe r
Black-throated Loon c	American Bittern
Red-throated Loon c	Whistling Swan

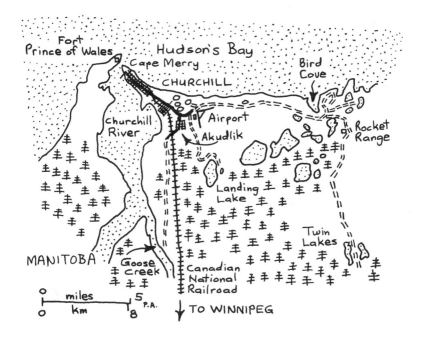

Canada Goose c
White-fronted Goose c M
Snow Goose c M, S
Mallard
American Black Duck
Northern Pintail c
Green-winged Teal c
Blue-winged Teal r
American Wigeon
Northern Shoveler
Greater Scaup c
Lesser Scaup r M
Common Goldeneye c
Bufflehead r
Long-tailed Duck c
Harlequin Duck r
Common Eider c
King Eider r
White-winged Scoter c
Surf Scoter
Black Scoter c
Goosander r
Red-breasted Merganser c
Rough-legged Buzzard
Northern Harrier c
Osprey r
Peregrine Falcon r M
Merlin
American Kestrel r
Spruce Grouse r
Willow Ptarmigan r M
Rock Ptarmigan r M
Whooping Crane r M
Sandhill Crane c M
Sora Crake
Yellow Crake
Semipalmated Plover c
Killdeer c
Lesser Golden Plover c
Gray Plover c M
Hudsonian Godwit c
Whimbrel c
Greater Yellowlegs r
Lesser Yellowlegs c
Solitary Sandpiper r
Ruddy Turnstone
Common Snipe c

Short-billed Dowitcher c
Red Knot r
Sanderling c M
Semipalmated Sandpiper c
Least Sandpiper c
White-rumped Sandpiper c M, r
 S
Baird's Sandpiper M
Pectoral Sandpiper c M
Dunlin c
Stilt Sandpiper c
Buff-breasted Sandpiper M
Red Phalarope r M
Little Phalarope c
Wilson's Phalarope r
Pomarine Jaeger r M
Parasitic Jaeger c
Long-tailed Jaeger M
Glaucous Gull
Kumlien's (Iceland) Gull
Great Black-backed Gull r
Lesser Black-backed Gull r M
Herring Gull c
Thayer's Gull c
Mew Gull r
Ring-billed Gull r
Bonaparte's Gull c
Ross's Gull r M
Sabine's Gull M
Arctic Tern c
Caspian Tern r
Snowy Owl r M
Northern Hawk-Owl r
Short-eared Owl c
Northern Flicker
Northern Three-toed Woodpecker r
Yellow-bellied Flycatcher r
Horned Lark c
Tree Swallow c
Sand Martin r
Barn Swallow r
Cliff Martin r
Gray Jay
Northern Raven c
American Crow
Boreal Chickadee r
American Robin c

Gray-cheeked Thrush
Ruby-crowned Kinglet
Water Pipit   c
Bohemian Waxwing
Great Gray Shrike
European Starling   c
Tennessee Warbler
Orange-crowned Warbler
Yellow Warbler   c
Yellow-rumped (Myrtle) Warbler
Blackpoll Warbler   c
Northern Waterthrush
Wilson's Warbler   r
House Sparrow
Western Meadowlark   r
Red-winged Blackbird   r
Rusty Blackbird   c

Pine Grosbeak   r
Hoary Redpoll   r
Common Redpoll   c
Savannah Sparrow   c
Northern (Slate-colored) Junco
Tree Sparrow   c
Harris's Sparrow   c
White-crowned Sparrow   c
White-throated Sparrow
Fox Sparrow
Lincoln's Sparrow   r
Swamp Sparrow   r
Song Sparrow   r
Lapland Longspur   c
Smith's Longspur   c
Snow Bunting   c M, r S

6

Point Pelee National Park, Ontario

ALTHOUGH POINT PELEE, situated on the north shore of Lake Erie, 35 miles (56 km) southeast of Windsor, Ontario (opposite Detroit, Michigan), is one of Canada's smallest national parks, it has outstanding attractions for visiting birders.

Within the mere six square miles (15.6 km^2) of the park is a diversity of environments, including 12 miles (19 km) of sandy beaches, a large freshwater marsh, and one of the few remaining Carolinian deciduous forests in Canada. The marsh is a migratory stopover for thousands of ducks, geese, and Whistling Swans. Nesting species include Least Bittern, Common and Black Terns, Common Gallinule, and rails. Many species of shorebirds can be seen on the beaches in spring and autumn.

An excellent place to observe shorebirds, gulls, and ducks is the tip of the point itself. Thousands of Red-breasted Mergansers winter here. In the Pelee woodland Orchard Oriole, Carolina Wren, Blue-gray Gnatcatcher and Yellow-breasted Chat nest in summer.

The park is open year-round, but the best birding time is during migration. In spring the period extends from March 15 to June 1, and in the autumn from August 15 to November 30. Over 100 species of birds can be seen in a day during the peak times in mid-May and mid-September.

There is a fine network of roads to the park. The nearest airport is in Windsor, Ontario. Motel accommodation is available in Leamington and other areas near the park.

CHECKLIST

Common Loon	M		Green Heron	S
Horned Grebe	c M		Great Egret	r M
Pied-billed Grebe	S		Black-crowned Night-Heron	c S
Double-crested Cormorant	M		Least Bittern	S
Great Blue Heron	M		American Bittern	S

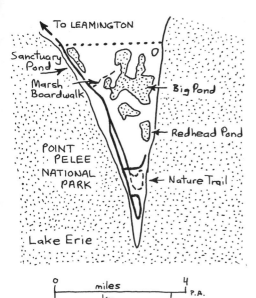

TO LEAMINGTON

Sanctuary Pond

Marsh Boardwalk

Big Pond

Redhead Pond

POINT PELEE NATIONAL PARK

Nature Trail

Lake Erie

miles

km

P.A.

Whistling Swan c M	Cooper's Sparrowhawk M
Canada Goose c M	Red-tailed Hawk
Mallard	Red-shouldered Hawk M
American Black Duck c	Broad-winged Hawk M
Gadwall M	Northern Harrier
Northern Pintail c M	American Kestrel S
Green-winged Teal c S	Northern Bobwhite r
American Wigeon c M	Common Pheasant c
Northern Shoveler M	Virginia Rail r S
Wood Duck c S	Sora Crake r S
Redhead M	Common Gallinule c S
Ring-necked Duck M	American Coot S
Canvasback M	Semipalmated Plover M
Greater Scaup M	Killdeer c S
Lesser Scaup M	Gray Plover M
Common Goldeneye c W	Ruddy Turnstone M
Bufflehead M	American Woodcock S
White-winged Scoter M	Common Snipe M
Surf Scoter M	Spotted Sandpiper S
Ruddy Duck M	Solitary Sandpiper M
Hooded Merganser M	Greater Yellowlegs M
Goosander c W	Lesser Yellowlegs M
Red-breasted Merganser c W	Pectoral Sandpiper M
Turkey Vulture r M	Least Sandpiper c M
Bald Sea-Eagle r	Dunlin M
Sharp-shinned Sparrowhawk c M	Short-billed Dowitcher M

Semipalmated Sandpiper   M
Sanderling   c M
Great Black-backed Gull   M
Herring Gull   c
Ring-billed Gull   c
Bonaparte's Gull   c W
Common Tern   c S
Caspian Tern   r S
Black Tern   c S
Rock Pigeon   c
Mourning Dove   c
Yellow-billed Cuckoo   S
Black-billed Cuckoo   S
Northern Screech-Owl
Great Horned Owl
Long-eared Owl   r W
Whip-poor-will   M
Common Nighthawk   S
Chimney Swift   c S
Ruby-throated Hummingbird   S
Belted Kingfisher   M
Northern (Yellow-shafted) Flicker
   S
Red-headed Woodpecker   S
Yellow-bellied Sapsucker   M
Hairy Woodpecker   M
Downy Woodpecker
Eastern Kingbird   c S
Great Crested Flycatcher   S
Eastern Phoebe   S
Yellow-bellied Flycatcher   M
Alder Flycatcher   S
Willow Flycatcher   r S
Wood Pewee   S
Horned Lark
Tree Swallow   c S
Sand Martin   S
Rough-winged Swallow   S
Barn Swallow   c S
Cliff Martin   S
Purple Martin   c S
Blue Jay
American Crow   c
Black-capped Chickadee
White-breasted Nuthatch
Red-breasted Nuthatch   M
Northern Treecreeper   W

House Wren   c S
Northern Wren   M
Carolina Wren   r S
Marsh Wren   c S
Sedge Wren   r S
Northern Mockingbird   r S
Gray Catbird   c S
Brown Thrasher   c S
American Robin   c S
Wood Thrush   S
Hermit Thrush   c M
Swainson's Thrush   c M
Gray-cheeked Thrush   r M
Veery   c M
Eastern Bluebird   M
Blue-gray Gnatcatcher   S
Golden-crowned Kinglet   W
Ruby-crowned Kinglet   c M
Water Pipit   M
Cedar Waxwing   S
Loggerhead Shrike   r M
European Starling
Yellow-throated Vireo   r M
Solitary Vireo   c M
Red-eyed Vireo   c S
Philadelphia Vireo   M
Warbling Vireo   S
Black-and-white Warbler   M
Prothonotary Warbler   r M
Golden-winged Warbler   r M
Blue-winged Warbler   r M
Tennessee Warbler   c M
Orange-crowned Warbler   r M
Nashville Warbler   c M
Northern Parula   M
Yellow Warbler   c S
Magnolia Warbler   c M
Cape May Warbler   M
Black-throated Blue Warbler   M
Yellow-rumped (Myrtle) Warbler
   c M
Black-throated Green Warbler   c
   M
Cerulean Warbler   r M
Blackburnian Warbler   M
Chestnut-sided Warbler   c M
Bay-breasted Warbler   c M

Blackpoll Warbler   c M
Pine Warbler   M
Palm Warbler   M
Ovenbird   M
Northern Waterthrush   M
Mourning Warbler   r M
Northern Yellowthroat   c S
Yellow-breasted Chat   S
Wilson's Warbler   M
Canada Warbler   M
American Redstart   c S
House Sparrow   c
Bobolink   S
Eastern Meadowlark   S
Red-winged Blackbird   c S
Orchard Oriole   S
Northern (Baltimore) Oriole   c S
Rusty Blackbird   M
Eastern Grackle   c S
Brown-headed Cowbird   c S
Scarlet Tanager   M
Rose-breasted Grosbeak   M
Indigo Bunting   c S

Evening Grosbeak   M
Purple Finch   M
Common Redpoll   W
Pine Siskin   r M
American Goldfinch   c
Rufous-sided Towhee   M
Savannah Sparrow   S
Grasshopper Sparrow   r M
Henslow's Sparrow   r M
Vesper Sparrow   M
Northern (Slate-colored) Junco   c W
Winter Sparrow   c W
Chipping Sparrow   c S
Clay-colored Sparrow   M
Field Sparrow   c S
White-crowned Sparrow   M
White-throated Sparrow   c M
Fox Sparrow   M
Lincoln's Sparrow   M
Swamp Sparrow   S
Song Sparrow   c S
Snow Bunting   W

7
Boston — New York — Washington, D.C.

THE NORTHEASTERN UNITED STATES, with the possible exception of Britain, is home to more birders than any other part of the world. Despite huge residential and industrial pressure, numerous forests, beaches, marshes, mountains, and migration "traps" can be reached within a few hours' drive from each major city.

The refuges and points along the ocean are popular in winter due to massive winter waterfowl and gull concentrations. In the late spring, city parks and cemeteries with large plantings often have large migrant warbler waves (after southwest winds). In the summer many specialties can be found in the mountains and along the wilder barrier beaches. In the autumn visits to lonely promontories and offshore islands often produce excellent birding (after northwest winds).

The top birding area north of Boston is Newburyport Harbor and Plum Island (the Parker River National Wildlife Refuge [NWR]). The road flanking the south side of the harbor offers many vantage points to scan for ducks, shorebirds, gulls, and Snowy Owl. The same road crosses a bridge to Plum Island, with its extensive salt marshes and migration "traps."

Gloucester and Rockport occupy Cape Ann, a rocky promontory northeast of Boston, which features a circling shore road. This area is noted for loons, grebes, eiders, alcids, Black-legged Kittiwake, and Northern Gannet in winter, particularly after northeasterly storms.

Near Boston, the Mt. Auburn Cemetery in Cambridge (just west of Harvard University) is excellent during migration in May. The Drumlin Farm Sanctuary, 15 miles (24 km) northwest of Boston, is the headquarters of the Massachusetts Audubon Society — Lincoln, MA 01773; (617) 259-9500. It is served by the South Lincoln stop on the Boston and Maine Railroad and features typical woodland birds and an active winter bird-feeding operation. When in the area, dial (617) 259-8805 for the Voice of Audubon to find out where the rare birds are each day. In nearby Concord, the Great Meadows NWR preserves a freshwater marsh and riverine habitats.

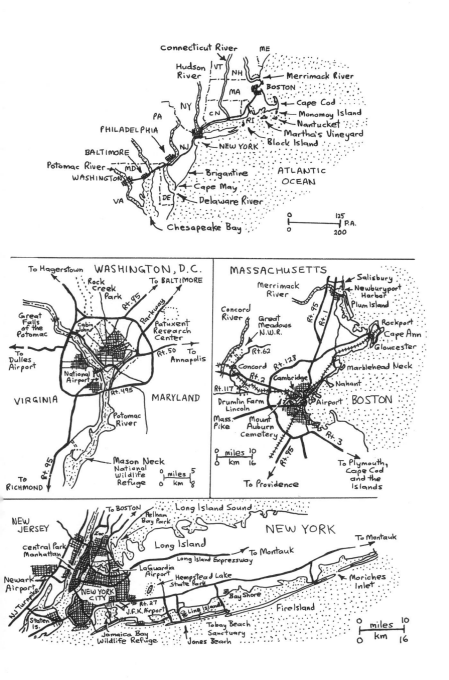

Plymouth Beach, an hour south of Boston, has a large colony of nesting terns, including Common, Arctic, Little, and Roseate. The Manomet Bird Observatory nearby has resident ornithologists and a large banding program.

Cape Cod is well-known for its late summer shorebirds (which include Hudsonian Godwit at the north end of Monomoy Island), autumn rarities, and massive wintering concentrations of Common Eider. A visit to the Wellfleet Bay Sanctuary in South Wellfleet provides good nature trails and birding tips. There is excellent ferry service from Woods Hole, Massachusetts, to the "birdy" islands of Nantucket and Martha's Vineyard, which, along with Block Island (off Rhode Island), are magnets for migrants in late summer and autumn. Hotels, rental cars, and bicycles are available on all three islands.

*

On Manhattan Island, the best birding is to be found in "The Ramble," in Central Park between 72nd and 79th Streets, opposite the American Museum of Natural History. During migration it is often alive with flycatchers, thrushes, vireos, warblers, and finches. In the Bronx visitors should see the World of Birds at the New York Zoological Gardens.

The National Audubon Society, with headquarters at 950 Third Avenue, NY 10022, is the home of *American Birds* magazine. This society and the Linnaean Society of New York offer a taped rare-bird alert — dial (212) 832-6523.

Jamaica Bay Wildlife Refuge (near JFK Airport) has many species of breeding herons, egrets, Glossy Ibis, ducks, terns, and Black Skimmer. Shorebirds are good from July through September. Open-country birds and waterfowl are present all winter. Located on the Cross Bay Boulevard, it can be reached via public transport on the IND Rockaway Line to Broad Channel, and then by walking north for one mile (1.6 km).

The south shore of Long Island, to the east, features many good birding spots such as Fire Island, Jones Beach, Moriches Inlet, and Montauk Point.

In New Jersey, to the south, the two best known areas are Brigantine NWR and Cape May — both famous for hawks, waterbirds, and migrants. Visitors can base at Atlantic City.

*

The shores of Chesapeake Bay and the Ocean City area of Maryland are attractive to wintering waterfowl and have a number of "southern" specialties breeding such as Swainson's, Yellow-throated, and Prothonotary Warblers.

In the vicinity of Washington, D.C., top spots to visit include Glover-Archbold Park (44th Street and Reservoir Road, NW), Dunbarton Oaks, and Montrose Parks in Georgetown, and the towpath along the C and O Canal in Maryland (Cabin John and Great Falls areas).

The Mason Neck NWR, 18 miles (29 km) from Washington on the Potomac River in Virginia, is a good place to see swans, ducks, and gamebirds.

The Patuxent Research Center, headquarters for many research activities for the U.S. Fish and Wildlife Service, is located in Maryland on Laurel–Bowie Road off State Route 197 and is open weekdays.

CHECKLIST

Common Loon   c W
Red-throated Loon   c W
Red-necked Grebe   r W
Horned Grebe   c W
Pied-billed Grebe
Cory's Shearwater   M
Greater Shearwater   M
Sooty Shearwater   M
Manx Shearwater   r S
Leach's Storm-Petrel   r S
Wilson's Storm-Petrel   c M
Northern Gannet   W
Great Cormorant   W
Double-crested Cormorant   c S
Great Blue Heron
Green Heron   c S
Little Blue Heron   S
Cattle Heron   S
Great Egret   S
Snowy Egret   S
Louisiana Heron   r S
Black-crowned Night-Heron   S
Yellow-crowned Night-Heron   r S
Least Bittern   r S
American Bittern   S
Glossy Ibis   S
Mute Swan
Whistling Swan   r W
Canada Goose   c

Brent Goose   W
Snow Goose   M
Mallard   c
Black Duck   c
Gadwall
Northern Pintail   M
Green-winged Teal   c M
Blue-winged Teal   c M
American Wigeon   c M
Northern Shoveler   r M
Wood Duck   c S
Redhead   W
Ring-necked Duck   M
Canvasback   W
Greater Scaup   c W
Lesser Scaup   c M
Common Goldeneye   c W
Barrow's Goldeneye   r W
Bufflehead   c W
Long-tailed Duck   W
Harlequin Duck   r W
Common Eider   c W
King Eider   r W
White-winged Scoter   c W
Surf Scoter   c W
Black Scoter   c W
Ruddy Duck   W, r S
Hooded Merganser   W
Goosander   W

Red-breasted Merganser   c W
Turkey Vulture   S
Black Vulture   r
Bald Sea-Eagle   r
Northern Goshawk   r
Sharp-shinned Sparrowhawk
Cooper's Sparrowhawk   r
Red-tailed Hawk   c
Red-shouldered Hawk   r
Broad-winged Hawk   c S
Rough-legged Buzzard   W
Northern Harrier   W
Osprey   S
Peregrine Falcon   M
Merlin   M
American Kestrel   c
Ruffed Grouse   r
Northern Bobwhite
Common Pheasant   c
Wild Turkey   r
King Rail   r S
Clapper Rail
Virginia Rail   S
Sora Crake   S
Common Gallinule   S
American Coot   c M
American Oystercatcher   r S
Semipalmated Plover   c M
Killdeer   c S
Piping Plover   r S
Lesser Golden Plover   M
Gray Plover   c M
Hudsonian Godwit   M
Whimbrel   M
Upland Sandpiper   r S
Greater Yellowlegs   c M
Lesser Yellowlegs   c M
Solitary Sandpiper   M
Willet   S
Spotted Sandpiper   S
Ruddy Turnstone   M
Wilson's Phalarope   r M
Little Phalarope   r M
Red Phalarope   r M
American Woodcock   S
Common Snipe   M
Short-billed Dowitcher   c M

Long-billed Dowitcher   M
Red Knot   M
Sanderling   c M
Semipalmated Sandpiper   c M
Western Sandpiper   c M
Least Sandpiper   c M
White-rumped Sandpiper   M
Baird's Sandpiper   r M
Pectoral Sandpiper   M
Purple Sandpiper   c W
Dunlin   c M
Stilt Sandpiper   M
Buff-breasted Sandpiper   r M
Ruff   r M
Pomarine Jaeger   M
Parasitic Jaeger   M
Great Skua   r W
Glaucous Gull   r W
Iceland Gull   W
Lesser Black-backed Gull   r W
Great Black-backed Gull   c
Herring Gull   c
Ring-billed Gull   c
Black-headed Gull   r W
Laughing Gull   c S
Bonaparte's Gull   c W
Little Gull   r W
Black-legged Kittiwake   W
Forster's Tern   S
Common Tern   c S
Arctic Tern   r S
Roseate Tern   S
Little Tern   S
Royal Tern   S
Caspian Tern   r M
Black Tern   M
Black Skimmer   S   .
Razorbill   r W
Thick-billed Murre   r W
Artic Auklet
Black Guillemot   W
Rock Pigeon   c
Mourning Dove   c
Yellow-billed Cuckoo   S
Black-billed Cuckoo   S
Barn Owl   r
Northern Screech-Owl

Great Horned Owl
Snowy Owl   r W
Barred Owl
Long-eared Owl   r W
Short-eared Owl   r
Saw-whet Owl   r W
Chuck-will's-widow   r S
Whip-poor-will   S
Common Nighthawk   c S
Chimney Swift   c S
Ruby-throated Hummingbird   S
Belted Kingfisher
Northern (Yellow-shafted) Flicker
  c
Pileated Woodpecker   r
Red-bellied Woodpecker
Red-headed Woodpecker   r
Yellow-bellied Sapsucker   M
Hairy Woodpecker   c
Downy Woodpecker   c
Eastern Kingbird   c S
Great Crested Flycatcher   S
Eastern Phoebe
Yellow-bellied Flycatcher   r M
Acadian Flycatcher   S
Willow Flycatcher   S
Alder Flycatcher   r M
Least Flycatcher   S
Wood Pewee   S
Olive-sided Pewee   r M
Horned Lark
Tree Swallow   c S
Sand Martin   S
Rough-winged Swallow   S
Barn Swallow   c S
Cliff Martin   S
Purple Martin   S
Blue Jay   c
American Crow   c
Fish Crow
Black-capped Chickadee   c
Carolina Chickadee   c
  (New Jersey south)
Tufted Titmouse   c
White-breasted Nuthatch   c
Red-breasted Nuthatch   W
Northern Treecreeper   W

House Wren   c S
Northern Wren   r W
Carolina Wren
Marsh Wren   S
Sedge Wren   r S
Northern Mockingbird   c
Gray Catbird · c S
Brown Thrasher   c S
American Robin   c
Wood Thrush   c S
Hermit Thrush
Swainson's Thrush   M
Gray-cheeked Thrush   r M
Veery   S
Eastern Bluebird   r
Blue-gray Gnatcatcher   S
Golden-crowned Kinglet   W
Ruby-crowned Kinglet   c M
Water Pipit   M
Cedar Waxwing
Great Gray Shrike   r W
Loggerhead Shrike   r M
European Starling   c
White-eyed Vireo   S
Yellow-throated Vireo   S
Solitary Vireo   S
Philadelphia Vireo   r M
Red-eyed Vireo   c S
Warbling Vireo   S
Black-and-white Warbler   S
Prothonotary Warbler   S
Worm-eating Warbler   r S
Golden-winged Warbler   r S
Blue-winged Warbler   S
Tennessee Warbler   M
Orange-crowned Warbler   r M
Nashville Warbler   S
Northern Parula   S
Yellow Warbler   c S
Magnolia Warbler   c M
Cape May Warbler   M
Black-throated Blue Warbler   M
Yellow-rumped (Myrtle) Warbler
  W, c M
Black-throated Green Warbler   c
  S
Cerulean Warbler   r S

Blackburnian Warbler   M
Yellow-throated Warbler   S
Chestnut-sided Warbler   c S
Bay-breasted Warbler   M
Blackpoll Warbler   c M
Pine Warbler   S
Prairie Warbler   c S
Palm Warbler   c M
Ovenbird   c S
Northern Waterthrush   S
Louisiana Waterthrush   S
Kentucky Warbler   r S
Connecticut Warbler   r M
Mourning Warbler   r M
Northern Yellowthroat   c S
Yellow-breasted Chat   S
Hooded Warbler   S
Wilson's Warbler   M
Canada Warbler   M
American Redstart   c S
House Sparrow   c
Bobolink   S
Eastern Meadowlark
Red-winged Blackbird   c
Orchard Oriole   S
Northern (Baltimore) Oriole   c S
Rusty Blackbird   M
Eastern Grackle   c
Brown-headed Cowbird   c
Scarlet Tanager   c S
Summer Tanager   r S
Northern Cardinal   c
Rose-breasted Grosbeak   c S

Blue Grosbeak   r S
Indigo Bunting   c S
Dickcissel   r M
Evening Grosbeak   W
Purple Finch
House Finch
Common Redpoll   W
Pine Siskin   W
American Goldfinch   c
Red Crossbill   W
White-winged Crossbill   r W
Rufous-sided Towhee   c
Savannah Sparrow
Grasshopper Sparrow   r S
Henslow's Sparrow   r S
Sharp-tailed Sparrow
Seaside Sparrow
Vesper Sparrow   r S
Lark Sparrow   r M
Northern (Slate-colored) Junco   c
   W
Winter Sparrow   c W
Chipping Sparrow   c S
Clay-colored Sparrow   r M
Field Sparrow
White-crowned Sparrow   M
White-throated Sparrow   c W
Fox Sparrow   M
Lincoln's Sparrow   M
Swamp Sparrow
Song Sparrow   c
Lapland Longspur   W
Snow Bunting   W

8
Miami, Florida

THE EVERGLADES NATIONAL PARK is of great interest due to the abundance, variety, and tameness of its birdlife, particularly water-birds. Only a few hours' drive from Miami, the park can be reached by following U.S. Route 1, turning west just south of Homestead on State Route 27, and observing signs. A paved road runs through the park for 39 miles (62.4 km), ending at Flamingo on Florida Bay.

Several miles past the entrance is the Royal Palm area with palms, oaks, and ferns where Pileated Woodpeckers and other woodland birds can be seen. Nearby is Anhinga Trail, a boardwalk that passes over ponds, sawgrass, and shrubs, where there are excellent opportunities to photograph the very tame birds, which include Purple Gallinule, Anhinga, egrets, herons, White Ibis, and Limpkin.

Continuing toward Flamingo, the attractions are the Mangrove Trail and the numerous wintering waterfowl at West Lake. The Flamingo Lodge at Flamingo is a modern hotel with guided tours and wildlife programs. The many habitats near Flamingo provide chances to see Bald Sea-Eagle, Osprey, many shorebirds including Long-billed Curlew and Marbled Godwit, and passerines. At Bear Lake, several miles northwest, there are American White Pelican, many herons, Wood Stork, and Roseate Spoonbill. Boat trips can be arranged to Cuthbert Lake rookery from February to June. Swallow-tailed Kite are often seen along the main road from late winter to early fall. Everglades National Park offers comfortable birding in fall, winter, and early spring before the mosquitoes take over the summer air.

Numerous other areas in south Florida are attractive to birders. In the Homestead region there is a mass of roads around the farms, lakes, swamps, and pinelands, in which Smooth-billed Ani and many wintering western birds are found.

The Florida Keys are a chain of islands connected by bridges all the way to Key West. Key Largo, 51 miles (82 km) south of Miami, and Big Pine Key, 126 miles (200 km) south of Miami, are particularly attractive to bird watchers. White-crowned Pigeon are seen all year, and Black-whiskered Vireo and Gray Kingbird are common from April through October.

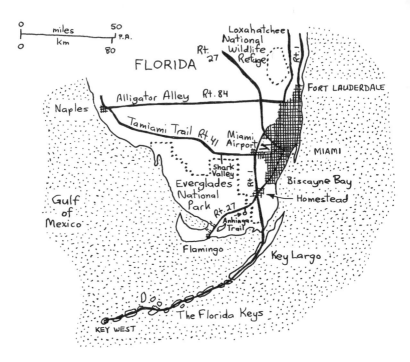

Miami itself is surprisingly rich in birds. The causeways to Miami Beach have numerous shorebirds, herons, terns, and ducks. Key Biscayne has Reddish Egret and Roseate Spoonbill at times. Greynolds Park, the University of Miami, and Parrot Jungle have most of the "garden" birds, including the introduced Spotted Oriole.

The Tamiami Trail (U.S. 41), a paved road running west through the Everglades, has bordering canals, with waterbirds in profusion and often a few Everglade Kites.

The kites and other forms of wildlife are best seen from the Shark Valley swamp tour organized by the National Park entrance station on U.S. 41. Loxahatchee NWR, 50 miles (80 km) from Miami, is rich in waterfowl and has a breeding population of Everglade Kite.

The Lake Okeechobee area has numerous back roads, along which birders may find Crested Caracara, Sandhill Crane, Burrowing Owl, and Scrub Jay.

The Dry Tortugas, a group of small islands 70 miles (112 km) west of Key West, have a summer breeding colony of Sooty Tern and Brown Noddy, with occasional Black Noddy, but there are no tourist accommodations. Visitors may charter boats themselves, join the occasional chartered boat party of birders, or fly over from the Key West Airport on a seaplane owned by Island City Flying Service.

CHECKLIST

Common Loon   W
Horned Grebe   W
Pied-billed Grebe   c
American White Pelican   c
Brown Pelican   c
Northern Gannet   W
Double-crested Cormorant   c
Anhinga   c
Magnificent Frigatebird
Great Blue Heron   c
Great Egret   c
Snowy Egret   c
Reddish Egret   r
Cattle Heron   c
Louisiana Heron   c
Little Blue Heron   c
Green Heron   c
Black-crowned Night-Heron
Yellow-crowned Night-Heron
American Bittern   r W
Least Bittern
Wood Stork   c
Glossy Ibis
White Ibis   c
Roseate Spoonbill
Mottled Duck   c
Gadwall   r W
Northern Pintail   W
American Wigeon   c W
Green-winged Teal   W
Blue-winged Teal   c W
Northern Shoveler   c W
Wood Duck   r
Ring-necked Duck   c W
Lesser Scaup   c W
Ruddy Duck   W
Hooded Merganser   W
Red-breasted Merganser   c W
Turkey Vulture   c
Black Vulture   c
Swallow-tailed Kite   c S
Everglade Kite
Bald Sea-Eagle   c

Sharp-shinned Sparrowhawk   W
Red-tailed Hawk
Red-shouldered Hawk   c
Broad-winged Hawk   W
Swainson's Hawk   W
Short-tailed Hawk   r
Northern Harrier   c W
Osprey   c
Crested Caracara   r
Peregrine Falcon   r W
Merlin   r W
American Kestrel   c
Northern Bobwhite   c
Wild Turkey   r
Sandhill Crane
Limpkin
King Rail
Clapper Rail
Sora Crake   W
Purple Gallinule   c
Common Gallinule   c
American Coot   c W, r S
American Oystercatcher   r
Semipalmated Plover   c W
Piping Plover   W
Snowy Plover   r
Wilson's Plover   c
Killdeer   c W, r S
Gray Plover   c W
Ruddy Turnstone   c W
Common Snipe   W
Long-billed Curlew   W
Whimbrel   r W
Upland Sandpiper   r M
Spotted Sandpiper   c W
Solitary Sandpiper   M
Willet   c W, S
Greater Yellowlegs   c W
Lesser Yellowlegs   c W
Red Knot   W
Pectoral Sandpiper   M
White-rumped Sandpiper   r M
Least Sandpiper   c W

Dunlin   c W
Short-billed Dowitcher   c W
Long-billed Dowitcher   M
Stilt Sandpiper   M
Semipalmated Sandpiper   c W
Western Sandpiper   c W
Marbled Godwit   W
Sanderling   c W
American Avocet   W
Black-necked Stilt   S
Herring Gull
Ring-billed Gull   W
Laughing Gull   c
Bonaparte's Gull   c W
Gull-billed Tern
Forster's Tern   c W, r S
Common Tern   W
Roseate Tern   r S
Little Tern   c S
Royal Tern   c
Sandwich Tern
Caspian Tern
Black Tern   M
Black Skimmer   c
White-crowned Pigeon
Rock Pigeon
White-winged Dove   r W
Mourning Dove   c
Common Ground-Dove   c
Mangrove Cuckoo   r
Yellow-billed Cuckoo   c S
Smooth-billed Ani
Barn Owl
Northern Screech-Owl
Great Horned Owl
Burrowing Owl
Barred Owl
Chuck-will's-widow
Whip-poor-will   W
Common Nighthawk   c S
Ruby-throated Hummingbird
Belted Kingfisher   c W
Northern (Yellow-shafted) Flicker
Pileated Woodpecker
Red-bellied Woodpecker   c
Red-headed Woodpecker   r
Yellow-bellied Sapsucker   c W

Hairy Woodpecker   r
Downy Woodpecker
Red-cockaded Woodpecker   r
Eastern Kingbird   c S
Gray Kingbird   c S
Western Kingbird   W
Scissor-tailed Flycatcher   W
Great Crested Flycatcher   c
Eastern Phoebe   c W
Empidonax, species   M, W
Wood Pewee   M
Tree Swallow   W
Sand Martin   M
Rough-winged Swallow   M
Barn Swallow   c M
Cliff Martin   M
Purple Martin   c S
Blue Jay   c
Scrub Jay
American Crow   c
Fish Crow
Tufted Titmouse   r
Brown-headed Nuthatch
House Wren   c W
Carolina Wren   c
Marsh Wren   W
Sedge Wren   W
Northern Mockingbird   c
Gray Catbird   c W
Brown Thrasher   W
American Robin   c W
Wood Thrush   r M
Hermit Thrush   W
Swainson's Thrush   r M
Gray-cheeked Thrush   r M
Veery   M
Eastern Bluebird
Blue-gray Gnatcatcher   c W
Ruby-crowned Kinglet   W
Cedar Waxwing   W
Loggerhead Shrike   c W
European Starling
White-eyed Vireo   c
Yellow-throated Vireo   W
Solitary Vireo   W
Black-whiskered Vireo   c S
Red-eyed Vireo   M

Black-and-white Warbler   W
Prothonotary Warbler   M
Worm-eating Warbler   W
Tennessee Warbler   M
Orange-crowned Warbler   W
Northern Parula   c   W
Yellow Warbler   S, r   W
Magnolia Warbler   r   W
Cape May Warbler   M, r   W
Black-throated Blue Warbler   M,
   r   W
Yellow-rumped (Myrtle) Warbler
   c   W
Black-throated Gray Warbler   r
   W
Black-throated Green Warbler   r
   W
Blackburnian Warbler   r   M
Yellow-throated Warbler
Chestnut-sided Warbler   r   M
Blackpoll Warbler   c   M (Spring)
Pine Warbler   c
Prairie Warbler   c
Palm Warbler   c   W
Ovenbird   W
Northern Waterthrush   W
Louisiana Waterthrush   M
Kentucky Warbler   r   M
Connecticut Warbler   r   M
Northern Yellowthroat   c
Yellow-breasted Chat   W
Hooded Warbler   M
Wilson's Warbler   M
American Redstart   W, c   M
House Sparrow   c

Bobolink   c   M
Eastern Meadowlark   c
Yellow-headed Blackbird   W
Red-winged Blackbird   c
Orchard Oriole   M
Spotted Oriole
Northern Oriole   W
Boat-tailed Grackle   c
Eastern Grackle   c
Brown-headed Cowbird   W
Western Tanager   r   W
Scarlet Tanager   M
Summer Tanager   M
Northern Cardinal   c
Rose-breasted Grosbeak   r   M
Blue Grosbeak   M
Indigo Bunting   W
Painted Bunting   W
American Goldfinch   W
Rufous-sided Towhee
Savannah Sparrow   c   W
Grasshopper Sparrow   W
Sharp-tailed Sparrow   W
Seaside Sparrow   r
Vesper Sparrow   r   W
Lark Sparrow   r   W
Bachman's Sparrow
Chipping Sparrow   W
Clay-colored Sparrow   r   W
Field Sparrow   W
White-throated Sparrow   r   W
Lincoln's Sparrow   W
Swamp Sparrow   c   W
Song Sparrow   r   W

9
Texas Coast

THIS SECTION BRINGS TOGETHER the highlights of a vast stretch of heavily birded areas from Houston all the way down to the subtropical Rio Grande Valley on the Mexican border. The checklist of birds that follows will aid visitors to most of the localities, although the abundance and seasonal symbols will not be entirely accurate for any one place.

The chief centers for arriving air passengers, each with rental car and motel facilities, are Houston, Austin, San Antonio, Corpus Christi, Harlingen, Brownsville, and McAllen. Birds are plentiful year-round, although most visiting birders come during March and April to catch the northward migrations of birds in breeding plumage and song, see the wildflowers, and avoid the summer heat. Advance reservations are useful in those months near birding hot spots such as High Island, Rockport, and McAllen.

Memorial Park, on the west side of Houston, has many woodland birds, including Pileated Woodpecker. Twenty miles (32 km) northeast of Houston there are trails through heavy forest and lakeshore at the Sheldon Reservoir Wildlife Management Area and at the south end of nearby Lake Houston. Ducks are a feature in winter, while in summer the area is home to Anhinga, Wood Duck, Purple Gallinule, and many warblers, including Prothonotary, Hooded, Kentucky, and Swainson's.

Jones State Forest, 35 miles (56 km) north of Houston (on Farm Road 1488, off Interstate 45), has Red-cockaded Woodpecker in old diseased pines (short-leafed and loblolly pines). Brown-headed Nuthatch, Chuck-will's-widow, Acadian Flycatcher, Pine Warbler, and Painted Bunting also breed here.

High Island is on the coast east of Houston. The Boy Scout Woods and Smith Woods here are small patches of trees surrounded by miles of salt marsh and prairies. Impressive numbers of migrant land birds swarm here in April if forced down by northerly winds. Vast numbers of Snow and other geese and ducks winter in nearby Anahuac NWR, in the heart of wet prairies and coastal marshes, along with Yellow and American Black Crakes.

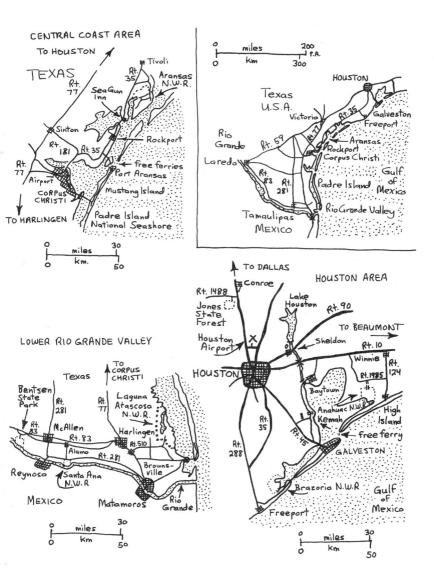

CENTRAL COAST AREA

To Houston

TEXAS

Tivoli

Rt. 35

Aransas N.W.R.

Rt. 77

SeaGun Inn

Sinton

Rockport

Rt. 181

Rt. 35

Rt. 77

Airport

free ferries

Port Aransas

CORPUS CHRISTI

Mustang Island

TO HARLINGEN

Padre Island National Seashore

miles

km.

30

50

miles

km

200

300

P.A.

HOUSTON

Texas U.S.A.

Victoria

Rt. 35

Galveston

Freeport

Rt. 77

Rt. 59

Aransas

Rockport

Corpus Christi

Rio Grande

Laredo

Rt. 83

Rt. 281

Padre Island

Gulf of Mexico

Rio Grande Valley

Tamaulipas MEXICO

LOWER RIO GRANDE VALLEY

Texas

TO CORPUS CHRISTI

Bentsen State Park

Rt. 281

Rt. 77

Laguna Atascosa N.W.R.

Rt. 83

McAllen

Rt. 83

Harlingen

Rt. 510

Alamo

Rt. 281

Brownsville

Reynosa

Santa Ana N.W.R.

MEXICO

Matamoros

Rio Grande

miles

km

30

50

TO DALLAS

Rt. 1488

Conroe

HOUSTON AREA

Jones State Forest

Lake Houston

Rt. 90

TO BEAUMONT

Houston Airport

Sheldon

Rt. 10

Winnie

Rt. 124

HOUSTON

Rt. 1985

Baytown

Rt. 35

Anahuac N.W.R.

Kemah

High Island

free ferry

Rt. 45

GALVESTON

Rt. 288

Brazoria N.W.R.

Gulf of Mexico

Freeport

miles

km

30

50

To the southeast of Houston, cars are permitted on the runway at Spaceland Airport, south of Kemah, up to an hour after dawn. Booming Greater Prairie Chickens can be seen here from January 1 through April.

Galveston Island is linked by bridge to Houston, and by ferry to points north and south on the coast. Migrant land birds drop into Kempner Park (which has Inca Dove), while migrant shorebirds are often abundant in the pastures and ponds on the southwestern end of the island.

The Sea-Gun Sports Inn (Route 1, Box 85, Rockport, TX 78382), just north of Rockport, is superbly situated for birders. The MV *Whooping Crane* (an excursion boat) makes half-day trips from the inn up to Aransas NWR, offering the best chances to see Whooping Crane (from mid-October until early April), as well as pelicans, Reddish Egret, American Oystercatcher, and Gull-billed Tern. Aransas NWR is an hour's drive north of Rockport. Visitors are restricted to their vehicles except at specified observation points. Sandhill and Whooping Cranes, Roseate Spoonbill, ibises, herons, egrets, waders, Wild Turkey, white-tailed deer, javelina, and armadillo are frequently seen.

Rockport, particularly the north end of Live Oak Peninsula (just south of the Sea-Gun), is another of Texas's famous March–April land bird traps. Look for WELCOME BIRD WATCHERS signs.

The Laguna Atascosa NWR east of Harlingen is worth visiting for coastal, prairie, and shore birding. Specialties here include White-tailed Kite, White-tailed Hawk, Botteri's and Cassin's Sparrows.

The McAllen area is a good base for visiting three famous birding areas where widespread Mexican birds have their only U.S. outposts.

Santa Ana NWR preserves 3.1 square miles (8 km²) of dry subtropical forest on the Rio Grande off U.S. Highway 281, 13 miles (21 km) southeast of McAllen. There are six miles (9.6 km) of roads, 12 miles (19 km) of footpaths, plus photoblinds, bird feeders, and ponds. Outstanding attractions include American Dabchick, Black-bellied Whistling-Duck, Plain Chachalaca (much tamer than in Mexico), Red-billed Pigeon, White-tipped Dove, Common Pauraque, Great Kiskadee, Green Jay, Long-billed Thrasher, Green-backed and Altamira Orioles, and Olive Sparrow.

Bentsen State Park, to the southwest of McAllen (five miles [8 km] from Mission on Route 2062), is similar to Santa Ana, but since it does not close at dusk, it is best for such nocturnal birds as nightjars and Elf Owl.

Falcon Dam State Park, 77 miles (132 km) west of McAllen, features xerophytic (desert) vegetation where Scaled Quail, Greater Roadrunner, Hooded Oriole, and Black-throated Sparrow can be seen. The dirt road downstream from the dam along the river sometimes has Green and Ringed Kingfishers.

The Golden-cheeked Warbler and Black-capped Vireo breed in the hills just west of Austin. The American Birding Association, a novel organization for active North American bird listers (tickers), is based here (PO Box 4335, Austin, TX 78765).

CHECKLIST

Common Loon W	Cinnamon Teal W
Black-necked Grebe c W	American Wigeon c W
American Dabchick r	Northern Shoveler c W
Pied-billed Grebe c	Wood Duck r
American White Pelican	Redhead c W
Brown Pelican	Ring-necked Duck W
Double-crested Cormorant c W	Canvasback W
Neotropic Cormorant	Lesser Scaup c W
Anhinga	Bufflehead W
Great Blue Heron c	Ruddy Duck W
Green Heron	Masked Duck r
Little Blue Heron	Hooded Merganser r W
Cattle Heron c	Red-breasted Merganser W
Reddish Egret	Turkey Vulture c
Great Egret c	Black Vulture c
Snowy Egret c	White-tailed Kite
Louisiana Heron c	Mississippi Kite M
Black-crowned Night-Heron	Bald Sea-Eagle W
Yellow-crowned Night-Heron r	Sharp-shinned Sparrowhawk W
Least Bittern r	Cooper's Sparrowhawk W
American Bittern r W	Red-tailed Hawk c W
Wood Stork S	Red-shouldered Hawk c W
White-faced Ibis	Broad-winged Hawk c M
White Ibis	Swainson's Hawk c M.
Roseate Spoonbill	White-tailed Hawk
Canada Goose c W	Harris's Hawk
White-fronted Goose c W	Northern Harrier c W
Snow Goose c W	Osprey M
Black-bellied Whistling-Duck	Crested Caracara
Fulvous Whistling-Duck r	American Kestrel c W
Mallard r W	Plain Chachalaca
Mottled Duck c	Greater Prairie Chicken
Gadwall c W	Northern Bobwhite
Northern Pintail c W	Scaled Quail
Green-winged Teal c W	Wild Turkey
Blue-winged Teal c	Whooping Crane W

Sandhill Crane   W
King Rail   r
Clapper Rail
Virginia Rail   r W
Sora Crake   W
Yellow Crake   r W
American Black Crake   r
Purple Gallinule   S
Common Gallinule
American Coot   c
Northern Jacana   r
American Oystercatcher   r
Semipalmated Plover   W
Piping Plover
Snowy Plover
Wilson's Plover
Killdeer   c
Lesser Golden Plover   M
Gray Plover   c W
Ruddy Turnstone   c W
Common Snipe   W
Long-billed Curlew   W
Whimbrel   M
Upland Sandpiper   M
Spotted Sandpiper   W
Solitary Sandpiper   M
Willet   c
Greater Yellowlegs   c W
Lesser Yellowlegs   W
Red Knot   W
Pectoral Sandpiper   M
White-rumped Sandpiper   c M
Baird's Sandpiper   r M
Least Sandpiper   c W
Dunlin   c W
Short-billed Dowitcher   c W
Long-billed Dowitcher   c W
Stilt Sandpiper   M
Semipalmated Sandpiper   W
Western Sandpiper   W
Buff-breasted Sandpiper   r M
Marbled Godwit   W
Hudsonian Godwit   r M
Sanderling   c W
American Avocet
Black-necked Stilt   c S
Wilson's Phalarope   M

Herring Gull   c W, r S
Ring-billed Gull   c W, r S
Laughing Gull   c
Franklin's Gull   c M
Bonaparte's Gull   r W
Gull-billed Tern
Forster's Tern   c
Common Tern   W
Little Tern   c S
Royal Tern   c
Sandwich Tern   S
Caspian Tern
Black Tern   c M
Black Skimmer   c S, r W
Red-billed Pigeon   r
Rock Pigeon   c
White-winged Dove   c S
Mourning Dove   c
Common Ground Dove
Inca Dove
White-tipped Dove
Yellow-billed Cuckoo   S
Greater Roadrunner
Groove-billed Ani
Barn Owl
Northern Screech-Owl
Great Horned Owl
Barred Owl   c
Elf Owl   r S
Chuck-will's widow   M
Whip-poor-will   M
Common Pauraque
Common Nighthawk   c S
Lesser Nighthawk   S
Chimney Swift   c S
Ruby-throated Hummingbird   c
   M
Black-chinned Hummingbird   M
Buff-bellied Hummingbird   S
Rufous Hummingbird   r W
Belted Kingfisher   W
Ringed Kingfisher   r
Green Kingfisher   r
Northern Flicker   c W
Pileated Woodpecker
Red-bellied Woodpecker
Golden-fronted Woodpecker   c

Red-headed Woodpecker   S
Yellow-bellied Sapsucker   W
Downy Woodpecker   r
Ladder-backed Woodpecker
Red-cockaded Woodpecker   r
Eastern Kingbird   c S
Tropical (Couch's) Kingbird
Western Kingbird   r S
Scissor-tailed Flycatcher   c S
Great Kiskadee
Great Crested Flycatcher   c S
Brown-crested Flycatcher   S
Eastern Phoebe   c W
Yellow-bellied Flycatcher   r M
Acadian Flycatcher   r S
Traill's Flycatcher   r M
Least Flycatcher   r M
Wood Pewee   S
Olive-sided Pewee   r M
Vermilion Flycatcher   r W
Horned Lark   c
Tree Swallow   c M, r W
Sand Martin   M
Rough-winged Swallow   M
Barn Swallow   c M, S
Cliff Martin   r S
Purple Martin   r S
Blue Jay   c
Green Jay   r
Chihuahuan Raven   r W
American Crow   c
Mexican Crow   r
Carolina Chickadee
Tufted (and Black-crested)
  Titmouse
Verdin
Brown-headed Nuthatch   r
Northern Treecreeper   r W
House Wren   r W
Bewick's Wren
Carolina Wren
Cactus Wren
Marsh Wren
Sedge Wren   W
Northern Mockingbird   c
Gray Catbird   M
Brown Thrasher   W

Long-billed Thrasher   r
Curve-billed Thrasher
American Robin   c W
Wood Thrush   S
Hermit Thrush   W
Swainson's Thrush   M
Gray-cheeked Thrush   r M
Veery   r M
Eastern Bluebird   r W
Blue-gray Gnatcatcher   c W
Golden-crowned Kinglet   r W
Ruby-crowned Kinglet   c W
Water Pipit   W
Sprague's Pipit   r W
Cedar Waxwing   W
Loggerhead Shrike   c
European Starling   c W
White-eyed Vireo
Bell's Vireo   r M
Yellow-throated Vireo   S
Solitary Vireo   W
Red-eyed Vireo   S
Philadelphia Vireo   r M
Warbling Vireo   r M
Black-and-white Warbler   r M
Worm-eating Warbler   r M
Prothonotary Warbler   S
Swainson's Warbler   r S
Golden-winged Warbler   r M
Blue-winged Warbler   r M
Tennessee Warbler   M
Orange-crowned Warbler   W
Nashville Warbler   M
Northern Parula   S
Tropical Parula   r
Yellow Warbler   M
Magnolia Warbler   M
Yellow-rumped (Myrtle) Warbler
Black-throated Green Warbler   M
Cerulean Warbler   r M
Blackburnian Warbler   M
Yellow-throated Warbler   r M
Chestnut-sided Warbler   M
Bay-breasted Warbler   M
Blackpoll Warbler   r M
Pine Warbler
Ovenbird   M

Northern Waterthrush   r M
Louisiana Waterthrush   r M
Kentucky Warbler   r S
Northern Yellowthroat
Yellow-breasted Chat   M
Hooded Warbler   S
Wilson's Warbler   M
Canada Warbler   M
American Redstart   c M
House Sparrow   c
Eastern Meadowlark   c
Western Meadowlark   r W
Yellow-headed Blackbird   r M
Red-winged Blackbird   c
Orchard Oriole   S
Green-backed Oriole   r
Hooded Oriole   S
Altamira Oriole
Northern Oriole   M
Rusty Blackbird   r W
Brewer's Blackbird   c W
Boat-tailed Grackle
Great-tailed Grackle   c
Eastern Grackle
Brown-headed Cowbird   c
Bronzed Cowbird
Scarlet Tanager   r M
Summer Tanager   W
Northern Cardinal   c
Pyrrhuloxia

Rose-breasted Grosbeak   M
Blue Grosbeak   S
Indigo Bunting   M
Painted Bunting   S
Dickcissel   S
White-collared Seedeater   r
Pine Siskin   r W
American Goldfinch   W
Olive Sparrow
Rufous-sided Towhee   r W
Savannah Sparrow   c W
Grasshopper Sparrow   r W
Le Conte's Sparrow   r W
Sharp-tailed Sparrow   r W
Seaside Sparrow
Vesper Sparrow   W
Lark Sparrow   W
Bachman's Sparrow   r
Botteri's Sparrow   r S
Cassin's Sparrow
Black-throated Sparrow   r
Northern Junco   r W
Chipping Sparrow   r W
Clay-colored Sparrow   M
Field Sparrow   r W
White-crowned Sparrow   r W
White-throated Sparrow   c W
Lincoln's Sparrow   W
Swamp Sparrow   W
Song Sparrow   r W

10
Yellowstone National Park, Wyoming

LOCATED IN NORTHWEST WYOMING on the Idaho-Montana border, the granddaddy of national parks still ranks with the best in the world for scenic attractions, size, and wildlife. Transportation and tourist facilities are abundant, with airports on all sides (West Yellowstone and Bozeman, Montana; Jackson and Cody, Wyoming) and motels at the park entrances — West Yellowstone, Silver Gate, Gardiner, and Cooke City. Within the park itself there are lodges, including the Mammoth Motor Inn, which is open all year round (seasons vary at other lodges). All are open from mid-June to early September, some from mid-May, some until mid-October. For latest details and for reservations write to the Yellowstone Park Company, Reservations Department, Yellowstone National Park, Wyoming 83020. There are ample campgrounds.

Lodgepole pine forests dominate the park at middle elevations, with meadows and sagebrush grassland in some areas. Elevations vary from 5000 to 11,360 feet (1524 to 3462 m) in the Absaroka Range. Yellowstone Lake is good for American White Pelican, Bald Sea-Eagle, Osprey, and gulls. The Yellowstone River flows northward from the lake through meadows where herons, shorebirds, and ducks can be seen including Cinnamon Teal and Barrow's Goldeneye. The canyon area is good for viewing Gray Jay, Pine Grosbeak, and woodpeckers.

The road from Tower Junction to Silver Gate provides access to ponds and winds up high into the hills. Trumpeter Swan, Ruddy Duck, Swainson's Hawk, Golden Eagle, and Yellow-headed Blackbird can be seen.

The Mammoth area near park headquarters is perhaps best for birds. The road north to Gardiner follows river valleys and is good for hawks, North American Dipper, Mountain Bluebird, Lazuli Bunting, and Green-tailed Towhee. The Upper Terrace Loop road to the southwest of Mammoth is also worth exploring. The trail from the New Highland Terrace parking lot passes through suitable habitat for Northern Raven, Clark's Nutcracker,

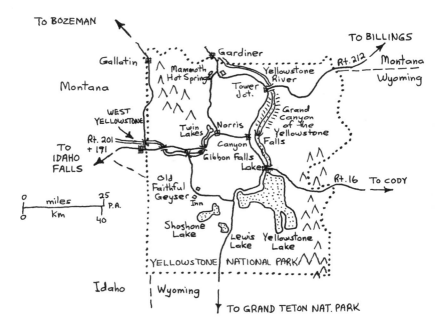

Mountain Chickadee, Townsend's Solitaire, and Cassin's Finch.

If you are driving from Mammoth to West Yellowstone you may find several good points for birds. On the Swan Lake flats there should be ducks, Wilson's Phalarope, and blackbirds. Around Twin Lakes, near Norris, Sandhill Crane are sometimes seen. Gibbon Falls area is good for Clark's Nutcracker and Western Tanager. The Madison River has occasional Trumpeter Swan.

There are three lodges at Old Faithful Geyser (May 15–October 15). Many birds can be seen in the vicinity although diligent searching is needed to find Ruffed Grouse, Northern Goshawk, and the rare Great Gray Owl.

During the winter only the north and northeast entrance roads are kept open.

CHECKLIST

Common Loon r S	Trumpeter Swan c
Black-necked Grebe c S	Canada Goose c
Pied-billed Grebe r S	Gadwall c
American White Pelican c S	Mallard c
Great Blue Heron c S	Northern Pintail c M
Whistling Swan c W	Green-winged Teal c

44

American Wigeon   c M
Northern Shoveler   r S
Redhead   M
Ring-necked Duck   r S
Canvasback   M
Greater Scaup   c W
Lesser Scaup   S
Common Goldeneye   c W
Barrow's Goldeneye   c
Bufflehead   r S, c W
Harlequin Duck   r
Ruddy Duck   s
Goosander   c
Bald Sea-Eagle   c
Northern Goshawk   r
Sharp-shinned Sparrowhawk   r
Cooper's Sparrowhawk   r
Northern Harrier   c S
Red-tailed Hawk   c S
Swainson's Hawk   c S
Rough-legged Buzzard   r
Golden Eagle   c
Osprey   c S
Peregrine Falcon   r S
American Kestrel   c S
Blue Grouse
Ruffed Grouse   r
Sandhill Crane   c S
Sora Crake   r S
American Coot   c S
Killdeer   c S
Common Snipe   S
Long-billed Curlew   r S
Spotted Sandpiper   c S
Solitary Sandpiper   M
Willet   r S
Greater Yellowlegs   M
Lesser Yellowlegs   M
Least Sandpiper   c M
Western Sandpiper   M
American Avocet   S
Wilson's Phalarope   S
California Gull   c S
Ring-billed Gull   S
Franklin's Gull   r S
Caspian Tern   r S
Black Tern   r S

Mourning Dove   S
Great Horned Owl
Great Gray Owl   r
Short-eared Owl   r
Saw-whet Owl   S
Common Nighthawk   r S
White-throated Swift   r S
Rufous Hummingbird   r S
Calliope Hummingbird   r S
Belted Kingfisher
Northern (Red-shafted) Flicker   c
Yellow-bellied Sapsucker   S
Williamson's Sapsucker   c S
Hairy Woodpecker   c
Downy Woodpecker   c
Black-backed Three-toed
   Woodpecker
Northern Three-toed Woodpecker
Eastern Kingbird   S
Western Kingbird   M
Say's Phoebe   S
Traill's Flycatcher   S
Hammond's Flycatcher   S
Dusky Flycatcher   S
Western Flycatcher   S
Western Pewee   S
Olive-sided Pewee   r S
Horned Lark
Violet-green Swallow   c S
Tree Swallow   c S
Sand Martin   c S
Barn Swallow   S
Cliff Martin   c S
Gray Jay   c
Steller's Jay   c
Black-billed Magpie   c
Northern Raven   c
American Crow   r
Clark's Nutcracker   c
Black-capped Chickadee
Mountain Chickadee   c
White-breasted Nuthatch
Red-breasted Nuthatch   c
North American Dipper   c
Northern Treecreeper
House Wren   c S
Rock Wren   S

Gray Catbird   r S
American Robin   c
Hermit Thrush   c S
Swainson's Thrush   S
Veery   r S
Mountain Bluebird   c S
Townsend's Solitaire   c
Ruby-crowned Kinglet   c S
Water Pipit   c S
Sprague's Pipit   c M
Bohemian Waxwing   c W
Great Gray Shrike   c W
European Starling
Warbling Vireo   c S
Yellow Warbler   c S
Yellow-rumped (Audubon's)
   Warbler   c S
Townsend's Warbler   S
McGillivray's Warbler   S
Northern Yellowthroat   S
Wilson's Warbler   c S
House Sparrow
Bobolink   S
Western Meadowlark   c
Yellow-headed Blackbird   S
Red-winged Blackbird   c S

Brewer's Blackbird   c
Brown-headed Cowbird
Western Tanager   c S
Evening Grosbeak   S
Cassin's Finch   c S
Pine Grosbeak
Gray-crowned Rosy-Finch   c W
Black Rosy-Finch   r S
Common Redpoll   W
Pine Siskin   c
American Goldfinch   S
Red Crossbill
White-winged Crossbill   r W
Green-tailed Towhee   S
Lark Bunting   S
Savannah Sparrow   c S
Vesper Sparrow   c S
Northern (Oregon) Junco   c
Winter Sparrow   W
Chipping Sparrow   c S
Brewer's Sparrow   c S
White-crowned Sparrow   c S
Lincoln's Sparrow   S
Song Sparrow   c
Snow Bunting   c W
Lapland Longspur   W

11
Bear River Refuge, Utah

THE BEAR RIVER MARSH AREA, perhaps the best known of all waterbird haunts in inland America, is a National Wildlife Refuge created in 1928 and covers 101 square miles (263 km²). The marshlands and lakes are impoundments created by damming the Bear River at its delta as it enters the Great Salt Lake. Most birders visit the marsh during the summer months in connection with visits to other national parks of the West, at which time up to sixty nesting species can be seen quite easily, many in large numbers. Canada Geese are common, as are Gadwall, Cinnamon Teal, Mallard, Northern Pintail, and Redhead. When one is driving the dykes and watching the marshes, islands, and alkali flats many western specialties can be seen, particularly during June and July. Highlights include Western Grebe, Snowy Egret, White-faced Ibis, Cinnamon Teal, Ruddy Duck, Long-billed Curlew, Willet, American Avocet, Black-necked Stilt, Wilson's Phalarope, California and Franklin's Gulls, Forster's, Caspian, and Black Terns, and Yellow-headed Blackbird.

Northern Pintail and Green-winged Teal are the most common in the fall, with large numbers of American Wigeon, Mallard, Redhead, and Northern Shoveler. Shorebirds are much commoner in the early autumn than in spring. The fabulous show of a million ducks converging here from the north begins in August and peaks in September. Unfortunately, parts of the refuge are open to hunting in the autumn, and cars are prohibited on the dykes at this season.

Whistling Swans are present through the late fall and winter, with numbers of up to 20,000. Bald Sea-Eagle, Golden Eagle, Canvasback, Bufflehead, and Common Goldeneye winter here. Other ducks linger into winter until heavy freezes occur.

The nearest town is Brigham City, which has several motels and can be easily reached by road from Salt Lake City. At refuge headquarters, located 15 miles (24 km) west on a paved road, there is a hundred-foot (30.5 m) tower that provides fine views of the refuge

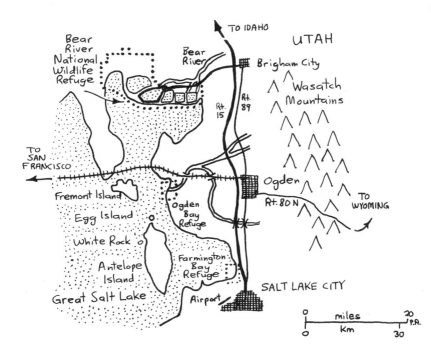

itself, the Promontory Mountains to the west, and the Wasatch Range to the east. Private cars are allowed to drive around Unit 2, a twelve-mile (19 km) circuit. Photography can be excellent on this route, and no special permits are needed.

CHECKLIST

Black-necked Grebe c M, r S	Gadwall c S
Western Grebe c S	Northern Pintail c S
Pied-billed Grebe c S	Green-winged Teal
American White Pelican c S	Blue-winged Teal c S
Double-crested Cormorant c S	Cinnamon Teal c S
Great Blue Heron c	American Wigeon c M
Cattle Heron r S	Northern Shoveler c S
Snowy Egret c S	Redhead c S
Black-crowned Night-Heron c S	Canvasback c M
American Bittern r S	Lesser Scaup c M
White-faced Ibis c S	Common Goldeneye c M
Whistling Swan c W	Barrow's Goldeneye r M
Canada Goose c M	Bufflehead c M
Snow Goose c M	Ruddy Duck c S
Mallard c	Goosander c M, r W

Red-breasted Merganser   M, r W
Turkey Vulture   r S
Bald Sea-Eagle   c W
Northern Harrier   c
Rough-legged Buzzard   c W
Ferruginous Buzzard   r
Golden Eagle   c W
Prairie Falcon   r
American Kestrel   r
Common Pheasant   c
American Coot   c
Semipalmated Plover   M
Snowy Plover   S
Killdeer   c S
Ruddy Turnstone   r M
Common Snipe   r S
Long-billed Curlew   c S
Spotted Sandpiper   c S
Willet   c S
Greater Yellowlegs   c M
Lesser Yellowlegs   c M
Baird's Sandpiper   c M
Least Sandpiper   c M
dowitcher, species   c M
Western Sandpiper   c M
Marbled Godwit   c M
American Avocet   c S
Black-necked Stilt   c S
Wilson's Phalarope   c S
Little Phalarope   c M
Herring Gull   r W
California Gull   c S
Ring-billed Gull   c W
Franklin's Gull   c S
Forster's Tern   c S
Caspian Tern   c S
Black Tern   c S
Mourning Dove   r S
Burrowing Owl   r S
Long-eared Owl   r S
Short-eared Owl   S

Northern (Red-shafted) Flicker   r
Eastern Kingbird   c S
Western Kingbird   c S
Horned Lark   c
Violet-green Swallow   c M
  (Spring)
Tree Swallow   c M (Spring)
Sand Martin   c S
Rough-winged Swallow   c M
Barn Swallow   c S
Cliff Martin   c S
Black-billed Magpie   c
Northern Raven   c
Marsh Wren   c S
Sage Thrasher   r S
American Robin   r S
Water Pipit   c
Loggerhead Shrike   r M
Starling   c
Nashville Warbler   r M
Yellow Warbler   c S
Yellow-rumped (Audubon's)
  Warbler   r S
MacGillivray's Warbler   r M
Wilson's Warbler   r M (fall)
House Sparrow   c
Western Meadowlark   c
Yellow-headed Blackbird   c S
Red-winged Blackbird   c
Brewer's Blackbird   c S
Brown-headed Cowbird   c S
Lazuli Bunting   r S
American Goldfinch   c W
Savannah Sparrow   c S
Vesper Sparrow   c M, r S
Lark Sparrow   c M
Sage Sparrow   r S
Northern Junco   c M, r W
White-crowned Sparrow   r W
Song Sparrow   r W

12

Tucson, Arizona

THE CHIEF BIRDING FAME of the Tucson area arises from the numerous birds typical of the Sierra Madre Occidental that have their northern limits in a half-dozen forested mountain ranges of southeastern Arizona.

Despite its 500,000 population, international airport, and urban sprawl, Tucson's residential areas, parks like Randolph, and the University of Arizona campus have many birds, of which Inca Dove, Black-chinned Hummingbird, Gila Woodpecker, Verdin, Cactus Wren, Curve-billed Thrasher, Northern Mockingbird, Northern Cardinal, and House Finch are characteristic species.

The nearby Saguaro National Monument — with two sections, one due east, another due west of Tucson — preserves fine desert flora, including extensive stands of the huge saguaro cactus. In the Monument and around the Arizona-Sonora Desert Museum (to the west) look for Gambel's Quail, Greater Roadrunner, Costa's Hummingbird (in red-flowering Ocotillo), Gilded Flicker, Gila Woodpecker, Brown-crested Flycatcher, Cactus Wren, and Black-throated Sparrow.

Sabino Canyon, an impressive gorge that has running water throughout the year, is about a half-hour's drive northeast of Tucson. Cottonwood and Sycamore trees line the bank, with riparian brush on the lower reaches. Elf Owl and Broad-billed Hummingbird are present in summer, North American Dipper in winter. Residents include White-throated Swift, Black Phoebe, Canyon and Rock Wrens, Phainopepla, and Abert's Towhee. There is a new shuttle bus service into the canyon.

To the northwest of Tucson on the Interstate Highway toward Phoenix, there are two ponds to the west of the road (one at Ruthrauff Road, the other at Ina Road). Although they are part of the water and sewage systems of the city, they often attract interesting waterbirds on migration and in winter. Grebes, ducks (including Redhead and Canvasback), shorebirds, Wilson's Phalarope, and gulls may be seen. Along Ina Road east of the freeway the Bendire's Thrasher may be found.

Southwest of Tucson on the San Xavier Indian Reservation is the

famous San Xavier Mission. The edges of fields and brush nearby are good for White-winged Dove, Vermilion Flycatcher, Verdin, Crissal Thrasher, Black-tailed Gnatcatcher, and Abert's Towhee.

Madera Canyon is located about halfway to the Mexican border in the Santa Rita Mountains, which, like all the other ranges, are part of the Coronado National Forest. Here desert vegetation is left behind and replaced by oak and pines. Several trails lead high into the mountains from the end of the road. Most birds can be seen within the first mile of the trail or along the paved road near the Santa Rita Lodge, which has several active hummingbird feeders. Some of Arizona's best birds can be found here between April and October, including Zone-tailed Hawk, Whiskered Owl, Elf Owl, many hummingbirds, Elegant Trogon, Sulfur-bellied Flycatcher, Dusky-capped Flycatcher, Mexican Jay, Bridled Titmouse, Red-faced Warbler, Painted Whitestart, Hepatic Tanager, and Yellow-eyed Junco.

Mt. Lemmon, in the Santa Catalina range just north of Tucson, is the only mountain with a paved road right to the top, through the life zones. For those wishing to stay at 9000 feet (2744 m), a hotel is near the top in heavy pine and fir forest. Although there are few birds in winter, in late spring and summer they abound. Look for Zone-tailed Hawk, Golden Eagle, Band-tailed Pigeon, Flammulated Scops-Owl (commonly heard at night), Coues's Pewee, Steller's Jay, Mountain Chickadee, Virginia's, Olive, and Red-faced Warblers. In late summer and early fall the mountain tops are rich with migrant Rufous Hummingbird, Hermit, Townsend's, and MacGillivray's Warblers.

The Sonoita grasslands (an hour's drive southeast of Tucson) are traversed by several paved roads. Swainson's Hawk can be seen in summer and in winter there are numerous sparrows and longspurs. Eastern Bluebird and Eastern Meadowlark have isolated populations here.

Sonoita Creek Sanctuary contains a cottonwood forest along a permanent stream just west of the town of Patagonia, which has a hotel and some expensive guest ranches. The unpaved road on the north side of the stream offers good access. Specialties here in spring and summer include Gray Hawk, Lesser Black Hawk, Broad-billed Hummingbird, Rose-throated Becard, Thick-billed Kingbird, Northern Beardless Tyrannulet, Lucy's Warbler, Summer Tanager, Varied Bunting, and Five-striped Sparrow.

The hummingbird feeders in Ramsey Canyon in the Huachuca Mountains south of Sierra Vista (which has motels) are well known and attract up to ten species of hummingbirds, including Rivoli's and Blue-throated, and Painted Whitestart, Arizona Woodpecker, and other mountain birds also occur. The Mile-Hi Lodge and the upper canyon have been purchased by the Nature Conservancy.

The Chiricahua Mountains are the most easterly and well worth visiting. The Southwestern Research Station and some guest cottages in Cave Creek allow birders to stay overnight to search for Elegant Trogon and hummingbirds near the creek. A dirt road goes high into the mountains to Rustler Park where Wild Turkey and Mexican Chickadee occur.

Willcox Lake on the Twin Lakes Golf Club near Willcox, 90 miles (144 km) east of Tucson, features breeding Snowy Plover, American Avocet, and a race of the Mallard known as Mexican Duck. Sandhill Cranes winter in the valley from Willcox south to Kansas Settlement.

The intensity of Tucson's two rainy seasons, one in winter and another in summer, governs the flowers that follow and some of the birdlife.

CHECKLIST

Black-necked Grebe W	Black-bellied Whistling-Duck r S
Pied-billed Grebe c W	Mallard
Double-crested Cormorant r W	Gadwall c W
Great Blue Heron W	Northern Pintail W
Green Heron	Green-winged Teal c S
White-faced Ibis r M	Blue-winged Teal r W

Cinnamon Teal   W
American Wigeon   c W
Northern Shoveler   W
Redhead   W
Ring-necked Duck   c W
Canvasback   W
Lesser Scaup   c W
Bufflehead   r W
Ruddy Duck   c W
Turkey Vulture   c S
Black Vulture   r W
Northern Goshawk   r H
Sharp-shinned Sparrowhawk   r S
   H, c W
Cooper's Sparrowhawk   c
Red-tailed Hawk   c
Swainson's Hawk   c S
Zone-tailed Hawk   S H
Rough-legged Buzzard   r W
Ferruginous Buzzard   r W
Gray Hawk   S
Harris's Hawk   r
Lesser Black Hawk   r S
Golden Eagle
Northern Harrier   c W
Crested Caracara   r
Prairie Falcon   r
Peregrine Falcon   r W
Merlin   r W
American Kestrel   c
Scaled Quail
Gambel's Quail   c
Montezuma Quail   r H
Wild Turkey   H
Sandhill Crane   W
Sora Crake   W
Common Gallinule   r
American Coot   c
Killdeer   c
Snowy Plover   S
Common Snipe   c W
Spotted Sandpiper
Greater Yellowlegs   M
Long-billed Dowitcher   M
Least Sandpiper   W
Western Sandpiper   M
American Avocet   S

Black-necked Stilt   M
Wilson's Phalarope   M
Ring-billed Gull   r M
Bonaparte's Gull   r M
Black Tern   r M
Band-tailed Pigeon   S H
Rock Pigeon   c
White-winged Dove   c S, r W
Mourning Dove   c
Common Ground-Dove   c
Inca Dove   c
Yellow-billed Cuckoo   r S
Greater Roadrunner   c
Barn Owl
Northern Screech-Owl
Whiskered Screech-Owl   H
Flammulated Scops-Owl   H
Great Horned Owl
Northern Pygmy-Owl   r H
Ferruginous Pygmy-Owl   r
Elf Owl   c S
Burrowing Owl   r
Spotted Owl   r H
Whip-poor-will   c S, H
Western Poor-will   c S
Common Nighthawk   r S, H
Lesser Nighthawk   c S
White-throated Swift
Vaux's Swift   r M
Black-chinned Hummingbird   c S
Costa's Hummingbird   c S
Anna's Hummingbird   W
Broad-tailed Hummingbird   S H
Rufous Hummingbird   c M, H
Rivoli's Hummingbird   S H
Blue-throated Mountaingem   S H
Violet-crowned Hummingbird   r
   S, H
White-eared Hummingbird   r S,
   H
Broad-billed Hummingbird   c S
Elegant Trogon   S H
Belted Kingfisher   c W
Green Kingfisher   r
Northern (Red-shafted) Flicker   S
   H, W L
Northern (Gilded) Flicker   c

Gila Woodpecker   c
Acorn Woodpecker   c H
Lewis's Woodpecker   r W
Yellow-bellied Sapsucker   c W
Williamson's Sapsucker   r W, H
Hairy Woodpecker   H
Ladder-backed Woodpecker   c
Arizona Woodpecker   H
Rose-throated Becard   r S
Thick-billed Kingbird   r S
Tropical Kingbird   r S
Western Kingbird   c S
Cassin's Kingbird   c S
Sulfur-bellied Flycatcher   S H
Brown-crested Flycatcher   c S
Ash-throated Flycatcher   c S
Dusky-capped Flycatcher   c S, H
Black Phoebe   c
Say's Phoebe   c
Willow Flycatcher   r S
Hammond's Flycatcher   c M
Dusky Flycatcher   c M, r W
Western Flycatcher   c S H
Gray Flycatcher   W
Buff-breasted Flycatcher   r S
Coues's Pewee   c S H
Western Pewee   c S, H
Olive-sided Pewee   r M
Vermilion Flycatcher   c
Northern Beardless Tyrannulet   S,
   r W
Horned Lark   c
Violet-green Swallow   c S, c M
Tree Swallow   c M
Sand Martin   r M
Rough-winged Swallow   c S
Barn Swallow   c S
Cliff Martin   c S
Purple Martin   c S
Steller's Jay   c H
Scrub Jay   r H
Mexican Jay   c H
Northern Raven
Chihuahuan Raven   c
Mexican Chickadee
Mountain Chickadee
Plain Titmouse   r

Bridled Titmouse   c H
Verdin   c
Bushtit   c H
White-breasted Nuthatch   c
Red-breasted Nuthatch   r
Pygmy Nuthatch   c H
Northern Treecreeper
North American Dipper   r W
House Wren
Brown-throated Wren   H
Bewick's Wren   c
Cactus Wren   c
Canyon Wren   H
Rock Wren   c
Northern Mockingbird   c
Bendire's Thrasher   r S, c W
Curve-billed Thrasher   c
Crissal Thrasher
Sage Thrasher   r W
American Robin
Rufous-backed Thrush   r W
Hermit Thrush
Swainson's Thrush   r M
Eastern Bluebird
Western Bluebird
Mountain Bluebird   W
Townsend's Solitaire   W
Blue-gray Gnatcatcher   c
Black-tailed Gnatcatcher
Golden-crowned Kinglet   r H
Ruby-crowned Kinglet   c W, r S
   H
Water Pipit   c W
Sprague's Pipit   r W
Cedar Waxwing   W
Phainopepla   c
Loggerhead Shrike   c
European Starling   c
Hutton's Vireo   c
Bell's Vireo   c S
Gray Vireo   r S
Solitary Vireo   S H
Warbling Vireo   S
Orange-crowned Warbler   c M, r
   W
Nashville Warbler   M
Virginia's Warbler   c S, H

Lucy's Warbler   c S
Olive Warbler   H
Yellow Warbler   c S
Yellow-rumped (Audubon's)
  Warbler   c W, c S H
Black-throated Gray Warbler   c S
  H, r W
Townsend's Warbler   c M, H
Hermit Warbler   c M, H
Grace's Warbler   c S, H
MacGillivray's Warbler   M
Northern Yellowthroat
Yellow-breasted Chat   S
Red-faced Warbler   S H
Wilson's Warbler   c M
American Redstart   r M
Painted Whitestart   c S, H
House Sparrow   c
Eastern Meadowlark   c
Western Meadowlark   c W
Yellow-headed Blackbird   W
Red-winged Blackbird   c
Hooded Oriole   c S
Scott's Oriole   c S
Northern (Bullock's) Oriole   c S
Brewer's Blackbird   c W
Great-tailed Grackle   c
Brown-headed Cowbird   c
Bronzed Cowbird
Western Tanager   c M; S H
Hepatic Tanager   S H
Summer Tanager   S
Northern Cardinal   c
Pyrrhuloxia   c
Rose-breasted Grosbeak   r M
Black-headed Grosbeak   c S, H
Blue Grosbeak   S
Lazuli Bunting   r W
Varied Bunting   r S

Evening Grosbeak   r H
Purple Finch   r W
Cassin's Finch   r W
House Finch   c
Pine Siskin   W
American Goldfinch   r W
Lesser Goldfinch
Lawrence's Goldfinch   r W
Red Crossbill   r W
Green-tailed Towhee   c W
Rufous-sided Towhee   S H, r W
Brown Towhee   c
Abert's Towhee   c
Lark Bunting   c W
Savannah Sparrow   W
Baird's Sparrow   r W
Grasshopper Sparrow
Vesper Sparrow   c W
Lark Sparrow   c
Five-striped Sparrow   r
Rufous-winged Sparrow   r
Rufous-crowned Sparrow
Botteri's Sparrow   r S
Cassin's Sparrow   r
Black-throated Sparrow   c
Sage Sparrow   r W
Northern (Oregon) Junco   c W
Gray-headed Junco   c W
Yellow-eyed Junco   c H
Chipping Sparrow   c
Brewer's Sparrow   c W
Black-chinned Sparrow   r
White-crowned Sparrow   c W
White-throated Sparrow   r W
Lincoln's Sparrow   c W
Song Sparrow
McCown's Longspur   r W
Chestnut-collared Longspur   W

13
Los Angeles, California

SOUTHERN CALIFORNIA is another extremely varied area with rich oceanic birding, high mountains, deserts, forests, cities, and grasslands. There is an abundance of literature on the area, and birders are constantly finding more and more rarities.

The city itself has some fine residential areas with extensive plantings attractive to birds. The mountains that separate the city from the San Fernando Valley still have wild areas. Griffith Park, just five miles (8 km) north of the city center, has chaparral-covered hillsides where California Quail, Anna's Hummingbird, Acorn and Nuttall's Woodpecker, Scrub Jay, Plain Titmouse, Bushtit, and Hutton's Vireo live. During migration look for Allen's and Rufous Hummingbirds, warblers, and Western Tanager.

Palos Verdes Peninsula west of Long Beach is good for cormorants and other seabirds. The lagoon and ocean front at Newport Beach has a variety of waterbirds.

The Tucker Bird Sanctuary lies in the mountains east of Santa Ana, south of Silverado off Route S18. Anna's, Black-chinned, Rufous, and Allen's Hummingbirds are common with peak abundance in late July and August.

High mountain birds can be found easily in many of the ranges. The Angeles Crest Drive in the San Gabriel Mountains starts at La Canada on Highway 2. Some 12 miles (19 km) up, at Switser's Camp in oak, sycamore, and spruce forest, Band-tailed Pigeon, woodpeckers, jays, wrens, nuthatches, and Western Bluebirds are found. Whiteheaded Woodpeckers occur in the pines and cedars of Charlton Flats, 35 miles (56 km) from La Canada. Three miles (4.8 km) on, at Chilao Reservation area (5200 feet), there may be Calliope Hummingbird and Lawrence's Goldfinch. The Buckthorn Flats area at 6500 feet (1981 m) is in white fir country and should be checked for Williamson's Sapsucker, Clark's Nutcracker, Olive-sided Pewee, and Green-tailed Towhee. Campers may find Western Poor-will and Flammulated Scops-Owl.

Although California Condors are difficult to see, there are three sites for those wishing to try: One is Mt. Pinos, about 75 miles (120 km) north of Los Angeles off Interstate Highway 5. Take the Frazer Park turnoff in Tejon Pass and follow the Mt. Pinos Road to its end at a large parking lot. Immediately before reaching the parking lot take the 1 mile (1.6 km) dirt road left to the west end of the summit of Mt. Pinos which is 8831 feet (2774 m) high. The optimum months are July through September. If you miss condors at Mt. Pinos, return to Interstate 5 and travel north 9 miles (14.4 km) to the Grapevine Exit and turn east for 6 miles to the Edmonston Pump Station's observation platform. California Condor, Golden Eagle, and Prairie Falcon occur with many Red-tailed Hawks.

The Sespe Condor Sanctuary is the best winter site for condors. Follow Highway 126 to Fillmore. Go north on A street in Fillmore for 3 miles (4.8 km), and take a right on a dirt road to Dough Flats, which is a rough one-hour (15 miles, 24 km) trip. Try to be there before 9:30 A.M. Note that this rocky road is often impassable during and after the winter rains.

CHECKLIST

Common Loon   W
Black-throated Loon   W
Red-throated Loon   W
Horned Grebe   r W
Black-necked Grebe   c W
Western Grebe   W
Pied-billed Grebe   c
Black-footed Albatross   r S
Northern Fulmar   r M
Pink-footed Shearwater   C
Sooty Shearwater   c S
Manx Shearwater   S
Leach's Storm-Petrel   M
Ashy Storm-Petrel   M
Black Storm-Petrel   c S
American White Pelican   r W
Brown Pelican   c
Double-crested Cormorant   c
Brandt's Cormorant   c
Pelagic Cormorant   c
Great Blue Heron   c
Green Heron
Great Egret   c
Snowy Egret   c
Black-crowned Night-Heron
Least Bittern   r S
American Bittern   r
Canada Goose   r W
Brent Goose   W
Mallard
Gadwall   W
Northern Pintail   c W
Green-winged Teal   c W
Cinnamon Teal
American Wigeon   c W
Northern Shoveler   c W
Redhead   W
Ring-necked Duck   W
Canvasback   W
Lesser Scaup   c W
Common Goldeneye   r W
Bufflehead   W
White-winged Scoter   W

Surf Scoter   W
Ruddy Duck   c
Red-breasted Merganser   c W
Turkey Vulture   c
California Condor   r H
White-tailed Kite
Sharp-shinned Sparrowhawk   W
Cooper's Sparrowhawk
Swainson's Hawk   r M
Red-tailed Hawk   c
Red-shouldered Hawk   r
Golden Eagle   H
Northern Harrier   c W
American Kestrel   c
California Quail   c
Mountain Quail   H
Common Pheasant
Clapper Rail
Virginia Rail   r
Sora Crake
Common Gallinule
American Coot   c
Black Oystercatcher   r
Semipalmated Plover   W
Snowy Plover
Killdeer . c
Mountain Plover   r W
Gray Plover   c W
Surfbird   W
Ruddy Turnstone   W
Black Turnstone   W
Common Snipe   W
Long-billed Curlew   c W
Whimbrel   c W
Spotted Sandpiper   c W
Wandering Tattler   r W
Willet   c
Greater Yellowlegs   c W
Lesser Yellowlegs   r M
Red Knot   r M
Least Sandpiper   c W
Dunlin   W
Short-billed Dowitcher   c M

Long-billed Dowitcher   c W
Western Sandpiper   c W
Marbled Godwit   c W
Sanderling   c W
American Avocet   c
Black-necked Stilt   c
Red Phalarope   c M
Wilson's Phalarope   c M
Little Phalarope   c M
Pomarine Jaeger   M
Parasitic Jaeger   M
Glaucous-winged Gull   r W
Western Gull   c
Herring Gull   c W
Thayer's Gull   r W
Ring-billed Gull   c
Mew Gull   r W
Bonaparte's Gull   c W
Heermann's Gull   c
Black-legged Kittiwake   r W
Sabine's Gull   M
Forster's Tern   c
Common Tern   c M
Arctic Tern   r M
Little Tern   S
Royal Tern   M
Elegant Tern   M
Caspian Tern   M
Black Tern   M
Xantus's Murrelet   r
Ancient Murrelet   r W
Cassin's Auklet
Band-tailed Pigeon   H
Rock Pigeon   c
Mourning Dove   c
Spotted Turtle-Dove
Greater Roadrunner
Barn Owl
Northern Screech-Owl
Flammulated Scops-Owl   r H
Great Horned Owl
Northern Pygmy-Owl   r H
Burrowing Owl
Short-eared Owl   r W
Western Poor-will   S
Common Nighthawk   S H
Lesser Nighthawk

Vaux's Swift   M
White-throated Swift
Black-chinned Hummingbird   c S
Anna's Hummingbird   c
Rufous Hummingbird   M
Allen's Hummingbird
Calliope Hummingbird   M H
Belted Kingfisher
Northern (Red-shafted) Flicker   c
Acorn Woodpecker   c
Yellow-bellied Sapsucker   H
Williamson's Sapsucker   r M
Hairy Woodpecker   H
Downy Woodpecker   r
Nuttall's Woodpecker   H
White-headed Woodpecker   H
Western Kingbird   c S
Cassin's Kingbird
Ash-throated Flycatcher   S
Black Phoebe
Say's Phoebe   W
Willow Flycatcher   r S
Dusky Flycatcher   S H
Western Flycatcher   S
Western Pewee   s H
Olive-sided Pewee   S H
Horned Lark   c
Violet-green Swallow   S H
Tree Swallow
Rough-winged Swallow   S
Barn Swallow   S
Cliff Martin   c S
Purple Martin   r S H
Steller's Jay   c H
Scrub Jay   c
Northern Raven   c
American Crow   c
Pinyon Jay   r H
Clark's Nutcracker   r H
Mountain Chickadee   c H
Plain Titmouse   c
Bushtit   c
White-breasted Nuthatch   H
Red-breasted Nuthatch   r H
Pygmy Nuthatch   c H
Northern Treecreeper   H
Wrentit

North American Dipper   r H
House Wren   c
Bewick's Wren
Marsh Wren
Canyon Wren
Rock Wren   r
Northern Mockingbird   c
California Thrasher
American Robin   c H
Hermit Thrush   W
Swainson's Thrush   S H
Western Bluebird   H
Mountain Bluebird   r H
Townsend's Solitaire   r H
Blue-gray Gnatcatcher
Ruby-crowned Kinglet   c W
Water Pipit   c W
Cedar Waxwing   W
Phainopepla
Loggerhead Shrike   c
European Starling   c
Hutton's Vireo
Bell's Vireo   S
Gray Vireo   r S
Solitary Vireo   S
Warbling Vireo   S
Orange-crowned Warbler
Nashville Warbler   c M
Yellow Warbler   c S
Yellow-rumped (Audubon's)
   Warbler   c W, S H
Black-throated Gray Warbler   S
Townsend's Warbler   M
Hermit Warbler   r M
MacGillivray's Warbler   r M
Northern Yellowthroat

Yellow-breasted Chat   r S
Wilson's Warbler
House Sparrow   c
Western Meadowlark   c
Yellow-headed Blackbird
Red-winged Blackbird   c
Tricolored Blackbird   r
Hooded Oriole   S
Northern (Bullock's) Oriole   S
Brewer's Blackbird   c
Brown-headed Cowbird   c
Western Tanager   S H
Black-headed Grosbeak   S
Blue Grosbeak   r S
Lazuli Bunting   S
Purple Finch   H
Cassin's Finch   H
House Finch   c
Pine Siskin   H
American Goldfinch
Lesser Goldfinch   c
Lawrence's Goldfinch   r
Green-tailed Towhee   H
Rufous-sided Towhee   c
Brown Towhee   c
Savannah Sparrow   r S, c W
Lark Sparrow   c W
Rufous-crowned Sparrow   r
Northern (Oregon) Junco   c H
Chipping Sparrow
Black-chinned Sparrow   r S
White-crowned Sparrow   c W
Golden-crowned Sparrow   W
Fox Sparrow   c H
Lincoln's Sparrow   H
Song Sparrow   c

14

San Francisco, California

ONE OF THE WORLD'S most attractive cities is also the hub of a great variety of bird habitats. The Pacific Ocean here is cold, often rough, and produces fog for much of the year. The fog, the winter rains, and a pleasant year-round climate have nurtured magnificent forests on the western face of the coast ranges. The coast redwood grows in great stands in Marin County (for example, Muir Woods), north of the Golden Gate Bridge, and in many places south of the city on the west side of the peninsula. The redwoods themselves have few birds, although the nearby forests of conifers, oaks, and others have Band-tailed Pigeon, Steller's Jay, Chestnut-backed Chickadee, Northern Treecreeper, and thrushes.

Golden Gate Park in San Francisco and the parks behind the University of California campus in Berkeley are good for many of the hummingbirds and passerines of the Bay Area.

Habitat for waterbirds in the Bay Area is under considerable pressure and is often difficult of access. Bolinas Lagoon, located in Marin County about 20 miles (32 km) from San Francisco, is a good spot. Adjacent is Audubon Canyon Ranch (Route 1, Stinson Beach), famous for its colony of Great Egrets and Great Blue Herons nesting high in the redwoods. The Point Reyes Bird Observatory (Box 321, Bolinas, CA 94924) is located nearby at the southern edge of the Point Reyes National Seashore. Tomales Bay, east of Inverness, is particularly good for wintering waterfowl. Point Reyes and Drake's beaches are good for oceanic birds in late summer and fall.

The Monterey Peninsula is a superb area for birds and includes the well-known Carmel and Pebble Beach. Some birds of the drier interior of California, such as Yellow-billed Magpie, are found nearby. The chief attractions are the many seabirds in Monterey Harbor, particularly in winter. Pelagic boat trips are arranged regularly for birders, although visiting birders often arrange to join a deep-sea sports fishing boat here (or at Santa Cruz or San Francisco). Take your seasick remedies and be prepared for spectacular numbers of shearwaters in summer and fall. September and October offer the best variety, although Black-footed Albatross are more common in summer. The

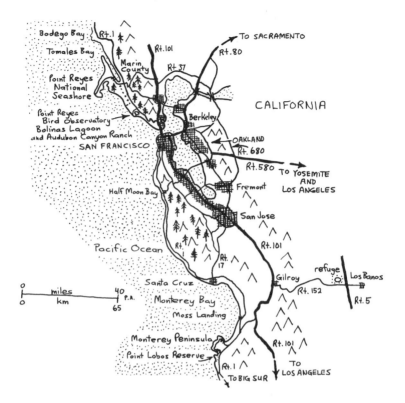

17-mile (27.2 km) drive around the peninsula is good for Black Oyster-catcher and other rock shorebirds.

Point Lobos State Reserve has stands of Monterey and Gowen cypress and Monterey pine where Wrentit and Chestnut-backed Chickadee can be seen. Sea otter, sea lion, killer whale, and harbor seal are often seen from shore. Brandt's and Pelagic Cormorants, Western Gull, and Brown Pelican often roost on Bird Rock. Point Lobos can be reached by car on Route 101, about 7 miles (11.2 km) south of Carmel.

Those with more time should consider visiting Yosemite National Park, a five-hour drive east of San Francisco. Located in the Sierra Nevada and famous for its high waterfalls, great sculptured peaks and domes, groves of giant sequoias, and boreal scenery, Yosemite has some birds of interest. Birders should try to arrange visits from late April until June, before the overcrowding begins. Facilities include fine hotels (such as the Ahwahnee and Yosemite Village), camp-grounds (reservations mandatory), and a new shuttle transportation system eliminating private vehicles from some popular roads.

Bridalveil Campground on Perigay Meadows off the Glacier Point road is home to the occasional Great Gray Owl, Black-backed Three-toed Woodpecker, and Pine Grosbeak. In the vast coniferous forests in the mountains of the park there are Blue Grouse, Williamson's Sapsucker, White-headed Woodpecker, Clark's Nutcracker, Mountain Chickadee, Pygmy Nuthatch, Mountain Bluebird, and Western Tanager. Steller's Jay is abundant near the hotels, and North American Dipper live on streams in Yosemite Valley.

Note: The following bird list does not include Yosemite National Park, and the central valley.

CHECKLIST

Common Loon c W	Green-winged Teal W
Black-throated Loon c W	Cinnamon Teal
Red-throated Loon c W	American Wigeon c W
Horned Grebe c W	Northern Shoveler c W
Black-necked Grebe c W	Redhead
Western Grebe c W	Ring-necked Duck r W
Pied-billed Grebe c W, r S	Canvasback W
Black-footed Albatross c S, r W	Greater Scaup c W
Northern Fulmar W	Lesser Scaup c W
Pink-footed Shearwater M	Common Goldeneye c W
Buller's Shearwater r M	Bufflehead c W
Sooty Shearwater c S, M	Harlequin Duck r W
Short-tailed Shearwater r M	White-winged Scoter c W
Ashy Storm-Petrel S	Surf Scoter c W
Black Storm-Petrel M	Black Scoter r W
American White Pelican W	Ruddy Duck c W, r S
Brown Pelican	Red-breasted Merganser c W
Double-crested Cormorant c	Turkey Vulture c
Brandt's Cormorant c	Sharp-shinned Sparrowhawk
Pelagic Cormorant c	Cooper's Sparrowhawk
Great Blue Heron c	Red-tailed Hawk c
Green Heron S	Red-shouldered Hawk r
Great Egret c	Swainson's Hawk S
Snowy Egret	Northern Harrier r W
Black-crowned Night-Heron	Peregrine Falcon r
Canada Goose W	American Kestrel
Brent Goose W	California Quail c
White-fronted Goose W	Virginia Rail r
Snow Goose W	Sora Crake r
Mallard	American Black Crake r
Gadwall W	American Coot c W, r S
Northern Pintail c W	Black Oystercatcher

Semipalmated Plover   M
Snowy Plover   r
Killdeer
Gray Plover   W
Surfbird   W
Ruddy Turnstone   M
Black Turnstone   W
Common Snipe   W
Long-billed Curlew   M
Whimbrel   M
Wandering Tattler   M
Willet   c
Greater Yellowlegs   M
Spotted Sandpiper
Least Sandpiper   c W
Dunlin   c W
Short-billed Dowitcher   r M
Long-billed Dowitcher   r M
Western Sandpiper   c W
Marbled Godwit   W
Sanderling   c W
Red Phalarope   M
Little Phalarope   M
American Avocet
Black-necked Stilt
Pomarine Jaeger   M
Parasitic Jaeger   M
Glaucous-winged Gull   c
Western Gull   c
Herring Gull   c W
California Gull   c W
Ring-billed Gull   W
Mew Gull   c W
Bonaparte's Gull   r W
Heermann's Gull   c W
Black-legged Kittiwake   r W
Sabine's Gull   r M
Forster's Tern   M
Common Tern   r M
Elegant Tern   r M
Caspian Tern   M
Common Murre   c
Pigeon Guillemot
Marbled Murrelet   r
Ancient Murrelet   W
Cassin's Auklet   c W
Rhinoceros Auklet   W

Tufted Puffin   r
Band-tailed Pigeon
Rock Pigeon   c
Mourning Dove
Barn Owl
Northern Screech-Owl
Great Horned Owl
Northern Pygmy-Owl
Spotted Owl   r
Saw-whet Owl
Western Poor-will   r S
Vaux's Swift   S
White-throated Swift
Anna's Hummingbird   c
Rufous Hummingbird   c M
Allen's Hummingbird   c S
Belted Kingfisher   c
Northern (Red-shafted) Flicker   c
Acorn Woodpecker   c
Yellow-bellied Sapsucker   r W
Hairy Woodpecker
Downy Woodpecker
Nuttall's Woodpecker   r
Black Phoebe   c
Say's Phoebe   W
Ash-throated Flycatcher   c S
Western Flycatcher   c S
Western Pewee   S
Olive-sided Pewee   S
Horned Lark
Violet-green Swallow   S
Tree Swallow   c S
Bank Swallow   r S
Rough-winged Swallow   S
Barn Swallow   S
Cliff Martin   c S
Purple Martin   r S
Steller's Jay   c
Scrub Jay   c
Yellow-billed Magpie   r
American Crow   c
Chestnut-backed Chickadee   c
Plain Titmouse
Bushtit   c
White-breasted Nuthatch
Red-breasted Nuthatch   r
Pygmy Nuthatch

64

Northern Treecreeper   c
Wrentit   c
House Wren   r
Northern Wren
Bewick's Wren   c
Marsh Wren
Northern Mockingbird   r
California Thrasher   r
American Robin   c
Varied Thrush   W
Hermit Thrush   c W, r S
Swainson's Thrush   c S
Western Bluebird   c
Golden-crowned Kinglet   W
Ruby-crowned Kinglet   c W
Water Pipit   W
Cedar Waxwing   W
Loggerhead Shrike   W, r S
European Starling   c
Hutton's Vireo   c
Warbling Vireo   S
Orange-crowned Warbler   c S, r
   W
Yellow Warbler   S
Yellow-rumped (Audubon's)
   Warbler   c W
Black-throated Gray Warbler   r S
Townsend's Warbler   W
Hermit Warbler   r
MacGillivray's Warbler   r S
Northern Yellowthroat

Wilson's Warbler   c S
House Sparrow   c
Western Meadowlark   c
Red-winged Blackbird   c
Tricolored Blackbird   W
Hooded Oriole   r S
Northern (Bullock's) Oriole   r S
Brewer's Blackbird   c
Brown-headed Cowbird   S, r W
Western Tanager   M
Black-headed Grosbeak   c S
Lazuli Bunting   S
Purple Finch
House Finch   c
Pine Siskin
American Goldfinch
Lesser Goldfinch
Rufous-sided Towhee   c
Brown Towhee   c
Savannah Sparrow   r S, c W
Grasshopper Sparrow   r S
Rufous-crowned Sparrow   r
Northern (Oregon) Junco   c
Chipping Sparrow   r S
Black-chinned Sparrow   r S
White-crowned Sparrow   c
Golden-crowned Sparrow   c W
Fox Sparrow   c W
Lincoln's Sparrow   r W
Song Sparrow   c

65

15
Hawaii

THE HAWAIIAN ISLANDS have a unique avifauna, with their endemic honeycreepers, other specialties, seabirds, and large numbers of introduced species. In Honolulu and around beach hotels on the outer islands there are seabirds and mainly introduced species. Airlines have frequent flights between the islands and to mainland United States and the western Pacific. Rental cars and four-wheel-drive vehicles are available at many locations.

Oahu, home island of much of the populace, and the main airport, has relatively few endemic birds but the largest variety of introduced ones. The grounds of the hotels on Waikiki Beach, Honolulu, and such places as the zoo, botanical gardens, Pearl Harbor, and the Diamond Head area are full of Indian Myna, Red-crested Cardinal, Spotted Turtle-Dove, and Peaceful Dove.

Outside of Honolulu is the Keaiwa Heiau State Park, above Aiea. Walking along the Aiea Trail in the park, visitors may see Elepaio, Amakihi, Apapane, Hwamei Laughing-Thrush, Shama, and Japanese Bush Warbler. To see oceanic birds on Oahu one must drive to Ulupau Head on the Kaneohe Military Base (an hour to the northeast of Honolulu via Route 61 or 63). The base usually accepts visitors (particularly on Saturdays), and the rocky promontory has a large nesting colony of Red-footed Boobies. Great Frigatebirds are often to be seen here, and one can catch glimpses of other species that nest on offshore islands. Permits and boats for visits to such islands as Moku Manu, Manana, and Popoia are difficult to arrange (inquire at the Bishop Museum in Honolulu). Wedge-tailed Shearwater, Christmas Shearwater, Bulwer's Petrel, boobies, Spectacled and Sooty Terns, Brown and Lesser Noddy breed on these islands.

Kauai is a large, very wet island west of Oahu. The airport and most hotels are located in the relatively dry southeast corner, around Lihue. Kokee State Park lies in the west beyond Wiamea Canyon, a dramatic gorge with White-tailed Tropicbirds. Although the park's forests can be worked into a day's trip from the coast, some visitors will want to stay at Kokee Lodge. Lunches are served to the public, but other meals must be prepared in the kitchenettes (reservations c/o PO Box

518, Kekaha, HI 96752). The maze of dirt roads and trails in Kokee are good for viewing Iiwi, Apapane, Elepaio, Amakihi, Hawaiian Creeper, Anianiau, Red Junglefowl, Shama, and Hwamei Laughing-Thrush. These, plus the Akepa, may be found on the trail east along the ridge from the last lookout on the Kalalau Valley Road. Hawaiian Duck may be found west of Kekaha on your return.

Hard-core birders will attempt to visit the Alakai Swamp in the highest part of Kauai. Here live some of the rarest birds such as the Small Kauai Thrush, Kauai Oo, Kauai Akialoa, Nukupuu, and Ou. Getting there is not easy. An elusive permit may now be required, you must rent an expensive helicopter at Lihue, and you should bring food and gear for the several days you are likely to be stranded. It is one of the wettest places in the world, with many hundreds of inches of rain. The area is so steep and slippery, with the lushest forest tangles and absolutely no facilities, that visits are discouraged.

Maui is located between Oahu and the island of Hawaii. Stilt and various shorebirds can be seen at the Kanaha ponds near the airport.

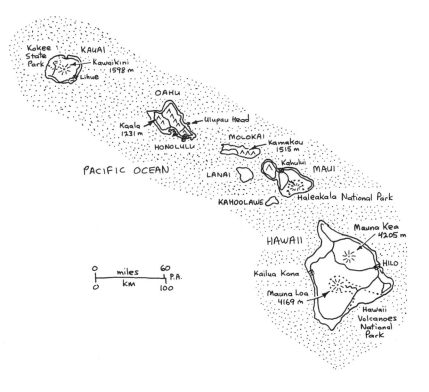

Hosmer Grove is a forested site on the road up to Haleakala National Park. Iiwi, Amakihi, and Apapane can be seen in the forest. Higher up in the grasslands look for Chukar and Northern Skylark. Horses can be rented to visit the crater where one can see the rare silversword plant, and look for Nene Goose. In the nearly inaccessible forests over on the eastern slope of Haleakala Crater live such rarities as Crested Honeycreeper and the recently discovered Poo-uli.

On the island of Hawaii there are two huge volcanoes. Mauna Loa dominates the Hawaii Volcanoes National Park, about an hour's drive south of Hilo. The Volcano House is a fine hotel located at 4000 feet (1220 m). Around the hotel and in the forests around the nearby Thurston Lava Tube look for Amakihi, Apapane, Iiwi, Japanese White-eye, Elepaio, Red-billed Leiothrox, and the highly local Hawaiian Thrush. Along the Mauna Loa Strip Road, which climbs up much higher, look for Nene Goose and Hawaiian Hawk.

The Palila occurs on the slopes of Mauna Kea about 9000 feet (2743 m), while the very endangered Hawaiian Crow is restricted to private ranches in the southwest. On the main road west from Hilo the Powerline Road veers southward toward Kulani. A four-wheel-drive vehicle or a hike of four miles takes you to patches of forest which have Akepa and Hawaiian Creeper.

CHECKLIST

(The checklist covers the four main islands only. Species restricted to one or more islands will be followed with these symbols: KA = Kauai, OA = Oahu, MA = Maui, and HA = Hawaii)

Black-footed Albatross   M
Laysan Albatross   r M
Wedge-tailed Shearwater
Sooty Shearwater   M
Christmas Shearwater   r
Manx (Newell's) Shearwater
Dark-rumped Petrel
Bulwer's Petrel
Band-rumped Storm-Petrel   r
Tristam's Storm-Petrel   r
White-tailed Tropicbird   c
Red-tailed Tropicbird
Masked Booby   r
Brown Booby   c
Red-footed Booby   c
Great Frigatebird   c

Cattle Heron
Black-crowned Night-Heron
Nene Goose   MA HA
Hawaiian Duck   KA
Northern Pintail   W
American Wigeon   W
Northern Shoveler   W
Hawaiian Hawk   HA
California Quail   MA, HA
Chukar   c MA, HA
Common Quail   r
Red Junglefowl   c KA
Common Pheasant
Indian Peafowl
Wild Turkey   HA
Common Gallinule   KA, OA

American Coot
Lesser Golden Plover   c W
Gray Plover   r W
Ruddy Turnstone   c W
Bristle-thighed Curlew   M
Wandering Tattler   W
Sharp-tailed Sandpiper   r M
Sanderling   W
Black-necked Stilt
Red Phalarope   r M
Pomarine Jaeger   c
Sooty Tern
Spectacled Tern
Brown Noddy
Lesser Noddy
Fairy Tern   r M
Rock Pigeon   c
Spotted Turtle-Dove   c
Peaceful Dove   c
Barn Owl   OA HA
Short-eared Owl
Northern Skylark   c
Hawaiian Crow   r HA
Varied Tit   r KA
Hwamei Laughing-Thrush   OA,
  KA
Red-billed Leiothrix   MA, HA
Red-vented Bulbul   OA
Northern Mockingbird   OA, HA
White-rumped Shama   KA, OA
Hawaiian Thrush   c HA, r KA

Small Kauai Thrush   r KA
Japanese Bush Warbler   OA
Elepaio   c KA, OA, c HA
Kauai Oo   r KA
Amakihi   c KA, MA, HA; r OA
Anianiau   KA
Hawaiian Creeper   r
Akepa   r KA, MA, HA
Kauai Akialoa   r KA
Poo-uli   r MA
Nukupuu   r KA, MA
Akiapolaau   r HA
Maui Parrotbill   r MA
Ou   r KA, MA
Palila   r HA
Apapane   c
Crested Honeycreeper   r MA
Iiwi   c KA, MA, HA; r OA
Indian Myna   c
Japanese White-eye   c
Western Meadowlark   c KA
Strawberry Finch   OA
Orange-cheeked Waxbill   OA
Spotted Munia   c
Black-headed Munia   OA
House Sparrow   c
Java Sparrow   OA
Northern Cardinal   c
Red-crested Cardinal   c OA, MA;
  r KA
House Finch   c

16
Mazatlan and San Blas, Mexico

MAZATLÁN IS A THRIVING BEACH RESORT on the Pacific coast of Mexico, just south of the Tropic of Cancer. The new airport is connected by frequent jets from Los Angeles, Tucson, Denver, Houston, and many Mexican cities. Inexpensive transportation is available in daily overnight train service from Nogales (south of Tucson, Arizona), and there are dozens of hotels in many price ranges.

The lagoons lining the paved road along the coast north of town are rich in resident and migratory waterbirds. Wave-washed rocky promontories often have Surfbird and Wandering Tattlers. The tropical deciduous forest on the extreme north edge has parrots, Gray Hawk, Magpie-Jay, Yellow Grosbeak, and occasional Lesser Roadrunner. Excursion boats can be rented at the "Star Fleet" on the sports fishing docks for an hour and a half cruise around the Dos Hermanos booby rocks. Here thousands of Brown Booby, dozens of Blue-footed Booby, Magnificent Frigatebird, and Brown Pelican can be seen. In winter there are usually a few Brandt's Cormorants as well.

The paved Durango Highway climbs the Sierra Madre Occidental from Villa Union (a half-hour south of Mazatlán, near the airport). This road climbs from seasonal tropical thorn forest up into pine-oak woodland and passes near some moist *barrancas* (canyons). This long excursion can be accomplished with an early departure from Mazatlán. Alternatively you may arrange to stay in the mountains at the small Hotel Villa Blanca, 46.3 miles (74 km) above Villa Union at Santa Lucia, in the pines (reservations: San Luis Potosi No. 1-B PTE, Mazatlán, Sinaloa [Tel. 2-16-28]). The general area has a number of mountain warblers, solitaires, and flycatchers, plus occasional flocks of the rare Thick-billed Parrot.

The Barranca Rancho Liebre is located 2 miles (3 km) west of El Palmito, Sinaloa, near the Durango border. There is a trail and a steep dirt road west off the highway which rises into pine-oaks, eventually reaching (within 1.2 miles [2 kilometers]) a steep canyon with subtropical broadleafs and sacred firs. This is the home of the rare Tufted

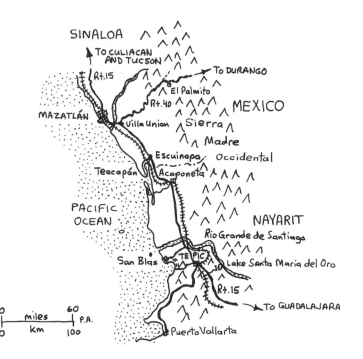

Jay, as well as such highland birds as Mountain Trogon, White-striped Woodcreeper, nightingale-thrushes, Red Warbler, and Slate-throated Whitestart.

The city of Tepic, at 3000 feet (915 m) is about a five hours' drive south of Mazatlán. The Mirador El Águila is a fine vantage point overlooking a large canyon (with a signpost on Highway 15, 7 miles [11.2 km] after the junction of the San Blas road). Here Military Macaws and other parrots can often be seen and heard in the morning and late afternoon. The Great Swallow-tailed Swift has been seen here. The Jalcocotán road from Tepic passes the slopes of Cerro San Juan, where broadleaf and coniferous forest patches mix in a bizarre intermingling of tropical and temperate birds. Lake Santa Maria del Oro is another fine side trip out of Tepic (an hour in the direction of Guadalajara). Western Grebe are resident on the lake, Great Swallow-tailed Swift are occasionally seen overhead, and many foothill birds live in the woods.

San Blas, on the Pacific west of Tepic, is a birder's mecca, with a variety of moderately comfortable hotels, such as Las Brisas, Casa Morales, and Bucanero. Here you can take boat trips with birder-trained boatmen up the Estero San Cristobel, a mangrove-lined river that eventually reaches open marshes that gradually dry up during the winter. Look for Boat-billed Heron, Bare-throated Tiger-Heron, Anhinga, Rufous-necked Wood-Rail, and Green Kingfisher among approximately 100 species you'll see. Another time, take an afternoon boat trip up to La Tovara Spring. After dusk and with strong flashlights, you may see a dozen or so Common Potoo as they sit on trees along the channel. Some dawn you may want to take a boat trip out in the ocean to Piedra Blanca (about two hours each way) to see Red-billed Tropicbird and Bridled Tern (best in the spring and summer).

The richest birding area around San Blas is in the luxuriant forest of Singaita (along the main road into town), where tall oil-nut palms, gumbo limbos, and kapok trees are alive with birds in the early morning hours. Specialties include Collared Forest-Falcon, pigeons, Orange-fronted Parakeet, parrots, Squirrel Cuckoo, Long-tailed Hermit, Russet-crowned Motmot, Gray-crowned and both large woodpeckers, Greenish Elaenia, Happy and Sinaloa Wrens, robins, Golden Vireo, warblers, and Red-crowned Ant-Tanager. Similar forest can be found along the old *camino real* (royal highway) around La Palma to the southeast of Matanchen Bay. Above La Palma there is a maze of roads in coffee plantations, shaded by huge broadleaf trees.

CHECKLIST

(H = Highlands chiefly)

Thicket Tinamou r	Little Blue Heron c
Black-throated Loon r W	Cattle Heron
American Dabchick	Reddish Egret r
Pied-billed Grebe W	Great Egret c
Black-necked Grebe W	Snowy Egret c
Western Grebe	Louisiana Heron c
Red-billed Tropicbird	Black-crowned Night-Heron
American White Pelican W	Yellow-crowned Night-Heron
Brown Pelican c	Bare-throated Tiger-Heron
Blue-footed Booby c	Least Bittern r W
Brown Booby c	American Bittern r W
Double-crested Cormorant W	Boat-billed Heron
Neotropic Cormorant c	Wood Stork
Brandt's Cormorant r W	White-faced Ibis c W
Anhinga c	White Ibis c
Magnificent Frigatebird c	Roseate Spoonbill
Great Blue Heron c	Black-bellied Whistling-Duck
Green Heron c	Fulvous Whistling-Duck r

Muscovy Duck   r
Gadwall   c W
Northern Pintail   c W
Green-winged Teal   c W
Blue-winged Teal   c W
Cinnamon Teal   c W
American Wigeon   c W
Northern Shoveler   c W
Redhead   W
Ring-necked Duck   r W
Canvasback   W
Lesser Scaup   c W
Ruddy Duck   c W
Masked Duck   r
Turkey Vulture   c
Black Vulture   c
White-tailed Kite   r
Cooper's Hawk   W
Sharp-shinned Sparrowhawk   W
Red-tailed Sparrowhawk
Swainson's Hawk   M
Zone-tailed Hawk
White-tailed Hawk
Short-tailed Hawk
Gray Hawk
Harris's Hawk   r
Great Black Hawk   r
Lesser Black Hawk   c
Crane Hawk   r
Osprey   c
Laughing Falcon   r
Collared Forest-Falcon   r
Crested Caracara
Peregrine Falcon   r W
American Kestrel
West Mexican Chachalaca   r
Elegant Quail
Montezuma Quail   r H
Clapper Rail
Rufous-necked Wood-Rail
Sora Crake   W
Common Gallinule   c
Purple Gallinule   r
American Coot   c W
Northern Jacana   c
American Oystercatcher
Semipalmated Plover   c W

Snowy Plover   r
Collared Plover   r
Wilson's Plover   c
Killdeer   c W
Gray Plover   c W
Surfbird   c M
Ruddy Turnstone   c W
Black Turnstone   r W
Common Snipe   W
Long-billed Curlew   c W
Whimbrel   c W
Spotted Sandpiper   c W
Solitary Sandpiper   r W
Wandering Tattler   r W
Willet   c
Greater Yellowlegs   c W
Lesser Yellowlegs   c W
Red Knot   W
Least Sandpiper   c W
Dunlin   r W
Long-billed Dowitcher   c W
Short-billed Dowitcher   c W
Stilt Sandpiper   c W
Western Sandpiper   c W
Marbled Godwit   c W
Sanderling   c W
American Avocet   c W
Black-necked Stilt   c
Wilson's Phalarope   c M
Herring Gull   r W
California Gull   r W
Ring-billed Gull   c W
Laughing Gull   c
Franklin's Gull   r M
Bonaparte's Gull   c W
Heerman's Gull   c W
Gull-billed Tern   c
Forster's Tern   c W
Common Tern   W
Little Tern   c S
Royal Tern   c
Elegant Tern   c M
Caspian Tern   c
Black Tern   M
Black Skimmer
Band-tailed Pigeon   H
Red-billed Pigeon

White-winged Dove   c
Mourning Dove   W
Common Ground-Dove   c
Ruddy Ground-Dove
Inca Dove
White-tipped Dove
Ruddy Quail-Dove   r
Military Macaw
Orange-fronted Parakeet
Thick-billed Parrot   r H
Blue-rumped Parrotlet
White-fronted Parrot   c
Lilac-crowned Parrot
Mangrove Cuckoo   r
Squirrel Cuckoo
Lesser Ground-Cuckoo   r
Lesser Roadrunner   r
Groove-billed Ani   c
Barn Owl
Whiskered Screech-Owl   H
Least Pygmy-Owl   r
Ferruginous Pygmy-Owl   c
Mottled Owl
Common Potoo
Lesser Nighthawk   c
Common Pauraque   c
Buff-collared Nightjar   r
Whip-poor-will   H
White-naped Swift
Chestnut-collared Swift   r
Vaux's Swift   W
White-throated Swift   H
Great Swallow-tailed Swift   r H
Long-tailed Hermit
Fork-tailed Emerald
Broad-billed Hummingbird   c
Common Woodnymph   r
White-eared Hummingbird   c H
Berylline Hummingbird   H
Cinnamon Hummingbird   c
Violet-crowned Hummingbird
Blue-throated Mountaingem   H
Rivoli's Hummingbird   H
Plain-capped Starthroat
Ruby-throated Hummingbird   W
Calliope Hummingbird   r M
Rufous Hummingbird   r W

Mountain Trogon   H
Citreoline Trogon
Elegant Trogon
Belted Kingfisher   c W
Ringed Kingfisher
Green Kingfisher
Russet-crowned Motmot
Northern (Red-shafted) Flicker   H
Gray-crowned Woodpecker
Lineated Woodpecker
Gila Woodpecker   c
Golden-cheeked Woodpecker   c
Acorn Woodpecker   c H
Yellow-bellied Sapsucker   r W
Ladder-backed Woodpecker
Arizona Woodpecker   H
Pale-billed Woodpecker
Ivory-billed Woodcreeper
White-striped Woodcreeper   H
Bright-rumped Attila   r
Gray-collared Becard   r
Rose-throated Becard   c
Masked Tityra   c
Vermilion Flycatcher   c
Black Phoebe
Western Kingbird   r M
Cassin's Kingbird   M
Tropical Kingbird   c
Thick-billed Kingbird   c
Sulfur-bellied Flycatcher   S
Boat-billed Flycatcher
Social Flycatcher   c
Great Kiskadee   c
Ash-throated Flycatcher   W
Nutting's Flycatcher
Brown-crested Flycatcher
Dusky-capped Flycatcher   c
Flammulated Flycatcher   r
Coues's Pewee
Tufted Flycatcher   W, H
Willow Flycatcher   W
Least Flycatcher   W
Western Flycatcher   c W
Greenish Elaenia
Northern Beardless Tyrannulet
Purple Martin   M
Gray-breasted Martin

74

Violet-green Swallow   H
Tree Swallow   M
Mangrove Swallow   c
Sand Martin   M
Rough-winged Swallow   c
Barn Swallow   M
Cliff Martin   r M
Steller's Jay   c H
Tufted Jay   H
Green Jay   r
San Blas Jay
Purplish-backed Jay
Magpie-Jay   c
Northern Raven
Mexican Crow   c
Mexican Chickadee   H
Bridled Titmouse   H
Bushtit   c H
Northern Treecreeper   H
House Wren   W
Brown-throated Wren   H
Spotted Wren   H
Sinaloa Wren   c
Happy Wren   c
Canyon Wren
Marsh Wren   r W
Northern Mockingbird   c
Blue Mockingbird
Curve-billed Thrasher
American Robin   c H
Rufous-backed Thrush
White-throated Thrush   c
Brown-backed Solitaire   H
Hermit Thrush
Swainson's Thrush   W
Russet Nightingale-Thrush   H
Orange-billed Nightingale-Thrush
   W H
Blue-gray Gnatcatcher   c W
Ruby-crowned Kinglet   W H
Water Pipit   W
Gray Silky-flycatcher   H
Loggerhead Shrike   W
Black-capped Vireo   W
Mangrove Vireo   r
Hutton's Vireo   c H
Bell's Vireo   c W

Golden Vireo
Solitary Vireo   c W, H
Red-eyed Vireo   S
Warbling Vireo   c W
Black-and-white Warbler   W
Worm-eating Warbler   r W
Orange-crowned Warbler   c W
Nashville Warbler   c W
Lucy's Warbler   W
Crescent-chested Warbler   H
Tropical Parula   c
Olive Warbler   H
Yellow (and Mangrove) Warbler
   c
Yellow-rumped (Audubon's)
   Warbler   c W, H
Black-throated Gray Warbler   c
   W, H
Townsend's Warbler   c H, W
Hermit Warbler   c H, W
Grace's Warbler   H
Ovenbird   r W
Northern Waterthrush   c W
Kentucky Warbler   r W
MacGillivray's Warbler   c W
Northern Yellowthroat   W
Gray-crowned Yellowthroat
Yellow-breasted Chat   W
Red-breasted Chat   r
Hooded Warbler   r W
Wilson's Warbler   c W
Red-faced Warbler   H
American Redstart   c W
Painted Whitestart   H
Slate-throated Whitestart   c H
Fan-tailed Warbler   r
Red Warbler   H
Golden-browed Warbler   H
Rufous-capped Warbler   c H
House Sparrow   c
Yellow-winged Cacique   c
Bronzed Cowbird   c
Brown-headed Cowbird   W
Great-tailed Grackle   c
Orchard Oriole   c W
Black-vented Oriole
Scott's Oriole   H

Hooded Oriole
Northern (Bullock's) Oriole   W
Northern (Baltimore) Oriole   r W
Streak-backed Oriole   c
Red-winged Blackbird
Yellow-headed Blackbird   M
meadowlark, species   W
Scrub Euphonia
Red-headed Tanager   H
Flame-colored Tanager   r H
Western Tanager   c M
Summer Tanager   c W
Hepatic Tanager   c H
Red-crowned Ant-Tanager
Rosy Thrush-Tanager   r
Grayish Saltator   c
Pyrrhuloxia
Yellow Grosbeak
Rose-breasted Grosbeak   r W
Black-headed Grosbeak   W
Blue Grosbeak   c W
Blue Bunting
Indigo Bunting   W
Lazuli Bunting   W
Varied Bunting   c

Painted Bunting   c W
House Finch   c
Dickcissel   M
White-collared Seedeater   c
Blue-black Grassquit   c
Pine Siskin   H
Black-headed Siskin   H
Lesser Goldfinch   W
Rufous-capped Brush-Finch   H
Green-striped Brush-Finch   r H
Green-tailed Towhee   c W
Rufous-sided Towhee   c H
Rusty-crowned Ground-Sparrow
Savannah Sparrow   W
Grasshopper Sparrow   W
Vesper Sparrow   W
Lark Sparrow   c W
Stripe-headed Sparrow
Botteri's Sparrow   r
Yellow-eyed Junco   c H
Chipping Sparrow   c H
Clay-colored Sparrow   W
White-crowned Sparrow   c W
Lincoln's Sparrow   W

17
Mexico City and
Valle de Bravo, Mexico

THE CAPITAL OF MEXICO is a huge metropolis of some eight million people occupying a valley at 7350 feet (2240 m). It has numerous attractions for visitors, ample accommodation, and is the air hub of the country. In the city itself, in parks like Chapultepec Park (somewhat removed from the pollution and noise), some birds can be seen, including Inca Dove, Bewick's and Canyon Wren, American Robin, Rufous-backed Thrush, Black-headed Grosbeak, and House Finch.

Visitors to the pyramids at Teotihuacan will see such desert birds as Vermilion Flycatcher, Bewick's Wren, Curve-billed Thrasher, Brown Towhee, and many wintering sparrows. But far and away the best birding can be done in the surprisingly rich and extensive pine, oak, and fir forests that blanket the mountains to the south, west, and east. The Desierto de los Leones National Park (to the west at 9000 feet [2743 m]) can be reached by car, taxi, or buses on the Toluca run. There is a paved road south from Route 15 at La Venta (near the pass). The richest area is about 3.7 miles (6 km) south, at a major picnic area on the right and a pump station in a valley to the left. There is an excellent trail down this valley with many broadleaf trees and shrubs adding diversity. Birds here include Mexican Chickadee, Brown-throated and Gray-barred Wren, Gray Silky-flycatcher, Crescent-chested, Red, and Golden-browed Warblers, Slate-throated White-start, and two brush-finches.

A dirt road climbs the saddle between Popocatepetl and Ixtac-cihuatl, the two huge snow-capped volcanoes east of Amecameca. The road is drivable and penetrates extensive forests. At the junction on the saddle, roads fork going into the bunch grass where Striped Sparrow is common. On the Popocatepetl spur there are some pine woods to the right where Brown-barred Woodpecker, Pygmy Nuthatch, and Red Crossbill are found.

Valle de Bravo is 90 miles (145 km) from Mexico City (via Toluca). It is 5900 feet (1800 m) above sea level and, due to lack of air pollution, much easier on the lungs than the capital. The beautiful small town

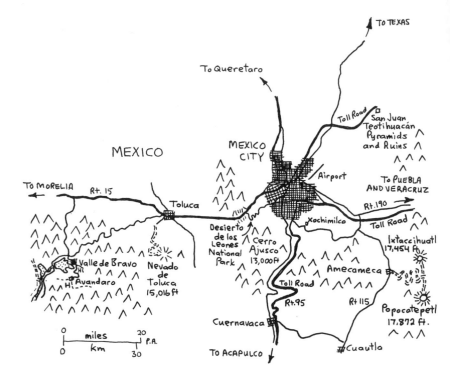

is located on the east side of an artificial lake nestled among the mountains with pine-clad hills nearby.

The grounds of the Hotel Refugio del Salto 3 miles (4 km) south of Valle de Bravo feature White-naped Swifts roosting under the bridge above the falls and occasional Aztec Thrushes. The Avandaro Motel and Golf Club 4 miles (6 km) south of Valle de Bravo offers excellent birding. Garden birds include Acorn Woodpecker, Vermilion Flycatcher, Eastern Bluebird, Red-headed, Flame-colored, and Hepatic Tanagers, Red Crossbill, and Striped Sparrow. The edges of the golf course (with riparian vegetation along the streams) have Green Violetear, White-eared and Bumblebee Hummingbirds, Buff-breasted Flycatcher, Greenish Elaenia, Blue Mockingbird, and Garden Flower-piercer. The pine-oak woodland south and west of the golf course has a number of good trails. Look for Blue-throated Mountain-gem, Rivoli's Hummingbird, Mountain Trogon, White-striped Woodcreeper, Chestnut-sided Shrike-Vireo, Red-faced Warbler, Slate-throated Whitestart, and Hooded Grosbeak.

The lakes often have many wintering diving ducks. In the strikingly different vegetation below the dam (deciduous arid scrub) look for Banded Quail, Lesser Roadrunner, Dusky Hummingbird, Thick-billed Kingbird, Boucard's and Banded Wrens, Golden Vireo, Gray-crowned Yellowthroat, Black-vented Oriole, Varied Bunting, and Stripe-headed Sparrow.

CHECKLIST

Black-necked Grebe   W
Pied-billed Grebe   W
Great Blue Heron   W
Cattle Heron
Gadwall   c   W
Northern Pintail   r   W
Green-winged Teal   W
Blue-winged Teal   W
American Wigeon   W
Northern Shoveler   W
Redhead   c   W
Ring-necked Duck   c   W
Canvasback   c   W
Lesser Scaup   c   W
Ruddy Duck   W
Turkey Vulture   c
Black Vulture
Cooper's Sparrowhawk   W
Sharp-shinned Sparrowhawk
Red-tailed Hawk
American Kestrel
Long-tailed Wood-Partridge
Banded Quail
Common Gallinule   W
American Coot   c   W
Solitary Sandpiper   M
Spotted Sandpiper   W
Least Sandpiper   W
Mourning Dove   W
Inca Dove   c
Northern Pygmy-Owl   r
White-naped Swift
Vaux's Swift   W
White-throated Swift
Green Violetear
Fork-tailed Emerald   r
Dusky Hummingbird
Broad-billed Hummingbird

White-eared Hummingbird   c
Violet-crowned Hummingbird
Berylline Hummingbird   c
Blue-throated Mountaingem
Rivoli's Hummingbird   r
Rufous Hummingbird   r   W
Broad-tailed Hummingbird
Bumblebee Hummingbird   r
Mountain Trogon   r
Belted Kingfisher   r   W
Green Kingfisher
Northern (Red-shafted) Flicker
Acorn Woodpecker   c
Yellow-bellied Sapsucker   W
Hairy Woodpecker
Ladder-backed Woodpecker
Brown-barred Woodpecker
White-striped Woodcreeper
Rose-throated Becard   r
Eastern Phoebe   r   W
Black Phoebe   c
Say's Phoebe
Vermilion Flycatcher   c
Cassin's Kingbird   c   W
Western Kingbird   W
Thick-billed Kingbird
Coues's Pewee   c
Tufted Flycatcher   c
Empidonax, species
Western Flycatcher
Buff-breasted Flycatcher
Greenish Elaenia
Horned Lark
Violet-green Swallow
Rough-winged Swallow
Barn Swallow   S
Cliff Martin   S
Steller's Jay

Mexican Jay
Northern Raven
Mexican Chickadee
Bridled Titmouse
Bushtit
White-breasted Nuthatch
Pygmy Nuthatch
Northern Treecreeper
American Dipper
House Wren   W
Brown-throated Wren
Gray-barred Wren
Boucard's Wren
Sedge Wren   r
Bewick's Wren
Banded Wren
Canyon Wren
Blue Mockingbird
Northern Mockingbird
Curve-billed Thrasher   c
American Robin   c
Rufous-backed Thrush
White-throated Thrush
Aztec Thrush   r
Hermit Thrush
Swainson's Thrush   r W
Russet Nightingale-Thrush
Orange-billed Nightingale-Thrush
Eastern Bluebird   c
Western Bluebird   W
Brown-backed Solitaire
Blue-gray Gnatcatcher   W
Golden-crowned Kinglet
Ruby-crowned Kinglet   c W
Water Pipit   W
Cedar Waxwing   W
Gray Silky-flycatcher
Loggerhead Shrike   c
Chestnut-sided Shrike-Vireo
Hutton's Vireo   c
Golden Vireo
Solitary Vireo   c W
Warbling Vireo   c W
Garden Flower-piercer
Black-and-white Warbler   W
Tennessee Warbler   W
Orange-crowned Warbler   W

Nashville Warbler   W
Virginia's Warbler   W
Colima Warbler   W
Crescent-chested Warbler
Olive Warbler
Yellow Warbler
Yellow-rumped (Audubon's)
   Warbler
Black-throated Gray Warbler   W
Townsend's Warbler   W
Black-throated Green Warbler   r
   W
Hermit Warbler   W
Grace's Warbler
Louisiana Waterthrush   W
MacGillivray's Warbler   W
Gray-crowned Yellowthroat   r
Wilson's Warbler   c W
Red-faced Warbler
Painted Whitestart
Slate-throated Whitestart   c
Red Warbler
Golden-browed Warbler
Rufous-capped Warbler   c
House Sparrow   c
Bronzed Cowbird
Brown-headed Cowbird   W
Great-tailed Grackle
Orchard Oriole   r W
Black-vented Oriole
Scott's Oriole   r W
Hooded Oriole   W
Northern Oriole
Red-winged Blackbird
Blue-hooded Euphonia   r
Red-headed Tanager
Flame-colored Tanager
Hepatic Tanager
Summer Tanager   W
Black-headed Grosbeak   c
Blue Grosbeak
Indigo Bunting   W
Varied Bunting
Evening Grosbeak
Hooded Grosbeak
House Finch   c
White-collared Seedeater   r

Blue-black Grassquit
Pine Siskin
Black-headed Siskin
Lesser Goldfinch
Red Crossbill
Rufous-capped Brush-Finch
Green-striped Brush-Finch
Rufous-sided Towhee
Olive-backed Towhee
Brown Towhee   c
Stripe-headed Sparrow
Striped Sparrow   c

Sierra Madre Sparrow   r
Lark Sparrow   c   W
Vesper Sparrow   W
Rusty Sparrow
Rufous-crowned Sparrow
Yellow-eyed Junco   c
Chipping Sparrow   c   W
Clay-colored Sparrow   W
Brewer's Sparrow   W
Lincoln's Sparrow   c   W
Song Sparrow   r

18
Merida, Yucatan, Mexico

THE YUCATAN IS A SURPRISINGLY DRY PENINSULA in eastern Mexico that separates the Gulf of Mexico from the Caribbean Sea. The original vegetation of xerophytic scrub in the north gradually gives way to tropical deciduous forest and eventually tropical evergreen forest as one moves south.

On the coast there are many pelicans, frigatebirds, herons, shorebirds, and terns. The top waterbird area is around Rio Lagartos, which has a modest hotel. Take the road east just past Los Colorados (17.5 miles [28 km] east of Rio Lagartos) where a maze of impoundments is host to many American Flamingo, shorebirds, and terns. In barren beach habitats near Los Colorados and other beach towns such as Progresso and Telchac Puerto, look for Black-throated Bobwhite, Mexican Sheartail, Yucatan Wren, and White-lored Gnatcatcher.

The two great Mayan ruins of Uxmal and Chichen Itza are located in tropical deciduous forest, each with fine hotels and trails into nearby woodlands. Uxmal is located 60 miles (96 km) south of Mérida, and Chichen Itza is 80 miles (128 km) east of Mérida. Birds regularly seen behind both ruins include Plain Chachalaca, hummingbirds, Golden-fronted and Yucatan Jay, wrens (Yucatan, Spotbreasted, Carolina, and White-bellied), Mangrove Vireo, Gray-throated Chat, Orange Oriole, and Blue Bunting.

There are three other fine birding areas reachable from Mérida. Additional species not found in northern Yucatan do not appear on the list.

Cozumel Island, lying to the east of Cancún in the Caribbean Sea, can be reached by ferry and air from the mainland. Visitors are always amazed that so many endemics, as well as Caribbean species not found elsewhere in Mexico, live on an island so close to the peninsula. Most of these can be found along the trail around the lagoon just east of Puerto de Abrigo, just north of the airport. In this area look for Ruddy Crake, White-crowned Pigeon, Zenaida and White-bellied Doves, Caribbean Elaenia, Cozumel Thrasher, Black Catbird, Cozumel and Yucatan Vireos, and Stripe-headed Tanager. Bridled and Roseate Terns roost seasonally on rocks

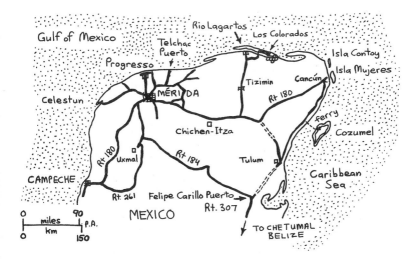

near the Punta Celarain lighthouse at the south tip of the island.

Visitors driving south to Chetumal will find two good trails leading east of the road, one at Km 8 and another at Km 25 south of Felipe Carillo Puerto. Birds of interest include Yellow-lored Parrot, Citreoline, Violaceous, and Slaty-tailed Trogons, toucans, Pale-billed Woodpecker, Gray-throated Chat, Green Shrike-Vireo, Rose-throated Tanager, and two ant-tanagers.

Palenque, located in northern Chiapas, has the wettest rain forest of any Mayan ruin area, including Tikal. There are several hotels, trails into hilly jungles, and excellent rain forest birds. Specialties include White Hawk, Black Hawk-Eagle, Stripe-tailed Hummingbird, Black-crested Coquette, Purple-crowned Fairy, Lovely Cotinga, Rufous Piha, Northern Royal Flycatcher, Black-throated Shrike-Tanager, Scarlet-rumped Tanager, and Orange-billed Sparrow.

Birds of the wetter areas south of Chetumal and around Palenque have not been added to the following list.

CHECKLIST

Thicket Tinamou r	Reddish Egret
American White Pelican W	Cattle Heron
Brown Pelican c	Great Egret
Magnificent Frigatebird c	Snowy Egret c
Neotropic Cormorant c	Green Heron
Great Blue Heron W	Louisiana Heron
Little Blue Heron c	Yellow-crowned Night-Heron

White Ibis
Roseate Spoonbill   r
American Flamingo
Blue-winged Teal   W
Gadwall   W
Northern Shoveler   W
American Wigeon   W
Ring-necked Duck   W
Lesser Scaup   W
Black Vulture   c
Turkey Vulture   c
Hook-billed Kite   r
Roadside Hawk
Gray Hawk
Osprey   W
Crested Caracara
Plain Chachalaca
Black-throated Bobwhite
Gray-necked Wood-Rail
American Coot   W
Ruddy Crake
Northern Jacana
Gray Plover   W
Killdeer   W
Ruddy Turnstone
Spotted Sandpiper   c W
Lesser Yellowlegs   W
Greater Yellowlegs   W
Willet   W
Western Sandpiper   W
Least Sandpiper   c W
Sanderling   W
Black-necked Stilt
Laughing Gull   c
Herring Gull   W
Black Tern   M
Roseate Tern   S
Royal Tern   c
Little Tern   S
Bridled Tern   S
White-winged Dove   c
Common Ground-Dove   c
Ruddy Ground-Dove   c
White-tipped Dove   c
Olive-throated Parakeet
Yellow-lored Parrot
White-fronted Parrot

Squirrel Cuckoo
Groove-billed Ani   c
Lesser Roadrunner   r
Ferruginous Pygmy-Owl
Lesser Nighthawk
Common Pauraque
Yucatan Poorwill
Vaux's Swift   c
Wedge-tailed Sabrewing   r
Green-breasted Mango
Fork-tailed Emerald   r
Cinnamon Hummingbird
Buff-bellied Hummingbird
Mexican Sheartail
Ruby-throated Hummingbird   W
Citreoline Trogon
Belted Kingfisher   c W
Green Kingfisher
Blue-crowned Motmot   r
Turquoise-browed Motmot   c
Lineated Woodpecker
Golden-fronted Woodpecker   c
Yucatan Woodpecker   r
Ladder-backed Woodpecker
Ivory-billed Woodcreeper
Barred Antshrike
Rose-throated Becard
Masked Tityra
Vermilion Flycatcher
Tropical Kingbird   c
Eastern Kingbird   M
Boat-billed Flycatcher
Social Flycatcher   c
Great Kiskadee
Brown-crested Flycatcher
Dusky-capped Flycatcher   c
Yucatan Flycatcher
Wood Pewee   M
Tropical Pewee
Yellow-olive Flycatcher   r
Yellow-bellied Elaenia
Greenish Elaenia
Gray-breasted Martin   c S
Purple Martin   M
Barn Swallow   M
Mangrove Swallow
Cave Martin   c

Rough-winged Swallow   c
Brown Jay
Yucatan Jay   c
House Wren   c
Spot-breasted Wren
Carolina Wren
Yucatan Wren
White-bellied Wren
Gray Catbird   c W
Tropical Mockingbird   c
Clay-colored Thrush   c
Wood Thrush   W
Blue-gray Gnatcatcher   c
White-lored Gnatcatcher
Rufous-browed Peppershrike   c
White-eyed Vireo   W
Mangrove Vireo
Yucatan Vireo
Red-eyed Vireo
Black-and-white Warbler   W
Prothonotary Warbler   W
Northern Parula   W
Tennessee Warbler   W
Mangrove Warbler
Yellow Warbler   W
Magnolia Warbler   W
Yellow-rumped Warbler   W
Black-throated Green Warbler   W
Yellow-throated Warbler   W
Bay-breasted Warbler   W
Palm Warbler   W

Northern Waterthrush   W
Kentucky Warbler   r W
Northern Yellowthroat
Gray-crowned Yellowthroat
Gray-throated Chat   r
Hooded Warbler   W
American Redstart   W
Orchard Oriole   W
Orange Oriole
Hooded Oriole   c
Altamira Oriole   c
Bronzed Cowbird
Great-tailed Grackle   c
Melodious Blackbird   c
Scrub Euphonia
Yellow-throated Euphonia
Blue-gray Tanager
Summer Tanager   W
Scarlet Tanager   M
Rose-throated Tanager   r
Grayish Saltator   c
Black-headed Saltator
Northern Cardinal   c
Blue Grosbeak   c
Blue Bunting   c
Indigo Bunting   W
Painted Bunting   W
Yellow-faced Grassquit
White-collared Seedeater   c
Blue-black Grassquit   c
Olive Sparrow

19
Belize City–Belmopan, Belize

BELIZE IS A FORMER BRITISH COLONY, just east of Guatemala, on the Caribbean. The capital is being moved from seaside Belize City to Belmopan in the interior. The offshore cays and reefs are among the most spectacular in the world and remain somewhat difficult of access. Visiting birders tend to spend most of their time inland in the tropical forests, lagoons, and rivers.

Many birds are found in the gardens, mangroves, and lawns of St. John's College campus, located in the Landivar section of Belize City. The gardens have Cinnamon and Rufous-tailed Hummingbirds, Hooded and Black-cowled Orioles, the mangroves have Clapper Rail, Mangrove Vireo, and Yellow (Mangrove) Warbler, while the lawns serve as resting areas for many migrant shorebirds.

Crooked Tree lagoons to the northwest of Belize City is an exceptionally rich area for birds. Along with nearby lagoons (Western, Spanish Creek, and Southern) it is home to vast numbers of waterbirds from February through May as the dry season progresses. Around a thousand Limpkins nest here in March, flocks of hundreds of Everglade Kite can be seen, and Jabiru Storks are not rare.

There are two ways to "attack" the area. Take the Northern Highway 16.2 miles (26 km) out from Belcan Bridge, and turn left on a small farm road to Double Run Landing on the Belize River. Arrangements for a boat to meet you should be made in advance via a local travel agency or contact in the Audubon Society. The woods along the road at Double Run have Yucatan Woodpecker, White-collared Manakin, and Northern Royal Flycatcher. The banks of the Belize River and Black Creek to the lagoon are partially lined with forest, good for Sungrebe, kingfishers, and jungle birds. The lagoon can also be reached via the Crooked Tree Road, which leaves the Northern Highway westward, a few miles north of Double Run and the village of Sand Hill. It is hard going for 18 miles (29 km).

The 50-mile (80 km) route along Western Highway to Belmopan traverses a number of good birding habitats. The first 12 miles (19.2

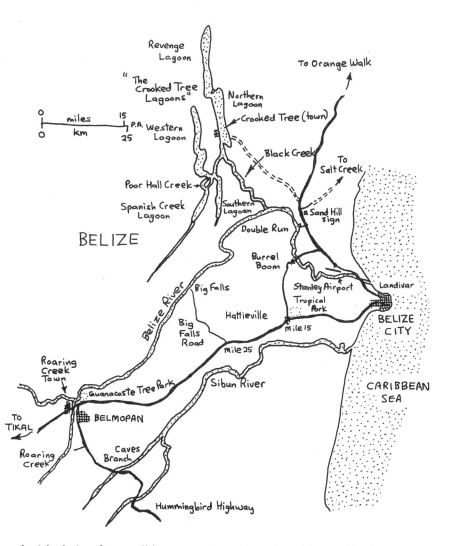

km) include a few small lagoons and marshes where kites, gallinules, jacanas, ibises, kingfishers, and Marsh Vulture can be seen. At Mile 15 (24 km) a road goes north into "Tropical Park," a good place for savanna species. The large pond at the end of the road often has a pair of Jabiru Stork. At Mile 25 (40 km) another road north enters the Big Falls Ranch (get permission by phoning their office in Belize City: 2018). This area features such raptors as kites, Laughing Falcon, and Great Black Hawk, waterbirds like Bare-throated Tiger-Heron and Roseate Spoonbill, and cowbirds.

The Hummingbird Highway, wandering off to the southeast of Belmopan, is good for King Vulture, White Hawk, Black Hawk-Eagle, and Bat Falcon. A number of side roads and trails enter the tropical forest. Five miles (8 km) south a road goes west to the Roaring River Estates. The first two miles (3.2 km) may yield forest-falcons, curassow, chachalaca, and Keel-billed Toucan. Black howler monkeys may be heard in this area.

Caves Branch Bridge (12 ½ miles [20 km] south of Belmopan) and the nearby trail west to St. Herman's Cave are worth visiting. Near the bridge look for Collared Aracari, Scarlet-rumped and Crimson-collared Tanager. Around the entrance to the cave you may find Rufous-tailed Jacamar, Sulfur-rumped Flycatcher, and interesting finches.

A mile (1.6 km) beyond the cave trail, a sign on the right marks the footpath to Blue Hole. If you walk the stairs quietly you may find both hermits, Blue-crowned and the rare Keel-billed Motmots, White-whiskered Puffbird, Bright-rumped Attila, and Orange-billed Sparrow. The cacao plantation just to the north often has three kinds of trogons, and many woodpeckers, woodcreepers, honeycreepers, warblers, and now and then a pair of Scarlet Macaws screaming overhead.

CHECKLIST

Little Tinamou   r
Slaty-breasted Tinamou   r
American Dabchick
Pied-billed Grebe   W
Brown Pelican   c
Neotropic Cormorant   c
Anhinga   c
Magnificent Frigatebird
Great Blue Heron   c W
Green Heron   c
Little Blue Heron   c
Great Egret   c
Snowy Egret   c
Cattle Heron   c
Louisiana Heron   c
Black-crowned Night-Heron   r W
Yellow-crowned Night-Heron   c
Bare-throated Tiger-Heron
Boat-billed Heron
Wood Stork   c
Jabiru Stork

White Ibis
Roseate Spoonbill
Black-bellied Whistling-Duck
Blue-winged Teal   c W
Northern Shoveler   r W
American Wigeon   r W
Lesser Scaup   W
Muscovy Duck
King Vulture
Black Vulture   c
Marsh Vulture
Turkey Vulture   c
White-tailed Kite   c
Swallow-tailed Kite   S
Gray-headed Kite   r
Double-toothed Kite   r
Plumbeous Kite   c S
Everglade Kite   c
White-tailed Hawk
Roadside Hawk   c
Short-tailed Hawk

Gray Hawk   c
White Hawk
Black-collared Hawk
Lesser Black Hawk   c
Great Black Hawk
Black Hawk-Eagle
Osprey   c
Laughing Falcon   c
Barred Forest-Falcon   r
Collared Forest-Falcon   r
Peregrine Falcon   W
American Kestrel   c W
Great Curassow   r
Plain Chachalaca   c
Black-throated Bobwhite   c
Limpkin   c
Clapper Rail   r
Gray-necked Wood-Rail   c
Ruddy Crake
Common Gallinule   c W
Purple Gallinule
American Coot   c W
Sungrebe
Northern Jacana   c
Gray Plover   c W
Semipalmated Plover   c W
Killdeer   c W
Wilson's Plover
Long-billed Curlew   W
Whimbrel   W
Lesser Yellowlegs   W
Greater Yellowlegs   W
Solitary Sandpiper   c W
Spotted Sandpiper   c W
Willet
Ruddy Turnstone   r W
Common Snipe   W
Western Sandpiper   W
Least Sandpiper   W
White-rumped Sandpiper   r M
Pectoral Sandpiper   W
Stilt Sandpiper   W
Black-necked Stilt
Caspian Tern
Royal Tern
Red-billed Pigeon
Pale-vented Pigeon   c

Scaled Pigeon   r
Short-billed Pigeon   c
Plain-breasted Ground-Dove   c
Ruddy Ground-Dove   c
Blue Ground-Dove   c
White-tipped Dove   c
Gray-headed Dove   r
Gray-chested Dove
Scarlet Macaw   r
Olive-throated Parakeet   c
Brown-hooded Parrot
White-crowned Parrot
Yellow-lored Parrot
White-fronted Parrot   c
Red-lored Parrot   c
Yellow-headed Parrot
Mealy Parrot
Mangrove Cuckoo   r
Squirrel Cuckoo   c
Groove-billed Ani   c
Common Potoo
Lesser Nighthawk   W
Common Nighthawk   M
Common Pauraque   c
Yucatan Poorwill
White-collared Swift
Vaux's Swift   c
Lesser Swallow-tailed Swift   r
Long-tailed Hermit
Little Hermit   c
Wedge-tailed Sabrewing
White-necked Jacobin   r
Green-breasted Mango
Fork-tailed Emerald
White-bellied Emerald   c
Red-billed Azurecrown
Cinnamon Hummingbird   c
Buff-bellied Hummingbird   c
Slaty-tailed Trogon
Citreoline Trogon   c
Violaceous Trogon
Ringed Kingfisher   c
Belted Kingfisher   c W
Amazon Kingfisher
Green Kingfisher
American Pygmy Kingfisher
Keel-billed Motmot   r

Blue-crowned Motmot
Rufous-tailed Jacamar
White-necked Puffbird
White-whiskered Puffbird
Collared Aracari   c
Keel-billed Toucan
Golden-olive Woodpecker   c
Chestnut-colored Woodpecker
Lineated Woodpecker   c
Acorn Woodpecker   c
Golden-fronted Woodpecker   c
Yucatan Woodpecker
Black-cheeked Woodpecker
Smoky-brown Woodpecker
Pale-billed Woodpecker
Tawny-winged Woodcreeper   r
Ruddy Woodcreeper
Olivaceous Woodcreeper   c
Wedge-billed Woodcreeper
Ivory-billed Woodcreeper   c
Streak-headed Woodcreeper
Rufous-breasted Spinetail   c
Barred Antshrike   c
Plain Antvireo
Dusky Antbird
Black-faced Ant-thrush
Red-capped Manakin
White-collared Manakin
Bright-rumped Attila
Cinnamon Becard
Rose-throated Becard   c
Masked Tityra   c
Black-crowned Tityra
Black Phoebe
Vermilion Flycatcher   c
Fork-tailed Flycatcher   c
Eastern Kingbird   M
Tropical Kingbird   c
Piratic Flycatcher   S
Sulfur-bellied Flycatcher   S
Streaked Flycatcher   S
Boat-billed Flycatcher   c
Social Flycatcher   c
Great Kiskadee   c
Brown-crested Flycatcher   c
Dusky-capped Flycatcher   c
Wood Pewee   M

Tropical Pewee   c
Empidonax, species   c W
Sulfur-rumped Flycatcher   r
Northern Royal Flycatcher
Yellow-olive Flycatcher
Common Tody-Flycatcher   c
Yellow-bellied Elaenia   c
Greenish Elaenia
Ochre-bellied Flycatcher   r
Purple Martin   c M
Gray-breasted Martin   c S
Barn Swallow   c M
Rough-winged Swallow   c
Tree Swallow   c W
Mangrove Swallow   c
Brown Jay   c
Green Jay
Yucatan Jay
Band-backed Wren
Spot-breasted Wren   c
House Wren
White-breasted Wood-Wren
White-bellied Wren   r
Gray Catbird   c W
Tropical Mockingbird   c
White-throated Thrush
Clay-colored Thrush   c
Wood Thrush   c W
Blue-gray Gnatcatcher   c W
Tropical Gnatcatcher
Long-billed Gnatwren
Rufous-browed Peppershrike
White-eyed Vireo   c W
Mangrove Vireo
Yellow-throated Vireo   W
Red-eyed Vireo
Lesser Greenlet
Montezuma's Oropendola   c
Yellow-billed Cacique   c
Giant Cowbird
Bronzed Cowbird
Great-tailed Grackle   c
Melodious Blackbird   c
Orchard Oriole   c W
Black-cowled Oriole   c
Hooded Oriole   c
Yellow-tailed Oriole   c

Yellow-backed Oriole
Northern (Baltimore) Oriole   c W
Red-winged Blackbird
Eastern Meadowlark   c
Black-and-white Warbler   c W
Prothonotary Warbler   W
Swainson's Warbler   r W
Worm-eating Warbler   r W
Golden-winged Warbler   r M
Blue-winged Warbler   W
Tennessee Warbler   c W
Northern Parula   W
Yellow Warbler   c
Magnolia Warbler   c W
Yellow-rumped (Myrtle) Warbler
   W
Black-throated Green Warbler   W
Yellow-throated Warbler   W
Chestnut-sided Warbler   r W
Ovenbird   W
Northern Waterthrush   c W
Louisiana Waterthrush   W
Kentucky Warbler   W
Northern Yellowthroat   c W
Gray-crowned Yellowthroat
Yellow-breasted Chat   W
Hooded Warbler   c W
Wilson's Warbler   c W
American Redstart   c W
Bananaquit   r
Green Honeycreeper

Red-legged Honeycreeper   c
Scrub Euphonia
Yellow-throated Euphonia   c
Olive-backed Euphonia   r
Golden-hooded Tanager
Blue-gray Tanager   c
Yellow-winged Tanager   c
Scarlet-rumped Tanager
Crimson-collared Tanager
Summer Tanager   c W
Hepatic Tanager
Red-crowned Ant-Tanager   r
Red-throated Ant-Tanager   c
Gray-headed Tanager
Black-headed Saltator   c
Buff-throated Saltator
Grayish Saltator   c
Black-faced Grosbeak   r
Northern Cardinal
Rose-breasted Grosbeak   W
Blue Grosbeak   W
Blue-black Grosbeak
Blue Bunting
Indigo Bunting   W
White-collared Seedeater   c
Variable Seedeater
Lesser Seed-Finch
Blue-black Grassquit   c
Orange-billed Sparrow   r
Black-striped Sparrow
Grasshopper Sparrow

20

Tikal National Park, Guatemala

TIKAL IS THE FINEST tropical forest birding area north of Panama. It has an excellent list of birds, a book in English and Spanish editions on the area, an airport, inexpensive hotels, unspoiled forest on all sides, good walking roads, and an excellent selection of such neotropical families as motmots, toucans, antbirds, hummingbirds, cotingas, and manakins. The Jungle Lodge is a little primitive, but food is good. There is a campground for those arriving overland. No vehicles need be rented since the airstrip, hotels, ruins, and forest are all in a compact area.

Daily flights connect with Guatemala City, and the more adventuresome can often get there by the dirt road system from Guatemala City or Belize.

Most of Tikal's birds can be seen right from the roads between the hotel and the Great Plaza, which pass through rich forest. Birding around the hotel and the nearby pond (called Aguada Tikal) is best in early morning and late afternoon. Roving bands of nectivorous, frugivorous, and insectivorous birds move through the forest during the warmer parts of the day.

Larger birds are most active at dawn and dusk. Occelated Turkeys are common and tame, parrots and toucans are frequently encountered at dawn, dusk, and after rains. Look for trails into the forest to see shyer birds such as tinamous, antbirds, and manakins.

The magnificent Mayan ruins centered on the Great Plaza may have flowering trees that attract icterids and warblers. Orange-breasted Falcon and Lesser Swallow-tailed Swift often nest in the temples.

Most birders stay at least two nights. Do bring chigger repellent, particularly if you plan to go off the roads into the grass.

The Tikal National Park was one of the first four parks approved to be on the World Heritage List for both cultural and natural characteristics. Its protection in the future seems secure, unlike Palenque and other Mayan sites.

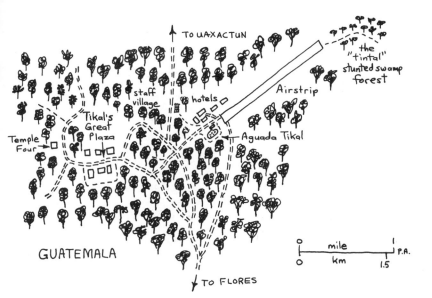

To UAXACTUN

the "tintal" stunted swamp forest

Airstrip

staff village

hotels

Tikal's Great Plaza

Temple Four

Aguada Tikal

GUATEMALA

mile

km

P.A.

1.5

TO FLORES

CHECKLIST

Great Tinamou
Slaty-breasted Tinamou
American Dabchick
Pied-billed Grebe   r W
Green Heron   W
Little Blue Heron   M
Cattle Heron
Yellow-crowned Night-Heron
Boat-billed Heron
Turkey Vulture   c
Black Vulture   c
King Vulture
Swallow-tailed Kite   S
Hook-billed Kite   r
Double-toothed Kite
Gray-headed Kite   r
Plumbeous Kite   S
Bicolored Sparrowhawk   r
Roadside Hawk   c
Short-tailed Hawk
White Hawk   r

Ornate Hawk-Eagle   r
Black Hawk-Eagle   r
Crane Hawk   r
Laughing Falcon
Collared Forest-Falcon   r
Barred Forest-Falcon   r
Orange-breasted Falcon
Bat Falcon
American Kestrel   W
Great Curassow   r
Crested Guan
Plain Chachalaca   c
Spotted Wood-Quail   r
Occelated Turkey   c
Limpkin   M
Gray-necked Wood-Rail
Common Gallinule
Northern Jacana
Solitary Sandpiper   W
Scaled Pigeon
Short-billed Pigeon   c

93

Ruddy Ground-Dove   c
Blue Ground-Dove
Gray-headed Dove
Ruddy Quail-Dove
Olive-throated Parakeet   c
Brown-hooded Parrot
White-crowned Parrot   c
White-fronted Parrot
Red-lored Parrot   c
Mealy Parrot   c
Squirrel Cuckoo   c
Groove-billed Ani   c
Pheasant Cuckoo   r
Vermiculated Screech-Owl
Mottled Owl
Common Potoo   r
Common Pauraque   c
Common Nighthawk   M
Yucatan Poorwill   r
Vaux's Swift   c
White-collared Swift   r
Lesser Swallow-tailed Swift
Long-tailed Hermit   r
Little Hermit   c
Scaly-breasted Hummingbird   c
Wedge-tailed Sabrewing
Green-breasted Mango   r
Fork-tailed Emerald   r
White-bellied Emerald   c
Buff-bellied Hummingbird   r
Rufous-tailed Hummingbird   c
Black-crested Coquette   r
Purple-crowned Fairy
White-necked Jacobin
Slaty-tailed Trogon   c
Citreoline Trogon   c
Collared Trogon
Violaceous Trogon   c
Belted Kingfisher   W
Tody Motmot   r
Blue-crowned Motmot   c
Rufous-tailed Jacamar   c
White-necked Puffbird   r
White-whiskered Puffbird
Emerald Toucanet
Collared Aracari   c
Keel-billed Toucan   c

Chestnut-colored Woodpecker
Lineated Woodpecker   c
Golden-fronted Woodpecker   c
Black-cheeked Woodpecker   c
Smoky-brown Woodpecker
Pale-billed Woodpecker   c
Tawny-winged Woodcreeper
Ruddy Woodcreeper
Olivaceous Woodcreeper   c
Wedge-billed Woodcreeper   r
Strong-billed Woodcreeper   r
Barred Woodcreeper
Ivory-billed Woodcreeper   c
Plain Xenops   c
Scaly-throated Leaftosser   r
Barred Antshrike
Russet Antshrike   r
Plain Antvireo   c
Dot-winged Antwren   c
Dusky Antbird
Black-faced Ant-thrush
Bright-rumped Attila
Rufous Mourner   r
Rufous Piha   r
Cinnamon Becard   c
Gray-collared Becard   r
Rose-throated Becard
Masked Tityra   c
Black-crowned Tityra
Red-capped Manakin   c
White-collared Manakin   c
Thrush-like Manakin   c
Eastern Kingbird   M
Tropical Kingbird   c
Piratic Flycatcher   S
Sulfur-bellied Flycatcher   S
Streaked Flycatcher   S
Boat-billed Flycatcher
Social Flycatcher   c
Great Kiskadee
Brown-crested Flycatcher
Great-crested Flycatcher   W
Dusky-capped Flycatcher   c
Wood Pewee   M
Tropical Pewee   S
Empidonax, species   c W
Ruddy-tailed Flycatcher   r

Sulfur-rumped Flycatcher c
Northern Royal Flycatcher
White-throated Spadebill c
Yellow-olive Flycatcher
Eye-ringed Flatbill
Slate-headed Tody-Flycatcher r
Northern Bentbill
Greenish Elaenia
Paltry Tyrannulet r
Yellow-bellied Tyrannulet r
Sepia-capped Flycatcher c
Ochre-bellied Flycatcher
Purple Martin M
Gray-breasted Martin S
Rough-winged Swallow c
Green Jay r
Brown Jay c
Spot-breasted Wren
Carolina Wren
White-breasted Wood-Wren c
White-bellied Wren
Gray Catbird c W
Clay-colored Thrush c
White-throated Thrush r
Wood Thrush c W
Swainson's Thrush M
Veery M (fall)
Tropical Gnatcatcher
Long-billed Gnatwren
Green Shrike-Vireo
White-eyed Vireo
Mangrove Vireo c
Yellow-throated Vireo r W
Red-eyed (Yellow-Green) Vireo
  M S
Tawny-crowned Greenlet
Lesser Greenlet c
Green Honeycreeper r
Red-legged Honeycreeper c
Bananaquit r
Black-and-white Warbler c W
Tropical Parula r
Prothonotary Warbler M
Worm-eating Warbler W
Blue-winged Warbler M
Tennessee Warbler c M
Yellow Warbler W

Magnolia Warbler c W
Yellow-rumped (Myrtle) Warbler
  c W
Black-throated Green Warbler W
Yellow-throated Warbler r W
Chestnut-sided Warbler W
Ovenbird W
Northern Waterthrush
Louisiana Waterthrush W
Kentucky Warbler W
Northern Yellowthroat W
Yellow-breasted Chat W
Hooded Warbler W
Wilson's Warbler c W
American Redstart c W
Golden-crowned Warbler c
Montezuma Oropendola c
Giant Cowbird c
Melodious Blackbird c
Great-tailed Grackle
Orchard Oriole c W
Black-cowled Oriole c
Northern (Baltimore) Oriole W
Scrub Euphonia
Yellow-throated Euphonia c
Olive-backed Euphonia c
Golden-hooded Tanager
Yellow-winged Tanager c
Summer Tanager W
White-winged Tanager r
Red-crowned Ant-Tanager c
Red-throated Ant-Tanager c
Gray-headed Tanager
Black-throated Shrike-Tanager
Black-headed Saltator c
Grayish Saltator
Black-faced Grosbeak
Blue Grosbeak W
Blue-black Grosbeak
Blue Bunting
Indigo Bunting W
Painted Bunting r W
White-collared Seedeater c
Blue-black Grassquit
Orange-billed Sparrow r
Black-striped Sparrow

21
Guatemala City – Lake Atitlan, Guatemala

THE HIGHLANDS OF GUATEMALA are one of the most pleasant places in the world to bird, with high volcanoes at every turn, extensive pine forests mixed with cornfields, colorful Indians, and fine accommodation in small towns. The jewel of it all is famous Lake Atitlan.

The lake is a three- or four-hour drive from Guatemala City over paved roads (some rather narrow with many curves). Panajachel is the tourist center with several superb hotels adjacent to the lake. In the bottlebrush trees in the town's many gardens Sparkling-tailed and White-eared Hummingbirds, Red-billed Azurecrown, and various warblers (including Cape May) and orioles can be easily seen. In coffee plantations around Panajachel and the Hotel Atitlan, one finds the Rufous Sabrewing, Bushy-crested Jay, and Golden-olive Woodpecker. The wooded hillsides on the road to Sololá are broadleaf deciduous and have birds not found in the extensive pine-oak woodlands. Listen for Whiskered Screech-Owl and Whip-poor-will at night near Panajachel. The rare Belted Flycatcher has been found near Panajachel in the summer, and the white-breasted form of the Sharp-shinned Sparrowhawk is not rare.

The most famous bird here is the Atitlan Grebe, a larger, flightless version of the Pied-billed (common here in winter). It is usually absent near Panajachel, but with luck, one might be seen near the south shore of the lake from the daily boat that goes over to Santiago Atitlan from the Hotel Tzanjuyu.

Pine-oak woodland birds can be seen easily at innumerable places on the road to Patzun between 3 and 9.5 miles (5 and 15 kilometers) from Panajachel. Birds to look for include Tufted Flycatcher, Rufous-collared Thrush, Brown-backed Solitaire, Gray Silky-flycatcher, Chestnut-sided Shrike-Vireo, Townsend's, Hermit, and Olive Warblers.

At Kilometer Post 149 on the Pan American Highway to the east of Nahuala, a trail leads up onto slopes of mixed pine, oak, and cypress. The area is being rapidly deforested, although Pink-headed

Warblers are common not far from the highway. By taking several of the rougher, steeper side trails you may find Blue-throated Motmot, Mountain Trogon, Blue-and-white Mockingbird, Ruddy-capped Nightingale-Thrush, and Chestnut-capped Brush-Finch.

CHECKLIST

American Dabchick
Black-necked Grebe   W
Pied-billed Grebe   c   W
Atitlan Grebe
Brown Pelican   r   W
Great Blue Heron   W
Green Heron   W
Least Bittern   r
Blue-winged Teal   W
Northern Shoveler   W
Northern Pintail   W
American Wigeon   W
Redhead   W
Ring-necked Duck   W
Lesser Scaup   c   W
Ruddy Duck   W
Turkey Vulture   c

Black Vulture   c
Sharp-shinned Sparrowhawk   W
Red-tailed Hawk   c
Swainson's Hawk   c   M
Broad-winged Hawk   c   M
Zone-tailed Hawk   r
American Kestrel
Singing Quail   r
Ocellated Quail   r
Sora Crake   W
Common Gallinule   c   W
American Coot   c   W
Northern Jacana
Spotted Sandpiper   c   W
Laughing Gull   W
Franklin's Gull   M
Band-tailed Pigeon

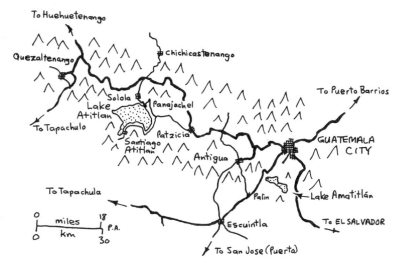

White-winged Dove   c
Mourning Dove   W
Common Ground-Dove
Inca Dove
White-tipped Dove   c
Green Parakeet
Barn Owl
Whiskered Screech-Owl   c
Northern Pygmy-Owl   r
Whip-poor-will   c
Common Nighthawk   M
White-collared Swift   c
White-throated Swift   c
Rufous Sabrewing
Green Violetear
White-eared Hummingbird   c
Red-billed Azurecrown   c
Amethyst-throated Mountaingem
Garnet-throated Mountaingem
Green-throated Mountaingem
Rivoli's Hummingbird
Slender Sheartail   r
Sparkling-tailed Hummingbird   c
Ruby-throated Hummingbird   c
   W
Wine-throated Hummingbird
Mountain Trogon
Blue-throated Motmot
Northern (Red-shafted) Flicker   c
Golden-olive Woodpecker   c
Golden-fronted Woodpecker   c
Acorn Woodpecker   c
Yellow-bellied Sapsucker   W
Hairy Woodpecker
Spot-crowned Woodcreeper
Rose-throated Becard   r
Western Kingbird   W
Great Kiskadee
Social Flycatcher
Brown-crested Flycatcher
Dusky-capped Flycatcher
Black Phoebe
Scissor-tailed Flycatcher   M
Coues's Pewee   c
Olive-sided Pewee   W
Western Pewee   r
Tufted Flycatcher   c

Belted Flycatcher
Empidonax, species   W
Yellowish Flycatcher   r
Buff-breasted Flycatcher
Yellow-bellied Elaenia
Paltry Tyrannulet   r
Rough-winged Swallow   c
Black-capped Swallow   c
Violet-green Swallow   c W
Bushy-crested Jay   c
Unicolored Jay   r
Steller's Jay   c
Bushtit   c
Northern Treecreeper
Band-backed Wren   c
Gray-breasted Wood-Wren
Plain Wren
House Wren   c
Rock Wren
Rufous-browed Wren   r
Blue-and-white Mockingbird   c
Tropical Mockingbird
Rufous-collared Thrush   c
Clay-colored Thrush
Black Thrush   r
Brown-backed Solitaire   c
Hermit Thrush   W
Ruddy-capped Nightingale-Thrush
Orange-billed Nightingale-Thrush
Eastern Bluebird   c
Blue-gray Gnatcatcher   W
Cedar Waxwing   c W
Gray Silky-flycatcher
Rufous-browed Peppershrike
Chestnut-sided Shrike-Vireo   r
Hutton's Vireo
Solitary Vireo   c
Warbling Vireo   c W
Red-legged Honeycreeper   M
Garden Flower-piercer   r
Black-and-white Warbler   W
Tennessee Warbler   c W
Orange-crowned Warbler   r W
Nashville Warbler   W
Crescent-chested Warbler
Olive Warbler
Yellow Warbler   W

Magnolia Warbler   W
Cape May Warbler   r W
Yellow-rumped (Audubon's)
   Warbler   c W
Townsend's Warbler   c W
Black-throated Green Warbler   W
Hermit Warbler   W
Grace's Warbler   r
MacGillivray's Warbler   c W
Northern Yellowthroat   W
Red-faced Warbler
Pink-headed Warbler
Golden-browed Warbler
Rufous-capped Warbler   c
Wilson's Warbler   c W
Painted Whitestart
Slate-throated Whitestart   c
House Sparrow   c
Yellow-billed Cacique   r
Bronzed Cowbird   c
Great-tailed Grackle   c
Melodious Blackbird   c
Orchard Oriole   c W
Black-vented Oriole   c
Altamira Oriole
Yellow-backed Oriole
Northern (Baltimore) Oriole   c W
Northern (Bullock's) Oriole   r W

Blue-hooded Euphonia   r
Blue-gray Tanager
Yellow-winged Tanager
Flame-colored Tanager
Summer Tanager   W
Western Tanager   c W
Hepatic Tanager   r
Common Bush-Tanager   r
Grayish Saltator   r
Rose-breasted Grosbeak   c W
Black-headed Grosbeak   r
Indigo Bunting   c W
Hooded Grosbeak   r
White-collared Seedeater   c
Black-capped Siskin
Black-headed Siskin   c
Lesser Goldfinch
Yellow-throated Brush-Finch   c
Chestnut-capped Brush-Finch
Yellow-faced Grassquit   r
Rufous-sided Towhee
Prevost Ground-Sparrow
Rusty Sparrow   c
Yellow-eyed Junco   r
Rufous-collared Sparrow   c
Lincoln's Sparrow   W
Red Crossbill   r

22
San Jose, Costa Rica

SAN JOSE, THE CAPITAL, with an international airport, many fine hotels, and car rental agencies, is situated at about 3000 feet (915 m) on the Meseta Central, a large montane valley now largely deforested and intensively cultivated. The Blue-and-white Swallow and Rufous-collared Sparrow are common in the city. Look for White-faced and White-eared Ground-Sparrows and Yellow-throated Brush-Finch in bushy coffee groves. For greater variety, one must ascend into the mountains or drop down to the lowlands. This writeup includes only montane areas, generally above 3000 feet (915 m).

The road up Volcan Irazu, beginning at Cartago, is paved and has a small hotel (the Robert) on it. Destruction of vegetation by both man and volcano has left little natural habitat intact although the Peg-billed Finch lives near the summit.

The Poas Volcano National Park, 15.6 square miles (40 km²), contains significantly more forest. North of San Jose, the park is reached via Route 9, going through Heredia. At the top of the divide just before Vara Blanca (22.5 miles [36 km] from San Jose), turn left on Route 120, which leads up to the park. The mountain is often shrouded with clouds and drizzle, especially in the afternoon. Careful observation in the high forests here may reveal Resplendent Quetzal (not common), Rivoli's, Fiery-throated and the endemic Cerise-throated Hummingbirds, Ruddy Treerunner, Buffy Tuftedcheek, Spot-crowned Woodcreeper, Dark Pewee, Black-capped Flycatcher, Sooty Thrush, Black-billed Nightingale-Thrush, Phainoptila, Garden Flower-piercer, Collared Whitestart, Black-cheeked Warbler, Sooty-capped Bush-Tanager, and Large-footed and Yellow-thighed Finches. Inside the crater is a lagoon, and small geyserlike eruptions often occur.

The highest section of the Pan American Highway is in southern Costa Rica, where it provides access to a barren but interesting páramo area at 11,000 feet (3491 m) on Cerro de la Muerte. From Cartago (east of San Jose) the road goes uphill southward. There are still patches of high-altitude forest where among the bamboo and the trees drenched with bromeliad live Resplendent Quetzal, Wren-

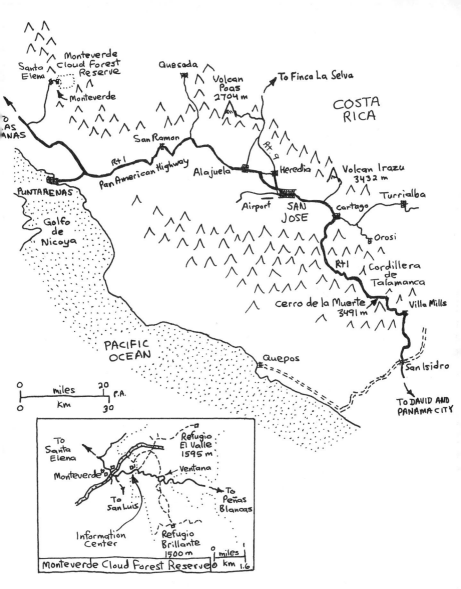

thrush, Black Guan, Long-tailed Silky-flycatcher, and Phainoptila.
The Timberline Wren is fairly common just below the open páramo,
and the local Volcano Junco is easily seen. Primitive accommodations
are available at La Georgina Inn, several miles south of the top.

The Monteverde Cloud Forest Reserve is home to a great variety
of birds. It can be reached via the Pan American Highway northwest
toward Nicaragua. After the turnoff to Puntarenas (Route 17), con-

tinue north until you reach the Rio Lagarto bridge (the third steel bridge with an overhead structure). Just before the bridge turn east onto a road that passes through Guacimal and Santa Elena. The forest reserve is 2 miles (3 km) beyond Monteverde. Visitors may book rooms at the Hotel de Montana Monteverde by writing Apto. 70, Plaza G. Víquez, San Jose, Costa Rica, or book rooms at the pension in the reserve at Apartado 10165, San Jose, Costa Rica.

The birdlife here is often rich and there are good chances for viewing such notables as Black Guan, Resplendent Quetzal, and Three-wattled Bellbird. Lower elevation species reach up to the Monteverde Pension, where Streak-headed Woodcreeper, Long-tailed Manakin, and White-eared Ground-Sparrow occur (most species occurring below 3000 feet [915 m] have been purposely left off this list to avoid confusion). The quetzals are most vocal and conspicuous from March through June and often nest near the Information Center. Cloud forest birding involves much time and patience due to weather and visibility problems. This exceptional area with its superb network of trails is the best place in Central America for mountain birds. Stay awhile.

CHECKLIST

Highland Tinamou
Blue-winged Teal   W
Black Vulture
Turkey Vulture
Swallow-tailed Kite
Double-toothed Kite   r
Bicolored Sparrowhawk   r
Cooper's Sparrowhawk   r W
Sharp-shinned Sparrowhawk   W
Red-tailed Hawk   r W
Swainson's Hawk   M
Broad-winged Hawk   W
White Hawk   r
Barred Hawk
Ornate Hawk-Eagle   r
Barred Forest-Falcon
American Kestrel
Black Guan
Spot-bellied Bobwhite   r
White-throated Wood-Quail
Band-tailed Pigeon   c
Red-billed Pigeon

Ruddy Pigeon
Short-billed Pigeon
White-tipped Dove
Costa Rican Quail-Dove
Ruddy Quail-Dove   r
Great Green Macaw   r
Crimson-fronted Parakeet
Sulfur-winged Parakeet
Barred Parakeet   r
Brown-hooded Parrot
White-fronted Parrot
Red-lored Parrot
Squirrel Cuckoo
Groove-billed Ani
Bare-shanked Screech-Owl
Spectacled Owl
Cheer-for-will   r
White-collared Swift
Vaux's Swift
Green-fronted Lancebill   r
Green Hermit
Little Hermit   r

Violet Sabrewing
Brown Violetear   r
Green Violetear   c
Emerald *(Chlorostilbon)*, sp.
Fiery-throated Hummingbird
Rufous-tailed Hummingbird
Steely-vented Hummingbird   c
Stripe-tailed Hummingbird
Variable Mountaingem
Rivoli's Hummingbird
Green-crowned Brilliant
Costa Rican Woodstar
Volcano Hummingbird
Scintillant Hummingbird
Ruby-throated Hummingbird   W
Resplendent Quetzal
Collared Trogon
Blue-crowned Motmot
Prong-billed Barbet
Red-headed Barbet   r
Emerald Toucanet
Golden-olive Woodpecker
Acorn Woodpecker
Golden-fronted Woodpecker
Yellow-bellied Sapsucker   r W
Smoky-brown Woodpecker
Hairy Woodpecker
Ruddy Woodcreeper
Olivaceous Woodcreeper
Wedge-billed Woodcreeper
Spotted Woodcreeper
Spot-crowned Woodcreeper
Red-faced Spinetail   c
Ruddy Treerunner
Spotted Barbtail
Buffy Tuftedcheek   r
Streak-breasted Treehunter   r
Gray-throated Leaftosser
Plain Antvireo   r
Slaty Antwren   r
Immaculate Antbird   r
Black-faced Ant-thrush   r
Scaled Antpitta   r
Silver-fronted Tapaculo
Long-tailed Manakin
Bright-rumped Attila
Barred Becard   r

Masked Tityra
Bare-necked Umbrellabird   r
Three-wattled Bellbird
Eastern Kingbird   M
Tropical Kingbird
Sulfur-bellied Flycatcher   S
Golden-bellied Flycatcher
Social Flycatcher
Great Kiskadee
Dusky-capped Flycatcher
Olive-sided Pewee   W
Wood Pewee   W
Western Pewee   r W
Dark Pewee   c
Ochraceous Pewee   r
Yellowish Flycatcher   c
Least Flycatcher   r W
Black-capped Flycatcher   c
Tufted Flycatcher   c
White-throated Spadebill
Eye-ringed Flatbill
Common Tody-Flycatcher   r
Scale-crested Pygmy-Tyrant   r
Mountain Elaenia   c
Paltry Tyrannulet   c
White-fronted Tyrannulet   r
Olive-striped Flycatcher
Rough-winged Swallow   c
Blue-and-white Swallow   c
Brown Jay
Silver-throated Jay
Azure-hooded Jay
Rufous-and-white Wren
Plain Wren
House Wren   c
Timberline Wren
Ochraceous Wren   c
Gray-breasted Wood-Wren   c
White-throated Thrush
Sooty Thrush
Mountain Thrush   c
Clay-colored Thrush
Black-faced Solitaire
Wood Thrush   W
Swainson's Thrush   W
Slaty-backed Nightingale-Thrush
Ruddy-capped Nightingale-Thrush

Black-billed Nightingale-Thrush
Long-tailed Silky-flycatcher
Phainoptila
Rufous-browed Peppershrike
Green Shrike-Vireo
Yellow-winged Vireo
Yellow-throated Vireo   r W
Red-eyed Vireo   r M
Yellow-green Vireo   S
Philadelphia Vireo   r W
Brown-capped Vireo
Lesser Greenlet
Yellow-billed Cacique   r
Northern (Baltimore) Oriole   r W
Eastern Meadowlark
Black-and-white Warbler   W
Golden-winged Warbler   W
Tennessee Warbler   W
Flame-throated Warbler
Tropical Parula
Yellow Warbler   W
Townsend's Warbler   W
Black-throated Green Warbler   c
   W
Blackburnian Warbler   r W
Chestnut-sided Warbler   r W
Ovenbird   W
Kentucky Warbler   W
Gray-crowned Yellowthroat
Wilson's Warbler   c W
Canada Warbler   r W
Slate-throated Whitestart   c
Collared Whitestart   c
Three-striped Warbler

Golden-crowned Warbler
Rufous-capped Warbler   r
Black-cheeked Warbler
Wrenthrush
Bananaquit
Scarlet-thighed Dacnis
Garden Flower-piercer   c
Golden-browed Chlorophonia
Blue-hooded Euphonia
Tawny-capped Euphonia   r
Spangle-cheeked Tanager
Silver-throated Tanager
Blue-gray Tanager
Summer Tanager   W
Hepatic Tanager   r
Scarlet Tanager   r M
White-winged Tanager   r
Common Bush-Tanager   c
Sooty-capped Bush-Tanager   c
Buff-throated Saltator
Yellow Grosbeak
Rose-breasted Grosbeak   W
Yellow-faced Grassquit   c
Yellow-throated Brush-Finch   c
Chestnut-capped Brush-Finch
White-eared Ground-Sparrow
Large-footed Finch
Slaty Finch   r
Peg-billed Finch   r
Yellow-thighed Finch   c
Sooty-faced Finch   r
Rufous-collared Sparrow   c
Volcano Junco
Yellow-bellied Siskin

23
Chiriqui Highlands, Panama

IN THE WESTERNMOST PROVINCE OF PANAMA, bordering Costa Rica, are high, cool mountains that are home to the world's most elegant bird, the Resplendent Quetzal, as well as a large number of endemic species.

Visitors can either drive to David from Panama City (7 or 8 hours through savanna habitats) or fly on the twice-daily flight between the two cities and rent a car in David. David is located at sea level in hot, cattle country. Two paved roads go into the mountains, and small hotels are available on both.

Boquette is a charming town at 3500 feet (1067 m) in a river valley east of Volcan Barú (11,300 feet [3445 m]). Gardens around town, such as the Hotel Panamonte garden, provide a habitat for many birds, but the best birding is in the remaining forest areas on the slopes above town. Finca Lerida, a private farm owned by the Collins family, is the best; permission to enter the farm property should be obtained at the Panamonte Hotel, which can also give you directions. Arrangements for special vehicles and drivers can be made. The road uphill is steep and rocky, and passes groves of coffee and patches of forest. Birds found in the Finca Lerida forest include Resplendent Quetzal, Three-wattled Bellbird, Black Guan, Spotted Wood-Quail, and Silvery-fronted Tapaculo. Quetzals are most easily found at El Mirador, a spot overlooking a spectacular ravine. Here, as elsewhere in cloud forests, clouds often descend in the afternoon, drenching the mountains with fog and heavy drizzle.

On the west side of Volcan Barú a paved road leads up to Cerro Punta. This side of the mountain is drier, and more forest has been cut down. Some birds can be found around the Hotel Dos Rios in Volcan, among them the Blue-crowned Motmot, Buff-rumped Warbler, and the endemic Chiriqui Yellowthroat. Fiery-billed Aracaris can sometimes be seen in woods along the road west toward the Costa Rican border.

After crossing the old lava flow north of Volcan, the road passes through woods along the Chiriqui Viejo River. Woodland patches above the Florida Audubon Society Cabin and along the little road

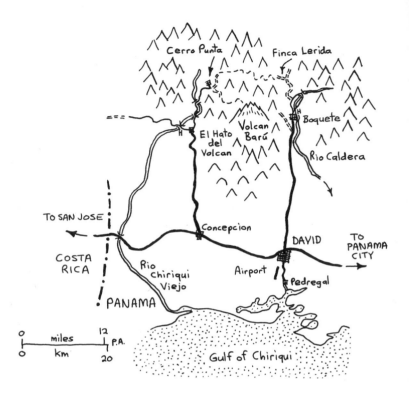

leading left to a Methodist Camp are among the most productive. Along the river Torrent Tyrannulets are common. Long-tailed Silky-flycatchers, hummingbirds, tanagers, and finches are conspicuous in the woods and clearings.

Cerro Punta is an agricultural town with a small Chinese pension. Energetic birders should drive through town on the main road for a half mile past a horse farm on the right, then across a wooden bridge. The Boquette Trail starts there (going to the right); cars can sometimes make it a mile or so beyond here. The trail itself winds up to about 8000 feet (2438 m) through forested areas and clearings. Featured birds would include Resplendent Quetzal, Volcano Hummingbird, Black-capped Flycatcher, Silvery-throated Jay, Sooty Robin, Black-billed and Ruddy-capped Nightingale-Thrushes, Black-thighed Grosbeak, and Large-footed Finch.

CHECKLIST

(In the following checklist *V* indicates birds found chiefly near El Hato del Volcan, *CP* = birds found best near Cerro Punta and the Chiriqui Viejo

River, and *B* is often used after species seen chiefly on the Boquette side)

Cattle Heron
Black Vulture
Turkey Vulture
White-tailed Kite
Swallow-tailed Kite
White-tailed Hawk   V
Swainson's Hawk   c M
Red-tailed Hawk   W
Broad-winged Hawk   W
Roadside Hawk   V
Black Guan   r B
Spotted Wood-Quail
White-throated Crake   V
Common Snipe   V W
Band-tailed Pigeon   c
Ruddy Pigeon
Ruddy Ground-Dove
Maroon-chested Ground-Dove   r
White-tipped Dove
Costa Rican Quail-Dove   B
Rufous-breasted Quail-Dove   CP
Crimson-fronted Parakeet
Sulfur-winged Parakeet   c
Barred Parakeet   r
White-crowned Parrot   V
Blue-headed Parrot   V
Squirrel Cuckoo
Andean Pygmy-Owl   r
Mottled Owl
Common Pauraque
Cheer-for-will   r
White-collared Swift
Vaux's Swift   c
Green Hermit   c
Green-fronted Lancebill   r CP
Violet Sabrewing
Green Violetear   c
Fiery-throated Hummingbird   r
  CP
Snowy-breasted Hummingbird   c
Rufous-tailed Hummingbird
Stripe-tailed Hummingbird
White-tailed Emerald
Variable Mountaingem   c
Green-crowned Brilliant

Rivoli's Hummingbird
Purple-crowned Fairy
Costa Rican Woodstar   r B
Volcano Hummingbird   CP
Scintillant Hummingbird   c
Resplendent Quetzal
Collared Trogon
Orange-bellied Trogon
Red-headed Barbet
Prong-billed Barbet   r
Emerald Toucanet   c
Fiery-billed Aracari   r V
Golden-olive Woodpecker
Acorn Woodpecker
Smoky-brown Woodpecker   r
Hairy Woodpecker   c
Spot-crowned Woodcreeper   c
Slaty Spinetail   V
Red-faced Spinetail   c
Ruddy Treerunner
Spotted Barbtail
Buffy Tuftedcheek   CP
Lineated Foliage-gleaner
Scaly-throated Foliage-gleaner
Buff-fronted Foliage-gleaner
Streak-breasted Treehunter
Scaled Antpitta   r B
Silvery-fronted Tapaculo
Bright-rumped Attila
Barred Becard
Black-and-white Becard   r B
Masked Tityra
Bare-necked Umbrellabird   r B
Three-wattled Bellbird   B
Black Phoebe
Tropical Kingbird
Streaked Flycatcher
Golden-bellied Flycatcher   CP
Boat-billed Flycatcher
Social Flycatcher
Gray-capped Flycatcher
Dusky-capped Flycatcher   c
Olive-sided Pewee   W
Dark Pewee
Tufted Flycatcher   c

Yellow-bellied Flycatcher W
Yellowish Flycatcher
Black-capped Flycatcher CP
White-throated Spadebill
Eye-ringed Flatbill
Common Tody-Flycatcher V
Torrent Tyrannulet
Yellow-bellied Elaenia c
Lesser Elaenia
Mountain Elaenia c
Paltry Tyrannulet c
White-fronted Tyrannulet r
Gray-breasted Martin
Blue-and-white Swallow c
Rough-winged Swallow
Silvery-throated Jay r
North American Dipper
Plain Wren V
House Wren c
Ochraceous Wren
Gray-breasted Wood-Wren c
Black-faced Solitaire
Clay-colored Thrush
Mountain Thrush
Sooty Thrush CP
Swainson's Thrush W
Ruddy-capped Nightingale-Thrush
Orange-billed Nightingale-Thrush
Black-billed Nightingale-Thrush
  CP
Long-tailed Silky-flycatcher c
Phainoptila r
Rufous-browed Peppershrike
Yellow-winged Vireo
Yellow-throated Vireo W
Philadelphia Vireo W
Brown-capped Vireo
Garden Flower-piercer c
Scarlet-thighed Dacnis V
Wrenthrush r
Black-and-white Warbler W
Golden-winged Warbler W
Tennessee Warbler c W
Flame-throated Warbler
Tropical Parula
Yellow-rumped Warbler W

Black-throated Green Warbler c
  W
Blackburnian Warbler W
Chestnut-sided Warbler W
Ovenbird W
Northern Waterthrush W
Kentucky Warbler W
Mourning Warbler W
Chiriqui Yellowthroat V
Wilson's Warbler c W
Canada Warbler W
American Redstart W
Slate-throated Whitestart
Collared Whitestart c
Golden-crowned Warbler
Black-cheeked Warbler
Rufous-capped Warbler
Yellow-billed Cacique
Northern (Baltimore) Oriole W
Golden-browed Chlorophonia
Blue-hooded Euphonia
Silver-throated Tanager c
Bay-headed Tanager
Golden-hooded Tanager
Blue-gray Tanager c
Scarlet-rumped Tanager V
Summer Tanager W
Flame-colored Tanager
White-winged Tanager
Common Bush-Tanager c
Sooty-capped Bush-Tanager
Buff-throated Saltator
Streaked Saltator
Black-thighed Grosbeak
Rose-breasted Grosbeak W
Indigo Bunting W
Yellow-faced Grassquit c
Blue Seedeater CP
Large-footed Finch CP
Yellow-thighed Finch c
Yellow-throated Brush-Finch c
Chestnut-capped Brush-Finch
Black-headed Brush-Finch V
Black-striped Sparrow
Rufous-collared Sparrow c
Yellow-bellied Siskin
Lesser Goldfinch

24
Panama City, Panama

THE PANAMA CANAL is the heart of one of the finest birding areas in the world. For 5 miles (8 km) on either side of the canal the United States preserved magnificent tropical forests and waters. Birdlife is exceptionally rich here since many South American forms meet those from Central America, and the drier forests and savannas of the Pacific slope merge into the taller humid forests of the Caribbean slope.

Paved roads and good all-weather dirt roads provide access to many good areas. Visitors usually arrive at Tocumen Airport east of Panama City. Accommodations include the La Siesta Hotel near the airport, many luxurious hotels in Panama City (be sure yours has a 24-hour coffee shop), and the Hotel Washington in Colon. Rental cars are easily obtained, and English is widely spoken. Food and water are much safer here than in many other countries.

In Panama City itself a good variety of birds can be found at Panama Viejo, the ruins of the old city about 5 miles (8 km) east of the center of town. Brown Pelican, Magnificent Frigatebird, Neotropic Cormorant, egrets, herons, countless shorebirds (with many Willet and Whimbrel), and Laughing Gulls are common.

Fort Amador lies between Panama City and the Pacific entrance to the canal. Collared Plover and many migratory shorebirds can be seen on the beaches there, particularly at high tide. The Farfan area on the west side of the canal entrance is good for Mangrove Warblers and has much dawn and dusk bird activity near woodland edge. To reach Farfan take the Bridge of the Americas over the canal, and turn left on the first road on the other side, then right at the only fork.

Summit Gardens and the Madden Forest Preserve are good areas for "jungle" birding. They are located near the Summit stop on the Panama railroad and are reached within an hour from Balboa or Panama City by road. Summit Gardens is an excellent area for a late afternoon trip and features a colony of Chestnut-headed Oropendola nesting in royal palms. A paved road runs through Madden Forest, with plenty of parking available. Although many forest birds occur

here, Purple-throated Fruitcrow and three species of trogons being common, there are few good trails and traffic is a nuisance.

Pipeline Road is a long (part dirt, part paved) road that runs northwest from Gamboa on the east side of the canal through heavy tropical forest. To reach it turn left on a gravel road a half mile (1 km) beyond Gamboa (a marshy pond appears on the right). The best birding is between 5 and 12 miles out. There is very little traffic since it is a dead end. The area would make a superb national park. Its rich avifauna includes such species as King Vulture, Swallow-tailed Kite, White Hawk, Black and Ornate Hawk-Eagles, parrots, hummingbirds, trogons, motmots, puffbirds, woodcreepers, antbirds, manakins, cotingas, countless flycatchers, honeycreepers, and tanagers. Wading through forest streams provides good access into the forest interior. Several days are needed to cover the area adequately.

Barro Colorado is a famous island in the middle of Gatun Lake. A permit is needed to make the day trip (obtainable from the Smithsonian Tropical Research Institute, Box 2072, Balboa, Panama). Visitors must take the morning train to Frijoles, be met by a prearranged boat, and return in the afternoon. Overnights are possible, though quite difficult to arrange. The island is really a hilltop, with many steps and steep trails, and most of the birds can be seen more easily elsewhere. Those who make the trip will find many birds in the clearing around the laboratory and occasional flocks of birds along the trails. Mammals are the highlight, with black howler, Central American spider and white-faced monkeys, Geoffrey's marmoset, coatimundi, two-toed and three-toed Sloths, tamandua anteater, agouti, collared peccary, and Baird's tapir all present.

Moving to the Caribbean slope in the Colon area, many shorebirds, jaegers, gulls, and terns can be found by visiting Coco Solo east of Manzanillo Bay. The grassy fields and the tidal pool near the huge abandoned hangars are good. Collared Plover and Saffron Finch are numerous on lawns throughout the area.

The Gatun Locks and Dam southwest of Margarita are also excellent for shorebirds, particularly in the fall. The wide greens on the west side are excellent for Upland, Pectoral, Buff-breasted, and Baird's Sandpipers.

The drawbridge over the canal (which is opened and closed constantly with the ship traffic) provides access to several outstanding forest areas. The road to the right goes to Fort Sherman and Fort San Lorenzo. The main road passes through heavy forest with many fine side roads begging to be birded. The roads to the left (away from the coast) are best. Toucans and Black-chested Jay are particularly numerous. Fort San Lorenzo is a picturesque ruin, perched on a promontory overlooking the mouth of the Rio Chagres.

The Piña and Escobal areas are reached by turning left after the drawbridge at Gatun Lock. After several miles, an intersection is reached where the right-hand fork leads eventually to Piña on the coast. Continue straight (left) for 5 ¼ miles (toward Escobal), to the Achiote Road, which branches off to the right. A superb variety of humid forest and swamp birds can be seen here with highlights including Hook-billed Kite, Crane Hawk, Red-throated Caracara, Spot-crowned Barbet, Pygmy and Streaked Antwrens, White-headed Wren, and Dusky-faced Tanager.

CHECKLIST

Great Tinamou	Pied-billed Grebe
Little Tinamou	Brown Pelican c
American Dabchick	Brown Booby

Neotropic Cormorant   c
Anhinga
Magnificent Frigatebird   c
Great Blue Heron   W
Great Egret   c
Snowy Egret
Little Blue Heron   c
Louisiana Heron
Green Heron   c
Cattle Heron
Black-crowned Night-Heron
Yellow-crowned Night-Heron
Wood Stork
White Ibis
Blue-winged Teal   W
King Vulture
Black Vulture   c
Turkey Vulture   c
White-tailed Kite
Swallow-tailed Kite
Hook-billed Kite   r
Double-toothed Kite
Plumbeous Kite
Tiny Sparrowhawk   r
Swainson's Hawk   M
Zone-tailed Hawk
Gray Hawk
Roadside Hawk
Short-tailed Hawk
Broad-winged Hawk   c M
White Hawk
Semiplumbeous Hawk
Plumbeous Hawk   r
Lesser Black Hawk
Ornate Hawk-Eagle
Black Hawk-Eagle
Osprey   W
Collared Forest-Falcon
Slaty-backed Forest-Falcon   r
Barred Forest-Falcon   r
Yellow-headed Caracara
Red-throated Caracara   r
Peregrine Falcon   W
American Kestrel   W
Great Curassow   r
Crested Guan   r
Gray-headed Chachalaca

Gray-necked Wood-Rail
White-throated Crake
Common Gallinule
Purple Gallinule
American Coot   W
Sungrebe
Wattled Jacana   c
Gray Plover   c W
Lesser Golden Plover   M
Semipalmated Plover   c W
Collared Plover
Killdeer   W
Wilson's Plover
Solitary Sandpiper   W
Lesser Yellowlegs   W
Greater Yellowlegs   W
Spotted Sandpiper   c W
Willet   c W
Ruddy Turnstone   W
Surfbird   W
Red Knot   W
Least Sandpiper   c W
Baird's Sandpiper   M
Pectoral Sandpiper   M
Sanderling   W
Semipalmated Sandpiper   W
Western Sandpiper   c W
Stilt Sandpiper   W
Buff-breasted Sandpiper   W
Upland Sandpiper   M
Whimbrel   c W
Marbled Godwit   W
Short-billed Dowticher   W
Common Snipe   W
Pomarine Jaeger   W
Parasitic Jaeger   W
Laughing Gull   W
Franklin's Gull   W
Black Tern   c W
Gull-billed Tern   W
Common Tern   c W
Little Tern   W
Royal Tern   W
Sandwich Tern   c W
Pale-vented Pigeon   c
Scaled Pigeon
Short-billed Pigeon   c

Ruddy Ground-Dove   c
Blue Ground-Dove
White-tipped Dove   c
Gray-chested Dove
Ruddy Quail-Dove   r
Orange-chinned Parakeet   c
Brown-hooded Parrot
Blue-hooded Parrot   c
Red-lored Parrot
Mealy Parrot
Yellow-billed Cuckoo   W
Squirrel Cuckoo   c
Little Cuckoo   r
Greater Ani
Smooth-billed Ani   c
Groove-billed Ani
Striped Cuckoo
Barn Owl
Tropical Screech-Owl
Spectacled Owl
Mottled Owl
Striped Owl
Common Potoo
Lesser Nighthawk
Common Nighthawk   M
Common Pauraque   c
Rufous Nightjar
White-collared Swift
Band-rumped Swift
Short-tailed Swift
Lesser Swallow-tailed Swift
Rufous-breasted Hermit
Band-tailed Barbthroat
Long-tailed Hermit   c
Little Hermit   c
Scaly-breasted Hummingbird
White-necked Jacobin
Black-throated Mango
Blue-tailed Emerald
Crowned Woodnymph
Violet-bellied Hummingbird
Sapphire-throated Hummingbird
Blue-chested Hummingbird
Snowy-breasted Hummingbird   c
Rufous-tailed Hummingbird   c
White-vented Plumeleteer
Purple-crowned Fairy

Long-billed Starthroat
Slaty-tailed Trogon   c
Black-tailed Trogon   r
White-tailed Trogon
Violaceous Trogon
Black-throated Trogon
Ringed Kingfisher
Belted Kingfisher   W
Amazon Kingfisher   r
Green Kingfisher
Rufous Motmot
Broad-billed Motmot
Blue-crowned Motmot
White-necked Puffbird
Black-breasted Puffbird
Pied Puffbird
White-whiskered Puffbird
Spot-crowned Barbet   r
Collared Aracari   c
Yellow-eared Toucanet   r
Keel-billed Toucan   c
Yellow-throated Toucan   c
Cinnamon Woodpecker
Lineated Woodpecker
Red-crowned Woodpecker   c
Black-cheeked Woodpecker
Crimson-crested Woodpecker
Plain-brown Woodcreeper
Long-tailed Woodcreeper
Wedge-billed Woodcreeper   c
Black-striped Woodcreeper
Streak-headed Woodcreeper
Buff-throated Foliage-gleaner
Plain Xenops   c
Fasciated Antshrike
Great Antshrike
Barred Antshrike   c
Slaty Antshrike   c
Spot-crowned Antvireo
Pygmy Antwren   r
Streaked Antwren
White-flanked Antwren   c
Checker-throated Antwren   c
Dot-winged Antwren   c
Dusky Antbird
White-bellied Antbird
Bare-crowned Antbird   r

Chestnut-backed Antbird
Dull-mantled Antbird   r
Bicolored Antbird
Spotted Antbird
Ocellated Antbird
Black-faced Ant-thrush
Streak-chested Antpitta   r
Blue Cotinga
Bright-rumped Attila
Speckled Mourner   r
Rufous Mourner
Rufous Piha
Cinnamon Becard
White-winged Becard
Masked Tityra   c
Black-crowned Tityra
Purple-throated Fruitcrow   c
Blue-crowned Manakin
Red-capped Manakin   c
Lance-tailed Manakin
Golden-collared Manakin   c
Thrush-like Manakin
Sirystes   r
Long-tailed Tyrant
Fork-tailed Flycatcher   c
Eastern Kingbird   M
Tropical Kingbird   c
Gray Kingbird   W
Piratic Flycatcher
Streaked Flycatcher   c
Boat-billed Flycatcher   c
White-ringed Flycatcher
Social Flycatcher   c
Rusty-margined Flycatcher
Great Kiskadee
Lesser Kiskadee
Great Crested Flycatcher   W
Panama Flycatcher
Dusky-capped Flycatcher
Olive-sided Pewee   W
Wood Pewee   c M
Tropical Pewee
Acadian Flycatcher   W
Traill's Flycatcher   W
Ruddy-tailed Flycatcher
Sulfur-rumped Flycatcher
Black-tailed Flycatcher

Northern Royal Flycatcher
Golden-crowned Spadebill   r
Brownish Flycatcher
Yellow-olive Flycatcher
Yellow-margined Flycatcher
Olivaceous Flatbill
Black-headed Tody-Flycatcher   r
Common Tody-Flycatcher
Southern Bentbill
Pale-eyed Pygmy-Tyrant
Yellow Tyrannulet
Yellow-bellied Elaenia   c
Lesser Elaenia
Greenish Elaenia   r
Scrub Flycatcher
Southern Beardless Tyrannulet
Paltry Tyrannulet
Yellow-crowned Tyrannulet
Brown-capped Tyrannulet
Olive-striped Flycatcher
Ochre-bellied Flycatcher
Sand Martin   M
Mangrove Swallow   c
Barn Swallow   W
Cliff Martin   M
Gray-breasted Martin   c
Purple Martin   M
Brown-chested Martin   S
White-thighed Swallow
Rough-winged Swallow
Black-chested Jay
White-headed Wren   r
Buff-breasted Wren
Plain Wren   c
Rufous-and-white Wren
Bay Wren
Black-bellied Wren
Rufous-breasted Wren
House Wren
White-breasted Wood-Wren
Song Wren
Nightingale Wren
Gray Catbird   W
Tropical Mockingbird   c
Clay-colored Thrush   c
Swainson's Thrush   W
Tropical Gnatcatcher

Long-billed Gnatwren
Green Shrike-Vireo
Yellow-throated Vireo   W
Red-eyed Vireo
Golden-fronted Greenlet
Lesser Greenlet   c
Scrub Greenlet
Bananaquit
Red-legged Honeycreeper   c
Shining Honeycreeper
Green Honeycreeper
Blue Dacnis
Scarlet-thighed Dacnis
Black-and-white Warbler   W
Prothonotary Warbler   W
Golden-winged Warbler   W
Tennessee Warbler   c W
Yellow Warbler
Magnolia Warbler
Blackburnian Warbler
Chestnut-sided Warbler   c W
Bay-breasted Warbler   c W
Northern Waterthrush   W
Kentucky Warbler   W
Mourning Warbler   W
Canada Warbler   W
American Redstart   W
Rufous-capped Warbler
Buff-rumped Warbler
Montezuma Oropendola
Chestnut-headed Oropendola   c
Crested Oropendola
Yellow-rumped Cacique
Scarlet-rumped Cacique
Yellow-billed Cacique
Giant Cowbird
Great-tailed Grackle   c
Orchard Oriole   c W
Yellow-tailed Oriole

Yellow-backed Oriole   c
Northern (Baltimore) Oriole   c W
Red-breasted Blackbird
Fulvous-vented Euphonia
White-vented Euphonia
Yellow-crowned Euphonia
Thick-billed Euphonia   c
Golden-hooded Tanager   c
Plain-colored Tanager   c
Bay-headed Tanager
Blue-gray Tanager   c
Palm Tanager   c
Crimson-backed Tanager   c
Bright-rumped Tanager
Summer Tanager   c W
Scarlet Tanager   M
Carmiol's Tanager
Red-throated Ant-Tanager
White-lined Tanager
White-shouldered Tanager   c
Tawny-crested Tanager
Sulfur-rumped Tanager
Gray-headed Tanager
Dusky-faced Tanager
Rosy Thrush-Tanager
Black-headed Saltator
Buff-throated Saltator   c
Streaked Saltator   c
Slate-colored Grosbeak
Rose-breasted Grosbeak   W
Blue-black Grosbeak   c
Blue-black Grassquit   c
Yellow-faced Grassquit
Variable Seedeater   c
Yellow-bellied Seedeater   c
Lesser Seed-Finch
Saffron Finch   c
Orange-billed Sparrow
Black-striped Sparrow

25
Greater Antilles (West Indies)

THE LARGE ISLANDS of Cuba, Hispaniola, Jamaica, and Puerto Rico, along with many nearby smaller island groups such as the Bahamas, Cayman Islands, and the Virgin Islands, make up the Greater Antilles. Despite rather close proximity to each other a rather high degree of endemism has evolved, particularly on the larger, more diversified islands. Each group is well worth a visit. This section treats all of them briefly, although each one deserves its own chapter. Students of zoogeography and would-be travelers will find the species list of great interest.

Cuba, the largest island, has been closed to most of us for nearly two decades. It was a hot spot for birders of yesteryear, and before jets was the only tropical birding exposure available to many. Despite a huge acreage under sugar cane and tobacco production, Cuba has enough wild country left to maintain its birdlife. Most readers will be pleased to learn that dozens of nature reserves have been established.

West of Havana, in Pinar del Rio Province, the Palm Crow lives near Matahambre, and Giant Kingbirds live in the pines of the Sierra del Rosario. There are two tropical forest reserves — Cabo Corrientes and El Cabo. El Cabo reserve features three species of quail-dove and the Cuban Trogon.

The Zapata Swamp is located about 100 miles (160 km) southeast of Havana on the south coast. The Cienaga de Zapata National Park has been created, and cabins, reached by motor launch, are available. This single swamp has three endemic birds, a rail, a wren, and a sparrow.

In Oriente province of eastern Cuba, visitors can stay at the Sierra de Cristal National Park with its mixed conifer and broadleaf forests. Specialties of eastern Cuba include the last populations of the famous Ivory-billed Woodpecker (near Moa), as well as Gundlach's Sparrowhawk, Cuban Solitaire, and Cuban Parakeet.

On Hispaniola, destruction of habitat is exceedingly severe in Haiti. In the gardens of Port-au-Prince visitors should find Antillean Palm-

Swift, Antillean Mango, Vervain Hummingbird, Hispaniolan Wood-pecker, and Palmchat. The Kyona Beach area, an hour north of the capital, is good for White-necked Crow, Broad-billed Tody, and the introduced Village Weaver. To the south of the capital, there are many hotels in Petionville. Above, around Kenscoff, the Hispaniolan Emerald, Golden Swallow, and Antillean Siskin can be found. If you can ride a horse or do extensive hiking up into the remnants of montane forest you may find Hispaniolan Trogon, Narrow-billed Tody, LaSelle Thrush, and several endemic warblers.

The Dominican Republic, with less pressure on its birds and habi-tat, is rapidly becoming a good birding destination. Most of the sights and developed beach resorts are in Santo Domingo and to the east. The best birding is to the west in the lakes and mountains west of Barahona (visitors may stay at the Hotel Guarocuya).

West of Barahona at Cabral, a road leads south to Polo. In the coffee plantations near the crest of the road there may be Red-necked Pigeon, Gray-headed Quail-Dove, Hispaniolan Lizard-Cuckoo, and Antillean Piculet. Lake Enriquillo, near the Haitian border, some-times has flamingo and spoonbill. The road from the southern shore of the lake south to Pedernales passes an abandoned sawmill near Aguacate. In the woods here look for Hispaniolan Parrot and Para-keet, Hispaniolan Trogon, Narrow-billed Tody, White-necked Crow, Rufous-throated Solitaire, warblers, and White-winged Crossbill.

Most visitors to Jamaica stay on the northwest coast at Montego Bay or on the northeast coast at Ocho Rios. Many of Jamaica's birds are so widespread that almost anyplace is interesting. The Rocklands Feeding Station run by Lisa Salmon is just south of Montego Bay at Anchovy. The feeders and nearby walks are good for Streamertail, Jamaican Mango, doves, cuckoos, Jamaican Owl, Jamaican Becard, and Orangequit. The farms and woods of the Cockpit country (such as around Windsor Cave), can be reached via a road due south of Falmouth (along the coast east of Montego Bay). This area is known for Jamaican Crow, both endemic parrots, Chestnut-bellied Cuckoo, and Golden Swallow.

The Blue Mountains between Ocho Rios and Kingston are still covered with heavy forest. The best birding is on trails near the Forest Service cabins at Hardwar Gap, on the older, twisting road through the mountains. In this area look for Ring-tailed and Plain Pigeons, Crested Quail-Dove, Jamaican Tody, White-eyed Thrush, Rufous-throated Solitaire, several vireos, and Arrow-headed Warbler.

The most *famous* place for birds in Puerto Rico is the heavy, damp forests of El Yunque east of San Juan, although birds are much more common elsewhere on the island in less misty areas. Take Route 3 east from San Juan 27 miles (43 km) to Mameyes, and turn south on Route 191, which passes through the Luquillo Experimental Forest where El Yunque peak is located. This is the only existing locality for the endangered Puerto Rican Parrot. It can best be seen around Kilometer Post 12 (7.5 miles) on Route 191. The recently discovered Elfin Woods Warbler moves quickly through the woods, uttering a high trill, particularly along East Peak Road.

Southwestern Puerto Rico is less congested than San Juan and has an excellent variety of habitats. There is an air service and fine hotels in Mayaguez, as well as more modest motels near Boqueron, La Parguera, and Guanica. Most of Puerto Rico's forest birds can be seen in the Maricao State Forest along Route 120, north of Sabana Grande (east of Mayaguez). This area consists of mountains covered with forest and coffee plantations. As usual, look for birds along side roads and trails. Waterbirds of many varieties can be found at three points on the southwest tip of Puerto Rico: Boqueron refuge, Cartagena Lagoon, and Cabo Rojo. Guanica State Forest, an arid woodland with much acacia and cactus, lies on the south shore east of Cabo Rojo. Plan to visit Guanica by dawn, since it becomes hot and windy later in the morning. Features here include two quail-doves, all Puerto Rican cuckoos, Whip-poor-will, vireos, Adelaide's Warbler, and Troupial.

The Cayman Islands, just south of Cuba, are very pleasant, fun to bird, and have the highest standard of living in the Greater Antilles. There are dozens of fine hotels, excellent roads, and few problems. The best forest birding on Grand Cayman is along a dirt road going south from Connolly's Variety Store, at Northside (3 miles [4.8 km] east of Cayman-Kai Resort, an hour east of Georgetown). Northside is good for Cuban Parrot, flycatchers, Thick-billed Vireo, Yucatan Vireo, Vitelline and wintering warblers, Stripe-headed Tanager, and Cuban Bullfinch.

The two outer islands of the Caymans are interesting to visit, as each has large numbers of Vitelline and wintering warblers, mangrove-lined ponds, and extensive dry forests. On Cayman Brac (stay at the Brac Reef or Buccaneer Inn) many Brown Boobies nest around the bluff at the end of the southside road. White-tailed Tropicbirds nest around the Bluff at Spot Bay on the north side road. Little Cayman has daily flights from Cayman Brac and one fishing lodge (Kingston Bight Lodge). The woods behind the lagoon just east of the airport contain an impressive colony of the beautiful tame Red-footed Booby as well as Magnificent Frigatebird.

The Bahamas are located a short distance east of Florida, and north of Cuba. Despite a number of endemics, the most interesting bird there is Kirtland's Warbler. Supposedly the entire population of a thousand or so winters in the Bahamas, yet it goes largely unobserved. The grounds of the Grand Bahama Hotel at the west end of Grand Bahama are a wildlife sanctuary. Look there for White-cheeked Pintail, Bahama Swallow (summer), Thick-billed Vireo, Bahama Yellowthroat, and Greater Antillean Bullfinch. Bahama Woodstar and Cuban Emerald are the common hummingbirds. The Pinelands Wildlife Sanctuary, 25 miles (40 km) east of West End, preserves a forest of Caribbean pines and is home to Olive-capped Warbler, Brownheaded Nuthatch, and Stripe-headed Tanager.

Adventurers may wish to visit the Great Inagua National Park on the southernmost island of the Bahamas. The Main House is a small hotel in tiny Matthew Town. The center of the island of Great Inagua is a vast salt lake, home to up to 10,000 pairs of American Flamingo. The lake, coasts, and reefs are home to many fine waterbirds, and Cuban Parrot and Giant Kingbird live in the woods.

The Virgin Islands have no endemics, but do have an interesting mix of Greater and Lesser Antillean birds, plus many White-tailed Tropicbirds. Green-throated Carib and Crested Hummingbirds are common. Anegada, in the British Virgins, has impressive shorebird concentrations in late summer.

CHECKLIST

(Special Symbols: BA = Bahamas, CU = Cuba, CI = Cayman Islands, JA = Jamaica, HI = Hispaniola, PR = Puerto Rico, VI = Virgin Islands)

American Dabchick
Pied-billed Grebe
Audubon's Shearwater
Black-capped Petrel   r (local)
Red-billed Tropicbird   (VI)
White-tailed Tropicbird
Brown Pelican
Masked Booby   (BA, VI)
Red-footed Booby
Brown Booby
Double-crested Cormorant   (BA, CU)
Neotropic Cormorant   (CU, BA)
Anhinga   (CU)
Magnificent Frigatebird
Great Blue Heron
Green Heron   c
Little Blue Heron   c

Cattle Heron   c
Reddish Egret
Great Egret
Snowy Egret   c
Louisiana Heron   c
Black-crowned Night-Heron
Yellow-crowned Night-Heron
Least Bittern
American Bittern   W
Wood Stork   (CU, HI)
Glossy Ibis
White Ibis   (not CI)
Roseate Spoonbill   (CU, HI, BA)
American Flamingo   (BA, CU, HI)
Fulvous Whistling-Duck   (CU)
West Indian Whistling-Duck
Gadwall   W

Northern Pintail   W
White-cheeked Pintail
Green-winged Teal   r W
Blue-winged Teal   c W
American Wigeon   W
Northern Shoveler   W
Wood Duck   (CU)
Redhead   W (BA, CU, JA)
Ring-necked Duck   W
Lesser Scaup   c W
Ruddy Duck
Masked Duck
Hooded Merganser   r W
Red-breasted Merganser   r W
Turkey Vulture   (not CI, VI)
Swallow-tailed Kite   M (CU, JA)
Cuban Kite   (CU)
Everglade Kite   (CU)
Sharp-shinned Sparrowhawk   (CU, HI, PR)
Gundlach's Sparrowhawk   (CU)
Red-tailed Hawk   (not CI)
Broad-winged Hawk   (CU, rPR)
Ridgway's Hawk   (HI)
Lesser Black Hawk   (CU)
Northern Harrier   W
Osprey
Crested Caracara   (CU)
Peregrine Falcon   W
Merlin   W
American Kestrel   c
Northern Bobwhite   (CU)
   (introduced on some other islands)
Helmeted Guineafowl   (CU, HI)
Sandhill Crane   (CU)
Limpkin   (CU, JA, HI)
King Rail   (CU)
Clapper Rail
Spotted Rail   (CU)
Zapata Rail   r (CU)
Sora Crake   W
Yellow-breasted Crake   (CU, JA, HI, PR)
American Black Crake   W (local)
Purple Gallinule
Common Gallinule   c

American Coot
Caribbean Coot   (local)
Northern Jacana   (CU, JA, HI)
American Oystercatcher   (local)
Semipalmated Plover   W
Piping Plover   r W
Snowy Plover   (local)
Wilson's Plover
Killdeer
Lesser Golden Plover   M
Gray Plover   W
Ruddy Turnstone   W
Black-necked Stilt   c
Common Snipe   W
Whimbrel   W
Upland Sandpiper   r M
Spotted Sandpiper   W
Solitary Sandpiper   M
Greater Yellowlegs   W
Lesser Yellowlegs   W
Willet   (local)
Red Knot   r M
Pectoral Sandpiper   M
White-rumped Sandpiper   M
Least Sandpiper   W
Semipalmated Sandpiper   W
Western Sandpiper   W
Sanderling   W
Short-billed Dowitcher   W
Stilt Sandpiper   M
Buff-breasted Sandpiper   r M
Marbled Godwit   r W
Hudsonian Godwit   M
Double-striped Thick-knee   (HI)
Parasitic Jaeger   r W
Herring Gull   W
Ring-billed Gull   W
Laughing Gull
Bonaparte's Gull   W
Gull-billed Tern   (local)
Forster's Tern   W
Common Tern   (local)
Roseate Tern   (local)
Bridled Tern   (local)
Sooty Tern   (local)
Little Tern   S
Royal Tern

Sandwich Tern
Caspian Tern
Black Tern   r M
Brown Noddy   (local)
Black Skimmer   W (not CI, JA)
White-crowned Pigeon
Red-necked Pigeon   (not CI, BA)
Ring-tailed Pigeon   (JA)
Plain Pigeon   (CU, JA, HI, PR)
Mourning Dove   (not CI, VI)
Zenaida Dove   c
White-winged Dove   c (rBA, VI)
Common Ground-Dove   c
White-bellied Dove   (JA, CI, Nassau)
Crested Quail-Dove   (JA)
Gray-headed Quail-Dove   (CU, HI)
Ruddy Quail-Dove   (CU, HI, JA, PR)
Key West Quail-Dove   (BA, CU, HI, PR)
Bridled Quail-Dove   (VI, Culebra)
Blue-headed Quail-Dove   CU
Cuban Parrot   (CU, CI, local BA)
Hispaniolan Parrot   (HI, PR)
Yellow-billed Parrot   (JA)
Puerto Rican Parrot   r (PR)
Black-billed Parrot   (JA)
Hispaniolan Parakeet   (HI)
Cuban Parakeet   (CU)
Olive-throated Parakeet   (JA)
Brown-throated Parakeet   (St. Thomas)
Green-rumped Parrotlet   (JA)
Mangrove Cuckoo
Yellow-billed Cuckoo   M
Chestnut-bellied Cuckoo   (JA)
Bay-breasted Cuckoo   (HI)
Great Lizard-Cuckoo   (BA, CU)
Hispaniolan Lizard-Cuckoo   (HI)
Jamaican Lizard-Cuckoo   (JA)
Puerto Rican Lizard-Cuckoo   (PR)
Smooth-billed Ani   c
Barn Owl   (CU, BA, HI, CI)
Puerto Rican Screech-Owl   (PR, VI)

Cuban Screech-Owl   (CU)
Burrowing Owl   (BA, HI)
Cuban Pygmy-Owl   (CU)
Short-eared Owl   (HI, PR)
Stygian Owl   (CU, HI)
Jamaican Owl   (JA)
Common Potoo   (JA, HI)
Chuck-will's-widow   W
Whip-poor-will   (PR)
Greater Antillean Nightjar   (CU, HI)
Least Pauraque   (HI)
Common (Antillean) Nighthawk
Chimney Swift   M
White-collared Swift   (CU, HI, JA)
American Black Swift   (CU, JA, HI, PR)
Antillean Palm-Swift   (CU, JA, HI)
Puerto Rican Emerald   (PR)
Hispaniolan Emerald   (HI)
Cuban Emerald   (BA, CU)
Jamaican Mango   (JA)
Antillean Mango   (HI, PR, St. Thomas)
Green Mango   (PR)
Green-throated Carib   (PR, VI)
Crested Hummingbird   (PR, VI)
Streamertail   c (JA)
Bahama Woodstar   c (BA)
Ruby-throated Hummingbird   W (BA, CU)
Bee Hummingbird   (CU)
Vervain Hummingbird   (HI, JA)
Hispaniolan Trogon   (CU)
Cuban Trogon   (CU)
Belted Kingfisher
Cuban Tody   (CU)
Narrow-billed Tody   (HI)
Puerto Rican Tody   (PR)
Jamaican Tody   (JA)
Broad-billed Tody   (HI)
Antillean Piculet   (HI)
Northern (Yellow-shafted) Flicker   (CU, CI)
Fernandina's Flicker   (CU)

Puerto Rican Woodpecker (PR)
Antillean Woodpecker (BA, CU, CI)
Jamaican Woodpecker (JA)
Hispaniolan Woodpecker (HI)
Yellow-bellied Sapsucker W
Cuban Green Woodpecker (CU)
Hairy Woodpecker (BA)
Ivory-billed Woodpecker r (CU)
Jamaican Becard (JA)
Eastern Kingbird r M(local)
Gray Kingbird c, (S only in west)
Giant Kingbird (CU, BA)
Loggerhead Kingbird (not VI)
Great Crested Flycatcher r W
Dark-capped Flycatcher (JA)
Jamaican Flycatcher (JA)
Stolid Flycatcher c
Wood Pewee M (west)
Lesser Antillean Pewee (PR)
Greater Antillean Pewee (BA, CU, JA, HI)
Caribbean Elaenia (CI, PR, VI)
Greater Antillean Elaenia (HI, JA)
Yellow-crowned Elaenia (JA)
Golden Swallow (HI, JA)
Bahama Swallow (BA), W (CU)
Tree Swallow W (west)
Purple Martin S, M
Sand Martin M
Rough-winged Swallow M
Barn Swallow M, W(PR, VI)
Cliff Martin M
Cave Martin (CU, HI, JA, PR)
Cuban Crow (CU, Caicos)
White-necked Crow (HI, PR)
Jamaican Crow (JA)
Palm Crow (CU, HI)
Brown-headed Nuthatch (Grand Bahama)
Zapata Wren (CU)
Northern Mockingbird c
Bahama Mockingbird (BA, JA)
Pearly-eyed Thrasher (BA, PR, VI)

Gray Catbird W (BA, CU, JA, CI)
American Robin W (BA, CU, JA)
White-eyed Thrush (JA)
LaSelle Thrush (HI)
White-chinned Thrush (JA)
Red-legged Thrush (BA, CU, HI, PR, CI)
Swainson's Thrush r M (west)
Gray-cheeked Thrush r M
Veery r M (west)
Cuban Solitaire (CU)
Rufous-throated Solitaire (JA, HI)
Blue-gray Gnatcatcher (BA), W (CU, CI)
Cuban Gnatcatcher (CU)
Cedar Waxwing r W (west)
Palmchat (HI)
European Starling (JA), W (BA)
Flat-billed Vireo (HI)
Jamaican White-eyed Vireo (JA)
Thick-billed Vireo (BA, CI)
White-eyed Vireo W (BA, CU, CI)
Cuban Vireo (CU)
Puerto Rican Vireo (PR)
Blue Mountain Vireo (JA)
Yellow-throated Vireo r W (west)
Black-whiskered Vireo S, resident (HI)
Yucatan Vireo (CI)
Black-and-white Warbler c W
Prothonotary Warbler W
Swainson's Warbler r W (CU, BA, CI)
Worm-eating Warbler W
Golden-winged Warbler r M
Blue-winged Warbler r W
Bachman's Warbler r W (CU)
Tennessee Warbler M (west)
Northern Parula c W
Yellow Warbler c
Magnolia Warbler W
Cape May Warbler c W

Black-throated Blue Warbler   W
Yellow-rumped (Myrtle) Warbler
  W
Black-throated Green Warbler   W
Yellow-throated Warbler   W
Adelaide's Warbler   (PR)
Olive-capped Warbler   (CU, BA)
Pine Warbler   (BA, HI)
Bay-breasted Warbler   M (west)
Blackpoll Warbler   M
Prairie Warbler   c W
Vitelline Warbler   c (CI)
Kirtland's Warbler   r W (BA)
Palm Warbler   c W
Arrow-headed Warbler   (JA)
Elfin Woods Warbler   (PR)
Ovenbird   W
Northern Waterthrush   c W
Louisiana Waterthrush   W
Northern Yellowthroat   c W, r
  W (PR, VI)
Bahama Yellowthroat   (BI)
Hooded Warbler   r M
Wilson's Warbler   r W (west)
Ground Warbler   (HI)
White-winged Warbler   (HI)
Yellow-headed Warbler   (CU)
Oriente Warbler   (CU)
American Redstart   c W
Bananaquit   c (not CU)
Red-legged Honeycreeper   (CU)
Orangequit   (JA)
Blue-hooded Euphonia   (HI, PR)
Jamaican Euphonia   (JA)
Stripe-headed Tanager   (not VI)
Scarlet Tanager   r M (west)
Summer Tanager   r M (west)
Black-crowned Tanager   (s. Haiti)
Gray-crowned Tanager   (s. Haiti)
Puerto Rican Tanager   (PR)
Chat-Tanager   (HI)
Shiny Cowbird   (PR)
Greater Antillean Grackle   (not
  BA, VI)
Cuban Blackbird   (CU)

Black-cowled Oriole   (BA, CU,
  HI, PR)
Jamaican Oriole   (JA)
Troupial   (PR, St. Thomas)
Red-winged Blackbird   (BA, west
  CU)
Tawny-shouldered Blackbird
  (CU, Haiti)
Yellow-shouldered Blackbird
  (PR)
Jamaican Blackbird   (JA)
Eastern Meadowlark   (CU)
Bobolink   M
House Sparrow   (CU, BA, JA,
  St. Thomas)
Java Sparrow   (PR)
Orange-cheeked Waxbill   (PR)
Bronze Munia   (PR)
Village Weaver   (HI)
Lesser Goldfinch   (CU)
Antillean Siskin   (HI)
White-winged Crossbill   (HI)
Saffron Finch   (JA)
Cuban Bullfinch   (CU, CI)
Puerto Rican Bullfinch   (CU, CI)
Greater Antillean Bullfinch   (BA,
  HI, JA)
Yellow-faced Grassquit   (Nassau,
  CU, CI, HI, JA, PR)
Black-faced Grassquit   (not CU,
  CI)
Cuban Grassquit   (Nassau, CU)
Yellow-shouldered Grassquit   (JA)
Rose-breasted Grosbeak   W
Blue Grosbeak   r W
Indigo Bunting   W
Painted Bunting   W (CU, BA)
Dickcissel   M (BA, CU, JA)
Zapata Sparrow   (CU)
Savannah Sparrow   W (BA, CU,
  CI)
Grasshopper Sparrow   S (HI, JA,
  PR) W (BA, CU, CI)
Rufous-collared Sparrow   (HI)

Florida
USA

Grand Bahama

Nassau

BAHAMAS

ATLANTIC
OCEAN

Andros

Havana

CUBA

Great
Inagua

Isle
of
Pines

Zapata
Swamp

Little
Grand Cayman

Cayman
Brac

Santiago
de Cuba

HAITI

DOMINICAN
REPUBLIC

San
Juan

Virgin
Islands

Antigua

Grand
Cayman

Swan Island

Montego
Bay

Kingston

Port-
au-
Prince

Santo
Domingo

PUERTO
RICO

Guadeloupe

JAMAICA

GREATER ANTILLES

LESSER
ANTILLES

Dominica

Martinique

St. Lucia
Barbados

CARIBBEAN SEA

St. Vincent

Old Providence

Grenada

St Andrew

Dutch West
Indies

miles   300

0

km   500

P.A.

Santa
Marta

Mara-
caibo

Chichiriviche

CARACAS

TRINIDAD

COLOMBIA

Rancho Grande

VENEZUELA

Orinoco
River

26
Lesser Antilles (West Indies)

THE NUMEROUS ISLES OF THE LESSER ANTILLES stretch from Anguilla and Barbuda southward to Grenada and the Barbados. Most
ornithological attention has been given to the five larger, central
islands, with tall peaks covered (until recently) with heavy tropical
forest; running from north to south, they are Guadeloupe, Dominica,
Martinique, St. Lucia, and St. Vincent. The French islands have been
heavily promoted for tourism, while Dominica, St. Lucia, and St.
Vincent are still fairly quiet. Fortunately for birders, the ecologically
less interesting islands of Barbados, Antigua, and to some degree St.
Martin have siphoned off the lion's share of visitors.

Of the smaller, drier islands Antigua is fairly typical. South of St.
John there is a dead end road up Christian Valley on the north slope
of Boggy Peak. This is the most humid forest area on Antigua and
is home to Bridled and Ruddy Quail-Doves, Purple-throated Carib,
Scaly-breasted and Pearly-eyed Thrashers.

Guadeloupe is essentially two islands. The eastern half, called
Grande-Terre, is relatively dry and level, with much sugar cane.
There, east of the capital Pointe-a-Pitre with its airport, live such birds
as Crested Hummingbird, Green-throated Carib, Lesser Antillean
Grackle, and Lesser Antillean Bullfinch. Western Guadeloupe,
known as Basse-Terre, is lush and consists of many mountains in the
3000- to 5000-foot (915 to 1525 m) range. A number of roads climb
into heavy forest, including the Les Mamelles road that bisects the
island east-west and a road that goes high up onto Soufriere Peak
above St. Claude and the city of Basse-Terre. These forests contain the
endemic Guadeloupe Woodpecker, Purple-throated Carib, Forest
Thrush, Brown Trembler, and Plumbeous Warbler.

Dominica, with an English-speaking population, is perhaps the
most verdant island of the chain and lies between Guadeloupe and
Martinique. It has two endemic parrots, both of which can be considered endangered. The Red-necked Parrot occupies lowland forest,
and although fairly common, is losing to habitat destruction and
hunting. The Imperial Parrot occupies mountain forest, principally
above 1970 feet (600 m). It is scarce, but may still be found on trails

on the west side of Morne Diablotin, the island's tallest peak. The new Central Forest Preserve is home to the Forest Thrush and Plumbeous Warbler.

Martinique, 40 miles (64 km) long, is a rugged lush island with a French flair. Like Haiti, Martinique is overpopulated and suffers from misuse of land and intense bird hunting (for the pot) by local children with small-bore rifles. The forests on the steep slopes of Mount Pelee (accessible by road) have Blue-headed Hummingbird, Lesser Antillean Swift, and Rufous-throated Solitaire. The exceedingly rare colonial White-breasted Trembler may still be seen around Ferret Point on La Caravelle Peninsula, which juts out five miles (8 km) into the Atlantic east of La Trinite. The endangered Martinique Oriole occurs in the southwest between Le Diamant (with a hotel and an hour by road from Fort-de-France) and Les Anses-D'Arlets.

St. Lucia is the northernmost of a string of English-speaking islands. The St. Lucia Parrot is now restricted to the central and southern mountains from Barre de L'Isle to Grand Magasin. The Grand Anse area due east of the capital, Castries, may be the top birding area on St. Lucia. It is home to the rare White-breasted Trembler, Brown Trembler, Streaked Saltator, and two of the four endemics — the St. Lucia Oriole and the St. Lucia Black Finch. The Semper's Warbler may now be extinct.

St. Vincent is the only home of the elegant St. Vincent Parrot. This parrot is considered endangered, although it survives in reasonable numbers in the mountain forests at the headwaters of the Buccament, Colonarie, and other rivers in the center of the island, and north of the Rabacca Dry River on the slopes of Soufriere Volcano in the north. Lowland seasonal forest survives at King's Hill Wood in the southeast, where the Lesser Antillean Tanager is found. The endemic Whistling Warbler of the montane rain forests is very scarce.

Grenada, the southernmost of the Lesser Antilles, is heavily cultivated. The island's only endemic bird, the Grenada Dove, lives in scrubby woodland in the west around Beausejour and behind the tourist developments at Grand Anse (which may destroy its restricted habitat). A variety of shorebirds occur on the salt pans at Point Salines at the southwest tip of the island. Some rain forest remains intact around Grand Etang (1970 feet [600 m] above sea level) where Red-necked Pigeon, Ruddy Quail-Dove, and Cocoa Thrush may be found. The Rufous-breasted Hermit is often seen near Annandale Falls.

The Barbados have a number of widespread Lesser Antillean birds but are noted for the remarkable variety of European vagrants that have been detected over the years.

CHECKLIST

(Special Symbols: AA = Antigua — Anguilla and islands inbetween, GU = Guadeloupe Islands, DO = Dominica, MA = Martinique, SL = St. Lucia, BA = Barbados, SV = St. Vincent, GR = Grenada and/or Grenadines)

Pied-billed Grebe
Audubon's Shearwater
Black-capped Petrel   r (local)
Red-billed Tropicbird
White-tailed Tropicbird
Brown Pelican
Masked Booby   (GR)
Brown Booby
Red-footed Booby   (local)
Magnificent Frigatebird
Great Blue Heron   W
Green Heron   c
Little Blue Heron   c
Cattle Heron
Great Egret   r
Snowy Egret   r
Louisiana Heron   r
Black-crowned Night-Heron
Yellow-crowned Night-Heron
Black-bellied Whistling-Duck
West Indian Whistling-Duck
   (AA)
White-cheeked Pintail   (AA, GU)
Blue-winged Teal   W
American Wigeon   W
Northern Shoveler   W
Ring-necked Duck   W
Lesser Scaup   r W
Masked Duck   r
Hook-billed Kite   (GR)
Broad-winged Hawk   (local)
Lesser Black Hawk   (SV)
Northern Harrier   W
Osprey   W
Peregrine Falcon   W
Merlin   W
American Kestrel
Rufous-vented Chachalaca   (GR)
Clapper Rail   (local)

Sora Crake   W
Purple Gallinule   (local)
Common Gallinule   c
Caribbean Coot   (local)
Semipalmated Plover   W
Snowy Plover   (local)
Collared Plover   (GR, BA)
Wilson's Plover   (AA)
Killdeer   W
Lesser Golden Plover   M
Gray Plover   W
Ruddy Turnstone   W
Black-necked Stilt   (local)
Common Snipe   W
Whimbrel   M
Upland Sandpiper   r M
Spotted Sandpiper   W
Solitary Sandpiper   M
Greater Yellowlegs   M
Lesser Yellowlegs   M
Willet   (local)
Red Knot   r M
Pectoral Sandpiper   M
White-rumped Sandpiper   M
Least Sandpiper   W
Semipalmated Sandpiper   W
Western Sandpiper   W
Sanderling   W
Short-billed Dowitcher   W
Stilt Sandpiper   M
Buff-breasted Sandpiper   M
Hudsonian Godwit   M
Ruff   r M
Parasitic Jaeger   r W
Laughing Gull
Common Tern   (local)
Roseate Tern   (local)
Bridled Tern   (local)
Sooty Tern   (local)

Little Tern   S
Royal Tern
Sandwich Tern
Black Tern   r M
Brown Noddy   (local)
White-crowned Pigeon   (local)
Red-necked Pigeon   (local)
Spot-eared Dove   (SL, SV, GR)
Zenaida Dove   c
Common Ground-Dove   c
Grenada Dove   (GR)
Ruddy Quail-Dove   (not AA, BA)
Bridled Quail-Dove   (Saba, Barbuda to SL)
Imperial Parrot   (DO)
St. Vincent Parrot   (SV)
St. Lucia Parrot   (SL)
Red-necked Parrot   (DO)
Green-rumped Parrotlet   (BA)
Mangrove Cuckoo   (local)
Yellow-billed Cuckoo   M
Black-billed Cuckoo   M
Smooth-billed Ani   (local)
Barn Owl   (DO, SV, GR)
Rufous Nightjar   (SL)
White-tailed Nightjar   (MA)
Short-tailed Swift   (SV)
Gray-rumped Swift   (GR)
Lesser Antillean Swift   (GU, DO, MA, SL, SV)
White-collared Swift   S (GR)
American Black Swift   S (GU, DO, MA, SL, SV)
Rufous-breasted Hermit   (GR)
Blue-headed Hummingbird   (DO, MA)
Purple-throated Carib   (not BA)
Green-throated Carib   c
Crested Hummingbird   c
Ringed Kingfisher   (GU, DO, MA)
Belted Kingfisher
Guadeloupe Woodpecker   (GU)
Tropical Kingbird   (GR)
Gray Kingbird   c
Fork-tailed Flycatcher   W (GR)

Brown-crested Flycatcher   (GR, SV)
Stolid Flycatcher   (GU, DO, MA, SL, local AA)
Lesser Antillean Pewee   (GU, DO, MA, SL)
Yellow-bellied Elaenia   (SV, GR)
Caribbean Elaenia   c
Purple Martin   S, M
Sand Martin   M
Barn Swallow   W
Cliff Martin   M
House Wren   (DO, SV, GR)
Tropical Mockingbird   (DO, MA, SL, SV, GR)
Scaly-breasted Thrasher   (most islands)
Pearly-eyed Thrasher   (not BA, GR, SV)
Brown Trembler   (not BA, GR)
White-breasted Trembler   (MA, SL)
Bare-eyed Thrush   (MA, SL, SV, GR)
Cocoa Thrush   (SV, GR)
Red-legged Thrush   (DO)
Forest Thrush   (Montserrat, GU, DO, SL)
Black-whiskered Vireo
Black-and-white Warbler   W
Prothonotary Warbler   W
Northern Parula   W (AA, GU)
Yellow Warbler   c
Cape May Warbler   r W
Adelaide's Warbler   (Barbuda, SL)
Blackpoll Warbler   M
Prairie Warbler   W
Plumbeous Warbler   (GU, DO)
Whistling Warbler   (SV)
Semper's Warbler   r (SL)
Ovenbird   r W
Northern Waterthrush   c W
American Redstart   W
Bananaquit   c
Blue-hooded Euphonia   (not BA)

Lesser Antillean Tanager   (SV, GR)
Shiny Cowbird   (MA south)
Carib Grackle
Montserrat Oriole   (Montserrat)
St. Lucia Oriole   (SL)
Martinique Oriole   (MA)
Grassland Yellow-Finch   (GU, MA, SL, BA)

Blue-black Grassquit   (GR)
Yellow-bellied Seedeater   (GR)
Lesser Antillean Bullfinch   c
St. Lucia Black Finch   (SL)
Streaked Saltator   (GU, DO, MA, SL)
Rose-breasted Grosbeak   r W

27
Trinidad and Tobago

TRINIDAD, THE MOST SOUTHERLY ISLAND in the Caribbean, is just 7 miles (11.2 km) from Venezuela. Its avifauna is essentially South American, not West Indian. Although it has more species than any other island in the Caribbean, there are no endemics. Port-of-Spain, the capital, has numerous hotels and the airport has many flights to and from the United States, London, Caracas, and the West Indies.

Spring Hill Estate, site of the Asa Wright Nature Center, is situated in the rich forests of the northern range at 1200 feet (365 m). Located just off the Blanchisseuse road, 7 miles (11.2 km) north of Arima, the estate serves as an ideal hotel for up to 20 guests. Reservations for lodging, meals, and Oilbird treks should be made via GPO Bag No. 10, Port-of-Spain, Trinidad, W.I., or c/o Wonder Bird Tours, 500 Fifth Ave., New York, NY 10036 (212) 279-7301. The trek to the Oilbird caves requires a guide, a key, and old tennis shoes for wading. Hummingbirds, trogons, toucans, manakins, honeycreepers, and tanagers are all regular residents at Spring Hill, while the calls of Bearded Bellbirds ring through the woods. Visitors not wishing to rent a car can take a taxi to Spring Hill, where bird tours with guides and cars can be organized by prior arrangement. The road uphill to the pass is good for higher species, while downhill north of the pass to Blanchisseuse more forest is accessible. The highest peaks reach 3000 feet (915 m).

Scarlet Ibis can be seen by taking the Caroni Swamp boat trips, which leave about 3 P.M. for the evening flight of these exotic birds to an island roost. Reservations for the trip can be made at Spring Hill. By hiring your own boat with a guide recommended at Spring Hill, many additional species can be seen in the marshes and mangroves.

The Arena Forest is a large forest with logging roads in flat country featuring many hawks, parrots, hummingbirds, Rufous-tailed Jacamar, woodcreepers, antbirds, and flycatchers. It is reached by taking the Balata road south, 1.5 miles (2.5 km) west of Cumoto.

Red-bellied Macaw, as well as marsh and savanna birds, are best

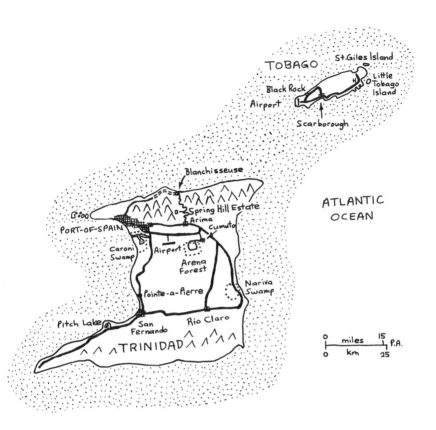

TOBAGO
St. Giles Island
Black Rock
Airport
Little Tobago Island
Scarborough

Blanchisseuse
Spring Hill Estate
B°oo
Arima
PORT-OF-SPAIN
Cumuto
Caroni Swamp
Airport
Arena Forest
Pointe-a-Pierre
Nariva Swamp
Pitch Lake
San Fernando
Rio Claro
TRINIDAD

ATLANTIC OCEAN

miles   15
km   25   P.A.

seen in the Nariva Swamp area on the east coast. Details and a guide are available at Spring Hill.

Tobago, a smaller island (116 square miles [301 km^2]) to the northeast, is reached by air from Piarco Airport. It is a beautiful island with mountains in the north and has 13 species of breeding birds not found in Trinidad. The Grafton Estate has a great bird-feeding program, and excellent birding trails have been laid out around the Bird of Paradise Inn at Speyside. Transport on the island is usually via taxi. Boats can be arranged there to visit Little Tobago Island, home of the Red-billed Tropicbird, terns, and a few introduced Greater Bird-of-Paradise.

CHECKLIST

(TR = Trinidad only, TO = Tobago and/or islets only)

Little Tinamou TR	Pied-billed Grebe
American Dabchick TR	Audubon's Shearwater TO

Leach's Storm-Petrel   r W
Red-billed Tropicbird   TO
Brown Pelican   c
Red-footed Booby   TO
Brown Booby
Neotropic Cormorant   TR
Anhinga
Magnificent Frigatebird   c
Great Blue Heron   W
Cocoi Heron   TR
Great Egret
Snowy Egret
Little Blue Heron   c
Louisiana Heron   c
Green Heron   c
Cattle Heron   c
Black-crowned Night-Heron
Yellow-crowned Night-Heron
Rufescent Tiger-Heron   r TR
Stripe-backed Bittern   TR
Least Bittern   TR
Pinnated Bittern   r TR
Boat-billed Heron   r TR
Scarlet Ibis   c TR
Glossy Ibis   r W TR
Roseate Spoonbill   r M TR
Fulvous Whistling-Duck   r M TR
Black-bellied Whistling-Duck   r
American Wigeon   W
White-cheeked Pintail   r
Blue-winged Teal   c W
Masked Duck   r TR
Black Vulture   c TR
Turkey Vulture   c TR
White-tailed Kite   r TR
Pearl Kite   r TR
Swallow-tailed Kite   S TR
Gray-headed Kite   r TR
Double-toothed Kite   TR
Plumbeous Kite   S TR
White-tailed Hawk   r TR
Zone-tailed Hawk   r TR
Broad-winged Hawk   TO
Short-tailed Hawk   TR
Gray Hawk   TR
White Hawk   TR
Black-collared Hawk   r TR

Savanna Hawk   r TR
Lesser Black Hawk   TR
Great Black Hawk   r TR
Ornate Hawk-Eagle   r
Long-winged Harrier   r TR
Osprey
Yellow-headed Caracara   r TR
Peregrine Falcon   W
Bat Falcon   TR
Aplomado Falcon   r TR
Merlin   W
Rufous-vented Chachalaca   TO
Blue-throated Piping-Guan   r TR
Limpkin   TR
Clapper Rail   TR
Spotted Rail   r
Gray-necked Wood-Rail   TR
Rufous-necked Wood-Rail   r TR
Sora Crake   W
Ash-throated Crake   r TR
Yellow-breasted Crake   r TR
Gray-breasted Crake   TR
Common Gallinule   c
Purple Gallinule
Caribbean Coot   r
Wattled Jacana   c TR
Southern Lapwing   M TR
Gray Plover   W
Lesser Golden Plover   c M
Semipalmated Plover   c W
Collared Plover   S
Killdeer   r W
Wilson's Plover   r
Ruddy Turnstone   W
Solitary Sandpiper   W
Lesser Yellowlegs   W
Greater Yellowlegs   c W
Spotted Sandpiper   c W
Willet   W
Red Knot   M
Least Sandpiper   W
White-rumped Sandpiper   M
Pectoral Sandpiper   M
Semipalmated Sandpiper   c W
Western Sandpiper   c W
Sanderling   c W
Stilt Sandpiper   M TR

Upland Sandpiper   r M
Whimbrel   W
Hudsonian Godwit   r M
Short-billed Dowitcher   c W
Common Snipe
Black-necked Stilt   W
Laughing Gull
Black Tern   M (fall)
Large-billed Tern   S TR
Gull-billed Tern   r W
Common Tern   c M
Roseate Tern   M
Bridled Tern   S TO
Sooty Tern   S TO
Yellow-billed Tern   S TR
Little Tern   TR
Royal Tern
Sandwich Tern   S
Brown Noddy   TO
Black Skimmer   M
Band-tailed Pigeon   r TR
Scaled Pigeon   TR
Pale-vented Pigeon
Spot-eared Dove
Common Ground-Dove   TR
Plain-breasted Ground-Dove   TR
Ruddy Ground-Dove   c
Blue Ground-Dove   r TR
White-tipped Dove   c
Gray-fronted Dove   TR
Ruddy Quail-Dove   TR
Lined Quail-Dove
Blue-and-yellow Macaw   r TR
Red-bellied Macaw   TR
Green-rumped Parrotlet
Lilac-tailed Parrotlet   TR
Blue-headed Parrot   c TR
Orange-winged Parrot
Yellow-billed Cuckoo   M
Mangrove Cuckoo   r TR
Dark-billed Cuckoo   r TR
Squirrel Cuckoo   TR
Little Cuckoo   TR
Greater Ani   TR
Smooth-billed Ani   c
Striped Cuckoo   TR
Barn Owl

Tropical Screech-Owl   c TR
Spectacled Owl   TR
Ferruginous Pygmy-Owl   c TR
Mottled Owl   TR
Striped Owl   TO
Oilbird   TR
Common Potoo
Short-tailed Nighthawk   TR
Lesser Nighthawk
Nacunda Nighthawk   S TR
Common Pauraque   c TR
Rufous Nightjar   TR
White-tailed Nightjar
White-collared Swift   M TR
Chestnut-collared Swift   TR
Chapman's Swift   r TR
Gray-rumped Swift   c
Band-rumped Swift   c TR
Short-tailed Swift   c
Lesser Swallow-tailed Swift   TR
Amazonian Palm-Swift   r TR
Rufous-breasted Hermit   c
Green Hermit   TR
Little Hermit   TR
White-tailed Sabrewing   r TO
White-necked Jacobin
Brown Violetear   TR
Green-throated Mango   TR
Black-throated Mango
Ruby-topaz Hummingbird   M
Tufted Coquette   TR
Blue-chinned Sapphire   c TR
Blue-tailed Emerald   r TR
White-tailed Goldenthroat   TR
White-chested Emerald   c TR
Copper-rumped Hummingbird   c
Long-billed Starthroat   TR
White-tailed Trogon   c TR
Collared Trogon
Violaceous Trogon   c TR
Belted Kingfisher   W
Green Kingfisher
American Pygmy Kingfisher   TR
Blue-crowned Motmot
Rufous-tailed Jacamar
Channel-billed Toucan   c TR
Golden-olive Woodpecker

133

Chestnut Woodpecker   TR
Lineated Woodpecker   TR
Red-crowned Woodpecker   c   TO
Red-rumped Woodpecker
Crimson-crested Woodpecker   TR
Plain-brown Woodcreeper
Olivaceous Woodcreeper   TO
Straight-billed Woodcreeper   TR
Buff-throated Woodcreeper   c
Streak-headed Woodcreeper   TR
Pale-breasted Spinetail   TR
Stripe-breasted Spinetail
Yellow-throated Spinetail   TR
Streaked Xenops   TR
Gray-throated Leaftosser
Great Antshrike   TR
Black-crested Antshrike   TR
Barred Antshrike   c
Plain Antvireo
White-flanked Antwren   TR
White-fringed Antwren   c   TO
Silvered Antbird   TR
White-bellied Antbird   TR
Black-faced Ant-thrush   TR
Scaled Antpitta   r   TR
Bright-rumped Attila   TR
White-winged Becard
Black-tailed Tityra   TR
White Bellbird   r   TR
Bearded Bellbird   TR
Golden-headed Manakin   c   TR
Blue-backed Manakin   TO
White-bearded Manakin   c   TR
Pied Water-Tyrant   c   TR
White-headed Marsh-Tyrant   c
   TR
Fork-tailed Flycatcher
Tropical Kingbird   c
Gray Kingbird
Sulfury Flycatcher   r   TR
Piratic Flycatcher   TR
Boat-billed Flycatcher   c   TR
Streaked Flycatcher
Great Kiskadee   c   TR
Brown-crested Flycatcher
Venezuelan Flycatcher   TO
Swainson's Flycatcher   r   S   TR

Dusky-capped Flycatcher   TR
Olive-sided Pewee   W   TR
Tropical Pewee   c   TR
Euler's Flycatcher   c   TR
Fuscous Flycatcher
Bran-colored Flycatcher   TR
White-throated Spadebill
Yellow-olive Flycatcher   c   TR
Yellow-breasted Flycatcher   c
Short-tailed Pygmy-Tyrant   TR
Crested Doradito   r
Yellow-bellied Elaenia   c
Lesser Elaenia   r   TR
Forest Elaenia   TR
Scrub Flycatcher   TR
Mouse-colored Tyrannulet   (islets)
Southern Beardless Tyrannulet   c
   TR
Slaty-capped Flycatcher   TR
Olive-striped Flycatcher   r   TR
Ochre-bellied Flycatcher   c
White-winged Swallow   TR
Purple (Caribbean) Martin   TO
Gray-breasted Martin   c   TR
Blue-and-white Swallow   S   TR
Rough-winged Swallow   TR
Sand Martin   r   M
Barn Swallow   c   W
Greater Bird-of-Paradise   (Little
   Tobago)
Rufous-breasted Wren
House Wren   c
Tropical Mockingbird   c
Orange-billed Nightingale-Thrush
   r   TR
Yellow-legged Thrush
Cocoa Thrush   c   TR
Bare-eyed Thrush   c
White-necked Thrush
Long-billed Gnatwren   TR
Rufous-browed Peppershrike   c
   TR
Red-eyed (Chivi) Vireo   c   S
Black-whiskered Vireo   r   M
Golden-fronted Greenlet   c   TR
Scrub Greenlet   c   TO
Shiny Cowbird   c

Giant Cowbird
Crested Oropendola   c
Yellow-rumped Cacique   TR
Carib Grackle   c
Yellow-hooded Blackbird   c TR
Moriche Oriole   r TR
Yellow Oriole   c TR
Red-breasted Meadowlark   c TR
Black-and-white Warbler   r W
Prothonotary Warbler   r W
Tropical Parula   TR
Yellow Warbler   c W
Cape May Warbler   r W TO
Blackpoll Warbler   M
Northern Waterthrush   c W
Masked Yellowthroat   TR
American Redstart   c W
Golden-crowned Warbler   TR
Bananaquit   c
Bicolored Conebill   TR
Purple Honeycreeper   c TR
Red-legged Honeycreeper
Green Honeycreeper   c TR
Blue Dacnis   TR
Swallow-Tanager   TR
Blue-hooded Euphonia   r TR
Trinidad Euphonia   TR
Violaceous Euphonia

Speckled Tanager   c TR
Turquoise Tanager   c TR
Bay-headed Tanager   c TR
Blue-gray Tanager   c
Palm Tanager   c TR
Blue-capped Tanager   TR
Silver-beaked Tanager   c TR
Hepatic Tanager   r TR
Summer Tanager   W
Red-crowned Ant-Tanager   TR
White-lined Tanager   c
White-shouldered Tanager   TR
Grayish Saltator   c TR
Streaked Saltator   TR
Red-capped Cardinal   r TR
Dickcissel   r W
Blue-black Grassquit   c
Black-faced Grassquit   c TO
Sooty Grassquit   TR
Slate-colored Seedeater   r TR
Gray Seedeater   TR
Variable Seedeater   r TO
Lined Seedeater
Yellow-bellied Seedeater
Ruddy-breasted Seedeater   c
Large-billed Seed-Finch   r TR
Lesser Seed-Finch   r TR
Saffron Yellow-Finch   TR

28

Henri Pittier (Rancho Grande) National Park, Aragua, Venezuela

OVER 500 BIRDS HAVE BEEN RECORDED in this superb national park, one of the longest lists for any park in the New World. Named after a famous botanist, the park is nevertheless usually referred to as Rancho Grande. A large building at Portachuelo Pass (about 3000 feet [915 m]) was initiated by a previous dictator as a retreat but is now headquarters of the Rancho Grande Biological Station. Scientists may be able to arrange to stay (taking their own provisions). Most birders stay in Maracay, near the park entrance, and spend several days stopping at various points along the paved road that winds through the park.

There is a variety of hotels in Maracay, including the elegant Hotel Maracay, which is only about 6.2 miles (10 km) from the park entrance. There are Rufous-vented Chachalaca, Common Potoo, Amazonian Palm-Swift, and Tropical Screech-Owl on the grounds. Tourists without rent-a-cars and not on a bird tour can travel by second-class bus from Maracay on the Turiamo and Ocumare routes, two towns on the Caribbean side of the park, each with modest hotel facilities.

The park covers a large section of the coastal range of Venezuela, about 69 miles (110 km) west of Caracas, Maracay being two hours' drive away via a four-lane paved toll road. The paved road through the park is 31 miles (50 km) long from the park entrance to the Caribbean. The police checkpoint at the park entrance is 5 miles (8 km) from Maracay. The southern face of the range is drier with tropical deciduous woodland in the ravines. The wet subtropical forest begins about Puente Rio Grande 7 miles (11 km) up the hill and Rancho Grande is a kilometer farther. Many of the best birds are seen around Rancho Grande, and along the main paved road from that point over nearby Portachuelo Pass, and for the next 1 ¼ miles (2 km) to a huge curve. Band-tailed Guan, the rare Helmeted Curassow,

White-tipped Quetzal, Collared Trogon, many hummingbirds, Handsome Fruiteater, Golden and Rufous-cheeked Tanagers are best seen here. Heavy clouds are a problem, and mornings offer the best visibility. If it is clear high up, save the lower elevations for times when it is clouded. Birding is excellent in light cloud (fog), however.

The road downhill on the Caribbean face passes through some of the finest subtropical forests left in the world with huge lianas, trees covered with epiphytes and orchids, the eerie calls of red howler monkeys, and pockets of exceedingly diverse birdlife. Black and Ornate Hawk-Eagles can often be seen soaring overhead, and Broadwinged Hawk are common in winter. Continuing downhill the forest gradually thins out due to lower rainfall. As you reach the lowlands there is a zone of settlements, where residents grow a rich variety of tropical crops such as cacao, chicle, bananas, citrus, and breadfruit. Along the river look for Amazon and Green Kingfishers. The road forks after crossing the river. The straight road leads to the Caribbean, where there are fine beaches, xerophytic shrubs and cactus, and some seabirds. The left fork leads through cocoa plantations with tropical birds not found in the cool forests of Rancho Grande.

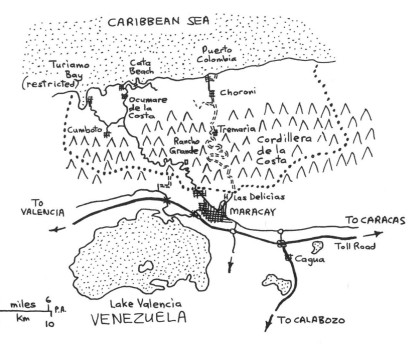

Birdlife moves about in feeding parties, and trees fruit randomly through the forest so that (unlike in many other localities) good spots are hard to pinpoint. There are ample parking areas and birders should plan to do a lot of walking along the road and hope to run into feeding parties. There are (most unfortunately) no nature trails into the forest so one is forced to stick to the main road. Avoid weekends and holidays, since half of Maracay empties into the park with fast cars and plenty of beer, and generally makes things dangerous. Weekdays are pleasant and rewarding. No permits or fees required.

An alternate poor — but usually passable — road winds through the eastern sector of the park from Maracay to Choroni. It reaches higher elevations, has extensive forests, and over 150 birds have been seen along it in one day (no waterbirds). Timid drivers and those with little time should avoid it.

CHECKLIST

Gray Tinamou   r H
Little Tinamou
Red-legged Tinamou   r L
Brown Pelican   c
Brown Booby
Magnificent Frigatebird   c
Snowy Egret
Black Vulture   c
Turkey Vulture   c
Gray-headed Kite
Broad-winged Hawk   c W
Roadside Hawk
Short-tailed Hawk
Gray Hawk
White Hawk   H
Lesser Black Hawk
Solitary Eagle   r H
Black-and-white Hawk-Eagle   r
Black Hawk-Eagle
Ornate Hawk-Eagle
Yellow-headed Caracara
Bat Falcon
Rufous-vented Chachalaca
Band-tailed Guan   H
Helmeted Curassow   r H
Royal Tern
Bridled Tern   M

Ruddy Pigeon   H
Common Ground-Dove
Ruddy Ground-Dove   c
Blue Ground-Dove   r
White-tipped Dove   c
Ruddy Quail-Dove   r
Lined Quail-Dove   r H
Scarlet-fronted Parakeet   M
Brown-throated Parakeet   c
Blood-eared Parakeet   H
Green-rumped Parrotlet   c
Lilac-tailed Parrotlet   r H
Blue-headed Parrot   r
Red-billed Parrot   c H
Orange-winged Parrot
Squirrel Cuckoo
Pavonine Cuckoo   r H
Smooth-billed Ani
Groove-billed Ani
Vermiculated Screech-Owl
Ferruginous Pygmy-Owl
Spectacled Owl
Mottled Owl
Common Potoo
Short-tailed Nighthawk   H
Band-winged Nightjar
Common Pauraque

White-collared Swift   c
Chestnut-collared Swift   H
Vaux's Swift
Gray-rumped Swift   c
Short-tailed Swift
White-tipped Swift   c H
Lesser Swallow-tailed Swift
Rufous-breasted Hermit
Pale-bellied Hermit
Sooty-capped Hermit
Little Hermit
Lazuline Sabrewing   r
White-necked Jacobin
Brown Violetear   H
Green Violetear   H
Black-throated Mango
Violet-headed Hummingbird   H
Spangled Coquette   r
Blue-tailed Emerald
Golden-tailed Sapphire
Glittering-throated Emerald
Copper-rumped Hummingbird
White-vented Plumeleteer
Speckled Hummingbird   H
Violet-fronted Brilliant   H
Violet-chested Hummingbird   H
Bronzy Inca   H
Booted Rackettail   H
Long-tailed Sylph   c H
Long-billed Starthroat   r
White-tipped Quetzal   H
Collared Trogon   c
Amazon Kingfisher
Green Kingfisher
Rufous-tailed Jacamar   c
Russet-throated Puffbird
White-necked Puffbird
Moustached Puffbird   r
Groove-billed Toucanet   c H
Scaled Piculet
Golden-olive Woodpecker   c H
Lineated Woodpecker
Red-crowned Woodpecker   c
Smoky-brown Woodpecker   H
Red-rumped Woodpecker
Crimson-crested Woodpecker   r
Plain-brown Woodcreeper

Olivaceous Woodcreeper   c
Strong-billed Woodcreeper   r H
Black-banded Woodcreeper   r
Buff-throated Woodcreeper
Olive-backed Woodcreeper
Straight-billed Woodcreeper
Streak-headed Woodcreeper   c
Red-billed Scythebill
Pale-breasted Spinetail
Stripe-breasted Spinetail
Rufous (Rusty) Spinetail   H
Crested Spinetail   H
Spotted Barbtail   r H
Streaked Tuftedcheek   H
Guttulated Foliage-gleaner   r H
Montane Foilage-gleaner   c H
Buff-fronted Foilage-gleaner   c H
Streak-capped Treehunter   r H
Streaked Xenops   r H
Plain Xenops
Black-crested Antshrike
Black-backed Antshrike
Barred Antshrike
Plain Antvireo
Plumbeous Antshrike   H
Slaty Antwren   H
Rufous-winged Antwren
White-fringed Antwren   c
Long-tailed Antbird   r
White-bellied Antbird
Short-tailed Ant-thrush
Black-faced Ant-thrush   r H
Rufous-tailed Ant-thrush
Plain-backed Antpitta   r H
Golden-breasted Fruiteater   r H
Handsome Fruiteater   H
Cinereous Becard
Chestnut-crowned Becard   H
Black-and-white Becard
Masked Tityra
Bearded Bellbird   r
Wire-tailed Manakin
Golden-headed Manakin   r
Lance-tailed Manakin
Wing-barred Manakin
Black Phoebe   c
Cattle Tyrant

Tropical Kingbird   c
Piratic Flycatcher   S
Boat-billed Flycatcher   c
Streaked Flycatcher
Golden-crowned Flycatcher   H
Rusty-margined Flycatcher   c
Social Flycatcher   c
Great Kiskadee   c
Bright-rumped Attila
Venezuelan Flycatcher
Brown-crested Flycatcher
Pale-edged Flycatcher   H
Dusky-capped Flycatcher   H
Olive-sided Pewee   W H
Tropical Pewee
Greater Pewee   c H
Cinnamon Flycatcher   H
Flavescent Flycatcher   r H
Bran-colored Flycatcher
Yellow-olive Flycatcher   c
Yellow-breasted Flycatcher
Common Tody-Flycatcher
Slate-headed Tody-Flycatcher
Pearly-vented Tody-Tyrant
Scale-crested Pygmy-Tyrant
Pale-eyed Pygmy-Tyrant   r
Marble-faced Bristle-Tyrant
   c H
Venezuelan Bristle-Tyrant   r H
Yellow-bellied Bristle-Tyrant   H
Yellow Tyrannulet
White-throated Tyrannulet   H
Yellow-bellied Elaenia
Forest Elaenia
Scrub Flycatcher
Mouse-colored Tyrannulet
Southern Beardless Tyrannulet
Paltry Tyrannulet   H
Brown-capped Tyrannulet
Slaty-capped Flycatcher   H
Olive-striped Flycatcher   H
Gray-breasted Martin   c
Blue-and-white Swallow   c H
Rough-winged Swallow   c
Green Jay   c H
Moustached Wren   H
Rufous-breasted Wren   c

Buff-breasted Wren
Rufous-and-white Wren
House Wren   c
Gray-breasted Wood-Wren   c H
Nightingale Wren
Andean Solitaire   H
Orange-billed Nightingale-Thrush
   r
Yellow-legged Thrush   H
Glossy-black Thrush   H
Black-hooded Thrush
Pale-breasted Thrush   c
Cocoa Thrush
Bare-eyed Thrush   c
White-necked Thrush   c H
Long-billed Gnatwren
Tropical Gnatcatcher
Rufous-browed Peppershrike   c
Red-eyed Vireo   M
Brown-capped Vireo   c H
Golden-fronted Greenlet
Scrub Greenlet
Shiny Cowbird
Giant Cowbird
Crested Oropendola   c
Russet-backed Oropendola   c H
Yellow-rumped Cacique
Carib Grackle   c
Orange-crowned Oriole
Yellow Oriole
Yellow-backed Oriole
Black-and-white Warbler   c W
Golden-winged Warbler   H W
Tennessee Warbler   c W
Tropical Parula   c
Yellow Warbler   r W
Cerulean Warbler   W
Blackburnian Warbler   W
Chestnut-sided Warbler   r W
Bay-breasted Warbler   r W
Blackpoll Warbler   W
Northern Waterthrush   c W
Masked Yellowthroat   r
American Redstart   c W
Slate-throated Whitestart   c H
Flavescent Warbler
Three-striped Warbler   c H

Golden-crowned Warbler   c
Bananaquit   c
White-eared Conebill
Green Honeycreeper
Purple Honeycreeper   M
Red-legged Honeycreeper   M
Blue Dacnis
Bluish Flower-piercer   r H
Swallow-Tanager
Blue-hooded Euphonia
Orange-bellied Euphonia   c H
Trinidad Euphonia
Thick-billed Euphonia
Fawn-breasted Tanager   r H
Speckled Tanager   c H
Golden Tanager   c H
Rufous-cheeked Tanager   H
Bay-headed Tanager   c
Burnished-buff Tanager
Beryl-spangled Tanager   H
Black-capped Tanager   r H
Black-headed Tanager   r
Blue-winged Mountain-Tanager   c
   H
Palm Tanager
Blue-gray Tanager   c

Glaucous (Sayaca) Tanager   r
Blue-capped Tanager   H
Silver-beaked Tanager   c
Hepatic Tanager
Summer Tanager   W
White-winged Tanager   H
White-lined Tanager   c
Gray-headed Tanager
Guira Tanager   r
Rosy Thrush-Tanager   r
Fulvous-headed Tanager   r
Oleaginous Hemispingus   r H
Common Bush-Tanager   c H
Buff-throated Saltator
Grayish Saltator
Streaked Saltator
Blue-black Grosbeak
Ultramarine Grosbeak
Blue-black Grassquit
Dull-colored Grassquit   r
Gray Seedeater
Yellow-bellied Seedeater
Ruddy-breasted Seedeater
Stripe-headed Brush-Finch   r H
Ochre-breasted Brush-Finch   H
Yellow-bellied Siskin   H

29
Calabozo, Venezuela

ONE OF THE WORLD'S TOP BIRD LOCALITIES is the flat Llanos of interior Venezuela, which is accessible between Calabozo and San Fernando in the state of Guarico.

The town of Calabozo is situated 170 miles (272 km) south of Caracas, about a four-hour drive on paved roads. The Motel Tiuna is one of several modest hotels in Calabozo with air-conditioning and a good restaurant. Another, for those wishing to do more exploring, is the Hotel La Fuente in San Fernando. A fine paved road runs south from Calabozo to San Fernando, and most of the birds of the Llanos can be seen and photographed from the road despite speeding traffic.

Leaving Calabozo the road soon crosses the Rio Guarico where Pale-headed Jacamar may be seen. It then passes through irrigated rice fields, with an abundance of side roads, where birds are variable in number and species. Savanna Hawks are abundant at all times. In the wet months, June through September, thousands of whistling-duck and Everglade Kite may be seen. Jabiru Stork flocks of up to 350 have been noted, although in the dry season they become scarce. Several million Dickcissels have been seen migrating in the evening in early March, and Scarlet Ibis are irregularly common. The very last rice fields are best for Whistling Herons and Bare-faced Ibis. Pesticides, though, are beginning to reduce some bird populations, and there has been much hunting.

South of this area the road passes through grazing country, including several famous ranches such as Flores Moradas and Hato Masaguaral, which are not open to the public. Along the road, particularly the few miles south of the Canaguaro CAN-TV tower, there are continuous roadside ponds with marshes and trees. This area often has Hoatzin, Sunbittern, Maguari Stork, and ducks in the dry season. Southward to the village of Camaguan are more ranches where, from the road, such birds as Buff-necked, Green, and Sharp-tailed Ibises, Jabiru Stork, Double-striped Thick-knee, and Hoatzin may be found.

The estuary on the west side of the road just before Camaguan is often alive with whistling-ducks, Brazilian Teal, Bare-faced and Scar-

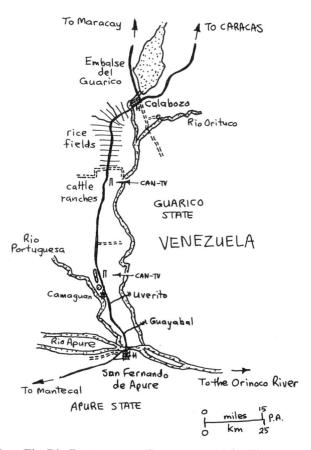

To Maracay
TO CARACAS

Embalse del Guarico

Calabozo

Rio Orituco

rice fields

cattle ranches

CAN-TV

GUARICO STATE

VENEZUELA

Rio Portuguesa

CAN-TV

Camaguan

Uverito

Guayabal

Rio Apure

San Fernando de Apure

To Mantecal

To the Orinoco River

APURE STATE

0 miles 15 P.A.
0 km 25

let Ibises. The Rio Portuguesa at Camaguan and the Rio Apure at San Fernando are good for Large-billed and Yellow-billed Tern.

CHECKLIST

Red-legged Tinamou   r
American Dabchick   r
Neotropic Cormorant   c
Anhinga
Cocoi Heron   c
Great Egret   c
Snowy Egret   c
Little Blue Heron   c
Green Heron   c
Cattle Heron   c
Whistling Heron
Capped Heron   r
Black-crowned Night-Heron

Yellow-crowned Night-Heron
Rufescent Tiger-Heron   c
Boat-billed Heron   r
Wood Stork   c
Maguari Stork
Jabiru Stork
Buff-necked Ibis
Sharp-tailed Ibis
Green Ibis
Bare-faced Ibis
White Ibis   r
Scarlet Ibis
Glossy Ibis

Roseate Spoonbill
Horned Screamer   r
Fulvous Whistling-Duck
White-faced Whistling-Duck
Black-bellied Whistling-Duck
Blue-winged Teal   W
Brazilian Teal   r
Comb Duck
Muscovy Duck
Masked Duck   r
King Vulture   r
Black Vulture   c
Turkey Vulture   c
Marsh Vulture
White-tailed Kite   c
Pearl Kite
Gray-headed Kite   r
Plumbeous Kite   S
Everglade Kite   c
Slender-billed Kite   r S
White-tailed Hawk   c
Zone-tailed Hawk   r
Roadside Hawk   c
Short-tailed Hawk
Gray Hawk
Swainson's Hawk   r W
Harris's Hawk   r
Black-collared Hawk
Savanna Hawk   c
Great Black Hawk   c
Crane Hawk
Osprey   W
Laughing Falcon
Yellow-headed Caracara   c
Crested Caracara   c
Aplomado Falcon
Merlin   W
American Kestrel
Rufous-vented Chachalaca   c
Yellow-knobbed Curassow   r
Crested Bobwhite
Hoatzin
Limpkin   c
Gray-necked Wood-Rail   c
Common Gallinule   r
Purple Gallinule
Azure Gallinule   r

Sunbittern
Wattled Jacana   c
Southern Lapwing   c
Pied Lapwing   r M
Lesser Golden Plover   M
Collared Plover   r
Solitary Sandpiper   c W
Greater Yellowlegs   W
Lesser Yellowlegs   W
Spotted Sandpiper   W
Least Sandpiper   W
Short-billed Dowitcher   r W
Stilt Sandpiper   M
Common Snipe
Black-necked Stilt
Double-striped Thick-knee
Large-billed Tern
Yellow-billed Tern
Black Skimmer
Bare-eyed Pigeon   r
Pale-vented Pigeon   c
Spot-eared Dove   c
Common Ground-Dove   (n. of
   Calabozo)
Plain-breasted Ground-Dove   c (s.
   of Calabozo)
Ruddy Ground-Dove   c
Blue Ground-Dove
Scaled Dove   c
White-tipped Dove   c
Scarlet Macaw   r
Brown-throated Parakeet   c
Green-rumped Parrotlet   c
Orange-chinned Parakeet   c
Yellow-crowned Parrot
Dwarf Cuckoo   r
Squirrel Cuckoo
Greater Ani   c
Smooth-billed Ani   c
Groove-billed Ani   c
Striped Cuckoo
Great Horned Owl
Ferruginous Pygmy-Owl
Burrowing Owl
Common Potoo
Great Potoo   r
Nacunda Nighthawk

Common Pauraque
White-tailed Nightjar
Amazonian Palm-Swift
Black-throated Mango
Ruby-topaz Hummingbird
Blue-tailed Emerald
Glittering-throated Emerald   c
Coppery-rumped Hummingbird
White-tailed Goldenthroat
Amethyst Woodstar   r
Ringed Kingfisher
Amazon Kingfisher
Green Kingfisher
American Pygmy Kingfisher   r
Rufous-tailed Jacamar
Pale-headed Jacamar   r
Russet-throated Puffbird   r
Aerial Puffbird   r
Scaled Piculet
Spot-breasted Flicker
Lineated Woodpecker
Red-crowned Woodpecker   c
Red-rumped Woodpecker
Crimson-crested Woodpecker
Straight-billed Woodcreeper
Streak-headed Woodcreeper
Pale-breasted Spinetail   c
Yellow-throated Spinetail   c
Rufous-fronted Thornbird
Xenops, species
Great Antshrike
Black-crested Antshrike   c
Barred Antshrike
White-fringed Antwren
Lance-tailed Manakin
Black-crowned Tityra   r
Pied Water-Tyrant   c
White-headed Marsh-Tyrant   c
Vermilion Flycatcher
Cattle Tyrant   c
Fork-tailed Flycatcher   c
Tropical Kingbird   c
Gray Kingbird   c
Boat-billed Flycatcher
Streaked Flycatcher
Variegated Flycatcher   S
Rusty-margined Flycatcher   c

Social Flycatcher   c
White-bearded Flycatcher
Great Kiskadee   c
Lesser Kiskadee
Short-crested Flycatcher
Brown-crested Flycatcher
Bran-colored Flycatcher
Yellow-olive Flycatcher
Yellow-breasted Flycatcher
Common Tody-Flycatcher
Slate-headed Tody-Flycatcher
Pale-eyed Pygmy-Tyrant
Yellow Tyrannulet
Pale-tipped Tyrannulet   c
Yellow-bellied Elaenia
Lesser Elaenia
Mouse-colored Tyrannulet
Southern Beardless Tyrannulet
Scrub Flycatcher
White-winged Swallow   c
Rough-winged Swallow
Gray-breasted Martin
Barn Swallow   W
Sand Martin   W
Bicolored Wren
Stripe-backed Wren   c
Buff-breasted Wren
House Wren   c
Tropical Mockingbird   c
Pale-breasted Thrush
Bare-eyed Thrush
Tropical Gnatcatcher
Yellowish Pipit   r
Rufous-browed Peppershrike
Golden-fronted Greenlet
Scrub Greenlet
Shiny Cowbird   c
Yellow-rumped Cacique   c
Carib Grackle   c
Yellow-hooded Blackbird   c
Orange-crowned Oriole   r
Troupial
Yellow Oriole   c
Oriole-Blackbird   c
Red-breasted Blackbird
Eastern Meadowlark
Bobolink   M

Tropical Parula
Yellow Warbler   c W
Northern Waterthrush   c W
Bananaquit   c
Chestnut-vented Conebill
Trinidad Euphonia
Thick-billed Euphonia
Burnished-buff Tanager   r
Palm Tanager
Blue-gray Tanager   c
Glaucous (Sayaca) Tanager
Hooded Tanager
Grayish Saltator   c

Orinocan Saltator
Pileated Finch
Red-capped Cardinal   c
Dickcissel   c W
Blue-black Grassquit   c
Gray Seedeater   c
Yellow-bellied Seedeater
Ruddy-breasted Seedeater
Large-billed Seed-Finch
Saffron Yellow-Finch   c
Black-striped Sparrow
Grassland Sparrow

30
Santa Marta, Colombia

SANTA MARTA IS A HISTORIC SMALL CITY on the Caribbean, with many resort hotels, against a backdrop of tall mountains. There is an airport with jet services to Bogota and Cartagena. Most of the inexpensive hotels are south of the city at Rodadero Beach, while the more luxurious hotels, such as the Irotama, are between Rodadero and the airport. The area is wettest in the summer and autumn.

The centerpiece of the region is the massive Sierra Nevada de Santa Marta, whose snowy summits reach 19,000 feet (5800 m) above sea level (they are rarely seen due to the tall foothills and tropical haze). These mountains are virtually inaccessible, except for the road up to the TV towers on San Lorenzo ridge, which passes through forests containing 11 of the 13 endemic birds. The vegetation on the lower slopes of the mountains is complicated. To the northwest (as around Santa Marta and Cienaga) it is rather arid woodland. To the southwest, toward the Rio Sevilla and Fundacion, it becomes more humid. North of the mountains against the Caribbean (Tayrona area) is another band of wetter lowland forest. To the northeast, toward Riohacha and the Guajira Peninsula, the countryside becomes remarkably dry and desertlike. West of Cienaga, the road to Barranquilla goes through dry areas with mangroves and seasonal lagoons.

Tayrona National Park, located at the kilometer post 30 (about 19 miles) east of Santa Marta, offers the most comfortable access and birding. The road north from the guard house (small entrance charge) to Canaveral Beach is paved, quiet (except on weekends), and passes through tropical deciduous forest often alive with birds. Military Macaws can be seen overhead, while the woods are alive with hummingbirds, antbirds, Lance-tailed and other manakins, hordes of flycatchers, wrens, and Crimson-backed Tanager. Golden-winged and Black-striped Sparrows are often attracted to taped calls of the Ferruginous Pygmy-Owl (an excellent aid in the lowlands throughout its range). The beach at the end of the road is beautiful, and there is a small restaurant though no hotel as yet.

Finding the birds of the mountains requires a strong constitution and a certain amount of luck. The road is often in miserable condition

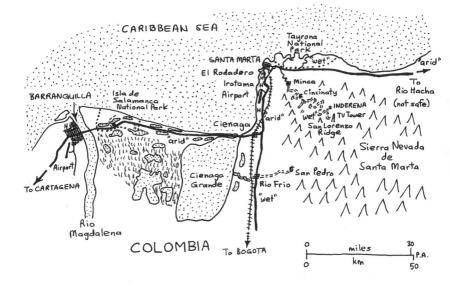

CARIBBEAN SEA

Tayrona National Park

SANTA MARTA
El Rodadero
Irotama Airport

"wet"
"arid"

BARRANQUILLA
Isla de Salamanca National Park

Minca
Cincinaty
INDERENA
TV Tower
San Lorenzo Ridge

To Rio Hacha (not safe)

Cienaga

"arid"

"arid"
"wet"

Sierra Nevada de Santa Marta

Airport

To CARTAGENA

Cienaga Grande

San Pedro
Rio Frio
"wet"

Rio Magdalena

COLOMBIA   To BOGOTA

0   miles   30
|———————————| P.A.
0   km   50

(rutted, dusty, or muddy) and at times impassable. Good drivers can usually make it in the local rent-a-cars, although a 4-wheel-drive vehicle or truck (with high clearance) is better.

The road to the TV towers on San Lorenzo ridge is marked MINCA, and departs the Riohacha highway immediately east of the police checkpoint east of Santa Marta. The first 8 miles (13 km) to Minca is partly paved, with good lowland birding in the early morning. The next 8 miles (13 km) to El Kampano store (Cincinaty) goes through coffee plantations in the hills and has not been heavily birded. Another 3.7 miles (6 km) uphill (keep left at all forks) brings you to a 2.5-mile (4-km) stretch with attractive weekend estates set in the forest (named Cabañas de Ziruma, Palo Alto, and Refugios de la Sierra). This area is often rich in activity, and is good for guans, White-tailed Starfrontlet, the rare Blossomcrown, White-tipped Quetzal, and warblers. The forest thickens during the final 3.7 miles (6 km) to the TV stations at the treeline. There is an Inderena (National Park Service) station along this stretch, where sometimes a few scientists work. These high forests are home to such attractions as Santa Marta Parakeet, Black-backed Thornbill, Mountain Velvetbreast, Masked 'Trogon, Rusty-headed and Streak-capped Spinetails, Santa Marta Antpitta, Red-crested Cotinga, Yellow-crowned Whitestart, Santa Marta Warbler, flower-piercers, Black-cheeked Mountain-Tanager, and Santa Marta Brush-Finch. Unfortunately there are no hotels here so visitors have to commute and bring their own food.

148

It takes about 3 hours of tough roads to get up and most birding is done from the road as there are few trails.

To the southwest of Santa Marta at Cienaga there is a road fork. The road south to the Rio Sevilla and Fundacion traverses increasingly wet country with a few birds not found to the north. As much of the area has been cleared, this day trip is recommended only for those with excess time. West of Cienaga the road to Barranquilla crosses a long sliver of land with the Caribbean to the north and the huge lake Cienaga Grande to the south. Hotels like the Irotama and Tamaca Inn now organize boat trips on the lake from Cienaga that offer easy waterbirding. Many shorebirds, herons, ducks, and hawks line the roads wherever water levels are right. In the mangroves the Chestnut Piculet and the extremely rare and local Sapphire-bellied Hummingbird live.

The Isla de Salamanca National Park has a visitors' center on the north side of the road called "Los Cocos." It is about 6.3 miles (10 km) east of the bridge over the Rio Magdalena at Barranquilla. A boardwalk over several lagoons offers easy shorebirding. The marshes on the south side of the road are richer, with Black-necked Screamer, Everglade Kite, and whistling-ducks, but there is no access except from the busy road, so be careful.

A number of desert-zone birds live in the scrub both west and east of Riohacha about a 4-hour drive east of Santa Marta. Due to the general lawlessness of the area (drug exporting schemes) it is recommended that most birders avoid this area. Such specialties as White-whiskered Spinetail, Vermilion Cardinal, and Tocuyo Sparrow occur also in northwestern Venezuela, a far safer area for single travelers.

The grounds of the Hotel Irotama (just north of the Santa Marta airport) are good for Bicolored Wren, Russet-throated Puffbird, Yellow Oriole, and Slender-billed Tyrannulet.

CHECKLIST

Little Tinamou r	Little Blue Heron c
Pied-billed Grebe	Reddish Egret r
American Dabchick	Louisiana Heron c
Brown Pelican c	Green Heron c
Neotropic Cormorant c	Cattle Heron c
Anhinga	Capped Heron r
Magnificent Frigatebird c	Black-crowned Night-Heron
Great Blue Heron W	Yellow-crowned Night-Heron
Cocoi Heron c	Rufescent Tiger-Heron r
Great Egret c	Boat-billed Heron r

Wood Stork
Bare-faced Ibis
White Ibis
Green Ibis   r
American Flamingo   r
Black-necked Screamer
Black-bellied Whistling-Duck
Fulvous Whistling-Duck
White-faced Whistling-Duck   r
White-cheeked Pintail   r
American Wigeon   W
Blue-winged Teal   c W
Northern Shoveler   r W
Lesser Scaup   r W
Muscovy Duck   r
Andean Condor   r H
King Vulture
Black Vulture   c
Turkey Vulture   c
Marsh Vulture
White-tailed Kite
Pearl Kite   c
Double-toothed Kite
Gray-headed Kite
Everglade Kite
Sharp-shinned Sparrowhawk   r H
White-tailed Hawk
Zone-tailed Hawk
Broad-winged Hawk   c W
Roadside Hawk   c
Short-tailed Hawk
Gray Hawk
White-rumped Hawk   H
Harris's Hawk
Lesser Black Hawk   c
Great Black Hawk   r
Savanna Hawk
Black-collared Hawk
Black-and-chestnut Eagle   r H
Black Hawk-Eagle
Osprey   W
Laughing Falcon
Collared Forest-Falcon   r
Barred Forest-Falcon   r
Yellow-headed Caracara   c
Crested Caracara   c
Bat Falcon

Peregrine Falcon   W
American Kestrel
Chestnut-winged Chachalaca
Band-tailed Guan   H
Crested Guan   r
Sickle-winged Guan   H
Crested Bobwhite
Black-fronted Wood-Quail   r H
Limpkin
Gray-necked Wood-Rail
Purple Gallinule
American Coot   W
Wattled Jacana   c
American Oystercatcher   r
Southern Lapwing
Gray Plover   c W
Semipalmated Plover   c W
Collared Plover
Wilson's Plover   c W
Whimbrel   W
Lesser Yellowlegs   c W
Greater Yellowlegs   c W
Solitary Sandpiper   W
Spotted Sandpiper   c ·W
Willet   W
Red Knot   r M
Ruddy Turnstone   c W
Short-billed Dowitcher   c W
Long-billed Dowitcher   r W
Common Snipe   W
Sanderling   c W
Western Sandpiper   c W
Least Sandpiper   c W
Pectoral Sandpiper   M
Black-necked Stilt   c
Laughing Gull   c W
Black Tern   W
Gull-billed Tern   c
Large-billed Tern   r
Caspian Tern   W
Common Tern   W
Little Tern   W
Royal Tern   c
Sandwich Tern   W
Band-tailed Pigeon   c H
Scaled Pigeon
Bare-eyed Pigeon

Pale-vented Pigeon
Spot-eared Dove
Common Ground-Dove   c
Ruddy Ground-Dove   c
Blue Ground-Dove
Scaled Dove   c
White-tipped Dove   c
Lined Quail-Dove   H
Ruddy Quail-Dove
Military Macaw
Scarlet-fronted Parakeet   c H
Brown-throated Parakeet   c
Santa Marta Parakeet   H
Green-rumped Parrotlet   (east)
Blue-winged Parrotlet   (west)
Orange-chinned Parakeet   c
Blue-headed Parrot   c
Red-billed Parrot   c H
Orange-winged Parrot
Yellow-billed Cuckoo   M
Squirrel Cuckoo
Greater Ani
Smooth-billed Ani   c
Groove-billed Ani
Striped Cuckoo
Tropical Screech-Owl
Spectacled Owl
Ferruginous Pygmy-Owl   c
Striped Owl
Lesser Nighthawk
Common Pauraque
Band-winged Nightjar
White-tailed Nightjar
White-collared Swift   c
Chestnut-collared Swift
White-tipped Swift   r H
Ashy-tailed Swift   r
Band-rumped Swift
Rufous-breasted Hermit
Band-tailed Barbthroat
Long-tailed Hermit
Pale-bellied Hermit   c
Little Hermit
White-necked Jacobin
Brown Violetear   r H
Green Violetear   c H
Sparkling Violetear   c H

Black-throated Mango
Ruby-topaz Hummingbird
Red-billed Emerald   r
Blue-tailed Emerald   c
Coppery Emerald   H
Common Woodnymph
Sapphire-bellied Hummingbird   r
White-chinned Sapphire   c
Steely-vented Hummingbird   c
Buffy Hummingbird   r
Rufous-tailed Hummingbird   c
White-vented Plumeleteer
Blossomcrown   r H
Mountain Velvetbreast   c H
White-tailed Starfrontlet   H
Black-backed Thornbill   r H
Tyrian Metaltail   c H
Long-billed Starthroat   r
Gorgeted Woodstar   r H
White-tipped Quetzal   c H
Masked Trogon   H
Violaceous Trogon
Ringed Kingfisher
Belted Kingfisher   W
Amazon Kingfisher
Green Kingfisher
American Pygmy Kingfisher   r
Blue-crowned Motmot
Rufous-tailed Jacamar   c
White-necked Puffbird
Pied Puffbird
Russet-throated Puffbird   c
Emerald Toucanet   c H
Groove-billed Toucanet   r H
Collared Aracari
Keel-billed Toucan
Chestnut Piculet
Spot-breasted Flicker
Golden-olive Woodpecker   c H
Lineated Woodpecker
Red-crowned Woodpecker   c
Smoky-brown Woodpecker   r H
Red-rumped Woodpecker
Crimson-crested Woodpecker
Plain-brown Woodcreeper   r
Strong-billed Woodcreeper   H
Straight-billed Woodcreeper   c

Buff-throated Woodcreeper
Spot-crowned Woodcreeper   c H
Pale-legged Hornero
Pale-breasted Spinetail
Rusty-headed Spinetail   c H
White-whiskered Spinetail
Yellow-throated Spinetail   c
Streak-capped Spinetail   c H
Spotted Barbtail   r H
Montane Foliage-gleaner   c H
Plain Xenops
Streaked Xenops   r H
Barred Antshrike
Black-crested Antshrike
Black-backed Antshrike
Slaty Antshrike
Slaty Antwren
White-fringed Antwren   c
Long-tailed Antbird   r H
Jet Antbird   r
White-bellied Antbird
Black-faced Ant-thrush
Santa Marta Antpitta   H
Brown-rumped Tapaculo   H
Red-crested Cotinga   H
Golden-breasted Fruiteater   H
Bright-rumped Attila   r
Cinnamon Becard
Barred Becard   r H
Cinereous Becard
White-winged Becard
Masked Tityra
Golden-headed Manakin   r
Lance-tailed Manakin   c
White-bearded Manakin   c
Thrush-like Manakin
Streak-throated Bush-Tyrant   H
Santa Marta Bush-Tyrant   r H
Yellow-bellied Chat-Tyrant   H
Black Phoebe
Pied Water-Tyrant   c
White-headed Marsh-Tyrant
Vermilion Flycatcher   r
Cattle Tyrant   c
Fork-tailed Flycatcher
Eastern Kingbird   M
Tropical Kingbird   c

Gray Kingbird   c W
Piratic Flycatcher
Streaked Flycatcher   c
Golden-crowned Flycatcher   H
Boat-billed Flycatcher
Rusty-margined Flycatcher
Social Flycatcher   c
Great Kiskadee   c
Lesser Kiskadee
Great-crested Flycatcher   r W
Brown-crested Flycatcher   c
Panama Flycatcher
Dusky-capped Flycatcher
Olive-sided Pewee   W H
Acadian Flycatcher   W
Wood Pewee   W
Tropical Pewee
Ruddy-tailed Flycatcher   r
Cinnamon Flycatcher   c H
Yellow-breasted Flycatcher
Yellow-olive Flycatcher
Olivaceous Flatbill   r
Black-headed Tody-Flycatcher
Common Tody-Flycatcher   c
Slate-headed Tody-Flycatcher
Southern Bentbill   c
Black-throated Tody-Tyrant   c H
Pearly-vented Tody-Tyrant   c
Pale-eyed Pygmy-Tyrant   c
Pale-tipped Tyrannulet
Yellow Tyrannulet
Slender-billed Tyrannulet
White-throated Tyrannulet   c H
Yellow-bellied Elaenia   c
Lesser Elaenia
Mountain Elaenia   c H
Forest Elaenia
Greenish Elaenia
Scrub Flycatcher   c
Mouse-colored Tyrannulet   c
Southern Beardless Tyrannulet   c
Paltry Tyrannulet   H
Black-capped Tyrannulet   H
Yellow-crowned Tyrannulet   c
Brown-capped Tyrannulet
Sepia-capped Flycatcher   c
Olive-striped Flycatcher   c H

Ochre-bellied Flycatcher   c
Brown-chested Martin   M
Gray-breasted Martin   c
Brown-bellied Swallow   H
Tree Swallow   r W
White-winged Swallow
Blue-and-white Swallow
Rough-winged Swallow   c
Sand Martin   M
Barn Swallow   W
Black-chested Jay   c
Bicolored Wren   c
Stripe-backed Wren
Rufous-breasted Wren
Rufous-and-white Wren
Buff-breasted Wren
House Wren   c
Gray-breasted Wood-Wren   H
Nightingale Wren
Tropical Mockingbird   c
Orange-billed Nightingale-Thrush
   c H
Slaty-backed Nightingale-Thrush
   H
Gray-cheeked Thrush   r W H
Swainson's Thrush   W
Yellow-legged Thrush   H
Great Thrush   c H
Black-hooded Thrush   H
Pale-breasted Thrush   c
Clay-colored Thrush
Long-billed Gnatwren
Tropical Gnatcatcher
Rufous-browed Peppershrike
Yellow-throated Vireo   W
Red-eyed Vireo
Brown-capped Vireo   H
Golden-fronted Greenlet
Scrub Greenlet   c
Crested Oropendola
Yellow-rumped Cacique
Giant Cowbird   r
Shiny Cowbird   c
Great-tailed Grackle   c
Northern (Baltimore) Oriole   W
Orchard Oriole   r W
Yellow-tailed Oriole

Orange-crowned Oriole
Yellow-backed Oriole   c H
Yellow Oriole   c
Troupial   r
Yellow-hooded Blackbird
Red-breasted Blackbird
Black-and-white Warbler   W
Prothonotary Warbler   W
Golden-winged Warbler   W
Tennessee Warbler   c W
Tropical Parula
Yellow Warbler   c W
Black-throated Green Warbler   r
   W
Cerulean Warbler   W
Blackburnian Warbler   c W
Bay-breasted Warbler   W
Ovenbird   r W
Louisiana Waterthrush   W
Northern Waterthrush   c W
Hooded Warbler   r W
Mourning Warbler   r W
Masked Yellowthroat   r
American Redstart   W
Slate-throated Whitestart   c H
Yellow-crowned Whitestart   c H
Santa Marta Warbler   H
Golden-crowned Warbler   H
Rufous-capped Warbler
White-lored Warbler   H
Bananaquit   c
Bicolored Conebill
Carbonated Flower-piercer   c H
White-sided Flower-piercer   c H
Garden Flower-piercer   H
Purple Honeycreeper
Red-legged Honeycreeper
Blue Dacnis
Swallow-Tanager
Blue-naped Chlorophonia
Thick-billed Euphonia   c
Trinidad Euphonia   c
Bay-headed Tanager   c
Black-capped Tanager   H
Black-headed Tanager   H
Black-cheeked Mountain-Tanager
   c

Blue-gray Tanager   c
Glaucous (Sayaca) Tanager
Palm Tanager   c
Blue-capped Tanager   c H
Crimson-backed Tanager   c
Summer Tanager   W
Hepatic Tanager   r
Scarlet Tanager   W
White-lined Tanager
Gray-headed Tanager
Plush-capped Finch   r H
Buff-throated Saltator   c
Grayish Saltator   c
Orinocan Saltator
Streaked Saltator   c
Vermilion Cardinal
Yellow Grosbeak
Rose-breasted Grosbeak   W
Blue-black Grosbeak
Indigo Bunting   r W

Blue-black Grassquit   c
Black-faced Grassquit
Gray Seedeater
Black-and-white Seedeater
Yellow-bellied Seedeater
Ruddy-breasted Seedeater
Lesser Seed-Finch
Pileated Finch   c
Saffron Yellow-Finch
Slaty Finch   r H
Santa Marta Brush-Finch   c H
Stripe-headed Brush-Finch   r H
Golden-winged Sparrow
Orange-billed Sparrow   r
Tocuyo Sparrow
Black-striped Sparrow
Rufous-collared Sparrow   c H
Andean Siskin   H
Lesser Goldfinch

31

Cali–Buenaventura, Colombia

CALI IS A LARGE CITY located at 3000 feet (915 m) in the Cauca Valley of western Colombia. Its international airport is served by major airlines from Miami, Panama City, Quito, and Lima. There is a variety of hotels, the most expensive being the Cali Intercontinental. Unfortunately there are no hotels in the western Andes where the birds are. There are a few simple hotels in Buenaventura for the dedicated.

There are some birds in Cali, such as Spectacled Parrotlet, but, as in much of Latin America, one must commute out to the birds. Those not on an organized birding tour will have to reserve a rent-a-car and find their own way around. Cali is at the western edge of the rather dry Cauca Valley flanking the western Andes. The valley is about 20 miles (32 km) wide and is covered with sugar cane fields and pastures, while off to the east the tall Central Andes form a wall. The best birding in the valley is around the Laguna de Sonso Reserve. It can be reached by taking the main road northeast to Palmira 17.5 miles (28 km) and then north 10.6 miles (17 km) to the town of Buga. From Buga the paved road west to the Cauca River passes by the north shore of the lake. Just before the bridge a short dirt road south offers traffic-free opportunities to see freshwater marsh birds including Horned Screamer, ibises, herons, rails, and riparian landbirds.

The western Andes are relatively low in elevation, and extremely verdant, with rainfall on the Pacific slope reaching 200 inches (5000 mm) a year, and with an incredibly long list of birds, including many rather local specialties. There is a paved road going west from Cali over the west crest of the Andes, and down a rain-shadow valley before reaching the wet lowlands near Buenaventura. Apical Flycatcher and Bar-crested Antshrike can be found along a short dirt road (south) in the arid Dagua Valley, 2 miles (3 km) before the toll booth (opposite the roadside chapel).

A large number of highland birds can be found on short side roads at the west crest. The San Antonio road goes off south at Kilometer

post 15 ¾ (about 9 miles west of Cali) up to a TV tower. The actual west crest at Kilometer post 18 (about 11.3 miles) has roads both north (good for Multicolored Tanager) and south through patches of cloud forest.

The Old Buenaventura Road branches off to the southwest (marked Boyero Ay.) six-tenths of a mile (1 km) beyond the west crest, passing through miles of rich bird habitat, and eventually rejoining the fast new road just east of Buenaventura. It passes through a dry valley before reaching Queremal at 5790 feet (1460 m), about an hour from Cali and 3 ½ hours above Buenaventura. There is fine roadside birding for the next few miles downhill.

Fine highland birding, complete with a wooden log trail through 1.9 miles (3 km) of virgin cloud forest, can be had by visiting Parque Nacional Farallones. To reach it take the rough dirt road south through Queremal plaza, and uphill to the Tokio Microwave Towers. Red-ruffed Fruitcrow, Purple-mantled, Moss-backed, and Grassgreen Tanagers, and Brown Inca are regularly seen.

Birds are usually in flocks or absent along this road, most activity being at dawn, during a light fog (the clouds pour in most days), and after rain. Nothing moves (so to speak) in the midday heat. There are innumerable places to stop when one is going downhill, despite increasing settlement. Hundreds of subtropical birds live in the area below Danubio (where a private road goes south to the Rio Anchicaya hydroelectric project). There is a banquet of cliffs, clouds, waterfalls, and rain-drenched forest for the next 12.5 miles (20 km), where Golden-chested and Scarlet-and-white Tanagers and Golden-collared Chlorophonia live.

The best birding near Buenaventura is in the cutover forests along the Bajo Calima road. This road runs northward from km 100, a few miles east of the Aduana (customs) stop where the old road branches off to the southeast. Birds include Yellow-throated Toucan, White Cotinga, Slate-throated Gnatcatcher, Blue-whiskered and Scarlet-and-white Tanagers.

For those with less time, the Pichinde Valley in the western Andes just southwest of Cali has a variety of birds, including some not found along the Buenaventura roads (plus another chance to miss Andean Cock-of-the-Rock).

While the people in the countryside are usually pleasant and helpful, visitors should exercise caution with personal belongings in central Cali and Buenaventura due to clever thieves.

CHECKLIST

(L = Buenaventura lowlands [chiefly below 3000 feet (915 m)]; H = Highlands of western Andes [chiefly above 3000 feet (915 m)]; V = Cauca Valley [incl. Cali, Buga Marsh] and arid portions of Dagua Valley [drier country])

Great Tinamou   r L
Tawny-breasted Tinamou   r H
Little Tinamou   r L
American Dabchick
Pied-billed Grebe
Brown Pelican   c L
Neotropic Cormorant
Anhinga
Magnificent Frigatebird
Great Blue Heron   W
Cocoi Heron   c V
Great Egret   c
Snowy Egret   c
Little Blue Heron
Louisiana Heron   L
Green Heron
Cattle Heron   c
Black-crowned Night-Heron
Least Bittern   V

Pinnated Bittern   r V
Buff-necked Ibis   V
Bare-faced Ibis   V
Horned Screamer   V
Fulvous Whistling-Duck   c V
Black-bellied Whistling-Duck   c V
American Wigeon   r W
Blue-winged Teal   W
Cinnamon Teal   W
Masked Duck   r
Black Vulture   c
Turkey Vulture   c
Swallow-tailed Kite   W
Double-toothed Kite   L
Plumbeous Kite   c M
Everglade Kite   V M
Tiny Sparrowhawk   r L
Roadside Hawk
White Hawk   L

Semiplumbeous Hawk   L
Barred Hawk   L
Savanna Hawk   V
Lesser Black Hawk   r L
Ornate Hawk-Eagle   L
Long-winged Harrier   V
Crane Hawk   r L
Osprey   W
Laughing Falcon
Barred Forest-Falcon   r L
Yellow-headed Caracara
Crested Caracara   V
Bat Falcon   L
American Kestrel
Speckled Chachalaca   V
Sickle-winged Guan   r H
Crested Bobwhite   c V
Rufous-fronted Wood-Quail   r L
Blackish Rail   V
Sora Crake   W
Gray-breasted Crake   V
Rufous-sided Crake   r L
Common Gallinule   c
Purple Gallinule   c
American Coot   V
Wattled Jacana   c
Southern Lapwing   V
Gray Plover   W
Semipalmated Plover   W
Collared Plover   r
Wilson's Plover
Ruddy Turnstone   W L
Solitary Sandpiper   W
Lesser Yellowlegs   W
Greater Yellowlegs   W
Spotted Sandpiper   W
Least Sandpiper   W
Western Sandpiper   W
Whimbrel   W L
Short-billed Dowitcher   W L
Common Snipe   W
Black-necked Stilt
Ring-billed Gull   r W L
Laughing Gull   c W L
Franklin's Gull   W L
Black Tern   W L
Large-billed Tern

Gull-billed Tern   W L
Royal Tern   W L
Sandwich Tern   W L
Band-tailed Pigeon   H
Scaled Pigeon   c L
Pale-vented Pigeon
Plumbeous Pigeon   L
Dusky Pigeon   L
Spot-eared Dove   c V
Common Ground-Dove   V
Ruddy Ground-Dove   c V
White-tipped Dove   V
Gray-headed Dove   V
Pallid Dove   L
Sapphire Quail-Dove   r L
White-throated Quail-Dove   r L
Scarlet-fronted Parakeet   v H
Spectacled Parrotlet   c V
Barred Parakeet   H
Red-winged Parrotlet   r L
Brown-headed (Beautiful) Parrot
   r L
Blue-headed Parrot   c L
Dwarf Cuckoo   V
Squirrel Cuckoo
Little Cuckoo
Greater Ani   V
Smooth-billed Ani   c
Striped Cuckoo   V
Tropical Screech-Owl   V
Mottled Owl   r L
Common Potoo   r
Lesser Nighthawk
Common Pauraque
White-collared Swift   c
Chestnut-collared Swift
Chimney Swift   M
Gray-rumped Swift
Band-rumped Swift   c L
Lesser Swallow-tailed Swift   L
Green-fronted Lancebill   r H
Tooth-billed Hummingbird   L
Band-tailed Barbthroat   L
White-whiskered Hermit   c L
Green Hermit   r L
Tawny-bellied Hermit   H
Little Hermit

White-tipped Sicklebill L
White-necked Jacobin V
Brown Violetear r H
Green Violetear H
Sparkling Violetear H
Black-throated Mango c V
Green Thorntail c L
Blue-tailed Emerald
Common Woodnymph L
Blue-headed Sapphire L
Blue-chested Hummingbird r L
Purple-chested Hummingbird r L
Andean Emerald H
Steely-vented Hummingbird c V
Rufous-tailed Hummingbird c
Speckled Hummingbird H
(Purple-bibbed) Whitetip r H
Fawn-breasted Brilliant r H
Empress Brilliant r H
White-tailed Hillstar H
Bronzy Inca H
Brown Inca r H
Collared Inca H
Buff-tailed Coronet H
Velvet-purple Coronet H
Greenish Puffleg r H
Booted Rackettail
Purple-backed Thornbill r H
Violet-tailed Sylph H
Wedge-billed Hummingbird r H
Purple-crowned Fairy c L
Long-billed Starthroat r
Purple-throated Woodstar r
Crested Quetzal H
Slaty-tailed Trogon L
Blue-tailed Trogon L
White-tailed Trogon r L
Collared Trogon L
Masked Trogon H
Violaceous Trogon c L
Ringed Kingfisher
Amazon Kingfisher L
Green Kingfisher
Broad-billed Motmot L
Rufous Motmot L
Blue-crowned Motmot H
Rufous-tailed Jacamar L

Black-breasted Puffbird L
Pied Puffbird L
Barred Puffbird r L
White-whiskered Puffbird r L
Moustached Puffbird r H
Lanceolated Monklet r L
Spot-crowned Barbet c L
Red-headed Barbet c H
Toucan Barbet r H
Emerald Toucanet H
Crimson-rumped Toucanet
Stripe-billed Aracari c L
Yellow-throated Toucan c L
Olivaceous Piculet L
Grayish Piculet H V
Spot-breasted Flicker V
Golden-olive Woodpecker c
White-throated Woodpecker L
Cinnamon Woodpecker L
Acorn Woodpecker H V
Lineated Woodpecker
Black-cheeked Woodpecker c L
Smoky-brown Woodpecker H
Yellow-vented Woodpecker H
Crimson-crested Woodpecker L
Crimson-bellied Woodpecker r L
Plain-brown Woodcreeper
Wedge-billed Woodcreeper c L
Barred Woodcreeper r L
Spotted Woodcreeper L
Olive-backed Woodcreeper L
Spot-crowned Woodcreeper H
Red-billed Scythebill r L
Brown-billed Scythebill
Azara's Spinetail c H
Pale-breasted Spinetail c V
Slaty Spinetail
Rufous Spinetail H
Red-faced Spinetail c H
Fulvous-dotted Treerunner r H
Spotted Barbtail r H
Lineated Foliage-gleaner H
Scaly-throated Foliage-gleaner r
Montane Foliage-gleaner c H
Buff-fronted Foliage-gleaner H
Ruddy Foliage-gleaner L
Streak-capped Treehunter H

Uniform Treehunter   r H
Streaked Xenops   H
Plain Xenops   c L
Tawny-throated Leaftosser   r H
Great Antshrike   L
Bar-crested Antshrike   V
Uniform Antshrike   H
Slaty Antshrike   c L
Russet Antshrike   r H
Plain Antvireo   H
Spot-crowned Antvireo   L
Streaked Antwren   c L
Slaty Antwren
Dot-winged Antwren   L
Rufous-rumped Antwren   r H
Dusky Antbird   r
Jet Antbird
Stub-tailed Antbird   r L
Esmeraldas Antbird   r L
Chestnut-backed Antbird   c L
Dull-mantled Antbird   L
Immaculate Antbird   c
Bicolored Antbird   r L
Undulated Antpitta (?)   H
Chestnut-crowned Antpitta   H
Fulvous-bellied Antpitta   L
Ochre-breasted Antpitta   H
Chestnut-crowned Gnateater   r H
Rufous-vented Tapaculo   r H
Unicolored Tapaculo   H
Blue Cotinga   L
White Cotinga   L
Green-and-black Fruiteater   H
Orange-breasted Fruiteater   r H
Scaled Fruiteater   r H
Barred Becard   c H
Cinnamon Becard   c L
White-winged Becard   c L
Masked Tityra   c L
Purple-throated Fruitcrow   L
Red-ruffed Fruitcrow   r H
Long-wattled Umbrellabird   r L
Andean Cock-of-the-Rock   r H
Red-capped Manakin   r L
White-crowned Manakin   L
Blue-crowned Manakin   c L
Golden-winged Manakin   r H

Golden-collared Manakin   c L
Club-winged Manakin   r H
Yellow-headed Manakin   r H
Thrush-like Manakin   L
Black Phoebe
Long-tailed Tyrant   L
Rufous-tailed Tyrant   H
Pied Water-Tyrant   V
Vermilion Flycatcher   c V
Fork-tailed Flycatcher   V
Tropical Kingbird   c
Gray Kingbird   L W
Piratic Flycatcher   L
Lemon-browed Flycatcher   H
Streaked Flycatcher
Golden-crowned Flycatcher
Rusty-margined Flycatcher   c
Gray-capped Flycatcher   c L
Great Kiskadee   c V
Bright-rumped Attila
Rufous Mourner   L
Panama Flycatcher   c L
Apical Flycatcher   V
Dusky-capped Flycatcher
Olive-sided Pewee   W
Wood Pewee   W
Greater Pewee   H
Acadian Flycatcher   c W
Tufted Flycatcher   L
Tawny-breasted Flycatcher   H
Sulfur-rumped Flycatcher   L
Ornate Flycatcher   H
Cinnamon Flycatcher   c H
Handsome Flycatcher   H
Bran-colored Flycatcher   H
White-throated Spadebill   H
Golden-crowned Spadebill   L
Yellow-olive Flycatcher   L
Eye-ringed Flatbill   L
Fulvous-breasted Flatbill   r L
Black-headed Tody-Flycatcher
Common Tody-Flycatcher   c
Slate-headed Tody-Flycatcher   V
Scale-crested Pygmy-Tyrant   c
Short-tailed Pygmy-Tyrant   L
Bronze-olive Pygmy-Tyrant   L
Marble-faced Bristle-Tyrant   H

Variegated Bristle-Tyrant   H
Torrent Tyrannulet   H
Yellow-bellied Elaenia   c
Lesser Elaenia   c H
Sooty-headed Tyrannulet   V
Southern Beardless Tyrannulet
Golden-faced Tyrannulet   c
Mouse-colored Tyrannulet   V
Brown-capped Tyrannulet   L
Slaty-capped Flycatcher   c H
Olive-striped Flycatcher   c
Gray-breasted Martin   c
Blue-and-white Swallow   c
White-thighed Swallow   L
Rough-winged Swallow   c
Sand Martin   M V
Barn Swallow   c W
Black-chested Jay   L
White-capped Dipper   H
White-headed Wren   L
Sooty-headed Wren   H
Black-bellied Wren   L
Moustached Wren   H
Bay Wren   c L
Stripe-throated Wren   L
House Wren   c
White-breasted Wood-Wren   L
Gray-breasted Wood-Wren   H
Nightingale Wren   L
Chestnut-breasted Wren   r H
Andean Solitaire   c H
Black Solitaire   r H
Orange-billed Nightingale-Thrush
   H
Swainson's Thrush   c W
Pale-eyed Thrush
Glossy-black Thrush   H
Black-billed Thrush   c
Pale-vented Thrush   r H
White-throated Thrush   c L
Slate-throated Gnatcatcher   L
Black-billed Peppershrike   H
Slaty-capped Shrike-Vireo   L
Red-eyed Vireo
Brown-capped Vireo   c H
Rufous-naped Greenlet   H
Tawny-crowned Greenlet   L

Shiny Cowbird   c
Giant Cowbird
Chestnut-headed Oropendola   L
Russet-backed Oropendola   L
Scarlet-rumped Cacique   c L
Yellow-billed Cacique   r L
Great-tailed Grackle   c L
Yellow-hooded Blackbird   c V
Yellow-backed Oriole   r L
Yellow-tailed Oriole   L
Red-breasted Blackbird
Black-and-white Warbler   W
Golden-winged Warbler   W H
Tennessee Warbler   W
Tropical Parula
Yellow Warbler   W
Blackburnian Warbler   c W
Bay-breasted Warbler   c W
Northern Waterthrush   W
Mourning Warbler   W
Olive-crowned Yellowthroat   L
Canada Warbler   c W
American Redstart   W
Slate-throated Whitestart   c H
Three-striped Warbler   c
Golden-crowned Warbler   c L
Russet-crowned Warbler   H
Buff-rumped Warbler   c L
Bananaquit
Garden Flower-piercer   H
White-sided Flower-piercer   H
Indigo Flower-piercer   r H
Purple Honeycreeper   L
Red-legged Honeycreeper   L
Green Honeycreeper   L
Blue Dacnis   c L
Scarlet-thighed Dacnis   L
Blue-naped Chlorophonia   H
Yellow-collared Chlorophonia   L
Chestnut-breasted Chlorophonia
   H
Blue-headed Euphonia   H
Orange-bellied Euphonia   c
Fulvous-vented Euphonia   L
White-vented Euphonia   c L
Fawn-breasted Tanager   H
Glistening-green Tanager   r H

Multicolored Tanager   H
Emerald Tanager   L
Blue-whiskered Tanager   L
Rufous-throated Tanager   H
Golden Tanager   c H
Silver-throated Tanager   c H
Saffron-crowned Tanager   c H
Flame-faced Tanager   r H
Metallic-green Tanager   c H
Blue-necked Tanager   H
Golden-hooded Tanager   c L
Golden-naped Tanager   c H
Gray-and-gold Tanager   L
Bay-headed Tanager   H
Rufous-winged Tanager   c L
Scrub Tanager   c V
Beryl-spangled Tanager   c H
Blue-and-black Tanager   r H
Black-capped Tanager   H
Purplish-mantled Tanager   H
Blue-winged Mountain-Tanager   H
Golden-chested Tanager   L
Moss-backed Tanager   H
Blue-gray Tanager   c
Palm Tanager   c
Blue-capped Tanager   H
Crimson-backed Tanager   V
Bright-rumped Tanager   c
Hepatic Tanager   H
Summer Tanager   r W
White-winged Tanager   r H
Lemon-browed Tanager   L
Ochre-breasted Tanager   H
Crested Ant-Tanager   H
White-lined Tanager   c
White-shouldered Tanager   c L
Tawny-crested Tanager   c L

Scarlet-browed Tanager   c L
Dusky-faced Tanager   c L
Scarlet-and-white Tanager   c L
Yellow-throated Bush-Tanager   H
Ash-throated Bush-Tanager   H
Dusky-bellied Bush-Tanager   c H
Grass-green Tanager   r H
House Sparrow   L
Buff-throated Saltator   c L
Black-winged Saltator   H
Streaked Saltator   H
Slate-colored Grosbeak   L
Rose-breasted Grosbeak   W
Blue-black Grosbeak   L
Ultramarine Grosbeak   V
Blue-black Grassquit   c
Yellow-faced Grassquit   c
Slate-colored Seedeater   H
Gray Seedeater   c
Variable Seedeater
Yellow-bellied Seedeater   c
Ruddy-breasted Seedeater   c
Saffron Yellow-Finch   V
Lesser Seed-Finch
Yellow-throated Brush-Finch   H
Tricolored Brush-Finch   H
Slaty Brush-Finch   H
Chestnut-capped Brush-Finch   H
Black-headed Brush-Finch   r H
Tanager-Finch   r H
Olive Finch   r H
Orange-billed Sparrow   c L
Rufous-collared Sparrow   c H
Andean Siskin   H
Yellow-bellied Siskin   H
Lesser Goldfinch   H

32

Quito, Ecuador

QUITO, THE CAPITAL OF ECUADOR, at 9300 feet (2835 m) has many fine hotels and an international airport. Wooded gullies and parks in town may have Black-tailed Trainbearer, Sparkling Violetear, Giant Hummingbird, flower-piercers, Rufous-naped Brush-Finch, Hooded Siskin, and Rufous-collared Sparrow.

The slopes of Volcan Pichincha can be reached by taking Avenida Naciones Unidas (from the stadium next to Colegio Aleman), then the first right after Avenida America. This puts you on Villa-lengua Avenida which should be taken up to Hacienda Mi Cielo, at 10,000 feet (3050 m). In the brush and eucalyptus nearby look for Speckled Hummingbird, Azara's Spinetail, Tawny Antpitta, Tufted Tit-Tyrant, and four flower-piercers. The road continues higher to 13,000 feet (3962 m) with occasional scrubby thickets. In the higher areas look for Curve-billed Tinamou, hawks, Shining Sunbeam, Sapphire-vented Puffleg, Great Sapphirewing, Giant and Sword-billed Hummingbird, Band-winged Nightjar, Red-rumped Bush-Tyrant, Red-crested Cotinga, and seedeaters. Superb views of snow-capped peaks can be had on clear days.

To see Andean Condors soaring by beautiful Volcan Cotopaxi pick a clear day. Follow the Pan American Highway south for 17 miles (27 km) to Machachi then continue on for 18 miles (29 km) farther on. Look for a dirt road going east (local inquiry may be needed to find the right road). In areas with good cover (much is rather barren and eroded) such as near an isolated hacienda, look for Andean Snipe, Great Thrush, Andean Tit-Spinetail, Black-bellied Shrike-Tyrant, two bush-tyrants, Citrine Warbler, Blue-and-yellow Tanager, and many finches.

There is a pond farther up the Cotapaxi road, located in the Paramo Zone. In this high country occur specialties such as the Andean Condor, Carunculated Caracara, Puna Hawk, Andean Lapwing, Slate-colored Coot, several ground-tyrants and cinclodes, and Plumbeous Sierra-Finch.

Additional highland birding can be undertaken by staying in Ibarra to the north (the Hotel Cusin is superb). In the vicinity of nearby

163

Cuicocha Lagoon look for grebes, Slate-colored Coot, Andean Gull, and White-capped Dipper. A rough road turns west (opposite the waterworks between San Pablo and Otavalo — great Indian market) to the Mojanda Lakes, where Andean Condor, Sword-billed Hummingbird, and Turquoise Jay can be found.

One of the finest day trips out of Quito is the main road to Papallacta, over the paramo to the east (this road eventually reaches the Amazon). From Transformer Circle north of the Quito Intercontinental Hotel, take the paved road east for 15 miles (24 km) to Pito (whereupon it serves northward). The unmarked Papallacta road continues straight for 1.8 miles (3 km) then bears right at a fork just before some chalky cliffs (Giant Hummingbird, brush-finches). There are three worthwhile stops along the road east to the pass: one where some stunted woods cover the slopes of a mountain to the north; another at a bog on the north side, and finally a pond to the south of the road surrounded by woods (home to Black-backed Bush-Finch). This pond is 14 miles (23 km) from Pito and 2 miles (3 km) from the top of the pass. The countryside is paramo/puna grassland with

164

occasional patches of trees for the next 7.5 miles (12 km) down to Papallacta (no facilities). The river below Papallacta along the road has several pairs of Torrent Duck and White-capped Dipper.

The old route to Santo Domingo via Chillogallo and Chiriboga is a dirt road going off to the southwest. Hire a car with driver for the day if not on a birding tour, as the directions for getting out of Quito are very complicated. The countryside is intensively farmed between Chillagallo and the top of the pass. After the pass take a left turn at the fork. This road gradually enters superb temperate (and subtropical lower down) forest. In the early morning and in light fog hordes of colorful tanagers (including mountain-tanagers and Grass-green) plus Andean Guans can be seen. It is about 1 ½ hours' drive to get to the forest.

The Nono–Nanegalito road to the northwest also offers fairly good mountain forest birding (beyond Nono).

The following bird list covers birds found chiefly above 6000 feet (1828 m).

CHECKLIST

Curve-billed Tinamou
Silvery Grebe
Pied-billed Grebe
Great Egret
Snowy Egret
Cattle Heron
Black-crowned Night-Heron
Speckled Teal
Yellow-billed Pintail
Blue-winged Teal   W
Torrent Duck
Ruddy Duck
Andean Condor
Black Vulture   c
Turkey Vulture
Swallow-tailed Kite   M
Sharp-shinned Sparrowhawk
Black-chested Buzzard-Eagle
Red-backed Hawk
Puna Hawk   c
Cinereous Harrier
Osprey   W
Carunculated Caracara
Peregrine Falcon   r W

Aplomado Falcon   r
Merlin   r W
American Kestrel   c
Andean Guan
Virginia Rail
Sora Crake   W
Purple Gallinule
American Coot   c
Slate-colored Coot   r
Andean Lapwing
Lesser Yellowlegs   W
Greater Yellowlegs   W
Spotted Sandpiper   W
Baird's Sandpiper   M
Pectoral Sandpiper   M
Andean Snipe
Rufous-bellied Seedsnipe   r
Andean Gull
Band-tailed Pigeon   c
Spot-eared Dove   c
Common Ground-Dove
Black-winged Ground-Dove
White-tipped Dove   c
Barn Owl

Great Horned Owl
Andean Pygmy-Owl
Burrowing Owl
Short-eared Owl
Band-winged Nightjar
White-collared Swift
White-tipped Swift
Green Violetear
Sparkling Violetear   c
Blue-tailed Emerald
Speckled Hummingbird
Andean Hillstar
Giant Hummingbird
Shining Sunbeam   c
Mountain Velvetbreast
Great Sapphirewing
Collared Inca
Buff-winged Starfrontlet
Sword-billed Hummingbird
Buff-tailed Coronet   r
Purple-throated Sunangel   r
Sapphire-vented Puffleg   c
Black-tailed Trainbearer   c
Green-tailed Trainbearer
Purple-backed Thornbill   r
Tyrian Metaltail   c
Blue-mantled Thornbill
White-bellied Woodstar
Plate-billed Mountain-Toucan
   (west)
Crimson-mantled Woodpecker
Stout-billed Cinclodes
Bar-winged Cinclodes
Andean Tit-Spinetail
Azara's Spinetail
Rufous Spinetail
White-browed Spinetail
White-chinned Thistletail
Many-striped Canostero
Pearled Treerunner
Streaked Tuftedcheek   r
Flammulated (?) Treehunter   r
Undulated Antpitta
Tawny Antpitta   c
Unicolored Tapaculo
Red-crested Cotinga
Barred Fruiteater   r

Andean Cock-of-the-Rock   r
Black-billed Shrike-Tyrant
Plain-capped Ground-Tyrant
Spot-billed Ground-Tyrant
Streak-throated Bush-Tyrant
Smoky Bush-Tyrant   r
Red-rumped Bush-Tyrant
Brown-backed Chat-Tyrant   c
Rufous-breasted Chat-Tyrant
Crowned Chat-Tyrant
Black Phoebe
Vermilion Flycatcher   c
Tropical Kingbird
Greater Pewee
Cinnamon Flycatcher
Tufted Tit-Tyrant   c
Torrent Tyrannulet
White-throated Tyrannulet
White-banded Tyrannulet
White-crested Elaenia   c
Brown-bellied Swallow   c
Blue-and-white Swallow   c
Turquoise Jay
White-capped Dipper
Rufous Wren
Plain-tailed Wren
Mountain Wren
Great Thrush   c
Paramo Pipit
Peruvian Red-breasted Meadowlark
Blackburnian Warbler   W
Slate-throated Whitestart
Spectacled Whitestart   c
Black-crested Warbler   c
Citrine Warbler   r
Cinereous Conebill   c
Blue-backed Conebill
Bluish Flower-piercer
Garden Flower-piercer
Glossy Flower-piercer   c
Carbonated Flower-piercer   c
White-sided Flower-piercer
Masked Flower-piercer
Blue-hooded Euphonia
Fawn-breasted Tanager   r
Scrub Tanager   (north)
Blue-and-black Tanager

Golden-crowned Tanager
Scarlet-bellied Mountain-Tanager
  c
Blue-winged Mountain-Tanager
Hooded Mountain-Tanager
Buff-breasted Mountain-Tanager
Blue-capped Tanager
Blue-and-yellow Tanager   c
Black-capped Hemispingus
Superciliaried Hemispingus
Grass-green Tanager
Plush-capped Finch
Yellow Grosbeak   c
Black-backed Grosbeak
Band-tailed Seedeater   c

Plain-colored Seedeater   c
Paramo Seedeater
Black-backed Bush-Finch
Grassland Yellow-Finch   c
Plumbeous Sierra-Finch   c
Ash-breasted Sierra-Finch
Band-tailed Sierra-Finch
Pale-naped Brush-Finch
Rufous-naped Brush-Finch   c
Tricolored Brush-Finch   r
White-winged Brush-Finch
Stripe-headed Brush-Finch
Rufous-collared Sparrow   c
Hooded Siskin   c

33
Rio Napo, Ecuador

ONE OF THE FINEST WAYS to see the birds of the Amazonian forest
has been established in Ecuador, east of the Andes on the Rio Napo.
A very well-run operation by Metropolitan Touring of Quito and the
management of the Flotel Orellana works approximately as follows.
Your travel agent (or birding tour organizer) obtains your reservations. Twice weekly chartered planes fly between Quito and the airstrip at Coca on the Rio Napo. Trucks take you to the port and for
three or four days the floating hotel is your clean home, serving fine
meals in spotless (by Amazon standards) comfort. Each day long
dugout canoes with motors take you out to the trails in the forest,
lonely tributaries, missionary camps, and even a tree house in the
jungle.

The flotel usually docks overnight at Primavera (which has a trail
into the forest behind the few houses). One side trip goes to Limonco-
cha, a missionary center of the Summer School of Linguistics. There
are some narrow trails into heavy forest there (despite clearing),
although the real highlight is the small lake. Boats are sometimes
available to go along the lake shore, which is attractive to freshwater
marsh birds and edge birds (Everglade Kite, Hoatzin, Azure Gallinule, Sungrebe, Wattled Jacana, and Pale-eyed Blackbird).

Taracoa "national park" is on the south bank opposite Primavera.
The very tall rain forest is bisected by trails to the Taracoa stream and
lake, where short boat trips are made. A really excellent strong new
"tree house" has been built high up in the crown of a giant tree. Steady
steps have been built, and there is room for a dozen or so people.
Seventy-two species were seen from the tree house by one of the
authors during part of a morning, and at eye level. These included
hawks, Blue-throated Piping-Guan, parrots and parakeets, nunbirds,
barbets, aracaris, toucans, Speckled Spinetail, Plum-throated
Cotinga, White-browed Purpletuft, Bare-necked Fruitcrow, a manakin, over a dozen tyrants, oropendolas, and flocks of honeycreepers,
euphonias, and tanagers.

Another fruitful trip is the dugout canoe trip from the flotel up the
Rio Indillama (downstream, and then south). This is a quiet tributary

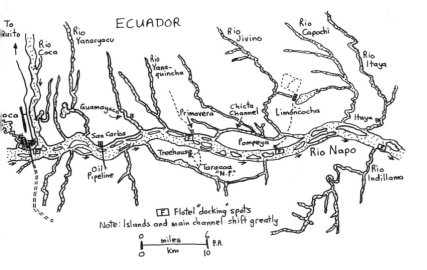

Note: Islands and main channel shift greatly

□ Flotel "docking" spots

that is often good for large raptors, puffbirds, aracaris, toucans, and some of the large macaws.

The Rio Napo is rather fast-flowing and very variable from day to day in water level affecting where the boats can opperate.

Congratulations are in order for this marvelous operation in the hope that other countries in the Amazon and the tropics will emulate this success. Here they have succeeded in setting aside a reserve, they have designed and built a great tree house, they have paid for local and foreign guides trained in biology to accompany each sailing and give lectures, and they provide hot water and clean food.

Amazon addicts may wish to visit other spots, such as the Anaconda Lodge or Jaguar Lodge located upstream below Tena. The river is even faster and more rocky, and a little higher in elevation. There is forest left in a number of places, and it is a little more scenic, but does not offer as many birds. Package tours to these hotels fly from Quito to Tena, or take in an overland drive, that itself can be spectacular and rewarding.

CHECKLIST

Great Tinamou
Little Tinamou
Undulated Tinamou
Variegated Tinamou
Anhinga   c

Neotropic Cormorant
Cocoi Heron
Great Egret
Snowy Egret
Little Blue Heron

Green Heron
Cattle Heron   c
Capped Heron   r
Rufescent Tiger-Heron   r
Green Ibis   r
Horned Screamer   r
Blue-winged Teal   W
Masked Duck   r
King Vulture
Black Vulture   c
Turkey Vulture   c
Jungle Vulture   c
Swallow-tailed Kite   c
Gray-headed Kite   r
Plumbeous Kite   c
Everglade Kite
Slender-billed Kite
Bicolored Sparrowhawk   r
Gray-bellied Goshawk   r
Roadside Hawk   c
Short-tailed Hawk
Slate-colored Hawk
Ornate Hawk-Eagle   r
Black Hawk-Eagle
Osprey
Laughing Falcon
Forest-falcons, species   r
Yellow-headed Caracara
Black Caracara   c
Red-throated Caracara
Orange-breasted Falcon
Bat Falcon   c
Speckled Chachalaca
Spix's Guan
Blue-throated Piping-Guan
Marbled Wood-Quail   r
Hoatzin
Limpkin
Gray-winged Trumpeter   r
Gray-breasted Crake
Purple Gallinule   c
Azure Gallinule
Sungrebe
Sunbittern   r
Wattled Jacana   c
Pied Lapwing
Collared Plover

Lesser Yellowlegs   M
Greater Yellowlegs   M
Solitary Sandpiper   W
Spotted Sandpiper   c W
Pectoral Sandpiper   M
Large-billed Tern
Yellow-billed Tern
Pale-vented Pigeon
Plumbeous Pigeon   c
Blue Ground-Dove   r
Gray-fronted Dove
Sapphire Quail-Dove   r
Ruddy Quail-Dove
Blue-and-yellow Macaw
Scarlet Macaw
Red-and-green Macaw
Chestnut-fronted Macaw   c
White-eyed Parakeet   c
Dusky-headed Parakeet   c
Maroon-tailed Parakeet
Dusky-billed Parrotlet
Blue-winged Parrotlet   r
Cobalt-winged Parakeet   c
Black-headed Parrot
Blue-headed Parrot
Yellow-crowned Parrot
Orange-winged Parrot
Mealy Parrot
Dark-billed Cuckoo   S
Squirrel Cuckoo   c
Little Cuckoo   r
Greater Ani
Smooth-billed Ani   c
Tropical Screech-Owl
Tawny-bellied Screech-Owl
Spectacled Owl
Ferruginous Pygmy-Owl
Black-banded Owl   r
Great Potoo   r
Common Potoo
nighthawk, species
Common Pauraque
Ladder-tailed Nightjar
White-collared Swift   c
Gray-rumped Swift
Short-tailed Swift   c
Fork-tailed Palm-Swift   c

Lesser Swallow-tailed Swift
Rufous-breasted Hermit
Pale-tailed Barbthroat
Long-tailed Hermit
White-bearded Hermit
Straight-billed Hermit
Little Hermit   r
Gray-breasted Sabrewing
Blue-tailed Emerald
Fiery Topaz   r
Common Woodnymph
Golden-tailed Sapphire
Glittering-throated Emerald
Gould's Jewelfront   r
Black-eared Fairy   r
White-tailed Trogon   c
Black-tailed Trogon
Blue-crowned Trogon   r
Violaceous Trogon
Ringed Kingfisher   c
Amazon Kingfisher   c
Green Kingfisher   c
Green-and-rufous Kingfisher
American Pygmy Kingfisher   r
Broad-billed Motmot
Rufous Motmot
Blue-crowned Motmot
Chestnut Jacamar   c
Brown Jacamer
White-chinned Jacamer
Bronzy Jacamar
White-necked Puffbird
Chestnut-capped Puffbird
Collared Puffbird   r
White-chested Puffbird
Lanceolated Monklet   r
Brown Nunlet   r
Black-fronted Nunbird   c
White-fronted Nunbird
Yellow-billed Nunbird   r
Aerial Puffbird   c
Scarlet-crowned Barbet   c
Black-spotted Barbet   c
Lemon-throated Barbet   r
Chestnut-eared Aracari
Many-banded Aracari   c
Lettered Aracari

Ivory-billed Aracari   c
Golden-collared Toucanet
Yellow-ridged Toucan
Cuvier's Toucan   c
Rufous-breasted Piculet
Gold-fronted Piculet   r
Spot-breasted Flicker
White-throated Woodpecker   r
Chestnut Woodpecker
Scale-breasted Woodpecker   r
Cream-colored Woodpecker
Lineated Woodpecker
Yellow-tufted Woodpecker   c
Red-stained Woodpecker
Crimson-crested Woodpecker   c
Plain-brown Woodcreeper   r
Olivaceous Woodcreeper   r
Wedge-billed Woodcreeper
Long-billed Woodcreeper   r
Cinnamon-throated Woodcreeper
   r
Barred Woodcreeper   c
Straight-billed Woodcreeper   c
Ocellated Woodcreeper
Buff-throated Woodcreeper   c
Curve-billed Scythebill   r
Hornero, species
Dark-breasted Spinetail
Speckled Spinetail
Orange-fronted Plushcrown
Chestnut-winged Hookbill
Rufous-rumped Foliage-gleaner
Cinnamon-rumped Foliage-gleaner
Chestnut-winged Foliage-gleaner
Olive-backed Foliage-gleaner
Ruddy Foliage-gleaner
Brown-rumped Foliage-gleaner
Chestnut-crowned Foliage-gleaner
   r
Plain Xenops   c
Black-tailed Leaftosser   r
Fasciated Antshrike
Undulated Antshrike   r
Great Antshrike
Black-capped Antshrike
Spot-winged Antshrike   c
Dusky-throated Antshrike   c

Cinereous Antshrike   c
Pygmy Antwren   r
Streaked Antwren
Plain-throated Antwren   c
Ornate Antwren
Rufous-tailed Antwren   r
White-flanked Antwren   c
Gray Antwren   c
Gray Antbird   c
Black-faced Antbird
Warbling Antbird
Spot-winged Antbird
Silvered Antbird
Plumbeous Antbird
White-shouldered Antbird
Sooty Antbird   r
Bicolored Antbird   c
Spot-backed Antbird
Scale-backed Antbird   r
Black-spotted Bare-eye
Reddish-winged Bare-eye   r
Striated Ant-thrush
Rufous-capped Ant-thrush   r
Black-faced Ant-thrush
Thrush-like Antpitta
Chestnut-belted Gnateater   r
Rusty-belted Tapaculo
Purple-throated Cotinga   r
Plum-throated Cotinga
White-browed Purpletuft
White-winged Becard
Black-capped Becard   r
Pink-throated Becard
Black-tailed Tityra   c
Black-crowned Tityra
Purple-throated Fruitcrow   c
Amazonian Umbrellabird   r
Bare-necked Fruitcrow   c
Golden-headed Manakin   r
Blue-crowned Manakin
Wire-tailed Manakin
White-bearded Manakin   r
Green Manakin
Dwarf Tyrant-Manakin   r
Wing-barred Manakin
Drab Water-Tyrant   c
Sirystes   c

Eastern Kingbird   c M
Tropical Kingbird   c
Fork-tailed Flycatcher   M
Crowned Slaty Flycatcher
Variegated Flycatcher   c
Piratic Flycatcher
Streaked Flycatcher   c
Sulfur-bellied Flycatcher   M
Boat-billed Flycatcher   c
Gray-capped Flycatcher   c
Social Flycatcher   c
Great Kiskadee   c
Lesser Kiskadee   c
Bright-rumped Attila
Cinnamon Attila
Grayish Mourner
Short-crested Flycatcher
Dusky-capped Flycatcher
Olive-sided Pewee   r M
Wood Pewee   W
Ruddy-tailed Flycatcher
Whiskered Flycatcher
Black-tailed Flycatcher
Bran-colored Flycatcher
Amazonian Royal Flycatcher   r
Brownish Flycatcher   r
Yellow-margined Flycatcher
Gray-crowned Flycatcher
Yellow-breasted Flycatcher
Painted Tody-Flycatcher   r
Golden-winged Tody-Flycatcher
Rusty-fronted Tody-Flycatcher   r
Mottle-backed Elaenia   r
Southern Beardless Tyrannulet   r
Yellow-crowned Tyrannulet
Sepia-capped Flycatcher
Ochre-bellied Flycatcher   c
White-winged Swallow   c
Brown-chested Martin   W
Gray-breasted Martin   c
Blue-and-white Swallow   c
White-banded Swallow   c
Rough-winged Swallow   c
Barn Swallow   c W
Sand Martin   M
Cliff Martin   M
Thrush-like Wren   c

Coraya Wren
Buff-breasted Wren
House Wren   r
White-breasted Wood-Wren
Nightingale Wren
Musician Wren
Black-capped Mockingthrush   c
Swainson's Thrush   W
Black-billed Thrush   c W
Lawrence's Thrush   r
Pale-vented Thrush   r
White-necked Thrush
Long-billed Gnatwren
Red-eyed Vireo   c
Tawny-crowned Greenlet
Bananaquit   r
Purple Honeycreeper   c
Green Honeycreeper
Blue Dacnis
Black-faced Dacnis
Yellow-bellied Dacnis
Yellow Warbler   c W
Cerulean Warbler   r M
Blackpoll Warbler   c W
Northern Waterthrush   r W
Canada Warbler   M
River Warbler
Shiny Cowbird
Giant Cowbird   c
Crested Oropendola   c
Russet-backed Oropendola   c
Olive Oropendola   r
Yellow-rumped Cacique   c
Solitary Black Cacique
Pale-eyed Blackbird
Moriche Oriole   r
Troupial
Oriole-Blackbird
Red-breasted Blackbird
Bobolink   M
Swallow-Tanager

Orange-bellied Euphonia   c
Thick-billed Euphonia   c
Rufous-bellied Euphonia
Golden-bellied Euphonia
Opal-rumped Tanager
Opal-crowned Tanager   r
Paradise Tanager
Green-and-gold Tanager   c
Yellow-bellied Tanager
Masked Tanager   r
Turquoise Tanager   c
Blue-gray Tanager   c
Palm Tanager   c
Silver-beaked Tanager   c
Masked Crimson Tanager   c
Summer Tanager   r W
Scarlet Tanager   W
Red-crowned Ant-Tanager
Fulvous Shrike-Tanager   r
Fulvous-crested Tanager
White-shouldered Tanager
Gray-headed Tanager
Guira Tanager   r
Yellow-backed Tanager   r
Magpie-Tanager   c
Buff-throated Saltator   c
Grayish Saltator   c
Slate-colored Grosbeak   r
Red-capped Cardinal   c
Blue-black Grosbeak   r
Blue-black Grassquit
Variable Seedeater
Lined Seedeater
Black-and-white Seedeater
Yellow-bellied Seedeater
Chestnut-bellied Seedeater   c
Great-billed Seed-Finch   r
Lesser Seed-Finch
Orange-billed Sparrow
Yellow-browed Sparrow   c

34
Galápagos, Ecuador

OFTEN CALLED THE ENCHANTED ISLES and known officially as the Archipélago de Colón, the Galápagos lie some 600 miles (960 km) from the Ecuadorian mainland directly on the Equator. The impression of a group of tiny specks in the great Pacific Ocean is misleading, for the archipelago extends for some 200 miles (320 km) from northwest to southeast and the largest island, Isabella, is nearly 70 miles (112 km) long. The islands were made famous by the visit of the young Charles Darwin aboard the *Beagle* in 1835, and, though colonized and settled, the hostile environment does not encourage development. The human population now numbers some 4000 persons, increased periodically by tourists since the early 1960s. Feral populations of goats, pigs, cats, dogs, and donkeys have interfered radically with the unique fauna and flora. Wildlife tourists (limited to 12,000 per year) are a major factor in efforts to preserve the unique fauna. The earlier killings by whaling crews, and now the feral mammals, have cut down the wild populations of the giant tortoise; yet the animals and birds of Galápagos remain innocently trusting and approachable.

The Ecuadorians deserve praise for their intelligent conviction that each boat must employ trained naturalist guides to both protect wildlife and inform the tourists. Cruises (boats limited to no more than 100 passengers) continuously visit most of the best areas. Most tours last for about a week, including flights to and from Guayaquil, some with one-way ocean crossings. Small boats may be rented with crews. There is one hotel at Academy Bay. Reserve all in advance with an organized birding tour, or on your own with a travel agent. Most tours visit Hood, Santa Cruz, Plaza, James, Isabella, and Fernandina, where many of the most interesting birds can be seen. Waved Albatross, Flightless Cormorant, Galápagos Penguin, and Swallow-tailed Gull, as well as Darwin's finches and the various species of mockingbirds, are endemic. The colonies of tropical boobies are immensely attractive. Most visitors will wish to savor Galápagos for itself, to sit surrounded by rugged landscapes and wild creatures, and to think. They will want to see the albatrosses on Hood, the cormorants and penguins at Punta Espinosa and Tagus Cove, the Swallow-tailed Gulls at several spots, and the boobies, frigatebirds, and others at places like Plaza and Seymour.

The trail uphill behind North James Bay's Flamingo Lagoon on James is the richest place on the islands for finches, including Sharp-beaked Ground-Finch, Vegetarian Finch, Small Tree-Finch, and Woodpecker Finch. The Floreana (or Medium) Tree-Finch can be seen easily about an hour's hike up the trail to the wet zone above Black Beach on Floreana. The San Cristobal Mockingbird is rare, but a few can sometimes be found in the town of Puerto Moreno. The Galápagos Crake is best found at Media Luna Crater Lake above Bellavista, west of Academy Bay on Santa Cruz. Most unfortunately, the normal cruise boats do not offer a morning trip by road up to the highlands of Santa Cruz for its wet-zone vegetation and wild tortoises.

CHECKLIST

(F I) = Fernandina and Isabella only.

Galápagos Penguin   c (F I)
Pied-billed Grebe   r
Galápagos Albatross   c S (Hood)
Dark-rumped Petrel
Parkinson's Petrel   r M
Audubon's Shearwater   c
White-vented Storm-Petrel   c
Band-rumped Storm-Petrel   r
Wedge-rumped Storm-Petrel   c
Red-billed Tropicbird   c
Brown Pelican   c
Blue-footed Booby   c
Masked Booby   c
Red-footed Booby   (local)
Flightless Cormorant   c (F I)
Great Frigatebird   c
Magnificent Frigatebird   c
Great Blue Heron
Great Egret
Snowy Egret   r M
Cattle Heron   M
Green (Lava) Heron   c
Yellow-crowned Night-Heron
American Flamingo
White-cheeked Pintail
Blue-winged Teal   W
Galápagos Hawk   c (local)

Osprey   r W
Peregrine Falcon   r W
Galápagos Crake
Paint-billed Crake
Common Gallinule
American Oystercatcher
Gray Plover   W
Semipalmated Plover   W
Ruddy Turnstone   c W
Spotted Sandpiper   W
Wandering Tattler   c W
Willet   W
Sanderling   c W
Whimbrel   c W
Short-billed Dowitcher   W
Black-necked Stilt
Little Phalarope   W
Red Phalarope   W
Wilson's Phalarope   r W
Pomarine Jaeger   W
Swallow-tailed Gull   c
Sabine's Gull   M
Lava Gull   c
Laughing Gull   W
Franklin's Gull   M
Common Tern   r W
Royal Tern   r W

Brown Noddy   c
Sooty Tern   (Culpepper only)
Galápagos Dove   c
Dark-billed Cuckoo
Barn Owl
Short-eared Owl
Vermilion Flycatcher
Galápagos Flycatcher   c
Southern (Galápagos) Martin
Sand Martin   r W
Galápagos Mockingbird   c
Charles Mockingbird   r (Floreana islets)
Hood Mockingbird   c (Hood)
San Cristobal Mockingbird   (S. Cristobal)

Yellow Warbler   c
Bobolink   r M
Small Ground-Finch   c
Medium Ground-Finch   c
Large Ground-Finch   r
Sharp-beaked Ground-Finch (local)
Cactus Finch   c
Large Cactus Finch   c (Hood)
Vegetarian Finch
Small Tree-Finch
Floreana Tree-Finch   (Floreana)
Large Tree-Finch   r
Woodpecker Finch
Mangrove Finch   (F I)
Warbler Finch   c (Hood chiefly)

176

35
Lima, Peru

LIMA, THE CAPITAL OF PERU, lies on the Pacific coast in the zone of constant winter fog and overcast. Its proximity to the Humboldt Current makes for exceptionally good oceanic birding. Many seabirds can be seen easily from shore on the Callao waterfront at the north end of Calle Paz Soldan and along the breakwaters. Boats can be engaged quite inexpensively (open top and no life jackets) at the public dock to go out toward Isla San Lorenzo. The waters here are calmed by the presence of the island, and the fishing boats attract many birds. Shearwaters, storm-petrels, prions, the three local cormorants, boobies, terns (including Inca), gulls, skuas, and jaegers are easily seen over the water. The island is a prison and landings are not permitted.

The parks and nicer residential areas of Lima have Croaking Ground-Dove, Amazilia Hummingbird, House Wren, and Rufous-collared Sparrow. Marsh birds can be seen easily near the entrance to the Villa Country Club and inside the grounds (no permit). Plumbeous Rail, Least Bittern, Wren-like Rushbird, and Many-colored Rush-Tyrant are regular. The beach is a fine spot for seabirds, and Peruvian Red-breasted Meadowlark and occasionally Tawny-throated Dotterel live in the fields. Irrigated river valleys, north and south of Lima, have Red-backed Hawk, doves, Burrowing Owl, hummingbirds, Long-tailed Mockingbird, and seedeaters.

The Hotel Paracas (one of Peru's finest) is situated alongside the water south of Pisco via paved roads. Daily boat trips leave for the Islas Ballestas in the morning. The usual seabirds can be seen, and there are chances for views of Ringed Storm-Petrel and Swallow-tailed Gull. Around the islands there are clouds of Peruvian Boobies, cormorants, gulls, and terns; a few Humboldt Penguin and Peruvian Diving-Petrel are usually seen near the islands (landings are not permitted).

The grounds of the Hotel Paracas are good for Oasis Hummingbird, Seaside Cinclodes, and Coastal Miner. The Bay of Paracas has extensive mudflats often used by migrant shorebirds (many stay all year), wintering Chilean Flamingoes, and masses of roosting gulls, terns, and skimmers. The mudflats can be easily approached from the

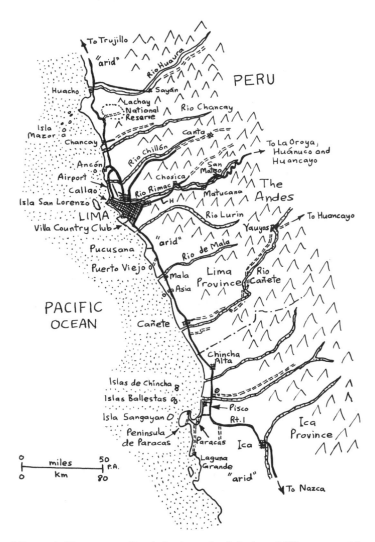

Museo de Paracas 2 miles (3 km) south of the hotel. The rare and local Slender-billed Finch (all slaty, with a long, thin yellow bill) occurs in several areas south of Pisco along the Pan American Highway. The best spot is in the mesquite woods in the sand dunes reached via a dirt road west off the highway between Kilometer posts 252 and 253.

Some Andean species can be found alongside the main highway east toward Chosica and La Oroya. The road is paved up to about 10,000 feet (3050 m) and may eventually be paved higher. The restaurants and gas stations at San Mateo (about 2 hours from Lima) are set amid

178

gardens full of hummingbirds. Andean Condor can sometimes be seen. Higher up Giant Hummingbird and White-capped Dipper may be noted near streams.

Most Lima hotels are located in the birdless center of the city (Crillon, Gran Bolivar, Sheraton, and Savoy). An excellent alternative is the El Pueblo Hyatt located 40 minutes' drive inland off the trans-Andean highway to Chosica. Collared Warbling-Finch live in the trees around the nearby Granja Azul Restaurant.

The following checklist covers species that can be found at or near sea level only.

CHECKLIST

Humboldt Penguin   r
Great Grebe
White-tufted Grebe   c
Pied-billed Grebe
Giant Petrel   M
Sooty Shearwater   c M
Cape Petrel   M
Prion *species*   r M
Ringed Storm-Petrel   r
Markham's Storm-Petrel   r
Wedge-rumped Storm-Petrel   r M
White-vented Storm-Petrel   c M
Wilson's Storm-Petrel   c M
Peruvian Diving-Petrel
Peruvian Pelican   c
Peruvian Booby   c
Guanay Cormorant   c
Red-legged Cormorant   c
Neotropic Cormorant   c
Snowy Egret
Cattle Heron   c
Great Egret
Green Heron
Least Bittern
Black-crowned Night-Heron   r
Chilean Flamingo
Blue-winged Teal   M
Cinnamon Teal
White-cheeked Pintail
Black Vulture   c
Turkey Vulture
Andean Condor   r

Red-backed Hawk
Bay-winged Hawk   r
Osprey   M
American Kestrel   c
Peregrine Falcon   r M
Plumbeous Rail
Sora Crake   r M
Common Gallinule   c
American Coot
American Oystercatcher
Blackish Oystercatcher
Gray Plover   c M
Tawny-throated Dotterel
Killdeer   c
Snowy Plover   c
Semipalmated Plover   c M
Puna Plover   r M
Ruddy Turnstone   c M
Surfbird   M
Hudsonian Godwit   r M
Solitary Sandpiper   M
Lesser Yellowlegs   M
Greater Yellowlegs   c M
Spotted Sandpiper   c M
Sanderling   c M
Western Sandpiper   c M
Semipalmated Sandpiper   r M
Least Sandpiper   M
Baird's Sandpiper   M
Pectoral Sandpiper   M
Red Knot   M
Short-billed Dowitcher   c M

Willet   r M
Whimbrel   M
Wilson's Phalarope   M
Little Phalarope   M
Black-necked Stilt   r
Peruvian Thick-knee   r
Least Seedsnipe
Great (Chilean) Skua   c M
Pomarine Jaeger   r M
Parasitic Jaeger   r M
Long-tailed Jaeger   r M
Kelp Gull   c
Band-tailed Gull   c
Gray-hooded Gull
Gray Gull   c
Franklin's Gull   c M
Laughing Gull   c M
Andean Gull   r M
Swallow-tailed Gull   r M
Sabine's Gull   r M
South American Tern   c S
Common Tern   M
Arctic Tern   M
Peruvian Tern   c
Elegant Tern   c M
Royal Tern   M
Inca Tern   c
Black Skimmer   c M
White-winged Dove   c
Spot-eared Dove
Croaking Ground-Dove   c
Bare-faced Ground-Dove
Plain-breasted Ground-Dove
White-tipped Dove
Groove-billed Ani   c
Barn Owl
Burrowing Owl
Ferruginous Pygmy-Owl   r
Short-eared Owl   r
Lesser Nighthawk
Band-winged Nightjar   r
White-collared Swift   r M
Chimney Swift   M
Amazilia Hummingbird   c
Purple-collared Woodstar   r
Peruvian Sheartail   r
Oasis Hummingbird   c

Coastal Miner   c
Grayish Miner   r
Cactus Canastero   r
Seaside Cinclodes
Wren-like Rushbird   c
Vermilion Flycatcher   c
Dark-faced Ground-Tyrant   W
Short-tailed Field-Tyrant
White-browed Chat-Tyrant
Tropical Kingbird
Tropical Pewee
Bran-colored Flycatcher
Many-colored Rush-Tyrant   c
Southern Beardless Tyrannulet
Tawny-crowned Pygmy-Tyrant
Pied-crested Tit-Tyrant   r
White-crested Elaenia   r W
Blue-and-white Swallow   c
Barn Swallow   M
Cave Martin
House Wren   c
Long-tailed Mockingbird   c
Chiguanco Thrush
Yellowish Pipit
Cinereous Conebill   c
Bobolink   M
Shiny Cowbird   c
Scrub Blackbird
Peruvian Red-breasted Meadowlark
Yellow-hooded Blackbird   r
Hepatic Tanager
Blue-and-yellow Tanager
Streaked Saltator
Band-tailed Seedeater   r
Slender-billed Finch   r
Blue-black Grassquit   c
Chestnut-throated Seedeater   c
Drab Seedeater
Dull-colored Grassquit   r
Parrot-billed Seedeater
Hooded Siskin   c
Grassland Yellow-Finch
Raimondi's Yellow-Finch   W
Rufous-collared Sparrow   c
Collared Warbling-Finch   r
House Sparrow   c

36
Cuzco, Peru

CUZCO, AN ATTRACTIVE ANCIENT CITY high in the Andes, at 11,400 feet (3475 m) has many hotels (reservations usually necessary) and an airport with frequent jets from Lima. It is connected by rail to Puno, while roads to Puno (and Lima) are terrible (bumpy and dusty).

The city itself has few birds except Andean Swift. The hilltop ruins of Sacsahuaman overlooking the city are most impressive, and sometimes have Andean Lapwing and Cinereous Conebill.

Near Huacarpay, 18 miles (29 km) to the west of Cuzco via a paved road, are several lakes that have many birds: grebes, ducks, Puna Hawk, Puna Plover, shorebirds, Bearded Mountaineer, White-winged Cinclodes, Rufous-backed Negrito, and Yellow-winged Blackbirds.

To see birds of the high Andes one should overnight at one of the hotels near Urubamba, located in a dry valley two hours northwest by car. There are numerous spots in the area with spectacular backdrops of snowy peaks. The best birding is northeast of Urubamba along the Abra Malaga road via Ollantaitambo, where Andean Condor can often be seen in the afternoon. The dirt road winds uphill beyond Ollantaitambo with some patches of woodland. Black-chested Buzzard-Eagle, Giant Hummingbird, White-tufted Sunbeam, flowerpiercers, Creamy-crested Spinetail, and Chestnut-breasted Warbling-Finch should be seen by stopping frequently.

Above the treeline such birds as Crested Duck, Andean Condor, Mountain Caracara, White-fronted and Plain-capped Ground-Tyrants, and White-winged Diuca-Finch may be seen. Fantastic views of the snowy heights of Veronica and other peaks, as well as herds of llamas and alpacas, can be seen near Abra Malaga pass. It can be cold at 13,000 feet (3963 m), particularly at dawn and when clouds obscure the sun.

Excellent temperate forest is entered on the wetter northern slope as the road winds downhill toward Quillabamba. Birding the area requires an early start from Urubamba. Among the more sought-after birds are Violet-throated Starfrontlet, Marcapata Spinetail, Puna Thistletail, Unstreaked Tit-Tyrant, Pale-footed Swallow, White-browed Conebill, Tit-like Dacnis, and Scarlet-bellied and Chestnut-

bellied Mountain-Tanagers. Many of these are barely known to science. There is a small pension at Quillabamba among cutover subtropical habitat. Most birders return to Urubamba (which is closer). Visitors may take the train directly to Machupicchu from Pisac junction station near Urubamba.

Machupicchu is certainly one of the world's most magnificent sites. Almost every tourist (hundreds a day) must take the predawn train from Cuzco, scramble into buses, and take the evening train back to Cuzco. Rumors of a new hotel are heartening since there is some birding here as well, and the present small hotel (with a fine restaurant) is notorious for overbooking and unreliability with reservations. The ruins and scenery are a delight in the morning and evening when the masses are gone, and well worth a night out.

Andean Cock-of-the-Rock may be seen at dawn and dusk from

the railroad tracks a half mile below the station (beware of quiet rail cars going downhill at high speeds). Noisy workers' homes and playgrounds have been built in their haunts. The disgusting habit of shooting them to sell stuffed as souvenirs is widespread in Peru. Mid-morning birding (it takes a long time for light to reach down into these magnificent canyons) can be quite good if one is walking the bottom third of the road between the hotel and the station. The museum area has some fruiting trees where Andean Cock-of-the-Rock occur at times.

The following list of birds has been gathered during the months of July and August only (relatively dry and cool). Visitors in the wetter southern summer will find a somewhat different avifauna.

CHECKLIST

(AM = Abra Malaga area; MP = Machupicchu)

White-tufted Grebe   c
Silvery Grebe   r
Green Heron
Snowy Egret   r
Black-crowned Night-Heron   c
Fasciated Tiger-Heron   MP
Buff-necked Ibis   r
Puna Ibis   c   .
Andean Goose   r H
Crested Duck   r H
Speckled Teal   c
Yellow-billed Pintail   c
Puna Teal   c
Blue-winged Teal   r M
Cinnamon Teal   c
Torrent Duck   c MP
Ruddy Duck   c
Andean Condor
Black-chested Buzzard-Eagle
Roadside Hawk   MP
Puna Hawk
White-throated Hawk
Cinereous Harrier
Mountain Caracara   c
Peregrine Falcon   r
Aplomado Falcon   r
American Kestrel   c
Speckled Chachalaca   MP

Andean Guan   MP
Plumbeous Rail
Common Gallinule   c
American Coot   c
Andean Lapwing   c
Puna Plover
Greater Yellowlegs   M
Pectoral Sandpiper   M
Black-necked Stilt   r
Gray-breasted Seedsnipe   H
Andean Gull   c
Band-tailed Pigeon
Spot-eared Dove   c
Bare-faced Ground-Dove
Black-winged Ground-Dove
Gray-fronted Dove   MP
Mitred/Scarlet-fronted Parakeet
   MP
Andean Parakeet
Burrowing Owl
Chestnut-collared Swift   MP
White-tipped Swift   MP
Andean Swift   c
Buff-tailed Sicklebill   r MP
Sparkling Violetear
Green Violetear
Green-and-white Hummingbird   c
Speckled Hummingbird   MP

Andean Hillstar   r
Black-breasted Hillstar   r
Giant Hummingbird   c
Shining Sunbeam   c
White-tufted Sunbeam   AM
Great Sapphirewing   AM
Violet-throated Starfrontlet
   r AM
Sword-billed Hummingbird
   r AM
Chestnut-breasted Coronet   MP
Amethyst-throated Sunangel
Sapphire-vented Puffleg   AM
Green-tailed Trainbearer
Black-tailed Trainbearer
Purple-backed Thornbill   AM
Scaled Metaltail   AM
Tyrian Metaltail   c AM
Blue-mantled Thornbill   AM
Bearded Mountaineer
White-bellied Woodstar   MP
Blue-crowned Motmot   MP
Andean Flicker
Crimson-mantled Woodpecker   r
   AM
Bar-bellied Woodpecker   AM
Wedge-billed Woodcreeper   MP
Common Miner
Bar-winged Cinclodes   c
White-winged Cinclodes   r
Wren-like Rushbird   c
Azara's Spinetail   MP
Marcapata Spinetail   c AM
Creamy-crested Spinetail   AM
Puna Thistletail   AM
Rusty-fronted Canastero
Streak-backed Canastero   AM
Streak-throated Canastero   AM
Many-striped Canastero   r AM
Line-fronted Canastero   AM
Pearled Treerunner   c AM
Streaked Xenops   MP
Variable Antshrike   MP
Andean Tapaculo   AM
Red-crested Cotinga   AM
White-winged Becard   r MP
Andean Cock-of-the-Rock   MP

White-tailed Shrike-Tyrant   r
Rufous-naped Ground-Tyrant   c
   W
White-browed Ground-Tyrant   r
   AM
White-fronted Ground-Tyrant
   AM
Plain-capped Ground-Tyrant   AM
Spot-billed Ground-Tyrant
Little Ground-Tyrant   MP
Rufous-backed Negrito   c
Streak-throated Bush-Tyrant   AM
Smoky Bush-Tyrant   AM
Brown-backed Chat-Tyrant   c
   AM
White-browed Chat-Tyrant   c
Rufous-breasted Chat-Tyrant   c
   AM
Black Phoebe   c
Tropical Kingbird   c MP
White-winged Black-Tyrant   c
   MP
Golden-crowned Flycatcher   MP
Social Flycatcher   MP
Greater Pewee   c MP
Dusky-capped Flycatcher
Mottle-cheeked Tyrannulet   MP
Many-colored Rush-Tyrant   c
Common Tody-Flycatcher   MP
Cinnamon Flycatcher   MP
Tufted Tit-Tyrant
Yellow-billed Tit-Tyrant
Ash-breasted Tit-Tyrant   r H
Unstreaked Tit-Tyrant   c H
White-crested Elaenia
Elaenia, species   MP
White-throated Tyrannulet   AM
White-tailed Tyrannulet   AM
Torrent Tyrannulet   c MP
Streak-necked Flycatcher   MP
Blue-and-white Swallow
Brown-bellied Swallow   c AM
Pale-footed Swallow   r AM
Andean Martin
White-capped Dipper   c MP
House Wren   c
Mountain Wren   AM

Plain-tailed Wren   c MP
Andean Solitaire   MP
Chiguanco Thrush   c
Great Thrush   c AM
Pale-eyed Thrush   r MP
Dusky-green Oropendola   c MP
Yellow-winged Blackbird
Red-eyed Vireo   MP
Brown-capped Vireo   MP
Tropical Parula   MP
Masked Yellowthroat   MP
Pale-legged Warbler   MP
Russet-crowned Warbler   MP
Citrine Warbler
Spectacled Whitestart   c MP, AM
Slate-throated Whitestart   c MP
Cinereous Conebill   c
Giant Conebill   r AM
White-browed Conebill   c AM
Capped Conebill   r MP
Garden Flower-piercer   MP
Glossy Flower-piercer   c AM
Carbonated Flower-piercer   AM
Masked Flower-piercer   AM
Tit-like Dacnis   r AM
Fawn-breasted Tanager   MP
Beryl-spangled Tanager   MP
Silvery Tanager   MP
Blue-and-black Tanager   MP
Saffron-crowned Tanager   c MP
Blue-gray Tanager   c MP

Scarlet-bellied Mountain-Tanager
   c AM
Chestnut-bellied Mountain-Tanager
   AM
Blue-capped Tanager   MP
Blue-and-yellow Tanager
Rust-and-yellow Tanager   AM
Black-capped Hemispingus   AM
Superciliared Hemispingus   AM
Three-striped Hemispingus   AM
Golden-billed Saltator
Black-backed Grosbeak
Black-and-white Seedwater   MP
Band-tailed Seedeater   c
Plain-colored Seedeater
Paramo Seedeater   AM
Greenish Yellow-Finch   c
Yellow-Finch, species
White-winged Diuca-Finch   AM
Gray-hooded Sierra-Finch
Mourning Sierra-Finch
Ash-breasted Sierra-Finch
Plumbeous Sierra-Finch   AM
Band-tailed Sierra-Finch
Slaty Brush-Finch
Rufous-collared Sparrow   c
Chestnut-breasted Warbling-Finch
Black Siskin   AM
Hooded Siskin   c
Lesser Goldfinch

37
Puerto Maldonado, Peru

THIS IS A GENUINELY NEW DESTINATION for globe-trotting birders. Located in southeastern Peru, east of the Andes, this small town is now served by several jets a week from Cuzco with connections from Lima.

Puerto Maldonado is an isolated port on the Madre de Dios River in the southwest corner of the huge Amazon basin. There is a long tedious dirt road from Cuzco but little road development around town. The Hotel de Turistas overlooking the river is quite comfortable by Amazonian standards. Visitors can reach some good tropical forest out along the Cuzco road west of town (by taxi; no rental cars are available yet). The main highways are the rivers, and several jungle lodges are located several hours away by boat.

One of the best of all the lodges anywhere in the Amazon basin is the Explorer's Inn, located on the Tambopata River, south of town. Reservations may be made through your travel agent or c/o Peruvian Safaris, PO Box 10088, Lima, Peru (telephone 31-30-47). The site was selected by biologists for its wildlife richness — a low Indian population and the presence of large mammals and birds that have been hunted out of most other accessible Amazonian centers.

On the boat trip to the lodge the birdlife will vary depending on the time of day, the weather, and whether the river is high or low. Among the larger conspicuous birds one might find are Horned Screamer, raptors, plovers, terns, macaws, parrots, kingfishers, toucans, and oropendolas.

Around Explorer's Inn itself there are toucans at dawn, hummingbirds and tanager flocks during the day, a procession of colorful macaws in the late afternoon, and owls at night.

The real richness lies in the vast forest behind the lodge. A wide trail extends for 3 miles (4.8 km) offering good visibility for up to several dozen birders. Tinamou are often heard, and Pale-winged Trumpeter can sometimes be found feeding on fallen fruit. Hummingbirds are relatively rare, but trogons, including the rarely noted Pavonine Quetzal, are regular. Screaming Piha and Band-tailed Manakin carry on with their group displays. One of the world's greatest mim-

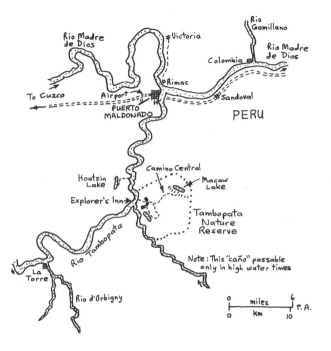

ics, Lawrence's Thrush, is often heard imitating many dozens of Amazonian species. Most visitors will have a lot of difficulty identifying the bewildering array of woodcreepers, furnariids, antbirds, and tyrant-flycatchers. The management of the Inn has very wisely recruited bilingual ornithologists to stay at the lodge for periods of several months. In addition to carrying on research projects they help groups of visiting naturalists.

There are three ponds (with canoes available) that can be visited for a quiet search for Hoatzin, Sungrebe, Sunbittern, Silvered Antbird, and Pale-eyed Blackbird. One pond is located at the end of the two-mile main trail behind the lodge, another on the west side of the Tambopata River, and the third just south of the lodge.

CHECKLIST

Gray Tinamou r	Neotropic Cormorant
Great Tinamou	Anhinga c
Cinereous Tinamou	Cocoi Heron c
Little Tinamou	Great Egret r
Undulated Tinamou c	Green Heron
Bartlett's Tinamou	Capped Heron

Rufescent Tiger-Heron
Boat-billed Heron
Wood Stork
Jabiru Stork r
Green Ibis
Horned Screamer c
Orinoco Goose r M
Muscovy Duck
King Vulture
Black Vulture c
Turkey Vulture r
Jungle Vulture c
Pearl Kite
Swallow-tailed Kite
Gray-headed Kite
Double-toothed Kite
Plumbeous Kite c M
Bicolored Sparrowhawk
Broad-winged Hawk M
Roadside Hawk c
Short-tailed Hawk
Great Black Hawk c
Harpy Eagle r
Ornate Hawk-Eagle
Black Hawk-Eagle r
Osprey M
Laughing Falcon
Barred Forest-Falcon
Black Caracara c
Red-throated Caracara
Bat Falcon c
Speckled Chachalaca c
Spix's Guan c
Blue-throated Piping-Guan r
Razor-billed Curassow r
Starred Wood-Quail
Hoatzin c
Pale-winged Trumpeter
Gray-necked Wood-Rail
Rufous-sided Crake
Purple Gallinule r
Azure Gallinule
Sungrebe r
Sunbittern r
Wattled Jacana
Pied Lapwing
Collared Plover

Solitary Sandpiper M
Spotted Sandpiper c M
White-rumped Sandpiper r M
Pectoral Sandpiper r M
Large-billed Tern
Yellow-billed Tern
Black Skimmer
Pale-vented Pigeon c
Ruddy Pigeon r
Plumbeous Pigeon c
Ruddy Ground-Dove r
Picui Ground-Dove W
Gray-fronted Dove c
White-tipped Dove r
Ruddy Quail-Dove
Blue-and-yellow Macaw c
Scarlet Macaw c
Red-and-green Macaw c
Red-bellied Macaw r
Blue-headed Macaw r
Chestnut-fronted Macaw c
White-eyed Parakeet
Dusky-headed Parakeet c
Rock Parakeet c
Dusky-billed Parrotlet r
Cobalt-winged Parakeet c
White-bellied Parrot c
Orange-cheeked Parrot
Blue-headed Parrot
Yellow-crowned Parrot
Mealy Parrot c
Ash-colored Cuckoo r W
Yellow-billed Cuckoo S
Dark-billed Cuckoo
Squirrel Cuckoo
Black-bellied Cuckoo
Greater Ani
Smooth-billed Ani c
Striped Cuckoo r
Tropical Screech-Owl c
Tawny-bellied Screech-Owl c
Spectacled Owl c
Least Pygmy-Owl
Ferruginous Pygmy-Owl
Mottled Owl r
Great Potoo r
Common Potoo r

Rufous Potoo   r
Common Nighthawk   M
Common Pauraque
Ocellated Poorwill
Sand-colored Nighthawk
Ladder-tailed Nightjar
White-collared Swift   c M
Chaetura Swift, sp.
Short-tailed Swift
Amazonian Palm-Swift   c
Rufous-breasted Hermit   c
Pale-tailed Barbthroat
Long-tailed Hermit   r
White-bearded Hermit
Needle-billed Hermit
Reddish Hermit   c
White-necked Jacobin
Gray-breasted Sabrewing   r
Common Woodnymph
White-chinned Sapphire
Golden-tailed Sapphire   r
Sapphire-spangled Emerald
Gould's Jewelfront   r
Black-eared Fairy   r
Pavonine Quetzal
Black-tailed Trogon
White-tailed Trogon   c
Blue-crowned Trogon   r
Collared Trogon   c
Violaceous Trogon   r
Ringed Kingfisher   c
Amazon Kingfisher
Green Kingfisher
Green-and-rufous Kingfisher   c
American Pygmy Kingfisher
Broad-billed Motmot   c
Rufous Motmot
Blue-crowned Motmot
Bluish-fronted Jacamar   c
Paradise Jacamar   r
Great Jacamar   r
White-necked Puffbird   r
Striolated Puffbird   r
Semicollared Puffbird
Black-fronted Nunbird   c
White-fronted Nunbird   c
Aerial Puffbird   c

Black-spotted Barbet   c
Lemon-throated Barbet
Emerald Toucanet   r
Chestnut-eared Aracari   c
Lettered Aracari   r
Brown-mandibled Aracari   c
Curl-crested Aracari   r
Golden-collared Toucanet
Yellow-ridged Toucan
Cuvier's Toucan   c
Gold-fronted Piculet
Yellow-throated Woodpecker   r
White-throated Woodpecker   r
Rufous-headed Woodpecker   r
Chestnut Woodpecker
Scale-breasted Woodpecker   r
Cream-colored Woodpecker   r
Lineated Woodpecker
Yellow-tufted Woodpecker   c
Little Woodpecker   r
Red-stained Woodpecker   c
Crimson-crested Woodpecker   c
Red-necked Woodpecker   c
Plain-brown Woodcreeper
White-chinned Woodcreeper   r
Long-tailed Woodcreeper   r
Olivaceous Woodcreeper   c
Wedge-billed Woodcreeper   c
Cinnamon-throated Woodcreeper
Bar-bellied Woodcreeper   r
Barred Woodcreeper
Black-banded Woodcreeper   r
Straight-billed Woodcreeper
Ocellated Woodcreeper   r
Spix's Woodcreeper   c
Buff-throated Woodcreeper   c
Lineated Woodcreeper   c
Red-billed Scythebill   r
Pale-legged Hornero   r
Plain-crowned Spinetail
Ruddy Spinetail
Speckled Spinetail   r
Striped Woodhaunter   r
Chestnut-winged Hookbill   c
Peruvian Recurvebill   r
Rufous-rumped Foliage-gleaner   c
Cinnamon-rumped Foliage-gleaner

Chestnut-winged Foliage-gleaner
  c
Olive-backed Foliage-gleaner
Chestnut-crowned Foliage-gleaner
Rufous-tailed Xenops   c
Plain Xenops
Black-tailed Leaftosser   r
Fasciated Antshrike
Great Antshrike   c
Barred Antshrike   c
White-shouldered Antshrike   r
Black-capped Antshrike   c
Spot-winged Antshrike   c
Dusky-throated Antshrike
Bluish-slate Antshrike   c
Pygmy Antwren   c
Sclater's Antwren   r
Plain-throated Antwren   c
White-eyed Antwren
Ornate Antwren
White-flanked Antwren   c
Long-winged Antwren
Gray Antwren
Banded Antbird   r
Striated Antbird
Chestnut-shouldered Antwren   r
Gray Antbird   c
White-browed Antbird   c
Black-faced Antbird   c
Warbling Antbird   c
Band-tailed Antbird
White-lined Antbird
Silvered Antbird
Chestnut-tailed Antbird   c
Plumbeous Antbird
Goeldi's Antbird
Black-throated Antbird
White-throated Antbird
Scale-backed Antbird
Black-spotted Bare-eye
Rufous-capped Ant-thrush
Black-faced Ant-thrush   c
Thrush-like Antpitta
Ash-throated Gnateater   r
Plum-throated Cotinga   r
Spangled Cotinga   r
Screaming Piha   c
White-winged Becard

Black-capped Becard   c
Pink-throated Becard
Black-tailed Tityra
Masked Tityra
Black-crowned Tityra
Purple-throated Fruitcrow   c
Bare-necked Fruitcrow   c
Red-headed Manakin   r
Round-tailed Manakin   c
Band-tailed Manakin   c
Blue-crowned Manakin   r
Fiery-capped Manakin
Cinnamon Manakin
Dwarf Tyrant-Manakin
Wing-barred Manakin
Greater Manakin   r
Thrush-like Manakin   r
Vermilion Flycatcher   c W
Drab Water-Tyrant   c
Sirystes   r
Eastern Kingbird   M
Tropical Kingbird   c
Dusky-chested Flycatcher   r
Variegated Flycatcher   r
Crowned Slaty Flycatcher   W
Piratic Flycatcher   M
Boat-billed Flycatcher
Sulfur-bellied Flycatcher   r M
Streaked Flycatcher
Rusty-margined Flycatcher   r
Gray-capped Flycatcher
Social Flycatcher   c
Great Kiskadee   c
Lesser Kiskadee
Bright-rumped Attila
Dull-capped Attila   c
Cinereous Mourner
Grayish Mourner
Short-crested Flycatcher   c
Swainson's Flycatcher   W
Wood Pewee   r M
Alder Flycatcher   r M
Ruddy-tailed Flycatcher
Bran-colored Flycatcher   r
Amazonian Royal Flycatcher   r
Golden-crowned Spadebill
Yellow-margined Flycatcher   r
Gray-crowned Flycatcher   c

Yellow-breasted Flycatcher r
Olivaceous Flatbill
Rufous-tailed Flatbill c
Large-headed Flatbill
Common Tody-Flycatcher r
Painted Tody-Flycatcher r
Rusty-fronted Tody-Flycatcher r
White-eyed Tody-Tyrant
Flammulated Pygmy-Tyrant
Elaenia, species W
Forest Elaenia
Yellow-crowned Tyrannulet
Sepia-capped Flycatcher
Ochre-bellied Flycatcher c
McConnell's Flycatcher r
Ringed Antpipit
White-winged Swallow c
Gray-breasted Martin r
Brown-chested Martin S
White-banded Swallow c
Rough-winged Swallow c
Barn Swallow M
Violaceous Jay c
Thrush-like Wren c
Moustached Wren
House Wren c
Nightingale Wren c
Musician Wren
Black-capped Mockingthrush c
Swainson's Thrush r
Creamy-bellied Thrush r W
Black-billed Thrush r
Cocoa Thrush r
Lawrence's Thrush c
White-necked Thrush c
Red-eyed Vireo c
Dusky-capped Greenlet c
Lemon-chested Greenlet
Giant Cowbird c
Casqued Oropendola
Crested Oropendola
Russet-backed Oropendola c
Olive Oropendola
Yellow-rumped Cacique c
Red-rumped Cacique
Solitary Black Cacique r
Pale-eyed Blackbird
Epaulet Oriole

Troupial r
Connecticut Warbler r M
Masked Yellowthroat r
Canada Warbler r M
River Warbler
Purple Honeycreeper c
Green Honeycreeper c
Blue Dacnis c
Black-faced Dacnis r
Swallow-Tanager r M
Orange-bellied Euphonia c
White-vented Euphonia r
Thick-billed Euphonia r
Rufous-bellied Euphonia
Golden-bellied Euphonia r
Opal-rumped Tanager
Opal-crowned Tanager
Paradise Tanager c
Yellow-bellied Tanager r
Green-and-gold Tanager c
Masked Tanager r
Turquoise Tanager c
Blue-gray Tanager
Palm Tanager c
Silver-beaked Tanager c
Masked Crimson Tanager c
Scarlet Tanager r M
Red-crowned Ant-Tanager c
White-winged Shrike-Tanager
Flame-crested Tanager c
White-shouldered Tanager c
Yellow-backed Tanager
Red-billed Pied Tanager r
Magpie Tanager
Buff-throated Saltator
Grayish Saltator
Slate-colored Grosbeak c
Red-capped Cardinal c
Blue-black Grosbeak
Blue-black Grassquit
Lined Seedeater c M
Yellow-bellied Seedeater r
Double-collared Seedeater c W
Chestnut-bellied Seedeater S
Lesser Seed-Finch r
Pectoral Sparrow
Yellow-browed Sparrow c

38
Puno and Arequipa, Peru

THE VAST MARSHES FLANKING LAKE TITICACA have large numbers of birds. Most tourists include a short boat trip from Puno to an Uro Indian village on a manmade floating reed island on the lake. The local Titicaca Grebe may be seen from the tour boat, from a number of spots along the lakeshore road, and from the new Tambo Titicaca Hotel. In the reedbeds look for the Plumbeous Rail, Wren-like Rushbird, Many-colored Rush-Tyrant, and Yellow-winged Blackbird. In Puno Harbor and along the lake edge characteristic waterbirds (at least June–August) include White-tufted Grebe, Black-crowned Night-Heron, Puna Ibis, Chilean Flamingo, Yellow-billed Pintail, teal, Ruddy Duck, Common Gallinule, American Coot, and Puna Plover.

Fine Puna grassland birding is available around Tiquilaca, a town reached via a dirt road east of Puno (Note: Puna is a term for Andean grassland, Puno is a town name). Darwin's Nothura, Puna Hawk, Cinereous Harrier, Aplomado Falcon, ground-doves, canasteros, miners, and finches are often in evidence. Titicaca Grebes are common on Laguna Umayo nearby.

Puno—12,650 feet (3856 m)—has a fine Hotel de Turistas (as does Juliaca), and some inexpensive hotels. Reservations are essential. There is an every-other-day train service to Cuzco, and every-other-night to Arequipa. In the wild country near Abra La Raya (pass) on the Cuzco train look for Crested Duck, Andean Condor, and Giant Coot. Although Peru is generally safe, be very careful of personal property at stations on this train.

Arequipa is a large and attractive city at 7500 feet (2286 m) with many fine hotels and daily jets from Lima, and Cuzco. Croaking Ground-Dove, Least Seedsnipe (near the airport), Peruvian Sheartail, and Chiguanco Thrush occur around the city. A fine day trip can be made up to Salinas Lake (about 14,000 feet [4267 m] elevation), for those who wish to hire a car and driver.

On the Salinas road, above the police checkpoint and below Chihuata, check the washes with shrubbery for ground-doves, hill-stars, Giant Hummingbird, tit-spinetails, Creamy-breasted Canas-

To CUZCO

La Raya Pass

PERU

Ayaviri

Airport

JULIACA

Lagunillas

Lake Titicaca

reeds

Tiquilaca PUNO

Volcan El Misti

Airport

AREQUIPA

Salinas Lake

TO LIMA

TO MOLLENDO

0	miles	45
0	km	75	P.A.

tero, and tit-tyrants. Between Kilometer posts 84 and 92 (52 and 58 miles from Arequipa) above the town of Chihuata there is a zone of dwarf polylepsis shrubs. Footwork in this arid area may yield treasures such as Giant Conebill, Tit-like Dacnis, Black-hooded Sierra-Finch, and the newly described Tamarugo Conebill. Just beyond the pass (about three hours' slow drive above Arequipa) you will see the great salt lagoon of Salinas. Its water level varies greatly as in most flamingo lagoons (when totally dry the birds desert it). It has all three mountain flamingo species (James's, Andean, and Chilean), Andean Goose, Crested Duck, Andean Avocet, Gray-breasted Seedsnipe, and on nearby hilltops the Rufous-bellied Seedsnipe.

The road onward to Puno is dramatic in places, very arid, and it features wild vicuña and Giant Coot. Unfortunately it seems endless, very dusty, rough, has no signs, no restaurants, no gas, and is all over 14,000 feet (4267 m). Birding can be a challenge.

193

CHECKLIST

(A = birds found only between Arequipa and Salinas, chiefly below 11,000 feet [3353 m])

Darwin's (Lesser) Rhea   r
Ornate Tinamou
Andean Tinamou
Darwin's Nothura   c
White-tufted Grebe   c
Silvery Grebe
Titicaca Grebe   c
Neotropic Cormorant   r
Black-crowned Night-Heron   c
Buff-necked Ibis
Puna Ibis   c
Chilean Flamingo
Andean Flamingo
James's Flamingo
Andean Goose   c
Crested Duck
Speckled Teal   c
Yellow-billed Pintail   c
Puna Teal   c
Cinnamon Teal   c
Ruddy Duck   c
Torrent Duck   r
Turkey Vulture   A
Red-backed Hawk   r A
Puna Hawk   c
Cinereous Harrier
Mountain Caracara   c
Aplomado Falcon
American Kestrel   c
Plumbeous Rail
Common Gallinule   c
American Coot
Slate-colored Coot   r
Giant Coot
Andean Lapwing   c
Puna Plover   c
Tawny-throated Dotterel
Diademed Sandpiper-Plover   r
Greater Yellowlegs   c M
Lesser Yellowlegs   M

Baird's Sandpiper   c M
Pectoral Sandpiper   M
Puna Snipe
Wilson's Phalarope   c M
Black-necked Stilt
Andean Avocet
Rufous-bellied Seedsnipe   r
Gray-breasted Seedsnipe
Least Seedsnipe   A
Andean Gull   c
Spot-eared Dove   c
Croaking Ground-Dove   c A
Bare-faced Ground-Dove   c
Golden-spotted Ground-Dove
Black-winged Ground-Dove
Mountain Parakeet
Burrowing Owl
Band-winged Nightjar
Andean Swift   A
Andean Hillstar
Giant Hummingbird   A
Bronze-tailed Comet   r A
Black Metaltail   A
Oasis Humingbird   A
Peruvian Sheartail   A
Purple-collared Woodstar   r A
Andean Flicker   c
Thick-billed Miner   r A
Puna Miner
Common Miner   c
Slender-billed Miner
Scale-throated Earthcreeper   A
White-throated Earthcreeper   A
Buff-breasted Earthcreeper
Straight-billed Earthcreeper   A
Bar-winged Cinclodes   c
White-winged Cinclodes
Wren-like Rushbird   c
Plain-mantled Tit-Spinetail   c A
Andean Tit-Spinetail   c A

Streaked Tit-Spinetail   A
Creamy-breasted Canastero   c A
Cordilleran Canastero
Streak-throated Canastero
Cactus Canastero   r A
Canyon Canastero   A
Black-billed Shrike-Tyrant
White-tailed Shrike-Tyrant
Rufous-naped Ground-Tyrant   c
Puna Ground-Tyrant
Ochre-naped Ground-Tyrant
White-fronted Ground-Tyrant   r
Plain-capped Ground-Tyrant
Spot-billed Ground-Tyrant
Rufous-backed Negrito   c
D'Orbigny's Chat-Tyrant   A
White-browed Chat-Tyrant   A
Many-colored Rush-Tyrant   c
Yellow-billed Tit-Tyrant
Brown-bellied Swallow   A
Blue-and-white Swallow   A
Andean Martin   c
White-capped Dipper   r
House Wren   c
Chiguanco Thrush   c
Yellow-winged Blackbird   c

Tamarugo Conebill   A
Carbonated Flower-piercer   r A
Giant Conebill   r A
Tit-like Dacnis   r A
Blue-and-yellow Tanager   r A
House Sparrow   A
Golden-billed Saltator   r A
Band-tailed Seedeater   r A
Plain-colored Seedeater   A
Puna Yellow-Finch
Bright-rumped Yellow-Finch   c
Greenish Yellow-Finch   c
White-winged Diuca-Finch
Gray-hooded Sierra-Finch   c
Black-hooded Sierra-Finch   r A
Mourning Sierra-Finch   c A
Plumbeous Sierra-Finch
Ash-breasted Sierra-Finch   c
Band-tailed Sierra-Finch   c
White-throated Sierra-Finch   r
Rusty-bellied Brush-Finch   r A
Rufous-collared Sparrow   c
Thick-billed Siskin   r A
Hooded Siskin   c A
Black Siskin   c
Yellow-rumped Siskin

39
Santiago, Chile

THE CENTRAL VALLEY OF CHILE enjoys a Mediterranean climate with the Pacific rollers to the west and some of the most spectacular snow-capped peaks of the Andes to the east. Chile is now a safe place for visitors, and the capital, Santiago, has all the usual amenities (international airport, fine hotels, and rental vehicles).

A fine day trip (although the rocky road is rough at the end) is to the southeast up the gorge of the Rio Maipo into the Andes. Take Route 73 south to Puente Alto then a road (G-25) east to San Jose de Maipo. A fork is reached in 15 miles (24 km) just beyond San Gabriel. The road left goes up to El Yeso Lake, a top area for Diademed Sandpiper-Plover. Unfortunately there is a barrier, and a permit, which is sometimes available at the water department in Puente Alto (or Santiago), is needed. Regardless, the main road continues 12 miles (19 km) uphill to Refugio Lo Valdes, a fine ski lodge run by a German alpine club. It would make a fine place to stay for a night or two on weekdays in the southern summer and has fine meals. Birds found in this area on a recent scouting trip included Andean Condor, Torrent Duck, White-sided Hillstar, Rufous-banded Miner, Gray-flanked Cinclodes, Des Mur's Wiretail, Moustached Turca, ground-tyrants, sierra-finches, and siskins.

The height of the ski season is July and August in midwinter. Birding and room availability are best in October and November; the coast gets crowded from Christmas on during summer.

Valparaiso is the port city for Santiago and is reached via a fast 4-lane toll road. The Hotel Miramar in swanky Viña del Mar perches on a headland over the Pacific. From a room here one can see shearwaters, pelicans, boobies, cormorants, Red Phalarope, gulls, and terns. Small boats can be rented by the hour at the main pier opposite the Valparaiso railroad station. One need not go out for more than a few hours or a morning to see a wealth of fine pelagics such as Wandering, Royal, Black-browed, and Shy Albatrosses, Sooty and Pink-footed Shearwaters, Wilson's Storm-Petrel, Southern Fulmar, White-chinned Petrel, and Great Skua.

The Concon area to the north of Viña del Mar along the ocean is farming country where a little bush-beating may produce Chilean Tinamou, ground-doves, Giant Hummingbird, Plain-mantled Tit-Spinetail, and Tufted Tit-Tyrant.

The Cerro La Campana National Park is reached via a dirt road going east from Olmué, an hour due east of Viña del Mar. This forested park is good for Austral Pygmy-Owl, Green-backed Fire-crown, Chilean Flicker, Striped Woodpecker, Thorn-tailed Rayadito, Fire-eyed Diucon, White-crested Elaenia, Chilean Swallow, Austral Thrush, Austral Blackbird, and Black-chinned Siskin.

The road north and east of Santiago toward Mendoza, Argentina, offers additional high-Andean birding below Aconcagua, the highest peak in South America at 21,212 feet (6959 m).

CHECKLIST

Humboldt Penguin
Chilean Tinamou
Great Grebe   c
Silvery Grebe
White-tufted Grebe
Pied-billed Grebe
Wandering Albatross   W
Royal Albatross   c W
Gray-headed Albatross   r W
Yellow-nosed Albatross   r W
Black-browed Albatross   c W
Shy Albatross   c W
Giant Petrel   W
Southern Fulmar   c W
Cape Petrel   c W
Dove Prion   r W
Slender-billed Prion   W
White-chinned Petrel   W
Sooty Shearwater   c W
Pink-footed Shearwater   c W
Blue-footed Petrel   r W
Wilson's Storm-Petrel   c W
Peruvian Diving-Petrel   c
Peruvian Pelican   c
Peruvian Booby   c
Guanay Cormorant   c
Neotropic Cormorant   c
Red-legged Cormorant
Great Egret
Snowy Egret
Black-crowned Night-Heron
Stripe-backed Bittern   r
Buff-necked Ibis
White-faced Ibis   r
Black-necked Swan
Andean Goose
Crested Duck
Bronze-winged Duck   r W
Yellow-billed Pintail   c
Chiloe Wigeon   c
Red Shoveler
Speckled Teal
Silver Teal   W

Cinnamon Teal
Torrent Duck
Rosy-billed Pochard   r
Ruddy Duck
Lake Duck
Black-headed Duck
Andean Condor
Black Vulture
Turkey Vulture
White-tailed Kite
Black-chested Buzzard-Eagle
Red-backed Hawk
White-throated Hawk
Harris's Hawk
Cinereous Harrier
Osprey   r M
Chimango Caracara   r
Mountain Caracara
Crested Caracara   r
Peregrine Falcon   r W
Aplomado Falcon   r
American Kestrel   c
California Quail   c
Plumbeous Rail
American Black Crake   r
Spot-flanked Gallinule
Red-gartered Coot   c
Red-fronted Coot
White-winged Coot   c
Argentine Painted-snipe   r
American Oystercatcher
Blackish Oystercatcher
Southern Lapwing   c
Gray Plover   M
Lesser Golden Plover   M
Snowy Plover
Semipalmated Plover   M
Two-banded Plover
Collared Plover   M
Tawny-throated Dotterel   S
Diademed Sandpiper-Plover
Greater Yellowlegs   M
Lesser Yellowlegs   M

Spotted Sandpiper   M
Ruddy Turnstone   c
Surfbird   c M
Baird's Sandpiper   M
White-rumped Sandpiper   M
Pectoral Sandpiper   M
Sanderling   M
Whimbrel   M
Common Snipe
Black-necked Stilt
Red Phalarope   c M
Least Seedsnipe
Gray-breasted Seedsnipe
Rufous-bellied Seedsnipe
Great Skua
Parasitic Jaeger   M
Gray Gull   S
Kelp Gull
Andean Gull
Brown-hooded Gull   S
Franklin's Gull   c M
Sabine's Gull   M
South American Tern   c
Trudeau's Tern
Elegant Tern   c M
Arctic Tern   M
Inca Tern   r
Black Skimmer   M
Chilean Pigeon   r
Spot-eared Dove
Picui Ground-Dove   c
Black-winged Ground-Dove   c
Slender-billed Parakeet   r
Mountain Parakeet   r
Barn Owl
Great Horned Owl
Austral Pygmy-Owl
Burrowing Owl
Rufous-legged Owl   r
Short-eared Owl
Band-winged Nightjar
White-sided Hillstar   c
Giant Hummingbird
Green-backed Firecrown   c
Chilean Flicker
Striped Woodpecker
Creamy-rumped Miner

Rufous-banded Miner   c
Common Miner   c
Scale-throated Earthcreeper   W
Straight-billed Earthcreeper   r
Crag Chilia
Dark-bellied Cinclodes   c
Gray-flanked Cinclodes   c
Bar-winged Cinclodes   c
White-winged Cinclodes
Seaside Cinclodes
Des Mur's Wiretail
Thorn-tailed Rayadito   c
Wren-like Rushbird
Plain-mantled Tit-Spinetail
Lesser Canastero
Dusky-tailed Canastero
Cordilleran Canastero
White-throated Treerunner
Moustached Turca   c
White-throated Tapaculo
Great Shrike-Tyrant
Black-billed Shrike-Tyrant
Fire-eyed Diucon   c
Ochre-naped Ground-Tyrant   c S
Rufous-naped Ground-Tyrant   S
White-browed Ground-Tyrant   c
   S
Plain-capped Ground-Tyrant
Black-fronted Ground-Tyrant   S
Spot-billed Ground-Tyrant
Dark-faced Ground-Tyrant   S
Cinnamon-bellied Ground-Tyrant
   S
Rufous-backed Negrito
Spectacled Tyrant   S
Warbling Doradito   S
Many-colored Rush-Tyrant
Tufted Tit-Tyrant   c
White-crested Elaenia   c S
Rufous-tailed Plantcutter
Chilean Swallow   c
Blue-and-white Swallow   c
Barn Swallow   M
House Wren   c
Sedge Wren
Chilean Mockingbird   c
Austral Thrush   c

Correndera Pipit
Shiny Cowbird   c
Yellow-winged Blackbird
Austral Blackbird   c
Long-tailed Meadowlark   c
House Sparrow   c
Grassland Yellow-Finch   c
Greater Yellow-Finch   c
Common Diuca-Finch   c
Gray-hooded Sierra-Finch   c

Patagonian Sierra-Finch   W
Mourning Sierra-Finch   c
Plumbeous Sierra-Finch   c
Band-tailed Sierra-Finch   c
Yellow-bridled Finch   r
Rufous-collared Sparrow   c
Thick-billed Siskin   r
Yellow-rumped Siskin   c
Black-chinned Siskin   c

40
Falkland Islands

THESE TREELESS ISLANDS IN THE SOUTH ATLANTIC are 300 miles (480 km) east of southern Argentina. Accessible only by occasional ships for many years, air service is now beginning from Commodoro Rividavia, Argentina (connected often with Buenos Aires). The islands are British, although Argentina claims them. The comfortable *Lindblad Explorer* often visits these islands, a most efficient means of reaching out-of-the-way bird islands. The principal industry is sheep farming.

The climate is of the "Cape Horn" variety with many days of winds, frequent gales, sunny periods, and calms interspersed. Rainfall amounts to only 30 inches (762 mm) a year, but the rain falls frequently. High seas and winds build up quickly and without warning. Most tourists will find the summer months from November to February the best.

In Stanley, the main town where half the population lives, the Upland Goose Hotel makes a good base. Transport, permits, and guides can be arranged on the spot. In Stanley Harbor be sure to visit the slaughterhouse when offal is discarded, attracting Giant Fulmar, Great Skua, Kelp and Dolphin Gulls. Along the shore look for Falkland Flightless Steamer-Duck, Black-crowned Night-Heron, Rock Shag, and South American Tern. In the gardens, trees, and fields around Stanley look for Dark-faced Ground-Tyrant, Austral Thrush, Correndera Pipit, Long-tailed Meadowlark, House Sparrow, Black-throated Finch, and Black-chinned Siskin.

The road to the airstrip near Cape Pembroke crosses desolate moors where snipe, Rufous-chested Dotterel, Two-banded Plover, pipits, and finches can be seen. Magellanic and Gentoo Penguins sometimes loiter on nearby beaches.

Kidney Island is an 80-acre (32 hectare) tussock-covered reserve in Berkeley Sound. Government permission must be obtained, as well as a competent guide and transport, for the day trip. It is 1 ½ hours by boat or ten minutes by air. No facilities other than a simple hut are available. Birds numbering 28 species are known to breed and many are tame and easily photographed. Rockhopper Penguins (mixed with

a few Macaroni) have a large colony here. Other birds to look for are Magellanic Penguin, King Shag, Blackish Oystercatcher, Short-eared Owl, Blackish Cinclodes, and both wrens. At night White-chinned Petrel, Sooty Shearwater, and Gray-backed Storm-Petrel come to their burrows in great numbers.

Gentoo and King Penguins can be seen by arranging permission and travel details with the manager of Johnson Harbor to use the house near the colony on Volunteer Beach. Other birds to look for en route to the penguins are Upland and Ruddy-headed Geese, Speckled Teal, Great Skua, and Magellanic Oystercatcher.

New Island, in the west, can be reached by chartered light aircraft or by cruise ship. Overnight guests will be accepted in the future either by an inn or in private farm houses. Rockhopper Penguins come ashore in droves late in the afternoon. Magellanic, Rockhopper, and Gentoo Penguins are all abundant, with Macaroni and King Penguins uncommon. Black-browed Albatross and King Shag nest in Rockhopper colonies. New Island is also of interest because of sea-lions, fur seals, an old whaling station, and its mussels, crabs, and mushrooms.

CHECKLIST

King Penguin r	Rockhopper Penguin c
Gentoo Penguin c	Macaroni Penguin r

Magellanic Penguin   c
White-tufted Grebe
Silvery Grebe
Wandering Albatross
Black-browed Albatross
Gray-headed Albatross   r W
Sooty Albatross   r W
Greater Shearwater   r
Sooty Shearwater
White-chinned Petrel
Southern Fulmar
Giant Petrel   c
Cape Petrel   W
Slender-billed Prion
Fairy Prion   r
Wilson's Storm-Petrel
Gray-backed Storm-Petrel   c
Common Diving-Petrel   c
Rock Cormorant   c
King Cormorant   c
Black-crowned Night-Heron   c
Black-necked Swan
Coscoroba Swan   r
Kelp Goose   c
Upland Goose   c
Ruddy-headed Goose   c
Ashy-headed Goose   r
Crested Duck   c
Mallard   r
Chiloe Wigeon
Speckled Teal   c
Yellow-billed Pintail   r
Silver Teal
Cinnamon Teal   r

Flightless Steamer-Duck   c
Flying Steamer-Duck
Turkey Vulture   c
Red-backed Hawk
Cinereous Harrier   r
Crested Caracara
Striated (Forster's) Caracara
Peregrine Falcon
American Kestrel   r
Red-gartered Coot   r M
Magellanic Oystercatcher   c
Blackish Oystercatcher   c
Rufous-chested Dotterel
Two-banded Plover   c
White-rumped Sandpiper   c M
Common Snipe
Cordilleran Snipe   r
Snowy Sheathbill   c W
Great Skua
Dolphin Gull   c
Kelp Gull   c
Brown-hooded Gull
South American Tern
Short-eared Owl
Blackish Cinclodes (Tussockbird)
Dark-faced Ground-Tyrant   c
Sedge Wren
House Wren
Austral Thrush   c
Correndera Pipit   c
Long-tailed Meadowlark   c
House Sparrow   c (Stanley only)
Black-throated Finch   c

41
Trelew and Bariloche, Argentina

WITHOUT GOING TO ANTARCTICA or Tierra del Fuego, birders can see many of the birds of the southern oceans, Patagonian desert, and southern Andes. There are daily jets from Buenos Aires south to Trelew where there are several hotels, including the Rayentray and the Cetenario, plus hotels in Puerto Madryn, an hour's drive to the north on the Golfo Nuevo. The chief logistic problem is the lack of rental cars so that most visitors have to spend fortunes on taxis (so take your friends, or join an organized birding tour, which saves you money and hassles).

To the north of Puerto Madryn is Peninsula Valdez, where mammals like guanaco and mara are common and birds include Elegant Crested Tinamou, Darwin's Rhea, and many ovenbirds. Sea elephants live in a large colony at Punta Norte, and tours are organized there from Madryn. Mating ends in September, after which time it is home to chiefly the cows. At Punto Pyramides there is a bird colony called Isla de los Pajaros where Sandwich (Cayenne) and South American Terns, Neotropic Cormorant, and Black-crowned Night-Heron nest. Crested Duck and Chilean Flamingo can also be seen nearby. Visitors can walk at low tide although access is restricted by a warden.

In the Trelew area there is a large pond just northeast of the town where many southward-ranging pampas species can be seen, including many ducks, Silvery Grebe, coot, Many-colored Rush-Tyrant, and Rufous-backed Negrito.

Punta Tombo is home to 450,000 Magellanic Penguin, plus skuas, Dolphin Gull, three species of cormorants, sheathbills, steamer ducks, and Giant Fulmar. The sea and shore teem with birds, perhaps one of the greatest spectacles in South America. By November days are hot, nights still cool, and, at intervals, strong winds build up for several days at a time. To reach the area, drive south on provincial Route 1 for several hours to the gate marked Estancia La Perla. The penguin show (marvelous photography) is attracting many nonbirders, and more detailed directions can be had in Trelew at hotels.

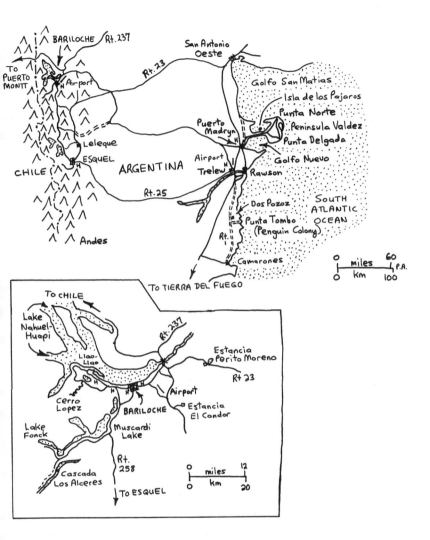

Although most birds can be seen easily enough from the visitors' trails, a permit must be obtained in advance from the government (check at your hotel) to go out to the cormorant colony. The road to Punta Tombo is excellent for guanaco and mara, as well as rhea, tinamou, Burrowing Parrot, earthcreepers, White-throated Cacholote, and Mourning Sierra-Finch.

Bariloche on Lake Nahuel-Huapi is a famous ski and mountain

resort at the base of the Andes in Rio Negro province. The dramatic snow-capped peaks, deep blue waters, and the tall nothofagus forests make a fabulous background. There is an airport with daily jets from Buenos Aires, an abundance of hotels (the top ones are the El Casco, Llao-llao, and Tunquelen) and inns in all price ranges, and several car rental agencies. Unfortunately, there is no way to fly direct from Trelew to Bariloche, although there are buses available, via Esquel.

The best time for a visit is from October to December, when wild-flowers are out and off-season prices are in effect. Weather at this time of year alternates between fine sunny days and several days of cold, wind, and rain, which is typical of temperate areas at this latitude.

A fine day's trip out of Bariloche is one to Cascada Los Alerces. Take Route 258 southwest past snowy peaks where Andean Condor may be seen. Look for Ashy-headed Geese in pastures. Turn right (west) on Route 254 to the waterfall where Torrent Duck are often seen in the morning. Exploring downriver is recommended to observe them. A side road leads to Lago Fonck, where the loud "Wok-wok-wok" call of the Magellanic Woodpecker may reveal its presence in older, decaying nothofagus forests.

Another day should be spent going east to the arid "Arizona-like" country of desert vegetation and colorful buttes. The best area is around Estancia Perito Moreno and beyond on Route 23. Finches, ovenbirds, and Upland Geese are common in the grasslands; and Black-chested Buzzard-Eagle and Andean Condor fly over the buttes. At the ranch (Estancia) there is a mucky pond that is good for ducks, grebes, and coots. The rare Bronze-winged Duck occurs in the fast-flowing streams about 6.2 miles (10 km) down the road to the east, although side roads may have to be used to find them.

Some high altitude species can be seen by driving up Cerro Lopez near Colonia Suiza. The road climbs through forest where at 4.5 miles (7 km) Black-throated Huet-Huet occur near a viewpoint. Above the treeline visitors may walk into snow fields where Andean Condor, sierra-finches, and ground-tyrants can be seen. The forest is somewhat wetter on the north side of the lake and may be worth visiting by boat or car.

CHECKLIST

T = Trelew (coast); B = Bariloche (Andes)

Magellanic Penguin c T	White-tufted Grebe c
Darwin's Rhea c T	Silvery Grebe c
Elegant Crested-Tinamou c T	Great Grebe c

Pied-billed Grebe   B
Black-browed Albatross   c T
Giant Petrel   c T
Neotropic Cormorant   c
Rock Cormorant   c T
Guanay Cormorant   T
Blue-eyed Cormorant   B
King Cormorant   c T
Great Egret   T
Black-crowned Night-Heron
Buff-necked Ibis   B
Chilean Flamingo   T
Coscoroba Swan   r
Black-necked Swan
Ashy-headed Goose   B
Upland Goose   T, c B
Crested Duck   T
Flying Steamer-Duck
Bronze-winged Duck   r B
Speckled Teal   B
Chiloe Wigeon   c
Yellow-billed Pintail   c
Silver Teal   r
Cinnamon Teal   T
Red Shoveler
Torrent Duck   B
Ruddy Duck
Andean Condor   B
Black Vulture   B
Turkey Vulture   T
Black-chested Buzzard-Eagle
Red-backed Hawk   c
Cinereous Harrier   c
Chimango Caracara   c
Crested Caracara   B
Peregrine Falcon   r B
American Kestrel   c
California Quail
Plumbeous Rail   B
Red-gartered Coot   c
White-winged Coot   c
American Oystercatcher   T
Blackish Oystercatcher   T
Southern Lapwing   c
Gray Plover   T
Two-banded Plover   c T
Tawny-throated Dotterel   c T

Ruddy Turnstone   c M T
Lesser Yellowlegs   T M
Red Knot   T M
Baird's Sandpiper   c M T
White-rumped Sandpiper   c M T
Semipalmated Sandpiper   M T
Sanderling   c M T
Hudsonian Godwit   M T
Black-necked Stilt   T
Least Seedsnipe   T
Snowy Sheathbill   T
Great Skua   T
Parasitic Jaeger   T
Dolphin Gull   T
Band-tailed Gull   r
Kelp Gull   c
Brown-hooded Gull   c
South American Tern   M
Arctic/Common Tern   M T
Royal Tern   c S T
Sandwich (Cayenne) Tern   S T
Spot-eared Dove   c
Burrowing Parrot   T
Burrowing Owl   T
Short-eared Owl   T
Green-backed Firecrown   B
Chilean Flicker   B
Magellanic Woodpecker   B
Common Miner   c
Scale-throated Earthcreeper   c
Band-tailed Earthcreeper   T
Dark-bellied Cinclodes   B
Bar-winged Cinclodes   B
Des Mur's Wiretail   B
Thorn-tailed Rayadito   B
Plain-mantled Tit-Spinetail
Lesser Canastero
Patagonian Canastero
White-throated Cacholote   T
White-throated Treerunner   B
Black-throated Huet-Huet   r B
shrike-tyrant, species
Mouse-brown Monjita   T
Rusty-backed Monjita   T
Fire-eyed Diucon   c B
White-browed Ground-Tyrant   B
Dark-faced Ground-Tyrant   c B

Rufous-backed Negrito   c
Spectacled Tyrant   c
Great Kiskadee   c T
Many-colored Rush-Tyrant   T
Tufted Tit-Tyrant   T
White-crested Elaenia   c B
Rufous-tailed Plantcutter   B
Chilean Swallow   c B
Southern Martin   T
Blue-and-white Swallow   c
Barn Swallow   T
House Wren   B
Patagonian Mockingbird   c T
White-banded Mockingbird   T
Austral Thrush   c B

Correndera Pipit   c
Shiny Cowbird   c
Austral Blackbird   B
Long-tailed Meadowlark   c
House Sparrow   c
Patagonian Yellow-Finch   T
Grassland Yellow-Finch   B
Common Diuca-Finch   c
Patagonian Sierra-Finch   B
Gray-hooded Sierra-Finch   B
Mourning Sierra-Finch   c
Plumbeous Sierra-Finch   B
Rufous-collared Sparrow   c
Black-chinned Siskin

42

Buenos Aires–Pampas, Argentina

BUENOS AIRES IS A VAST CITY on the banks of the muddy Rio de la Plata, the wide estuary of the Parana and Uruguay Rivers. Everglade Kite, Guira Cuckoo, and Rufous Hornero are conspicuous in nearby open areas.

The best birding is out on the plains, marshes, and ponds of the famous Argentine pampas to the southeast on Cabo (Cape) San Antonio. There is a fast paved road via Chascomus (75 miles [120 km]) and Dolores (130 miles [210 km]) to the seaside town of San Clemente del Tuyu (206 miles [330 km]) on Cabo San Antonio. Chascomus is situated on a huge lake with roads along the shore that offer views of herons, Black-necked Swan, gallinules, coots, and the elusive Bay-capped Wren-Spinetail. Dolores is a nice town, and its small Hotel Plaza makes a suitable base if hotels at San Clemente are full (which they often are from December on). Most birders will want to come here in the spring (October, November), although birding is fine all year round.

Greater Rhea survive only in protected ranches such as those southwest of San Clemente (Los Ingleses and El Palenque), and permission must be arranged. The rheas can also be seen from the alternate route back to Buenos Aires (Rte. 11), a dirt road up to Magdalena (thence paved via La Plata to Buenos Aires).

The real thrill of the pampas is the clouds of distinctive waterbirds most of which do not live elsewhere in the world. In just a day or two of driving backroads and along canals here you should have ample opportunity to see and photograph such delights as White-tufted Grebe, Stripe-backed Bittern, Southern Screamer, Coscoroba Swan, Chiloe Wigeon, Silver Teal, Red Shoveler, Rosy-billed Pochard, the parasitic and rare Black-headed Duck, hundreds of Everglade Kites, Long-winged Harrier, Spot-flanked Gallinule, three exotic coots, Brown-hooded Gull, and Trudeau's Tern. Smaller marshbirds in this area include Wren-like Rushbird, Spectacled and Yellow-browed Tyrants, Many-colored Rush-Tyrant, Scarlet-headed Blackbird, Brown-

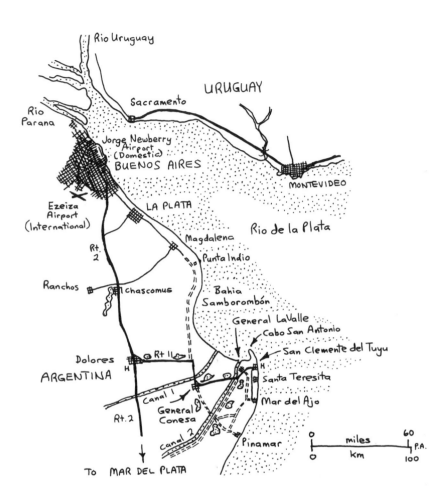

and-yellow Marshbird, and Great Pampa-Finch. These and more can be easily seen along Route 11 west of San Clemente near General LaValle. A fine circuit would be to take the road along Canal 2 to the southwest, thence north to General Conesa, and return to your hotel on Route 11.

The dunes, mud flats, and beaches of the tip of Cabo San Antonio just north of San Clemente are worth visiting on the dirt track. Look for Chilean Flamingo, Hudsonian Godwit, Freckle-breasted Thornbird, Warbling Doradito, and mockingbirds.

Species listed below have been noted on October and November (only) visits to the area.

CHECKLIST

Greater Rhea
Red-winged Tinamou
Spotted Nothura
White-tufted Grebe   c
Great Grebe   c
Pied-billed Grebe
Neotropic Cormorant   c
Cocoi Heron   c
Great Egret   c
Snowy Egret   c
Green Heron
Cattle Heron
Whistling Heron   r
Black-crowned Night-Heron
Stripe-backed Bittern
Maguari Stork   c
Buff-necked Ibis   W
White-faced Ibis   c
Roseate Spoonbill   c
Chilean Flamingo
Southern Screamer   c
Fulvous Whistling-Duck   c
Coscoroba Swan
Black-necked Swan   c
Speckled Teal   c
Chiloe Wigeon   c
Yellow-billed Pintail   c
Silver Teal   c
Cinnamon Teal
Red Shoveler
Rosy-billed Pochard
Lake Duck
Black-headed Duck
Black Vulture
Turkey Vulture
White-tailed Kite
Everglade Kite   c
Swainson's Hawk   M
Roadside Hawk
Cinereous Harrier
Long-winged Harrier   c
Crested Caracara
Chimango Caracara   c

Limpkin   c
Plumbeous Rail
Giant Wood-Rail   r
Spot-flanked Gallinule
White-winged Coot   c
Red-fronted Coot   c
Red-gartered Coot   c
Common Gallinule
Wattled Jacana
Argentine Painted-Snipe
American Oystercatcher   c
Southern Lapwing   c
Gray Plover   M
Lesser Golden Plover   c M
Semipalmated Plover   M
Two-banded Plover
Ruddy Turnstone   M
Lesser Yellowlegs   M
Greater Yellowlegs   M
Baird's Sandpiper   M
White-rumped Sandpiper   c M
Pectoral Sandpiper   c M
Sanderling   M
Stilt Sandpiper   c M
Buff-breasted Sandpiper   M
Upland Sandpiper   M
Whimbrel   M
Hudsonian Godwit   M
Common Snipe
Black-necked Stilt   c
Wilson's Phalarope   M
Parasitic Jaeger   M
Band-tailed Gull   c
Kelp Gull   c
Gray-hooded Gull
Brown-hooded Gull   c
Royal Tern   c
Sandwich Tern   c
Common Tern
South American Tern
Trudeau's Tern   c
Black Skimmer   c
Picazuro Pigeon   c

Spot-eared Dove   c
Picui Ground-Dove
White-tipped Dove
Monk Parakeet   r
Dark-billed Cuckoo
Guira Cuckoo   c
Barn Owl
Burrowing Owl   c
Short-eared Owl
Glittering-bellied Emerald
Ringed Kingfisher
Green Kingfisher
Campo Flicker
Golden-breasted Flicker   c
Narrow-billed Woodcreeper
Common Miner
Rufous Hornero   c
Curve-billed Reedhaunter   r
Wren-like Rushbird   c
Plain-mantled Tit-Spinetail
Tufted Tit-Spinetail
Chotoy Spinetail
Hudson's Canastero
Bay-capped Wren-Spinetail
Little Thornbird
Freckle-breasted Thornbird   c
Firewood-gatherer
White Monjita
Spectacled Tyrant   c
Vermilion Flycatcher   c
Yellow-browed Tyrant
Cattle Tyrant   c
Fork-tailed Flycatcher   c
Tropical Kingbird   c
Great Kiskadee   c
Euler's Flycatcher
Warbling Doradito
Many-colored Rush-Tyrant
Sooty Tyrannulet

White-crested Tyrannulet
Small-billed Elaenia
White-rumped Swallow   c
Brown-chested Martin   c
Gray-breasted Martin   c
Blue-and-white Swallow
Barn Swallow   M
Sedge Wren
House Wren   c
Chalk-browed Mockingbird   c
White-banded Mockingbird
Rufous-bellied Thrush   c
Creamy-bellied Thrush
Masked Gnatcatcher
Correndera Pipit   c
Short-billed Pipit
Shiny Cowbird   c
Bay-winged Cowbird   c
Screaming Cowbird   c
Yellow-winged Blackbird   c
Epaulet Oriole
Scarlet-headed Blackbird
Brown-and-yellow Marshbird   c
White-browed Blackbird
Lesser Red-breasted Meadowlark
Tropical Parula
Masked Yellowthroat
Diademed Tanager
Blue-and-yellow Tanager   c
House Sparrow
Red-crested Cardinal   c
Grassland Yellow Finch   c
Saffron Yellow-Finch   c
Rufous-collared Sparrow   c
Black-and-rufous Warbling-Finch
  c
Long-tailed Reed-Finch
Great Pampa-Finch   c
Hooded Siskin

43
Asuncion, Paraguay

ASUNCION IS THE CAPITAL OF THE COUNTRY, site of its international airport, and hub of its road system. The city is attractive, with few visible poor districts, and there is a variety of good hotels, good drinking water, and clean food.

Car rental is quite expensive, so one-day visitors and those spending the first day of their trip here should use taxis or buses. The best birding near town is around the botanical gardens, zoo, and golf course located on the northeast side of town, about 3.1 miles (5 km) from the center. Birds include Reddish-bellied and Canary-winged Parakeets, White-barred Piculet, Purplish Jay, Chestnut-vented Conebill, and Hooded Tanager.

The quickest way to see a good variety of Chaco birds is to take one of the hourly small-vehicle ferries from Asuncion to Chaco-I on the west bank of the Rio Paraguay. The Pilcomayo road (Rte. 12) leads northwest through excellent open country with ponds. The road from Chaco-I to Villa Hayes also offers good birding. Any or all of the Chaco roads are closed and impassable during and after rains, often for several days.

The most exciting birding is on the road deep into the Chaco, which is the name given to Paraguay west of the Rio Paraguay. There are several organized "safaris" that can be arranged in Asuncion, although they cater chiefly to hunters. The road runs northwest to the Bolivian border (unpaved), and simple accommodation is available en route in Filadelphia (a long, long day's drive). Much can be seen in one long day by car from Asuncion by catching the first ferry to Villa Hayes from Piquete Cue, a half hour's drive north. Ferries run every two hours roughly; times are published daily in city newspapers. Scissor-tailed Nightjars can be seen in the road before dawn just west of the ferry landing.

On leaving Villa Hayes, one sees a small cattle impoundment near a pond on the left. Nacunda Nighthawks often roost here. The Chaco-I road branches left 3.1 miles (5 km) from the ferry and passes through open grasslands where Black-hooded Parakeet, White Monjita, Spectacled Tyrant, and Great Pampa-Finch are found.

From the junction of the Chaco-I road it is 5.6 miles (9 km) to Benjamin Aceval. The countryside beyond the last town consists of scrub, palm savanna, some marshy areas, and occasional woods, and birds are plentiful. Highlights on a dry season visit (May through October) could include Whistling Heron, Maguari Stork, Jabiru Stork, Plumbeous and Buff-necked Ibises, Southern Screamer, hawks, Giant Wood-Rail, Monk Parakeet, Firewood-gatherer, Strange-tailed Tyrant, Suiriri Flycatcher, and White-banded Mockingbird. The more common birds include Guira Cuckoo, Campo Flicker, White Monjita, Cattle Tyrant, Great Kiskadee, and Red-crested Cardinal.

Forty-two miles (68 km) from Benjamin Aceval is the first store of any kind (Tacuara) and there gasoline (sometimes), beer, soft drinks, and emergency meals can be obtained. Another 4.5 miles (7 km) farther is the bridge over the Rio Aguaray Gauzu. The gallery forest has Scaly-headed and Turquoise-fronted Parrots, Blue-crowned Trogon, Rufous Casiornis, Golden-winged Cacique, Epaulet Oriole, and parrots. The entire road is said to be often impassable in the wet season, and sometimes even in the dry season. Bring food and water.

Lake Ypacarai, about an hour's drive east on paved roads, can be recommended for the less adventurous. The marshes along Route 2, before the turnoff to San Bernardino, have many Limpkin and Yellow-billed Cardinal. The grasslands after the turnoff have Guira Cuckoo, Gray Monjita, Chotoy Spinetail, and others. There are several good hotels in a resort setting. The drive east to Iguassu Falls is of at least 5 hours' duration.

CHECKLIST

Greater Rhea r	Stripe-backed Bittern r
Tataupa Tinamou r	Least Bittern r
Red-winged Tinamou r	Wood Stork
Spotted Nothura	Maguari Stork c
American Dabchick	Jabiru Stork c
Pied-billed Grebe	Plumbeous Ibis c
Neotropic Cormorant	Buff-necked Ibis c
Cocoi Heron c	Bare-faced Ibis r
Great Egret c	White-faced Ibis
Snowy Egret c	Roseate Spoonbill
Green Heron	Southern Screamer
Whistling Heron c	White-faced Whistling-Duck
Black-crowned Night-Heron	Black-bellied Whistling-Duck
Rufescent Tiger-Heron	Brazilian Duck

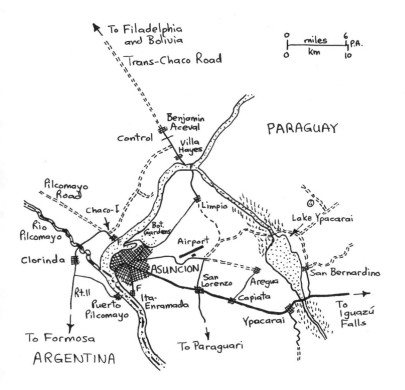

To Filadelphia and Bolivia

Trans-Chaco Road

miles
km
P.A.

Benjamin Aceval

Control

Villa Hayes

PARAGUAY

Pilcomayo Road

Chaco-I

Limpio

Lake Ypacarai

Rio Pilcomayo

Bot. Gardens

Airport

Clorinda

San Bernardino

ASUNCION

San Lorenzo

Aregua

Rt.11

Ita-Enramada

Capiata

To Iguazú Falls

Puerto Pilcomayo

Ypacarai

To Formosa

To Paraguari

ARGENTINA

Comb Duck r	American Kestrel c
Muscovy Duck	Chaco Chachalaca
Black Vulture c	Limpkin c
Turkey Vulture c	Plumbeous Rail
Marsh Vulture c	Blackish Rail r
Everglade Kite c	Spotted Rail r
Zone-tailed Hawk r	Gray-necked Wood-Rail
Swainson's Hawk M	Giant Wood-Rail c
Roadside Hawk c	Ash-throated Crake r
Black-collared Hawk c	Rufous-sided Crake r
Savanna Hawk c	Paint-billed Crake r
Great Black Hawk	Purple Gallinule
Long-winged Harrier r	Red-gartered Coot r
Crane Hawk	Wattled Jacana c
Laughing Falcon	Red-legged Seriema r
Yellow-headed Caracara	Argentine Painted-snipe r
Chimango Caracara	Southern Lapwing c
Crested Caracara c	Collared Plover
Aplomado Falcon r	Lesser Golden Plover M

Solitary Sandpiper   M
Lesser Yellowledgs   M
Pectoral Sandpiper   M
Common Snipe   r
Black-necked Stilt
Black Skimmer
Spot-winged Pigeon
Picazuro Pigeon
Spot-eared Dove   c
Ruddy Ground-Dove
Picui Ground-Dove   c
White-tipped Dove
Blue-crowned Parakeet
Black-hooded Parakeet   c
Reddish-bellied Parakeet
Monk Parakeet   c
Canary-winged Parakeet   c
Scaly-headed Parrot
Turquoise-fronted Parrot
Yellow-billed Cuckoo   M
Dark-billed Cuckoo
Squirrel Cuckoo
Greater Ani   r
Smooth-billed Ani   c
Guira Cuckoo   c
Striped Cuckoo
Burrowing Owl
Nacunda Nighthawk
Scissor-tailed Nightjar
Glittering-bellied Emerald   c
Gilded Hummingbird
Blue-crowned Trogon
Ringed Kingfisher
Amazon Kingfisher
Green Kingfisher   r
Toco Toucan
White-barred Piculet   c
Campo Flicker   c
Green-barred Flicker
Pale-crested Woodpecker
White Woodpecker   c
Checkered Woodpecker   r
Little Woodpecker
Cream-backed Woodpecker   r
Crimson-crested Woodpecker   r
Olivaceous Woodcreeper
Great Rufous Woodcreeper

Narrow-billed Woodcreeper   c
Red-billed Scythebill
Rufous Hornero   c
Chotoy Spinetail   c
Pale-breasted Spinetail
Sooty-fronted Spinetail   c
Yellow-throated Spinetail
Stripe-crowned Spinetail
Greater Thornbird
Rufous-fronted Thornbird   r
Little Thornbird
Great Antshrike
Barred Antshrike   c
Variable Antshrike
Black-capped Antwren   r
Rusty-backed Antwren   r
Olive-crowned Crescentchest   r
White-naped Xenopsaris
Green-backed Becard
White-winged Becard
Crested Becard
White-tipped Plantcutter
Gray Monjita   c
Black-and-white Monjita   r
White Monjita
Streamer-tailed Tyrant
Strange-tailed Tyrant   r
Hudson's Black-Tyrant   W
Spectacled Tyrant   W
Pied Water-Tyrant   c
White-headed Marsh-Tyrant
Vermilion Flycatcher   c
Yellow-browed Tyrant
Cattle Tyrant   c
Fork-tailed Flycatcher   c S
Tropical Kingbird   S
Crowned Slaty Flycatcher   S
Streaked Flycatcher   S
Great Kiskadee   c
Rufous Casiornis
Brown-crested Flycatcher
Short-crested Flycatcher
Swainson's Flycatcher   r
Yellow-olive Flycatcher
Pearly-vented Tody-Tyrant   c
Tawny-crowned Pygmy-Tyrant
Bearded Tachuri   r

Warbling Doradito   r S
Sharp-tailed Tyrant   r
White-crested Tyrannulet   c
Sooty Tyrannulet   r S
White-crested Elaenia   S
Small-billed Elaenia   S
Suiriri Flycatcher   c
Mouse-colored Tyrannulet
Southern Beardless Tyrannulet
White-rumped Swallow
Gray-breasted Martin   S
Tawny-headed Swallow   r
Purplish Jay
Plush-crested Jay
House Wren   c
Chalk-browed Mockingbird   c
White-banded Mockingbird   c
Rufous-bellied Thrush
Creamy-bellied Thrush
Masked Gnatcatcher
Yellowish Pipit
Rufous-browed Peppershrike   c
Red-eyed Vireo   S
Shiny Cowbird   c
Bay-winged Cowbird   c
Golden-winged Cacique
Chopi Blackbird   c
Chestnut-capped Blackbird
Unicolored Blackbird
Epaulet Oriole   c

Yellow-rumped Marshbird
White-browed Blackbird
Bobolink   M
Tropical Parula   c
Masked Yellowthroat
Golden-crowned Warbler
White-browed Warbler
Chestnut-vented Conebill   c
Purple-throated Euphonia
Sayaca Tanager   c
White-lined Tanager
Ruby-crowned Tanager
Hooded Tanager   c
Grayish Saltator
Red-crested Cardinal   c
Yellow-billed Cardinal
Blue-black Grassquit   S
Rusty-collared Seedeater
White-bellied Seedeater
Tawny-bellied Seedeater
Lesser Seed-Finch
Saffron Yellow-Finch   c
Red-crested Finch
Grassland Sparrow   c
Rufous-collared Sparrow   c
Wedge-tailed Grass-Finch
Black-capped Warbling-Finch   c
Great Pampa-Finch   c
Hooded Siskin   W
House Sparrow   c

44

Iguassu Falls,
Argentina and Brazil

THESE FALLS ARE IMPRESSIVE (wider than Niagara, taller than Victoria) and are the focal point of much tourist and commercial activity in the border region of three countries — Argentina, Brazil, and nearby Paraguay.

National parks have been set aside on the Brazilian and Argentine sides, both of which contain extensive forest. The Argentine side has more roads into the forest than the Brazilian side.

There is an airport on the Brazilian side with flights daily to Rio de Janiero and Asuncion. Rental cars may be available, and taxis and buses are easily engaged. Lodging on the Brazilian side includes the plush but crowded Hotel Das Cataratas at the Falls, the San Martin near the park entrance, and the excellent Bourbon along the road to Foz do Iguaçu, a rather large town. Green-headed Tanagers are common along the road in the park, and the heavy forest is good for birding, particularly the environs of the museum.

The Argentine side also has an airport with daily flights from Buenos Aires. Taxis are the chief mode of transport here and are expensive. There is a fine hotel, the recently expanded Cataratas, on the Argentine side, and another hotel in Puerto Iguazú. Birding from the boardwalk near the falls can be productive. Great Dusky Swifts nest under the falls in large numbers. Good birding can be had along the dirt road around the falls, which ends at a picnic area (from which boats take you to the end of the boardwalk for a one-way walk to the hotel). The dirt road continues into the forest away from the crowds, where Black-fronted Piping-Guans and other fine birds can be seen. Unfortunately a permit (available only in Buenos Aires) is necessary for use of this road. The various roads south lead through much good forest, particularly along lumbering tracks off Route 12, where Red-ruffed Fruit-Crows occur. The old airstrip near the hotel is excellent for early morning walks when birds are conspicuous in the cecropia trees.

On the Paraguay side there are the Hotel-Casino Acaray and the

Hotel Catedral, and a paved road leading to Asuncion in six hours. The best birding on that side is in the Reserva Forestal, 6.2 miles (12 km) west. There is a pond there, surrounded by some tall forest with several good trails. Birds include Red-breasted Toucan, Blond-crested and Robust Woodpeckers, White-shouldered Fire-eye, Green-backed Becard, Three-striped Flycatcher, Eared Pygmy-Tyrant, and Chestnut-bellied Euphonia.

CHECKLIST

Solitary Tinamou   r
Brown Tinamou
Small-billed Tinamou   r
Tataupa Tinamou
American Dabchick
Pied-billed Grebe

Neotropic Cormorant
Green Heron
Whistling Heron   r
Rufescent Tiger-Heron
Plumbeous Ibis   r
Green Ibis   r

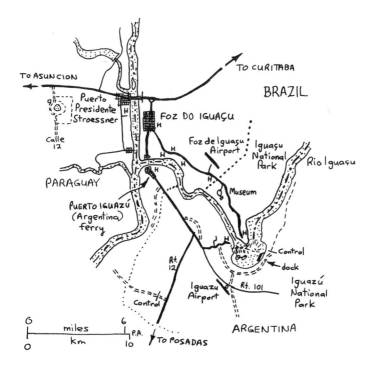

Muscovy Duck
Brazilian Duck
Black Vulture   c
Turkey Vulture
Marsh Vulture
White-tailed Kite
Swallow-tailed Kite   c
Rufous-thighed Kite
Plumbeous Kite   c S
Everglade Kite
Bicolored Sparrowhawk   r
Roadside Hawk   c
Mantled Hawk   r
Yellow-headed Caracara   r
Crested Caracara
American Kestrel   c
Peregrine Falcon   r W
Dusky-legged Guan
Black-fronted Piping-Guan
Limpkin
Wattled Jacana
Southern Lapwing
Lesser Yellowlegs   M
Solitary Sandpiper   M
Spotted Sandpiper   M
White-rumped Sandpiper   M
Picazuro Pigeon
Pale-vented Pigeon   c
Spot-eared Dove
Ruddy Ground-Dove   c
Blue Ground-Dove
White-tipped Dove
White-eyed Parakeet   c
Reddish-bellied Parakeet   c
Blue-winged Parrotlet   c
Red-capped Parrot
Scaly-headed Parrot
Turquoise-fronted Parrot
Dark-billed Cuckoo
Squirrel Cuckoo   c
Greater Ani   c
Smooth-billed Ani   c
Guira Cuckoo   c
Striped Cuckoo
Tropical Screech-Owl
Ferruginous Pygmy-Owl
Nacunda Nighthawk   r

White-collared Swift
Great Dusky Swift   c
Ashy-tailed Swift
Scale-throated Hermit
Black-throated Mango
Glittering-bellied Emerald   c
Violet-capped Woodnymph
Black-throated Trogon
Surucua Trogon   c
Ringed Kingfisher   c
Amazon Kingfisher
Rufous Motmot
White-necked Puffbird
White-eared Puffbird   r
Rusty-breasted Nunlet   r
Toco Toucan
Red-breasted Toucan   c
Chestnut-eared Aracari
Saffron Toucanet   r
Ochre-collared Piculet   r
Green-barred Flicker   r
White-browed Woodpecker   r
Blond-crested Woodpecker   r
Lineated Woodpecker
Yellow-fronted Woodpecker
White-spotted Woodpecker   c
Cream-backed Woodpecker   r
Robust Woodpecker
Plain-brown Woodcreeper
Olivaceous Woodcreeper   c
White-throated Woodcreeper
Rufous-capped Spinetail   c
Gray-bellied Spinetail
Yellow-throated Spinetail
Olive Spinetail
Ochre-breasted Foliage-gleaner   c
Buff-fronted Foliage-gleaner
Streaked Xenops
Spot-backed Antshrike
Tufted Antshrike
Variable Antshrike
Plain Antvireo
Rufous-winged Antwren   c
Ferruginous Antbird   c
Dusky-tailed Antbird
Streak-capped Antwren
White-shouldered Fire-eye   c

Short-tailed Ant-thrush
Variegated Antpitta
Rufous Gnateater   r
Green-backed Becard   c
Chestnut-crowned Becard
Black-tailed Tityra   c
Black-crowned Tityra   c
Red-ruffed Fruitcrow
Swallow-tailed Manakin
Wing-barred Manakin
Long-tailed Tyrant   c
Cattle Tyrant
Fork-tailed Flycatcher   c S
Eastern Kingbird   M
Tropical Kingbird   c S
Variegated Flycatcher
Piratic Flycatcher
Sirystes
Streaked Flycatcher   c
Boat-billed Flycatcher
Three-striped Flycatcher
Social Flycatcher   c
Great Kiskadee   c
Tropical Pewee
Euler's Flycatcher
Yellow-olive Flycatcher
Large-headed Flatbill
Eared Pygmy-Tyrant   c
Drab-breasted Pygmy-Tyrant
Bay-ringed Tyrannulet   c
Mottle-cheeked Tyrannulet
Sao Paulo Tyrannulet   c
Yellow Tyrannulet
Sooty Tyrannulet
Yellow-bellied Elaenia
Greenish Elaenia
Rough-legged Tyrannulet
Sepia-capped Flycatcher
Gray-hooded Flycatcher
Southern Antpipit
Gray-breasted Martin   c
Brown-chested Martin   c
Rough-winged Swallow
Blue-and-white Swallow   c
Barn Swallow   M
Sand Martin   M
White-winged Swallow   c

White-rumped Swallow
Plush-crested Jay   c
House Wren   c
White-necked Thrush
Creamy-bellied Thrush   c
Rufous-bellied Thrush
Pale-breasted Thrush
Cream-bellied Gnatcatcher
Rufous-browed Peppershrike
Red-eyed (Chivi) Vireo   c
Rufous-crowned Greenlet
Blue Dacnis
Bananaquit   c
Chestnut-vented Conebill
Tropical Parula   c
Masked Yellowthroat
Golden-crowned Warbler   c
White-browed Warbler
River Warbler   r
House Sparrow
Crested Oropendola
Red-rumped Cacique   c
Giant Cowbird
Shiny Cowbird   c
Screaming Cowbird
Epaulet Oriole
White-browed Blackbird
Swallow-Tanager   c
Blue-naped Chlorophonia
Purple-throated Euphonia
Violaceous Euphonia   c
Chestnut-bellied Euphonia
Green-throated Euphonia
Fawn-breasted Tanager
Green-headed Tanager   c
Chestnut-backed Tanager   r
Sayaca Tanager   c
Red-crowned Ant-Tanager
White-lined Tanager   c
Ruby-crowned Tanager   c
Black-goggled Tanager   c
Chestnut-headed Tanager
Guira Tanager   c
Magpie-Tanager   c
Green-winged Saltator
Ultramarine Grosbeak
Plumbeous Seedeater

Double-collared Seedeater
Temminck's Seedeater   r
Blackish-blue Seedeater
Lesser Seed-Finch
Blue-black Grassquit

Grassland Yellow-Finch
Saffron Yellow-Finch
Uniform Finch
Red-crested Finch   c
Rufous-collared Sparrow   c

45
Itatiaia National Park, Brazil

THIS GREAT PARK of 46 square miles (120 km²) includes some of the highest mountains in Brazil, with Itatiaia's peak reaching 8490 feet (2787 m). The main birding and hotel area of the park is located 8 miles (12.8 km) north of the town of Itatiaia. The paved access road runs northward from a point just east of the toll booth on the main Rio de Janeiro–Sao Paulo highway 97 miles (155 km) from Rio.

Unlike most Latin American parks, there are several hotels actually in the park (no commuting). The Hotel Simon, the largest and most expensive, is quite comfortable. The small Hotel do Ipe has good rooms and is run like a guest house, with family-style meals. The Ipe features active hummingbird feeders with woodnymphs, White-throated Hummingbird, and rubies dominating, although up to a dozen kinds occur. In the hotel area at various seasons Swallow-tailed Cotinga, Crested Becard, Purple-breasted Plovercrest, Reddish-bellied Parakeet, and many tanagers can be seen. Tawny-browed Owls sometimes come to lights around the hotels at night.

The subtropical forest here is rich in birdlife, including most of the species endemic to southeastern Brazil (a high percentage of which are not illustrated in any field guide). Birding is fine all along the main road downhill from Hotel do Ipe to the Museum (with an excellent bird collection), and uphill to Maromba bridge. The road peters out above the Maromba bridge and becomes a jeep track. Hiking uphill early in the day penetrates the habitat of a number of birds not found as low as the bridge. The Black-and-gold Cotinga occurs in the higher forests. Among the hundreds of birds living in the forests along the road and near the bridge are Saffron and Spot-billed Toucanets, Suru-cua Trogon, Red-breasted Toucan, Reddish-bellied Parakeet, White-throated Woodcreeper, Pallid Spinetail, Giant Antshrike (above bridge), Sharpbill (scarce) and Gilt-edged, Brassy-breasted, Golden-chevroned, and Brown Tanagers.

To reach the very high country take a circuitous route via the Sao Paulo toll road, turning north at Eng. Passos. The dry valley 3.7 miles

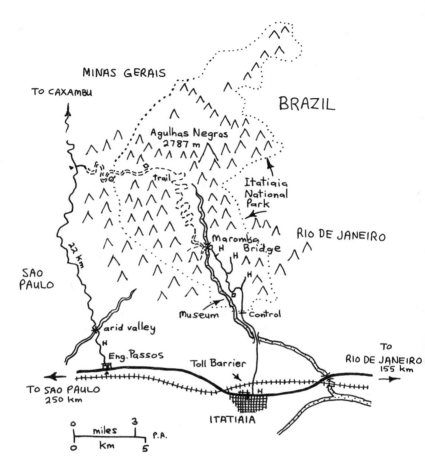

Agulhas Negras
2787 m

trail

Itatiaia
National
Park

RIO DE JANEIRO

Maromba
Bridge

SAO
PAULO

22 km

Museum

Control

arid valley

Eng. Passos

Toll Barrier

To
RIO DE JANEIRO
155 km

TO SAO PAULO
250 km

ITATIAIA

miles

km

P.A.

(6 km) up is good for birds not regularly seen in the park, such as
Rufous Hornero. At the top of the pass there is a marked road to the
right that winds up into the park. It goes through some forest where
plovercrest, White-browed Warbler, and warbling-finches may be
seen, and Black-and-gold Cotingas heard. The marsh at Kilometer
Post 8 sometimes features Slate-breasted Wood-Rail and Blackish
Rail. The high grasslands have many endemic plants and some local
birds including Itatiaia Spinetail, Crested Black-Tyrant, Hellmayr's
Pipit, and Great Pampa-Finch. No food or lodging is available in the
high country.

Book into either hotel on weeknights only. On weekends and in
holiday weeks the park is often full of raucous people and cars speed-

ing along the dusty roads. Weekdays (except in summer) are tranquil and relatively free of trouble.

CHECKLIST

Brown Tinamou   r
Black Vulture   c
Turkey Vulture
Rufous-thighed Kite
Sharp-shinned Sparrowhawk
Roadside Hawk   c
White-rumped Hawk
White-tailed Hawk
Short-tailed Hawk
Mantled Hawk
Black Hawk-Eagle   r
Harpy Eagle   r
Yellow-headed Caracara
Crested Caracara
American Kestrel
Dusky-legged Guan
Spot-winged Wood-Quail   r
Slate-breasted Wood-Rail
Blackish Rail
Plumbeous Pigeon   c
Ruddy Ground-Dove
Gray-fronted Dove
Reddish-bellied Parakeet   c
Blue-winged Parrotlet
Plain Parakeet
Scaly-headed Parrot
Red-capped Parrot
Squirrel Cuckoo   c
Smooth-billed Ani
Guira Cuckoo
Tawny-browed Owl
Rusty-barred Owl
Burrowing Owl
Ferruginous Pygmy-Owl
Short-tailed Nighthawk
Long-trained Nightjar
White-collared Swift   c
Gray-rumped Swift
Scale-throated Hermit   c
Planalto Hermit   r
Swallow-tailed Hummingbird

Black Jacobin   c
White-vented Violetear
Purple-breasted Plovercrest
Glittering-bellied Emerald
Violet-capped Woodnymph   c
White-throated Hummingbird   c
Brazilian Ruby   c
Amethyst Woodstar
Black-throated Trogon   r
Surucua Trogon   c
Rufous Motmot
White-eared Puffbird
Spot-billed Toucanet
Saffron Toucanet
Red-breasted Toucan
White-barred Piculet
Campo Flicker
Green-barred Flicker
Yellow-fronted Woodpecker
White-browed Woodpecker
White-spotted Woodpecker   c
Robust Woodpecker
Plain-brown Woodcreeper
Olivaceous Woodcreeper
White-throated Woodcreeper   c
Scaled Woodcreeper   c
Rufous Hornero
Itatiaia Spinetail
Rufous-capped Spinetail
Chicli Spinetail
Pallid Spinetail   c
Firewood-gatherer
White-collared Foliage-gleaner
Buff-browed Foliage-gleaner
White-browed Foliage-gleaner   r
Buff-fronted Foliage-gleaner   c
Pale-browed Treehunter   r
Sharp-billed Treehunter   r
Streaked Xenops
Sharp-tailed Streamcreeper   r
Giant Antshrike

225

Tufted Antshrike
White-bearded Antshrike   r
Variable Antshrike   c
Rufous-capped Antshrike
Plain Antvireo
Star-throated Antwren
Ferruginous Antbird   c
Rufous-tailed Antbird
Ochre-rumped Antbird
White-shouldered Fire-eye   c
White-bibbed Antbird
Short-tailed Ant-thrush
Rufous-tailed Ant-thrush
Variegated Antpitta   r
Rufous Gnateater   r
Slaty Bristlefront   r
Mouse-colored Tapaculo
Swallow-tailed Cotinga
Black-and-gold Cotinga   r
Gray-hooded Attila
Chestnut-crowned Becard   c
Crested Becard
Black-tailed Tityra   c
Sharpbill
Swallow-tailed Manakin
Pin-tailed Manakin   r
White-rumped Monjita
Long-tailed Tyrant   c
Streamer-tailed Tyrant
Crested Black-Tyrant
Velvety Black Tyrant   c
Blue-billed Black-Tyrant
Shear-tailed Gray-Tyrant
Sirystes
Yellow-browed Tyrant
Cattle Tyrant
Fork-tailed Flycatcher
Tropical Kingbird
Variegated Flycatcher
Piratic Flycatcher
Boat-billed Flycatcher
Streaked Flycatcher
Great Kiskadee   c
Social Flycatcher
Short-crested Flycatcher
Swainson's Flycatcher   ?
Tropical Pewee   c

Black-tailed Flycatcher
Euler's Flycatcher   c
Cliff Flycatcher   c
White-throated Spadebill
Yellow-olive Flycatcher   c
Large-headed Flatbill
Yellow-lored Tody-Flycatcher
Ochre-faced Tody-Flycatcher
Hang-nest Tody-Tyrant   r
Eared Pygmy-Tyrant   c
Drab-breasted Pygmy-Tyrant
Brown-breasted Pygmy-Tyrant
Mottle-cheeked Tyrannulet
Serra do Mar Tyrannulet
Yellow Tyrannulet
Sooty Tyrannulet
Olivaceous Elaenia
Greenish Tyrannulet
Planalto Tyrannulet
Gray-capped Tyrannulet
Sepia-capped Flycatcher
Gray-hooded Flycatcher   c
Gray-breasted Martin
White-rumped Swallow
Blue-and-white Swallow   c
White-thighed Swallow
Rough-winged Swallow
House Wren   c
Chalk-browed Mockingbird
Creamy-bellied Thrush   r
Rufous-bellied Thrush   c
Yellow-legged Thrush   c
Hellmayr's Pipit
Rufous-browed Peppershrike   c
Red-eyed (Chivi) Vireo   c
Rufous-crowned Greenlet   c
Lemon-chested Greenlet   r
Blue Dacnis   c
Bananaquit
Tropical Parula   c
White-browed Warbler   c
Golden-crowned Warbler   c
Red-rumped Cacique   c
Chopi Blackbird
Golden-winged Cacique
Shiny Cowbird   c
Blue-naped Chlorophonia

Chestnut-bellied Euphonia
Fawn-breasted Tanager
Gilt-edged Tanager   c
Brassy-breasted Tanager   c
Green-headed Tanager
Burnished-buff Tanager
Diademed Tanager   c
Palm Tanager   c
Sayaca Tanager   c
Golden-chevroned Tanager   c
Olive-green Tanager
Red-crowned Ant-Tanager
Ruby-crowned Tanager   c
Black-goggled Tanager
Rufous-headed Tanager
Orange-headed Tanager

Brown Tanager   c
Magpie-Tanager
Thick-billed Saltator
Green-winged Saltator   c
Black-throated Grosbeak
Blue-black Grassquit
Buffy-fronted Seedeater
Temminck's Seedeater
Double-collared Seedeater
Uniform Finch
Rufous-collared Sparrow   c
Long-tailed Reed-Finch   r
Bay-chested Warbling-Finch   c
Red-rumped Warbling-Finch   c
Great Pampa-Finch

46
Rio de Janeiro, Brazil

RIO IS ONE OF THE WORLD'S LARGEST AND MOST EXPENSIVE RE-
SORTS. Five million people crowd the beaches, roads, and hills, yet
there are many spots easily accessible to birders. Transportation,
lodging, and language problems must be met first. Rent-a-cars are
easy to get, but you need good luck with the maze of roads and the
impossible task of interpreting road signs (which always seem to point
to places other than your destination). Hotels are expensive, the
cheaper ones in the city center can be very noisy all night long, and
those on the beach are quite overpriced. The Hotel Painheiras (at 2500
feet [760 m] in the jungles of Tijuca National Park near the Corcovado
statue of Christ) is an alternative to the lowlands, but quite isolated.
The paved roads near the Painheiras, especially the one to the mountain town of Alto da Boa Vista, are rich with forest birds. Scaly-
headed Parrot, hummingbirds, woodcreepers, foliage-gleaners,
xenops, antbirds, Swallow-tailed and Pin-tailed Manakins, Eared
Pygmy-Tyrant, thrushes, Golden-crowned Warbler, and many tanagers can be seen.

The Botanical Gardens behind Ipanema Beach are attractive and
have many birds, including Plain Parakeet, piculet, Masked Water-
Tyrant, Yellow-lored Tody-Flycatcher, Rufous-bellied Thrush, and
Green-headed Tanager. The Parque da Cidade in the hills to the west
may still have Bare-throated Bellbird.

Water and marsh birds can be seen a half-hour west of the Botanical
Gardens. The Marapendi Lagoon behind Coq's Bar is good for ducks,
gallinules, hawks, and herons. The ocean has many Brown Boobies.
The north and west sides of Jacarepagna Lagoon (near the convention
center) consists of scrub, marshes, and grasslands. In morning or late
afternoon look for rails, shorebirds, Plain-breasted Ground-Dove,
Striped Cuckoo, flycatchers, Long-billed Wren, Yellowish Pipit,
Masked Yellowthroat, Brazilian Tanager, Unicolored, Chestnut-
capped, and White-browed Blackbirds, Wedge-tailed Grass-Finch,
and the introduced Common Waxbill.

For longer trips out of Rio de Janeiro try Itatiaia National Park (see
pages 223–227 in this book), the Serra dos Orgaos National Park just

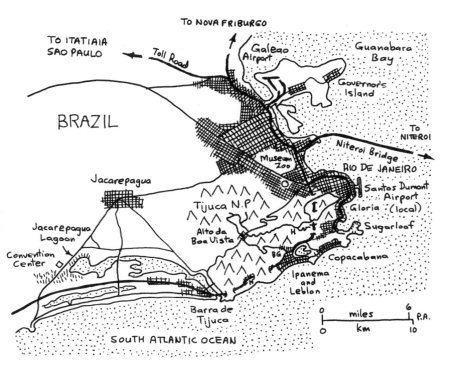

south of Teresopolis (cloud forest), and the Nova Friburgo area (also in the mountains). A fine welcome and fine hummingbird feeders await the visitor at the intimate remote Fazenda Sao Joao, a Swiss-style lodge east of Nova Friburgo (write: Caixa Postal 2566, Nova Friburgo 28.600 RJ, Brazil).

CHECKLIST

American Dabchick   r
Pied-billed Grebe   r
Black-browed Albatross   r W
Brown Booby   c
Neotropic Cormorant   c
Anhinga   r
Magnificent Frigatebird   c
Cocoi Heron
Great Egret   c
Snowy Egret   c
Little Blue Heron

Green Heron
Black-crowned Night-Heron
Roseate Spoonbill   r
White-faced Whistling-Duck   c
White-cheeked Pintail   c
Brazilian Duck
Black Vulture   c
Turkey Vulture   r
Marsh Vulture   r
White-tailed Kite
White-tailed Hawk

Roadside Hawk   c
Short-tailed Hawk
Harris's Hawk
Osprey   M
Yellow-headed Caracara
Crested Caracara
Aplomado Falcon   r
Rusty-margined Guan   r
Spot-winged Wood-Quail   r
Blackish Rail   r
Gray-necked Wood-Rail
Ash-throated Crake   c
Russet-crowned Crake
Common Gallinule   c
Purple Gallinule
Wattled Jacana
Semipalmated Plover   M
Collared Plover
Lesser Yellowlegs   M
Greater Yellowlegs   M
Spotted Sandpiper   M
Common Snipe
Sanderling   M
Semipalmated Sandpiper   M
White-rumped Sandpiper   r M
Kelp Gull   c
South American Tern
Royal Tern   S
Sandwich/Cayenne Tern   S
Ruddy Ground-Dove   c
Plain-breasted Ground-Dove
Ruddy Quail-Dove   r
Blue-winged Parrotlet
Plain Parakeet
Scaly-headed Parrot   c
Dark-billed Cuckoo   r
Striped Cuckoo
Smooth-billed Ani   c
Guira Cuckoo
Tropical Screech-Owl
Lesser Nighthawk
Scissor-tailed Nightjar   r
Common Pauraque
Band-winged Nightjar
Ashy-tailed Swift
Gray-rumped Swift
White-collared Swift   c

Biscutate Swift   r
Saw-billed Hermit   r
Dusky-throated Hermit
Planalto Hermit
Reddish Hermit
Black Jacobin
Swallow-tailed Hummingbird
Versicolored Emerald
Glittering-throated Emerald
Glittering-bellied Emerald
Violet-capped Woodnymph
White-vented Violetear
Black-bellied Thorntail   r
Ringed Kingfisher
Rufous Motmot
Crescent-chested Puffbird   r
White-barred Piculet   c
Campo (Field) Flicker
Yellow-throated Woodpecker   r
Yellow-fronted Woodpecker
Yellow-eared Woodpecker
Lesser Woodcreeper
Olivaceous Woodcreeper
Plain-brown Woodcreeper
Rufous Hornero
Yellow-throated Spinetail   c
Ochre-breasted Foliage-gleaner
Black-capped Foliage-gleaner
Buff-fronted Foliage-gleaner
White-eyed Foliage-gleaner
Plain Xenops
Streaked Xenops
Sharp-tailed Steamcreeper   r
Lined Antshrike
Slaty Antshrike
Spot-breasted Antvireo   c
Plain Antvireo   c
Cinereous Antshrike
White-flanked Antwren
Unicolored Antwren
Rufous-winged Antwren
Scaled Antbird
White-bibbed Antbird   r
Bare-throated Bellbird   r
Swallow-tailed Manakin   c
Pin-tailed Manakin
White-bearded Manakin

Greenish Manakin
White-rumped Monjita
Streamer-tailed Tyrant
Velvety Black-Tyrant
Masked Water-Tyrant   c
White-headed Marsh-Tyrant
Yellow-browed Tyrant   S
Cattle Tyrant   S
Tropical Kingbird   c
Streaked Flycatcher   S
Social Flycatcher   c
Great Kiskadee   c
Short-crested Flycatcher
Euler's Flycatcher
Bran-colored Flycatcher
Cliff Flycatcher
Yellow-olive Flycatcher   c
Yellow-breasted Flycatcher
Common Tody-Flycatcher
Eye-ringed Tody-Tyrant   r
Eared Pygmy-Tyrant
Yellow Tyrannulet
Tawny-crowned Pygmy-Tyrant
Yellow-bellied Elaenia   c
Southern Beardless Tyrannulet
Sepia-capped Flycatcher
Gray-hooded Flycatcher
Sharpbill   r
Gray-breasted Martin   c
Brown-chested Martin
Rough-winged Swallow
White-rumped Swallow
Blue-and-white Swallow   c
Barn Swallow   M
Long-billed Wren
House Wren   c
Tropical Mockingbird
Black-capped Mockingthrush
White-necked Thrush
Creamy-bellied Thrush
Pale-breasted Thrush
Rufous-bellied Thrush   c
Yellow-legged Thrush   c W
Yellowish Pipit

Rufous-browed Peppershrike   c
Red-eyed Vireo   c
Lemon-chested Greenlet
Shiny Cowbird   c
Unicolored Blackbird
Chestnut-capped Blackbird   W
White-browed Blackbird   W
Tropical Parula   c
Masked Yellowthroat   c
Golden-crowned Warbler   c
Blue Dacnis   c
Bananaquit   c
Chestnut-vented Conebill
Bicolored Conebill
Swallow-Tanager   S
Purple-throated Euphonia   c
Violaceous Euphonia
Chestnut-bellied Euphonia   r
Fawn-breasted Tanager
Green-headed Tanager   c
Red-necked Tanager   c
Sayaca Tanager   c
Palm Tanager   c
Golden-chevroned Tanager
Brazilian Tanager   c
Red-crowned Ant-Tanager   c
Ruby-crowned Tanager
Flame-crested Tanager   c
Rufous-headed Tanager   c
Black-goggled Tanager
Yellow-backed Tanager
Orange-headed Tanager
Buff-throated Saltator
Green-winged Saltator
Double-collared Seedeater   c
Yellow-bellied Seedeater
Blue-black Grassquit   c
Saffron Yellow-Finch
Grassland Yellow-Finch
Rufous-collared Sparrow   c
Wedge-tailed Grass-Finch   c
House Sparrow   c
Common Waxbill   c

47
Belem, Brazil

THE CITY OF BELEM, located near the mouth of the Amazon in Para, is an ideal base from which to search for many lower Amazonian birds. The attractive city, with numerous old buildings, now boasts a population of over half a million. There are many hotels (a good one, outside of town near the airport, is the Seltom), and good roads radiate in various directions. Rental cars are available at several agencies downtown. The climate is hot, but generally not unpleasantly so; January through April are the rainiest months, September through November the driest. Be prepared to get around with Portuguese, as there is little English spoken, and even Spanish is rarely understood.

In the city be sure to visit the Museu Paraense Emilio Goeldi with its fine zoo featuring representative birds; Spotted Tody-Flycatchers are numerous here.

The visiting birder will soon discover that a permit is needed to work almost all the worthwhile areas around Belem — allow some time for this tedious process. The best area near town is on the Guama Ecological Research Area owned by EMBRAPA, a large agricultural research organization. Inquire at the Instituto Evandro Chagas (on Av. Barroso; ask for Dr. Pinheiro, or Geraldo Ricardo Silva), or at the Museu Paraense (on Av. Independencia; ask for Dr. Skaff), for permits or guides. An adjacent area around Utinga Lake is owned by COSANPA as a watershed for Belem's water supply; another permit is needed to enter this forest area. The EMBRAPA director himself may be willing to help if the foregoing information becomes outdated.

Having acquired the necessary permits, you are ready to proceed as follows: Drive out past the bus station on what is the start of the Belem–Brazilia Highway. Continue past the Bosque Park (on the left) to the first traffic lights; here turn right. Proceed for about one-third of a mile (1/2 km) and follow the first paved road to the left until you reach the EMBRAPA gate on the left.

The first real forest reached along this road is at Igarape Catu (a black water stream), where toucans, aracaris, and other birds are often much in evidence (especially early in the day). The Mocambo Forest, a small patch of near-virgin growth, is on the left about a

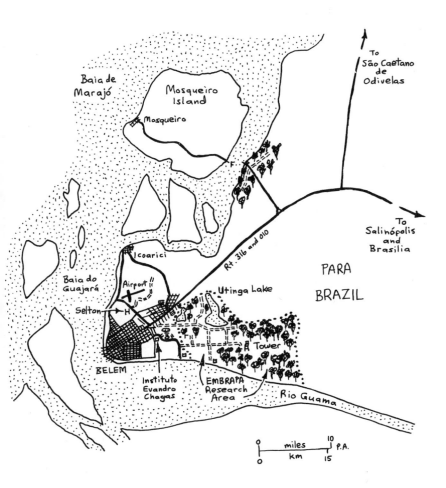

kilometer farther on; drive in the short dirt track, and then walk. Though beautiful, this area is often singularly devoid of bird activity; again, early morning is best. The next dirt road on the left leads to the Utinga Lake area; follow it for some distance over the dam itself and into the good forest beyond. Continue straight ahead on to the track leading into the extensive "Station A" Forest and to the tower (located past the forest hut, and to the right).

A visit to the tower will certainly be the highlight of your birding at EMBRAPA. Though quite sturdy, it is rather frightening and not recommended for those with a fear of heights. Plan to arrive near dawn, and climb to the upper level, over 100 feet (30.5 m) above the ground. As this platform is slightly above the forest canopy, visitors

233

will have a unique opportunity to view canopy birds at eye-level. Parrots and toucans should be much in evidence, while various hawks and many other smaller birds will also be seen. Paradise Jacamars and Spangled and White-tailed Cotingas are regulars, and with luck you might even see a Crimson Topaz. The calls of three species of tinamou (Cinereous, Brazilian, and Little, in that order of abundance) will echo from far below, while the ventriloquial "bark" of the Lined Forest-Falcon may be heard. By the time the vultures begin to soar (usually between 9 and 9:30 A.M.), general activity will have begun to decline and it will be time to leave. The tower can also be good in mid and late afternoon.

For ground-level forest birding, a permit should be obtained from the Director of the Museu Paraense to visit the fazenda (ranch) owned by Joaquim Borges Gomez. Drive along the Belem–Brazilia road for 17.5 miles (28 km), then turn left on the road to Mosqueiro. After 17 miles (27.2 km) on this paved road, look for a dirt road entering the forest on the left (which is just before reaching the waterfront where the ferry to Mosqueiro Island leaves). For those without a rental car, this area can be easily and cheaply reached by taking the bus to the Mosqueiro ferry, which leaves hourly from the main terminal in Belem (first departure at 5:30 or 6 A.M.).

Although most of the forest here has been selectively logged, it is still excellent for a large variety of interesting birds, particularly manakins. The Opal-crowned Manakin male utters a subdued "chiwrr," often repeated three or four times, and the obscure Dwarf Tyrant-Manakin constantly utters its loud "jew-pit." Antbirds are also a feature, including White-shouldered and Cinereous Antshrikes, Long-winged, Gray, and Rufous-winged Antwrens, White-backed Fire-eye, and Black-faced and Scale-backed Antbirds. Other notable birds to look for include: White-throated and Brazilian Tinamous, Red-throated Caracara, Sapphire-rumped Parrotlet, Vulturine Parrot, Collared Puffbird, White-fronted Nunbird, Gould's Toucanet, Yellow-throated, Waved, and Red-necked Woodpeckers, Rufous-rumped and Olive-backed Foliage-gleaners, Purple-breasted Cotinga, White-browed Purpletuft, Grayish Mourner, Black-capped Becard, Short-tailed Pygmy-Tyrant, McConnell's Flycatcher, Gray-chested Greenlet, Para Oropendola, Golden-sided Euphonia, and Opal-rumped and Spotted Tanagers.

The delightful seaside resort of Salinopolis is reached via a paved road 4 hours east of Belem. The Hotel Salinopolis provides excellent accommodation and superb seafood. Shore and wading birds are quite numerous near the hotel, and there are Clapper Rails in the marsh. Surely one of the finest beaches in South America, Atalaia, is only 7.5

miles (12 km) away, reached by paved road. Scarlet Ibis occur in mangroves to the east. The local specialty is the Point-tailed Palm-creeper, which may be found in the many small buriti palm swamps. Palmcreepers are inconspicuous birds, but their loud melodic wood-creeper-like calls often reveal their presence. They feed mostly at the base of the palm fronds, also on the fronds themselves, often hanging upside-down (like a nuthatch). Red-bellied Macaws also occur in these palm swamps, often going out to feed in the large cashew nut plantations nearby.

The following list *excludes* birds of Salinopolis (if they are found *only* there), as well as most migrant gulls, terns, and shorebirds (which are surprisingly rare).

CHECKLIST

White-throated Tinamou   r
Cinereous Tinamou   c
Little Tinamou
Variegated Tinamou   r
Brazilian Tinamou   c
American Dabchick
Pied-billed Grebe
Anhinga   r
Cocoi Heron
Great Egret
Snowy Egret
Green Heron
Cattle Heron
Rufescent Tiger-Heron   r
Black-crowned Night-Heron
Green Ibis   r
Black Vulture   c
Turkey Vulture
Jungle Vulture
Swallow-tailed Kite
Gray-headed Kite   r
Double-toothed Kite
Plumbeous Kite
Everglade Kite   r
Slender-billed Kite   r
Bicolored Sparrowhawk   r
Tiny Sparrowhawk   r
Roadside Hawk
Gray Hawk
White-browed Hawk   r

Slate-colored Hawk
Savanna Hawk   r
Black Hawk-Eagle   r
Crane Hawk   r
Laughing Falcon
Lined Forest-Falcon
Red-throated Caracara
Yellow-headed Caracara
Crested Caracara   r
Bat Falcon
Buff-browed Chachalaca
Gray-necked Wood-Rail
Gray-breasted Crake
Rufous-sided Crake
Sungrebe   r
Sunbittern   r
Wattled Jacana
Southern Lapwing
Pied Plover   r
Spotted Sandpiper   W
Solitary Sandpiper   W
Scaled Pigeon
Pale-vented Pigeon
Plumbeous Pigeon
Common Ground-Dove
Ruddy Ground-Dove
Blue Ground-Dove
Gray-fronted Dove
Ruddy Quail-Dove   r
Red-bellied Macaw   r

Peach-fronted Parakeet   r
Pearly Parakeet   r
Green-rumped Parrotlet
Golden-winged Parakeet
Sapphire-rumped Parrotlet
Scarlet-shouldered Parrotlet   r
White-bellied Parrot   c
Vulturine Parrot
Blue-headed Parrot   c
Dusky Parrot
Orange-winged Parrot   c
Mealy Parrot
Squirrel Cuckoo   c
Little Cuckoo
Greater Ani
Smooth-billed Ani   c
Striped Cuckoo
Tropical Screech-Owl
Spectacled Owl   r
Black-banded Owl   r
Mottled Owl   r
Striped Owl
Nacunda Nighthawk
Common Pauraque   c
Little Nightjar
Blackish Nightjar   r
Chapman's Swift
Band-rumped Swift
Short-tailed Swift
Lesser Swallow-tailed Swift
Amazonian Palm-Swift
Rufous-breasted Hermit
Pale-tailed Barbthroat   c
Long-tailed Hermit   c
Reddish Hermit   c
Gray-breasted Sabrewing
White-necked Jacobin   c
Green-throated Mango   r
Black-throated Mango
Dot-eared Coquette   r
Blue-chinned Sapphire
Common Woodnymph   c
Rufous-throated Sapphire   r
Green-tailed Goldenthroat
Plain-bellied Emerald
Crimson Topaz   r
Black-eared Fairy

Black-tailed Trogon
White-tailed Trogon   c
Black-throated Trogon
Violaceous Trogon
Ringed Kingfisher
Green Kingfisher
Green-and-rufous Kingfisher
American Pygmy Kingfisher
Blue-crowned Motmot
Yellow-billed Jacamar
Paradise Jacamar   c
White-necked Puffbird   r
Pied Puffbird
Collared Puffbird   r
Striolated Puffbird   r
Rufous-necked Puffbird
White-fronted Nunbird
Aerial Puffbird   c
Black-necked Aracari   c
Red-necked Aracari
Lettered Aracari   c
Spot-billed (Gould's) Toucanet
Channel-billed Toucan   c
Red-billed Toucan   c
Yellow-throated Woodpecker
Golden-green Woodpecker   r
Chestnut Woodpecker
Waved Woodpecker   c
Cream-colored Woodpecker
Ringed Woodpecker   r
Lineated Woodpecker
Yellow-tufted Woodpecker
Red-stained Woodpecker   c
Crimson-crested Woodpecker
Red-necked Woodpecker   c
Plain-brown Woodcreeper
Wedge-billed Woodcreeper   c
Long-billed Woodcreeper   r
Cinnamon-throated Woodcreeper
   r
Barred Woodcreeper
Straight-billed Woodcreeper
Striped Woodcreeper
Spix's Woodcreeper   c
Plain-crowned Spinetail
Ruddy Spinetail
Rufous-rumped Foliage-gleaner

Cinnamon-rumped Foliage-gleaner
Rufous-tailed Foliage-gleaner   r
Olive-backed Foliage-gleaner   c
Chestnut-crowned Foliage-gleaner
   r
Plain Xenops
Short-billed Leaftosser   r
Black-tailed Leaftosser   r
Great Antshrike
Lined Antshrike
White-shouldered Antshrike   c
Amazonian Antshrike
Spot-winged Antshrike
Plain Antvireo
Cinereous Antshrike   c
Streaked Antwren
Plain-throated Antwren   c
White-flanked Antwren   c
Long-winged Antwren
Gray Antwren
Rufous-winged Antwren
White-fringed Antwren
Gray Antbird
Dusky Antbird
White-backed Fire-eye   c
Ash-breasted Antbird   r
Black-faced Antbird   r
Band-tailed Antbird
Silvered Antbird
Scale-backed Antbird
Black-spotted Bare-eye
Rufous-capped Ant-thrush
Black-faced Ant-thrush
Wing-banded Antbird   r
Hooded Gnateater
Ringed Antpipit   r
Band-tailed Manakin   c
Red-headed Manakin   c
White-crowned Manakin
Opal-crowned Manakin
Blue-backed Manakin
White-bearded Manakin   c
Dwarf Tyrant-Manakin
Wing-barred Manakin   r
Thrush-like Manakin
Spangled Cotinga
Purple-breasted Cotinga   r

White-tailed Cotinga
White-browed Purpletuft
Bright-rumped Attila
Cinnamon Attila   r
Cinereous Mourner   r
Grayish Mourner
Screaming Piha
Cinereous Becard
Black-capped Becard
Pink-throated Becard   r
Black-tailed Tityra   c
Purple-throated Fruitcrow   c
White-headed Marsh-Tyrant
Fork-tailed Flycatcher
Tropical Kingbird   c
Sulfury Flycatcher   r
Variegated Flycatcher   c
Boat-billed Flycatcher
Streaked Flycatcher
Rusty-margined Flycatcher   c
Great Kiskadee   c
Lesser Kiskadee
Short-crested Flycatcher
Dusky-capped Flycatcher
Ruddy-tailed Flycatcher
Whiskered Flycatcher   r
Bran-colored Flycatcher
Amazonian Royal-Flycatcher
White-crested Spadebill   r
Cinnamon-crested Spadebill   r
Yellow-olive Flycatcher
Gray-crowned Flycatcher   r
Yellow-breasted Flycatcher
Olivaceous Flatbill
Rufous-tailed Flatbill
Painted Tody-Flycatcher
Spotted Tody-Flycatcher   c
Helmeted Pygmy-Tyrant   c
Black-chested Tyrant   r
Short-tailed Pygmy-Tyrant
Yellow-bellied Elaenia   c
Plain-crested Elaenia   r
Forest Elaenia   c
Yellow-crowned Elaenia   r
Mouse-colored Tyrannulet
Southern Beardless Tyrannulet
Slender-footed Tyrannulet

Yellow-crowned Tyrannulet
White-lored Tyrannulet   r
Ochre-bellied Flycatcher
McConnell's Flycatcher
Ringed Antpipit   r
White-winged Swallow
Gray-breasted Martin   c
Rough-winged Swallow   c
Barn Swallow   W
Moustached Wren   r
Coraya Wren
House Wren   c
Nightingale Wren
Black-capped Mockingthrush
Pale-breasted Thrush
Cocoa Thrush
Bare-eyed Thrush
White-necked Thrush
Tropical Gnatcatcher
Long-billed Gnatwren
Yellowish Pipit
Rufous-browed Peppershrike
Red-eyed (Chivi) Vireo
Lemon-chested Greenlet
Gray-chested Greenlet
Tawny-crowned Greenlet
Bananaquit
Purple Honeycreeper   c
Red-legged Honeycreeper
Green Honeycreeper
Blue Dacnis   c
Masked Yellowthroat
River Warbler
Green Oropendola

Para Oropendola
Yellow-rumped Cacique   c
Red-rumped Cacique
Giant Cowbird
Purple-throated Euphonia
Violaceous Euphonia
Golden-sided Euphonia
Opal-rumped Tanager
Spotted Tanager
Turquoise Tanager   c
Bay-headed Tanager
Blue-gray Tanager   c
Palm Tanager   c
Silver-beaked Tanager   c
White-lined Tanager
Fulvous-crested Tanager
Flame-crested Tanager
Gray-headed Tanager
Guira Tanager
Red-billed Pied Tanager
Black-faced Tanager
Buff-throated Saltator   c
Grayish Saltator
Yellow-green Grosbeak
Blue-black Grosbeak
Variable Seedeater
Lined Seedeater
Yellow-bellied Seedeater
Ruddy-breasted Seedeater
Lesser Seed-Finch
Large-billed Seed-Finch   r
Red-crested Finch   r
Pectoral Sparrow   c
Yellow-browed Sparrow

48
Paramaribo, Suriname

SURINAME (FORMERLY KNOWN AS DUTCH GUIANA IN ENGLISH) is a small country on the Atlantic coast of South America, located halfway between Trinidad and the mouth of the Amazon River. It has immense tropical forests and savannas, many protected reserves, a small population, and many English-speaking people.

The capital is connected by air with Amsterdam, Belem, Curacao, Cayenne, Georgetown, and Port-of-Spain (with connections to the United States). There are several fine hotels, such as the expensive downtown Toracica and the less expensive Riverclub Hotel in nearby Leonsberg. The botanic garden in town sometimes has Cinnamon Attila and Crimson-hooded Manakin. The Arrowhead Piculet and Blood-colored Woodpecker occur near the Riverclub.

Rental cars (when available) and taxis may be hired to reach nearby swampy habitats of the coastal plain. One good marsh can be reached by taking an early morning ferry across the Suriname River to Meerzog and driving 4 miles (6.4 km) to the east. That area is good for Slender-billed Kite, Azure Gallinule, and Finsch's Euphonia. Other places of interest near Paramaribo include the road to the Saramacca River bridge and the road southeast to Kraka. There are trails near stream junctures and good roadside birding when the weather is cool. In this savanna forest area look for Cream-colored and Yellow-tufted Woodpeckers, Pompadour and Spangled Cotingas, fruitcrows, Paradise Jacamar, White-bearded Manakin, and Cayenne Jay.

There are at least four reserves that can be visited with the help of STINASU, the government forestry agency located at 10 Cornelis Jongbawstraat, Paramaribo. The agency has been most helpful in aiding birding tours with transport, opening up rest houses in the reserves, and even arranging cooks to help larger parties.

The two coastal reserves require long boat trips and may not be of priority to visitors with little time. The Coppename-mouth reserve, which can be reached from the landing at Boskamp, west of Paramaribo, protects nesting colonies of Scarlet Ibis, Wood Stork, herons, and egrets. Eastward lies the Wia-Wia reserve with its important sea-turtle nesting beaches and waterbird havens.

The two most exciting reserves are inland and are covered with high tropical rain forest and hill forest: Brownsberg and Raleigh Falls. Arrangements must be made with STINASU long in advance of your visit to either reserve.

The Brownsberg reserve is located in the hills to the west of the huge lake and Afobaka Dam, a 3-hour drive over dirt roads south of Paramaribo. The guest house at Brownsberg has a kitchen and a few bedrooms. Several roads lead into the tall dark forest, which can be very quiet, with occasional bird parties and rarities. Do inspect the many wide foot trails in the hope of finding a raiding army-ant swarm with their attendant woodcreepers and White-plumed and Rufous-throated Antbirds. White Bellbirds are frustratingly difficult to see except at the summit lookout point. Specialties of Brownsberg include Marail Guan, Dusky Parrot, Guianan Toucanet, 20 antbirds, White-throated Pewee, Opal-rumped and Red-billed Pied Tanagers, as well as a small monkey named the red-headed tamarin. This reserve can be visited by rental vehicles entirely, though roads may become impassable during rains.

The Voltzberg–Raleigh Falls reserve, located to the west, up the Coppename River, is even richer and wilder. If you can get here

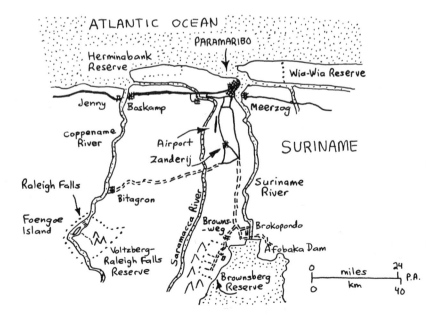

(either in a tour group or via your own arrangements with STINASU), you will take a four-hour bus trip to the village of Bitagron and then a four-hour dugout trip upriver to the reserve's guesthouse on Foengoe Island. It is also possible to charter light aircraft for the trip.

Foengoe Island offers outstanding birding. A little-used airstrip near the guesthouse is lined with tall trees offering nesting cavities for up to four species of macaws. Macaws are among the most spectacular of all birds, and it is becoming difficult to find them elsewhere due to the cage-bird trade and shooting. The Blue-and-yellow, Scarlet, Red-and-green, and Chestnut-fronted Macaws are all present and best seen early or late in the day. If you wander about the island you may see Hook-billed Kite, caracaras, Little Chachalaca, White-headed Piping-Guan, Caica and Red-fan Parrots, Straight-billed Hermit, Green-tailed Jacamar, toucans, three species of large woodpeckers, and Green Oropendola.

Hired guides take visitors across the river to the Mother's Falls trail. It is an hour's hike through the forest to an expanse of boulders below the falls where Blackish Nightjar, Pauraque, Black-collared Swallow, and herons are often seen.

Visitors with stamina may be able to organize a three-hour trek (each direction) to the 820-foot (250-m) granite dome of Voltzberg. It is best to take hammocks and stay overnight at the "rock." This area is full of primates, including red howler, weeper capuchin, and black spider monkey. Birds include Great Tinamou, Black Curassow, Gray-winged Trumpeter, a lek of the Guianan Cock-of-the-Rock, and the rare Sharpbill.

CHECKLIST

Great Tinamou	Louisiana Heron
Little Tinamou	Rufescent Tiger-Heron r
Variegated Tinamou	Least Bittern
Neotropic Cormorant r	Green Ibis r
Anhinga	Scarlet Ibis
Magnificent Frigatebird	Muscovy Duck r
Cocoi Heron	King Vulture
Capped Heron r	Black Vulture c
Green Heron c	Turkey Vulture c
Little Blue Heron c	Marsh Vulture
Cattle Heron c	Jungle Vulture c
Great Egret c	White-tailed Kite
Snowy Egret c	Swallow-tailed Kite c

Gray-headed Kite
Hook-billed Kite
Double-toothed Kite
Plumbeous Kite   c
Everglade Kite   c
Slender-billed Kite
White-tailed Hawk   r
Roadside Hawk   c
Short-tailed Hawk
Gray Hawk   c
White Hawk   c
Black-faced Hawk   r
Savanna Hawk   r
Great Black Hawk
Rufous Crab Hawk
Black-collared Hawk
Harpy Eagle   r
Black-and-white Hawk-Eagle   r
Ornate Hawk-Eagle
Black Hawk-Eagle
Long-winged Harrier
Osprey   W
Laughing Falcon
Lined Forest-Falcon
Black Caracara
Red-throated Caracara   c
Yellow-headed Caracara   c
Peregrine Falcon   r W
Bat Falcon   c
Black Curassow
Marail Guan
Little Chachalaca   c
Blue-throated Piping-Guan
Crested Bobwhite
Marbled Wood-Quail
Limpkin
Gray-winged Trumpeter
Gray-necked Wood-Rail
Ash-throated Crake   r
Yellow-breasted Crake   r
Gray-breasted Crake   r
Purple Gallinule
Azure Gallinule
Wattled Jacana   c
Gray Plover   W
Semipalmated Plover   c W
Collared Plover   r

Whimbrel   W
Lesser Yellowlegs   c W
Greater Yellowlegs   c W
Solitary Sandpiper   c W
Spotted Sandpiper   c W
Willet   W
Ruddy Turnstone   W
Short-billed Dowitcher   W
Common (Paraguayan) Snipe
Semipalmated Sandpiper   c W
Least Sandpiper   W
Laughing Gull   c W
Large-billed Tern   r
Gull-billed Tern   r W
Common Tern   W
Yellow-billed Tern
Little Tern   r W
Royal Tern   r W
Sandwich/Cayenne Tern
Black Skimmer
Scaled Pigeon
Pale-vented Pigeon   c
Plumbeous Pigeon   c
Common Ground-Dove   c
Plain-breasted Ground-Dove
Ruddy Ground-Dove   c
Blue Ground-Dove   r
White-tipped Dove   c
Gray-fronted Dove   c
Ruddy Quail-Dove
Blue-and-yellow Macaw
Scarlet Macaw
Red-and-green Macaw
Chestnut-fronted Macaw
Red-shouldered Macaw   r
Brown-throated Parakeet   c
Painted Parakeet   c
Green-rumped Parrotlet   c
Golden-winged Parakeet   c
Lilac-tailed Parrotlet
Black-headed Parrot
Caica Parrot
Blue-headed Parrot   c
Dusky Parrot
Orange-winged Parrot   c
Mealy Parrot
Red-fan Parrot   c

Squirrel Cuckoo   c
Black-bellied Cuckoo   r
Little Cuckoo   c
Greater Ani
Smooth-billed Ani   c
Striped Cuckoo
Spectacled Owl
Common Potoo
Short-tailed Nighthawk
Lesser Nighthawk
Common Pauraque   c
White-tailed Nightjar
Blackish Nightjar
Ladder-tailed Nightjar
Band-rumped Swift   c
Short-tailed Swift   c
Lesser Swallow-tailed Swift
Amazonian Palm-Swift   c
Rufous-breasted Hermit
Long-tailed Hermit   c
Straight-billed Hermit
Reddish Hermit   c
Little Hermit
Gray-breasted Sabrewing
White-necked Jacobin
Green-throated Mango
Black-throated Mango   c
Ruby Topaz   r
Tufted Coquette   r
Racquet-tailed Coquette   r
Blue-tailed Emerald
Common Woodnymph   c
Rufous-throated Sapphire   r
White-chinned Sapphire
White-tailed Goldenthroat
Green-tailed Goldenthroat
Glittering-throated Emerald   c
Plain-bellied Emerald
Crimson Topaz   r
Black-eared Fairy   c
Black-tailed Trogon
White-tailed Trogon   c
Collared Trogon
Black-throated Trogon
Violaceous Trogon   c
Ringed Kingfisher   c
Amazon Kingfisher   c

Green Kingfisher
Green-and-rufous Kingfisher
American Pygmy Kingfisher
Brown Jacamar   r
Paradise Jacamar
Yellow-billed Jacamar
Green-tailed Jacamar
Great Jacamar   r
White-necked Puffbird
Pied Puffbird
Spotted Puffbird   r
Collared Puffbird   r
White-chested Puffbird   r
Black Nunbird   c
Aerial Puffbird   c
Black-spotted Barbet   c
Black-necked Aracari   c
Green Aracari   c
Guianan Toucanet
Channel-billed Toucan
Red-billed Toucan   c
Golden-spangled Piculet
Arrowhead Piculet
Spot-breasted Flicker
Golden-olive Woodpecker   c
Yellow-throated Woodpecker   c
Golden-green Woodpecker
Chestnut Woodpecker
Waved Woodpecker
Cream-colored Woodpecker   r
Lineated Woodpecker   c
Yellow-tufted Woodpecker   c
Golden-collared Woodpecker   c
Blood-colored Woodpecker
Crimson-crested Woodpecker
Red-necked Woodpecker
Plain-brown Woodcreeper   c
Wedge-billed Woodcreeper   c
Barred Woodcreeper
Black-banded Woodcreeper
Straight-billed Woodcreeper   c
Buff-throated Woodcreeper   c
Chestnut-rumped Woodcreeper
Lineated Woodcreeper
Pale-breasted Spinetail   c
Plain-crowned Spinetail   c
Cabanis's Spinetail   r

Yellow-throated Spinetail   c
Ruddy Foliage-gleaner   r
Rufous-rumped Foliage-gleaner
Buff-throated Foliage-gleaner   r
Plain Xenops
Rufous-tailed Xenops   r
Fasciated Antshrike   c
Great Antshrike
Black-crested Antshrike
Barred Antshrike   c
Mouse-colored Antshrike   c
Slaty Antshrike
Amazonian Antshrike
Spot-winged Antshrike   r
Dusky-throated Antshrike
Cinereous Antshrike   c
Pygmy Antwren
Streaked Antwren
Rufous-bellied Antwren
Brown-bellied Antwren
White-flanked Antwren   c
Long-winged Antwren
Gray Antwren
Spot-tailed Antwren   r
Dot-winged Antwren
White-fringed Antwren   r
Gray Antbird
Dusky Antbird   c
White-browed Antbird   r
Warbling Antbird   r
Black-chinned Antbird   r
Black-headed Antbird   c
Silvered Antbird
Ferruginous-backed Antbird
Rufous-capped Ant-thrush
Black-faced Ant-thrush   r
White-plumed Antbird
Rufous-throated Antbird
Spot-backed Antbird
Scale-backed Antbird   r
Wing-banded Antbird   r
Thrush-like Antpitta   c
Spotted Antpitta   r
Chestnut-belted Gnateater   r
Guianan Red Cotinga   r
Spangled Cotinga
Pompadour Cotinga

Cinnamon Attila
Cinereous Mourner   r
Grayish Mourner
Screaming Piha   c
Pink-throated Becard   r
Cinereous Becard   c
White-winged Becard
Black-tailed Tityra   c
Black-crowned Tityra
Crimson Fruitcrow   r
Purple-throated Fruitcrow
Capuchinbird
Bare-necked Fruitcrow   r
White Bellbird
Guianan Cock-of-the-Rock   r
Crimson-hooded Manakin   r
Golden-headed Manakin   c
White-crowned Manakin
White-fronted Manakin   r
White-throated Manakin   r
White-bearded Manakin
Tiny Tyrant-Manakin   r
Wing-barred Manakin
Thrush-like Manakin
Sirystes   r
Long-tailed Tyrant
Pied Water-Tyrant   c
White-headed Marsh-Tyrant   c
Fork-tailed Flycatcher   M
Tropical Kingbird   c
Gray Kingbird
Variegated Flycatcher
Piratic Flycatcher   c
Boat-billed Flycatcher   c
White-ringed Flycatcher
Rusty-margined Flycatcher   c
Sulfury Flycatcher   r
Great Kiskadee   c
Lesser Kiskadee   c
Brown-crested Flycatcher   c
Swainson's Flycatcher   M
Dusky-capped Flycatcher
Cliff Flycatcher   r
Tropical Pewee   r
White-throated Pewee   c
Whiskered Flycatcher   c
Bran-colored Flycatcher

White-crested Spadebill   r
Cinnamon-crested Spadebill   r
Gray-crowned Flycatcher   r
Yellow-breasted Flycatcher   c
Yellow-olive Flycatcher
Painted Tody-Flycatcher
Common Tody-Flycatcher   c
Spotted Tody-Flycatcher   c
Double-banded Pygmy-Tyrant   r
Helmeted Pygmy-Tyrant
Short-tailed Pygmy-Tyrant   r
Pale-tipped Tyrannulet
Yellow-bellied Elaenia   c
Plain-crested Elaenia   c
Rufous-crowned Elaenia   r
Forest Elaenia
Mouse-colored Tyrannulet
Southern Beardless Tyrannulet
Slender-footed Tyrannulet
Yellow-crowned Tyrannulet   r
White-lored Tyrannulet   r
Ochre-bellied Flycatcher   r
McConnell's Flycatcher   c
Ringed Antpipit   r
Sharpbill   r
White-winged Swallow   c
Brown-chested Martin   c
Gray-breasted Martin   c
White-banded Swallow   c
Black-collared Swallow
Rough-winged Swallow   c
Barn Swallow   c W
Cayenne Jay
Coraya Wren   c
Buff-breasted Wren   c
House Wren   c
White-breasted Wood-Wren   c
Wing-banded Wren   r
Musician Wren   r
Tropical Mockingbird   c
Black-capped Mockingthrush   c
Pale-breasted Thrush   c
Cocoa Thrush
Bare-eyed Thrush
White-necked Thrush   c
Guianan Gnatcatcher   r
Tropical Gnatcatcher   c

Long-billed Gnatwren
Collared Gnatwren   r
Rufous-browed Peppershrike
Red-eyed Vireo   c
Lemon-chested Greenlet
Ashy-headed Greenlet   c
Crested Oropendola   c
Green Oropendola   c
Yellow-rumped Cacique   c
Red-rumped Cacique
Giant Cowbird   c
Shiny Cowbird
Carib Grackle
Epaulet Oriole
Moriche Oriole
Yellow Oriole
Yellow-hooded Blackbird   c
Red-breasted Blackbird   c
Eastern Meadowlark   r
Tropical Parula   c
Yellow Warbler   W
Northern Waterthrush   W
Masked Yellowthroat
Rose-breasted Chat   r
American Redstart   r W
Bananaquit   c
Bicolored Conebill
Purple Honeycreeper   c
Red-legged Honeycreeper   c
Blue Dacnis   c
Black-faced Dacnis
Green Honeycreeper   c
Swallow-Tanager
White-vented Euphonia
Finsch's Euphonia
Violaceous Euphonia   c
Golden-sided Euphonia
Golden-bellied Euphonia   r
Opal-rumped Tanager
Paradise Tanager
Spotted Tanager   r
Turquoise Tanager   c
Bay-headed Tanager   c
Burnished-buff Tanager   c
Blue-gray Tanager   c
Palm Tanager   c
Silver-beaked Tanager   c

Hepatic Tanager   r
Blue-backed Tanager   r
Fulvous Shrike-Tanager
White-lined Tanager   c
Flame-crested Tanager
Fulvous-crested Tanager   c
Red-shouldered Tanager
Hooded Tanager
Guira Tanager
Yellow-backed Tanager
Red-billed Pied Tanager
Magpie Tanager   r
Black-faced Tanager
Buff-throated Saltator   c

Grayish Saltator   c
Yellow-green Grosbeak   c
Slate-colored Grosbeak
Blue-black Grosbeak
Variable Seedeater   c
Lined Seedeater   r
Chestnut-bellied Seedeater
Ruddy-breasted Seedeater   c
Lesser Seed-Finch   r
Blue-black Grassquit   c
Pectoral Sparrow   r
Grassland Sparrow
Wedge-tailed Grass-Finch   r

49
Iceland

ICELAND IS AN EXCELLENT COUNTRY to see many Arctic birds in great abundance. The Keflavik airport near Reykjavik has daily flights to New York, London, and Scandinavia. A large, beautiful country with a low population density, Iceland has many tame birds and excellent photography, although photographing eagles, falcons, Snowy Owls, and Arctic Auklets at their nests is prohibited without a special permit. There are many vehicles and hotels available around the country. Costs for these services are high.

About 75 species of birds breed in Iceland, not a high number, but many of them are present in great numbers and include a number otherwise difficult to find in Europe or North America. Arctic Tern, ducks, geese, and occasionally Whooper Swan can be seen on the lake in the center of the capital.

The best birding is found around Lake Myvatn in the northeast, the Snaefellsnes Peninsula in the west, and the Vestmann Islands to the south.

Lake Myvatn is a waterfowl nursery without equal in Europe. Along the indented shoreline of lava flows, breed numbers of Greater Scaup, Tufted Duck, Eurasian Wigeon, Northern Shoveler, and Green-winged Teal. Along the Laxa River to the north the visitor should see the exciting Harlequin Duck and Barrow's Goldeneye. Other common birds in the area are loons, grebes, Little Phalarope, Arctic Tern, and Whooper Swan. Gyrfalcon and Merlin course the open moorlands. Many geese and waders can be seen here and at Sandvatn (to the northwest) during passage. There is a choice of accommodation, mostly simple but clean. However, midges and flies can be a real problem, particularly at Lake Myvatn.

The Vestmann Islands have suffered from the recent eruption of the volcano Helgafell. Visitors able to overcome transport and lodging problems may find the cliffs alive again with Northern Fulmar, Black-legged Kittiwake, Atlantic Puffin, and other alcids.

A huge Northern Gannet colony is to be found on Eldey off the Reykjanes Peninsula near Reykjavik.

Parasitic Jaegers are common and the Great Skua occurs in the

southeast coastal district. The rare White-tailed Sea-Eagle occurs in the northwest, while Rock Ptarmigan and Pink-footed Goose breed in the highlands. Common Eider, European Golden Plover, Whimbrel, Common Snipe, Common Redshank, and Common Oystercatcher are all widespread in the summer.

CHECKLIST

Common Loon   c
Red-throated Loon   c
Horned Grebe   c
Northern Fulmar
Manx Shearwater
European Storm-Petrel
Leach's Storm-Petrel
Northern Gannet   c
Great Cormorant
Shag
Gray Heron   r W
Whooper Swan
Brent Goose   M
Greylag Goose   S

Pink-footed Goose   S
White-fronted Goose   M
Mallard
Green-winged Teal
Gadwall   S
Eurasian Wigeon
American Wigeon   r S
Northern Pintail   S
Northern Shoveler   S
Northern Pochard   r S
Tufted Duck
Greater Scaup   c S
Common Eider   c
Black Scoter   c

248

Harlequin Duck   c S
Long-tailed Duck   c
Barrow's Goldeneye   c S
Goosander
Red-breasted Merganser
White-tailed Sea-Eagle   r
Gyrfalcon
Merlin
Rock Ptarmigan
Water Rail
Common Coot   S
Common Oystercatcher
Greater Ringed Plover   S
European Golden Plover   c S
Ruddy Turnstone   M
Purple Sandpiper
Red Knot   M
Dunlin   c S
Sanderling   M
Common Redshank
Black-tailed Godwit   S
Whimbrel   c S
Common Snipe   c S
Red Phalarope   S
Little Phalarope   c S
Great Skua
Parasitic Jaeger   c S
Black-headed Gull

Lesser Black-backed Gull   S
Herring Gull
Iceland Gull   W
Glaucous Gull
Great Black-backed Gull
Mew Gull
Black-legged Kittiwake   S
Arctic Tern   S
Black Guillemot
Arctic Auklet
Razorbill
Common Murre
Thick-billed Murre
Atlantic Puffin
Snowy Owl
Short-eared Owl
Barn Swallow   S
White Wagtail   c S
Northern Wren
Northern Wheatear   S
Fieldfare
Eurasian Blackbird   W
Redwing   W
Snow Bunting
Common Redpoll
House Sparrow
European Starling
Northern Raven

50

Shetland Islands,
United Kingdom

THE SHETLAND ISLES ARE NEARER BERGEN in Norway than Aberdeen on the Scottish mainland, a fact that helps to explain the pride and fervor with which the people maintain their Norse origins. The birds too are more akin to those of Scandinavia than to those of the rest of Britain, an important factor that brings many bird watchers to these island shores.

The Shetlands are a far-flung group extending for over 75 miles (120 km) from north to south, though only 19 of the hundred or more islands are inhabited. In winter they are a haven for Arctic trawlermen and birds alike, with Glaucous Gulls in the harbor and an outside chance of an Ivory Gull or Surf Scoter.

In late May and June, however, the islands are at their very best. Huge colonies of seabirds line the cliffs, while waders, Merlin, and skuas occupy the open moorlands. Much of Shetland consists of deep peat moors and impassable bogs that are short on animal life, but in the east there are green fields and fine pastures with a variety of birds. Transportation is easy by inter-island air services and ferries, and boats are numerous and well worth chartering. Each island is different, though the visitor would be well advised to concentrate his attentions on the major birding spots of Fair Isle, Fetlar, Unst, and the Out Skerries.

Fair Isle is a migration watch spot famous the world over for its remarkable ability to produce extreme rarities in late autumn. Visitors are welcome throughout the summer months, but book well in advance for autumn. Write to the Fair Isle Bird Observatory, 21 Regent Terrace, Edinburgh EH75BT (Tel 031-556 6042).

Fetlar, the green island, is a must for all visitors. It usually has Snowy Owl, Little Phalarope, Whimbrel, other waders and all the usual cliff-breeding seabirds. Try to see the northern cliffs from the sea by boat. Accommodation is available at a guest house (write to Mrs. Pattison, Fetlar, Shetland) and in other private houses.

Unst is the most northern and rugged of the islands. The great

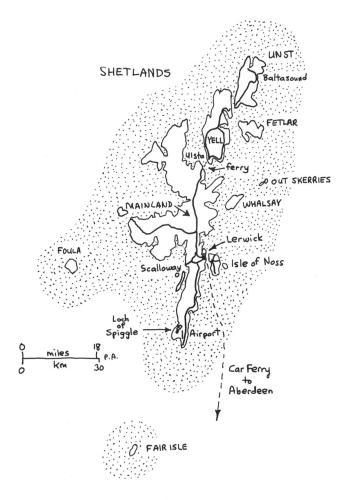

SHETLANDS

UNST
Baltasound

FETLAR

YELL

Ulsta

← ferry

OUT SKERRIES

MAINLAND

WHALSAY

← Lerwick

FOULA

Scalloway

Isle of Noss

Loch
of
Spiggle ⟶ Airport

miles 18
Km 30 P.A.

Car Ferry
to
Aberdeen

FAIR ISLE

promontory of Hermaness in the north is the headquarters of the Great Skua and there are seabirds galore on the cliffs including a fine gannetry. Two hotels are available and there is plenty of private accommodation.

The Out Skerries are another migration spot and can be particularly productive. The only accommodation is in private homes and transport is by charter boat. Two other fine general areas to bird are the Loch of Spiggle, just west of the airport on Mainland, and the Isle of Noss.

Due to the recent surge in oil-related business the costs and availability of services have made birding excursions difficult.

CHECKLIST

Red-throated Loon   c
Common Loon   W
Northern Fulmar   c
Manx Shearwater   S
European Storm-Petrel   S
Northern Gannet   c
Great Cormorant   c
Shag   c
Gray Heron   M
Whooper Swan   W
Common Shelduck   r
Green-winged Teal   c
Eurasian Wigeon
Northern Pintail   r
Northern Shoveler   r W
Northern Pochard   W
Tufted Duck
Greater Scaup   W
Common Eider   c
Black Scoter   c
White-winged Scoter   W
Common Goldeneye   W
Red-breasted Merganser   c
Peregrine Falcon   S
Merlin
Willow Ptarmigan (Red Grouse)
Common Quail   S
Water Rail   r W
Corn Crake   S
Common Gallinule
Common Coot
Common Oystercatcher
Greater Ringed Plover   S
European Golden Plover
Northern Lapwing
Ruddy Turnstone   W
Purple Sandpiper   W
Dunlin   c
Red Knot   M
Sanderling   M
Common Redshank
Common Sandpiper   S
Black-tailed Godwit   M

Eurasian Curlew
Whimbrel   S
Eurasian Woodcock   W
Common Snipe   c
Jack Snipe   r W
Little Phalarope   S
Great Skua   c S
Parasitic Jaeger   S
Black-headed Gull   c
Lesser Black-backed Gull   c S
Herring Gull   c
Iceland Gull   r W
Glaucous Gull   W
Great Black-backed Gull
Mew Gull   S
Black-legged Kittiwake   c S
Common Tern   S
Arctic Tern   c S
Black Guillemot
Arctic Auklet   W
Razorbill   c
Common Murre   c
Atlantic Puffin
Wood Pigeon   r
Rock Pigeon   c
Collared Turtle-Dove
Eurasian Cuckoo   S
Snowy Owl
Long-eared Owl   W
Short-eared Owl   r M
Common Swift   S
Eurasian Wryneck   r M
Great Spotted Woodpecker   r M
Northern Skylark
Barn Swallow   M
House Martin   M
Tree Pipit   M
Meadow Pipit
Water Pipit
White Wagtail   c M
Northern Wren
Barred Warbler   r M
Blackcap   M

Greater Whitethroat   M
Lesser Whitethroat   M
Willow Warbler   c M
Chiffchaff   M
Yellow-browed Warbler   r M
Goldcrest   W
Spotted Flycatcher   r M
Northern Wheatear   c S
Eurasian Redstart   M
European Robin   W
Fieldfare   W
Eurasian Blackbird
Redwing   W

Song Thrush
Corn Bunting
Reed Bunting   r S
Snow Bunting   W
Chaffinch   W
Brambling   M
Eurasian Siskin   r W
Twite   c
Common Redpoll   W
House Sparrow   c
European Starling
Eurasian Crow   c
Northern Raven   c

51
London, England

SOUTHEASTERN ENGLAND IS HOME to an intensively studied and loved avifauna. Many fine birding localities can be reached easily via public transport as well as with rental cars. Many visitors stop in London for quick business, shopping, or sightseeing trips and may be able to squeeze in a day or two of birding.

The many fine parks of London's West End such as Regent's, St. James', and Hyde Park plus Kensington Gardens have a good sample of British birds, and they are safe for strolling. The many ponds, woods, and lawns are host to exotic wildfowl as well as Tufted Duck, Common Gallinule, Black-headed Gull, Wood Pigeon, Song Thrush, Eurasian Blackbird, Dunnock, and tits.

Richmond Park on the southwest side of London is wilder, with red and fallow deer and a greater variety of woodland birds. Smew winter on the Stoke Newington Reservoirs in north London, off Lordship Road east of Manor House. Just west of Heathrow Airport are the Staines Reservoirs on B379 road. Stop at the pumping station and look for Great Crested Grebe and three species of wintering mergansers. Five miles (8 km) west of the Staines By-pass on A30 is a forest and lake area known as Virginia Water. Park just before the Wheatsheaf Hotel, and take the trail through the forest to the lake, looking for many woodland birds. Mandarin Duck, Great Crested Grebe, Hawfinch, and a variety of tits and warblers may be seen.

For those with a full day available we suggest a trip to the marshes of North Kent on the south side of the Thames estuary. Drive southeast on A2 until it becomes the M2, then turn off on A289 marked STROOD. A mile (1.6 km) later turn left onto B2000 and follow this to Cliffe. The entire area east from here to Yantlet Creek is pleasant for birding. Concentrate on the seawall along the Thames, watching for ducks in winter, waders on passage, and a good collection of breeding birds in summer.

The Minsmere reserve near Ipswich is famous for Black-capped Avocets, Marsh Harrier, Bearded Reedling, and other marsh birds. Permits must be obtained in advance from the Royal Society for the Protection of Birds, The Lodge, Sandy, Bedfordshire, SG19.

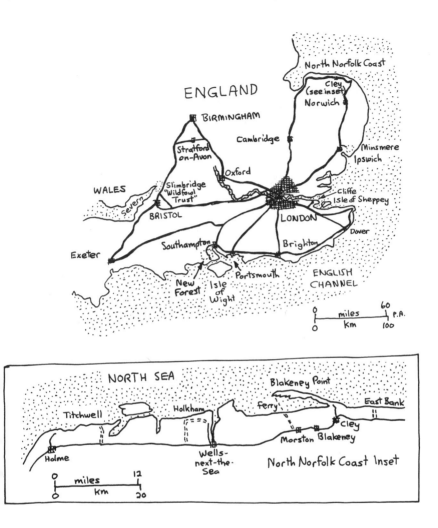

ENGLAND

BIRMINGHAM

Cambridge

North Norfolk Coast

Cley (see inset)

Norwich

Stratford on-Avon

Oxford

Minsmere

Ipswich

WALES

Slimbridge "Wildfowl Trust"

Severn

BRISTOL

Cliffe

Isle of Sheppey

LONDON

Exeter

Southampton

Brighton

Dover

New Forest

Isle of Wight

Portsmouth

ENGLISH CHANNEL

```
0          miles      60   P.A.
0          Km         100
```

NORTH SEA

Blakeney Point

East Bank

Titchwell

Holkham

Ferry

Cley

Morston Blakeney

Holme

Wells-next-the-Sea

North Norfolk Coast Inset

```
0     miles     12
0     Km        20
```

Farther to the west those with more time should visit the New Forest west of Southampton and the Severn Wildfowl Trust in Slimbridge, north of Bristol.

Along the coast of north Norfolk, three hours' drive northeast of London, stretches one of the prime birding areas of Europe. For thirty-odd miles there are marshes and saltings thronged with birds and birders alike. At the eastern end of this great wetland lies the picturesque village of Cley — the "Mecca" of British birders. The visitor would be well advised to cover the whole area. In summer the tern colonies of Blakeney Point can be studied from boats from Mor-

255

ston Quay. In winter he will enjoy the geese in Wells Harbor and the wildfowl on all the marshes; but in spring and autumn he should head for the East Bank at Cley.

The East Bank, lying to the east of Cley village, has a convenient car park. It runs between the coastal road and the beach and gives excellent views over Arnold's Marsh to the east and the Norfolk Naturalists' Trust Reserve to the west. This reserve is open to the public on a permit system. Here waders and terns abound, and the ability of this area to pick up rare migrants is quite uncanny. Eurasian Spoonbill and harriers may be easy to spot, and the waders have included almost every species to be seen in Britain. During these passage periods rare birds regularly occur in the village gardens, though most watchers head out to Blakeney Point when there is the slightest evidence of a "fall." They also inspect the pine woods at Holkham, the marshes of the Royal Society for the Protection of Birds reserve at Titchwell, and the marshes at Weybourne.

Since this is a migration spot it is often difficult to predict what will turn up, though in summer Bearded Reedling, Eurasian Bittern, Ruff, and Black-tailed Godwit may be seen.

Most areas are of open access, while a permit to visit the Cley marshes may be secured from either Norfolk Naturalists' Trust, 4 The Close, Norwich, NOR 16P, or through the warden in the village. "The George" in Cley is the Saturday evening haunt of all birders and the source of much information and merriment. It is a good place to stay, but book well in advance. Other accommodation is available at several small (and nice) hotels along the coast.

CHECKLIST

Common Loon	r W	Eurasian Spoonbill	r M
Red-throated Loon	W	Canada Goose	
Black-throated Loon	W	Brent Goose	W
Little Dabchick		Mute Swan	c
Black-necked Grebe	W	Common Shelduck	c
Horned Grebe	W	Egyptian Goose	
Red-necked Grebe	r W	Mallard	c
Great Crested Grebe	c	Green-winged Teal	c
Northern Fulmar	c	Gadwall	
Northern Gannet	c W	Eurasian Wigeon	c W
Great Cormorant	W	Northern Pintail	c W
Shag		Garganey	r S
Eurasian Bittern		Northern Shoveler	
Gray Heron	c	Northern Pochard	c

Tufted Duck   c
Greater Scaup   W
Mandarin Duck
Common Eider   W
Black Scoter   W
White-winged Scoter   W
Long-tailed Duck   W
Common Goldeneye   W
Smew   W
Red-breasted Merganser   W
Goosander   W
Eurasian Sparrowhawk   r
Common Buzzard   r M
Northern Harrier   W
Montagu's Harrier   r S
Marsh Harrier   r S
Merlin   M
Common Kestrel   c
Red-legged Partridge
Gray Partridge
Common Pheasant
Water Rail   c
Common Gallinule   c
Common Coot   c
Common Oystercatcher   c
Greater Ringed Plover
Little Ringed Plover   S
European Golden Plover   c W
Gray Plover   W
Northern Lapwing   c
Ruddy Turnstone   W
Little Stint   M
Temminck's Stint   r M
Dunlin   c W
Curlew Sandpiper   M
Red Knot   M
Sanderling   M
Ruff   c M, r S
Spotted Redshank   c M, r W
Common Redshank   c W
Common Greenshank   M
Green Sandpiper   W
Wood Sandpiper   M
Common Sandpiper   W
Black-tailed Godwit   W, r S
Bar-tailed Godwit   c W
Eurasian Curlew   W

Whimbrel   M
Eurasian Woodcock
Common Snipe
Jack Snipe   r W
Black-capped Avocet   r S
Parasitic Jaeger   M
Little Gull   M
Black-headed Gull   c
Lesser Black-backed Gull   c M
Herring Gull   c W
Glaucous Gull   r W
Great Black-backed Gull   c W
Mew Gull   c W
Black-legged Kittiwake   W
Black Tern   M
Sandwich Tern   c S
Common Tern   c S
Arctic Tern   c S
Little Tern   c S
Wood Pigeon   c
Stock Pigeon
Rock Pigeon   c
Collared Turtle-Dove   c
European Turtle-Dove
Eurasian Cuckoo   S
Barn Owl   r
Short-eared Owl
Little Owl
Tawny Owl   c
Common Swift   c S
Eurasian Kingfisher
Eurasian Wryneck   M
European Green Woodpecker
Great Spotted Woodpecker
Lesser Spotted Woodpecker   r
Horned Lark   W
Wood Lark   r
Northern Skylark
Sand Martin   S
Barn Swallow   S
House Martin   c S
Richard's Pipit   r M
Tree Pipit   S
Meadow Pipit   c
Yellow Wagtail   c S
Gray Wagtail
White Wagtail   c

Red-backed Shrike   r S
Great Gray Shrike   W
Bohemian Waxwing   r W
Northern Wren   c
Dunnock   c
Sedge Warbler   c S
European Reed-Warbler   c S
Icterine Warbler   r M
Barred Warbler   r M
Garden Warbler   S
Blackcap   S
Greater Whitethroat   c S
Lesser Whitethroat   r S
Willow Warbler   c S
Chiffchaff   c S
Wood Warbler   S
Yellow-browed Warbler   r M
Goldcrest
Pied Flycatcher   M
Spotted Flycatcher   S
Whinchat   M
Stonechat
Northern Wheatear   M
Black Redstart   S
Eurasian Redstart   S
European Robin   c
Nightingale   S
Bluethroat   r M
Fieldfare   c W
Eurasian Blackbird   c
Redwing   c W

Song Thrush   c
Mistle Thrush   c
Long-tailed Tit
Marsh Tit   c
Willow Tit
Coal Tit   c
Blue Tit   c
Great Tit   c
Eurasian Nuthatch   c
Northern Treecreeper
Corn Bunting   c
Yellowhammer   c
Cirl Bunting   r
Reed Bunting   c
Chaffinch   c
Brambling   W
Eurasian Greenfinch   c
Eurasian Siskin   W
Eurasian Goldfinch   c
Linnet   c
Common Redpoll
Eurasian Bullfinch
Hawfinch   r
House Sparrow   c
Tree Sparrow
European Starling   c
Eurasian Jay   c
Black-billed Magpie   c
Western Jackdaw   c
Rook   c
Eurasian Crow   c

52
Amsterdam, Holland

QUAINT OLD CANALS, the cultural charm of Amsterdam, and the international airport make the Dutch capital one of the tourist centers of Europe. Transport, car rental, hotels, and all the usual facilities are easily available, and within a short drive of the city, the visitor can be watching birds. Holland is primarily known as a major haunt of wetland birds. Species such as Eurasian Spoonbill, Purple Heron, Marsh Harrier, and Black Tern breed within 6.2 miles (10 km) of the city center.

Outstanding is the reserve of Naardermeer, which is reached by turning right on the Amsterdam–Amersfoort road 1.8 miles (3 km) after crossing the River Vecht. Here there is a viaduct, but after climbing the hill turn right, away from Muiderberg. After 0.6 miles (1 km) take a small road to the right to the warden's house. Boat trips should be booked in advance with Vereniging tot Behoud van Natuurmonumenten in Nederland, Herengradt 540, Amsterdam-C (phone 020246212). This superb reed-fringed lake is the home of Eurasian Spoonbill and Purple Heron, both scarce species in northern Europe, but there are hosts of other birds here as well.

Zuidelijk Flevoland, as well as the other polders in the former Zuiderzee, is a superb area. As each polder dries out part of the newly formed land is preserved as nature reserves while the rest is turned to agriculture. European Dotterel breed here at sea level. During construction virtually the whole polder is one gigantic wetland, full of birds. Oost Flevoland is now complete, Zuid Flevoland was drained in 1968, but still is being worked, and Markerwaard is in process of damming. All should be explored. The forests north of Arnhem are worth exploring for passerines and Black Woodpecker. Enter Hoge Veluwe at Otterlo or Hoenderloo.

South of Amsterdam is shallow Lake Niewkoop, a reed-fringed water that is best at its southwest corner where Little Bittern and Purple Heron are specialties. Northwest of the city is the reserve of Westzaan with its Ruff and Black-tailed Godwit. Both areas are nice and easy day trips.

Texel, pronounced "Tessel," is a small, low-lying island and the

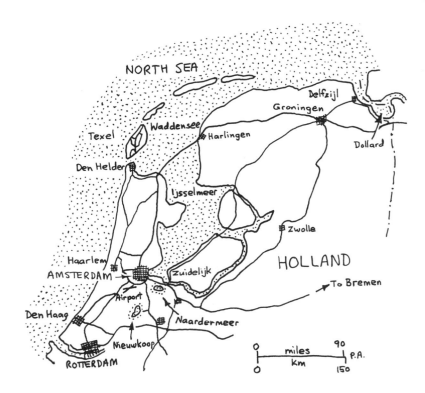

most southerly of the Friesian chain. There are 19 small bird reserves on this island, which is 10 miles (16 km) long. Most of the reserves are situated among the dunes of the seaward coast, and even the casual visitor should make sure that he sees one of them. The most famous reserve is Muy, which consists of a well-reeded lake with islands on which Eurasian Spoonbill breed. Harriers and warblers are the other attractions. The Geul Reserve in the south also holds Eurasian Spoonbill, along with Black-capped Avocet, Black-tailed Godwit, harriers, and Long-eared Owl. Slufter Creek has almost every European shorebird present at some time during the year. Black-capped Avocet, terns, and Snowy Plover all breed here.

In the heart of the island the splashy meadows of the Waalenburg attract vast hordes of wildfowl in winter. As they dry out, Ruff and Black-tailed Godwit move in to breed. A fine area and a great contrast to the coast. The island's woodland areas at Dennen, south of De Koog, are host to European Golden Oriole, Icterine Warbler, European Sparrowhawk, and Eurasian Woodcock.

Most of the Texel reserves can be visited only with permission. The Waalenburg area is strictly out of bounds, but can be well seen from the surrounding roads. For permits apply well in advance to Vereniging tot Behoud van Natuurmonumenten in Nederland, Herengracht 540, Amsterdam-C. Some permits can be obtained on the spot from the warden and your hotel will know his current address. This is an ideal area to do without a car, as one can take trains from Amsterdam to Denhelder, then a short ferry ride, and rent a bicycle for a few days.

Along the Waddensee coastline there are many outstanding bird haunts. The Dollard, at the mouth of the Ems on the Netherlands-Germany border, is the only nearby large area of fine particle silt remaining along the Waddensee. That it now faces enclosure and drainage together with industrial and marine development is a tragedy that must be avoided.

Geese are numerous in winter and include over 40 percent of the total Dutch population of Bean Goose. Greylags and White-fronts are abundant, and the air echoes to their calls. Flocks of surface-feeding duck are huge, while waders must be seen to be believed.

In an area so rich, most of the other birds of the tide lines of northern Europe can be found. Access to this borderland is via Groningen on Route 89 to Delfzijl, then southeastward on minor roads to Termunten. Tracks lead to Punt Van Reide and other vantage points. Write to Landelijke Vereniging tot Behoud van de Waddensee, Postbus 90, Harlingen, Netherlands, and express your support for the conservation of this unique area.

CHECKLIST

Red-throated Loon W	Bean Goose W
Black-throated Loon W	Pink-footed Goose c W
Little Dabchick	Mute Swan
Black-necked Grebe	Whooper Swan r W
Red-necked Grebe	Bewick's Swan W
Great Crested Grebe	Common Shelduck c
Northern Gannet W	Mallard c
Great Cormorant	Green-winged Teal c
Eurasian Bittern	Gadwall c
Little Bittern c S	Eurasian Wigeon c W
Gray Heron c	Northern Pintail
Purple Heron S	Garganey c S
White Stork r S	Northern Shoveler c
Eurasian Spoonbill S	Red-crested Pochard
Barnacle Goose W	Northern Pochard c
Brent Goose c W	Tufted Duck c
Greylag Goose c W	Greater Scaup W
White-fronted Goose c W	Common Eider

Black Scoter   W
White-winged Scoter   W
Common Goldeneye   W
Smew   W
Red-breasted Merganser   W
Goosander   W
Northern Goshawk   r
Eurasian Sparrowhawk
Common Buzzard
Northern Harrier   W
Montagu's Harrier   S
Marsh Harrier
European Hobby   S
Common Kestrel   c
Water Rail
Spotted Crake   S
Common Gallinule
Common Coot
Common Oystercatcher   c
Greater Ringed Plover   c
Little Ringed Plover   c S
Snowy Plover   S
European Golden Plover   c W
Gray Plover   W
European Dotterel   S
Northern Lapwing   c
Ruddy Turnstone   W
Little Stint   c M
Temminck's Stint   M
Dunlin   c W
Curlew Sandpiper   c M
Red Knot   c W
Sanderling   W
Ruff   c
Spotted Redshank   W
Common Redshank   c
Common Greenshank   c M
Green Sandpiper   c M
Wood Sandpiper   c M
Common Sandpiper   c M
Black-tailed Godwit   c S
Bar-tailed Godwit   W
Eurasian Curlew   c
Whimbrel   M
Eurasian Woodcock
Common Snipe
Great Snipe   r M

Jack Snipe   r W
Black-capped Avocet   c
Black-headed Gull   c
Lesser Black-backed Gull   S
Herring Gull   c
Great Black-backed Gull
Mew Gull   c
Black-legged Kittiwake   W
Black Tern   c S
Gull-billed Tern   M
Caspian Tern   M
Sandwich Tern   M
Common Tern   c S
Arctic Tern   S
Little Tern   S
Razorbill   W
Common Murre   W
Wood Pigeon   c
Stock Pigeon
Collared Turtle-Dove
European Turtle-Dove   S
Eurasian Cuckoo   c S
Barn Owl
Long-eared Owl
Short-eared Owl
Little Owl
Tawny Owl
Common Swift   S
Eurasian Kingfisher
European Green Woodpecker
Black Woodpecker
Great Spotted Woodpecker
Lesser Spotted Woodpecker
Crested Lark   c
Wood Lark
Northern Skylark   c
Sand Martin   c S
Barn Swallow   c S
House Martin   c S
Tree Pipit   c S
Meadow Pipit   c
Water Pipit   W
Yellow Wagtail   c S
White Wagtail   c
Red-backed Shrike   S
Great Gray Shrike   W
Northern Wren   c

Dunnock
Savi's Warbler   S
Western Grasshopper-Warbler   S
Sedge Warbler   c S
Marsh Warbler   S
European Reed-Warbler   c S
Great Reed-Warbler   S
Icterine Warbler   S
Garden Warbler   S
Blackcap   S
Greater Whitethroat   S
Lesser Whitethroat   c S
Willow Warbler   c S
Chiffchaff   c S
Wood Warbler   S
Goldcrest   c
Firecrest
Pied Flycatcher   M
Spotted Flycatcher   S
Whinchat
Stonechat   c S
Northern Wheatear   c S
Black Redstart   S
Eurasian Redstart   S
European Robin   c
Nightingale   S
Fieldfare   c W
Ring Thrush   W
Eurasian Blackbird   c
Redwing   c W
Song Thrush   c
Mistle Thrush

Bearded Reedling   r
Marsh Tit
Willow Tit
Crested Tit
Coal Tit   c
Blue Tit   c
Great Tit   c
Eurasian Nuthatch
Short-toed Treecreeper
Corn Bunting
Yellowhammer
Reed Bunting
Lapland Longspur   W
Snow Bunting   W
Chaffinch   c
Brambling   W
European Serin
Eurasian Greenfinch   c
Eurasian Siskin
Eurasian Goldfinch
Linnet   c
Common Redpoll
House Sparrow   c
Tree Sparrow
Eurasian Starling   c
Eurasian Golden Oriole   S
Eurasian Jay
Black-billed Magpie
Western Jackdaw   c
Rook
Eurasian Crow

53
Denmark and
Southern Sweden

THE FINEST BIRDING IN DENMARK is along the west coast from Esbjerg to Ålborg. Starting in the south there is the migration watchpoint of Blåvands Huk, a sand-dune area with a lighthouse and bird observatory. Eastward lies the Ho Bugt, a fine estuary with a regular post-breeding flock of Black-capped Avocet and the occasional Broad-billed Sandpiper and European Crane. Moving northward up the coast is the shallow inlet of Ringkobing Fjord with its bird sanctuary of Tipperne (see the warden for permission to enter). Wildfowl are numerous in winter, while Black-capped Avocet, Ruff, and Black-tailed Godwit breed along with Sandwich and Gull-billed Terns. The next area to the north is Stadil Fjord and beyond that Nissum Fjord, a major wintering ground of Brent Geese. Both areas hold passage and breeding waders, terns, and wildfowl in profusion in the late autumn when the area is a major staging post on the North Sea–Atlantic flyway.

Across the top of Denmark runs the huge Limfjorden, a maze of waterways, lakes, islands, and marshes. The whole area is worthy of attention, but most visitors start at the fine freshwater marsh at Vejlerne. Here, in the breeding season, visitors may see Black-necked Grebe, Eurasian Bittern, Eurasian Spoonbill (rarely), Marsh Harrier, Black-tailed Godwit, Ruff, Little Gull, and Gull-billed and Black Terns. As there is no admission to the reserve, visitors must view the area from the new road east of Östlös, from the road between Tistèd and Ålborg, and from a rough road between the main fjord and Österild Fjord.

The southernmost tip of Sweden near Falsterbo is a superb autumn migratory bird concentration point. Take the ferry from Copenhagen to Malmö and drive south. Immense numbers of passerines and raptors are features.

Out in the Baltic, south of Stockholm, are the two islands of Öland and Gotland. These islands are superb for both breeding and migrant birds, attracting many Scandinavian birders. Öland can be reached via a new bridge from Kalmar, while Gotland is connected with eastern Sweden via ferries.

South-central Sweden is more or less half water and half land. Roads twist this way and that across the landscape, and views of water and forests appear at every turn. Forest birds can be seen throughout the area, even in the environs of Stockholm itself. Visitors usually concentrate at the wetland sites with nearby forests. The nearest spot is Lake Hjälstaviken, some 37.5 miles (60 km) west of Stockholm along the E18. This lake, with its growth of reeds and sedges, is noted for Horned Grebe, Eurasian Bittern, Water Rail, Spotted Crake, Marsh Harrier, Eurasian Honey-Buzzard, Osprey, Icterine Warbler, and Red-backed Shrike. Waders are numerous on passage, and September brings Bluethroat and Red-throated Pipit. There is a car park and a yellow-marked footpath. Kvismaren, located to the southeast of Örebro, near Norrbyås, has huge reed beds, some open water, and a canal. There is a fine parking place on the north side of the bridge over Kvismare Kanal, 2 miles (3.2 km) southwest of Norrbyås, with nearby paths to west and east along the wetlands. The bird station, Kvismare Fågelstation, is located a half mile (1 km) southeast of

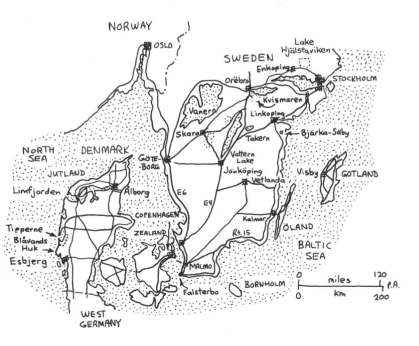

Norrbyäs. Breeding birds include Horned Grebe, Eurasian Bittern, ducks, Marsh Harrier, European Crane, Spotted Crake, Water Rail, Black-tailed Godwit, Short-eared Owl, Western Grasshopper-Warbler, and, in some years, Little and Baillon's Crakes and River Warbler. Nearby woods hold Eurasian Honey-Buzzard, European Hobby, Icterine Warbler, and Eurasian Wryneck. In the surrounding fields look for Ortolan Bunting and Common Quail. In winter the area is noted for Golden Eagle and Northern Goshawk.

There are two great spectacles awaiting visitors in late March and April. The annual gathering of European Cranes takes place on fields between Skara and Falköping along route 47, about 55 miles (88 km) northwest of Jönköping. Thousands of these great birds await the thaw of their Arctic breeding grounds while dancing and displaying with abandon. Visitors (including photographers) must stick to the road and car parks at this season. This spectacle takes place west of the reedy lake known as Hornborgasjön.

Östen, north-northeast of Hornborgasjön, is another reedy lake with noted concentrations of geese and swans in spring. In late March and April again, several thousand Whooper Swan and Bean Goose (also Greylag, White-fronted, and Barnacle) mix with even larger numbers of duck. This small lake can be reached by going east 16 miles (26 km) from Skara to Skövde, thence northward to Odensaker. There is a minor dirt road, 1300 feet (400 m) short of the church in Odensaker, which leads to Östen lake. The birds can be seen from the bird observation tower at the lake.

CHECKLIST

Black-throated Loon	Whooper Swan W
Little Dabchick S	Bewick's Swan M
Black-necked Grebe S	Common Shelduck
Great Crested Grebe c	Mallard c
Great Cormorant c	Green-winged Teal
Eurasian Bittern r S	Gadwall r S
Gray Heron c	Eurasian Wigeon
White Stork r S	Northern Pintail S
Canada Goose	Garganey S
Barnacle Goose W	Northern Shoveler
Brent Goose c W	Northern Pochard
Greylag Goose c	Tufted Duck c
White-fronted Goose W	Common Eider c
Bean Goose W	Black Scoter W
Pink-footed Goose W	White-winged Scoter W
Mute Swan	Long-tailed Duck W

Common Goldeneye
Smew W
Red-breasted Merganser
Goosander
Osprey S
Eurasian Honey-Buzzard S
White-tailed Sea-Eagle r
Northern Goshawk
Eurasian Sparrowhawk
Rough-legged Buzzard W
Common Buzzard
Golden Eagle r W
Greater Spotted Eagle r M
Northern Harrier
Montagu's Harrier S
Marsh Harrier c S
Peregrine Falcon
European Hobby S
Merlin
Common Kestrel
Hazel Grouse
Black Grouse
Capercaillie r
Gray Partridge
Common Quail r S
Common Pheasant
European Crane M, S
Water Rail
Little Crake r S
Baillon's Crake r S
Spotted Crake S
Corn Crake S
Common Gallinule
Common Coot
Common Oystercatcher c
Greater Ringed Plover c S
Little Ringed Plover S
Snowy Plover S
European Golden Plover
Gray Plover M
Northern Lapwing c
Ruddy Turnstone
Little Stint M
Temminck's Stint M
Purple Sandpiper W
Dunlin W
Curlew Sandpiper M

Red Knot M
Sanderling M
Broad-billed Sandpiper r M
Ruff S
Spotted Redshank M
Common Redshank S
Common Greenshank M
Green Sandpiper S
Wood Sandpiper S
Common Sandpiper S
Black-tailed Godwit S
Bar-tailed Godwit M
Eurasian Curlew S
Whimbrel M
Eurasian Woodcock
Common Snipe
Black-capped Avocet r S
Little Gull
Black-headed Gull c
Lesser Black-backed Gull c
Herring Gull c
Glaucous Gull r W
Great Black-backed Gull
Mew Gull c
Black Tern S
Gull-billed Tern S
Caspian Tern r S
Sandwich Tern S
Common Tern c S
Arctic Tern S
Little Tern S
Black Guillemot
Razorbill
Common Murre W
Wood Pigeon
Stock Pigeon S
Collared Turtle-Dove
Eurasian Cuckoo S
Barn Owl r
Long-eared Owl
Short-eared Owl
Tengmalm's Owl r
Eurasian Pygmy-Owl r
Tawny Owl
Eurasian Nightjar S
Common Swift c S
Eurasian Kingfisher

Eurasian Wryneck S
European Green Woodpecker
Black Woodpecker
Great Spotted Woodpecker
Middle Spotted Woodpecker r
Lesser Spotted Woodpecker
Horned Lark W
Crested Lark
Wood Lark
Northern Skylark
Sand Martin S
Barn Swallow c S
House Martin c S
Tree Pipit c S
Meadow Pipit
Red-throated Pipit M
Water Pipit
Yellow Wagtail S
Gray Wagtail r S
White Wagtail S
Red-backed Shrike S
Great Gray Shrike W
Bohemian Waxwing W
Eurasian Dipper r
Northern Wren
Dunnock
Western Grasshopper-Warbler S
Sedge Warbler S
Marsh Warbler S
European Reed-Warbler S
Great Reed-Warbler S
Icterine Warbler S
Barred Warbler r S
Garden Warbler c S
Blackcap S
Greater Whitethroat S
Lesser Whitethroat S
Willow Warbler c S
Chiffchaff M
Wood Warbler S
Goldcrest
Pied Flycatcher c S
Spotted Flycatcher c S
Whinchat S
Northern Wheatear c S
Eurasian Redstart S
European Robin

Thrush-Nightingale S
Bluethroat M
Fieldfare c S
Eurasian Blackbird c
Redwing
Song Thrush S
Mistle Thrush
Bearded Reedling r
Long-tailed Tit
Marsh Tit
Willow Tit
Crested Tit
Coal Tit
Blue Tit c
Great Tit c
Eurasian Nuthatch
Northern Treecreeper
Corn Bunting
Yellowhammer
Ortolan Bunting S
Reed Bunting
Lapland Longspur W
Snow Bunting W
Chaffinch
Brambling W
Eurasian Greenfinch c
Eurasian Siskin
Eurasian Goldfinch
Twite W
Linnet c S
Common Redpoll W
Scarlet Rosefinch r S
Pine Grosbeak W
Parrot Crossbill r
Red Crossbill
Eurasian Bullfinch
Hawfinch
House Sparrow
Tree Sparrow
European Starling c
Eurasian Jay
Black-billed Magpie c
Eurasian Nutcracker r
Western Jackdaw c
Rook
Eurasian Crow c
Northern Raven

54
Lapland, Norway, Sweden, and Finland

LAPLAND IS A VAST AREA. It is often many miles between birds, but some places stand out. There are vast fluctuations in numbers of lemmings (small arctic rodents) with far fewer birds during years with few lemmings.

The Varangerfjord is Europe's primary arctic birding area. Lying at 70°N, the huge fjord opens into the Arctic Sea to the east, and thus boasts a number of birds otherwise found only in prohibited areas of northern Russia and Siberia. Throughout its entire length the Varanger, with its adjacent marshes and fjells, is first class for birding, and interesting species can be found everywhere. Hosts of arctic breeding waders can be found, as well as a few species that breed nowhere else available to bird watchers. Steller's Eider, Bar-tailed Godwit in summer plumage, and occasional Yellow-billed Loon occur at Ekkeroy Island, east of Vadsö. A sandy causeway leads to the island village of Ekkeroy, where visitors will also see a huge colony of Black-legged Kittiwake, plus Red-throated Pipit and Lapland Longspur.

Vadsö itself is the center of the Varanger, and accommodation is available. The local garbage dump, on an island south of town, is noted for its gull flocks, which regularly include Glaucous and Iceland and have, on occasion, boasted Ross's and Ivory. Inland, the Kalkefjell is alive with many typical birds of the area including innumerable Temminck's Stint, Little Phalarope, Purple Sandpiper, and Longtailed Jaeger.

Vardö is an island town with frequent ferries from the mainland. Boats can be hired to circle a nearby island that has hundreds of Razorbill, both murres, and Black Guillemot. Varangerbotn, at the head of the fjord, has an interesting marsh that provides feeding for passage waders and has Arctic Warbler among the nearby birch scrub. Away to the south, the Pasvik Valley is surrounded on all sides by national boundaries and, in fact, virtually penetrates the Soviet Union. Birds include Bean Goose, Black-tailed Godwit, Yellow-

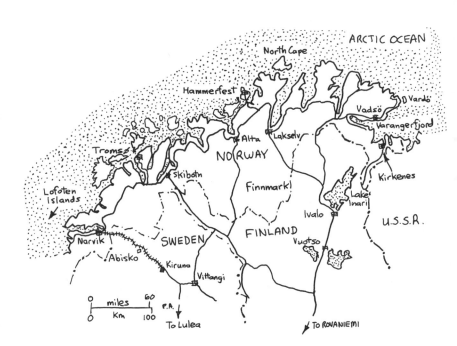

breasted Bunting, and Great Gray Owl. The airport is located near Kirkenes with daily flights from Oslo and other Norwegian cities. Unfortunately no flights connect the area with Finland and Sweden, and few rental cars are available in Lapland. Most visitors work the area in late June and early July, arriving overland via Finland. Accommodation is available at most of the main towns, particularly Vadsö.

Abisko, Sweden, with its dominant U-shaped valley, the Lapp Gate, is one of the most famous of Scandinavian bird localities. From far and near an international medley of bird watchers descend each summer in search of rare birds like Arctic Warbler and the peace that only lonely fjells can provide. Abisko lies on the tree line and, though the hillsides are covered with birch forest, the tops are open tundra and the valley floors have extensive marshland. This variety of habitat gives rise to an equally diverse avifauna.

Abisko cannot be reached by road. Instead, resort must be made to the railway that connects Kiruna, a Swedish town, to the Norwegian coast at Narvik. Kiruna's deposits of iron ore are moved in winter by this railway, when the Gulf of Bothnia is frozen solid. The visitor may fly from Stockholm to Kiruna or to Narvik, Norway, and take the train.

270

Having arrived, exploration is by foot, and rooms can be found at the excellent Abisko Turiststation. There is also accommodation at Abisko Lägerby, which is more modest in style and price. One should allow several days, up to a fortnight, for exploration.

On the hilltops, Rough-legged Buzzard, Long-tailed Jaeger, European Dotterel, Ring Thrush, and Snow Bunting can be found, while birch woodlands hold Bluethroat and Arctic Warbler. Waders in variety breed in the marshes, including such attractions as Little Phalarope, Temminck's Stint, and Whimbrel. There is a good chance of seeing Golden Eagle and a slight one of the White-tailed Sea-Eagle.

As in many other wild parts of Scandinavia, an excellent network of huts offers simple accommodation and cooking facilities. Thus the bird watcher can explore for considerable distances, using Abisko as a base and information center (write to the Abisko Turiststation, Abisko via Kiruna, for details and booking).

Northern Finland has a number of diverse areas to explore. Rental cars may be arranged at the cities of Oulu or Rovaniemi, where there are airports and hotels. The third largest lake in Finland lies in a superb region of open hills and pine-clad slopes in Lapland. Lake Inare is beautiful and has some fine birds, but it is not so remote as to be without facilities, transportation, and accommodation. There are, for instance, boats to be hired to facilitate exploration of the water, there is a network of dirt roads, and the Inari Tourist Hotel is set beside the rapids of the Juutuanjoke River. Arctic Warbler, Pine Grosbeak, Rustic Bunting, Siberian Jay, and European Crane are among the attractions.

CHECKLIST

Red-throated Loon S	Common Eider c
Black-throated Loon S	King Eider r
Yellow-billed Loon r	Steller's Eider
Great Cormorant	White-winged Scoter c
Shag	Long-tailed Duck
Greylag Goose r S	Common Goldeneye S
Lesser White-fronted Goose M	Smew S
Bean Goose S	Red-breasted Merganser c S
Whooper Swan S	Goosander r S
Mallard r S	Osprey r S
Green-winged Teal S	White-tailed Sea-Eagle r
Eurasian Wigeon S	Northern Goshawk s
Northern Pintail S	Eurasian Sparrowhawk r S
Greater Scaup	Rough-legged Buzzard c S

Northern Harrier r S
Gyrfalcon r
Peregrine Falcon r S
Merlin c S
Common Kestrel r S
Willow Ptarmigan
Rock Ptarmigan
Capercaillie
European Crane r S
Common Oystercatcher c S
Greater Ringed Plover c S
European Dotterel r S
European Golden Plover c S
Ruddy Turnstone S
Little Stint M
Temminck's Stint c S
Purple Sandpiper S
Dunlin S
Red Knot M
Sanderling M
Ruff S
Spotted Redshank S
Common Redshank c S
Common Greenshank S
Wood Sandpiper S
Common Sandpiper c S
Black-tailed Godwit S
Bar-tailed Godwit S
Eurasian Curlew r M
Whimbrel S
Common Snipe c S
Jack Snipe r S
Little Phalarope c S
Parasitic Jaeger c S
Long-tailed Jaeger c S
Black-headed Gull r S
Lesser Black-backed Gull r S
Herring Gull c
Glaucous Gull r
Great Black-backed Gull c S
Mew Gull c
Black-legged Kittiwake c S
Arctic Tern c S
Black Guillemot c
Arctic Auklet W
Razorbill c
Common Murre c

Thick-billed Murre
Atlantic Puffin c S
Eurasian Cuckoo S
Snowy Owl
Short-eared Owl
Tengmalm's Owl
Eurasian Pygmy-Owl
Northern Hawk-Owl r
Ural Owl
Great Gray Owl r
Common Swift r S
Great Spotted Woodpecker
Lesser Spotted Woodpecker
Northern Three-toed Woodpecker
Horned Lark S
Northern Skylark r S
Sand Martin S
Barn Swallow S
House Martin S
Tree Pipit c S
Meadow Pipit c S
Red-throated Pipit c S
Yellow Wagtail S
White Wagtail c S
Great Gray Shrike S
Bohemian Waxwing r
Eurasian Dipper r
Dunnock S
Sedge Warbler S
Garden Warbler r S
Willow Warbler c S
Arctic Warbler S
Goldcrest r S
Pied Flycatcher r S
Spotted Flycatcher r S
Northern Wheatear c S
Eurasian Redstart S
Bluethroat S
Fieldfare S
Ring Thrush S
Redwing S
Song Thrush S
Willow Tit
Siberian Tit
Great Tit S
Yellowhammer S
Little Bunting r S

Rustic Bunting   S
Yellow-breasted Bunting   r S
Reed Bunting   S
Lapland Longspur   S
Snow Bunting   S
Brambling   S
Eurasian Siskin   r S
Common Redpoll   c
Hoary Redpoll
Pine Grosbeak

Parrot Crossbill   r
Red Crossbill
Eurasian Bullfinch   r S
House Sparrow
European Starling   r S
Siberian Jay
Black-billed Magpie
Eurasian Crow
Northern Raven

55
Istanbul, Turkey

EVERY SPRING AND AUTUMN hundreds of thousands of soaring birds cross the narrow straits of the Bosphorus between Europe and Asia Minor. Dependent for movement on thermals of warm rising air over land, these birds are unable to make long sea crossings and concentrate instead at either end of the Mediterranean barrier. There are similar concentration points at Falsterbo in southern Sweden, where raptors pass from the Scandinavian peninsula to the European mainland via Denmark, and at Gibraltar, where they pass from Spain into Morocco. Though passage is sometimes heavier in Sweden, the Bosphorus has a reputation for producing the largest variety and most spectacular passage of all.

Different species have different passage periods. In late August peak numbers of Eurasian Honey-Buzzard pass through, while in September the air over Istanbul is full of White Storks. Later, Common Buzzard and Lesser Spotted Eagle are dominant. Mid-September is perhaps the best of all, with often a dozen different species in the air together. Eagles, vultures, kites, sparrowhawks, storks — all pass through at this time, and there is hardly a bird watcher who has not seen his or her first Levant Sparrowhawk at this site.

Though major attractions are in the air, the passage of Manx Shearwaters of the *yelkouan* race is heavy, and the gardens of Istanbul and the hills offer shelter to a wealth of birds that have migrated southeastward across Europe or southward along the western shore of the Black Sea. Icterine and Olivaceous Warblers, European Serin, and Eurasian Scops-Owl vie for attention among the numbers of Eurasian (Hooded) Crow, Alpine Swift, and Laughing Turtle-Dove. The airport at Istanbul invariably produces sights of a few raptors and Black-headed Bunting in summer.

Although spring passage is also interesting it is the autumn that is most spectacular. Some passage can be seen from the hotels of Istanbul, but it is best to go to the Camlica Hills on the Asian shore. If traveling by road, take the Bosphorus (toll) bridge and follow signs first to Kiskili and from there to Camlica. In the village take the road up Buyuk Camlica, where most birders gather (refreshments are avail-

able). Viewing from the smaller hill, Kucuk Camlica, is also good. Refreshments are available on both hills. If you travel by public transport from central Istanbul, take the ferry to Uskudar and then a number 1 or 9 bus up the hill. Peak passage is in midmorning, when the sun begins to warm the land.

Lake Manyas (or Manyas Gölü in Turkish) lies in Anatolia, just a few miles south of the Sea of Marmara, which separates Europe from Asia. Called "Kus Cenneti" or Bird Paradise by its prewar German discoverers, part of Manyas was declared a national park in 1959 and has since been effectively protected. Some 3000 pairs of herons, Eurasian Spoonbill, and Glossy Ibis breed here, although only about a third do so inside the protected area that lies on the northeastern shore. This area, which is equipped with hides, is approached via a branch road from Kilometer post 15 on the Bandirma–Balikesir road, which is signposted KUS CENNETI. A warden is often present near the gate to aid and control visitors.

Manyas is nowhere deeper than 30 feet (9 m) and for much of its shoreline is edged with belts of emergent vegetation. Though the majority of herons breed among the willow trees, the large reed beds are an attraction to many other birds. Plans to clear reeds and create pools to attract ducks have been discussed.

Eastern White Pelicans number up to 3500 during migration. Part of the population found in the Danube Delta, which passes through Anatolia, they can be seen from Manyas through to Lake Van in the east. Most visitors will be delighted by the breeding waterbirds, which include Black-crowned Night, Gray and Squacco Herons, Little Egret, Pygmy Cormorant, and large numbers of Eurasian Spoonbill. Purple Heron and Little Bittern can be found in the reeds along with European and Great Reed-Warblers. The Eastern White Pelican is most often found outside the reserve in the southeast, where they are joined by a few Dalmatian Pelican, flocks of Glossy Ibis, and Black-winged Stilt. Marsh terns are found along with a good passage of waders.

The nearby Lake Apolyont is similarly overgrown along the shoreline with reeds and lilies, which are used by large colonies of Whiskered and Black Terns. The River Kemelpasa runs into the lake in the southwestern corner and has created a delta of mud that is gradually being invaded by marshland vegetation. Here there are large colonies of Spur-winged Lapwing, Black-winged Stilt, and Stone-curlew. The lake is worked via a well-surfaced embankment that leads southward from the village of Ulnabat from the memorial to Hassau (the first to scale the walls of Istanbul in 1453 and whose birthplace is nearby). There are migrant passerines in willows and good views over the lake for Dalmatian Pelican, egrets, and herons, waders, raptors, and duck.

The great mountain of Uludag rises to 8341 feet (2543 m) and was known to the ancients as the Mountain of the Gods. By good fortune it can easily be reached from Bursa via a narrow road through beech and coniferous forests that leads to a ski resort. There are also cable cars. It is best visited in May or June, when the well-clothed bird watcher can explore the dwarf vegetation zone as well as the bare ridges. Lammergeier, Alpine Chough, Alpine Accentor, Kruper's Nuthatch, and Red-fronted Serin may be found.

CHECKLIST

Black-throated Loon W	Black-crowned Night-Heron c S
Little Dabchick c	Squacco Pond-Heron c S
Black-necked Grebe	Great Egret
Red-necked Grebe r S	Little Egret c S
Great Crested Grebe	Gray Heron c
Cory's Shearwater M	Purple Heron c S
Manx Shearwater	Eurasian Spoonbill c S
Eastern White Pelican c M	Glossy Ibis c S
Dalmatian Pelican S	White Stork c M
Great Cormorant c	Black Stork M
Pygmy Cormorant	Greylag Goose
Little Bittern S	White-fronted Goose c W
Eurasian Bittern	Mute Swan

Ruddy Shelduck   W
Common Shelduck   W
Mallard   c   W
Green-winged Teal   c   W
Gadwall   c   W
Eurasian Wigeon   c   W
Northern Pintail   c   W
Garganey   S
Northern Shoveler   c   W
Red-crested Pochard
Northern Pochard   c   W
Ferruginous Duck
Tufted Duck   c   W
Greater Scaup   W
Common Goldeneye   r   W
Smew   W
Eurasian Honey-Buzzard   c   M
Black Kite   c   S
White-tailed Sea-Eagle   r
Levant Sparrowhawk   c   M
European Sparrowhawk   W
Common Buzzard   c   M
Booted Eagle   r   M
Greater Spotted Eagle   r   W
Lesser Spotted Eagle   c   M
Imperial Eagle   r   W
Golden Eagle   H
Egyptian Vulture   S
Lammergeier   H
Griffon Vulture   S
Short-toed Snake-Eagle   r   W, c
   M
Northern Harrier   W
Montagu's Harrier   r·M
Marsh Harrier   c
Peregrine Falcon   r   W
European Hobby   c   S
Red-footed Falcon   r   M
Lesser Kestrel   c   S
Common Kestrel
Chukar
Common Quail   S
European Crane   W
Water Rail
Common Gallinule
Common Coot   c
Greater Ringed Plover   M

Little Ringed Plover   M
Snowy Plover   c
European Golden Plover   W
Gray Plover   r   M
Northern Lapwing   c   W
Spur-winged Lapwing   S
Little Stint   W
Dunlin   c   W
Curlew Sandpiper   M
Ruff   M
Common Redshank   c
Spotted Redshank   c   M
Common Greenshank   M
Green Sandpiper   M
Wood Sandpiper   M
Common Sandpiper   M
Black-tailed Godwit   M
Eurasian Curlew   W
Eurasian Woodcock   r   W
Common Snipe   c   W
Black-winged Stilt   c   S
Black-capped Avocet   M
Stone-curlew   S
Collared Pratincole   S
Mediterranean Gull   c   M
Little Gull   W
Black-headed Gull   c   W
Slender-billed Gull
Lesser Black-backed Gull   M
Herring Gull   c   M
Mew Gull   r   W
Audouin's Gull   r   M
Black Tern   S
White-winged Black Tern   c   S
Whiskered Tern   c   S
Caspian Tern   r   M
Sandwich Tern   M
Common Tern   c   S
Little Tern   S
Wood Pigeon   c   W
Stock Pigeon   W
Collared Turtle-Dove
European Turtle-Dove   c   S
Laughing Turtle-Dove
Eurasian Cuckoo   S
Great Spotted Cuckoo   S
Long-eared Owl

Short-eared Owl   W
Eurasian Scops-Owl   S
Little Owl
Tawny Owl
Eurasian Nightjar   S
Common Swift   c S
Alpine Swift   c S
Eurasian Roller   c S
Eurasian Kingfisher
Eurasian Bee-eater   c S
Hoopoe   S
Eurasian Wryneck   M
Black Woodpecker   r H
Great Spotted Woodpecker
Syrian Woodpecker   c
Middle Spotted Woodpecker   r
Lesser Spotted Woodpecker   r
Sand Martin   c M
Northern Crag Martin
Barn Swallow   c S
Red-rumped Swallow   S
House Martin   S
Short-toed Lark   S
Calandra Lark
Horned Lark   H
Crested Lark   c
Northern Skylark   c W
Tawny Pipit   S
Tree Pipit   M
Meadow Pipit   W
Red-throated Pipit   M
Water Pipit   W, S H
Yellow Wagtail   c S
Gray Wagtail   c W, S H
White Wagtail   c
Red-backed Shrike   c
Masked Shrike   r S
Woodchat Shrike   r W
Lesser Gray Shrike   S
Great Gray Shrike   r W
Eurasian Dipper   H
Northern Wren
Dunnock   W, S H
Alpine Accentor   H
Cetti's Bush-Warbler   c
Savi's Warbler   M
Moustached Warbler

Sedge Warbler   r M
European Reed-Warbler   M
Great Reed-Warbler   S
Icterine Warbler   M
Olivaceous Warbler   S
Garden Warbler   r M
Blackcap   M
Greater Whitethroat   M, S H
Lesser Whitethroat   M
Sardinian Warbler
Willow Warbler   c M
Chiffchaff   c W
Wood Warbler   r M
Goldcrest   r W
Firecrest   H
Pied Flycatcher   M
Collared Flycatcher   M
Red-breasted Flycatcher   M
Spotted Flycatcher   c M
Whinchat   c M
Stonechat   W, SH
Northern Wheatear   c S
Black-eared Wheatear   S H
Rufous Scrub-Robin   S
White-backed Rock-Thrush   S H
Blue Rock-Thrush   S H
Black Redstart   W, S H
Eurasian Redstart   M
European Robin   W, S H
Nightingale   S
Fieldfare   r W
Ring Thrush   M
Eurasian Blackbird   W
Song Thrush   W, S H
Mistle Thrush   H
Long-tailed Tit
Sombre Tit
Coal Tit
Blue Tit
Great Tit
Eurasian Penduline-Tit
Eurasian Nuthatch
Kruper's Nuthatch   H
Rock Nuthatch
Short-toed Treecreeper
House Sparrow   W
Spanish Sparrow   c S

Tree Sparrow   r
Rock Petronia   W
Chaffinch   c
Brambling   W
Red-fronted Serin   W, S H
European Serin
Eurasian Greenfinch   c
Eurasian Siskin   c W
Eurasian Goldfinch   c
Linnet   c W, S H
Red Crossbill   H
Eurasian Bullfinch   H
Hawfinch   r W
Corn Bunting
Yellowhammer   r W
Rock Bunting   W, S H

Ortolan Bunting   M
Cretzschmar's Bunting   r S
Cirl Bunting
Black-headed Bunting   c S
Reed Bunting   c W
Eurasian Golden Oriole   c M
Rose-colored Starling   r M
European Starling   c W
Eurasian Jay
Black-billed Magpie   c
Alpine Chough   H
Western Jackdaw   c
Rook   c W
Eurasian (Hooded) Crow   c
Northern Raven   H

56
Danube Delta, Romania

AT THE MOUTH OF EUROPE'S LARGEST RIVER on the Black Sea coast of Romania is one of that continent's richest bird areas — the Danube Delta. Tulcea, with its Hotel Delta, is the chief town of the region. Nearly 1930 square miles (5000 km²) of low-lying marshlands are intersected by numerous waterways and backwaters to form a truly huge wilderness area without parallel in Europe. Access is difficult and the government conservation policy seals off some of the most interesting of the breeding areas; nevertheless, there are frequent water buses penetrating the delta from Tulcea, and within the marshes small boats can be hired with an oarsman and guide. Though it is possible to take a wildlife cruise to explore the whole of the delta, this is really quite unnecessary. Most of the area consists of huge reed beds with tangled growths of willows, and one part is much like the next. Thus it is only necessary to visit three major areas to get the very best out of the region and see most of the significant birds.

Maliuc has a new hotel located on the Sulina Channel. Food and service are good, but back bedrooms overlook a noisy and smelly generator. Hire a rowboat and get up before dawn to watch the pelican flight — the delta is one of the few European breeding spots. Birds such as Pygmy Cormorant, Little Bittern, Glossy Ibis, Red-crested Pochard, and Ferruginous Duck are common.

Murighiol is a small village on the southern edge of the delta near the St. Georghe Channel. Boats can be hired to penetrate the channel and nearby lakes. This is an excellent spot for Pygmy Cormorant and offers good insight into the lives of the local inhabitants.

Sinoe and Razelm are two large lakes south of the main delta that are virtually alive with birds. The best spots are where the two join together and at the southern outlet of Sinoe. In these areas look for Greylag Goose, Ruddy Shelduck, and Collared Pratincole. Both areas can be reached via dirt roads near Istria. Cars can be rented in Mamaia, which is an international beach resort just north of Constanta and has some decent birding nearby. There is a busy airport at Constanta.

Information on the area is available from Romanian National

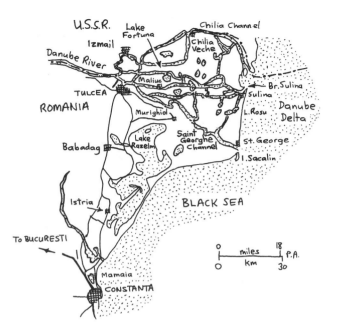

Tourist Offices, or write to Litoral National Tourist Office, Hotel Bucuresti B, Mamaia, Romania.

CHECKLIST

Great Crested Grebe c	Glossy Ibis c S
Red-necked Grebe c	White Stork c S
Black-necked Grebe	Black Stork r S
Little Dabchick	Mute Swan
Eastern White Pelican c S	Greylag Goose c
Dalmatian Pelican c S	Red-breasted Goose r W
Great Cormorant	Common Shelduck
Pygmy Cormorant c	Ruddy Shelduck S
Gray Heron	Mallard c
Purple Heron c S	Gadwall c
Great Egret c S	Eurasian Wigeon W
Little Egret c S	Green-winged Teal c
Squacco Pond-Heron c S	Garganey c S
Black-crowned Night-Heron S	Northern Pintail c W
Little Bittern c S	Northern Shoveler c
Eurasian Bittern	Red-crested Pochard c S
Eurasian Spoonbill S	Tufted Duck W

Greater Scaup W
Northern Pochard c
Ferruginous Duck c
Common Goldeneye W
White-headed Duck r
Goosander W
Red-breasted Merganser W
Smew W
Osprey S
Eurasian Honey-Buzzard S
Black Kite c S
Red Kite r
White-tailed Sea-Eagle r
Egyptian Vulture M
Griffon Vulture M
Short-toed Snake-Eagle r S
Marsh Harrier c
Northern Harrier W
Pallid Harrier
Montagu's Harrier S
Northern Goshawk
Eurasian Sparrowhawk
Levant Sparrowhawk S
Common Buzzard
Lesser Spotted Eagle S
Greater Spotted Eagle
Imperial Eagle r
Golden Eagle
Booted Eagle S
Lesser Kestrel S
Common Kestrel
Red-footed Falcon S
Merlin W
European Hobby S
Saker Falcon r
Peregrine Falcon r
Gray Partridge
Common Quail
Common Pheasant
European Crane S
Water Rail c
Spotted Crake S
Little Crake S
Baillon's Crake S
Corn Crake S
Common Gallinule c
Common Coot c

Common Oystercatcher
Northern Lapwing c
Little Ringed Plover c S
Snowy Plover c S
Eurasian Woodcock
Common Snipe W
Jack Snipe M
Eurasian Curlew S
Black-tailed Godwit S
Ruff M
Wood Sandpiper M
Green Sandpiper M
Common Redshank c S
Spotted Redshank M
Common Greenshank M
Marsh Sandpiper S
Common Sandpiper S
Dunlin M
Curlew Sandpiper M
Little Stint M
Temminck's Stint M
Black-winged Stilt S
Black-capped Avocet S
Stone-curlew S
Black-winged Pratincole r M
Collared Pratincole S
Slender-billed Gull S
Black-headed Gull c
Little Gull c S
Mediterranean Gull S
Herring Gull
Mew Gull W
Gull-billed Tern S
Caspian Tern S
Sandwich Tern S
Common Tern c S
Little Tern S
Black Tern c S
White-winged Black Tern c S
Whiskered Tern S
Rock Pigeon
Stock Pigeon S
Wood Pigeon
Collared Turtle-Dove c
European Turtle-Dove S
Eurasian Cuckoo c
Barn Owl

Eurasian Eagle-Owl   r
Short-eared Owl
Eurasian Scops-Owl
Little Owl
Tawny Owl
Eurasian Nightjar   S
Common Swift   c S
Eurasian Bee-eater   c S
Eurasian Roller   c S
Eurasian Kingfisher   c
Hoopoe   c S
Gray-headed Woodpecker
Great Spotted Woodpecker   c
Syrian Woodpecker
Middle Spotted Woodpecker
Lesser Spotted Woodpecker
Eurasian Wryneck   S
Short-toed Lark   S
Calandra Lark   c
Crested Lark
Northern Skylark
Sand Martin   c S
Barn Swallow   c S
House Martin   S
Tawny Pipit   S
Meadow Pipit   W
Water Pipit   W
Yellow Wagtail   c S
White Wagtail   c
Red-backed Shrike   S
Lesser Gray Shrike   S
Great Gray Shrike   r
Northern Wren
Cetti's Bush-Warbler
Savi's Warbler   c S
River Warbler   S
Moustached Warbler   S
Sedge Warbler   S
Marsh Warbler   S
European Reed-Warbler   c S
Great Reed-Warbler   c S
Icterine Warbler   S
Olivaceous Warbler   S
Barred Warbler   S
Garden Warbler   S
Blackcap

Greater Whitethroat   S
Lesser Whitethroat   S
Willow Warbler   M
Chiffchaff
Wood Warbler
Collared Flycatcher   S
Red-breasted Flycatcher   S
Spotted Flycatcher   c S
Whinchat   S
Stonechat   S
Northern Wheatear   S
Pied Wheatear   S
Eurasian Redstart   c S
European Robin
Thrush-Nightingale   S
Bluethroat   S
Eurasian Blackbird   c
Song Thrush   S
Mistle Thrush
Fieldfare   W
Bearded Reedling   c
Long-tailed Tit
Blue Tit   c
Great Tit   c
Eurasian Penduline Tit
Corn Bunting
Yellowhammer
Ortolan Bunting   S
Reed Bunting   c
Chaffinch   c
Brambling   W
Eurasian Greenfinch
Eurasian Goldfinch   c
Linnet
Common Redpoll   W
Hawfinch
House Sparrow   c
Tree Sparrow   c
Rose-colored Starling   c S
European Starling   c S
Eurasian Golden Oriole   c S
Black-billed Magpie   c
Western Jackdaw   c
Rook
Eurasian (Hooded) Crow   c
Northern Raven

57
Vienna, Austria

ONLY A TWO-HOUR DRIVE southeast of Vienna lies the inland sea of Lake Neusiedl. Although located in eastern Austria it is geographically part of the great Hungarian Plain. It is over 16 miles (25.6 km) long, shallow, and fringed with huge reed beds that provide a home for one of Central Europe's richest collections of birds. No more than half of the lake is open water and in exploration it seems more like a gigantic marsh. The total list of birds is some 280 species, many of which breed and can be seen to advantage. There is a good paved road system and several well-sited and acceptable hotels. Stay in Neusiedl-am-See at the Leiner Hotel, or one of the other smaller villages such as Rust, where good accommodation and food are available.

The lake itself is perhaps best approached via the single-track railway between Neusiedl and Weiden which proves an excellent vantage point over the marshes. Egrets, storks, harriers, warblers, Eurasian Penduline-Tit, and Bearded Reedling can be seen. The return to Neusiedl can be made along the ridge, with its vineyards and wooded gullies.

Pride of place goes to the Great Egret, which numbers some 200 pairs among the reeds (a bird remarkably rare in Europe, though abundant elsewhere in the world). Other herons are numerous, including large colonies of Purple Herons, plus Eurasian Bittern, Little Bittern, and Eurasian Spoonbill. White Stork breed on the village chimneys, and Black Stork in the nearby woodlands. But the keen watcher will be more taken with the opportunities to see elusive species like Spotted and Little Crakes, and River and Aquatic Warblers. Many other species of particular interest include Syrian Woodpecker and Red-necked Grebe.

Raptors can be seen flying over the forests of Kapuvarer Erlen Wald. It is just across the Hungarian border and can be viewed from the south of Tadten on the Tadten Plain east of the lake. A number of shy breeders find conditions in the sensitive no man's land dividing east and west a safe sanctuary. This area is noted as a good locality for Great Bustard, a species high on the wanted list of so many bird watchers. The raptor watcher can enjoy searching for Imperial,

Greater and Lesser Spotted Eagles, Eurasian Honey-Buzzard, Northern Goshawk, and Red-footed Falcon. In winter Neusiedl is a great wildfowl concentration point. Over 100,000 geese descend on it including Bean and White-fronted. Waders pass through in the thousands, with Marsh Sandpiper and Temminck's Stint regularly seen.

Seewinkel is a lake-dotted area north of Illmitz. Lange Lacke, Zick Lacke, Warmsee Darscholacke, and Oberstinkersee are the best, featuring herons, Eurasian Spoonbill, Ferruginous Duck, harriers, and waders in season. The Leitha Hills to the northwest of Schützen are

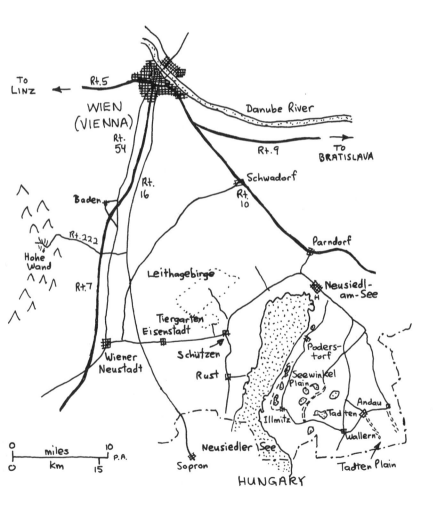

crisscrossed with paths leading from the Eisenstadt–Jois road; they are excellent for raptors as well as Syrian Woodpecker, Lesser Gray Shrike, Icterine Warbler, and Ortolan Bunting.

Visitors wishing to combine alpine birding with the great lake are advised to travel to Hohe Wand. It can be reached by taking the E7 motorway from Vienna toward Wiener Neustadt; from there, west on Route 222 for 8 kilometers, where there is a sign for Hohe Wand. It is a cliff-face where a plateau plunges down into a deep valley. The rocky cliff itself is home to the elusive Wallcreeper, White-backed Rock-Thrush, and Rock Bunting. There is also a road to the top that passes through coniferous forest. Hard work in the forests may yield views of Capercaillie, Bonelli's Warbler, Crested Tit, and Eurasian Nutcracker.

CHECKLIST

Great Crested Grebe   c
Red-necked Grebe   S
Black-necked Grebe   c
Little Dabchick   c
Gray Heron
Purple Heron   c S
Great Egret   c S
Little Egret   S
Squacco Pond-Heron   S
Black-crowned Night-Heron   S
Little Bittern   c S
Eurasian Bittern
Eurasian Spoonbill   S
White Stork   c S
Black Stork   r S
Greylag Goose   c S
Bean Goose   M
White-fronted Goose   W
Mallard   c
Gadwall
Eurasian Wigeon   c W
Green-winged Teal   c
Garganey   S
Northern Pintail   W
Northern Shoveler   M
Tufted Duck   c W
Northern Pochard
Ferruginous Duck
Common Goldeneye   W

Goosander   W
Red-breasted Merganser   W
Smew   W
Osprey   S
Eurasian Honey-Buzzard   S
Black Kite   S
Red Kite   r S
Short-toed Snake-Eagle   r S
Marsh Harrier   c S
Northern Harrier
Montagu's Harrier   c S
Northern Goshawk
Eurasian Sparrowhawk
Common Buzzard   c
Rough-legged Buzzard   W
Lesser Spotted Eagle   S
Greater Spotted Eagle   r S
Imperial Eagle   r
Common Kestrel
Red-footed Falcon   r S
European Hobby   S
Saker Falcon   r S
Peregrine Falcon
Black Grouse
Capercaillie
Gray Partridge
Common Quail   S
Common Pheasant
European Crane   M

Great Bustard
Water Rail
Spotted Crake   r S
Little Crake   r S
Corn Crake   S
Common Gallinule
Common Coot
Northern Lapwing
Gray Plover   M
European Dotterel   r M
Ringed Plover   M
Little Ringed Plover   S
Snowy Plover   S
Eurasian Woodcock
Ruddy Turnstone   r M
Common Snipe
Eurasian Curlew   S
Whimbrel   M
Black-tailed Godwit   c S
Ruff   S
Wood Sandpiper   M
Green Sandpiper   S
Little Redshank   S
Spotted Redshank   M
Common Greenshank   M
Common Sandpiper   S
Dunlin   M
Curlew Sandpiper   M
Little Stint   M
Temminck's Stint   M
Sanderling   M
Black-capped Avocet   S
Stone-curlew   S
Black-headed Gull   c
Little Gull   M
Mediterranean Gull   M
Herring Gull   W
Lesser Black-backed Gull   M
Mew Gull   W
Common Tern   c S
Black Tern   c S
White-winged Black Tern   r S
Stock Pigeon
Wood Pigeon
Collared Turtle-Dove
European Turtle-Dove   c S
Eurasian Cuckoo   S

Barn Owl
Eurasian Eagle-Owl   r
Long-eared Owl   r
Short-eared Owl   W
Eurasian Pygmy-Owl   r
Tengmalm's Owl   r
Little Owl
Tawny Owl
Eurasian Nightjar   S
Common Swift   c S
Eurasian Roller   S
Eurasian Kingfisher
Hoopoe   S
Gray-headed Woodpecker
European Green Woodpecker
Great Spotted Woodpecker
Syrian Woodpecker   c
Middle Spotted Woodpecker
Lesser Spotted Woodpecker
Black Woodpecker
Eurasian Wryneck   S
Crested Lark
Wood Lark   S
Northern Skylark
Sand Martin   c S
Barn Swallow   c S
House Martin   S
Tawny Pipit   S
Tree Pipit   S
Meadow Pipit
Red-throated Pipit   M
Water Pipit
Yellow Wagtail   c S
Gray Wagtail
White Wagtail
Red-backed Shrike   S
Woodchat Shrike   c S
Lesser Gray Shrike   c S
Great Gray Shrike
Bohemian Waxwing   W
Eurasian Dipper
Northern Wren
Alpine Accentor
Dunnock
Savi's Warbler   c S
River Warbler   r S
Western Grasshopper-Warbler   S

Moustached Warbler   S
Aquatic Warbler   S
Sedge Warbler   S
Marsh Warbler   c S
European Reed-Warbler   S
Great Reed-Warbler   S
Icterine Warbler   S
Barred Warbler   S
Garden Warbler   S
Blackcap   S
Greater Whitethroat   S
Lesser Whitethroat   S
Willow Warbler   S
Chiffchaff   S
Bonelli's Warbler   S
Wood Warbler   S
Goldcrest
Firecrest   S
Pied Flycatcher   S
Collared Flycatcher   S
Red-breasted Flycatcher   S
Spotted Flycatcher   S
Whinchat   S
Stonechat   S
Northern Wheatear   S
White-backed Rock Thrush   S
Eurasian Redstart   S
Black Redstart   S
European Robin
Nightingale   S
Bluethroat   S
Fieldfare   W
Ring Thrush   S
Eurasian Blackbird   c
Redwing   W
Song Thrush   c S
Mistle Thrush
Bearded Reedling
Long-tailed Tit
Marsh Tit

Willow Tit
Crested Tit
Coal Tit
Blue Tit
Great Tit
Eurasian Penduline Tit
Eurasian Nuthatch
Northern Treecreeper
Short-toed Treecreeper
Corn Bunting
Yellowhammer
Rock Bunting
Ortolan Bunting   S
Reed Bunting   S
Chaffinch   c
Brambling   W
Citril Finch
European Serin   S
Eurasian Greenfinch
Eurasian Siskin
Eurasian Goldfinch
Linnet
Common Redpoll   W
Red Crossbill
Eurasian Bullfinch
Hawfinch
House Sparrow   c
Tree Sparrow   c
Eurasian Snow-Finch
European Starling   c
Eurasian Golden Oriole   S
Eurasian Jay
Black-billed Magpie
Eurasian Nutcracker
Alpine Chough
Western Jackdaw
Rook
Eurasian (Hooded) Crow
Northern Raven

288

58
Camargue, France

No OTHER AREA OF EUROPE enjoys such a reputation for birds as does the Camargue, the delta of the Rhône on the Mediterranean coast of France. Here, sandwiched between the fleshpots of St. Tropez and the Côte d'Azur and the moneypots of the hyper-modern marinas along the coast of Languedoc, lies a wilderness of marshes and skies. The romantic sees the Camargue as a land of wild white horses, of splashing pools and gypsy festivals — a land where only cowboys roam to look after the fighting bulls that survive their encounters in the Roman arenas of Nimes and Arles. Realistically, the Camargue has not survived unscathed. Les Stes. Maries de la Mer is not just a gypsy town; it is a fully fledged candy-floss-and-deck-chair place that is best left behind, unless you can find lodging there. To the east, the owners of much of the Camargue, a salt-extraction company, continue to create salt pans from saline lagoons and cast their eyes enviously over the huge areas to the north that are the heart of the Camargue Reserve. In the north, freshwater marshes are being progressively changed over to a monoculture of rice, and this in turn is affecting the delicate salinity balance of the delta as a whole.

The Camargue is dominated by the Étang de Vaccares, a huge inland sea that can be whipped up into waves by the wind. It is a shallow water providing vast areas suitable for wading birds, with islands that dry out as the water level drops in summer. Here are the famous Camargue Greater Flamingoes, which nest to the south among the saline pools of the salt company. Lagoon links to lagoon and a maze of roads and tracks penetrate the farthest corners and crannies of the delta. There are stilts, bee-eaters, rollers, and other birds that are difficult to find in northern Europe. Egrets and herons haunt the lagoons and fly to the riverine forest along the arms of the Rhône to roost and breed. Passage waders are as impressive as anywhere with huge numbers of Wood Sandpiper regularly passing through. Overhead, Black Kite and Marsh Harrier are constantly beating, while high in the sky is a collection of raptors that frequently includes Short-toed Snake-Eagle and Osprey.

To the southeast of Arles lies Le Crau, a stony desert that was once

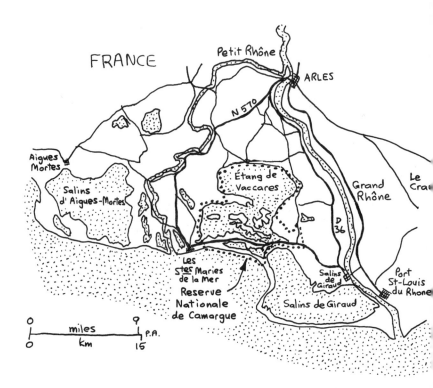

FRANCE
Petit Rhône
ARLES
N 570
Aigues Mortes
Salins d' Aigues-Mortes
Étang de Vaccares
Grand Rhône
Le Cra
D 36
Les Stes Maries de la Mer
Salins de Giraud
Port St-Louis du Rhone
Reserve Nationale de Camargue
Salins de Giraud
miles
P.A.
km
0   9   15

the delta of the River Durance. Here, in land seemingly fit only for sheep, live Lesser Kestrel, Little Bustard, Pin-tailed Sandgrouse, Black-eared Wheatear, and a wealth of larks. To the north, the hills of Les Baux are famous not only for their Roman remains but also as a notable haunt of Alpine Swift and a few vultures.

Some resourceful visitors find accommodation in one of the farms in the delta near the reserve where horses can sometimes be rented. There are several small hotels (a few rooms each), such as Hotel L'Estrambord, in the town of Le Sambuc to the east of the reserve. Well to the north, but within commuting distance, is the city of Arles, with a wide range of facilities.

For a permit (needed to enter some of the good areas in the reserve) write to the Directeur de la Reserve, Reserve Nationale de Camargue, La Capeliere, 13200 Arles, France (Telephone 97 00 97). Much, however, can be seen from the public highway and via unrestricted roads on dykes. Two finely detailed maps of the area are available in France: map No. 83 of the Michelin series, and the 1/100,000 map published by l'Institut Geographique National in Paris.

CHECKLIST

Red-throated Loon   W
Little Dabchick   c
Black-necked Grebe   r
Red-necked Grebe   r W
Great Crested Grebe   c
Northern Gannet   W
Great Cormorant   c W
Eurasian Bittern
Little Bittern   S
Black-crowned Night-Heron   c S
Squacco Pond-Heron   S
Little Egret   c
Gray Heron   c
Purple Heron   c S
White Stork   r S
Black Stork   r S
Greater Flamingo   c
Greylag Goose   r W
Bean Goose   r W
Common Shelduck
Mallard   c
Green-winged Teal   c W
Gadwall   r S, c W
Eurasian Wigeon   c W
Northern Pintail   c W
Garganey   r S, c M
Northern Shoveler   c W
Red-crested Pochard   c
Northern Pochard   c W
Ferruginous Duck   r W
Tufted Duck   c W
Greater Scaup   r W
Common Eider   r
Black Scoter   r W
White-winged Scoter   r W
Common Goldeneye   r W
Red-breasted Merganser   r W
Osprey   M
Eurasian Honey-Buzzard   M
Red Kite   r W
Black Kite   c S
Northern Goshawk   r
Eurasian Sparrowhawk

Common Buzzard   c W
Bonelli's Eagle   r
Egyptian Vulture   r S
Short-toed Snake-Eagle   r S
Northern Harrier   r W
Montagu's Harrier   S
Marsh Harrier   c
Peregrine Falcon   r
European Hobby   S
Merlin   r W
Lesser Kestrel   S
Common Kestrel   c
Common Pheasant
Red-legged Partridge
Common Quail
Water Rail   c
Spotted Crake   r
Little Crake   r S
Baillon's Crake   r S
Common Gallinule   c
Common Coot   c
Little Bustard
Common Oystercatcher
Greater Ringed Plover   c M
Little Ringed Plover   c M
Snowy Plover   c S
European Golden Plover   c W
Gray Plover   M
Northern Lapwing   c
Ruddy Turnstone   W
Little Stint   c M, r W
Temminck's Stint   c M
Dunlin   c W
Curlew Sandpiper   c M
Red Knot   M
Sanderling   M
Ruff   c M
Spotted Redshank   W
Common Redshank   c
Marsh Sandpiper   M
Common Greenshank   M
Green Sandpiper   c M, r W
Wood Sandpiper   c M, r W

Common Sandpiper   c M
Black-tailed Godwit   c M
Bar-tailed Godwit   W
Eurasian Curlew   c W
Whimbrel   M
Eurasian Woodcock   r W
Common Snipe   c W
Jack Snipe   r W
Black-winged Stilt   c S
Black-capped Avocet   c
Stone-curlew
Collared Pratincole   S
Parasitic Jaeger   r M
Mediterranean Gull   W, r S
Little Gull   M
Black-headed Gull   c
Slender-billed Gull   r S
Lesser Black-backed Gull   S
Herring Gull   c
Mew Gull   W
Black Tern   c M
White-winged Black Tern   M
Whiskered Tern   c S
Gull-billed Tern   S
Caspian Tern   M
Sandwich Tern
Common Tern   c S
Roseate Tern   r S
Little Tern   c S
Razorbill   r W
Pin-tailed Sandgrouse
Wood Pigeon   W
Stock Pigeon   W
European Turtle-Dove   c S
Eurasian Cuckoo   c S
Great Spotted Cuckoo   S
Barn Owl
Long-eared Owl
Eurasian Scops-Owl   S
Little Owl   c
Tawny Owl
Eurasian Nightjar   S
Common Swift   c S
Alpine Swift   M
Eurasian Kingfisher
Eurasian Bee-eater   c S
Eurasian Roller   S

Hoopoe   S
Eurasian Wryneck   M
European Green Woodpecker
Great Spotted Woodpecker
Lesser Spotted Woodpecker   r
Short-toed Lark   c S
Calandra Lark
Crested Lark   c
Wood Lark   c M
Northern Skylark   c
Sand Martin   c S
Barn Swallow   c S
House Martin   c S
Tawny Pipit   S
Tree Pipit   c M
Meadow Pipit   c W
Water Pipit   c S
Yellow Wagtail   c S
Gray Wagtail   W
White Wagtail   c M, r W
Red-backed Shrike   M
Woodchat Shrike   r S, c M
Lesser Gray Shrike   r S
Great Gray Shrike
Northern Wren   M
Dunnock   c M, r W
Cetti's Bush-Warbler   c
Savi's Warbler   S
Western Grasshopper-Warbler   r
   M
Moustached Warbler
Aquatic Warbler   r M
Sedge Warbler   M
European Reed-Warbler   c S
Great Reed-Warbler   c S
Icterine Warbler   r M
Melodious Warbler   c S
Orphean Warbler   M
Garden Warbler   c M
Blackcap   c
Greater Whitethroat   c S
Sardinian Warbler
Subalpine Warbler
Spectacled Warbler   c S
Dartford Warbler
Willow Warbler   c M
Chiffchaff   c W

Bonelli's Warbler   c M
Wood Warbler   M
Goldcrest   W
Firecrest   W
Zitting Cisticola   c S
Pied Flycatcher   c M
Spotted Flycatcher   S
Whinchat   c M
Stonechat   c W
Northern Wheatear   c M
Black-eared Wheatear   S
White-backed Rock Thrush   r M
Black Redstart   W, c M
Eurasian Redstart   c M
European Robin   c W
Nightingale   c S
Bluethroat   c M
Fieldfare   W
Ring Thrush   r M
Eurasian Blackbird   c
Redwing   c W
Song Thrush   c M
Mistle Thrush   W
Bearded Reedling
Long-tailed Tit
Blue Tit   c W

Great Tit   c
Eurasian Penduline Tit
Short-toed Treecreeper
Yellowhammer   r W
Cirl Bunting   W
Ortolan Bunting   M
Rock Bunting   r W
Reed Bunting   c
Corn Bunting   c
Brambling   W
Chaffinch   c W
Eurasian Siskin   r W
European Serin
Eurasian Greenfinch
Eurasian Goldfinch   c
Linnet
Hawfinch   r W
House Sparrow   c
Tree Sparrow   c
European Starling   c W
Eurasian Golden Oriole   S
Eurasian Jay   .
Black-billed Magpie   c
Western Jackdaw   c
Eurasian Crow

59
Andalucia, Spain

ANDALUCIA IS THAT ROMANTIC CORNER of southwestern Spain around Sevilla, Granada, Malaga, Jerez, and Cadiz with vast marshes, sand dunes, craggy mountains, cork-oak forests, and a fascinating aggregation of birds.

Far and away the most famous area for birds is the Coto Doñana, one of the last homes of the Spanish race of the Imperial Eagle. Permits to visit the Coto Doñana National Park in specially designated Land-Rovers should be made through: Jefe de Visitas del Parque Nacional Doñana, ICONA, Plaza de España No. 1, Sevilla, España. Once your date is confirmed you will be driven around the park to selected habitats.

Several paved roads lead west from Sevilla to Almonte, where a road leads south to El Rocio, a quiet town (except during the festival of the Virgin of the Dew in spring) at the edge of the *marismas* (marshes). A raised causeway and bridge are often good for sighting marsh birds. Land-Rover tours leave from the new visitors' center just south of El Rocio bridge. Continuing to the ocean, visitors arrive at the monstrous new seaside resort of Matalascañas which sprang up overnight (putting pressure on the Coto Doñana). There is, though, convenient accommodation nearby at the Hotel Tierra y Mar and Hotel Flamero.

The *marismas* of the mouth of the Guadalquivir, though still spectacular, have been greatly reduced by canals, clearing, and drainage schemes. The birdlife is still rich, probably more accessible than ever, but is declining due to liberal pesticide usage on the rice farms. This area can be visited by rented car from Sevilla via Coria to Venta de la Cruz, where the paved road to Villafranca makes a sharp left turn at a little country bar. Go straight onto a dirt road (left at a fork) until you reach a drainage canal (about 6 miles [9.6 km]). Turn left (south) and take the next right (unless it is flooded). Once upon the dyke on the other side, you are on a dyke-top road (impassable during and after winter rains) that penetrates far into the *marismas,* where sandgrouse, Lesser Short-toed Lark, and many waterbirds can be seen. The road to the new Coto Doñana *marisma* reserve and El Rocio makes

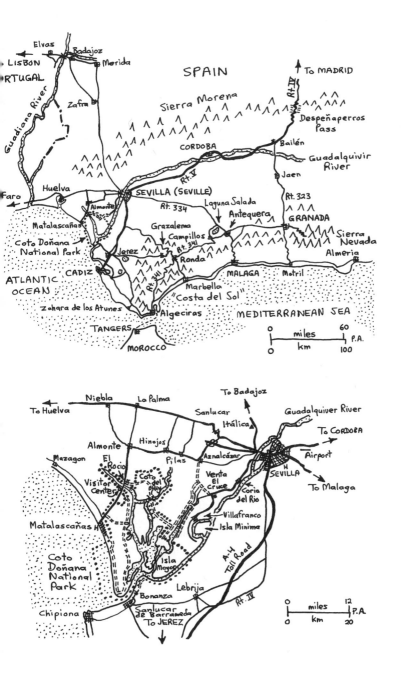

a sharp right at a gate and leaves the canal behind. This journey into the marshes is not recommended for timid drivers with poor senses of direction.

Ronda is a spectacular cliff-top town high in the mountains of southern Andalucia. The roads in all directions (i.e., to Algeciras, Malaga, Sevilla) pass by spectacular cliffs and verdant forests. Birding is rich on all roads, particularly on the Grazalema road (which branches south off the Sevilla highway, northwest of town). Egyptian Vulture, Bonelli's Eagle, Booted Eagle, Alpine Swift, Sardinian, Melodious, Subalpine, Dartford, and Bonelli's Warblers, Black Wheatear, Rock Petronia, and Red-billed Chough are all locally common.

The Laguna Salada, west of Fuente de Piedra, is a great mountain salt lake (3 hours' drive east of Ronda, north of Antequera) where Greater Flamingo breed in the thousands when water conditions are correct. The lake has no outlet and is fresh water in very wet years and dries up in drought years. Thus, the presence and numbers of waterbirds including flamingoes are variable. With a little organization and visitors' aids this could be a major attraction.

The snow-capped Sierra Nevada is reached via a fine paved road to the southeast of Granada. There are a number of ski lodges at the resort of Solynieve, as well as chair lifts. Alpine Accentor, White-backed Rock-Thrush, three wheatears, Northern Skylark, Northern Crag Martin, Black Redstart, Tawny Pipit, and Ortolan Bunting breed.

Algeciras, located opposite Gibraltar and Morocco, is the center of an area noted for its fine stork and raptor passage. The woods of Almoraima to the north have many fine areas for woodland and streamside birding. The ferry (not hydrofoil) to Tangiers can be good for viewing shearwaters, Northern Gannet, skuas, and alcids, and there is an outside chance of seeing Audouin's Gull. The recently discovered White-rumped Swift breeds in three or four mountain ranges north of Algeciras. There are several public and private ponds southeast of Jerez that from time to time feature breeding White-headed Duck, Purple Swamphen, and Red-knobbed Coot. Due to the irresponsibility of egg-collectors, exact details have to be withheld.

Elvas, Portugal, is located just west of Badajoz, Spain (a 4–5-hour drive from Sevilla). Several roads southeast from Elvas to the border area pass olive groves, wheat fields, and rice paddies. This area is home to Great and Little Bustards, Black-shouldered Kite, Black-bellied Sandgrouse, and Eurasian Roller; only the last-mentioned is common.

CHECKLIST

Little Dabchick
Black-necked Grebe
Great Crested Grebe
Cory's Shearwater   S
Manx Shearwater   S
Northern Gannet   W
Great Cormorant   W
Eurasian Bittern   r
Little Bittern   S
Black-crowned Night-Heron   S
Squacco Pond-Heron   S
Cattle Heron   c
Little Egret   c
Gray Heron   c
Purple Heron   S
White Stork   c S
Eurasian Spoonbill
Glossy Ibis   r W
Greater Flamingo
Greylag Goose   c W
Mallard   c
Green-winged Teal   c W
Gadwall
Eurasian Wigeon   W
Northern Pintail   M
Garganey   c W
Northern Shoveler
Marbled Teal   r S
Red-crested Pochard
Northern Pochard
Ferruginous Duck   r
Tufted Duck   W
Black Scoter   W
White-headed Duck   r
Black-shouldered Kite   r
Eurasian Honey-Buzzard   M
Red Kite   S
Black Kite   c S
Common Buzzard
Booted Eagle   c S
Bonelli's Eagle   H
Imperial Eagle   r
Golden Eagle   r

Egyptian Vulture   S
Cinereous Vulture   r W
Griffon Vulture   c
Short-toed Snake-Eagle   S
Northern Harrier   W
Montagu's Harrier   c S
Marsh Harrier
Peregrine Falcon   r
European Hobby   S
Lesser Kestrel   c S
Common Kestrel   c
Red-legged Partridge   c
Common Quail   S
Water Rail   r
Spotted Crake   r W
Baillon's Crake   r S
Purple Swamphen   r
Common Gallinule   c
Common Coot   c
Red-knobbed Coot   r
Great Bustard   r
Little Bustard
Common Oystercatcher   r W
Greater Ringed Plover   W
Little Ringed Plover   S
Snowy Plover
European Golden Plover   W
Gray Plover   W
Northern Lapwing
Ruddy Turnstone   W
Little Stint   W
Temminck's Stint   r M
Dunlin   c W
Curlew Sandpiper   M
Red Knot   r W
Sanderling   W
Ruff   c W
Broad-billed Sandpiper   r M
Spotted Redshank   W
Common Redshank   c
Marsh Sandpiper   r W
Common Greenshank   W
Green Sandpiper   W

Wood Sandpiper   W
Common Sandpiper   W
Black-tailed Godwit   c
Bar-tailed Godwit   c W
Eurasian Curlew   W
Whimbrel   W
Eurasian Woodcock   r W
Common Snipe   c W
Black-winged Stilt   c S
Black-capped Avocet
Stone-curlew
Collared Pratincole   c S
Parasitic Jaeger   M
Mediterranean Gull   r W
Little Gull   r M
Black-headed Gull   c
Slender-billed Gull   r S
Lesser Black-backed Gull
Herring Gull
Great Black-backed Gull   r W
Mew Gull   r W
Audouin's Gull   r W
Black-legged Kittiwake   W
Black Tern   M
White-winged Black Tern   r M
Whiskered Tern   c S
Gull-billed Tern   S
Caspian Tern   r M
Sandwich Tern
Common Tern   c M
Roseate Tern   r M
Little Tern   S
Razorbill   W
Atlantic Puffin   W
Black-bellied Sandgrouse   r
Pin-tailed Sandgrouse
Wood Pigeon   c
Stock Pigeon   r
Rock Pigeon   c
European Turtle-Dove   c S
Eurasian Cuckoo   S
Great Spotted Cuckoo   S
Barn Owl
Eurasian Scops-Owl
Little Owl   c
Tawny Owl
Eurasian Nightjar   S H

Red-necked Nightjar   S
White-rumped Swift   r S
Pallid Swift   c S
Common Swift   c S
Alpine Swift   S H
Eurasian Kingfisher
Eurasian Bee-eater   c S
Eurasian Roller   S
Hoopoe   c S
Eurasian Wryneck   M
European Green Woodpecker
Great Spotted Woodpecker
Short-toed Lark   c S
Lesser Short-toed Lark   r S
Calandra Lark
Crested Lark   c
Thekla Lark   r
Wood Lark
Northern Skylark   W
Sand Martin   S
Northern Crag-Martin
Barn Swallow   c S
Red-rumped Swallow   c S
House Martin   c S
Tawny Pipit   S
Tree Pipit   W
Meadow Pipit   W
Water Pipit   r W
Yellow Wagtail   c S
Gray Wagtail
White Wagtail   c W
Woodchat Shrike   c S
Great Gray Shrike
Eurasian Dipper   r H
Northern Wren
Alpine Accentor   H
Dunnock   r W
Cetti's Bush-Warbler
Savi's Warbler   S
Moustached Warbler   r
Sedge Warbler   M
European Reed-Warbler   S
Great Reed-Warbler   c S
Melodious Warbler   S
Olivaceous Warbler   S
Orphean Warbler   S
Garden Warbler   M

Blackcap   c
Greater Whitethroat   M
Sardinian Warbler   c
Subalpine Warbler   S
Spectacled Warbler   S
Dartford Warbler
Willow Warbler   c M
Chiffchaff
Bonelli's Warbler   S
Firecrest
Zitting Cisticola   c
Pied Flycatcher   M
Spotted Flycatcher   S
Whinchat   M
Stonechat   c
Northern Wheatear   S H
Black-eared Wheatear   c S
Black Wheatear
Rufous Scrub-Robin   S
White-backed Rock-Thrush   S H
Blue Rock-Thrush
Black Redstart   H
Eurasian Redstart   M
European Robin
Nightingale   S
Fieldfare   W
Ring Thrush   r W
Eurasian Blackbird   c
Redwing   W
Song Thrush   W
Mistle Thrush

Long-tailed Tit
Crested Tit
Coal Tit
Blue Tit   c
Great Tit   c
Eurasian Nuthatch
Short-toed Treecreeper
Corn Bunting   c
Rock Bunting   H
Cirl Bunting
Ortolan Bunting   H
Reed Bunting   W
Chaffinch   c
European Serin   c
Eurasian Greenfinch   c
Eurasian Siskin   W
Eurasian Goldfinch   c
Linnet
Red Crossbill   r W
Hawfinch   r
House Sparrow   c
Tree Sparrow
Rock Petronia
Spotless Starling   c
Eurasian Golden Oriole   S
Eurasian Jay
Azure-winged Magpie
Black-billed Magpie
Red-billed Chough   c H
Western Jackdaw   c
Northern Raven

60
Morocco

MOROCCO IS A FASCINATING COUNTRY, relatively close to both European and North American birders. Rainfall occurs chiefly in the winter months (with snow in the Atlas Mountains) with wetter areas being the north and west coasts. Very dry desert conditions exist to the south and east of the mountains. Some excellent wetlands line stretches of the Atlantic coast, with great waterbird and passerine migrations. The Rif Mountains in the north run to the east of Tangier and Tetouan. The Middle Atlas lie to the south of Fés and Meknès. East of Agadir are the parallel ranges of the High Atlas and Anti-Atlas. The Sahara reaches up to the east of these latter two ranges in the vicinity of Ouarzazate.

Ouarzazate is a well-watered oasis with various crops and palms, as well as a hotel. Around town look for Blue-cheeked Bee-eater, Long-legged Buzzard, and Moussier's Redstart. Outside of town the ground is covered with aromatic herbs, thorn bushes lining occasional wadis (creek beds), and odd goats. These rolling plains are penetrated by several roads along which Desert and Bar-tailed Larks, Desert, Black-eared, Mourning, and White-crowned Black Wheatear live.

Other desert specialties found near Ouarzazate are Crowned and Black-bellied Sandgrouse, Fulvous Babbler, Desert and Scrub Warblers, and House Bunting.

Even those without desert vehicles can venture from Ouarzazate out the Tinerhir road to Boumalne and from there explore tracks to the south. Lanner Falcon, Greater Red-rumped Wheatear, Temminck's Lark, Bifasciated Lark, Thick-billed Lark, and Trumpeter Finch all occur. Houbara Bustard live farther on at Tizi-n-Tazazert.

Mogador Island, lying a mile (1.6 km) off the city of Essaouira (where boats are available) on the Atlantic, is one of the few known Moroccan breeding sites of the colonial Eleonora's Falcon, which is here in the summer and fall feeding on migrants. A freshwater wadi just south of town with a shallow river is well worth visiting. Eleonora's Falcon leave the island to bathe here, sometimes beside Audouin's Gulls. Many waterbirds occur, while the nearby bushes are

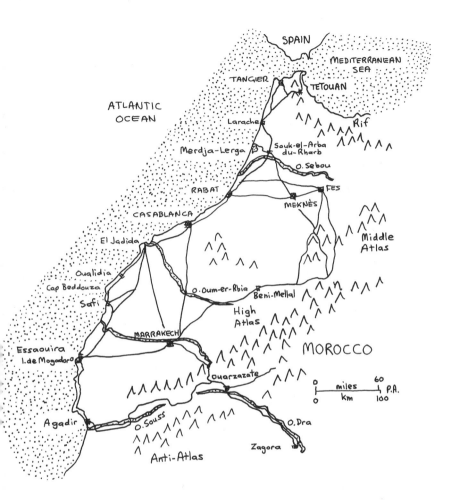

home to Rufous Bush-Chat and Black-crowned Bush-Shrike. Essaouira boasts of a fascinating old market quarter and bazaar and a choice of hotels. There is only one exit road south. To reach the wadi stay right at all forks, as it lies just behind the beach.

Oualidia is a modest resort town north of Essaouira and well south of Casablanca. Slender-billed Curlew and Audouin's Gull both winter near town. For 30 miles (48 km) to the north there are fascinating lagoons and salt pans created by a barrier beach. Various paths and drives to the shore of the lagoons are feasible, and huge numbers of wintering and migrant birds can be seen. Cap Beddouza just south of Oualidia is a fine sea-watching point, with numbers of Cory's and Manx Shearwaters, skuas, and Royal and Lesser Crested Terns.

The lagoons of Merdja Zerga, located between Tangier and Rabat, are flooded in winter and are good for birding at all seasons. From the town of Souk-el-Arba-du-Rharb take minor roads signposted MOULAY-BOU-SELHAM to the hotel that overlooks the lagoon entrance. Various rough roads circle the lagoon. This is the top wintering area for duck and coot in Morocco, and also has great numbers of herons, shorebirds and terns, including Royal and Lesser Crested. The Slender-billed Curlew and Greater Flamingo winter here, and Osprey and Long-legged Buzzard are regular. Just to the north, around Laranche, Black-shouldered Kite live in the groves of cork oaks.

There are several colonies of Bald Ibis in Morocco, including one at Timhadite in the Middle Atlas, and another near Talmeste.

CHECKLIST

Little Dabchick r	Garganey r M
Great Crested Grebe r	Northern Shoveler W
Black-necked Grebe r	Marbled Teal r
Cory's Shearwater r M	Red-crested Pochard r W
Manx Shearwater	Northern Pochard r W
Northern Gannet c W	Ferruginous Duck r W
Great Cormorant	Tufted Duck r W
Shag r	Black Scoter W
Long-tailed Cormorant r	Red-breasted Merganser r W
Little Bittern S	White-headed Duck r
Black-crowned Night-Heron r S	Eurasian Honey-Buzzard c M
Squacco Pond-Heron r S	Black-shouldered Kite r
Cattle Heron c	Black Kite c S
Little Egret c	Red Kite
Gray Heron c	Lammergeier r H
Purple Heron S	Egyptian Vulture S
White Stork S	Griffon Vulture
Glossy Ibis r W	Lappet-faced Vulture r
Bald Ibis S	Cinereous Vulture r W
Eurasian Spoonbill r W	Short-toed Snake-Eagle S
Greater Flamingo W	Marsh Harrier c
Greylag Goose r W	Northern Goshawk r
Ruddy Shelduck	European Sparrowhawk
Common Shelduck r W	Common Buzzard W
Eurasian Wigeon c W	Long-legged Buzzard
Gadwall r W	Tawny Eagle r
Green-winged Teal c W	Imperial Eagle r
Mallard	Golden Eagle r
Northern Pintail W	Booted Eagle S

Bonelli's Eagle
Osprey   r
Lesser Kestrel
Common Kestrel
European Hobby   S
Eleonora's Falcon   S
Lanner Falcon   c
Peregrine Falcon   r
Barbary Falcon
Barbary Partridge   c
Double-spurred Francolin   r
Common Quail
Helmeted Guineafowl   r
Common Buttonquail   r
Water Rail
Spotted Crake   r W
Common Gallinule
Purple Swamphen   r
Common Coot   c
Red-knobbed Coot   r
European Crane   r W
Demoiselle Crane   r S
Little Bustard   r
Houbara Bustard
Arabian Bustard   r
Great Bustard   r
Common Oystercatcher   W
Black-winged Stilt   c
Black-capped Avocet   c W
Stone-curlew
Cream-colored Courser
Collared Pratincole   S
Little Ringed Plover
Greater Ringed Plover   c W
Snowy Plover   c
European Dotterel   W
European Golden Plover   W
Gray Plover   c W
Northern Lapwing   c
Red Knot   W
Sanderling   c W
Little Stint   c W
Temminck's Stint   r M
Curlew Sandpiper   M
Dunlin   c W
Ruff   c W
Jack Snipe   r W

Common Snipe   c W
Black-tailed Godwit   c W
Bar-tailed Godwit   W
Whimbrel   W
Slender-billed Curlew   r W
Eurasian Curlew   c W
Spotted Redshank   W
Common Redshank   c W
Common Greenshank   W
Green Sandpiper   W
Wood Sandpiper   W
Common Sandpiper   W
Ruddy Turnstone   W
Parasitic Jaeger   W
Great Skua   r W
Mediterranean Gull   c W
Little Gull   W
Black-headed Gull   c W
Slender-billed Gull   r W
Audouin's Gull
Lesser Black-backed Gull   c W
Herring Gull   c
Great Black-backed Gull   r W
Black-legged Kittiwake   W
Gull-billed Tern   r W
Caspian Tern   r W
Royal Tern   r M
Lesser Crested Tern   M
Sandwich Tern   c W
Common Tern   c M
Arctic Tern   r M
Little Tern   S
Whiskered Tern   r M
Black Tern   c M
Razorbill   W
Atlantic Puffin   W
Crowned Sandgrouse
Spotted Sandgrouse
Black-bellied Sandgrouse
Pin-tailed Sandgrouse
Rock Pigeon   c
Stock Pigeon
Wood Pigeon
European Turtle-Dove   c S
Great Spotted Cuckoo
Eurasian Cuckoo   S
Barn Owl   r

Eurasian Scops-Owl
Eurasian Eagle-Owl   r
Little Owl
Tawny Owl
Long-eared Owl   r
Short-eared Owl   r W
Marsh Owl   r
Eurasian Nightjar   r S
Red-necked Nightjar   S
Plain Swift   r M
Common Swift   c S
Pallid Swift   c S
Alpine Swift   S
White-rumped Swift   r S
House Swift
Eurasian Kingfisher   r
Blue-cheeked Bee-eater   r S
Eurasian Bee-eater   c S
Eurasian Roller   r S
Hoopoe   S
Eurasian Wryneck   r W
European Green Woodpecker   r
Great Spotted Woodpecker
Bar-tailed Lark
Desert Lark
Bifasciated Lark
DuPont's Lark
Thick-billed Lark
Calandra Lark
Short-toed Lark   c S
Lesser Short-toed Lark
Crested Lark   c
Thekla Lark
Wood Lark
Northern Skylark
Horned Lark
Temminck's Lark
Plain Martin
Sand Martin   M
Pale Crag-Martin
Northern Crag-Martin
Barn Swallow   c S
Red-rumped Swallow   S
House Martin   c S
Tawny Pipit   S
Tree Pipit   M
Meadow Pipit   c W

Red-throated Pipit   r W
Water Pipit   r W
Yellow Wagtail   c
Gray Wagtail
White Wagtail
Garden Bulbul
Eurasian Dipper   r H
Northern Wren
Dunnock   r W
Alpine Accentor   H
Rufous Scrub-Robin   S
European Robin
Nightingale   c S
Bluethroat   W
Black Redstart
Eurasian Redstart   c M, r S
Moussier's Redstart
Whinchat   M
Stonechat   c
Northern Wheatear
Black-eared Wheatear   S
Desert Wheatear   c
Greater Red-rumped Wheatear
Mourning Wheatear
White-crowned Black Wheatear
Black Wheatear
White-rumped Rock-Thrush   S H
Blue Rock-Thrush
Ring Thrush   W
Eurasian Blackbird   c
Song Thrush   c W
Redwing   W
Mistle Thrush
Cetti's Bush-Warbler
Scrub Warbler
Western Grasshopper-Warbler   M
Sedge Warbler   M
European Reed-Warbler   S
Great Reed-Warbler   S
Olivaceous Warbler   S
Melodious Warbler   c S
Dartford Warbler   r
Tristam's Warbler   H
Spectacled Warbler
Subalpine Warbler   S
Sardinian Warbler   c
Desert Warbler

Orphean Warbler   S
Greater Whitethroat   S
Garden Warbler   M
Blackcap
Bonelli's Warbler   S
Chiffchaff   c W
Willow Warbler   c M
Firecrest
Zitting Cisticola
Spotted Flycatcher   S
Pied Flycatcher   S
Fulvous Babbler
Coal Tit
Blue Tit
Great Tit
Eurasian Nuthatch
Short-toed Treecreeper
Eurasian Golden Oriole   r S
Black-crowned Bush-Shrike
Great Gray Shrike
Woodchat Shrike   c S
Eurasian Jay
Black-billed Magpie
Alpine Chough   H
Red-billed Chough

Western Jackdaw
Brown-necked Crow
Northern Raven
European Starling   c W
Spotless Starling
House Sparrow   c
Spanish Sparrow
Desert Sparrow   r
Rock Petronia
Chaffinch   c
European Serin   c
Eurasian Greenfinch   c
Eurasian Goldfinch   c
Eurasian Siskin   r W
Linnet   c
Red Crossbill   r H
Crimson-winged Finch   H
Trumpeter Finch
Hawfinch   r
Cirl Bunting   c
Rock Bunting
House Bunting
Ortolan Bunting   r M
Reed Bunting   r W
Corn Bunting

61
Canary Islands, Spain

THE CANARY ISLANDS, lying off the coast of southern Morocco, boast of a few unique birds. Perhaps the space would be better taken by a section on Sulawesi (Celebes), but the truth is that many more birders are likely to visit the Canaries. Las Palmas airport on Gran Canaria has frequent flights from many European capitals, South America, and West Africa, while Tenerife has direct flights from Spain and elsewhere. There is a plethora of hotels and rental cars on most larger islands. Temperatures are moderate, with relatively warm winters and cool summers, compared with those of the continent. The western islands are relatively humid, while the eastern ones (and the southeastern corners of Gran Canaria and Tenerife) are much more arid.

Gran Canaria has the Jardin Canario in Tafira, just south of Las Palmas. This garden will help you understand why the islands are called the botanist's Galapágos. The adaptive radiation of huge succulents, giant buglosses, and other plants are well seen here. Laurel forests (of a type extinct on the mainland since the Pliocene) once covered much of Gran Canaria. A tiny stand still can be seen at Los Tiles, reachable by a dirt road above Moya in the north-center of the island. The Parador Cruz de Tejeda makes a fine mountain hotel base, and Berthelot's Pipit is common there. The Pinar de Tamadaba is a pine forest near Artenara, the highest village on the island. It can be reached by road going west from Cruz de Tejeda and is home to the rare Blue Chaffinch, Great Spotted Woodpecker, and Rock Petronia, all of which may also be searched for at Pinar Pajonal, southwest of Cruz de Tejeda. The south tip of the island around the Oasis de Maspalomas is good for Lesser Short-toed Lark, Spectacled Warbler, and Trumpeter Finch. This is the only Canary island with Red-legged Partridge.

Tenerife is a large island with a busy airport and the cities of Santa Cruz and Puerto de la Cruz. Firecrest and possibly the Long-toed Pigeon inhabit the laurel forests on Monte de las Mercedes, reachable via a 7-mile (11-km) road north of the airport. The Pico de Teide National Park contains the most impressive scenery in the islands

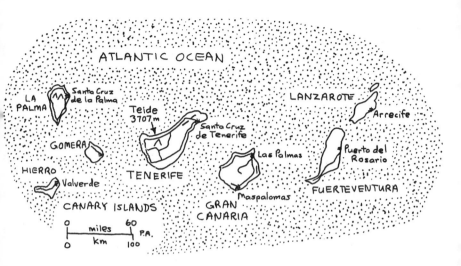

ATLANTIC OCEAN

LA PALMA
Santa Cruz de la Palma

Teide 3707m

GOMERA

HIERRO
Valverde

TENERIFE
Santa Cruz de Tenerife

CANARY ISLANDS

LANZAROTE
Arrecife

Las Palmas

Puerto del Rosario

FUERTEVENTURA

GRAN CANARIA
Maspalomas

miles 60
km 100
P.A.

with its 12,200-foot (3720 m) snow-capped centerpiece (reachable by cable car). The Parador de las Cañadas provides fine accommodation in the mountains, with many Plain Swift and Island Canary in evidence. West of the Parador the main road forks at Boca de Tauce. Barbary Partridge can be found near there in the morning. Seven miles (11 km) from Boca de Tauce on the road west to Guia is a locality known for Blue Chaffinch.

Fuerteventura, one of the eastern islands, is quite arid and is covered with rocky plains. A gully and nearby fields a half mile (1 km) north of the airport on the main road to Puerto del Rosario, the chief town, are good for the restricted Canary Islands Chat. Other birds found in the vicinity are Egyptian Vulture, Cream-colored Courser, Great Gray Shrike, Berthelot's Pipit, and Trumpeter Finch. This island and neighboring Lanzarote are home to Eleonora's Falcon, Houbara Bustard, and Black-bellied Sandgrouse.

The wetter western islands of La Palma and Gomera are the best places for the vanishing Laurel and Long-toed Pigeons, Eurasian Woodcock, Firecrest, and Red-billed Chough (Palma only).

CHECKLIST

Black-necked Grebe r W	Cory's Shearwater
Little Dabchick r W	Sooty Shearwater r M
Soft-plumaged Petrel r M	Manx Shearwater M
Bulwer's Petrel	Little Shearwater

Leach's Storm-Petrel   r W
European Storm-Petrel
Northern Gannet   r W
Gray Heron   r
Little Egret   r M
Eurasian Wigeon   W
Mallard   W
Green-winged Teal   W
Northern Shoveler   W
Red Kite   r
Egyptian Vulture
Eurasian Sparrowhawk   r
Common Buzzard
Osprey
Common Kestrel   c
European Hobby   r M
Eleonora's Falcon   S
Barbary Falcon
Red-legged Partridge
Barbary Partridge
Common Quail
Houbara Bustard
Common Coot   W
Common Gallinule   r W
African Oystercatcher   r
Stone-curlew
Cream-colored Courser
Snowy Plover   W
Ringed Plover   W
Little Ringed Plover   r W
Gray Plover   W
European Golden Plover   r W
Northern Lapwing   W
Sanderling   W
Curlew Sandpiper   r M
Dunlin   W
Ruff   W
Jack Snipe   r W
Common Snipe   W
Eurasian Woodcock
Eurasian Curlew   r M
Whimbrel   M
Black-tailed Godwit   W
Bar-tailed Godwit   r W
Common Redshank   r M
Green Sandpiper   r M
Wood Sandpiper   c W

Ruddy Turnstone   c W
Red Phalarope   M
Collared Pratincole   r M
Parasitic Jaeger   W
Black-headed Gull   W
Lesser Black-backed Gull   W
Herring Gull   c
Sandwich Tern   W
Common Tern   M
Razorbill   r W
Atlantic Puffin   r W
Black-bellied Sandgrouse   r
Rock Pigeon
Long-toed Pigeon   r
Laurel Pigeon
European Turtle-Dove   S
Barn Owl
Long-eared Owl
Common Swift   r M
Plain Swift   S H
Pallid Swift   S L
Eurasian Bee-eater   M
Eurasian Roller   r M
Hoopoe
Great Spotted Woodpecker   r
Northern Skylark   W
Lesser Short-toed Lark
Barn Swallow   c M
House Martin   M
Sand Martin   M
Northern Crag-Martin   r M
Tree Pipit   M
Berthelot's Pipit   c
White Wagtail   W
Yellow Wagtail   r W
Gray Wagtail
Northern Wheatear   r M
Eurasian Redstart   r M
Black Redstart   r M
European Robin
Bluethroat   r M
Canary Islands Chat
Stonechat   r M
Whinchat   r M
Eurasian Blackbird   c
Song Thrush   c W
Fieldfare   r W

Spectacled Warbler
Sardinian Warbler
Willow Warbler   M
Wood Warbler   M
Garden Warbler   M
Greater Whitethroat   M
Blackcap
Chiffchaff   c
Firecrest
Spotted Flycatcher   M
Pied Flycatcher   M
Blue Tit   c
Great Gray Shrike

Red-billed Chough   r
Northern Raven   c
European Starling   W
Spanish Sparrow   c
Rock Petronia
Chaffinch
Blue Chaffinch   r
Island Canary
Eurasian Goldfinch   r
Linnet
Trumpeter Finch
Corn Bunting

62
Senegal and Gambia

THESE TWO COUNTRIES are attracting a lot of attention from North American and European birders. They are located at the westernmost tip of Africa, only a 7-hour flight from New York or northern Europe. Along the lush banks of the Gambia River is Gambia, a narrow tongue of a country where English is spoken. It is encircled by French-speaking Senegal, a much larger country that is bordered on the north by the deserts of Mauritania and on the south by the jungles of Guinea-Bissau and Guinee. Birders can sample near-desert conditions, Sahelian steppes, Sudan savanna, and monsoonal forest as well as some fine coastal and wetland habitats in a relatively compact area.

Banjul (formerly Bathurst), Gambia, has a few international flights, some hotels, and a road system going upriver. The "romantic" boat trips upriver have ceased, but due to the popularity of *Roots* (book and TV series) there may well be organized, reliable trips soon. There are plenty of birds along the Gambia River, but we will concern ourselves with the much greater range of avifaunas and national parks found in Senegal.

Dakar is a surprisingly sophisticated capital city, located on the cliffs of Cape Verde. The Hotel Teranga in the center and various hotels on the coast are first class. Senegal offers fantastic food in almost every restaurant, probably the finest of any so-called Third World country. Its major roads are mostly paved and have remarkably little traffic. Its hotels are spotless and nights are calm. There is very little stealing and most of the country is safe. Yet it is expensive, very expensive compared to most other tropical countries, but worth the expense.

It should be stressed that Senegal has very wet summers and autumns (some roads are impassable and most parks closed), and dry winters and springs that get increasingly arid and hot. December through April are the best months. Also note that there are cycles of wetter and drier years. The birds have learned to be highly nomadic and thus unpredictable in their appearances at times.

A fine one-day trip out of Dakar lies northward to Mboro. Take the main road east (N1) to Rufisque (12 miles [19 km] east of the airport

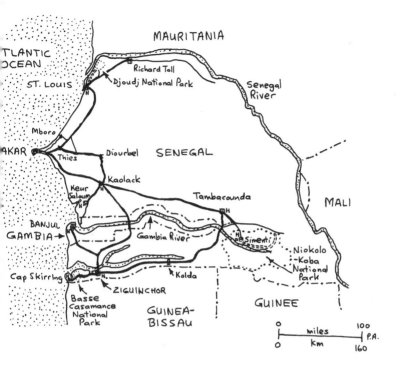

turnoff), thence left (north) on R70 for 3.7 miles (6 km) to a large forest of swollen baobabs. Strolling here one may see Senegal Parrot, Western Gray Plantain-eater, Green Wood-Hoopoe, Vieillot's Barbet, and Splendid Sunbird. Thirty-one miles (50 km) north of Rufisque, just before Mboro, a reedy lake lies to the left. The next dirt road left leads out to the ocean (beware of sand at the end of the road) and passes three ponds. A variety of fine birds can be seen here when water levels are up, including many herons, African Fish-Eagle, Purple Swamphen, Black Crake, African Jacana, and Little Bee-eater. The return can be made via Thies, or visitors may proceed north to St. Louis, which is 104 miles (166 km) north of Dakar.

The Djoudj National Park is located about two hours' drive (with stops) northeast of the city of St. Louis (several hotels). There is a small lodge in the Djoudj with 6 cabins and a restaurant (expensive). Boat trips are offered in winter to see huge masses of breeding Eastern White Pelicans. The reserve roads are good for seeing patas monkey and arid-zone birds, as are the two roads up from St. Louis. The waterbirds here put on a tremendous show, mixing northern migrants with resident African birds.

The Casamance region in the southwest can be reached via Air

Senegal to either the posh beach resort of Cap Skirring (with several fine hotels, including a Club Mediterranee) or the regional capital of Ziguinchor (with several fine hotels, including Aubert and Le Diola). One can also arrive by road, crossing the Gambia by ferry at Mansa Konko or Banjul. The verdant Casamance region is most attractive, with numerous Black Heron, Western Reef-Heron, Palm-nut Vulture, and Blue-bellied Roller. Hundreds of Yellow-billed Storks and Pink-backed Pelicans nest and/or roost in large trees all around central Ziguinchor, a remarkable sight. The Basse Casamance National Park is located halfway between Ziguinchor and Cap Skirring. There is a modest tourist camp in the park. The park preserves some of the tallest forest left in Senegal and is home to Crowned Hawk-Eagle (rare), Guinea Turaco, many hornbills, Red-bellied Gonolek, a variety of bulbuls and sunbirds, as well as other forest birds not found elsewhere in the country. Birding can be great or quiet, depending on many factors. Exploration on foot is unhindered after payment of a modest entry fee. The western red colobus monkeys are well worth the price of admission.

The premier park of Senegal is the huge Niokolo-Koba located to the east of Gambia in southeast Senegal. Here are vast tracts of light woodland, broken by hills, ponds, small plains, and rivers. The tourist lodge at Simenti has 30 rooms, a pool, and several open trucks for game drives. The park can be reached via road (in a long day) from Dakar and Ziguinchor or by occasional flights on small planes (seating up to 20). Walking outside of designated areas is prohibited. The big game is neither as rich nor as easy to see as in East Africa, yet you should see western baboon, hippopotamus, warthog, bushbuck, roan, defassa waterbuck, Buffon's kob, bubal hartebeest, and red-flanked duiker, among others. Elephants are easy to see late in the dry season. Birding can be very exciting, with Saddle-billed Stork, Hammerkop, Egyptian Courser, and Blue-breasted Kingfisher at the rivers. Overhead you may see Bateleur, three species of snake-eagles, and Martial Eagle. Running on the ground will be Helmeted Guineafowl, Stone Partridge, bustards, and Abyssinian Ground Hornbill. Look for Abyssinian Roller, Violet Turaco, many gorgeous bee-eaters, and Long-crested Helmet-Shrike in the trees.

CHECKLIST

(DJ = Djoudj N.P.; NK = Niokolo-Koba; DK = Dakar; NW = Northwest [n. and e. of Dakar]; SW = Southwest [w. Gambia, Casamance]; BC = Basse Casamance N.P.)

Little Dabchick
Red-billed Tropicbird   r DK
Pink-backed Pelican   c SW
Eastern White Pelican   c DJ
Northern Gannet   r W
Long-tailed Cormorant   c
Great Cormorant   c
Darter   c
Little Bittern   r
Black-crowned Night-Heron
Green Heron
Squacco Pond-Heron
Cattle Heron   c
Little Egret   c
Short-billed Egret
Black Heron
Western Reef-Heron   c
Great Egret   c
Black-headed Heron
Gray Heron   c
Purple Heron
Goliath Heron   r
White Stork   M
Black Stork   r M
Abdim's Stork   S
Woolly-necked Stork   SW, NK
Saddle-billed Stork   NK
Yellow-billed Stork   c
Marabou Stork
Sacred Ibis
Hadada Ibis
Glossy Ibis
African Spoonbill
Eurasian Spoonbill   W
Hammerkop   c
Greater Flamingo   c
Fulvous Whistling-Duck   DJ
White-faced Whistling-Duck   c
Egyptian Goose   c
Spur-winged Goose
Knob-billed Goose
African Pygmy-Goose   r
Northern Pintail   c W, DJ
Garganey   c W, DJ
Northern Shoveler   W, DJ
Northern Pochard   W, DJ
Tufted Duck   W, DJ

White-backed Duck   r
Osprey   W
Eurasian Honey-Buzzard   M
Bat Kite   r
Black-shouldered Kite   c
Scissor-tailed Kite
Black Kite   c
African Sea-Eagle
Palm-nut Vulture   c SW, NK
Hooded Vulture   c
African White-backed Vulture   c
Ruppell's Vulture
Lappet-faced Vulture
White-headed Vulture   r
Short-toed Snake-Eagle   W
Beaudouin's Snake-Eagle   NK
Brown Snake-Eagle   NK
Banded Snake-Eagle   r NK
Bateleur   c NK
African Harrier-Hawk   c
Montagu's Harrier   c W
Marsh Harrier   c W
Dark Chanting-Goshawk
Gabar Goshawk   NK
African Goshawk   SW
Shikra   c
Great Goshawk   r NK
Grasshopper Buzzard   c
Lizard Buzzard   c
Long-legged Buzzard   r W
Wahlberg's Eagle   c NK
African Hawk-Eagle   NK
Booted Eagle   W
Long-crested Eagle
Crowned Hawk-Eagle   r BC
Martial Eagle   NK
Lesser Kestrel   M
Common Kestrel   c W
Gray Kestrel   c SW, NK
Red-necked Falcon   r NK
African Hobby   NK
European Hobby   W
Peregrine Falcon   W
Double-spurred Francolin   c
Stone Partridge   c NK
Helmeted Guineafowl   c NK
African Black Crake

Common Gallinule
Purple Swamphen
Allen's Gallinule   r
Western Crowned Crane
Arabian Bustard   DJ
Black-bellied Bustard   NK
Common Buttonquail   NK
African Jacana   c
Greater Painted-snipe
Common Oystercatcher   r W
Black-winged Stilt   c
Black-capped Avocet
Spur-winged Lapwing   c
Black-headed Lapwing   c
White-crowned Lapwing   NK
Senegal Lapwing   r NK
Wattled Lapwing   c
Gray Plover   W
Kittlitz's Plover
Greater Ringed Plover   c W
Little Ringed Plover   r W
Snowy Plover   r W
Whimbrel   c W
Eurasian Curlew   r W
Black-tailed Godwit   c W
Bar-tailed Godwit   W
Common Greenshank   W
Marsh Sandpiper   W
Wood Sandpiper   c W
Green Sandpiper   W
Common Redshank   W
Spotted Redshank   M
Common Sandpiper   W
Ruddy Turnstone   W
Common Snipe   W
Great Snipe   r W
Curlew Sandpiper   c W
Dunlin   r W
Red Knot   r W
Little Stint   c W
Ruff   c W
Sanderling   W
Senegal Dikkop   c
Spotted Dikkop   r
Egyptian Courser   c NK
Cream-colored Courser   r DJ
Temminck's Courser

Collared Pratincole   M
Gray-headed Gull   c
Black-headed Gull   W
Slender-billed Gull
Lesser Black-backed Gull   c W
Black Tern   M
White-winged Black Tern   r M
Whiskered Tern   r M
Gull-billed Tern   c
Caspian Tern   c
Royal Tern   c
Sandwich Tern   c
Common Tern
Little Tern
African Skimmer   r
Chestnut-bellied Sandgrouse   DJ
Four-banded Sandgrouse   NK,
    SW
Speckled Pigeon   c
Red-eyed Dove   c
European Turtle-Dove   M
Mourning Turtle-Dove   c
Vinaceous Turtle-Dove   c
Pink-headed Turtle-Dove   NW
Laughing Turtle-Dove   c
Namaqua Dove   c
Blue-spotted Wood-Dove   SW,
    NK
Black-billed Wood-Dove
African Green-Pigeon
Yellow-bellied Green-Pigeon   r
Brown-necked Parrot   r
Senegal Parrot   c
Ring-necked Parakeet   c
Guinea Turaco   SW
Violet Turaco   NK, SW
Western Gray Plantain-eater   c
Great Spotted Cuckoo   M
Levaillant's Cuckoo   S
Klaas's Cuckoo   S
Green Cuckoo   S, SW
Senegal Coucal   c
African Scops-Owl   c
White-faced Scops-Owl   BC
Verreaux's Eagle-Owl   r
Pel's Fishing Owl   r NK
Pearl-spotted Owlet   NK

Egyptian Nightjar   r   DJ
Dusky Nightjar   BC
Long-tailed Nightjar   NW
Standard-winged Nightjar   NK
Common Swift   M
Pallid Swift   M
House Swift   c
African Palm-Swift   c
Mottle-throated Swift   NK
Blue-naped Mousebird   NW
Giant Kingfisher
Pied Kingfisher   c
Malachite Kingfisher
African Pygmy Kingfisher   r   NK
Woodland Kingfisher   r   NK
Blue-breasted Kingfisher   c   NK
Striped Kingfisher   c
Gray-headed Kingfisher   NK
Eurasian Bee-eater   c   W
Blue-cheeked Bee-eater   r   M
Northern Carmine Bee-eater   NK
White-throated Bee-eater   S
Green Bee-eater   S
Little Bee-eater   c
Red-throated Bee-eater   c   NK
Swallow-tailed Bee-eater
Abyssinian Roller   c
Rufous-crowned Roller
Blue-bellied Roller   c   SW, NK
Cinnamon Roller
Hoopoe
Green Wood-Hoopoe   c
Black Wood-Hoopoe   r
African Gray Hornbill   c
Red-billed Hornbill   c
African Pied Hornbill   c   SW
Yellow-casqued Hornbill   r   BC
Piping Hornbill   BC
Abyssinian Ground-Hornbill
Bearded Barbet
Vieillot's Barbet
Yellow-fronted Tinkerbird
Lemon-rumped Tinkerbird   r
Red-rumped Tinkerbird   r   SW
Greater Honeyguide   c   S
Spotted Honeyguide   BC
Eurasian Wryneck   r   M

Fine-spotted Woodpecker
Cardinal Woodpecker   NK
Little White-spotted Woodpecker
   NK
Gray Woodpecker
Black-crowned Finch-Lark   NW
Chestnut-backed Finch-Lark   c
Crested Lark   c
Sun Lark   NK
Sand Martin   W
Barn Swallow   W
Wire-tailed Swallow
Pied-winged Swallow   r
Mosque Swallow
Red-rumped Swallow
House Martin   c   M
Fanti Saw-wing   r
Yellow Wagtail   c   W
White Wagtail   c   W
African Pied Wagtail   S
Plain-backed Pipit
Tree Pipit   M
Red-throated Pipit   W, NW
Yellow-throated Longclaw   SW
White (Long-crested)
   Helmet-Shrike   NK, SW
Brubru Shrike   NK
Gambian Puffback Shrike
Black-crowned Tchagra
Red-bellied Gonolek
Sulfur-breasted Bush-Shrike   r
Gray-headed Bush-Shrike
Yellow-billed Shrike   c
Woodchat Shrike   c   W
African Golden Oriole
European Golden Oriole   W
African Drongo   c
Splendid Glossy-Starling   DK
Purple Glossy-Starling   c
Blue-eared Glossy-Starling   c
Lesser Blue-eared Glossy-Starling
   NK, SW
Bronze-tailed Glossy-Starling   NK
Northern Long-tailed
   Glossy-Starling   c
Amethyst Starling   S
Chestnut-bellied Starling   c   NW

Yellow-billed Oxpecker
Piapiac   c
Pied Crow   c
White-breasted Cuckoo-shrike   r
Red-shouldered Cuckoo-shrike   r
Garden Bulbul   c
Little Greenbul   SW
Yellow-throated Leaf-love   NK, SW
Swamp Palm Bulbul   BC
Leaf-love Greenbul   SW
Gray-headed Bristlebill   BC
Yellow-spotted Nicator   BC
Whinchat   W
Stonechat   NW
Northern Wheatear   c W
Black-eared Wheatear   W NW
Northern Ant-Chat
Eurasian Redstart   M
Rufous Scrub-Robin
Black Scrub-Robin   DJ
White-crowned Robin-Chat   NK
Snowy-crowned Robin-Chat   SW, NK
Fire-crested Alethe   BC
Bluethroat   M
African Thrush
Rufous-winged Akalat   BC
Sudan Babbler   c SW, NK
Capuchin Babbler   BC
Blackcap Babbler   NK
European Reed-Warbler   W
Sedge Warbler   W DJ
Melodious Warbler   c W
Olivaceous Warbler   c W
Garden Warbler   M
Orphean Warbler   r W
Sardinian Warbler   W
Greater Whitethroat   W
Subalpine Warbler   W
Bonelli's Warbler   W, NW
Willow Warbler   c W
Chiffchaff   W
Wood Warbler   W
Zitting Cisticola
Red-winged Warbler
Tawny-flanked Prinia   SW, NK

Moho   r NK
Gray-backed Camaroptera
Green-backed Eremomela
Senegal Crombec
Yellow-bellied Hyliota   r
Pallid Flycatcher
Swamp Flycatcher   NK
Northern Black Flycatcher   S
Gray Tit-Flycatcher   SW, NK
Senegal Batis
White-browed Forest-Flycatcher   BC
Northern Wattle-eye   BC, NK
Northern Fairy Flycatcher   NK
Black-headed Paradise-Flycatcher   S, SW, NK
African Paradise-Flycatcher   S, SW, NK
White-shouldered Black-Tit   NK
Sudan Penduline-Tit   r
Green Hylia   r BC
Western Violet-backed Sunbird
Collared Sunbird   SW
Pygmy Sunbird
Scarlet-chested Sunbird
Variable Sunbird   c
Copper Sunbird   r
Splendid Sunbird   DK, SW
Beautiful Sunbird
Yellow White-eye
White-rumped Canary   DK
Yellow-fronted Canary
White-billed Buffalo-Weaver   c
Gray-headed Sparrow   c
Golden Sparrow   c NW
Bush Petronia
Yellow-throated Petronia   NK
Speckle-fronted Weaver   DJ
Little Weaver
Vitelline Masked Weaver
Village Weaver
Gambian Black-headed Weaver
Black-necked Weaver
Blue-billed Malimbe   BC
Red-headed Malimbe   r NW
Red-billed Quelea   c NW
Yellow-crowned Bishop   S

Fire-crowned Bishop   S
Yellow-mantled Widowbird   S
Pin-tailed Whydah
Indigobird
Northern Broad-tailed Whydah
Chestnut-breasted Negro-Finch
   BC
Cut-throat Finch   NW
Orange-cheeked Waxbill   SW, NK

Green-winged Pytilia   NW
Common Waxbill
Western Lavender Waxbill
Red-cheeked Cordonbleu
Black-faced Fire-Finch   r NK
Red-billed Fire-Finch   c
Common Quail-Finch   DJ
White-throated Munia   NK
Bronze Munia

63
Lagos–Ibadan, Nigeria

MOST VISITORS TO NIGERIA arrive at the Lagos Ikeja International Airport in the southwestern corner of the country. Nigerian cities are vibrant crowded places with overpriced hotels and restaurants. Cars may be rented, but due to the conditions of vehicles and roads, most visitors not on organized birding tours should consider hiring a good Nigerian driver from a major travel agency.

The climate is tropical with the wettest months being March through June and September through November.

Most visitors to Lagos stay at hotels on Ikoyi Island connected by bridges with Lagos Island. Birding in Turnbull Road and nearby swamps can be good in the evening (White-crested Tiger-Herons have been noted here).

Victoria Island, which separates Lagos and Ikoyi from the sea, is worth a visit. Waders and passerines visit the sandy areas. The mangrove swamp by Kuramo Waters may have Moho and Mouse-brown Sunbird. A second-growth jungle and palm forest beyond Igbosere should produce views of Snowy-headed Robin-Chat and Carmelite Sunbird.

To the west of Lagos there are marshes near Apapa with many waders, rails, herons, and kingfishers. Farther west on the Ojo Road, about 15 miles (24 km) from Lagos, is a sandy area with savanna and swamp forest.

Just north of Lagos in the grasslands north of Ebute Metta (or in similar areas if these disappear) specialties such as Standard-winged Nightjar (December–March), Red-faced and Short-winged Cisticola, Chestnut-winged Starling, and Compact Weaver may be found.

About 20 miles (32 km) north of Lagos is the Ogun River, which can be reached by following the road toward the airport. At the circle in Ikeja bear right, and go past the Airport Hotel and Agidingki. There are many raptors and forest birds along the road and several paths into forest and to the Ogun River before entering Isieri. Exploring this area (perhaps via boat if it could be arranged) may reveal Palm-nut Vulture, Egyptian Courser, Guinea Turaco, Woodland Kingfisher, White-tailed Hornbill, Melancholy Woodpecker, Chest-

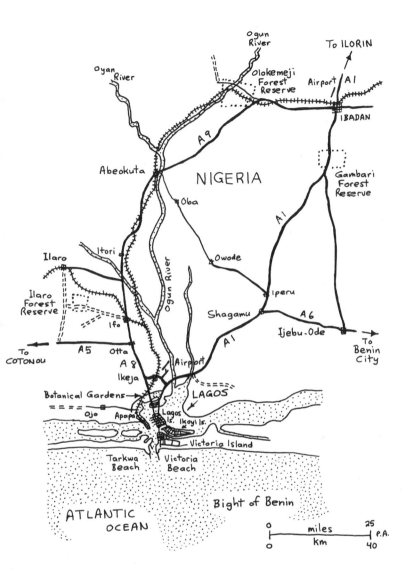

nut-capped and Cassin's Gray Flycatcher, Rufous Cane Warbler, Chattering Cisticola, West African Swallow (dry season), Velvet-headed Glossy-Starling, and Scarlet-tufted Sunbird.

Jungle birding can be good at the Ilaro Forest Reserve 50 miles (80 km) northwest of Lagos. Take the main road north toward Abeokuta and turn left at Ifo (35 miles) toward Cokers Market.

Ibadan is a good base to visit several fine areas. In town the Ibadan University grounds, suburban gardens, and nearby plantations are worthwhile visiting. The Ona River has been dammed to form the Eleiyele Reservoir, a major wetland. Many waterbirds live there, including African Finfoot.

There are two tall forests near Ibadan that can be visited. The Gambari Forest Reserve 15 miles (24 km) south has Gray Parrot and Red-chested Cuckoo. About 30 miles (48 km) west is the Olokemeji Forest Reserve, along the Lagos-Ibadan Railroad where the Afonrin River joins the Ogun River. Many spectacular forest birds live here (including some rare ones not on our list).

CHECKLIST

Pink-backed Pelican   r
Long-tailed Cormorant
Darter
Gray Heron
Black-headed Heron
Purple Heron
Great Egret
Cattle Heron
Little Egret
West African Reef-Heron   r
Green Heron
Black-crowned Night-Heron
White-crested Tiger-Heron   r
Little Bittern   W
Hammerkop   r
Sacred Ibis   r
White-faced Whistling-Duck
Hartlaub's Duck   r
African Pygmy Goose
Osprey   r W
African Baza
Black-shouldered Kite
Black Kite
Palm-nut Vulture
Harrier-Hawk
Marsh Harrier   W
African Goshawk
Shikra
Lizard Buzzard
Common Kestrel
Double-spurred Francolin

Blue Quail
African Crake   r
African Black Crake
Lesser Gallinule   r
African Finfoot
African Jacana   c
Greater Painted-snipe   r
White-crowned Lapwing
Senegal Lapwing
Gray Plover   r W
Ringed Plover   c W
Little Ringed Plover   c W
Forbes's Plover   r
White-fronted Plover   c
Whimbrel   W
Common Redshank   r W
Marsh Sandpiper   W
Common Greenshank   c W
Wood Sandpiper   c W
Common Sandpiper   W
Common Snipe   r W
Ethiopian Snipe   r
Great Snipe   r W
Sanderling   W
Little Stint   r W
Curlew Sandpiper   r W
Egyptian Courser
Gray Pratincole
Lesser Black-backed Gull   r W
Black Tern   c W
Common Tern   c W

Arctic Tern   M
Roseate Tern   W
Bridled Tern   M
Damara Tern   M
Little Tern   W
Royal Tern   M
Sandwich Tern   M
Red-eyed Turtle-Dove   c
Vinaceous Turtle-Dove   r
Laughing Turtle-Dove   c
Blue-spotted Wood-Dove   c
Tambourine Wood-Dove   r
African Green Pigeon   c
Guinea Turaco
Western Gray Plaintain-eater
Bare-faced Go-away-bird   c
Great Spotted Cuckoo   W
Levaillant's Cuckoo   r S
Red-chested Cuckoo   r S
Emerald Cuckoo   r
Klaas's Cuckoo   r
Didric Cuckoo   r
Green Coucal   r
Rufous-bellied Coucal
Black-throated Coucal
Blue-headed Coucal   r
Senegal Coucal   c
White-faced Scops-Owl   c
Dusky Nightjar
Natal Nightjar   r
Plain Nightjar   r
Standard-winged Nightjar
House Swift   c
African Palm-Swift   c
Giant Kingfisher   r
Pied Kingfisher   c
Shining Blue Kingfisher   r
Malachite Kingfisher   c
African Pygmy Kingfisher   r
Gray-headed Kingfisher   r
Woodland Kingfisher   c
Blue-breasted Kingfisher   r
Little Bee-eater
Black Bee-eater
White-throated Bee-eater
Rosy Bee-eater
Eurasian Roller   M

Cinnamon Roller
Blue-throated Roller
Black Wood-Hoopoe
African Gray Hornbill
Dwarf Hornbill   r
African Pied Hornbill   c
White-crested Hornbill
White-tailed Hornbill   r
Naked-faced Barbet
Bristle-nosed Barbet
Yellow-spotted Barbet   r
Speckled Tinkerbird
Lemon-throated Tinkerbird
Hairy-breasted Barbet
Double-toothed Barbet
Yellow-billed Barbet
Least Honeyguide   r
Lesser Honeyguide
Buff-spotted Woodpecker   r
Melancholy Woodpecker   r
Gray Woodpecker
Fire-bellied Woodpecker   c
Barn Swallow   W
Ethiopian Swallow
West African Swallow
Rufous-chested Swallow
Mosque Swallow
Fanti Saw-wing
Square-tailed Drongo
African Drongo   c
Black-winged Oriole   c
Chestnut-winged Starling
Purple-headed Glossy-Starling   r
Purple Glossy-Starling
Splendid Glossy-Starling   c
Amethyst Starling
Pied Crow   c
Black-winged Babbler
Red-shouldered Cuckoo-shrike
Garden Bulbul
Little Greenbul   c
Yellow-whiskered Greenbul
Slender-billed Greenbul
Honeyguide Greenbul
Spotted Greenbul   r
Simple Leaf-love   c
Yellow-throated Leaf-love

Swamp Palm Greenbul
White-throated Greenbul   r
Gray-headed Bristlebill   r
Yellow-spotted Nicator
Nightingale   W
Snowy-crowned Robin-Chat
Whinchat   c
African Thrush   c
Moustached Grassbird
Willow Warbler   W
Wood Warbler   r W
Zitting Cisticola   r
Red-faced Cisticola
Singing Cisticola
Whistling Cisticola
Chattering Cisticola
Winding Cisticola
Croaking Cisticola
Short-winged Cisticola
Moho
Gray-backed Camaroptera   c
Green Crombec
Rufous Reed-Warbler
Pied Flycatcher   W
Cassin's Gray Flycatcher   r
Spotted Flycatcher   W
White-browed Forest-Flycatcher
Common Forest-Flycatcher
Northern Black Flycatcher
Pallid Flycatcher
Black-and-white Flycatcher   r
Northern Wattle-eye   r
Chestnut Wattle-eye
Blisset's Wattle-eye
Chestnut-capped Flycatcher   r
Northern Fairy-Flycatcher
Blue-headed Crested-Flycatcher
African Paradise-Flycatcher
Black-headed Paradise-Flycatcher
Yellow Wagtail   c W
African Pied Wagtail   c
Yellow-throated Longclaw   c
Plain-backed Pipit
Gambian Puff-back Shrike
Black-capped Tchagra
Black-crowned Tchagra   c
Cape Boubou

Black-headed Gonolek
Sulfur-breasted Bush-Shrike
Fiery-breasted Bush-Shrike
Yellow-billed Shrike
Common Fiscal-Shrike   c
Woodchat Shrike   r
Red-billed Helmet-Shrike
Green Hylia
Mouse-brown Sunbird
Gray-headed Sunbird
Collared Sunbird   c
Olive Sunbird
Green-headed Sunbird
Carmelite Sunbird
Buff-throated Sunbird
Variable Sunbird
Olive-bellied Sunbird   c
Copper Sunbird
Splendid Sunbird
Superb Sunbird
Yellow White-eye   c
Chestnut-breasted Negro-Finch
Pale-fronted Negro-Finch   r
Gray Negro-Finch   c
Black-bellied Seedcracker   r
Bar-breasted Fire-Finch
Orange-cheeked Waxbill
Common Quail-Finch
Bronze Munia   c
Red-backed Munia
Gray-headed Sparrow
Thick-billed Weaver
Black-necked Weaver
Orange Weaver   r
Village Weaver   c
Vieillot's Black Weaver   c
Compact Weaver
Yellow-mantled Weaver
Red-vented Malimbe   c
Ibadan Malimbe
Blue-billed Malimbe
Red-headed Malimbe   c
Crested Malimbe   r
Red-headed Quelea   r
Yellow-crowned Bishop   r
Yellow-mantled Widowbird
Pin-tailed Whydah

64

Virunga National Park, Zaire

CREATED IN 1925 and covering 3124 square miles (8122 km²), Virunga is a candidate for the title "the most beautiful national park in the world." It is well protected, and provides birding opportunities in a variety of different habitats, from the "Mountains of the Moon" at Ruwenzori in the north to the shores at Lake Kivu, 150 miles (242 km) to the south. All of the usual species of African mammals abound, and hippopotamus are said to number over 20,000, perhaps the greatest concentration of this species in the world. The centerpiece of the park is Lake Edward, where hippos congregate and Eastern White Pelicans come to squabble around the fishing boats, along with Marabou Storks. With drainage and steep valleys running from the south to the north, the major park roads run along the same axis, but at least five major roads cut across from west to east, allowing access to most of the better areas.

Most visitors fly to Kinshasa, the capital of Zaïre, and then connect with a flight to the Lake Kivu area, where airports are located at Goma, Bukavu on the south side of the lake, and Kigali in Rwanda (transfering from there to Goma). One of the focal points of the park is at Rwindi, 62 miles (100 km) north of Goma. Accommodation at the Park Lodge at Rwindi is in comfortable rondavels (round native-style huts) with modern facilities. Meals are good and informal.

Most birding has been done around the plains area of Rwindi and nearby Lake Edward. Waterbirds abound, along with vultures and birds of prey, though a view of Whale-headed Stork is, as elsewhere, elusive. Migrant waders are quite excellent, and Greater Painted-snipe are not uncommon. The area is as far west as the Madagascar Blue-cheeked Bee-eater migrates, and other species include an excellent list of swallows, among them Mosque and White-headed Sawwing.

The famous volcano section around Goma and the shore of Lake Kivu is rewarding. Mountain Buzzard and Great Goshawk, a couple

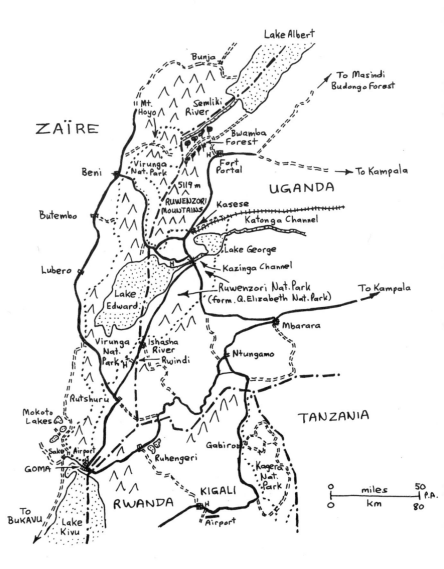

of the less widespread bee-eaters, African Broadbill, Abyssinian Hill-Babbler, Honeyguide Greenbul, a host of "difficult" flycatchers and warblers, and a few sunbirds can be seen.

From Rwindi it is a two-day drive north over dirt tracks to Mount Hoyo, where the Mount Hoyo Guest House is situated right at the Park boundary, northeast of Beni. This is an excellent area for forest-bird watching, including Great Blue Turaco, White-thighed and Black Casqued Hornbills, Gray Parrot, Square-tailed Saw-wing, and Sabine's Swift. These mountain forests are still home to the world's smallest race ("the pygmies") and mountain gorillas, as well. Spend at least three nights to enjoy the best of the area and break the journey at comfortable Kikyo Hotel at Butembo.

For booking write to Délégation Régionale du Commissariat Général au Tourism, PO Box 242, Goma, Zaïre; keep in mind that French is the preferred language.

CHECKLIST

Eastern White Pelican   c
Pink-backed Pelican   c
Great Cormorant   c
Long-tailed Cormorant   c
Black-headed Heron   c
Goliath Heron   c
Purple Heron   c
Great Egret   c
Black Heron   r
Short-billed Egret   c
Cattle Heron   c
Little Egret   c
Squacco Pond-Heron   c
Madagascar Pond-Heron   r M
Green Heron   r
Black-crowned Night-Heron
Whale-headed Stork   r
Hammerkop   c
Abdim's Stork   c M
Saddle-billed Stork   c
Black Open-billed Stork   r
Yellow-billed Stork   c
Marabou Stork   c
Sacred Ibis   c
Hadada Ibis   c
Glossy Ibis   r
African Spoonbill   c

Lesser Flamingo   c
White-faced Whistling-Duck   r
Egyptian Goose   c
Knob-billed Goose   c
Cape Teal   c
Yellow-billed Duck   c
Red-billed Duck   c
Hottentot Teal   c
Osprey   r W
Black-shouldered Kite   c
Black Kite   c
African Sea-Eagle
Palm-nut Vulture
Hooded Vulture   c
African White-backed Vulture   c
Lappet-faced Vulture
White-headed Vulture
Black-breasted Snake-Eagle   r
Brown Snake-Eagle   r
Bateleur   c
Marsh Harrier   r W
African Harrier   c
Pallid Harrier   c W
Montagu's Harrier   c W
Great Goshawk
Rufous-breasted Sparrowhawk   r
Lizard Buzzard

Common Buzzard   W
Mountain Buzzard
Augur Buzzard   c
Tawny Eagle
African Hawk-Eagle
Long-crested Eagle   c
Martial Eagle
Lesser Kestrel   r W
Common Kestrel   r W
Gray Kestrel
African Hobby
Lanner Falcon
Handsome Francolin   c
Red-necked Spurfowl   c
Harlequin Quail   r M
Helmeted Guineafowl   c
Crested Guineafowl   r
Eastern Crowned Crane   c
African Black Crake
Purple Swamphen   c
Common Gallinule   c
Red-knobbed Coot   r
Black-bellied Bustard
African Jacana   c
Greater Painted-snipe   r
Long-toed Lapwing
Spur-winged Lapwing   c
Senegal Lapwing   c
Crowned Lapwing   c
Wattled Lapwing
Kittlitz's Plover
Greater Ringed Plover   c W
Three-banded Plover
Marsh Sandpiper   c W
Common Greenshank   c W
Wood Sandpiper   c W
Common Sandpiper   c W
Common Snipe   c W
Little Stint   W
Temminck's Stint   r W
Dunlin   r W
Curlew Sandpiper   c W
Ruff   c W
Black-winged Stilt   c
Water Dikkop
Spotted Dikkop
Temminck's Courser

Collared Pratincole   c W
Black-winged Pratincole   r W
Lesser Black-backed Gull   c W
Gray-headed Gull   c
Gull-billed Tern   c
African Skimmer   c
Olive Pigeon
Red-eyed Turtle-Dove   c
Cape Turtle-Dove   c
Emerald-spotted Wood-Dove
Blue-spotted Wood-Dove
Tambourine Wood-Dove
African Green Pigeon   c
Gray Parrot
Black-billed Turaco   r
Ruwenzori Turaco   r
Ross's Turaco   c
Great Blue Turaco   r
White-bellied Go-away-bird   c
Great Spotted Cuckoo   c W
Levaillant's Cuckoo   r
Jacobin Cuckoo   c W
Red-chested Cuckoo
Eurasian Cuckoo   W
Emerald Cuckoo   r
Didric Cuckoo   r
White-browed Cuckoo   c
Verreaux's Eagle-Owl
Gabon Nightjar
Mottled Swift   r
Alpine Swift   r
White-rumped Swift   c
House Swift   c
Speckled Mousebird
Blue-naped Mousebird
Narina Trogon   r
Giant Kingfisher
Pied Kingfisher   c
Shining Blue Kingfisher
Malachite Kingfisher   c
Dwarf Kingfisher   r
African Pygmy Kingfisher
Chocolate-backed Kingfisher   r
Gray-headed Kingfisher
Woodland Kingfisher
Blue-breasted Kingfisher
Striped Kingfisher

Little Bee-eater   c
Cinnamon-chested Bee-eater
Black Bee-eater
White-throated Bee-eater
Blue-cheeked Bee-eater
Eurasian Roller
Cinnamon Roller
Blue-throated Roller
Hoopoe   c
Green Wood-Hoopoe   c
Southern Scimitarbill
African Gray Hornbill
Crowned Hornbill
Gray-cheeked Hornbill
Gray-throated Barbet
Speckled Tinkerbird
Yellow-fronted Tinkerbird
Lemon-rumped Tinkerbird
Yellow-throated Tinkerbird
Spot-flanked Barbet
Hairy-breasted Barbet
White-headed Barbet
Double-toothed Barbet
Yellow-billed Barbet
Cassin's Honeyguide
Lesser Honeyguide   c
Thick-billed Honeyguide
Greater Honeyguide
Red-breasted Wryneck
Nubian Woodpecker   r
African Spotted Woodpecker   r
Brown-eared Woodpecker
African Broadbill
Flappet Bush-Lark   c
Rufous-naped Bush-Lark   c
Red-capped Lark   c
Banded Martin   c
Plain Martin   c
Sand Martin   c W
Wire-tailed Swallow   c
Angola Swallow
Barn Swallow   c W
Red-rumped Swallow   r
Mosque Swallow   r
Rufous-chested Swallow
Lesser Striped Swallow   c
Rock Martin

Square-tailed Saw-wing   r
White-headed Saw-wing   r
Richard's Pipit   c
Golden Pipit
Yellow-throated Longclaw   c
Yellow Wagtail   c W
African Pied Wagtail   c
Mountain Wagtail
Black Cuckoo-shrike   r
Gray Cuckoo-shrike   r
Gambian Puffback Shrike   c
Black-crowned Tchagra   c
Black-headed Gonolek   c
Tropical Boubou   c
Doherty's Bush-Shrike
Lesser Gray Shrike   W
MacKinnon's Shrike
Common Fiscal Shrike   c
Garden Bulbul   c
Cameroon Sombre Greenbul
Mountain Greenbul   c
Yellow-whiskered Greenbul   c
Honeyguide Greenbul
Stonechat   c
Sooty Chat   c
Red-backed Scrub-Robin   c
Starred Robin
Snowy-crowned Robin-Chat
Heuglin's Robin-Chat   c
Cape Robin-Chat   c
Whiskered Akalat
Olive Thrush   c
Pale-breasted Akalat   r
Mountain Akalat   r
Black-lored Babbler   c
White-rumped Babbler   r
Arrow-marked Babbler   r
Abyssinian Hill-Babbler
Sedge Warbler   W
Marsh Warbler   r W
European Reed-Warbler   c W
Great Reed-Warbler   r W
Olive-tree Warbler   r W
Willow Warbler   c W
Zitting Cisticola   c
Stout Cisticola   r
Chubb's Cisticola

Winding Cisticola   c
Collared Apalis   c
Gray-backed Camaroptera   c
Gray-capped Warbler
White-browed Crombec
Green Crombec   c
Spotted Flycatcher   c W
Swamp Flycatcher   c
Pallid Flycatcher   c
White-eyed Slaty Flycatcher   c
Chin-spot Batis   c
Black-headed Batis
Northern Wattle-eye
White-tailed Crested Flycatcher
African Paradise Flycatcher   c
Collared Sunbird   c
Purple-banded Sunbird
Red-chested Sunbird   c
Lesser Double-collared Sunbird   c
Copper Sunbird   c
Regal Sunbird
Bronzy Sunbird   c
Scarlet-tufted Malachite Sunbird
Scarlet-chested Sunbird   c
Yellow White-eye   c
Golden-breasted Bunting   c
Yellow-crowned Canary   c
African Citril
Yellow-fronted Canary
Thick-billed Canary   c
Streaky Canary   c
Village Weaver   c
Vieillot's Black Weaver   c

Northern Brown-throated Weaver   c
Lesser Masked Weaver   c
Little Weaver   r
Slender-billed Weaver   c
Spectacled Weaver   c
Black-necked Weaver
Red Bishop   r
Fire-crowned Bishop
Yellow Bishop   c
Red-collared Widowbird   c
Fan-tailed Widowbird   c
Red-billed Quelea   c
Gray-headed Sparrow   c
Pin-tailed Whydah   c
Gray-headed Negro-Finch   r
Green-winged Pytilia   c
Dusky Crimsonwing
Red-billed Fire-Finch   c
Common Waxbill   c
Black-crowned Waxbill   r
Black-headed Waxbill   c
Bronze Munia
Ruppell's Long-tailed Starling   c
Chestnut-winged Starling   c
Amethyst Starling
Wattled Starling
Yellow-billed Oxpecker   c
African Drongo
Square-tailed Drongo   r
Black-winged Oriole   c
Pied Crow   c
White-necked Raven   c

65

Kakamega Forest, Kenya

THE KAKAMEGA FOREST is located 22 miles (33 km) north of Kisumu on the shore of Lake Victoria. On the lakeshore in Kisumu is the excellent new Sunset Hotel. The township of Kakamega lies along a paved road and now has the modest yet adequate Kakamega Highway Hotel (PO Box 677, Kakamega, Kenya). Most of the surrounding countryside is densely populated (unlike the Masai country) and intensively cultivated. To reach the remnants of Kenya's last "West African" wet forest take the dirt road due east 6.2 miles (10 km) then turn left on another major dirt road. After 3.7 miles (6 km) you enter heavy forest, where a smaller dirt road to the left takes you to the forest station and the pumphouse trail. Staying on the main road, you will pass the Rondo Mission grounds on the right in 1.3 miles (2 km) and 3.1 miles (5 km) farther you'll arrive at the Ikuywa River bridge.

This unique forest is being eaten away by timber and farming interests, depriving Kenya of its last stretch of "lowland" western forest full of zoological and botanical treasures. Rainfall averages close to 100 inches (2540 mm) a year, much of it falling between May and August. The elevation here is between 5000 and 6000 feet (1524 and 1830 m), whereas most of Kenya's surviving forests are much higher in elevation. Mammals here include three interesting primates — the black-and-white colobus, blue monkey, and copper-tailed monkey. Most of the larger mammals have been hunted out, and you are free to get lost or eaten. Birds are sometimes commonly seen in parties, and at other times the forest appears lifeless; in any case, you will see less here than in the savannas despite the high quality of individual species.

The Ikuywa River bridge is an excellent birding place during the first few hours of the day, and at dusk, due to good visibility and rich streamside forest. A wide trail just beyond the bridge to the right offers access into the forest, but with frequent human traffic. Among the birds found here are Gray Parrot (evenings), African Broadbill, Dusky Tit, Shrike-Flycatcher, Turner's Eremomela, and Gray-green Bush-Shrike.

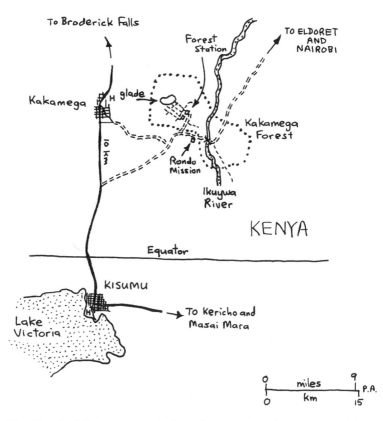

The Rondo Mission grounds have lawns under huge trees, with many flowering plants. Gray-cheeked Hornbill, Great Blue Turaco, Snowy-crowned Robin-Chat, and a variety of sunbirds are often seen there. The staff is quite friendly, there are rest rooms, and a little contribution is greatly appreciated.

The most intensively birded area is the Forest Station plot, where a maze of wide trails (with occasional fallen trunks) goes north into heavy forest and a natural grassy glade. The trails can be slippery and mud boots would be welcome at times of rain. Take care not to get lost. The forest itself is home to numerous birds, many of them shy, though you may see such gems as the Blue-headed Bee-eater, barbets, greenbuls, wattle-eyes, Red-headed Malimbe, and Brown-capped Weaver. The open grassy glade is about a twenty-minute walk through the forest and is a good spot to look for Crowned Hawk-Eagle, Moustached Grassbird, Stout Cisticola, and during the last few months of the year, the Orange-tufted Sunbird.

Birds can be numerous at the edge of the forest, in the clearing, and about the houses at the forest camp. You should also take the trail to the pumphouse to the southeast, which provides additional forest birding including White-tailed Rusty-Thrush.

CHECKLIST

Pink-backed Pelican   M
Black-headed Heron
Hammerkop
White Stork   M
Abdim's Stork   M
Marabou Stork   c
Hadada Ibis
Olive Ibis   r
Black Kite
Black-shouldered Kite
Eurasian Honey-Buzzard   W
African Baza
Bat Kite
Hooded Vulture
Pallid Harrier   W
African Harrier-Hawk
Bateleur
Banded Snake-Eagle
Great Goshawk   r
African Goshawk
Shikra
Little Sparrowhawk
Lizard Buzzard
Augur Buzzard
Common Buzzard   W
Mountain Buzzard
Long-crested Eagle   c
Crowned Hawk-Eagle
African Hawk-Eagle   r
Ayre's Hawk-Eagle   r
Wahlberg's Eagle
African Hobby
European Hobby   W
Gray Kestrel   r
Common Kestrel   W
Scaly Francolin
Common Quail
Harlequin Quail   M
Crested Guineafowl   r
Eastern Crowned Crane

Red-chested Flufftail   r
White-spotted Flufftail   r
Buff-spotted Flufftail   r
Wood Sandpiper   W
Green Sandpiper   W
Common Sandpiper   W
Olive Pigeon   r
Bronze-naped Pigeon
Red-eyed Turtle-Dove   c
Cape Turtle-Dove
Tambourine Wood-Dove   c
Blue-spotted Wood-Dove
Lemon Dove
African Green-Pigeon
Brown Parrot
Gray Parrot   r
Black-billed Turaco   c
Hartlaub's Turaco
Ross's Turaco   r
Great Blue Turaco
Levaillant's Cuckoo
Red-chested Cuckoo   r
Black Cuckoo
Klaas's Cuckoo   c
Didric Cuckoo   r
Emerald Cuckoo
Green Coucal
Black Coucal
Blue-headed Coucal
White-browed Coucal
Grass Owl
White-faced Scops-Owl
Verreaux's Eagle-Owl
Pearl-spotted Owlet
Red-chested Owlet   r
African Wood Owl
Eurasian Nightjar   W
Natal Nightjar
Mottled Swift
Common Swift   W

Nyanza Swift
Scarce Swift
White-rumped Swift
House Swift
Sabine's Swift
Speckled Mousebird
Narina's Trogon r
Bar-tailed Trogon
Giant Kingfisher
African Pygmy Kingfisher
Woodland Kingfisher
Striped Kingfisher
Eurasian Bee-eater W
Blue-cheeked Bee-eater M
White-throated Bee-eater
Little Bee-eater
Cinnamon-chested Bee-eater c
Blue-headed Bee-eater c
Cinnamon Roller
White-headed Wood-Hoopoe
Crowned Hornbill
Gray-cheeked Hornbill
Hairy-breasted Barbet r
Gray-throated Barbet
Yellow-spotted Barbet c
Speckled Tinkerbird r
Golden-rumped Tinkerbird c
Yellow-billed Barbet
Scaly Honeyguide r
Greater Honeyguide
Lesser Honeyguide
Thick-billed Honeyguide r
Least Honeyguide c
Chapin's Least Honeyguide r
Cassin's Honeyguide
Brown-eared Woodpecker
Buff-spotted Woodpecker
Fine-banded Woodpecker
Cardinal Woodpecker
Yellow-crested Woodpecker
African Broadbill r
Rufous-naped Bush-Lark
Plain Martin
Sand Martin c W
Barn Swallow c W
Angola Swallow
Wire-tailed Swallow

Rufous-chested Swallow
Mosque Swallow
Red-rumped Swallow
Lesser Striped Swallow
Gray-rumped Swallow
Black Saw-wing
White-headed Saw-wing c
African Drongo
Square-tailed Drongo
Eurasian Golden Oriole W
African Golden Oriole
Western Black-headed Oriole c
African Black-headed Oriole
Black-winged Oriole
Stuhlmann's Starling c
Splendid Glossy-Starling
Amethyst Starling r
Sharpe's Starling
Waller's Starling
Red-billed Oxpecker
Pied Crow
Cape Crow
White-bellied Tit
Dusky Tit c
Yellow Wagtail W
Gray Wagtail W
Mountain Wagtail
White Wagtail W
African Pied Wagtail
Richard's Pipit
Plain-backed Pipit
Tree Pipit W
Yellow-throated Longclaw
Rosy-breasted Longclaw
Abyssinian Hill Babbler
Gray-chested Akalat
Brown Akalat
Mountain Akalat
Pale-breasted Akalat
Scaly-breasted Akalat
Gray Cuckoo-shrike
Purple-throated Cuckoo-shrike r
Red-shouldered Cuckoo-shrike c
Black Cuckoo-shrike
Garden Bulbul c
Chestnut-tailed Bristlebill
Fischer's (Cabinis's) Greenbul

Toro Olive Greenbul   r
Joyful Leaf-love
Honeyguide Greenbul
Shelley's Greenbul
Cameroon Sombre Greenbul
Little Gray Greenbul
Ansorge's Greenbul
Slender-billed Greenbul
Little Greenbul
Yellow-whiskered Greenbul   c
Sooty Flycatcher
Ashy Flycatcher   r
Pied Flycatcher   W
White-eyed Slaty Flycatcher
Southern Hyliota
Shrike-Flycatcher
Chin-spot Batis
Common Wattle-eye
Chestnut Wattle-eye   c
Blissett's Wattle-eye   c
Yellow-bellied Wattle-eye
Northern Fairy-Flycatcher
Dusky Crested-Flycatcher
White-tailed Crested-Flycatcher
Black-headed Paradise-Flycatcher
African Paradise-Flycatcher
Stonechat
Northern Ant-Chat
Brown-chested Robin
Equatorial Robin
Forest Robin
Gray-winged Robin-Chat
Cape Robin-Chat
Blue-shouldered Robin-Chat
Snowy-crowned Robin-Chat
White-tailed Rusty-Thrush
African Thrush
Broad-tailed Grass-Warbler
Natal Chloropeta
Moustached Grassbird
Garden Warbler   W
Blackcap   W
Willow Warbler   W
Chiffchaff   W
Wood Warbler   W
Brown Leaf-Warbler
Uganda Leaf-Warbler

Red-faced Cisticola
Whistling Cisticola
Chubb's Cisticola
Rattling Cisticola
Winding Cisticola
Stout Cisticola
Croaking Cisticola
Tawny-flanked Prinia
White-chinned Prinia
Banded Prinia
Black-throated Apalis
Black-collared Apalis
Gray Apalis
Black-backed Apalis
Chestnut-throated Apalis
Black-faced Rufous Warbler
Olive-green Camaroptera   c
Bleating Camaroptera
Turner's Eremomela
White-browed Crombec
Gambian Puffback-Shrike
Pink-footed Puffback-Shrike
Blackcap Tchagra
Black-crowned Bush-Shrike
Brown-crowned Tchagra
Luhder's Boubou
Tropical Boubou
Gray-green Bush-Shrike
Fiery-breasted Bush-Shrike
Mackinnon's Shrike
Gray-backed Fiscal-Shrike
Common Fiscal-Shrike
Yellow White-eye   c
Green Hylia
Gray-chinned Sunbird
Collared Sunbird
Olive Sunbird   c
Green-headed Sunbird
Scarlet-chested Sunbird
Variable Sunbird
Northern Double-collared Sunbird
Olive-bellied Sunbird
Orange-tufted Sunbird
Copper Sunbird
Bronzy Sunbird
Thick-billed Weaver
Reichenow's Weaver

Holub's Golden Weaver
Village Weaver
Vieillot's Black Weaver
Gambian Black-headed Weaver
Golden-backed Weaver
Compact Weaver
Dark-backed Weaver
Yellow-mantled Weaver
Spectacled Weaver
Black-necked Weaver
Black-billed Weaver
Brown-capped Weaver
Red-headed Malimbe   c
Cardinal Quelea
Red-billed Quelea
White-winged Widowbird
Red-collared Widowbird
Black Bishop
Marsh Widowbird
Yellow-mantled Widowbird
Gray-headed Sparrow   c

Pin-tailed Whydah   c
Green Twin-spot
Gray-headed Negro-Finch
White-breasted Negro-Finch
Red-headed Bluebill   c
Yellow-bellied Waxbill
Fawn-breasted Waxbill
Black-crowned Waxbill
Common Waxbill
Red-cheeked Cordonbleu
Red-billed Fire-Finch
Blue-billed Fire-Finch
Bronze Munia
Red-backed Munia
Yellow-fronted Canary
Black-throated Canary
Brimstone Canary
African Citril
Thick-billed Canary
Oriole-Finch
Streaky Canary

66
Nairobi, Kenya

THE ENVIRONS OF NAIROBI and nearby northern Tanzania provide one of the premier birding grounds of the entire world. This is due partly to an abundance of rich savannas, deserts, lakes, mountains, and forests all within a day's drive from a pleasant modern city. The climate is superb, there are huge national parks, good field guides, superb transportation facilities, and efficient, well-located hotels with safe restaurants. Many tourists on big-game safari circuits who have never noticed birds before begin to notice the ostriches, bustards, bee-eaters, hornbills, eagles, and weavers and get hooked on bird watching.

There are so many excellent birding areas, a number of national park checklists available locally, and so many visitors touching down at almost all of these spots that we will here attempt only a view of the region as a whole. The comprehensive list that follows will be of great value to those following a safari circuit due to the relative abundance and seasonal symbols, as well as tips on where the more local species occur.

Political circumstances have, in the past, frequently closed the border between Kenya and Tanzania. If it is not open to through traffic at the time of a projected visit a decision must be made concerning which of the two countries will be visited. Tanzania, with its magnificent reserves of Serengeti, Ngorongoro Crater, Lake Manyara, and Tarangire, has been cut off from much tourism over the last few years. Lately it has shown signs of opening up and facilitating visits for those wishing to tour Tanzania by itself.

Over much of Kenya and Tanzania one can still taste the wild and be out of sight of people, although at some busy seasons some crowding does occur in a few parks. The busiest season is from Christmas through Easter and July–August. The most pleasant season is October through Christmas, during the short rains when things are green, temperatures are cooler, and one can have the pick of places to stay. There are dozens of packages to choose from, and very few people just arrive, rent a car, and hope to find a room. You will have to decide if the relatively inexpensive tour crams too many people into a vehicle and whether or not your leaders know about anything other than a few mammals. The drivers are generally excellent and friendly, but very few know any birds. The lodges and hotels are of such high standards here that it is difficult to judge tour quality on hotels alone.

The permanent tented camps are often every bit as comfortable as a lodge and offer an outstanding bush experience (they usually have hot water showers and you can walk around inside the tents). Think seriously about joining an organized tour led by experienced people who know their birds and mammals well and can offer the most efficient itinerary. Most travel is done in Volkswagen buses and Land Rovers, and on top-grade safaris there is a trained leader in every vehicle, which can make a great difference. On such tours it is not unusual to see over 600 species of birds in four weeks (500 in three), plus up to 70 species of mammals. You may also arrange a private car with a top local guide.

Nairobi continues to be the dominant center of wildlife tourism in the world. It has a fine airport, great hotels, a relatively green and uncongested center, and within a day's drive you can reach Samburu, Tsavo, the Rift Valley, or the Masai Mara in the northern Serengeti. Kenya is generally a very safe country with helpful citizens, but do not be careless with your belongings in Nairobi or Nakuru. The Westwood Park Hotel in Karen (near Nairobi National Park) has fine grounds for birds, but it is a long way from the city and cannot match the services and rooms of a dozen or more hotels in Nairobi — the Norfolk and New Stanley are the traditional homes of wildlife parties.

The only thorn in the otherwise outstanding experience in Africa is the fact that you cannot jump out of your vehicles whenever you see a bird you want to study. Most vehicles have a flip-top roof, and you must stay inside while in the parks. There are a few specific spots (such as at hippo pools or hilltops or around lodges) where you can stretch and work on small birds. Try to include time in places outside the parks where you can do some normal birding. Due to the presence of large predators, as well as the disturbing effect mobs of casual tourists would have in running up to herbivores, you will be restricted to vehicles in most parts of Tsavo, Amboseli, Meru, Samburu, Masai Mara, the Tanzanian parks, and at such places as the Ark and Tree-tops. Birders would do well to think about staying just outside some of these parks, in the tented camps, where not only can you bird on foot, but take night game drives for nocturnal species.

The glories of the wildlife need not be repeated here; suffice a few comments on ways to approach each area:

Nairobi National Park is well worthwhile — do not think of missing it. It is rich in cats, antelope, rhinoceros, and bustards, and it makes a great introduction. Try to get there early in the morning, since most tours come in the afternoon. From the Main Entrance follow the Songora Ridge road southeast to Rangers' Post No. 3. A trail is there along the Athi River to a hippo pool where you can walk among many riparian birds.

There are four major lakes strung out in the Rift Valley west of Nairobi. It is a 2-hour drive to Naivasha, 3- to Nakuru, and 6- to Baringo. Lake Naivasha is a freshwater lake, with several fine shoreline hotels with magnificent grounds that attract many birds. Boat trips can be easily arranged at the hotels. The ill-advised introduction of the South American nutria (coypu) by fur farmers has resulted in such wholesale destruction of much of the aquatic plantlife that a number of waterbirds can no longer use the lake. However, it is still good for others and worth a visit. Hell's Gate Gorge a few minutes to the south is excellent for swifts, Lammergeier (sometimes absent), eagles including Verreaux's, and francolins. Lake Nakuru has now lost most of its flamingoes. Again, an ill-advised introduction, in this case, of a fish *(Tilapia),* has so altered the ecology of the lake that the flamingoes have no food, while pelicans are having a field day. There are still thousands of less specialized waterbirds here, and the surrounding forests of fever trees are often rich and can be explored on foot. There is a fine new camp on the northeast side of the lake; the hotels of central Nakuru are poor.

Two delightful lakes off the tourist circuit in the northern Rift Valley at lower elevations are Lake Baringo and Lake Bogoria (formerly Hannington). The latter is reached via a rough track off the Baringo road and is now used heavily by vast numbers of flamingo. Lake Baringo is located in dry acacia forest with some fine cliffs just to the west where many local hornbills, starlings, and honeyguides live. The Lake Baringo Lodge on the shore is outstanding, as is the Island Camp on Kokwe Island in the middle of the lake. Birds are abundant along the shore, and boat trips are easily arranged. The water level varies greatly between wet and dry years.

The Masai Mara Game Reserve is in Kenya's section of the Serengeti Plains. It is in excellent condition, full of big game (often spilling out a long way beyond the reserve boundary), and proves a spectacular experience for visitors. The herds are migratory, so that there will always be relatively quiet months. Both the Keekorok Lodge and the new hilltop Serena Lodge are well run and offer good birding on the grounds. There are three tented camps along the Mara River, just north of the park, which are good bases. Unfortunately one can no longer continue south into Serengeti and Ngorongoro from Kenya in a logical sequence. Big game is commonest in the Mara in the latter half of the year.

Treetops and the Ark are two unique establishments located in the wet mountain forests of Nyandarua National Park (formerly Aberdare). Each has a pond, searchlights, salt licks, and a host of rarely seen semi-nocturnal mammals. Visitors usually stay only one night and some highland birds of note are invariably seen at both places.

Mt. Kenya rises to 17,058 feet (5200 m) with snow on the Equator. There are rough roads part way up on many sides, offering hikers a chance to find a few alpine endemics. The forests along the flanks, such as around the Naro Moru Lodge (rustic) and the Mt. Kenya Safari Club (luxurious), have a fairly good assortment of montane birds.

The Samburu and Buffalo Springs Game Reserves are located at the southern edge of the Northern Frontier desert, and north of the snows of Mt. Kenya. The Ewaso Nyiro River flows through the area, and there is a fine game lodge, and a number of tented camps strung out along the road. Distinctive mammals and birds are found here that are absent in the higher altitude savannas.

Tsavo West National Park is located halfway between Nairobi and the Indian Ocean. It has many of the mammals found in other parks (with more elephants) and a wide variety of birds. The three lodges in the north (Kilaguni, Ngulia, and Kitani), plus tented camps, offer access to Mzima Springs, where there is a short, but welcome, walking trail. It is sometimes a good spot to observe Peter's Finfoot. Golden-breasted Starlings and masses of hornbills and weavers visit the lodges for crumbs, and there is a waterhole at each that is good for game and bird viewing.

Lake Jipe is a fine freshwater lake located on the Tanzanian border south of Taveta at the southern edge of Tsavo West. It can best be reached by staying at either the Taita Hills or Salt Lick Lodges (both rather elegant). This lake holds many species of fine waterbirds, and sometimes a boat is available. Birding is best here in the dry season when other pools dry up. The plains between Lake Jipe and the hotels have many birds, plus interesting big game.

Almost every bird found in Ngorongoro Crater and the Serengeti of Tanzania also occurs in nearby Kenya and is included in the following list. At Tarangire National Park south of Arusha there are even more novelties, which have been left off the list.

CHECKLIST

(TS = Tsavo; SA = Samburu; RV = Rift Valley; SE = Serengeti)

Ostrich c
Little Dabchick c
Black-necked Grebe r
Great Crested Grebe c
Eastern White Pelican c
Pink-backed Pelican c
Great Cormorant c
Long-tailed Cormorant c
Darter c
Gray Heron c
Black-headed Heron c
Goliath Heron
Purple Heron
Little Egret c
Great Egret c
Short-billed Egret c
Black Heron r
Cattle Heron c
Squacco Pond-Heron c
Madagascar Pond-Heron r M
Green Heron
Black-crowned Night-Heron
Little Bittern r W
Hammerkop c
White Stork c M
Black Stork c M
Woolly-necked Stork r
Saddle-billed Stork
Black Open-billed Stork r
Marabou Stork c
Yellow-billed Stork c
Sacred Ibis c
Olive Ibis r H
Hadada Ibis c
Glossy Ibis
African Spoonbill c
Greater Flamingo
Lesser Flamingo
Fulvous Whistling-Duck
White-faced Whistling-Duck
Egyptian Goose c

Spur-winged Goose c
Knob-billed Goose
African Pygmy-Goose r TS
African Black Duck r H
Eurasian Wigeon r W
Green-winged Teal r W
Cape Teal
Yellow-billed Duck c
Northern Pintail r W
Red-billed Duck c
Hottentot Teal r
Garganey c W
Northern Shoveler r W
Southern Pochard
White-backed Duck
Maccoa Duck
Osprey W
African Baza r
Bat Kite r
Black-shouldered Kite c
Black Kite c
African Sea-Eagle c
Egyptian Vulture
Lammergeier r
Hooded Vulture c
African White-backed Vulture c
Ruppell's Vulture
Lappet-faced Vulture c
White-headed Vulture c
Black-breasted Snake-Eagle
Brown Snake-Eagle
Bateleur c
African Harrier-Hawk
Marsh Harrier W
African Harrier
Pallid Harrier c W
Montagu's Harrier c W
Dark Chanting-Goshawk SE
Pale Chanting-Goshawk c
Gabar Goshawk r
Great Goshawk

Rufous-breasted Sparrowhawk   H
Little Sparrowhawk   r
Ovampo Sparrowhawk   r
Shikra
African Goshawk
Grasshopper Buzzard   W TS, SA
Lizard Buzzard   r
Common Buzzard   W
Mountain Buzzard   H
Long-legged Buzzard   r W
Augur Buzzard   c
Lesser Spotted Eagle   r W
Tawny (Steppe) Eagle   c
Wahlberg's Eagle   c
Verreaux's Eagle
African Hawk-Eagle
Ayre's Hawk-Eagle   r H
Long-crested Eagle   c
Crowned Hawk-Eagle   r H
Martial Eagle   c
Secretarybird   c
Pygmy Falcon
Lesser Kestrel   M
Greater Kestrel
Common Kestrel
Amur Falcon   r M
European Hobby   W
Lanner Falcon
Peregrine Falcon   r W
Taita Falcon   r TS
Coqui Francolin
Crested Francolin
Shelley's Francolin   SE
Hildebrant's Francolin
Scaly Francolin   H
Jackson's Francolin   H
Gray-breasted Spurfowl   SE
Red-necked Spurfowl   SE
Yellow-necked Spurfowl   c
Common Quail   W
Harlequin Quail
Helmeted Guineafowl   c
Vulturine Guineafowl   c TS, SA
Common Buttonquail   r
Eastern Crowned Crane   c
Buff-spotted Flufftail
Corn Crake   r W

Kaffir Rail
African Black Crake   c
Purple Swamphen   c
Common Gallinule   c
Red-knobbed Coot   c
African Finfoot   r
Denham's Bustard   SE
Kori Bustard   c
Buff-crested Bustard
White-bellied Bustard   c
Black-bellied Bustard
Hartlaub's Bustard   c
Lesser Jacana   r TS
African Jacana   c
Greater Painted-snipe   r
Long-toed Lapwing   TS
Blacksmith Lapwing   c
Spur-winged Lapwing   c
Black-headed Lapwing   SA
Senegal Lapwing
Black-winged Lapwing   c
Crowned Lapwing   c
Wattled Lapwing   SE
Greater Ringed Plover   c W
Little Ringed Plover   W
Kittlitz's Plover   c
Three-banded Plover   c
White-fronted Plover
Chestnut-banded Plover   r
Mongolian Plover   r W
Caspian Plover   c W
Black-tailed Godwit   W
Eurasian Curlew   r W
Spotted Redshank   r W
Common Redshank   r W
Marsh Sandpiper   c W
Common Greenshank   c W
Green Sandpiper   c W
Wood Sandpiper   c W
Common Sandpiper   c W
Common Snipe   c W
Ethiopian Snipe
Great Snipe   W
Little Stint   c W
Temminck's Stint   r W
Curlew Sandpiper   c W
Ruff   c W

Black-winged Stilt   c
Black-capped Avocet
Water Dikkop
Spotted Dikkop
Two-banded Courser
Heuglin's Courser   r
Cream-colored Courser   SA
Temminck's Courser   c
Lesser Black-backed Gull   c W
Gray-headed Gull   c
Black-headed Gull   W
Whiskered Tern   W
White-winged Black Tern   c W
Gull-billed Tern   c
African Skimmer   r
Chestnut-bellied Sandgrouse
Yellow-throated Sandgrouse
Black-faced Sandgrouse   TS, SA
Lichtenstein's Sandgrouse   SA
Speckled Pigeon   c
Olive Pigeon   H
Bronze-naped Pigeon   r H
Pink-breasted Turtle-Dove   H
Mourning Turtle-Dove   c
Red-eyed Turtle-Dove   c
Cape Turtle-Dove   c
Laughing Turtle-Dove   c
Emerald-spotted Wood-Dove
Tambourine Wood-Dove
Namaqua Dove   c
Lemon Dove   r
African Green-Pigeon   c
Fischer's Lovebird   RV
Masked Lovebird   RV
Orange-bellied Parrot   SA, TS
Brown Parrot
Red-headed Parrot   H
Schalow's Turaco   SE
Hartlaub's Turaco   H
Ross's Turaco   H (west only)
White-bellied Go-away-bird
Bare-faced Go-away-bird
Great Spotted Cuckoo   W
Levaillant's Cuckoo   W
Jacobin Cuckoo   W
Red-chested Cuckoo
Black Cuckoo

Eurasian Cuckoo   W
African Cuckoo   c
Emerald Cuckoo   r
Klaas's Cuckoo   c
Didric Cuckoo
White-browed Coucal   c
Grass Owl   r H
African Scops-Owl
White-faced Scops-Owl
African Wood Owl   H
Spotted Eagle-Owl
Verreaux's Eagle-Owl   c
Pel's Fishing Owl   r
Pearl-spotted Owlet
Abyssinian Long-eared Owl   H
Marsh Owl
Eurasian Nightjar   W
Dusky Nightjar
Donaldson-Smith's Nightjar   SA
Abyssinian Nightjar   H
Freckled Nightjar
Gabon Nightjar
Alpine Swift   H
African Black Swift
Mottled Swift
Common Swift   W
Nyanza Swift   c
White-rumped Swift   c
House Swift   c
Horus Swift   r
African Palm-Swift   c
Speckled Mousebird   c
White-headed Mousebird   c SA
Blue-naped Mousebird   c
Narina Trogon   r
Bar-tailed Trogon   r H
Giant Kingfisher
Pied Kingfisher   c
Malachite Kingfisher   c
African Pygmy Kingfisher
Gray-headed Kingfisher   c
Woodland Kingfisher   SE
Striped Kingfisher   c
Somali Bee-eater   SA
Little Bee-eater   c
Cinnamon-chested Bee-eater   H
White-fronted Bee-eater

White-throated Bee-eater
Eurasian Bee-eater W
Northern Carmine Bee-eater S
Blue-cheeked Bee-eater
Eurasian Roller c W
Lilac-breasted Roller c
Rufous-crowned Roller c
Cinnamon Roller
Hoopoe c
Green Wood-Hoopoe c
White-headed Wood-Hoopoe H
Abyssinian Scimitarbill
Southern Scimitarbill
African Gray Hornbill c
Red-billed Hornbill c
Von der Decken's Hornbill TS,
  SA
Yellow-billed Hornbill TS, SA
Hemprich's Hornbill RV
Crowned Hornbill H
Gray-cheeked Hornbill SE
Silvery-cheeked Hornbill H
Southern Ground Hornbill
Red-fronted Tinkerbird H
Golden-rumped Tinkerbird
Spot-flanked Barbet
Red-fronted Barbet
Brown-throated Barbet SA
Black-collared Barbet r TS
White-headed Barbet r
Brown-breasted Barbet r SA
Double-toothed Barbet SE
Red-and-yellow Barbet
Black-billed (D'Arnaud's)
  Ground-Barbet c SE
Pale-billed (D'Arnaud's)
  Ground-Barbet c
Cassin's Honeyguide r H
Wahlberg's Honeyguide
Scaly Honeyguide r RV
Lesser Honeyguide
Greater Honeyguide
Eurasian Wryneck r W
Red-breasted Wryneck r
Nubian Woodpecker c
Fine-banded Woodpecker H
Green-backed Woodpecker r RV

Cardinal Woodpecker c
Little White-spotted Woodpecker
  r
Gray Woodpecker c
Bearded Woodpecker
Singing Bush-Lark TS
Red-winged Bush-Lark c TS, SA
Rufous-naped Bush-Lark c
Flappet Bush-Lark
Fawn-colored Bush-Lark
Pink-breasted Bush-Lark c TS,
  SA
Chestnut-headed Finch-Lark SA
Fischer's Finch-Lark c
Red-capped Lark c
Short-tailed Lark r
Plain Martin c
Sand Martin W
Banded Martin
Rock Martin
Gray-rumped Swallow
Barn Swallow c W
Wire-tailed Swallow c
Lesser Striped Swallow
Rufous-chested Swallow r H
Mosque Swallow
Red-rumped Swallow
House Martin c W
Black Saw-wing
African Drongo c
Eurasian Golden Oriole W
African Golden Oriole
African Black-headed Oriole
Black-winged Oriole H
Red-winged Starling RV
Waller's Starling
Slender-billed Starling H
Bristle-crowned Starling RV, SA
Blue-eared Glossy-Starling c
Lesser Blue-eared Glossy-Starling
  RV
Ruppell's Long-tailed Starling c
Abbott's Starling r TS
Sharpe's Starling r H
Amethyst Starling c M
Superb Starling c
Hildebrandt's Starling c

Golden-breasted Starling   TS, SA
Wattled Starling   c
Yellow-billed Oxpecker
Red-billed Oxpecker   c
Cape Crow   RV
Pied Crow   c
Fan-tailed Raven   RV, SA
White-necked Raven   H, TS
African Gray Tit
White-bellied Tit
Red-throated Tit   r
Gray Penduline-Tit
Mouse-colored Penduline-Tit   r
   RV
Spotted Creeper   r
Rufous Chatterer
Black-lored Babbler   RV
Arrow-marked Babbler
Northern Pied Babbler   H
Sudan Babbler   RV
Gray Cuckoo-shrike   H
Purple-throated Cuckoo-shrike   H
Black Cuckoo-shrike
Garden Bulbul   c
Slender-billed Greenbul   H
Yellow-whiskered Greenbul   H
Yellow-bellied Leaf-love   H
Fischer's (Placid) Greenbul   H
(Olive-breasted) Mountain
   Greenbul   H
Red-backed Scrub-Robin
Rufous Scrub-Robin   W
Brown-chested Alethe   r
Starred Robin   H
Thrush-Nightingale   W
Ruppell's Robin-Chat   H
Heuglin's Robin-Chat
Cape Robin-Chat   H, RV
Spotted Morning-Thrush   RV
Hill Chat   r H
Whinchat   r W
Stonechat   c H
Northern Ant-Chat   c H, RV
Sooty Chat   SE
Familiar Chat   SE
Mocking Cliff-Chat
Isabelline Wheatear   c W

Northern Wheatear   c W
Mourning Wheatear   RV
Pied Wheatear   c W
Capped Wheatear   c
Little Rock-Thrush   RV
White-backed Rock-Thrush   W
Abyssinian Ground-Thrush   r H
Olive Thrush   c H
Sedge Warbler   W
Great Reed-Warbler   r W
European Reed-Warbler   r W
Cape Reed-Warbler
Natal Chloropeta   r
Mountain Chloropeta   r H
Icterine Warbler   r W
Olive-tree Warbler   W
Olivaceous Warbler   W
Barred Warbler   r W
Garden Warbler   W
Blackcap   W
Greater Whitethroat   W
Willow Warbler   c W
Brown Leaf-Warbler   c H
Zitting Cisticola
Red-faced Cisticola
Singing Cisticola
Hunter's Cisticola   c H
Rattling Cisticola   c
Wailing Cisticola   RV
Lyne's Cisticola   RV
Winding Cisticola   c
Stout Cisticola   c
Croaking Cisticola   SE
Ashy Cisticola   TS
Tiny Cisticola
Desert Cisticola
Wing-snapping Cisticola   SE
Pectoral-patch Cisticola
Tawny-flanked Prinia   c
Pale Prinia   RV, SA
Bar-throated Apalis   H
Yellow-breasted Apalis   c
Black-collared Apalis
Chestnut-throated Apalis   H
Gray Apalis   H
Black-headed Apalis   r
Red-faced Apalis   SA

Acacia (Buff-bellied) Warbler
Gray-capped Warbler
Moustached Grassbird   r
Gray-backed Camaroptera
Green-backed Eremomela
Yellow-bellied Eremomela
White-browed Crombec   H
Senegal Crombec
Red-faced Crombec
Somali Crombec   TS
Banded Tit-Warbler   SE
Brown Tit-Warbler   H
African Dusky Flycatcher   c H,
   SE
Ashy Flycatcher
Pallid Flycatcher   c
Little Gray Flycatcher
Spotted Flycatcher   c W
Southern Black Flycatcher
Northern Black Flycatcher   r
White-eyed Slaty Flycatcher   c H,
   RV
Silverbird
Chin-spot Batis   c
Pygmy Batis   SA
Black-headed Batis   r
Northern Wattle-eye   SE
Black-throated Wattle-eye
Northern Fairy-Flycatcher   SE
African Paradise-Flycatcher
Yellow Wagtail   c W
Gray Wagtail   r W
White Wagtail   r W
African Pied Wagtail   c
Mountain Wagtail   H
Cape Wagtail   RV, H
Golden Pipit   TS
Yellow-throated Longclaw   c
Pangani Longclaw
Sharpe's Longclaw   TS
Rosy-breasted Longclaw
Richard's Pipit   c
Plain-backed Pipit
Long-billed Pipit
Tree Pipit   r W
Red-throated Pipit   W
Striped Pipit   TS

Northern White-crowned Shrike   c
White Helmet-Shrike
Gray-crested Helmet-Shrike   SE
Retz's Helmet-Shrike
Brubru Shrike
Pringle's Puffback-Shrike   r SA
Black-backed Puffback-Shrike
Black-crowned Tchagra
Brown-crowned Tchagra
Three-streaked Tchagra   RV
Rosy-patched Shrike   TS, SA
Tropical Boubou   c
Slate-colored Boubou
Sulfur-breasted Bush-Shrike   r
Black-fronted Bush-Shrike   r H
Doherty's Bush-Shrike   H
Red-tailed Shrike   W
Red-backed Shrike   W
Lesser Gray Shrike   W
Gray-backed Fiscal-Shrike   c RV
Long-tailed Fiscal-Shrike   H, TS
Common Fiscal-Shrike   c
Teita Fiscal-Shrike   TS, SA
Kenya Violet-backed Sunbird
Collared Sunbird   c
Green-headed Sunbird   H
Amethyst Sunbird
Scarlet-chested Sunbird   RV, H,
   SE
Hunter's Sunbird   RV, SA, TS
Variable Sunbird   c
Eastern Double-collared Sunbird
   c H
Northern Double-collared Sunbird
   H
Tacazze Sunbird   c H
Mariqua Sunbird   SE, RV
Violet-breasted Sunbird   TS
Beautiful Sunbird
Little Black-bellied Sunbird   r TS
Malachite Sunbird   H
Scarlet-tufted Malachite Sunbird   r
   H
Bronzy Sunbird   c
Golden-winged Sunbird   H
Yellow White-eye
Broad-ringed White-eye   H

Yellow-crowned Canary   H
African Citril   r
Black-throated Canary
Yellow-fronted Canary   RV, SE
Brimstone Canary   H, RV
Streaky Canary   H, RV
Thick-billed Canary   H
White-bellied Canary   RV, SA
Oriole-Finch   r H
Cinnamon-breasted Bunting
Somali Bunting   SA
Golden-breasted Bunting
Gray-headed Negro-Finch   r H
Green-winged Pytilia   RV
Green Twinspot   r H
Red-billed Fire-Finch
Blue-billed Fire-Finch
Red-cheeked Cordonbleu   c
Blue-capped Cordonbleu   r
Purple Grenadier
Yellow-bellied Waxbill   r H
Crimson-rumped Waxbill
Common Waxbill
Black-headed Waxbill   r H
Black-cheeked Waxbill   r SA
Common Quail-Finch   r
White-throated Munia   r
Gray-headed Munia   TS, SE
Bronze Munia   c
Rufous-backed Munia   H
White-billed Buffalo-Weaver   RV
Red-billed Buffalo-Weaver   SA,
   TS
White-headed Buffalo-Weaver
White-browed Sparrow-Weaver   c
Donaldson-Smith's Sparrow-
   Weaver   SA
Rufous-tailed Weaver   SE

Black-capped Social-Weaver   TS,
   SA
Gray-headed Social-Weaver
Great Sparrow
Gray-headed Sparrow
Chestnut Sparrow   RV, SA
Yellow-spotted Petronia
Speckle-fronted Weaver
Thick-billed Weaver
Reichenow's Weaver   c
Spectacled Weaver
Eastern Golden Weaver   SA, TS
Holub's Golden Weaver   SE
Golden Palm Weaver   SA
Taveta Golden Weaver   TS
Northern Masked Weaver   RV
Lesser Masked Weaver
Vitelline Masked Weaver
Speke's Weaver   H, RV
Village Weaver   c
Brown-capped Weaver   r H
Red-headed Weaver
Cardinal Quelea   M
Red-billed Quelea
Red Bishop   TS
Yellow-crowned Bishop   RV
Yellow Bishop
Indigobird
Fan-tailed Widowbird   SE
White-winged Widowbird   H
Red-collared Widowbird   H
Long-tailed Widowbird   H
Jackson's Widowbird   H
Steel-blue Whydah   r SA
Straw-tailed Whydah   TS, SA
Pin-tailed Whydah
Paradise Whydah

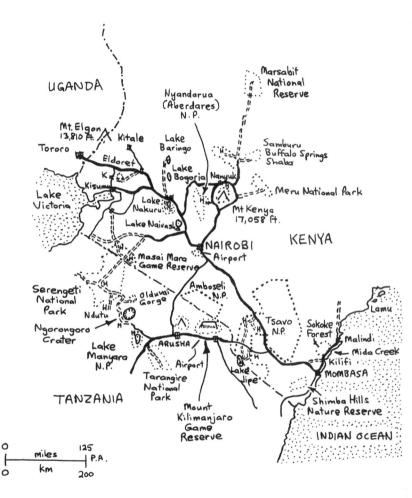

67
Mombasa, Kenya

MOMBASA IS A LARGE SEAPORT and resort center on the Indian Ocean. The airport links it to Nairobi, with direct flights to Europe as well. The road to Nairobi passes through Tsavo National Park, which makes a good stopover. The House Crow, introduced from India, is common around Mombasa.

The Shimba Hills, near Kwale, south of Mombasa, is home to Kenya's only sable antelopes and many interesting birds. Look for Palm-nut Vulture, Northern Carmine Bee-eater, Brown-breasted Barbet, and Cape Batis.

The three best places on the coast are located north of Mombasa. Those wishing to work these areas may base at the plush Mnarari Beach Club Hotel at Kilifi Creek, or near Mida Creek at the expensive Watamu Beach Hotel, or the down-to-earth Turtle Bay Hotel, or at a number of fine hotels on the beach at Malindi. Kilifi Creek has boats (two hours' round trip) to the evening roost of Northern Carmine Bee-eaters in winter and spring. Thousands of these red birds mix with Blue-cheeked Bee-eaters on a small mangrove island four miles inland.

About 10 miles (16 km) north of the ferry landing on Kilifi Creek, the coast road passes Sokoke Forest, which can be reached via a signposted dirt road to the left. The forest is tall, although dry in the spring. Many special birds occur here, and it is hoped that the Kenyan government will preserve this segment of the coastal forest. Specialties include Southern Snake-Eagle, Crowned Hawk-Eagle, Boehm's Needletail, Sokoke Scops-Owl, Sokoke Pipit, Retz's and Chestnut-fronted Helmet-Shrikes, Amani and Plain-backed Sunbirds, Clarke's Weaver, and Peter's Twinspot.

Mida Creek and Turtle Bay together are a good vacation spot with a fine beach and nearby coral reefs with good snorkeling. A few small boats are available to explore Mida Creek, a great area for waders. At low tide the extensive mud flats are often home to dozens of Crab-plover, a few Black Heron, and thousands of migrant shorebirds, including many Asian species, such as Terek Sandpiper. Those not wishing to rent boats can explore the back end of the lagoon from the main road.

The Galana River, 4 miles (6.4 km) north of Malindi, is crossed by a bridge. Just after the bridge there is an overgrown road to the right (on the north shore) which leads to chicken coops, and then downhill along the shore to the river mouth. This area is often superb for shorebirds (including Broad-billed Sandpiper); the intervening fields have various bishops and passerines, and the Malindi Pipit occurs.

CHECKLIST

Little Dabchick
Pink-backed Pelican   c
Great Cormorant
Darter
Gray Heron   c
Black-headed Heron   c
Goliath Heron   c
Purple Heron
Great Egret   c
Black Heron   c
Little Egret   c
Green Heron
Woolly-necked Stork
Yellow-billed Stork   c
Hadada Ibis
Glossy Ibis
White-faced Whistling-Duck
Knob-billed Goose
White-backed Duck
Eurasian Honey-Buzzard   W
Black-shouldered Kite   c
Black Kite   c
African Sea-Eagle   c
Palm-nut Vulture
Southern Snake-Eagle   r
Bateleur
African Harrier-Hawk
Great Sparrowhawk
Little Sparrowhawk
African Goshawk
Lizard Buzzard   c
Wahlberg's Eagle
African Hawk-Eagle
Long-crested Eagle
Crowned Hawk-Eagle
Peregrine Falcon   W

Crested Francolin
Kenya Guineafowl
African Jacana   c
Senegal Lapwing
Gray Plover   c W
Greater Ringed Plover   c W
White-fronted Plover
Mongolian Plover   c W
Great Sand Plover   c W
Whimbrel   c W
Eurasian Curlew   c W
Common Redshank   W
Marsh Sandpiper   W
Common Greenshank   c W
Terek Sandpiper   c W
Common Sandpiper   c W
Ruddy Turnstone   W
Broad-billed Sandpiper   r W
Sanderling   c W
Little Stint   c W
Curlew Sandpiper   c W
Black-winged Stilt
Black-capped Avocet
Water Dikkop
Crabplover   c W
Collared Pratincole   W
Sooty Gull
Lesser Black-backed Gull   W
Black-headed Gull   W
Gull-billed Tern   c
Lesser Crested Tern   c
Roseate Tern   W
Common Tern   W
African Skimmer   r
Mourning Turtle-Dove
Red-eyed Turtle-Dove   c

Cape Turtle-Dove   c
Laughing Turtle-Dove
Emerald-spotted Wood-Dove
Tambourine Wood-Dove
Namaqua Dove
African Brown-headed Parrot   c
Fischer's Turaco
Levaillant's Cuckoo
Jacobin Cuckoo
Thick-billed Cuckoo
Eurasian Cuckoo
Lesser Cuckoo   M
Klaas's Cuckoo
Didric Cuckoo
Green Cuckoo
Black Coucal
White-browed Coucal
African Scops-Owl
Sokoke Scops-Owl
Verreaux's Eagle-Owl
African Wood Owl
Dusky Nightjar
Fiery-necked Nightjar
Plain Nightjar
Gabon Nightjar
Mottle-throated Swift   c
Boehm's Needletail
Common Swift   W
House Swift
African Palm-Swift
Speckled Mousebird   c
Blue-naped Mousebird
Narina Trogon
Pied Kingfisher
Malachite Kingfisher
African Pygmy Kingfisher   r
Gray-headed Kingfisher
African Mangrove Kingfisher
Brown-hooded Kingfisher
Striped Kingfisher
Little Bee-eater
White-throated Bee-eater   c
Eurasian Bee-eater   W
Northern Carmine Bee-eater   c M
Blue-cheeked Bee-eater   M
Eurasian Roller   W
Lilac-breasted Roller

Rufous-crowned Roller
Cinnamon Roller   c
Green Wood-Hoopoe
Southern Scimitarbill
Crowned Hornbill
Trumpeter Hornbill
Gray-cheeked Hornbill
Silvery-cheeked Hornbill
Green Barbet   c
Green Tinkerbird
Golden-rumped Tinkerbird
Black-collared Barbet
Cassin's Honeyguide
Wahlberg's Honeyguide
Lesser Honeyguide
Scaly Honeyguide
Greater Honeyguide
Golden-tailed Woodpecker   c
Cardinal Woodpecker
Little White-spotted Woodpecker
African Pitta
Flappet Bush-Lark
Ethiopian Swallow
Barn Swallow   W
Mosque Swallow
Lesser Striped Swallow
Black Saw-wing
Malindi Pipit   r
Sokoke Pipit
Red-throated Pipit   W
Golden Pipit
Yellow Wagtail   W
African Pied Wagtail
Red-shouldered Cuckoo-shrike
Retz's Helmet-Shrike
Chestnut-fronted Helmet-Shrike
Black-backed Puffback-Shrike
Black-crowned Tchagra
Brown-crowned Tchagra
Tropical Boubou
Gorgeous Bush-Shrike
Red-tailed Shrike   c W
Red-backed Shrike   W
Long-tailed Fiscal-Shrike   c
Garden Bulbul
Little Greenbul
Eastern Sombre Greenbul   c

Yellow-bellied Leaf-love   c
Fischer's (Eastern) Greenbul
Terrestrial Greenbul
Northern Wheatear   W
White-backed Rock-Thrush   W
Eastern Bearded Scrub-Robin
Scrub Morning-Thrush
Spotted Morning-Thrush
Heuglin's Robin-Chat
Natal Robin-Chat
Red-tailed Rusty-Thrush
Thrush-Nightingale   W
African Bare-eyed Thrush
Spotted Ground-Thrush
Rufous Chatterer
Squamulated Babbler
Rattling Cisticola
Winding Cisticola
Tawny-flanked Prinia
Black-headed Prinia
Black-headed Apalis   c
Bleating Camaroptera
Spotted Flycatcher   c W
Ashy Flycatcher
Pallid Flycatcher   c
Cape Batis
Chin-spot Batis
Little Yellow Flycatcher   c
Blue-mantled Crested-Flycatcher
African Paradise-Flycatcher
Collared Sunbird   c
Blue-throated Sunbird
Amani Sunbird   c
Purple-banded Sunbird
Violet-breasted Sunbird

Olive Sunbird
Scarlet-chested Sunbird
Amethyst Sunbird
Mouse-colored Sunbird
Yellow-fronted Canary
Black-throated Canary
Village Weaver
Taveta Golden Weaver
Golden Palm Weaver   c
Eastern Golden Weaver
Clarke's Weaver
Spectacled Weaver
Dark-backed Weaver   c
Thick-billed Weaver
Zanzibar Red Bishop
White-winged Widowbird
Red-billed Quelea   c
Pin-tailed Whydah
Orange-winged Pytilia
Peter's Twinspot
Green Twinspot
Red-cheeked Cordonbleu
Common Waxbill
Bronze Munia   c
Red-backed Munia
Black-bellied Glossy-Starling
Blue-eared Glossy-Starling
Superb Starling
Amethyst Starling
African Drongo
African Black-headed Oriole   c
African Golden Oriole   c
Eurasian Golden Oriole   c W
House Crow
Pied Crow   c

68
Blantyre, Malawi

BLANTYRE IS THE COMMERCIAL CAPITAL of this small African country, formerly called Nyasaland. Lying among beautiful hills near the edge of the escarpment of the Great Rift Valley, the city boasts three fine hotels. A drive of forty miles (64 km) west over the all-weather gravel road to Chikwawa leads one down the Rift wall to the hot tropical valley of the Lower Shire River. There, in the Lengwe National Park, visitors can see nyala, kudu, bushbuck, and buffalo. Lengwe's dense thickets and huge dry-forest trees shelter Livingstone's Flycatcher, guineafowl, Hildebrant's, Kirk's, and Crested Francolins, Black-bellied Bustard, Trumpeter Hornbill, Purple-banded and White-bellied Sunbirds, and Cameroon Sombre Greenbul. The water holes attract not only game but a variety of doves, and Yellow-billed and Saddle-billed Storks, White-backed Duck, and Lizard Buzzard. North of the park, along the banks of the Shire, crocodiles bask on the open sand spits, along with herons, Three-banded Plover, and other waterbirds. The river bush is home to the Lilac-breasted Roller and to bee-eaters, including the Southern Carmine. The commoner raptors that hunt the surrounding bush country are Bonelli's Eagle, Martial Eagle, Brown and Banded Snake-Eagles, and the ever-present Bateleur.

Thyolo is only 25 miles (40 km) south of Blantyre over a tarmac road, an easy day trip from the city. Thyolo Mountain, with its extensive rain forest, must be approached through the grounds of the Satemwa Tea Estate, and it is perhaps wise to get the prior permission of the estate manager, though this has not always been necessary in the past. The manager can be reached by telephone from Blantyre. In the interior of the forest patience may result in glimpses of Lemon Dove, Tambourine Wood-Dove, Bar-tailed Trogon, Livingstone's Turaco, White-eared and Green Barbets, Starred Robin, Stripe-cheeked Greenbul, White-winged Apalis, Green-headed Oriole, and Black-fronted Bush-Shrike.

The Mulanje Plateau, 35 miles (56 km) east of Blantyre, has spectacular 10,000-foot (3000 m) peaks and is a paradise for the climber-cum-ornithologist. Trails ascend through rain and riparian forests,

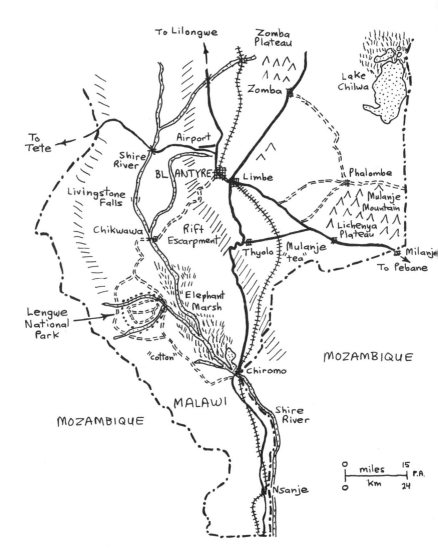

through a belt of dry brachystegia, and on to the open uplands of the plateau itself. Five forestry-department huts are scattered over the 180 square miles (468 km²) of the plateau below the high ragged peaks.

From the birder's viewpoint, the Lichenya Plateau, the south-western portion of the Mulanje system, offers the greatest variety of bird life in a remote wilderness of magnificent mountains. In the brachystegia forests of the escarpment slopes there are Rufous Tit, African Golden Oriole, Bearded Woodpecker, White-breasted

Cuckoo-shrike, and Long-billed Pipit. The open grasslands of the plateau itself shelter Wailing Cisticola, Red-necked Spurfowl, and Shelley's Francolin. Raptors of the open range include hobbies, kestrels, Augur Buzzard, Lanner Falcon, and Montagu's and Pallid Harriers. On the streams of the plateau live Mountain Wagtail and African Black Duck. Large patches of riparian rain forest fill the valleys and depressions; in them can be found Yellow-throated Leaf-Warbler, White-throated Robin-Chat, Olive Pigeon, White-tailed Crested-Flycatcher, Cholo (Thyolo) Alethe, African Broadbill, and Square-tailed Drongo. The open rock of the cliffs and peaks attracts not only raptors but White-necked Raven, Mocking Cliff-Chat, Mottled Swift, and Red-winged Starling.

Those wishing to give Mulanje its due ought first to contact the Secretary of the Mulanje Mountain Club at PO Box 240, Blantyre. Information about trails, huts, equipment, maps, and the like can be obtained from this source. The huts themselves, though, must be booked in advance through the Assistant Conservator of Forests, Mulanje Mountain, PO Box 50, Mulanje.

Anyone confined to the city itself will find that the rain forest covering the summit of Soche Hill in the southeastern quarter of the city offers nearly as many forest species as Thyolo Mountain. The open heights of Ndirande, another hill within the city's compass, is a fine place for Lanner Falcon, Verreaux's Eagle, and Rock Martin. The reed beds and open water of Coronation Dam (near Blantyre) attract migrant waterfowl, African Sea-Eagle, Short-billed Egret, African and Lesser Jacanas, Black Crake, Southern Pochard, and Hottentot Teal.

CHECKLIST

(BF = Brachystegia Forests)

Little Dabchick   c
Great Cormorant   r
Long-tailed Cormorant   c
Darter
Eastern White Pelican   r
Pink-backed Pelican
Gray Heron
Black-headed Heron
Goliath Heron   r
Purple Heron   c
Great Egret
Short-billed Egret   c

Black Heron   L
Little Egret
Cattle Heron   c
Squacco Pond-Heron
Green Heron   r
Rufous-bellied Heron   r
Black-crowned Night-Heron
Little Bittern   r
Dwarf Bittern
Hammerkop
White Stork   M
Woolly-necked Stork   r

Abdim's Stork   r S
Black Open-billed Stork
Saddle-billed Stork
Marabou Stork   L
Yellow-billed Stork
Sacred Ibis
Hadada Ibis   r L
Glossy Ibis
African Spoonbill   r
Greater Flamingo   r M
Fulvous Whistling-Duck   L
White-faced Whistling-Duck   L
Egyptian Goose   r
Spur-winged Goose
Knob-billed Goose
African Pygmy-Goose
African Black Duck
Yellow-billed Duck   H
Red-billed Duck
Hottentot Teal
Southern Pochard
White-backed Duck   r
Osprey   r
Eurasian Honey-Buzzard   r W
Bat Kite   r
Black-shouldered Kite
Black Kite   c
African Sea-Eagle   c
Hooded Vulture
Brown Snake-Eagle   L
Black-breasted Snake-Eagle
Banded Snake-Eagle
Bateleur   c
African Harrier-Hawk
African Harrier
Pallid Harrier   r M
Montagu's Harrier   r M
Dark Chanting-Goshawk
Gabar Goshawk
Great Goshawk
Little Sparrowhawk
African Goshawk
Shikra   c
Lizard Buzzard   c
Common Buzzard   M
Augur Buzzard   c H
Lesser Spotted Eagle   r M

Tawny (Steppe) Eagle
Wahlberg's Eagle   M
Verreaux's Eagle   H
African Hawk-Eagle
Ayre's Hawk-Eagle   r
Long-crested Eagle
Crowned Hawk-Eagle   r
Martial Eagle
Lesser Kestrel   M
Common Kestrel   c
Dickinson's Kestrel   L
Amur Falcon   M
Red-necked Falcon   L
European Hobby   W
Lanner Falcon   c
Peregrine Falcon   r H
Coqui Francolin   BF
Crested Francolin   L
Kirk's Francolin   L
Shelley's Francolin
Hildebrandt's Francolin
Red-necked Spurfowl   c
Common Quail   c H
Harlequin Quail   S
Blue Quail
Helmeted Guineafowl
Crested Guineafowl   L
Common Buttonquail   c
Kaffir Rail
Corn Crake   M
African Crake
African Black Crake   c
Spotted Crake   r M
Chestnut-tailed Flufftail   r H
Purple Swamphen   L
Allen's Gallinule   r
Common Gallinule
Lesser Gallinule   r
Red-knobbed Coot
African Finfoot   r
African Jacana   c
Lesser Jacana
Black-bellied Bustard
Greater Painted-snipe
Long-toed Lapwing
Blacksmith Lapwing
Senegal Lapwing   r

354

Wattled Lapwing
Greater Ringed Plover   M
Three-banded Plover
Caspian Plover   r M
Marsh Sandpiper   M
Common Greenshank   M
Green Sandpiper   M
Wood Sandpiper   c M
Common Sandpiper   c M
Ethiopian Snipe
Little Stint   M
Curlew Sandpiper   M
Ruff   M
Black-winged Stilt   r
Spotted Dikkop   r
Water Dikkop
Bronze-winged Courser   r
Temminck's Courser
Collared Pratincole   M
White-winged Black Tern   W
African Skimmer   r
Olive Pigeon   H
Bronze-naped Pigeon   r H
Red-eyed Turtle-Dove   c H
Mourning Turtle-Dove   L
Cape Turtle-Dove   c
Laughing Turtle-Dove
Namaqua Dove   L
Tambourine Wood-Dove   c H
Blue-spotted Wood-Dove   c
Emerald-spotted Wood-Dove   c
Lemon Dove   c H
African Green Pigeon
African Brown-headed Parrot   L
Brown-necked Parrot   L
Knysna Turaco   c H
Purple-crested Turaco   c
Gray Go-away-bird   c L
Eurasian Cuckoo   M
Red-chested Cuckoo   S
Black Cuckoo   S
Barred Long-tailed Cuckoo   L S
Thick-billed Cuckoo   r L S
Great Spotted Cuckoo   M
Jacobin Cuckoo   S
Levaillant's Cuckoo   S
Emerald Cuckoo   r H

Didric Cuckoo
Klaas's Cuckoo   c
Black Coucal
White-browed Coucal
Senegal Coucal
Green Cuckoo   L
Barn Owl
African Scops-Owl
White-faced Scops-Owl
Spotted Eagle-Owl   c BF
Verreaux's Eagle-Owl   r
Pel's Fishing Owl   r L
Pearl-spotted Owlet   c
African Barred Owlet
African Wood Owl   c
Marsh Owl   r
Eurasian Nightjar   r M
Dusky Nightjar   c BF
Freckled Nightjar
Gabon Nightjar   L
Pennant-winged Nightjar   c S
Mottled Swift   r H
Common Swift   c M
Scarce Swift   r M
White-rumped Swift
Horus Swift   L
Little Swift   L
African Palm-Swift   c
Speckled Mousebird   r
Red-faced Mousebird   L
Narina Trogon
Bar-tailed Trogon   r H
Giant Kingfisher
Pied Kingfisher   c
Half-collared Kingfisher   r
Malachite Kingfisher   c
African Pygmy Kingfisher
Woodland Kingfisher   M
Brown-headed Kingfisher   c
Gray-headed Kingfisher   M
Striped Kingfisher   c
Eurasian Bee-eater   c M
Blue-cheeked Bee-eater   L M
Southern Carmine Bee-eater   L M
Boehm's Bee-eater   L
Little Bee-eater   c
White-fronted Bee-eater   r L

355

Swallow-tailed Bee-eater   L
Eurasian Roller   M
Racquet-tailed Roller   L
Lilac-breasted Roller   c
Rufous-crowned Roller   r L
Cinnamon Roller   c M
Hoopoe
Green Wood-Hoopoe
Southern Scimitarbill   c
African Gray Hornbill   c
Yellow-billed Hornbill   L
Pale-billed Hornbill   r BF
Crowned Hornbill   c
Trumpeter Hornbill
Silvery-cheeked Hornbill   H
Southern Ground Hornbill
White-eared Barbet   H
Green Barbet   r H
Yellow-fronted Tinkerbird   BF
Golden-rumped Tinkerbird   c H
Black-collared Barbet   c
Crested Barbet   r
Cassin's Honeyguide   r
Least Honeyguide   r H
Lesser Honeyguide   r
Scaly Honeyguide   r
Greater Honeyguide
Bennett's Woodpecker   r BF
African Spotted Woodpecker   r
Golden-tailed Woodpecker
Cardinal Woodpecker   c
Stierling's Woodpecker   r BF
Bearded Woodpecker
African Broadbill   r
African Pitta   r M
Flappet Bush-Lark   c BF
Chestnut-backed Finch-Lark
Red-capped Lark
Barn Swallow   c M
Gray-rumped Swallow
Blue Swallow   H M
Wire-tailed Swallow   c
Red-rumped Swallow   H
Mosque Swallow   r
Lesser Striped Swallow   c
Sand Martin   r L M
Plain Martin   r

Rock Martin   H
House Martin   M
Black Saw-wing   c
African Drongo   c
Square-tailed Drongo   H
Eurasian Golden Oriole   r M
African Black-headed Oriole   c
   BF
Green-headed Oriole   r H
Red-winged Starling   c H
Blue-eared Glossy-Starling   c L
Lesser Blue-eared Glossy-Starling
   c L
Amethyst Starling   c M
Wattled Starling   r
Yellow-billed Oxpecker   r L
Pied Crow   c
White-necked Raven   c H
Rufous-breasted Tit   BF
Southern Black Tit   L
Gray Penduline Tit   BF
Spotted Creeper   r BF
Arrow-marked Babbler   c
Gray Cuckoo-shrike   r H
White-breasted Cuckoo-shrike   BF
Black Cuckoo-shrike
Garden Bulbul   c
Little Greenbul   H
Cameroon Sombre Greenbul   L
Mountain Greenbul   c H
Stripe-cheeked Greenbul   c H
Yellow-bellied Leaf-love   c L
Terrestrial Greenbul
Gray-olive Greenbul   H
Yellow-streaked Greenbul   H
Fischer's Greenbul   H
Red-backed Scrub-Robin   c
Eastern Bearded Scrub-Robin   L
Starred Robin   c H
Thrush-Nightingale   M
Natal Robin-Chat
Heuglin's Robin-Chat   c
Cape Robin-Chat   c H
White-throated Robin-Chat
Olive-flanked Robin-Chat   H
Scrub Morning-Thrush   c L
Cholo Alethe   H

Familiar Chat
Stonechat   H
Arnott's Chat   r BF
Mocking Cliff-Chat   c H
Angola Rock-Thrush   BF
Orange Ground Thrush   H
Spotted Ground-Thrush   r H
Olive Thrush   r H
Kurrichane Thrush   c BF
Cape Reed-Warbler   c
Rush Warbler   c
Barratt's Scrub-Warbler   c H
Cinnamon Bracken Warbler   H
Sedge Warbler   M
Marsh Warbler   M
Great Reed-Warbler   M
Moustached Grassbird
Garden Warbler   M
Yellow-throated Leaf-Warbler   c
  H
Zitting Cisticola
Red-faced Cisticola
Singing Cisticola
Lazy Cisticola   BF
Rattling Cisticola
Wailing Cisticola   H
Croaking Cisticola
Neddicky Cisticola   BF
Short-winged Cisticola
Winding Cisticola   ? L
Red-winged Warbler   BF
Tawny-flanked Prinia   c
Bar-throated Apalis
White-winged Apalis   r H
Yellow-breasted Apalis   H
Black-headed Apalis   c H
Gray-backed Camaroptera
Bleating Camaroptera
Stierling's Camaroptera
Yellow-bellied Eremomela
Green-capped Eremomela
Burnt-necked Eremomela
Cape Crombec   L
Red-faced Crombec   BF
Yellow-bellied Hyliota   BF
Mountain Chloropeta
African Dusky Flycatcher   c H

Ashy Flycatcher   H
Spotted Flycatcher   M
Gray Tit-Flycatcher   r
Southern Black-Flycatcher
Pallid Flycatcher   BF
Black-and-white Flycatcher   L
Cape Batis   c H
Chinspot Batis   c
Woodward's Batis   r L
Black-throated Wattle-eye
Livingstone's Flycatcher   c L
Blue-mantled Crested Flycatcher
White-tailed Crested Flycatcher   c
  H
African Paradise-Flycatcher   c S
African Pied Wagtail   c
Mountain Wagtail   c H
Yellow Wagtail   M
Long-billed Pipit   BF
Richard's Pipit   c
Tree Pipit   M
Striped Pipit   BF
Yellow-throated Longclaw
Brubru Shrike
Black-backed Puffback-Shrike   c
Black-crowned Tchagra   c
Brown-crowned Tchagra   c
Black-capped Tchagra
Tropical Boubou   c
Sulfur-breasted Bush-Shrike
Olive Bush-Shrike   H
Black-fronted Bush-Shrike   r H
Gorgeous Bush-Shrike   r L
Gray-headed Bush-Shrike   r
Yellow-spotted Nicator   r
Magpie Shrike   r L
Souza's Shrike   r BF
Red-backed Shrike   c M
Common Fiscal-Shrike   c
White Helmet-Shrike   c BF
Retz's Helmet-Shrike
Western Violet-backed Sunbird   r
Collared Sunbird   c H
Olive Sunbird
Amethyst Sunbird   BF
Scarlet-chested Sunbird   c
Variable Sunbird   c

357

White-bellied Sunbird   L
Lesser Double-collared Sunbird
Eastern Double-collared Sunbird
   H
Copper Sunbird   r
Shelley's Sunbird   r BF
Purple-banded Sunbird   r L
Yellow White-eye   c
Green White-eye   c H
African Citril   H
Yellow-fronted Canary   c
Brimstone Canary
Black-eared Canary   BF
Cinnamon-breasted Bunting   H
Cape Bunting   BF
Golden-breasted Bunting   BF
Cabinis's Bunting   BF
Orange-winged Pytilia
Green-winged Pytilia
Green Twin-spot   r
Red-faced Crimsonwing   H
Nyasa Seedcracker   r H
Peter's Twinspot
Red-billed Fire-Finch   c
Blue-billed Fire-Finch
Jameson's Fire-Finch
Southern Cordonbleu   c
Southern Lavender Waxbill   r L
Yellow-bellied Waxbill   c H
Common Waxbill   c
Orange-breasted Waxbill
Bronze Munia   c

Red-backed Munia
Pied Munia   r
Cut-throat Finch   r L
White-browed Sparrow-Weaver
Gray-headed Sparrow   c
Yellow-throated Petronia
Thick-billed Weaver
Bertram's Weaver
Eastern Golden Weaver
Holub's Golden Weaver
Southern Brown-throated Weaver
   c L
Lesser Masked Weaver   L
Vitelline Masked Weaver
Village Weaver   c
Dark-backed Weaver   c H
Usambara Weaver   r BF
Red-headed Weaver   BF
Red-headed Quelea
Red-billed Quelea   M
Red Bishop   c
Fire-crowned Bishop   c
Yellow Bishop   c
Fan-tailed Widowbird   L
White-winged Widowbird
Red-collared Widowbird   c
Parasitic Weaver   r
Indigobird
Pin-tailed Whydah   c
Paradise Whydah   c
Southern Broad-tailed Whydah   c

69
Luangwa Valley National Parks, Zambia

A STRING OF FOUR PARKS lies along either side of the Luangwa River in eastern Zambia, northeast of Lusaka, the capital. Zambia Airways has flights to Mfuwe Lodge's airstrip, and the area can also be reached by road.

The South Luangwa National Park is the centerpiece of the area, occupying 3494 square miles (9050 km²). The scenery is greatly varied, with tall escarpment cliffs to the west and an active meandering river that frequently changes its course. There is riparian forest and, away from the river, miombo and mopane woodland. There is open grassland in the north on the Chifungwe Plain, where the Short-wing Cisticola rules over the great beasts.

This park is renowned for its abundance of large mammals. In addition to over 30,000 elephants, there are large numbers of buffalo, hippo, impala, puku, zebra, waterbuck, warthog, baboon, and vervet monkeys. Other mammals that visitors may find are greater kudu, bushbuck, black rhinoceros, roan, eland, sable (rare), hartebeest, common duiker, and grysbok. Cookson's wildebeest is best seen in the Nsefu sector east of the river, while the local Thornicroft's giraffe is most regular in the area south of Luamfwa Lodge, south of the river. Lion are not rare, and visitors taking specially guided nocturnal tours may see leopard and hyena. Oxpeckers are common, with the Red-billed preferring giraffe, impala, and zebra, while the Yellow-billed prefers to search for ticks on kudu, eland, and warthog.

There are three fully catered lodges at Mfuwe, Chichele, and Luamfwa, as well as noncatered lodges at Nsefu, Lion Camp, and Big Lagoon. Vehicles are present in the park for guided tours with advance arrangements. The park is open all year, with the dry, cooler season from mid-May through October. It gets hot in October, and the rains come in November. Although the roads become less reliable in the summer wet season, a number of water-birds, European migrants, cuckoos, rails, kingfishers, and weavers are best found at this time. The Wattled Crane can sometimes be seen in such rivers as the Mupamadzi in the north of the park.

The North Luangwa National Park is famous for being a true wilderness with no roads. The only access is via organized wilderness-trail safaris. Clients walk with officially approved armed escorts, and bearers set up camps at designated sites. This is a woodland park with miombo woodland on the better drained sandy areas, and mopane woodland on the heavier soils. There is a complex of vegetation types along the river to the east and tall cliffs on the west along the Muchinga escarpment. Mammals as well as birds are profuse.

The Luambe National Park is a small park located east of the river, with a small, noncatering lodge. The park can be reached by road and features the largest herds of Cookson's wildebeest, many elephant, and several lagoons for birds. The Lukusuzi National Park to the east lies at higher elevations, and while it is good for klipspringer, it has no accommodation and roads are rough. There is fine plateau country in the east of the park and there are many mammals.

New lodges and a new airport in the area are planned to handle the increased numbers of visitors expected in the future.

CHECKLIST

Little Dabchick   r
Eastern White Pelican   c M
Darter   c
Dwarf Bittern   r
White-backed Night-Heron   r
Black-crowned Night-Heron   r
Squacco Pond-Heron   c
Rufous-bellied Heron   r M
Cattle Heron   c
Green Heron   c
Black Heron   r M
Little Egret
Short-billed Egret
Great Egret   c
Gray Heron
Black-headed Heron
Goliath Heron   c
Hammerkop   c
White Stork   M
Black Stork   r M
Abdim's Stork   c S
Woolly-necked Stork   S

Black Open-billed Stork
Saddle-billed Stork   c
Marabou Stork   c
Yellow-billed Stork   c
Sacred Ibis   c
Hadada Ibis   c
African Spoonbill
White-faced Whistling-Duck
Egyptian Goose   c
African Pygmy-Goose   r S
Knob-billed Goose   c
Spur-winged Goose
Secretarybird   r
Black Kite   c
African White-backed Vulture   c
Lappet-faced Vulture   r
White-headed Vulture
Hooded Vulture   c
Black-shouldered Kite   r
Bat Kite   r
Tawny Eagle   c
Wahlberg's Eagle   r S

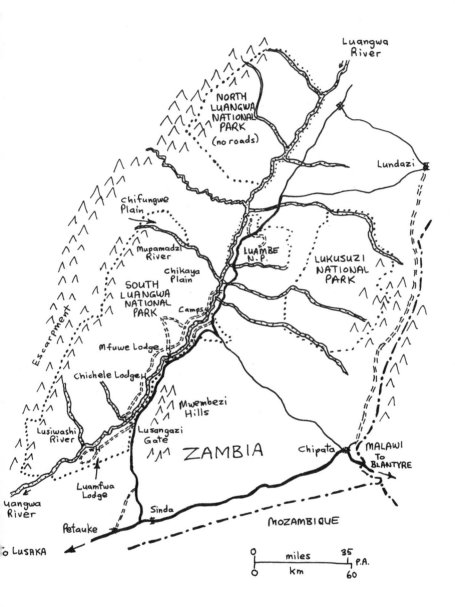

African Hawk-Eagle
Lesser Spotted Eagle   r M
Long-crested Hawk   r
Martial Eagle   c
Lizard Buzzard   c
Brown Snake-Eagle   r
Black-breasted Snake-Eagle   r
Banded Snake-Eagle   c
Bateleur   c
African Sea-Eagle   c
Common Buzzard   r M
Ovampo Sparrowhawk   r
Little Sparrowhawk   r
Shikra   c
African Goshawk   r
Dark Chanting-Goshawk   r
Gabar Goshawk   c
African Harrier-Hawk   r
Lanner Falcon   r
Red-necked Falcon   r
Dickinson's Kestrel   r
Hildebrant's Francolin
Natal Francolin
Red-necked Spurfowl   c
Swainson's Spurfowl   c
Harlequin Quail   r S
Helmeted Guineafowl   c
Crested Guineafowl   r
Common Buttonquail   r
Wattled Crane   r
Eastern Crowned Crane   c
Corn Crake   r M
African Crake   c S
African Black Crake   c
Lesser Gallinule   r S
Black-bellied Bustard   r
African Jacana   c
Lesser Jacana   r
Greater Painted-snipe   r S
White-fronted Plover   r
Caspian Plover   M
Kittlitz's Plover   r
Three-banded Plover   r
Senegal Lapwing   r
Blacksmith Lapwing
White-crowned Lapwing   c
Wattled Lapwing   c

Common Sandpiper   c M
Green Sandpiper   r M
Marsh Sandpiper   M
Common Greenshank   c M
Wood Sandpiper   c M
Little Stint   r M
Ruff   r M
Great Snipe   r M
Black-winged Stilt   r
Spotted Dikkop
Water Dikkop   c
Temminck's Courser   r S
Heuglin's Courser   c
Bronze-winged Courser   S
Gray-headed Gull   r S
White-winged Black Tern   r M
African Skimmer   c S
Double-banded Sandgrouse   c
Red-eyed Turtle-Dove   c
Mourning Turtle-Dove   c
Cape Turtle-Dove   c
Laughing Turtle-Dove   c
Namaqua Dove   r
Tambourine Wood-Dove
Emerald-spotted Wood-Dove   c
African Green-Pigeon   r
Brown-necked Parrot   r
Brown Parrot   r
Lilian's Lovebird   c
Purple-crested Turaco   c
Gray Go-away-bird   c
African Cuckoo   r S
Red-chested Cuckoo   c S
Black Cuckoo   r S
Great Spotted Cuckoo   r M
Jacobin Cuckoo   S
Thick-billed Cuckoo   r
Emerald Cuckoo   c S
Didric Cuckoo   c S
Black Coucal   r
Senegal Coucal   c
White-browed Coucal   c
African Wood-Owl   r
White-faced Scops-Owl   r
Pearl-spotted Owlet   c
African Barred Owlet   r
Verreaux's Eagle-Owl   r

Pel's Fishing Owl   r
Gabon Nightjar   c
Pennant-winged Nightjar   r S
Common Swift   M
Horus Swift
African Palm-Swift
Boehm's Needletail   r
Red-faced Mousebird   r
Pied Kingfisher   c
Giant Kingfisher   r
Half-collared Kingfisher   r
Malachite Kingfisher
African Pygmy Kingfisher   r S
Woodland Kingfisher   c S
Brown-hooded Kingfisher   c
Gray-headed Kingfisher   c S
Striped Kingfisher   r
Eurasian Bee-eater   r M
Blue-cheeked Bee-eater   r M
Southern Carmine Bee-eater   c
White-fronted Bee-eater
Little Bee-eater
Swallow-tailed Bee-eater   r S
Eurasian Roller   r M
Lilac-breasted Roller   c
Racquet-tailed Roller
Broad-billed Roller   c S
Hoopoe
Green Wood-Hoopoe   c
Southern Scimitarbill   r
Trumpeter Hornbill   r
African Gray Hornbill   c
Red-billed Hornbill   c
Crowned Hornbill   r
Southern Ground Hornbill
Black-collared Barbet   c
Yellow-fronted Tinkerbird   r
Crested Barbet
Greater Honeyguide   c
Lesser Honeyguide   r
Wahlberg's Honeyguide   r
Bennett's Woodpecker   r
Cardinal Woodpecker
Bearded Woodpecker   r
African Broadbill   r
Flappet Bush-Lark   r
Dusky Bush-Lark   r

Chestnut-backed Finch-Lark   r S
Barn Swallow   M
Wire-tailed Swallow   c
Mosque Swallow   r M
Lesser Striped Swallow   r
Sand Martin   r M
Plain Martin
White-breasted Cuckoo-shrike   r S
African Drongo   c
African Golden Oriole   r
African Black-headed Oriole   r
Southern Black Tit   r
Arrow-marked Babbler   c
Garden Bulbul   c
Terrestrial Greenbul   r
Yellow-bellied Leaf-love
Yellow-spotted Nicator   r
Kurrichane Thrush
Familiar Chat   r
Arnott's Chat
Heuglin's Robin-Chat   r
Natal Robin-Chat   r
Scrub Morning-Thrush
Thrush-Nightingale   r M
Red-backed Scrub-Robin   r
Garden Warbler   M
Greater Whitethroat   M
Great Reed-Warbler   M
Marsh Warbler   M
Sedge Warbler   M
Moustached Grassbird
Willow Warbler   c M
Burnt-necked Eremomela   r
Bleating Camaroptera
Zitting Cisticola   c
Short-winged Cisticola
Rattling Cisticola   r
Red-faced Cisticola   c
Neddicky Cisticola   r
Tawny-flanked Prinia   c
Spotted Flycatcher   r M
Ashy Flycatcher
Southern Black Flycatcher   r
Chin-spot Batis   r
African Paradise-Flycatcher   c
African Pied Wagtail   c
Richard's Pipit   r

Brubru Shrike   r
Black-backed Puffback-Shrike
Black-crowned Tchagra   c
Cape Boubou   c
Sulfur-breasted Bush-Shrike
Gray-headed Bush-Shrike
Red-backed Shrike   M
Lesser Gray Shrike   r M
White Helmet-Shrike   r
Red-billed Helmet-Shrike   r
Wattled Starling   r S
Amethyst Starling   r S
Blue-eared Glossy-Starling
Lesser Blue-eared Glossy-Starling
Southern Long-tailed Starling   c
Yellow-billed Oxpecker   c
Red-billed Oxpecker   c
Collared Sunbird
Amethyst Sunbird   r
Scarlet-chested Sunbird   c
White-bellied Sunbird   r
Red-billed Buffalo-Weaver   c
White-browed Sparrow-Weaver   c
Gray-headed Sparrow   c
Yellow-throated Petronia   r
Spectacled Weaver   r
Holub's Golden Weaver   r

Lesser Masked Weaver   r
Vitelline Masked Weaver
Village Weaver   r
Cardinal Quelea   r
Red-billed Quelea   c
Fire-crowned Bishop   c
Red Bishop   c
Yellow Bishop
White-winged Widowbird   c
Red-collared Widowbird   r
Peter's Twinspot   r
Green-winged Pytilia   r
Orange-winged Pytilia   r
Common Waxbill   r
Southern Cordonbleu   c
Red-billed Fire-Finch   c
Jameson's Fire-Finch
Orange-breasted Waxbill
Bronze Munia   r
Pin-tailed Whydah   r
Indigobird
Paradise Whydah
Southern Broad-tailed Whydah   r
Yellow-fronted Canary   r
Golden-breasted Bunting   r
Cinnamon-breasted Bunting   r

70
Victoria Falls, Zimbabwe (Rhodesia) and Zambia

THE LARGEST SHEET OF FALLING WATER in the world is the star attraction of two parks in northwestern Zimbabwe (Rhodesia) and southwestern Zambia. Victoria Falls National Park covers 230 square miles (598 km^2) and is located 231 miles (370 km) from Bulawayo via road. The Mosi-oa-Tunya National Park lines the river near Maramba (formerly Livingstone), Zambia (ten miles [16 km] north of the falls). There are fine hotels in both countries near the falls.

Two major game drives on the Zimbabwe side offer much birding, particularly at pans and observation points. The Zambezi Drive follows the river upstream. Along the river look for storks, Peter's Finfoot, Wattled Lapwing, Rock Pratincole, African Skimmer, kingfishers, and White-fronted Bee-eater. There are launch trips up the river above the falls, and outboard motorboats are for hire for viewing hippos and White-collared Pratincole.

The Chamabonda Drive takes in the plains and pans of the drier country and is noted for its sable antelope. Look for Wahlberg's Eagle, African Jacana, and Rufous-naped Lark.

The spray from the falls has created a miniature rain forest with many trees found in more humid areas. In this area look for African Goshawk, African Green-Pigeon, Trumpeter Hornbill, Yellow-bellied Bulbul, African Paradise-Flycatcher, and Collared Sunbird. The falls themselves are known as a breeding area for the rare Taita Falcon, a local specialty. In the gorges below the falls look for Gray-rumped Swallow, African Swift, Rock Martin, Familiar Chat, and Mocking Cliff-Chat.

The parks are at an elevation of about 3000 feet (915 m) and the rainfall is just under 30 inches (760 mm) a year, with hot rainy summers and drier, less humid winters. In the wet season the Pennant-winged Nightjar can be seen in mopane veld, a woodland on the plateau, and on ridges away from the river. Travel on most of the circuits is limited to May through November, before the rains begin.

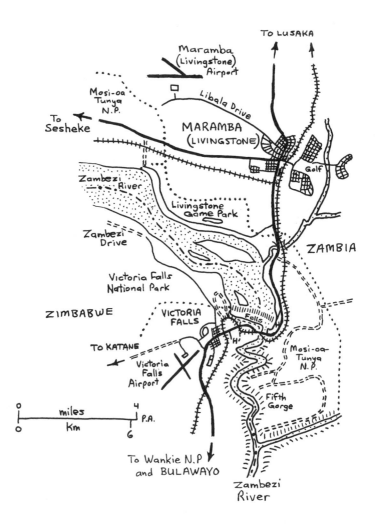

Ornithologically, the area has a large list, which is due to its location. It lies at the north edge of the south African zoogeographical area and is in the east-west convergence zone. Thus there is a mixing of species here on two fronts.

CHECKLIST

Great Cormorant r	Darter c
Long-tailed Cormorant c	Little Bittern r

Gray Heron
Goliath Heron   r
Purple Heron   r
Great Egret
Little Egret   r
Cattle Heron
Squacco Pond-Heron   r
Green Heron   c
Black Heron   r
Rufous-bellied Heron   r
Black-crowned Night-Heron
White-backed Night-Heron   r
Hammerkop   c
Marabou Stork   M
Black Open-billed Stork   r
Saddle-billed Stork
Yellow-billed Stork
Abdim's Stork   c S
Hadada Ibis   c M
Sacred Ibis   r
African Spoonbill
White-faced Whistling-Duck
Spur-winged Goose
Egyptian Goose
Knob-billed Goose   M
African Pygmy-Goose
Red-billed Duck
White-backed Duck   r
Lappet-faced Vulture
Hooded Vulture
Black Kite
Black-shouldered Kite
Bat Kite   r
African Goshawk
Shikra
Gabar Goshawk
Dark Chanting-Goshawk
Tawny Eagle
Wahlberg's Eagle   c
Long-crested Eagle
African Hawk-Eagle
Martial Eagle
Lizard Buzzard
Black-breasted Snake-Eagle
African Sea-Eagle   c
Bateleur   c
Augur Buzzard   r

Dickinson's Kestrel
Taita Falcon
European Hobby   M
Lanner Falcon
Coqui Francolin
Crested Francolin   c
Natal Francolin   r
Swainson's Spurfowl
Helmeted Guineafowl   c
Common Buttonquail
African Crake
African Black Crake
Purple Swamphen
African Finfoot
Black-bellied Bustard
African Jacana
White-fronted Plover
Three-banded Plover   c
Blacksmith Lapwing   c
White-crowned Lapwing
Wattled Lapwing
Common Sandpiper   M
Common Greenshank   M
Wood Sandpiper   M
Black-winged Stilt
Water Dikkop   c
Rock Pratincole
Gray-headed Gull
African Skimmer
Red-eyed Turtle-Dove   c
Cape Turtle-Dove   c
Laughing Turtle-Dove
Namaqua Dove   r
Emerald-spotted Wood-Dove   c
African Green-Pigeon
Brown-necked Parrot   r
Brown Parrot   c
Black-cheeked Lovebird   r
Knysna Turaco   r
Gray Go-away-bird   c
Red-chested Cuckoo   S
Black Cuckoo   r S
Levaillant's Cuckoo
Emerald Cuckoo   r
Klaas's Cuckoo
Didric Cuckoo
Senegal Coucal

African Wood Owl
Pel's Fishing Owl   r
Rufous-cheeked Nightjar
Dusky Nightjar
Pennant-winged Nightjar   S
African Black Swift
Horus Swift
African Palm-Swift
Red-faced Mousebird
Pied Kingfisher   c
Giant Kingfisher
Half-collared Kingfisher   r
Malachite Kingfisher
Gray-headed Kingfisher   c
Brown-hooded Kingfisher   c
Striped Kingfisher
Eurasian Bee-eater   M
White-fronted Bee-eater   c
Little Bee-eater   c
Swallow-tailed Bee-eater   c
Lilac-breasted Roller   c
Broad-billed Roller   c
Hoopoe
Green Wood-Hoopoe
Southern Scimitarbill
Trumpeter Hornbill   c
African Gray Hornbill   c
Yellow-billed Hornbill
Red-billed Hornbill
Black-collared Barbet
Pied Barbet   r
Yellow-fronted Tinkerbird   c
Greater Honeyguide
Golden-tailed Woodpecker
Cardinal Woodpecker   c
Bearded Woodpecker
Rufous-naped Bush-Lark
Dusky Bush-Lark   S
Flappet Bush-Lark
Barn Swallow   c M
Wire-tailed Swallow
Gray-rumped Swallow
Lesser Striped Swallow   c
Rock Martin   c
Black Cuckoo-Shrike
African Drongo   c
African Golden Oriole

African Black-headed Oriole
Southern Black-Tit   c
Arrow-marked Babbler   c
White-rumped Babbler   r
Garden Bulbul   c
Terrestrial Greenbul
Yellow-bellied Leaf-love
Kurrichane Thrush
Groundscraper Thrush
Familiar Chat
Mocking Cliff-Chat   r
Heuglin's Robin-Chat   c
Red-backed Scrub-Robin   c
Scrub Morning-Thrush
Willow Warbler   c M
Yellow-bellied Eremomela   r
Sedge Warbler   M
Rush Warbler
Gray-backed Camaroptera   c
Cape Crombec   c
Yellow-breasted Apalis
Zitting Cisticola
Neddicky Cisticola   c
Rattling Cisticola   c
Red-faced Cisticola
Croaking Cisticola
Tawny-flanked Prinia   c
Spotted Flycatcher
Ashy Flycatcher
Gray Tit-Flycatcher
Pallid Flycatcher
Southern Black Flycatcher
Chin-spot Batis   c
African Paradise-Flycatcher
African Pied Wagtail   c
Cape Wagtail
Mountain Wagtail
Richard's Pipit
Red-backed Shrike   c M
Cape Boubou   c
Black-backed Puffback-Shrike   c
Brown-crowned Tchagra   c
Sulfur-breasted Bush-Shrike   c
Gray-headed Bush-Shrike   c
Yellow-spotted Nicator   r
White Helmet-Shrike
Red-billed Helmet-Shrike

Brubru Shrike
Wattled Starling   S
Amethyst Starling   c
Glossy-Starling   sp.
Red-winged Starling   c
Red-billed Oxpecker   c
Copper Sunbird
Purple-banded Sunbird   r
White-bellied Sunbird
Collared Sunbird   c
Amethyst Sunbird   c
Scarlet-chested Sunbird   c
Yellow White-eye   c
White-browed Sparrow-Weaver   c
Gray-headed Sparrow   c
Yellow-throated Petronia   S

Holub's Golden Weaver   c
Vitelline Masked Weaver   c
Red-billed Quelea   c
Red Bishop   c
White-winged Widowbird   S
Cut-throat Finch
Bronze Munia
Jameson's Fire-Finch   c
Brown Fire-Finch   r
Southern Cordonbleu   c
Common Waxbill   r
Shaft-tailed Whydah   r
Paradise Whydah   r
Yellow-fronted Canary   c
Cinnamon-breasted Bunting
Golden-breasted Bunting   c

71
Cape Town, Cape Province

CAPE TOWN is a fascinating city at the southwestern tip of Africa. It enjoys a Mediterranean climate with winter rains, fine spring flowers in the hinterland, and a pleasing jumble of mountains, vineyards, desert, marshes, and bays. Birding is varied and exciting as it includes searching for many localized forms not found in the great game parks to the northeast, and birding on foot is possible most places.

From the Ambassador Hotel in Sea Point the casual visitor scanning the ocean may find penguins, lines of gannets and cormorants, flocks of terns, and continuous soaring Kelp and Silver Gulls. The National Botanical Gardens at Kirstenbosch are only eight miles (12.8 km) from the center, at the back of Table Mountain. Proteas bloom here from August through October, with their attendant Cape Sugarbirds and Orange-breasted Sunbirds. On weekdays look for Cape Batis in the woods.

The Cape of Good Hope Nature Reserve makes a fine day's outing as it combines flowers, great seascapes, such mammals as zebra, bontebok, and springbok, and a good variety of birds. The seas are often full of gannets, cormorants, and terns. The shore, as at Clifantsbosbai, has shorebirds that include oystercatchers. Birds commonly encountered inland include Cape Francolin, African Black and Alpine Swift, Cape Rock-Thrush, Cape Grassbird, Karoo Prinia, Red-winged Starling, Cape Sugarbird, sunbirds, and Cape Bunting.

The Strandfontein Sewage Farm, located east of Muizenburg, is a superb place for waterbirds. A permit must be secured from the Chemical Branch, City Engineer's Office, Athlone (Cape Town). Driving around the dykes great numbers of Eastern White Pelican, both flamingoes, ducks (including Cape Shoveler), and shorebirds can be seen. The nearby Rondevlei Bird Sanctuary is closed from July to December. Visitors during other months can enter on weekends, although a permit from the Nature Conservation Department, Provincial Administration, Wall Street, Cape Town, is needed on weekdays.

The closest spot for Rufous Rockjumper and the shy Victorin's Scrub Warbler is on the Elgin side of Sir Lowry's Pass. Considerable exploration on foot is called for.

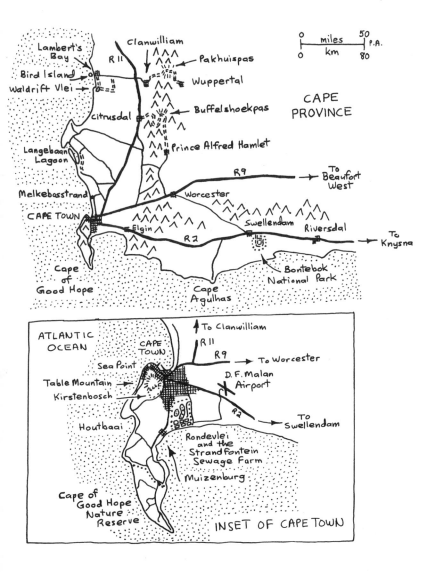

Photographers and seabird enthusiasts should not miss a visit to Bird Island at Lambert's Bay, to the north. Excellent accommodations can be secured at the Hotel Clanwilliam in Clanwilliam, and the Marine Hotel is right in Lambert's Bay. The island is now connected by a short breakwater over which visitors walk onto the island. From the paths one can approach breeding Cape Gannets, Jackass Penguins, and cormorants (including the rare Bank) at close range. No permit problem, and there are thousands of birds.

Just to the south (about seven miles [11.2 km]) is Waldrift Vlei, a lake with good numbers of flamingo, South African Shelduck, other ducks, and shorebirds. The countryside between here and Clanwilliam is good for Booted Eagle, Black Bustard, Karoo Scrub-Robin, Karoo Lark, Red and Cape Bishops, and Pin-tailed Whydah.

In the mountainsides around Pakhuispas, above Clanwilliam, look for Verreaux's Eagle, Ludwig's Bustard, Mountain Wheatear, Fairy Flycatcher, Pale-winged Starling, and Protea Seedeater. Around Buffelshoekpas above Citrusdal the Rufous Rockjumper, sugarbirds, and sunbirds are found.

The Bontebok National Park, just east of Swellendam (with several hotels), is a rolling plain dotted with the rare bontebok plus springbok. Birds can be seen on game drives from within cars and outside at the picnic area along the Breede River. Specialties include Gray-winged Francolin, Denham's Bustard, Black Bustard, Burchell's Coucal, Cape Crow, Fiscal Flycatcher, Cape Batis, Bar-throated Apalis, and Bokmakierie.

If you are driving east toward the Tsitsikamma Forest, look for Blue Cranes east of Riversdal.

CHECKLIST

Jackass Penguin	Eastern White Pelican c
Ostrich	Cape Gannet c
Black-necked Grebe r	Great Cormorant c
Little Dabchick	Cape Cormorant c
Wandering Albatross r W	Bank Cormorant
Black-browed Albatross c W	Long-tailed (Crowned) Cormorant
Shy Albatross r W	c
Giant Petrel W	Darter
Cape Petrel r W	Cattle Heron c
Great-winged Petrel r W	Little Egret
White-chinned Petrel c W	Short-billed Egret
Sooty Shearwater c W	Gray Heron
Wilson's Storm-Petrel W	Black-headed Heron

Hammerkop
Sacred Ibis
African Spoonbill
Greater Flamingo
Lesser Flamingo
Egyptian Goose   c
South African Shelduck
Yellow-billed Duck   c
Cape Teal   c
Red-billed Teal   c
Cape Shoveler   c
Southern Pochard
Spur-winged Goose
Maccoa Duck
Secretarybird   r
Black-shouldered Kite   c
Verreaux's Eagle
Booted Eagle   r
African Sea-Eagle   r
Common Buzzard   c M
Augur Buzzard
Pale Chanting-Goshawk   r
African Harrier
African Harrier-Hawk   r
Common Kestrel   c
Gray-winged Francolin
Cape Francolin   c
Common Quail
Helmeted Guineafowl   c
Blue Crane   r
Red-chested Flufftail   r
Purple Swamphen
Common Gallinule
Red-knobbed Coot   c
Denham's Bustard
Ludwig's Bustard   r
Black Bustard
Greater Painted-snipe   r
African Oystercatcher
Greater Ringed Plover   M
White-fronted Plover
Kittlitz's Plover
Three-banded Plover   c
Gray Plover   M
Crowned Lapwing   c
Blacksmith Lapwing   c
Ruddy Turnstone   M

Common Sandpiper   M
Marsh Sandpiper   M
Common Greenshank   M
Curlew Sandpiper   c M
Little Stint   c M
Red Knot   r M
Sanderling   c M
Ruff   c M
Ethiopian Snipe   r
Bar-tailed Godwit   M
Eurasian Curlew   M
Whimbrel   M
Black-winged Stilt   c
Black-capped Avocet   c
Spotted Dikkop
Great Skua   W
Parasitic Jaeger   M
Kelp Gull   c
Gray-headed Gull
Silver (Hartlaub's) Gull   c
Caspian Tern   c
Common/Arctic Terns   c M
Sandwich Tern
Greater Crested Tern
Damara Tern
White-winged Black Tern   c M
Namaqua Sandgrouse   r
Speckled Pigeon   c
Olive Pigeon   r
Red-eyed Turtle-Dove
Cape Turtle-Dove   c
Laughing Turtle-Dove   c
Namaqua Dove
Red-chested Cuckoo   r S
Klaas's Cuckoo   r
White-browed Coucal
Spotted Eagle-Owl   r
African Black Swift   c
Alpine Swift   c
White-rumped Swift   c
House Swift
Speckled Mousebird   c
White-backed Mousebird
Red-faced Mousebird
Giant Kingfisher
Eurasian Bee-eater   M
Hoopoe

373

Ground Woodpecker
Clapper Bush-Lark
Gray-backed Finch-Lark
Thick-billed Lark   c
Karoo Bush-Lark
Red-capped Lark
Stark's Lark
Barn Swallow   c M
White-throated Swallow
Greater Striped Swallow
Rock Martin   c
Plain Martin   c
Pied Crow   c
Cape Crow
White-necked Raven
Cape Bulbul   c
Eastern Sombre Greenbul   r
Olive Thrush   c
Cape Rock-Thrush
Mountain Wheatear
Capped Wheatear
Familiar Chat   c
Southern Ant-Chat
Stonechat   c
Cape Robin-Chat   c
Rockjumper   r
Karoo Scrub-Robin
Cape Reed-Warbler
Victorin's Scrub Warbler   r
Bar-throated Apalis
Cape Crombec
Cape Grassbird
Grey-backed Cisticola   c
Tinkling Cisticola
Neddicky Cisticola
Karoo Prinia   c

Fiscal Flycatcher   r
Cape Batis
Fairy Flycatcher
African Paradise-Flycatcher
Cape Wagtail   c
Richard's Pipit
Cape Longclaw
Cape Boubou
Bokmakierie   c
Common Fiscal Shrike   c
European Starling   c
Wattled Starling
Pale-winged Starling
Red-winged Starling   c
Pied Starling   c
Cape Sugarbird   c
Lesser Double-collared Sunbird   c
Orange-breasted Sunbird   c
Malachite Sunbird   c
Cape White-eye   c
House Sparrow
Cape Sparrow   c
Cape Weaver   c
Red Bishop   c
Yellow Bishop   c
Common Waxbill
Pin-tailed Whydah
Cape Siskin
Cape Canary   c
Yellow Canary
Brimstone Canary   r
White-throated Canary
Protea Canary   r
Streaky-headed Canary
Cape Bunting   c

72
Zululand Reserves, Natal

NORTHEAST OF DURBAN, NATAL, just south of the Swaziland and Mozambique borders, there is a string of four superb game reserves, Umfolozi, Hluhluwe (pronounced Shlu-shlu-we), Mkuzi, and Ndumu. All four can be reached via the major R2 paved highway and via gravel spur roads. There are several luxury hotels at the town of Hluhluwe (including the Zululand Safari Lodge), a hotel at Mtubatuba, and safari camps with rondavels in most of the reserves (run by the Natal Parks Board, PO Box 662, Pietermaritzburg). Mammals are the main attraction in each park, and excellent photo blinds are strategically placed at water holes. The white rhinoceros is relatively numerous in its Umfolozi stronghold, while the beautiful long-haired nyala is widespread, particularly common at Mkuzi. Other mammals visitors may find include chacma baboon, vervet monkey, side-striped jackal, banded mongoose, cheetah (Hluhluwe), zebra, hippopotamus, warthog, giraffe, greater kudu, bushbuck, common waterbuck, blue wildebeest, impala, steenbok, and African buffalo.

Visitors to each reserve must bring their own food along with them even if overnighting at one of the reserves' camps. Water is available. Each reserve has a network of dirt tracks, and with a few exceptions there is the usual African policy of no-walking outside of vehicles except in camps and photo-blind areas. The choice of which places to stop on which roads is left up to the observer. Stop wherever you see things of interest, wait, and surely other creatures of interest will appear. All four reserves have a mixture of rivers, riparian forest, woodland, water holes, and small grassy plains.

Ndumu requires more time and effort to visit than the other three, involving a much longer trip over back roads, but if you are chiefly interested in birds it is perhaps the richest of the four. The seven 3-bed huts have a nearby kitchen where the staff will cook the food you bring. Birding around the main camp can be good. Strollers may see Purple-crested Turaco and Sulfur-breasted Bush-Shrike. You can take longer hikes if a guard accompanies you. The Ulkhondo Forest would be a good target for birding on foot, with hornbills, trogons, and rare passerines.

A special vehicle runs daily tours around the Nyamiti Pan with expert ranger guidance. This and other water areas are home to pythons and numerous large birds, including Darter, Goliath Heron, Hammerkop, storks, ibis, ducks, African Sea-Eagle, plovers, and Water Dikkop. Near the easterly fence, not far from the Pongolo River, is a small patch of tropical sand forest where African Broadbill, Rudd's Apalis, and Neergaard's Sunbird live.

The Zululand reserves are most pleasant in the winter months of May through October. The summer brings strong heat and rains which may make some roads temporarily impassable.

CHECKLIST

(Special Symbols: UM = Umfolozi, HL = Hluhluwe, MK = Mkuzi, ND = Ndumu)

Ostrich   UM
Little Dabchick
Eastern White Pelican   r
Pink-backed Pelican   r
Long-tailed Cormorant   c
Darter   c
White-backed Night-Heron   r
Black-crowned Night-Heron
Squacco Pond-Heron
Cattle Heron   c
Green Heron
Black Heron   MK, ND
Little Egret   c
Short-billed Egret
Great Egret
Purple Heron   r
Gray Heron
Black-headed Heron
Goliath Heron
Hammerkop   c
White Stork   M
Black Stork   r M
Abdim's Stork   M
Woolly-necked Stork
Black Open-billed Stork   S
Saddle-billed Stork   r S
Marabou Stork   r S
Sacred Ibis
Glossy Ibis   r S

Hadada Ibis   c
African Spoonbill   r S
White-faced Whistling-Duck
Fulvous Whistling-Duck   r
Egyptian Goose   c
Yellow-billed Duck   MK
African Black Duck   r
Hottentot Teal   r ND
Southern Pochard   r S
African Pygmy-Goose
Knob-billed Goose
Spur-winged Goose   c
Maccoa Duck   r
Secretarybird   c
Cape Vulture
African White-backed Vulture   c
Lappet-faced Vulture   r
White-headed Vulture
Black Kite   c
Black-shouldered Kite   c
African Baza
Eurasian Honey-Buzzard   r M
Tawny Eagle
Wahlberg's Eagle   c
African Hawk-Eagle   r
Long-crested Eagle
Martial Eagle
Crowned Hawk-Eagle
Lizard Buzzard

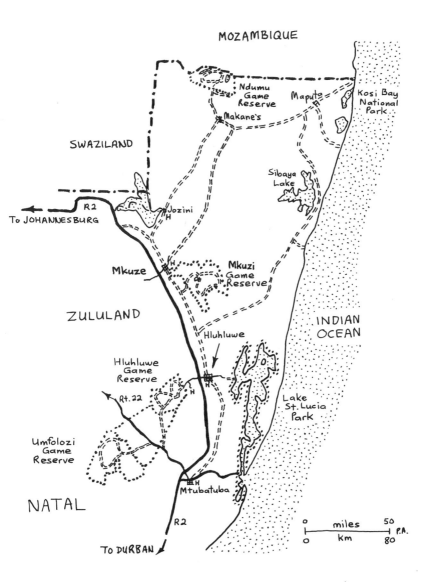

Brown Snake-Eagle
Black-breasted Snake-Eagle
Southern Snake-Eagle   r HL, UM
Bateleur   c
African Fish-Eagle   c
Common Buzzard   M
Jackal Buzzard
Little Sparrowhawk
Great Goshawk   r
Shikra   r
African Goshawk
African Harrier
African Harrier-Hawk
Osprey
Lanner Falcon
Common Kestrel
Greater Kestrel   r
Crested Francolin   c
Shelley's Francolin
Natal Francolin
Common Quail
Blue Quail   M
Helmeted Guineafowl   c
Crested Guineafowl   c
Common Buttonquail
African Black Crake
Buff-spotted Flufftail   r
Purple Swamphen
Common Gallinule
Lesser Gallinule   r
Red-knobbed Coot   ND
Peter's Finfoot   r
Black-bellied Bustard   c
African Jacana   c
Lesser Jacana   r ND, MK
Greater Painted-snipe   r
Greater Ringed Plover   M
Kittlitz's Plover   ND
Three-banded Plover
Crowned Lapwing   S
Senegal Lapwing   S
Blacksmith Lapwing
Wattled Lapwing   S
Common Sandpiper   c M
Marsh Sandpiper   c M
Common Greenshank   M
Wood Sandpiper   c M

Curlew Sandpiper   c M
Little Stint   c M
Ruff   c M
Black-winged Stilt   c
Spotted Dikkop
Water Dikkop
Temminck's Courser   UM, HL
Bronze-winged Courser   r
White-winged Black Tern   c M
Delagorgue's Pigeon   r UM, HL
Red-eyed Turtle-Dove   c
Cape Turtle-Dove
Laughing Turtle-Dove   r UM,
   HL
Namaqua Dove   r
Tambourine Wood-Dove
Emerald-spotted Wood-Dove
Lemon Dove   r
African Green-Pigeon
African Brown-headed Parrot
Purple-crested Turaco
Gray Go-away-bird   r
Red-chested Cuckoo   S
Black Cuckoo   r S
Great Spotted Cuckoo   r M
Jacobin Cuckoo   r M
Emerald Cuckoo   S
Klaas's Cuckoo   S
Didric Cuckoo   S
Green Cuckoo   r
White-browed Coucal   c
Barn Owl
Grass Owl
African Wood-Owl
Spotted Eagle-Owl
Pel's Fishing Owl   ND
Dusky Nightjar
Gabon Nightjar
African Black Swift
Alpine Swift   M
White-rumped Swift
House Swift
Speckled Mousebird   c
Red-faced Mousebird
Narina Trogon
Pied Kingfisher
Giant Kingfisher   r

African Pygmy Kingfisher   r
Malachite Kingfisher   r
Woodland Kingfisher   MK, ND
Brown-hooded Kingfisher
Striped Kingfisher
Eurasian Bee-eater   M
White-fronted Bee-eater
Little Bee-eater
Eurasian Roller   r M
Rufous-crowned Roller   r UM,
   HL
Cinnamon Roller   S
Hoopoe
Green Wood-Hoopoe   c
Southern Scimitarbill   c
Trumpeter Hornbill   c
Red-billed Hornbill   r
Yellow-billed Hornbill   UM, HL,
   MK
Crowned Hornbill   c
Southern Ground Hornbill   r
Black-collared Barbet
Pied Barbet   r
White-eared Barbet   c
Red-fronted Tinkerbird
Golden-rumped Tinkerbird
Crested Barbet
Greater Honeyguide   r
Scaly Honeyguide   r
Lesser Honeyguide
Golden-tailed Woodpecker
Cardinal Woodpecker   c
Olive Woodpecker   r HL, UM
Red-breasted Wryneck   r HL,
   UM
African Broadbill   r ND, MK
Rufous-naped Bush-Lark   c
Flappet Bush-Lark
Sabota Bush-Lark   c
Barn Swallow   c M
White-throated Swallow
Wire-tailed Swallow   c
Lesser Striped Swallow   c
Gray-rumped Swallow   r
Rock Martin
Plain Martin
Black Saw-wing

Black Cuckoo-Shrike   c
African Drongo   c
Square-tailed Drongo
African Golden Oriole   r
African Black-headed Oriole
Pied Crow   c
White-necked Raven
Southern Black-Tit   c
Gray Penduline-Tit   r
Arrow-marked Babbler   MK, ND
Garden Bulbul   c
Terrestrial Greenbul
Eastern Sombre Bulbul   c
Yellow-bellied Leaf-love
Yellow-spotted Nicator
Kurrichane Thrush
Sentinel Rock-Thrush   HL, UM
Familiar Chat
Stonechat
Chorister Robin-Chat   UM, HL
Heuglin's Robin-Chat   MK, ND
Natal Robin-Chat
Cape Robin-Chat
White-throated Robin-Chat
Starred Robin   r
Red-backed Scrub-Robin
Eastern Bearded Scrub-Robin
Garden Warbler   r M
Great Reed-Warbler   r M
Cape Reed-Warbler
Rush Warbler
Willow Warbler   c M
Bar-throated Apalis
Yellow-breasted Apalis   c
Rudd's Apalis   ND, MK
Green-capped Eremomela   r
Burnt-necked Eremomela   r
Bleating Camaroptera   c
Stierling's Camaroptera   MK
Zitting Cisticola
Desert Cisticola   r HL, UM
Rattling Cisticola   c
Red-faced Cisticola
Winding Cisticola   c ND, MK
Croaking Cisticola   HL, UM
Neddicky Cisticola
Tawny-flanked Prinia   c

African Dusky Flycatcher
Ashy Flycatcher
Gray Tit-Flycatcher
Pallid Flycatcher   c
Southern Black Flycatcher   c
Fiscal Flycatcher   S
Chin-spot Batis   c
Woodward's Batis   ND, MK
Black-throated Wattle-eye   MK, ND
Blue-mantled Crested Flycatcher
African Paradise-Flycatcher
African Pied Wagtail   c
Cape Wagtail
Richard's Pipit   c
Long-billed Pipit   HL, UM
Plain-backed Pipit   HL, UM
Bushveld Pipit
Cape Longclaw   HL, UM
Yellow-throated Longclaw   c
Brubru Shrike
Black-backed Puff-back Shrike   c
Brown-crowned Tchagra
Black-crowned Tchagra   c
Cape Tchagra   UM, HL
Cape Boubou   c
Sulfur-breasted Bush-Shrike   c
Gorgeous Bush-Shrike
Gray-headed Bush-Shrike
Red-backed Shrike   c M
Lesser Gray Shrike   M
Common Fiscal-Shrike
White Helmet-Shrike   c
Wattled Starling   S
Amethyst Starling   c S
Cape Glossy-Starling   c
Black-bellied Glossy-Starling
Red-winged Starling   c
Red-billed Oxpecker
Collared Sunbird   c
Olive Sunbird   r
Mouse-colored Sunbird   r
Amethyst Sunbird

Scarlet-chested Sunbird   c
White-bellied Sunbird   c
Neergaard's Sunbird   r ND, MK
Mariqua Sunbird
Purple-banded Sunbird   MK, ND
Yellow White-eye   MK, ND
Cape White-eye   UM, HL, MK
House Sparrow   c
Gray-headed Sparrow
Yellow-throated Petronia   c
Thick-billed Weaver
Spectacled Weaver
Eastern Golden Weaver   ND, MK
Southern Brown-throated Weaver   ND
Lesser Masked Weaver
Vitelline Masked Weaver   c
Village Weaver   c
Dark-backed Weaver
Red-billed Quelea   c S
Red Bishop
Fan-tailed Widowbird
White-winged Widowbird
Red-collared Widowbird
Pink-throated Twinspot   ND, MK
Green Twinspot   r
Green-winged Pytilia
Common Waxbill
Southern Cordonbleu   c
Red-billed Fire-Finch   c
Blue-billed Fire-Finch   c
Red-backed Munia
Bronze Munia
Pin-tailed Whydah
Indigobird
Paradise Whydah   S
Yellow-fronted Canary   c
Brimstone Canary   r
Streak-headed Canary
Golden-breasted Bunting   c
Cinnamon-breasted Bunting

73

Kruger National Park, Transvaal

KRUGER, ONE OF THE WORLD'S oldest, largest, and most famous national parks, is predominantly wooded savanna (known as "thornveld"), with grassland in patches and forests along the permanent rivers.

Most visitors will find the central and southern sections the most rewarding for game and bird viewing. The northern section has some special birds in the forested hills near Punta Milia Camp, and the dense shrubs of the sandy areas on the eastern border. This area is closed for periods and, due to logistic problems, not recommended for jet-set birders. In the Pretoriuskop Camp area there are some species usually found in slightly higher, moister conditions.

The mammals here are well worth the trip, with large numbers of impala, giraffe, lion, and so on. Remember that this is one of the many African parks where you cannot legally get out of your car, even for a quick picture or to check on an eagle overhead.

Those not on a guided bird-watching tour have two choices. Write to the National Parks Board, PO Box 787, Pretoria, giving your dates, the number of persons in your party, and preferred camps; and you can book a rental car in Johannesburg once your accommodation is secured. Alternatively you can have your travel agent book you on a general-interest (not stopping for birds) tour, or a private-chauffeur tour in your own vehicle. Comair Safaris has packages that can be individually tailored, including a Johannesburg–Skukuza flight (round trip), accommodations, meals, guides, and so on.

The camps are really rather fine hotels, with individual units boasting private baths and efficient well-run restaurants. The Skukuza Camp is now a city, and we recommend several days each in two or three of the more remote camps. Although the Satara Camp is away from any river, it is a good base for birding. The Olifants Camp is in a rich area for game, with several rivers nearby, including one you look down on from the camp. The Letaba Camp is adjacent to a river and has the best camp birding of all, due to its large trees. Good shops

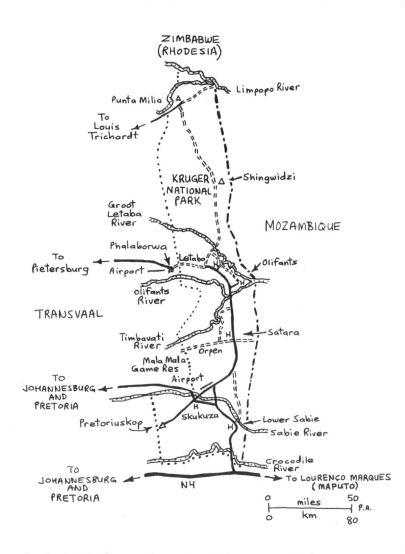

for food, drink, souvenirs, and medicines are at all these camps.

Kruger has a network of paved roads (unlike the dust-ridden parks elsewhere) and a large number of dirt roads open to touring. You are not allowed out of camps after dusk, and fines are imposed on those not back by gate closing. Reservations are crucial, as crowds are a problem in the June-July school holidays and during long weekends.

Many of the birds and mammals of the area can be seen in one of the private reserves just to the west such as the elegant Mala Mala Private Game Park, adjacent to Kruger. It has Comair flights to and

from Johannesburg, a swimming pool, special Land Rover and foot
excursions, and is a little more expensive — for bookings, write to PO
Box 3741, Durban, or work through your travel agent.

Due to the paved roads and wide variety of accommodation, there
is no real season. Game is best viewed late in the dry season, in August
through October. Later, when the rains come and the Palearctic
migrants appear, insect, plant, and animal life are at a peak, and
greater numbers of birds can be seen.

CHECKLIST

(Central and South)

Ostrich
Little Dabchick   r
Long-tailed Cormorant
Darter
Black-crowned Night-Heron
Cattle Heron
Green Heron   c
Little Egret   r
Short-billed Egret   r
Great Egret   r
Gray Heron
Goliath Heron
Hammerkop   c
White Stork   M
Black Stork   r
Abdim's Stork   S
Woolly-necked Stork
Black Open-billed Stork   r
Saddle-billed Stork
Marabou Stork   c
Yellow-billed Stork
Hadada Ibis
Egyptian Goose   c
African Black Duck
Knob-billed Goose   S
Spur-winged Goose   S
Secretarybird   c
Cape Vulture   c
African White-backed Vulture   c
Lappet-faced Vulture   c
White-headed Vulture   c
Hooded Vulture   c
Black Kite   c

Black-shouldered Kite
Tawny Eagle   c
Lesser Spotted Eagle   r M
Wahlberg's Eagle   c S
African Hawk-Eagle
Martial Eagle
Brown Snake-Eagle   c
Black-breasted Snake-Eagle   r
Bateleur   c
African Fish-Eagle   c
Little Sparrowhawk   r
Shikra
Gabar Goshawk
Dark Chanting-Goshawk
African Harrier-Hawk   r
Lanner Falcon   S
Amur Falcon   M
Red-footed Falcon   M
Lesser Kestrel   r M
Coqui Francolin
Crested Francolin   c
Natal Francolin   c
Swainson's Spurfowl   c
Common Quail   S
Harlequin Quail   S
Helmeted Guineafowl   c
Common Buttonquail
African Black Crake   c
Lesser Gallinule   S
Peter's Finfoot   r
Kori Bustard
Buff-crested Bustard   c
Black-bellied Bustard

African Jacana   c
Greater Painted-snipe   r S
White-fronted Plover   r
Three-banded Plover   c
Crowned Lapwing
Senegal Lapwing   S
Blacksmith Lapwing   c
Common Sandpiper   c M
Common Greenshank   M
Wood Sandpiper   c M
Ruff   M
Spotted Dikkop
Water Dikkop
Bronze-winged Courser   S
Double-banded Sandgrouse
Red-eyed Turtle-Dove
Mourning Turtle-Dove
Cape Turtle-Dove   c
Laughing Turtle-Dove   c
Namaqua Dove
Emerald-spotted Wood-Dove   c
African Green-Pigeon
African Brown-headed Parrot
Purple-crested Turaco   r
Gray Go-away-bird   c
Eurasian Cuckoo   M
Red-chested Cuckoo   S
Great Spotted Cuckoo   M
Didric Cuckoo   S
White-browed Coucal   c
Barn Owl
African Scops-Owl
Pearl-spotted Owlet   c
Verreaux's Eagle-Owl
White-rumped Swift
Horus Swift
House Swift   c
Alpine Swift   M
African Palm-Swift
Speckled Mousebird
Red-faced Mousebird   c
Pied Kingfisher   c
Giant Kingfisher
Malachite Kingfisher
Woodland Kingfisher   S
Brown-hooded Kingfisher
Striped Kingfisher

Eurasian Bee-eater   M
Southern Carmine Bee-eater   S
White-fronted Bee-eater   c
Little Bee-eater
Eurasian Roller   M
Lilac-breasted Roller   c
Rufous-crowned Roller   c
Hoopoe   c
Green Wood-Hoopoe
Southern Scimitarbill
African Gray Hornbill   c
Red-billed Hornbill   c
Yellow-billed Hornbill   c
Crowned Hornbill   r
Southern Ground Hornbill   c
Black-collared Barbet
Pied Barbet
Crested Barbet   c
Bennett's Woodpecker
Golden-tailed Woodpecker
Cardinal Woodpecker
Bearded Woodpecker
Monotonous Bush-Lark   S
Sabota Bush-Lark   c
Chestnut-backed Finch-Lark
Barn Swallow   c M
Wire-tailed Swallow   c
Rufous-chested Swallow   c
Lesser Striped Swallow   c
Black Cuckoo-shrike
African Drongo   c
Eurasian Golden Oriole   M
Eurasian Black-headed Oriole   c
Southern Black Tit   c
Arrow-marked Babbler   c
Garden Bulbul   c
Kurrichane Thrush
Groundscraper Thrush
Heuglin's Robin-Chat   r
Natal Robin-Chat   r
White-throated Robin-Chat
Red-backed Scrub-Robin   c
Cape Crombec   c
Yellow-bellied Eremomela
Green-capped Eremomela
Zitting Cisticola
Rattling Cisticola   c

Neddicky Cisticola
Tawny-flanked Prinia   c
Spotted Flycatcher   c **M**
Southern Black-Flycatcher   c
Chin-spot Batis   c
African Paradise Flycatcher
African Pied Wagtail   c
Richard's Pipit   **M**
White Helmet-Shrike
Southern White-crowned Shrike   c
Brubru Shrike   c
Black-backed Puffback-Shrike   c
Brown-crowned Tchagra
Black-crowned Tchagra
Sulfur-breasted Bush-Shrike
Gray-headed Bush-Shrike
Magpie Shrike   c
Red-backed Shrike   **M**
Wattled Starling   **S**
Amethyst Starling   **S**
Cape Starling   c
Blue-eared Glossy-Starling

Burchell's Glossy-Starling   c
Red-billed Oxpecker   c
Collared Sunbird
White-bellied Sunbird
Mariqua Sunbird   c
Red-billed Buffalo-Weaver   c **S**
House Sparrow   c
Gray-headed Sparrow   c
Spectacled Weaver   c
Lesser Masked Weaver
Vitelline Masked Weaver
Village Weaver
Red-headed Weaver
Red-billed Quelea   c **S**
White-winged Widowbird   c **S**
Green-winged Pytilia
Common Waxbill
Southern Cordonbleu   c
Red-billed Fire-Finch   c
Paradise Whydah   **S**
Yellow-fronted Canary   c
Golden-breasted Bunting   c

74
Madagascar

ISOLATION HAS RESULTED IN A HIGH PERCENTAGE of endemic species, and even families, of birds on this huge island in the southwest Indian Ocean. Now known as the Malagasy Republic, Madagascar is a birder's dream and nightmare rolled into one. It has some of the world's fanciest and rarest birds, but before rushing there it should be realized that there are no English field guides, no tourist facilities in most areas, that roads are often primitive, and that linguistic problems do not help with permits and logistic problems.

Antananarivo (formerly Tananarive), the capital, is a city of 350,-000 located in cool mountains. The Hotel de France and the Madagascar Hilton are good bases from which to work. The Tsimbazaza Botanical Gardens have many native plants, a zoo featuring lemurs, and some native birds. Around the city look for Great Egret, Cattle Heron, Western Reef-Heron, Black Heron, Madagascar Pond-Heron, Black Kite, Madagascar Kestrel, Common Gallinule, Malachite Kingfisher, Blue-cheeked Bee-eater, Madagascar Bush-Lark, Stonechat, Pied Crow, Madagascar Red-Fody, and Madagascar Wagtail.

The eastern side of the island is much wetter than the west. Most of the original forest has been cleared and only vestiges remain. One such forest is the Perinet Forest Reserve located near Perinet 89 miles (142 km) east of Tananarive. Rooms are available at the Hotel de la Gare. Many endemics occur here including both goshawks, White-throated Rail, Blue Pigeon, both vasa parrots, Blue and Red-fronted Couas, both nightjars, Madagascar Pygmy Kingfisher, Scaled and Pitta-like Ground-Rollers, Cuckoo-Roller, Velvet and Wattled Asities, tetrakas, Brush Warbler, Ward's and Newtonia Flycatchers, Souimanga's and Green Sunbirds, Madagascar White-eye, Nelicourvi Weaver, Saklava Fody, and the following vangas: Chabert's, Blue, Red-tailed, Hook-billed, White-headed, and the Nuthatch-Vanga.

Lake Aloatra and nearby ponds have grebes and ducks. In the agricultural areas look for Common Quail, Namaqua Dove, Black Coucal, Cinnamon Roller, and Hoopoe.

The Ankarafantsika Reserve protects dry lowland forest about 126 miles (200 km) southeast of Majunga (where there are airport and

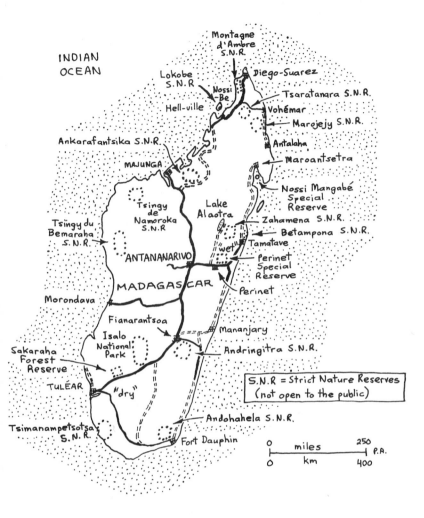

INDIAN
OCEAN

Montagne
d'Ambre
S.N.R.

Lokobe
S.N.R

Diego-Suarez

Nossi
-Be

Tsaratanara S.N.R.

Hell-ville

Vohémar

Marojejy S.N.R.

Ankarafantsika S.N.R.

Antalaha

MAJUNGA

Maroantsetra

Nossi Mangabé
Special
Reserve

Tsingy
de
Namoroka
S.N.R

Lake
Alaotra

Zahamena S.N.R.

Tsïngy du
Bemaraha
S.N.R.

Betampona S.N.R.

"wet"

Tamatave

ANTANANARIVO

Perinet
Special
Reserve

MADAGASCAR

Perinet

Morondava

Fianarantsoa

Mananjary

Isalo
National
Park

Andringitra S.N.R.

Sakaraha
Forest
Reserve

S.N.R = Strict Nature Reserves
(not open to the public)

TULÉAR

"dry"

Tsimanampetsotsa
S.N.R.

Andohahela S.N.R.

Fort Dauphin

0   miles   250
├────────────────────┤ P.A.
0   km   400

hotels). This reserve features Madagascar Crested Ibis, White-breasted Mesite, Giant Coua, Crested Coua, Coqueral's Coua, Cuckoo-Roller, and seven species of vangas. Camping is necessary, as is a permit from the park's board in the capital.

Tuléar is located in the arid deciduous forests of the southwest where, on the beach, is the fancy Le Capricorne Hotel. In the Tuléar region specialties include the Bensch's Monia, Gray-headed Lovebird, Long-tailed Ground-Roller, Common Jery, four couas (Crested, Running, Red-capped, and Verreaux's), and four vangas (Chabert, Lafresnaye's, Hook-billed, and the scarce Sickle-billed).

The Sakaraha Forest Reserve is located near Sakaraha, about 88 miles (140 kilometers) northeast of Tuléar. Among the rich birdlife are Madagascar Harrier-Hawk, Madagascar Buzzard, Madagascar Buttonquail, Cuckoo-Roller, Madagascar Paradise-Flycatcher, and Rufous Vanga.

Madagascar is one area in particular where prospective visitors should consider joining organized birding tours.

CHECKLIST

Madagascar Dabchick   c
Little Dabchick
Madagascar Red-necked Grebe
Wilson's Storm-Petrel   r W
Black-bellied Storm-Petrel   r W
Broad-billed Prion   W
Wedge-tailed Shearwater   r S
(Northern) Giant Petrel   r W
White-tailed Tropicbird   r
Red-tailed Tropicbird   r
Red-billed Tropicbird   r
Pink-backed Pelican
Red-footed Booby   r
Long-tailed Cormorant   c
Darter   c
Lesser Frigatebird
Great Frigatebird
Gray Heron   c
Purple Heron   c
Goliath Heron   r
Madagascar Heron
Great Egret   c
Western Reef-Heron   c
Black Heron
Cattle Heron   c
Squacco Pond-Heron   c
Madagascar Pond-Heron   c S
Black-crowned Night-Heron
Green Heron   c
Little Bittern
Hammerkop   c
Yellow-billed Stork   r
Black Open-billed Stork
Glossy Ibis   c
Sacred Ibis

Madagascar Crested Ibis
African Spoonbill
Greater Flamingo
Lesser Flamingo
Fulvous Whistling-Duck   c
White-faced Whistling-Duck   c
Hottentot Teal
Red-billed Pintail
Meller's Duck
Madagascar Teal   r
Madagascar Pochard
African Pygmy-Goose   r
Knob-billed Goose   c
White-backed Duck   c
Madagascar Baza   r
Bat Kite
Black Kite   c
Madagascar Sea-Eagle
Madagascar Serpent-Eagle   r
Madagascar Harrier-Hawk   c
Marsh Harrier
Madagascar Goshawk
Henst's Goshawk
Frances's Sparrowhawk   c
Madagascar Sparrowhawk
Madagascar Buzzard   c
Sooty Falcon   c M
Eleonora's Falcon   M
Madagascar Kestrel   c
Barred Kestrel
Peregrine Falcon
Madagascar Partridge   c
Harlequin Quail
Common Quail   r
Helmeted Guineafowl

White-breasted Mesite
Brown Mesite
Bensch's Monia
Madagascar Buttonquail   c
Madagascar Jacana   c
Madagascar Gray-throated Rail
White-throated Rail
Madagascar Rail
Baillon's Crake
Olivier's Rail   r
Madagascar Flufftail
Water's Flufftail
Common Gallinule   c
Allen's Gallinule
Red-knobbed Coot   c
Greater Painted-snipe
Crabplover   c
Gray Plover   c M
Lesser Golden Plover   r M
Greater Ringed Plover   c M
Black-banded Plover   r
Kittlitz's Plover   c
Three-banded Plover   c
White-fronted Plover   c
Great Sand Plover   c M
Black-tailed Godwit   r M
Bar-tailed Godwit   M
Whimbrel   c M
Eurasian Curlew   M
Marsh Sandpiper   M
Common Greenshank   c M
Green Sandpiper   r M
Wood Sandpiper   M
Common Sandpiper   c M
Terek Sandpiper   M
Ruddy Turnstone   c M
Madagascar Snipe
Sanderling   c M
Little Stint   M
Dunlin   r M
Curlew Sandpiper   c M
Ruff   M
Black-winged Stilt   c
Black-capped Avocet   r
Madagascar Pratincole
Great Skua   r W
Kelp Gull

Gray-headed Gull   r
Whiskered Tern   c
White-winged Black Tern   r M
Caspian Tern   r
Common Tern   c M
Roseate Tern
Bridled Tern
Sooty Tern   r
Little Tern
Greater Crested Tern   c
Lesser Crested Tern   c
Brown Noddy   r
Lesser Noddy   r
Fairy Tern   r
Masked Sandgrouse
Madagascar Blue-Pigeon   c
Madagascar Green-Pigeon
Madagascar Turtle-Dove   c
Namaqua Dove   c
Greater Vasa Parrot   c
Lesser Vasa Parrot   c
Gray-headed Lovebird   c
Lesser Cuckoo   c S
Thick-billed Cuckoo   r
Black Coucal   c
Blue Coua   c
Crested Coua   c
Verreaux's Coua
Red-fronted Coua
Red-breasted Coua
Delalande's Coua   r
Giant Coua
Red-capped Coua   c
Running Coua   c
Coquerel's Coua   c
Barn Owl
Madagascar Red Owl   r
Madagascar Scops-Owl
Madagascar Hawk-Owl   r
Madagascar Long-eared Owl
Marsh Owl
Madagascar Nightjar   c
Collared Nightjar
Common Swift
Alpine Swift
African Palm-Swift   c
Madagascar Needletail   c

Malachite Kingfisher   c
Madagascar Pygmy Kingfisher
Blue-cheeked Bee-eater   c
Cinnamon Roller   S
Cuckoo-Roller   c
Short-legged Ground-Roller   r
Scaled Ground-Roller   r
Pitta-like Ground-Roller
Crossley's Ground-Roller   r
Long-tailed Ground-Roller   c
Hoopoe
Velvety Asity
Schlegel's Asity
Wattled Asity
Madagascar Bush-Lark   c
Plain Martin   c
Sand Martin   r   M
Mascarene Martin   c
Barn Swallow   M
Crested Drongo
Madagascar Starling   c
Indian Myna   c
Pied Crow   c
Common Jery   c
Green Jery
Stripe-throated Jery   c
Wedge-tailed Jery   r
White-throated Oxylabes
Crossley's Babbler
Ashy Cuckoo-Shrike   c
Long-billed Greenbul   c
Dusky Greenbul
Spectacled Greenbul   c
Yellow-browed Greenbul
Gray-crowned Greenbul
Appert's Greenbul
Black Bulbul   c
Madagascar Magpie-Robin   c

Stonechat   c
Madagascar Rock-Thrush
Madagascar Cisticola   c
Madagascar Brush-Warbler   c
Kiritika Warbler   c
Rand's Warbler   r
Madagascar Swamp Warbler
Gray Emu-tail
Brown Emu-tail   r
Common Newtonia   c
Dark Newtonia
Archbold's Newtonia
Fanovana Newtonia   r
Ward's Flycatcher   c
Madagascar Paradise-Flycatcher   c
Madagascar Wagtail   c
White-headed Vanga   c
Bare-eyed Vanga   c
Blue Vanga   c
Rufous Vanga   c
Bernier's Vanga   r
Hook-billed Vanga   c
Southwestern Vanga
Pollen's Vanga   r
Van Dam's Vanga   r
Helmeted Vanga   r
Red-tailed Vanga   c
Sickle-billed Vanga
Nuthatch-Vanga
Kinkimavo Vanga
Souimanga Sunbird   c
Madagascar Green Sunbird   c
Madagascar White-eye   c
Madagascar Munia   c
Nelicourvi Weaver   c
Red Fody   c
Forest Fody   r
Sakalava Weaver   c

75
Mauritius and Reunion

THESE TWO ISLANDS are located in the southwestern Indian Ocean, east of Madagascar. Both are mountainous with tropical lowlands (covered with sugar cane), and each has endemic birds.

Mauritius was the home of the Dodo and other extinct birds, and today it is the home of several rarities and a large number of introduced species. It has a beautiful coastline, with fine hotels such as those at the southwest tip on Le Morne Brabant. There and in other lowland areas look for shorebirds, herons, swiftlets, martins, and introduced birds. The wetter mountains are in the southwest, and it is here that the best birds survive. The "Gorges de la Riviere Noire" is the last home of the Mauritius Kestrel. The woodlands here and in such nearby areas as the Plaine Champagne, the trail up Black River Peak, Bassin Blanc, and the Macabe-Mare Longue Reserve are home to the Pink Pigeon and the local endemic cuckoo-shrike, bulbul, paradise flycatcher, white-eyes, and fody.

The nearby resort of Curepipe at 1800 feet (550 m) is a good base. Both white-eyes occur in the gardens of the Park Hotel. Meller's Duck can be found at Piton de Milieu and Valetta lakes to the northeast.

Visitors arriving from October into summer may attempt to charter a boat from Grand Baie or Cap Malheureux to make the 14-mile (22.4 km) crossing to Round Island. This valuable island, off the north coast, is one of the two known breeding haunts of the rare Herald Petrel. It and the Wedge-tailed Shearwater nest in burrows here, while both tropicbirds nest in cubbyholes. Nearby Serpent Island (one mile from Round) features nesting Brown and Lesser Noddies, Sooty Tern, and Masked Booby.

Reunion is a department of France, much more mountainous than Mauritius, culminating in Piton des Neiges at 10,066 feet (3069 m), where snow is not uncommon. The airport and the capital are at St. Denis in the north, where many hotels are located. In the gorge above St. Denis look for White-tailed Tropicbird, Olive White-eye, and the local swiftlet and swallow. Higher up, trails lead to forest on the Plaine des Chicots and Plaine d'Affouches where the Reunion Cuckoo-Shrike survives. The Marsh Harrier and the Reunion Chat

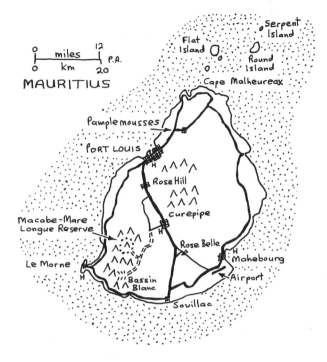

can be seen around Hellbourg. Most endemic birds and the local bulbul and paradise flycatcher prefer to live above 1640 feet (500 m), although they and the Madagascar Turtle-Dove live in the natural forests near sea level in the southeast, near St. Philippe (site of the Hotel le Maril). Barau's Petrel can be seen at many points around the coast, but is commonest off the mouth of the Riviere St. Etienne at St. Louis an hour before dusk where they congregate before flying inland as it gets dark.

Both islands are served by jets. Mauritius has the greatest variety of flights being linked with Africa and Europe, as well as Bombay, and Perth, Australia. French is important on both islands with English important only on Mauritius.

CHECKLIST

(MA = Mauritius, RE = Reunion)

Yellow-nosed Albatross r W	Wedge-tailed Shearwater
Giant Petrel r W	Audubon's Shearwater RE
Cape Petrel r W	Mascarene Petrel RE

Barau's Petrel   RE
Herald Petrel   MA
Wilson's Storm-Petrel   r W
Red-tailed Tropicbird   MA
White-tailed Tropicbird
Masked Booby   MA
Lesser Frigatebird   r S
Green Heron   c M
Cattle Heron
Dimorphic Egret   r M
Meller's Duck   MA
Marsh Harrier   c RE
Mauritius Kestrel   r MA
Chinese Francolin   RE
Gray Francolin   r
Madagascar Partridge   RE
Common Quail   c RE, r MA
Red Junglefowl   RE
Helmeted Guineafowl   r MA
Madagascar Buttonquail   RE
Common Gallinule   c
Greater Ringed Plover   M

Gray Plover   M
Great Sand Plover   M
Ruddy Turnstone   c M
Whimbrel   c M
Eurasian Curlew   M
Bar-tailed Godwit   M
Common Greenshank   M
Marsh Sandpiper   MA M
Common Sandpiper   c M
Terek Sandpiper   MA M
Sanderling   M
Curlew Sandpiper   M
Great Skua   M
Roseate Tern   r S
Common Tern   M
Little Tern   M
Sooty Tern   MA
Crested Tern   r M
Brown Noddy   c
Lesser Noddy   MA
Rock Pigeon
Mauritius Pink Pigeon   r MA

Madagascar Turtle-Dove   c MA;
   RE
Spotted Turtle-Dove   c MA
Peaceful Dove   c
Rose-ringed Parakeet   c MA; r
   RE
Gray-headed Lovebird   r RE
Mascarene Cave Swiftlet   c
Mascarene Martin   c MA; RE
House Crow   MA
Mauritius Cuckoo-shrike   MA
Reunion Cuckoo-shrike   RE
Red-whiskered Bulbul   c MA; RE
Mascarene Bulbul
Mascarene Paradise-Flycatcher

Reunion Chat   RE
Indian Myna   c
Olive White-eye   MA; c RE
Mascarene Gray White-eye   c
   MA; RE
House Sparrow   c
Village Weaver   c
Red Fody   c
Mauritius Fody   MA
Spotted Munia   c MA; r RE
Strawberry Finch   r RE
Common Waxbill   c
Yellow-crowned Canary   c RE
Yellow-fronted Canary   c

76
Seychelles

A THOUSAND MILES (1600 KM) EAST OF KENYA lie the granitic islands of the Seychelles. These beautiful islands of the western Indian Ocean are now served by jets from Europe, Africa, Asia, and Mauritius. There are several fine hotels near Victoria, the capital, on Mahe Island; and a hotel on Praslin Island, the Cote d'Or.

The botanical gardens near Victoria and the surrounding low country have Seychelles Kestrel, Thick-billed Bulbul, Seychelles White-eye, and Seychelles Sunbird, and the planted palm tree, coco de mer. The nearby mudflats on the Victoria waterfront are home to hundreds of migrant waders. Some of the rarer birds can be found in the higher, wetter forests, reached via three of the roads that cross the island. The Seychelles Blue Pigeon, Bare-legged Scops-Owl, the Seychelles White-eye, and others occur around Morne Blanc on the Foret Noire road in the Morne Seychellois National Park. The Souvenir Estate on the La Misere road, and the Montagne Posee road (above Anse aux Pins) both reach montane forest.

Praslin can be reached by daily boat from Victoria or by small aircraft. All visitors will want to see the only truly wild coco de mer *(Lodoicea maldivica)* forest in the world. This palm has huge leaves and the largest seed in the plant kingdom. It is protected in the Vallee de Mai National Park, along with the only Lesser Vasa Parrots in the Seychelles. Other birds here include the Seychelles Blue Pigeon, Mascarene Cave Swiftlet, Thick-billed Bulbul, and Seychelles Sunbird. Perhaps the local flying-fox will be noted. The Yellow Bittern occurs in the swamp behind L'Amitie, and Seychelles Paradise-Flycatcher and Bare-legged Scops-Owl may occur on Praslin, as well.

Cousin Island, the first sanctuary of the International Council for Bird Preservation, is located just west of Praslin. Only 70 acres (28.3 hectares) in size, Cousin Island has all of the world's breeding Seychelles Brush Warblers (about 70 in total). The increasingly rare Seychelles Fody has one of its last strongholds here, too. Introduced cats, rats, and Barn Owls (which have decimated birdlife on most of the other islands) have been carefully kept off this island. Other birds often seen on Cousin are two shearwaters, frigatebirds, and noddies,

INDIAN OCEAN

Bird Island

Denis Island — Edge of the Seychelles Bank

SEYCHELLES ISLANDS

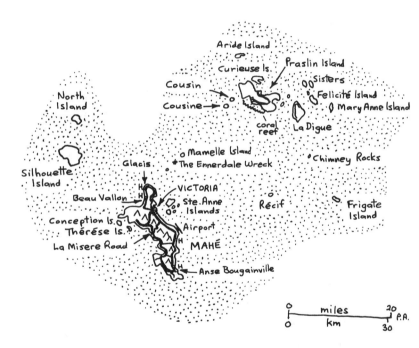

Aride Island

Curieuse Is.

Praslin Island

Cousin

Sisters

Cousine

Felicité Island

North Island

Mary Anne Island

coral reef

La Digue

Mamelle Island

Glacis

The Ennerdale Wreck

Chimney Rocks

Silhouette Island

VICTORIA

Beau Vallon

Ste. Anne Islands

Récif

Frigate Island

Conception Is.

Thérèse Is.

Airport

La Misere Road

MAHÉ

Anse Bougainville

miles

km

P.A.

plus Green Heron, Common Gallinule, Bridled and Fairy Terns, the local subspecies of the Madagascar Turtle-Dove, White-tailed Tropicbird, Barred Dove, Seychelles Sunbird, and Red Fody.

Also of interest are four other islands, some of which may require joining a Lindblad cruise or making other special arrangements. La Digue, 3.5 miles (5 ½ km) east of Praslin, is a steep forested island and the last home of the long-tailed Seychelles Paradise Flycatcher. Home to the last handful of the black-and-white Seychelles Magpie-

396

Robin is isolated Frigate Island (privately owned). Aride Island, 5 miles (8 km) north of Praslin, is home to 160,000 pairs of terns of six species. Two million Sooty Terns, one of the largest bird concentrations in the world, make their home on Bird Island, a low, flat sandy cay 58 miles (93 km) north of Victoria.

CHECKLIST

Wedge-tailed Shearwater	Great Skua r M
Audubon's Shearwater	Roseate Tern
White-tailed Tropicbird c	Bridled Tern
Red-tailed Tropicbird r S	Black-naped Tern r
Masked Booby	Sooty Tern
Red-footed Booby r S	Little Tern W
Great Frigatebird	Damara Tern
Lesser Frigatebird r S	Greater Crested Tern M
Gray Heron r W	Brown Noddy c
Green Heron	Lesser Noddy c
Cattle Heron	Fairy Tern c
Yellow Bittern r	Seychelles Blue Pigeon c
Seychelles Kestrel c	Madagascar Turtle-Dove c
Common Gallinule c	Peaceful Dove c
Grey Plover c W	Lesser Vasa Parrot
Greater Ringed Plover W	Gray-headed Lovebird
Little Ringed Plover r W	Barn Owl c
Great Sand Plover W	Bare-legged Scops-Owl
Mongolian Plover r W	Mascarene Cave Swiftlet
Ruddy Turnstone c W	European Roller r W
Bar-tailed Godwit W	Yellow Wagtail r W
Whimbrel c W	Tree Pipit r W
Common Greenshank W	Thick-billed Bulbul c
Terek Sandpiper r W	Seychelles Magpie-Robin
Common Sandpiper c W	Seychelles Paradise Flycatcher
Wood Sandpiper W	Indian Myna c
Little Stint W	Seychelles Sunbird c
Curlew Sandpiper c W	Seychelles White-eye
Sanderling W	Red Fody c
Crabplover r W	Seychelles Fody
	Common Waxbill c

77
Azraq, Jordan

DEEP IN THE EASTERN DESERT OF JORDAN, 70 miles (112 km) directly east of Amman, lies the shimmering oasis of Azraq, off a modern highway. This area has the only permanent water in the Jordanian Desert, water that wells up to the surface as part of an inland drainage basin. It spreads out to form marshes and channels, and it nurtures some farms. Plans are afoot to take most of this water for irrigation projects, which would ruin the reserve.

There are two small villages, a picturesque army fort, and a few cafes. Rooms can be secured at the Lodge of the Royal Society for the Conservation of Nature (PO Box 6354, Amman). Check in at the fort on arrival, and take great care not to get lost if you go out exploring.

The wetland reserve covers 38.6 square miles (100 km²), the adjacent desert reserve an additional 232 square miles (600 km²). It is gently contoured land with bare flint-and-basalt plains crossed by lightly vegetated wadis. The qas are depressions with water, the main one being the lush Qa el Azraq, where millions of gallons of water pour out to form one of the most important wetlands for thousands of miles. There are hilly areas, including the blindingly white chalky cliffs of Faidhat Edh Dhahikiya, 25 miles (40 km) southeast of Azraq. The migrants concentrate in the luxuriant wadis, but a number of larks and interesting breeders and residents prefer the hostile-looking barren areas with differing surfaces and ground cover, so it is necessary to get out into the desert on one of the tracks.

The role of Azraq as a critical migration resting and feeding area is staggering. Millions of birds that breed in Europe and Asia and winter in Africa use this oasis from March through May and September through November. With the winter rains and spring greenery, it boasts impressive migrations in the spring, every day new species dropping in, others departing.

The autumn migrations are less spectacular, due to harsher conditions. Some species have different migration routes at the different seasons, and abundance of any one species varies from year to year. Raptors prefer fine clear weather without strong winds. Migration is continual, without pronounced waves except

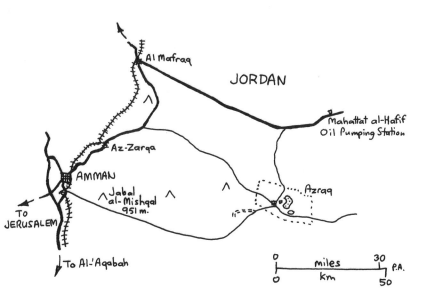

during inclement weather, when highfliers are forced down.

The winter months are noted for incredible waterfowl concentrations (up to a quarter of a million), chiefly Green-winged Teal, Northern Pintail, Common Coot, Eurasian Wigeon, Tufted Duck, and Mallard. Hunting has been going on for many years here, but with gradually improved protection (monitoring is hard, and the reserve is not on solid ground yet), the waterfowl may become tamer.

The breeding birds of most interest to visiting birders are Sand Partridge, Houbara Bustard, Great Sand Plover, Cream-colored Courser, sandgrouse, Egyptian Nightjar, Blue-cheeked Bee-eater, larks (Dunn's, Desert, Bar-tailed Desert, Bifasciated, and Temminck's), Brown-necked Raven, Graceful Prinia, Streaked Scrub Warbler, and Desert and Strickland's Wheatear.

Mammals of Azraq that will interest visitors include Ethiopian hedgehog, Asiatic jackal, red fox, striped hyena, Arabian gazelle (almost gone), Arabian hare, jerboas, and gerbils.

This area deserves support from conservationists worldwide. In the last fifty years the cheetah, Syrian ass, oryx, and Ostrich have been exterminated here. What's next?

CHECKLIST

Little Bittern S	Squacco Pond-Heron S
Black-crowned Night-Heron	Great Egret W

Little Egret   W
Gray Heron   W
Purple Heron   S
Glossy Ibis   r M
White Stork   c M
Black Stork   M
Ruddy Shelduck   W
Common Shelduck   W
Mallard   c
Green-winged Teal   c W
Gadwall   W
Eurasian Wigeon   c W
Northern Pintail   c W
Garganey   M
Northern Shoveler   c W
Northern Pochard   W
Tufted Duck   c W
Ferruginous Duck   W
Red-breasted Merganser   W
Smew   r W
Osprey   M
European Honey-Buzzard   M
Black Kite   c M
Levant Sparrowhawk   M
Eurasian Sparrowhawk   M
Common Buzzard   c M
Long-legged Buzzard   r W
Short-toed Snake-Eagle   M
Booted Eagle   r M
Steppe (Tawny) Eagle   M
Greater Spotted Eagle   M
Lesser Spotted Eagle   c M
Egyptian Vulture
Griffon Vulture   M
Northern Harrier   M
Pallid Harrier   r M
Marsh Harrier   c
Peregrine Falcon   M
Red-footed Falcon   M
Merlin   c W
Common Kestrel   S
Lesser Kestrel   c M
Sand Partridge
Chukar
Common Quail   M
European Crane   W
Houbara Bustard   S (?)

Water Rail
Baillon's Crake
Little Crake   r
Spotted Crake   r
Corn Crake   r M
Common Gallinule   S
Common Coot   c M
Snowy Plover
Greater Ringed Plover   W
Little Ringed Plover   W
Great Sand Plover   S
Caspian Plover   r M
White-tailed Lapwing   r M
Northern Lapwing   W
Sociable Lapwing   r W
Spur-winged Lapwing   S
Little Stint   M
Temminck's Stint   c M
Dunlin   c W
Curlew Sandpiper   r M
Ruff   c M
Spotted Redshank   M
Common Redshank   W
Marsh Sandpiper   M
Common Greenshank   c M
Green Sandpiper   c W
Wood Sandpiper   M
Common Sandpiper   M
Black-tailed Godwit   M
Eurasian Curlew   r M
Eurasian Woodcock   r W
Common Snipe   c W
Jack Snipe   W
Black-winged Stilt   S
Black-capped Avocet
Stonecurlew   c S
Cream-colored Courser   c S
Collared Pratincole   c S
Black-headed Gull   r M
Gull-billed Tern   M
White-winged Black Tern   c M
Whiskered Tern   M
Black-bellied Sandgrouse
Pin-tailed Sandgrouse   c
Spotted Sandgrouse
European Turtle-Dove   c M
Rock Pigeon

Little Owl
Egyptian Nightjar S
Common Swift M
Pied Kingfisher c M
Eurasian Kingfisher M
Eurasian Bee-eater c M
Blue-cheeked Bee-eater S
Eurasian Roller M
Hoopoe c M
Eurasian Wryneck M
Sand Martin c M
Barn Swallow c M
Red-rumped Swallow c M
House Martin r M
Dunn's Lark S
Desert Lark c S
Bar-tailed Lark c S
Bifasciated Lark c S
Short-toed Lark S
Lesser Short-toed Lark c S
Thick-billed Lark S
Temminck's Lark c S
Crested Lark c S
Tawny Pipit r M
Meadow Pipit W
Tree Pipit c M
Red-throated Pipit W, c M
Water Pipit c W
Yellow Wagtail c M
Gray Wagtail r W
White Wagtail c W
Red-backed Shrike c M
Red-tailed Shrike M
Masked Shrike M
Lesser Gray Shrike M
Great Gray Shrike
Eurasian Golden Oriole M
European Starling c W
Northern Raven
Brown-necked Crow
Savi's Warbler S
Moustached Warbler c S
Sedge Warbler c S
Marsh Warbler c M
European Reed-Warbler c S

Clamorous Reed-Warbler r S
Great Reed-Warbler c S
Barred Warbler M
Garden Warbler c M
Blackcap c M
Greater Whitethroat M
Lesser Whitethroat c M
Sardinian Warbler S
Willow Warbler c M
Chiffchaff c M
Booted Warbler c M
Olivaceous Warbler r M
Graceful Prinia S
Streaked Scrub Warbler
Zitting Cisticola S
Pied Flycatcher c M
Collared Flycatcher c M
Spotted Flycatcher M
Whinchat M
Stonechat c M
Northern Wheatear M
Black-eared Wheatear M
Pied Wheatear r M
Mourning Wheatear S
Variable Wheatear S
Desert Wheatear S
Greater Red-rumped Wheatear S
Isabelline Wheatear M
Rufous Scrub-Robin c S
Black Redstart M
Eurasian Redstart M
Nightingale M
Thrush-Nightingale M
Bluethroat M
Eurasian Blackbird r W
Song Thrush r M
Persian Robin r M
House Sparrow
Pale Petronia S
Eurasian Goldfinch S
Trumpeter Finch
Ortolan Bunting c M
Cretzschmar's Bunting r M
Black-headed Bunting M

78
Bahrain

BAHRAIN IS A SMALL GROUP OF ISLANDS IN THE PERSIAN GULF, 15 miles (24 km) to the east of Saudi Arabia. The main island of Bahrain is 30 miles (48 km) long by 10 miles (16 km) wide. Two of the neighboring islands are linked by causeways. Oil income has provided a jetport, hotels, and a good road system, all of which aid birders on a stopover, though to reach all the habitats a local driver who knows the dirt tracks may be necessary.

White-cheeked Bulbuls and Graceful Prinias mix with many migrants in the irrigated areas of northern Bahrain. A good area, particularly for migrating warblers, shrikes, pipits, and Hoopoe, is called the "green patch." It is located between the refinery and the Askar Road.

Several types of desert are found. Some of it is scrub-covered and the rest is a sandy and stony desert mixed with salt flats and dunes. This latter type can be visited south of Awali in the center of the island and features Cream-colored Courser and Desert Lark. The "Jebel-ad-Dhukan," a hilly area with cliffs, south of Awali, is attractive to Hooded and Mourning Wheatears, Blue Rock Thrush, and Northern Crag-Martin.

Despite pollution and rubbish problems, many fine waterbirds can be found near the airport and hotels on Muharraq Bay, with good road access. Waders, herons, gulls, and terns are commonly seen from the road and Sitra Island causeway. Socotra Cormorants and additional waders can be studied at the south tip of Sitra via a dirt track. Marshes near the sea can be reached near Manama. Take the road south from the mental hospital and a dirt track right after the cola plant for kingfishers, egrets, and marshbirds.

Fewer than 20 birds breed here, although many shorebirds are here over summer. From May until September temperatures are usually very hot. During the rest of the year the weather can be pleasant and the islands play host to a good list of migrants passing to and from Asia and Africa. A number of migrants pass through chiefly in the spring such as Great Black-headed Gull, Pallid Swift, Tree Pipit, Woodchat Shrike, White-backed Rock Thrush, most warblers, Collared Flycatcher, and Ortolan Bunting.

CHECKLIST

Great Cormorant   c W
Socotra Cormorant   c
Gray Heron   W
Purple Heron   r W
Western Reef-Heron
Little Egret   W
Squacco Pond-Heron   W
Greater Flamingo   r
Mallard   W
Osprey   M
Common Buzzard   M
Pallid Harrier   c M
Marsh Harrier   M
European Hobby   r M
Lesser Kestrel   M
Common Kestrel   M

Peregrine Falcon   r W
Houbara Bustard   r M
Common Oystercatcher   W
Greater Ringed Plover   W
Little Ringed Plover   M
Snowy Plover   c
Mongolian Plover   c W
Great Sand Plover   c W
Caspian Plover   r W
European Golden Plover   r M
Gray Plover   c W
Ruddy Turnstone   W
Common Snipe   M
Eurasian Curlew   W
Whimbrel   M
Bar-tailed Godwit   W

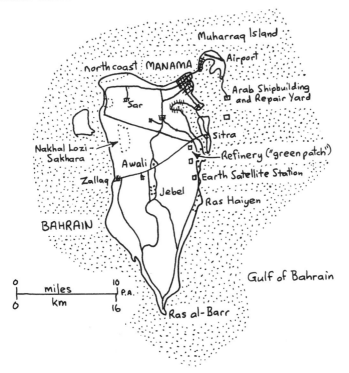

403

Ruff   W
Common Redshank   c W
Spotted Redshank   r M
Common Greenshank   W
Green Sandpiper   W
Marsh Sandpiper   r W
Wood Sandpiper   W
Common Sandpiper   W
Terek Sandpiper   M
Dunlin   W
Curlew Sandpiper   W
Broad-billed Sandpiper   r W
Little Stint   c W
Sanderling   W
Stonecurlew   r M
Cream-colored Courser
Herring Gull   c W
Lesser Black-backed Gull   c W
Great Black-headed Gull   r M
Slender-billed Gull   c
Black-headed Gull   c W
Gull-billed Tern
Lesser Crested Tern   r S
Common Tern   W
White-cheeked Tern   c S
Little Tern   c S
European Turtle-Dove   S
Collared Turtle-Dove   S
Rose-ringed Parakeet   c
Common Swift   M
Pallid Swift   M
Pied Kingfisher   W
Eurasian Kingfisher   W
Eurasian Bee-eater   c M
Blue-cheeked Bee-eater   M
Green Bee-eater   r
Eurasian Roller   M
Hoopoe   M
Northern Skylark   W
Crested Lark   c
Short-toed Lark   c W
Lesser Short-toed Lark   W
Bifasciated Lark   c
Desert Lark
Black-crowned Finch-Lark   r S
Barn Swallow   c M
Red-rumped Swallow   r M

Northern Crag-Martin   M
House Martin   M
Sand Martin   M
Tree Pipit   M
Richard's Pipit   M
Tawny Pipit   W
Water Pipit   c W
White Wagtail   c W
Yellow Wagtail   c M
Gray Wagtail   r W
White-cheeked Bulbul   c R
Lesser Gray Shrike   M
Masked Shrike   M
Great Gray Shrike   r W
Red-backed Shrike   M
Red-tailed Shrike   c M
Woodchat Shrike   M
Song Thrush   W
Black-throated Thrush   r W
White-backed Rock Thrush   M
Nightingale   r M
Eurasian Redstart   c M
Stonechat   M
Whinchat   M
Northern Wheatear   c M
Desert Wheatear   c W
Black-eared Wheatear   W
Pied Wheatear   c M
Isabelline Wheatear   W
Red-tailed Wheatear   r M
Mourning Wheatear   W
Hooded Wheatear   W
Rufous Scrub-Robin   c S
Sardinian Warbler   M
Willow Warbler   c M
Chiffchaff   r M
Olivaceous Warbler   M
Greater Whitethroat   M
Lesser Whitethroat   M
Desert Warbler   W
Graceful Prinia
Collared Flycatcher   M
Ortolan Bunting   M
House Sparrow   c
European Starling   c W
Northern Raven   r

79
Lahore, Pakistan

LAHORE is a city of 3 million in the fertile plains of the Punjab of northeastern Pakistan, with flights from Karachi and Delhi, plus fine hotels. It is 2000 years old and was the showcase for the glories of the Mogul emperors. The Lawrence Gardens (Bagh-I-Jinnah) lie just off the city's main road, the Mall, and only a few minutes' walk from the Intercontinental Hotel. The gardens boast a wealth of native and imported trees, mainly Australasian, and these in turn attract a variety of the more common species of birds, including Indian White-backed Vulture, Rose-ringed Parakeet, White-browed Fantail, and Common Tailorbird. These gardens are also a resort for migrant passerines, including many Palearctic warblers, such as Lesser White-throat and the abundant Blyth's Reed-Warbler. Some of these visitors stay to winter, including Black-throated Thrush and Yellow-browed Warbler; and occasionally they are joined by other Himalayan species such as Long-tailed Minivet, Slaty-blue Flycatcher, and Himalayan Treecreeper.

The Punjab's five main rivers offer excellent birding opportunities with a wealth of wetland habitats and impressive collections of species. Of the five, Balloki is the nearest to Lahore (about 40 miles [64 km] or one hour away by road). Take the main road south out of Lahore toward Multan and fork right at the village of Bhai Peru, 35 miles (56 km) south of Lahore. Embankments, called "bunds," flank both banks, enclosing extensive areas of marsh with reed beds and lotus swamp.

Resident species include the elusive Greater Painted-snipe, Pheasant-tailed Jacana, and Jungle Sparrow. Summer brings numbers of Chestnut, Yellow, and Black Bitterns, all of which are easy to see provided that you can stand the heat. Summer bird watching here is something of an ordeal in this respect. Cotton Pygmy-Goose, Lesser Whistling-Duck, Baya Weaver, and Strawberry Finch are all present at this time. Passage brings Palearctic crakes to join the resident Ruddy-breasted and Brown Crakes, and Red-headed Buntings pass through. Winter brings northern warblers and chats and Water Rail.

Changa Manga, a forest reserve about 10 miles (16 km) southeast of Balloki, is reached by continuing on the main Lahore–Multan road for some 5 miles (8 km) south of Bhai Peru, where you turn left. Forest species include resident Eurasian Honey-Buzzard, Shikra, the decidedly uncommon Sind Pied Woodpecker, with Asian Paradise-Flycatcher in summer and Red-breasted Flycatcher in winter.

A fine trip for the resourceful and adventurous would be the Lal Suhanna Sanctuary, about 200 miles (322 km) southwest of Lahore. Lal Suhanna is a small village to the east of the River Sutlej in the southern Punjab, on the main road and railway between Bahawalpur and Bahawalnagar. Here an extensive area of swamps and shallow lakes is flanked by an overgrown canal and by an area of scrub-covered semidesert. Access is across the railway line south of the village, where a dirt road leads to the first rest house. Cross the canal and follow the left bank for several miles with interesting marshes on the right. Just before the second rest house, which, from the road, is visible on a hill to the left of the canal, cross the canal and follow a difficult dirt track (four-wheel drive is advisable) to the third rest house. This is the main lake area. Rest houses may be booked through the Deputy Commissioner's Office, Bahawalpur.

A vast collection of aquatic species includes hordes of winter wild-fowl, though the Marbled Teal are by courtesy of a reintroduction scheme. Demoiselle Cranes pass through, and a good collection of raptors includes Pallas's Fishing Eagle. Desert fauna, close at hand, includes Dusky Eagle-Owl, Sind Nightjar, Black-crowned Finch-Lark, Black Partridge, and a desert race of the Stonecurlew. These species are best found by following the canal to just south of Yazman, from where a track crosses the Cholistan Desert to the Fort Abbas road. Here birds include Houbara Bustard and sandgrouse, and there are also a few Chinkara gazelles and blackbuck.

Due to rather sketchy reports, the following list is rather incomplete and has no abundance or seasonal symbols.

CHECKLIST

Little Cormorant	Intermediate Egret
Indian Cormorant	Little Egret
Darter	Purple Heron
Yellow Bittern	Lesser Whistling-Duck
Cinnamon Bittern	Garganey
Black Bittern	Northern Shoveler
Black-crowned Night-Heron	Northern Pintail
Indian Pond-Heron	Marbled Duck
Great Egret	Ferruginous Duck

Cotton Pygmy-Goose
Black Kite
Eurasian Honey-Buzzard
Brahminy Kite
Shikra
Tawny Eagle
Indian White-backed Vulture
White-eyed Buzzard
Marsh Harrier
Black Francolin
Gray Francolin
Demoiselle Crane
Water Rail
Baillon's Crake
Brown Crake
Ruddy-breasted Crake
Spotted Crake
Purple Swamphen
Pheasant-tailed Jacana
Houbara Bustard
White-tailed Lapwing
Red-wattled Lapwing
Greater Painted-snipe
Temminck's Stint
Wood Sandpiper
Ruff
Black-winged Stilt
Little Pratincole
Stonecurlew
River Tern
Black-bellied Tern
Chestnut-bellied Sandgrouse
Black-bellied Sandgrouse
Yellow-legged Green Pigeon
Spotted Turtle-Dove
Collared Turtle-Dove
Red Turtle-Dove
Laughing Turtle-Dove
Rose-ringed Parakeet
Common Koel
Greater Coucal
Dusky Eagle-Owl
Spotted Owlet
Syke's Nightjar
House Swift
Pied Kingfisher
White-breasted Kingfisher

Hoopoe
Indian Roller
Indian Gray Hornbill
Coppersmith Barbet
Eurasian Wryneck
Sind Pied Woodpecker
Common Golden-backed
    Woodpecker
Yellow-fronted Pied Woodpecker
Sand Lark
Oriental Skylark
Black-crowned Finch-Lark
Plain Martin
Wire-tailed Swallow
Olive-backed Pipit
Water Pipit
Richard's Pipit
Citrine Wagtail
Large Pied Wagtail
Small Minivet
Long-tailed Minivet
Bay-backed Shrike
Rufous-backed Shrike
Great Gray Shrike
Himalayan Treecreeper
Rufous Treepie
House Crow
Indian Myna
Rose-colored Starling
Red-vented Bulbul
White-cheeked Bulbul
Common Babbler
Jungle Babbler
Striated Babbler
Yellow-eyed Babbler
Purple Sunbird
Oriental White-eye
Eurasian Golden Oriole
Black Drongo
Clamorous Reed-Warbler
Blyth's Reed-Warbler
Paddyfield Warbler
Desert Warbler
Cetti's Bush-Warbler
Moustached Warbler
Lesser Whitethroat
Chiffchaff

Yellow-browed Warbler	Indian Robin
Plain Leaf-Warbler	Asian Magpie-Robin
Yellow-bellied Prinia	Pied Bushchat
Ashy Prinia	White-tailed Bushchat
Common Tailorbird	Bluethroat
Red-breasted Flycatcher	Jungle Sparrow
White-browed Fantail	Chestnut-shouldered Petronia
Slaty-blue Flycatcher	Red-headed Bunting
Asian Paradise-Flycatcher	Rock Bunting
Black Redstart	Strawberry Finch
Black-throated Thrush	Streaked Weaver

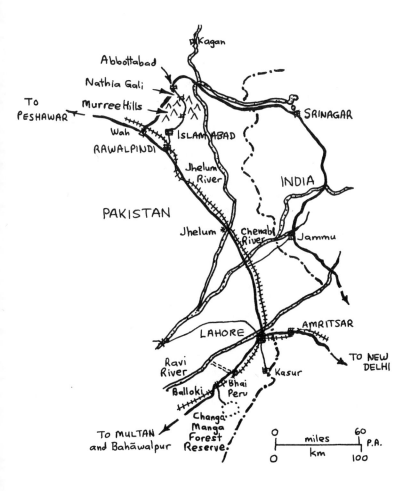

80
Islamabad, Pakistan

ISLAMABAD, which lies just north of Rawalpindi and due west of Srinigar, Kashmir, is a jumping off spot for some fine Himalayan birding.

The Murree Hills lie some 30 miles (48 km) north of Islamabad in the foothills of the Himalayan system and reach an altitude of some 7500 feet (2286 m). Above 5000 feet (1524 m) there are excellent stands of conifers and the area is rich in birdlife throughout the year. The zone between Murree itself and Bhurban, some 8 miles (12.8 km) to the northeast, is best of all and supports a good range of sub-Himalayan forest species including Large Crowned Leaf-Warbler, Blue-headed Rock-Thrush, Gray Bush-Chat, Long-tailed Minivet, and others. Winter brings a number of birds from higher altitudes and latitudes, including Himalayan Spectacled Finch, Great Himalayan Barbet, and Pink-browed Rosefinch.

Only 17 miles beyond Murree, Nathia Gali is a pine-covered valley along the Abbottabad road between 8000 and 9000 feet (2286 and 2743 m). Although it is inaccessible in winter, it holds a wealth of summer birds, including Slaty-blue, Verditer, and Ultramarine Flycatchers, Orange-flanked Bush-Robin, and Pallas's Leaf-Warbler.

In late spring, excursions even farther northward into the mountains are productive and the valleys of Swat, Gilgit, and Kagan are particularly appealing. Though on the verge of becoming a holiday area the Kagan Valley still boasts large unspoiled areas. The side valley, the Manoor Valley, still holds the extremely rare Western Tragopan, which may be sought at the villages of Beari and Behari between 8000 and 10,000 feet (2438 and 3048 m).

There are no abundance or seasonal symbols for this partial list, due to brief visits.

CHECKLIST

Eurasian Sparrowhawk
Northern Goshawk

Himalayan Vulture
Slaty-headed Parakeet

Blossom-headed Parakeet
Oriental Cuckoo
Great Himalayan Barbet
Brown-fronted Pied Woodpecker
Scaly-bellied Green Woodpecker
Himalayan Pied Woodpecker
Fulvous-breasted Pied Woodpecker
Red-rumped Swallow
Nepal Martin
Ashy Drongo
Yellow-billed Blue Magpie
Large-billed Crow
Black Bulbul
White-cheeked Bulbul
Pallas's Leaf-Warbler
Large Crowned Leaf-Warbler
Strong-footed Bush-Warbler
Striated Prinia
Ultramarine Flycatcher
Slaty-blue Flycatcher
Verditer Flycatcher
Rufous-bellied Niltava
Gray Bush-Chat

Blue-headed Rock-Thrush
Orange-flanked Bush-Robin
Indian Blue Robin
Gray-headed Thrush
Blue Whistling-Thrush
Black-throated Thrush
Streaked Laughing-thrush
Variegated Laughing-thrush
Spot-winged Black Tit
Simla Black Tit
Green-backed Tit
Great Tit
Red-headed Tit
White-cheeked Nuthatch
Chestnut-bellied Nuthatch
Himalayan Treecreeper
Cinnamon Sparrow
Himalayan Greenfinch
Pink-browed Rosefinch
Black-and-yellow Grosbeak
Red-browed Finch
White-capped Bunting

81

Srinagar, Kashmir, India

KASHMIR IS EASY TO GET TO, with daily jet service between Delhi and Srinagar, as well as buses that ply the very scenic 188 mile (300 km) mountain road connecting Kashmir with Jammu and the plains of the Punjab. Accommodation in Srinagar is readily obtainable, except during the peak tourist months of May and June. Rooms on the many houseboats are novel as well as comfortable. Taxis for birding trips can be arranged through the Government Tourist Center or directly with the individual drivers.

The Vale of Kashmir is a valley at an altitude of about 5000 feet (1524 m) between the Pir Panjal Range to the south and the Great Himalayan Range to the north. On the valley floor are urban settlements between extensive fields, as well as the Jhelum River and several lakes. North-facing slopes surrounding the Vale are covered with fine stands of conifers, mostly blue pines. South-facing slopes are generally exposed and appear grass-covered or rocky. Above the treeline, which is at about 11,000 feet (3353 m), are extensive meadows stretching up to the rock and snow. During the summer vast flocks of domestic livestock graze over these highland areas, leaving little vegetation undisturbed.

Bird watching in Kashmir may be divided into three general categories: water and marsh birds, birds of urban and cultivated areas, and birds of Himalayan forests and meadows.

Around Srinagar common birds include Western Jackdaw, European Starling, Eurasian Roller, White-cheeked Bulbul, and Eurasian Kingfisher. On a visit to the Shalimar Gardens, the famous beauty spot of the Moguls, look for Slaty-headed Parakeet in the Chinar and fruit trees while Tickell's Thrush may be seen hopping about on the lawns. A fine one-day taxi excursion can be made around Wular Lake via Manasbal Lake, Bandipur, Watlab, and Pattan.

For mountain birds we recommend a day's trip to Gulmarg (hotel accommodation is available here if you wish a longer stay), a meadow at 9000 feet (2743 m) in the Pir Panjal. In the meadow itself there are Himalayan Greenfinch, Eurasian Goldfinch, and Cinnamon Sparrow, as well as many Large-billed Crow. Look for Himalayan Griffon

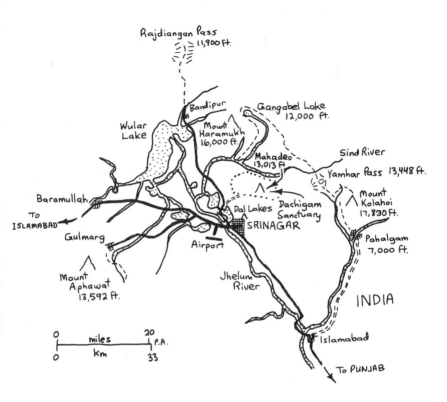

overhead. Once at the meadow, head for the northern rim where a "ring" road takes one around the periphery of the meadow. Here among the fir trees one may find Simla Black Tit, Himalayan Pied Woodpecker, and Himalayan Treecreeper, as well as several leaf-warblers (the Large Crowned and the Pallas's Leaf-Warblers are common). Streaked Laughing-thrush hop about bushes close to the ground. One may also note Asian Sooty Flycatcher on dead upright branches.

One may wish to continue above Gulmarg. The path ascends through fine fir forest and emerges at Khillenmarg in the scrub rhododendron *(R. companulatum)* zone.

In the intervening meadows look for Olive-backed Pipit. The Tickell's Leaf-Warbler stays close to low bushes. In the scrub above the treeline, watch for Tytler's Leaf-Warbler.

Permits to visit the Dachigam Sanctuary are obtainable from the office of the Director of Game Preservation at the Srinagar Tourist Center. Dachigam Sanctuary, northwest of Srinagar, one of four Himalayan wildlife sanctuaries presently established in the Himalayas of India, is fine for birding. Birds include Verditer Flycatcher, Asian Paradise-Flycatcher, Long-tailed Minivet, and Gray-headed Bunting, but many of the birds on the checklist withdraw southward for the winter.

CHECKLIST

(Summer only)

Little Dabchick   c
Gray Heron
Little Egret
Cattle Heron
Indian Pond-Heron   c
Black-crowned Night-Heron   c
Little Bittern   c
Eurasian Bittern
Himalayan Vulture   H
Lammergeier   r
Black Kite
Eurasian Sparrowhawk
Gray-headed Fishing-Eagle
Long-legged Buzzard
Golden Eagle   r H
Eurasian Kestrel   H
Chukar   r
Common Gallinule
Purple Swamphen
Pheasant-tailed Jacana
Common Sandpiper
Whiskered Tern
Rock Pigeon
Snow Pigeon   H
Collared Turtle-Dove
Oriental Turtle-Dove   H
Laughing Turtle-Dove
Slaty-headed Parakeet   H
Eurasian Cuckoo   H
Plaintive Cuckoo
White-breasted Kingfisher
   c
Eurasian Kingfisher   c
Pied Kingfisher
Eurasian Bee-eater
Eurasian Roller
Hoopoe

Brown-fronted Pied Woodpecker
   H
Striated Swallow   c
Barn Swallow   c
House Martin   H
Ashy Drongo   c
Black Drongo   c
Eurasian Golden-Oriole
Indian Myna   c
Jungle Myna
European Starling
Red-billed Chough   H
Eurasian Nutcracker   H
Yellow-billed Blue-Magpie   H
Western Jackdaw   c
Large-billed Crow   c
House Crow
Dark Cuckoo-shrike
Simla Black Tit   H
Green-backed Tit   H
Great Tit   c
White-cheeked Nuthatch   H
Eurasian Nuthatch   r H
Northern Treecreeper   H
Himalayan Treecreeper   H
Streaked Laughing-thrush   H
Variegated Laughing-thrush   H
Long-tailed Minivet   H
White-cheeked Bulbul   c
Red-vented Bulbul
Black Bulbul   H
Northern Wren   H
Blue Whistling-Thrush   H
Blue Rock-Thrush
Blue-headed Rock-Thrush
Mistle Thrush   H
Gray-headed Thrush

Tickell's Thrush
Little Forktail
Spotted Forktail
Eurasian Blackbird   r H
Orange-flanked Bush-Robin   H
Himalayan Rubythroat   r H
Plumbeous Water-Redstart
White-capped River-Chat
Black Redstart   c H
Blue-fronted Redstart   H
Pied Bushchat
Stonechat
Clamorous Reed-Warbler
Large Crowned Leaf-Warbler   c
   H
Yellow-browed Warbler   H
Tytler's Leaf-Warbler   H
Tickell's Leaf-Warbler   H
Pallas's Warbler   H
Gray-headed Flycatcher-Warbler
   c H
Goldcrest   H

Dark-sided Flycatcher   H
Verditer Flycatcher   H
Rufous-gorgeted Flycatcher   H
Rusty-tailed Flycatcher   H
Crested Gray-headed Flycatcher   r
   H
Asian Paradise-Flycatcher
Rufous-breasted Accentor   H
Alpine Accentor   H
Richard's Pipit
Olive-backed Pipit   c H
White Wagtail   c H
Oriental White-eye
Schach Shrike
Black-and-yellow Grosbeak   H
Eurasian Goldfinch   c H
Himalayan Greenfinch
Rock Bunting
Hodgson's Rosy-Finch   c H
Cinnamon Sparrow
House Sparrow   c

415

82
New Delhi–Agra, India

VISITORS TO INDIA'S CAPITAL and the nearby Taj Mahal in Agra are often impressed with the abundance, variety, and tameness of birds. Although summers are very hot and humid, it is dry and pleasant much of the rest of the year.

New Delhi is a city of trees and gardens. Even in the center at Connaught Place, thousands of roosting Ring-necked Parakeet can be seen. Probably more vultures, kites, hawks, eagles, and falcons cruise the skies over Delhi than over any other city in the world. The Delhi Zoological Park and the nearby golf links adjacent to the Hotel Oberoi Intercontinental are home to dozens of species of wild birds, such as Painted Stork, Coppersmith Barbet, babblers, shrikes, mynas, prinias, and Indian Robin.

Just to the northwest of the town of Gurgaon (southwest of the Delhi Airport on the Jaipur road) is a series of lagoons known as the Sultanpur Jheels. This is a fine waterbird sanctuary set in a bare, virtually tree-less landscape. All three cormorants, storks, egrets, ibises, lapwings, and sometimes, flamingo, occur here. During migration and winter the area is home to large flocks of Bar-headed Geese, ducks, waders, Greater Spotted Eagle, terns, and Citrine Wagtail.

Agra, about 85 miles (135 km) south of New Delhi, can be reached by road, rail, or air. Rich birding along the road includes chances for Black Ibis, Sarus Crane, raptors, River Terns, and woodland birds. The grounds of the Taj Mahal and the nearby hotels are good for seeing Egyptian Vulture, Indian Roller, Dusky Crag-Martin, Blue Rock-Thrush, Large Pied Wagtail, Brown Rock Chat, and Purple Sunbird.

One of the world's most famous bird sanctuaries, the Keoladeo Ghana, is located an hour-and-a-half drive west of Agra on the paved road to Jaipur. Wild peacocks can be seen in the vicinity of the remarkable ruins of Fatehpur Sikri, a royal city of the sixteenth century. The sanctuary is located just to the east of Bharatpur. It consists of a huge shallow lagoon, disected by numerous raised embankments that serve as viewing roads and walking trails. Boats are sometimes available for wildlife photography.

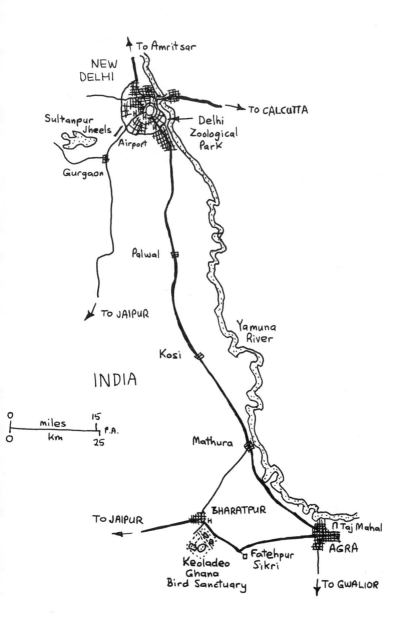

The "Ghana" is the main wintering ground of the endangered Siberian White Crane. During the rains thousands of storks, ibises, spoonbills, herons, and cormorants nest in the trees. All year long visitors will see many ducks, the elegant Pheasant-tailed and Bronze-winged Jacanas, waders, rails, and kingfishers. Many eagles and vultures occur, with Pallas's Sea-Eagle (nesting in trees in the marsh) and Imperial Eagle wintering. Part of the reserve is set aside for the blackbuck antelope, and this upland is good for Common Iora, Small Minivet, White-browed Woodshrike, and Red-breasted Flycatchers.

There are fine hotels in Bharatpur, Delhi, and Agra and a simple but clean and modern rest house within the sanctuary (write Divisional Forest Officer, Bharatpur, Rajasthan, for details).

Delhi and Agra both have jet airports. If you are not on an organized birding tour, be prepared to have to hire a taxi and driver for a few days (relatively inexpensive by world standards) since few rent-a-car services are willing to allow their cars on the slow roads covered with cattle, camels, people, and carts. Despite the crowded towns the people are friendly and pleasant.

CHECKLIST

Little Dabchick c	Eurasian Spoonbill c
Eastern White Pelican W	Greater Flamingo
Great Cormorant c	Greylag Goose W
Indian Cormorant	Bar-headed Goose c W
Little Cormorant c	Ruddy Shelduck c
Darter c	Green-winged Teal c W
Gray Heron c	Spot-billed Duck c
Purple Heron c	Gadwall W
Indian Pond-Heron c	Eurasian Wigeon W
Cattle Heron c	Garganey c W
Great Egret c	Northern Shoveler W
Short-billed Egret c	Red-crested Pochard W
Little Egret c	Northern Pochard W
Black-crowned Night-Heron	Ferruginous Duck W
Painted Stork c	Tufted Duck c W
White Open-billed Stork	Cotton Pygmy-Goose
Woolly-necked Stork	Knob-billed Goose
White Stork r W	Black-shouldered Kite
Black-necked Stork	Eurasian Honey-Buzzard
Greater Adjutant Stork r M	Black Kite c
Sacred Ibis c	Shikra
Black Ibis	Long-legged Buzzard r W
Glossy Ibis c	White-eyed Buzzard

Bonelli's Eagle   r
Imperial Eagle   W
Tawny Eagle   c
Steppe Eagle   W
Greater Spotted Eagle   W
Lesser Spotted Eagle   W
White-tailed Sea-Eagle   r W
Pallas's Sea-Eagle
Gray-headed Fishing-Eagle
Pondicherry Vulture
Griffon Vulture   W
Long-billed Vulture
Indian White-backed Vulture   c
Egyptian Vulture   c
Pallid Harrier   W
Montagu's Harrier   r W
Marsh Harrier   c W
Short-toed Snake-Eagle
Crested Serpent-Eagle
Lanner Falcon
Red-necked Falcon   r
Common Kestrel   W
Black Francolin
Gray Francolin
Common Quail   W
Jungle Bush-Quail
Indian Peacock   c
Barred Buttonquail
Sarus Crane   c
Siberian White Crane   W
Baillon's Crake   r
Ruddy-breasted Crake   r
Brown Crake
White-breasted Waterhen   c
Watercock   r
Common Gallinule   c
Purple Swamphen   c
Common Coot   c W
Pheasant-tailed Jacana   c
Bronze-winged Jacana   c
Greater Painted-snipe   r
White-tailed Lapwing   c
Red-wattled Lapwing   c
Yellow-wattled Lapwing   r
Sociable Lapwing   r W
Little Ringed Plover
Snowy Plover   M

Eurasian Curlew   W
Black-tailed Godwit   W
Spotted Redshank   W
Common Redshank   c W
Marsh Sandpiper   c W
Common Greenshank   W
Green Sandpiper   c W
Wood Sandpiper   c W
Common Sandpiper   W
Pintail Snipe   W
Common Snipe   c W
Jack Snipe   r W
Little Stint   W
Temminck's Stint   W
Dunlin   r W
Curlew Sandpiper   r W
Ruff   c W
Black-winged Stilt   c
Black-capped Avocet
Stonecurlew
Great Thick-knee   r
Indian Courser   r
Collared Pratincole   W
Little Pratincole   c
Brown-headed Gull   r W
Whiskered Tern   c
Gull-billed Tern   c
River Tern
Black-bellied Tern
Chestnut-bellied Sandgrouse   r
Yellow-legged Green-Pigeon
Rock Pigeon   c
Collared Turtle-Dove   c
Red Turtle-Dove
Laughing Turtle-Dove   c
Rose-ringed Parakeet   c
Jacobin Cuckoo   S
Common Hawk-Cuckoo   S
Common Koel
Greater Coucal   c
Eurasian Eagle-Owl
Dusky Eagle-Owl
Brown Fish-Owl
Spotted Owlet   c
Indian Nightjar
Franklin's Nightjar
House Swift   c

Asian Palm-Swift
Pied Kingfisher   c
Eurasian Kingfisher
White-breasted Kingfisher   c
Blue-cheeked Bee-eater   c S
Blue-tailed Bee-eater   c S
Green Bee-eater   c
Indian Roller   c
Hoopoe   c
Indian Gray Hornbill
Brown-headed Barbet   c
Coppersmith Barbet   c
Lesser Golden-backed Woodpecker
Yellow-fronted Pied Woodpecker
Gray-capped Woodpecker
Rufous-winged Bush-Lark
Ashy-crowned Finch-Lark
Rufous-tailed Lark
Short-toed Lark   c W
Sand Lark
Crested Lark   c
Oriental Skylark
Sand Martin
Plain Martin   c
Dusky Crag Martin
Barn Swallow   c W
Wire-tailed Swallow   c
Indian Swallow
Red-rumped Swallow
Great Gray Shrike   c
Bay-backed Shrike   c
Schach Shrike   c
Brown Shrike   W
Eurasian Golden Oriole   S
Black Drongo   c
White-bellied Drongo   r
Brahminy Myna   c
Rose-colored Starling   W
European Starling   W
Pied Myna   c
Indian Myna   c
Bank Myna   c
Rufous Treepie
House Crow   c
Large-billed Crow   c
White-browed Woodshrike
Small Minivet

Common Iora
Red-whiskered Bulbul
White-cheeked Bulbul   c
Red-vented Bulbul   c
Jungle Babbler
Common Babbler   c
Large Gray Babbler   c
Red-breasted Flycatcher   W
Zitting Cisticola
Gray-breasted Prinia
Rufous-fronted Prinia
Ashy Prinia
Tawny-flanked Prinia   c
Common Tailorbird   c
Blyth's Reed-Warbler   c W
Paddyfield Warbler   r W
Clamorous Reed-Warbler   c
Booted Warbler   W
Orphean Warbler   r W
Lesser Whitethroat   c W
Chiffchaff   W
Yellow-browed Warbler   W
Greenish Warbler   c W
Siberian Rubythroat   W
Bluethroat   c W
Asian Magpie-Robin   c
Black Redstart   c W
Brown Rock Chat   c
Stonechat   c W
Pied Bushchat   c
Indian Robin   c
Blue Rock-Thrush   W
Black-throated Thrush   r W
Great Tit   r
Chestnut-bellied Nuthatch   r
Yellow Wagtail   W
Citrine Wagtail   c W
Gray Wagtail   r W
White Wagtail   c W
Large Pied Wagtail   c
Richard's Pipit   W
Tree Pipit   W
Olive-backed Pipit   r W
Thick-billed Flowerpecker   r
Purple Sunbird   c
Oriental White-eye
Crested Bunting

White-capped Bunting   W
Black-headed Bunting   r W
Red-headed Bunting   W
White-throated Munia   c
House Sparrow   c

Chestnut-shouldered Petronia   c
Bengal Weaver
Streaked Weaver
Baya Weaver   c

83
Kathmandu, Nepal

THE KATHMANDU VALLEY is a roughly circular basin in the central Himalayas. The valley floor, of approximately 200 square miles (520 km²), lies between 4500 and 5000 feet (1372 and 1524 m) elevation and is almost entirely cultivated and dotted with villages and towns. The surrounding hill slopes exhibit cutover subtropical scrub growth up to an altitude of about 7000 feet (2133 m). The forest is thicker higher up so that ridge tops near 9000 feet (2743 m) have a covering of rhododendron forest and dense oak.

The valley floor supports a population of open-country birds somewhat similar to those of the Indian plains. Isolated forest preserves, such as Rani Bari, Gokarna, and Chapagoan, attract subtropical forest species. The greatest bird variety probably occurs at the edge of the valley where the scrub forest and forest proper meet. Thus Nagarjung (at the northwest edge of the valley), Sheopuri (north), and Godaveri (southeast) are the best areas for endemic Himalayan birds as well as visiting Palearctic species in winter.

Kathmandu is connected with daily jet service to several neighboring countries. Accommodation is always difficult outside the monsoon season so advance reservations are advisable; try the Soaltee-Oberoi, Annapurna, or Malla. Transportation around the valley is easy in metered taxis, which can wait for you (or arrange a pickup time) at the best bird areas. At Godaveri, Nagarjung, or Sheopuri one may walk about exploring the secluded ravines and forest cover. Birding trips to Kathmandu may be scheduled at any time of year, but one should expect leeches in the forest areas during the summer monsoons. The high Himalayan peaks are best visible from Kathmandu from mid-October to mid-February.

CHECKLIST

H = Highlands [birds found on upper slopes above 7000 feet (2153 m)]

Little Dabchick   r
Indian Pond-Heron   c

Cattle Heron   c S
Little Egret

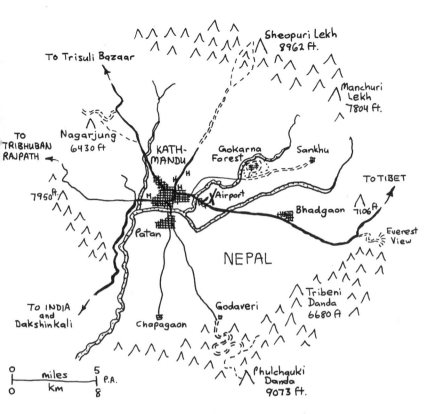

To Trisuli Bazaar

Sheopuri Lekh
8962 ft.

Manchuri
Lekh
7804 ft.

Nagarjung
6430 ft

KATH-
MANDU

Gokarna
Forest

Sankhu

TO
TRIBHUBAN
RAJPATH

To TIBET

7950 ft

Airport

Bhadgaon

7106 ft

Everest
View

Patan

NEPAL

To INDIA
and
Dakshinkali

Godaveri

Tribeni
Danda
6680 ft

Chapagaon

Phulchquki
Danda
9073 ft.

0   miles   5
|———————————| P.A.
0   km   8

Cinnamon Bittern   S
Black-crowned Night-Heron   S
Garganey   r M
Black Kite   c
Eurasian Sparrowhawk   W
Besra Sparrowhawk
Long-legged Buzzard   W
Common Buzzard   W
Black Eagle   H
Mountain Hawk-Eagle
Tawny Eagle   M
Indian White-backed Vulture   r S
Griffon Vulture   W
Long-billed Vulture   c S
Northern Harrier   r M
Marsh Harrier   M
Crested Serpent-Eagle   r S
European Hobby   r M
Oriental Hobby   r S
Common Kestrel   c

Black Francolin
Common Hill-Partridge
Kalij Pheasant
Ruddy-breasted Crake   S
White-breasted Waterhen   S
Gray-headed Lapwing   r W
Red-wattled Lapwing   S
Little Ringed Plover
Common Greenshank   W
Green Sandpiper   W
Common Sandpiper   c W
Ruff   M
Pintail Snipe   W
Common Snipe   W
Eurasian Woodcock   W
Temminck's Stint   W
Ibisbill   r M
Wedge-tailed Green Pigeon   H
Rock Pigeon   c
Ashy Pigeon

423

Oriental Turtle-Dove   c
Red Turtle-Dove   S
Spotted Turtle-Dove   c
Slaty-headed Parakeet   r S H
Jacobin Cuckoo   r M
Large Hawk-Cuckoo   S H
Indian Cuckoo   S
Eurasian Cuckoo   S H
Oriental Cuckoo   S H
Lesser Cuckoo   S H
Plaintive Cuckoo   S
Drongo Cuckoo   S
Common Koel   c S
Green-billed Malkoha   S
Spotted Scops-Owl
Eurasian Eagle-Owl
Collared Owlet
Barred Owlet
Spotted Owlet   c
Brown Hawk-Owl   r
Jungle Nightjar
House Swift   c S
White-breasted Kingfisher   c
Hoopoe   c S, r W
Great Himalayan Barbet   H
Golden-throated Barbet   H
Blue-throated Barbet   c
Coppersmith Barbet   S
Speckled Piculet
Rufous-bellied Woodpecker   H
Gray-headed Woodpecker
Lesser Yellow-naped Woodpecker
Darjeeling Pied Woodpecker   H
Brown-fronted Pied Woodpecker
   H
Fulvous-breasted Pied Woodpecker
   c
Oriental Skylark   W
Plain Martin   S
Barn Swallow   c
Red-rumped Swallow   c S
Tibetan Shrike   W
Schach Shrike   c
Brown Shrike   W
Maroon Oriole   H
Black Drongo   c
Ashy Drongo   c

Lesser Racquet-tailed Drongo   S
European Starling   M
Chestnut-tailed Starling   S
Indian Myna   c
Jungle Myna   c
Eurasian Jay   H
Red-billed Blue Magpie
Gray Treepie
House Crow   c
Large-billed Crow   c
Pied Woodshrike
Black-faced Cuckoo-shrike
Dark Cuckoo-shrike   S
Scarlet Minivet
Long-tailed Minivet   H
Short-billed Minivet   r
Yellow-throated Minivet   W
Orange-bellied Leafbird   H
White-cheeked Bulbul   c
Red-vented Bulbul   c
Striated Bulbul   W
Rufous-bellied Bulbul
Black Bulbul   c H
Puff-throated Babbler
Rufous-necked Scimitar-Babbler
Rusty-cheeked Scimitar-Babbler
Pygmy Wren-Babbler   r H
Lesser Scaly-breasted Wren-Babbler
   r W H
Black-chinned Babbler
Gray-throated Babbler
Black-throated Parrotbill   H
Spiny Babbler
White-throated Laughing-thrush
Striated Laughing-thrush
White-crested Laughing-thrush
Gray-sided Laughing-thrush   H
Chestnut-crowned Laughing-thrush
   H
Red-billed Leiothrix   H
Nepal Cutia   H
White-browed Shrike-Babbler   H
Green Shrike-Babbler   H
Hoary Barwing   H
Bar-throated Minla   c H
Blue-winged Minla
Red-tailed Minla   H

Yellow-naped Yuhina   c H
Stripe-throated Yuhina   H
Rufous-vented Yuhina   W H
White-bellied Yuhina
Rufous-winged Fulvetta   c H
White-browed Fulvetta   c H
Nepal Fulvetta   c H
Black-capped Sibia   c H
Dark-sided Flycatcher   S
Red-breasted Flycatcher   W
Rufous-gorgeted Flycatcher   W
Snowy-browed Flycatcher   S H
Slaty-backed Blue Flycatcher   W
Westermann's Flycatcher   S H
Ultramarine Flycatcher   S H
Small Niltava
Rufous-bellied Niltava
Blue-throated Niltava   S
Verditer Flycatcher   c
Gray-headed Flycatcher
Yellow-bellied Fantail   W
Chestnut-headed Tesia   H
Zitting Cisticola   S
Striated Prinia   S
Common Tailorbird   c
Chiffchaff   W
Orange-barred Leaf-Warbler   c H
Greenish Warbler   W
Gray-faced Leaf-Warbler   c W
Yellow-browed Warbler   c W
Pallas's Leaf-Warbler   c W
Blyth's Leaf-Warbler   S H
Eastern Crowned Warbler
Black-browed Warbler   r W
Gray-headed Flycatcher-Warbler
   c
Black-faced Warbler   H
Golden-spectacled Warbler
Indian Blue Robin   M H
Asian Magpie-Robin
Orange-flanked Bush-Robin   W
Golden Bush-Robin   W H
Blue-headed Redstart   W
Hodgson's Redstart   W
Blue-fronted Redstart   W
Plumbeous Water-Redstart   W
White-tailed Robin   S H

Asian Magpie-Robin   c
Slaty-backed Forktail   r S
Spotted Forktail
Stonechat   c W
Pied Bushchat
Gray Bushchat   c
White-capped River-Chat   W
Blue-headed Rock-Thrush   S H
Chestnut-bellied Rock-Thrush   W
   H
Blue Whistling-Thrush
Scaly Thrush
Plain-backed Thrush   W
White-collared Blackbird   W H
Gray-winged Blackbird   H
Black-throated Thrush   W
Brown Dipper   M
Maroon-backed Accentor   W H
Rufous-breasted Accentor   W H
Great Tit
Green-backed Tit   H
Yellow-cheeked Tit   c
Yellow-browed Tit   c H
Red-headed Tit
White-tailed Nuthatch   c H
Chestnut-bellied Nuthatch
Wallcreeper   W
Sikkim Treecreeper   H
Nepal Treecreeper   r
Hodgson's Pipit   W; S H
Richard's Pipit   c
Upland Pipit
Yellow Wagtail   M
Citrine Wagtail   W
Gray Wagtail   M
White Wagtail   c W
Indian Pied Wagtail   r M
Thick-billed Flowerpecker   S
Yellow-bellied Flowerpecker   W
Plain-breasted Flowerpecker   S
Fire-breasted Flowerpecker   c
Purple Sunbird
Nepal Sunbird   H
Black-throated Sunbird
Scarlet Sunbird   S
Fire-tailed Sunbird   W
Oriental White-eye   c

House Sparrow   c
Tree Sparrow   c
Baya Weaver   S
Spotted Munia   c
Himalayan Greenfinch   c W
Tibetan Siskin   W
Scarlet Rosefinch   W
Nepal Rosefinch   W H

Pink-browed Rosefinch   W H
Scarlet Finch   W
Golden-naped Black Finch   r W
Red-headed Bullfinch   r
Brown Bullfinch   H
Yellow-breasted Bunting   r W
Little Bunting   r W
Crested Bunting

84
Mt. Everest, Nepal

THE FINE NEW EVEREST NATIONAL PARK is an extremely rugged mountain region encompassing 320 square miles (832 km²) of the world's highest peaks. Much of the area is above the snowline and features ice pinnacles, snow cornices, avalanche channels, and wind-swept rock faces. In summer, however, between the snowline and the treeline, Himalayan meadows are carpeted with flowers and host numerous nesting birds. Descending below the treeline (about 13,000 feet) (3960 m), the forest changes from birch with rhododendron, to fir with rhododendron, and then to rhododendron with maples and other broad-leaved species. Much forest in the highlands of Nepal has been sacrificed for firewood, causing severe floods.

Most of the proposed park is not easily accessible except to those with considerable cold weather gear and climbing equipment. But from the birding point of view, there is no need to cover the entire park to adequately sample the bird population.

The park may be reached in three ways. The first route is to take a bus to Lamosangu and then walk for 12 days into the Sherpa village of Namche Bazaar at the edge of the park. The second is to fly by charter plane to Lukla at 9000 feet (2743 m) and then walk for two days along the Dudh Kosi River to Namche. This allows a little acclimatization en route. A final method is the quickest and easiest: by charter aircraft to the Sangboche strip at 12,000 feet (3658 m) elevation just above Namche. On this approach some people feel the effects of rapid altitude change. Do not plan too much birding im-mediately upon arrival. Accommodation is available at the (expen-sive) Everest View Hotel near Khumjung and adjacent to the Sang-boche strip.

The hotel is within the park and is one of the best areas for birds. Here are scattered fir trees with bushes and open meadows. Hedges and the surrounding fields of Khumjung-Kunde are also good. In addition, watch for large soaring birds overhead. Across the valley at Thyangboche Monastery is the best place for Blood and Impeyan Pheasants. The lamas protect the birds, so they are remarkably tame. Also note the tame rosefinches and Black-faced Laughing-thrush.

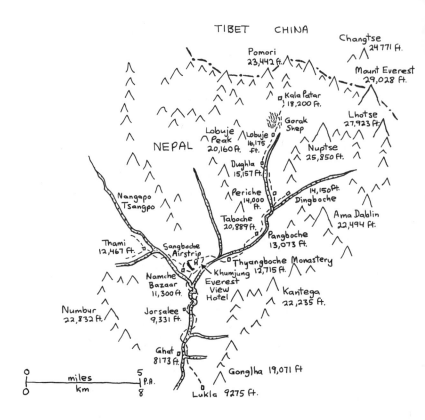

Above Thyangboche along the Everest base camp trail, there are not many birds except during the inaccessible summer monsoon months. If you do continue upward, however, be sure to look for Tibetan Snowcock near Dingboche. Early winter (October and November) and spring (April and May) are the best months for birding near Everest. Since most visitors will come during migration periods rather than at the height of the summer monsoon, or in the snows of winter, the following list has no seasonal symbols. There would be extensive altitudinal migration taking place here with many species simply retreating downhill for the winter, rather than undertaking long migrations.

CHECKLIST

Black Kite   Eurasian Sparrowhawk
Northern Goshawk   Golden Eagle

428

Tawny (Steppe) Eagle
Himalayan Vulture   c
Lammergeier   c
Northern Harrier
Common Kestrel
Snow Partridge
Tibetan Snowcock
Blood Pheasant
Impeyan Pheasant
Ibisbill   r
Eurasian Cuckoo
Oriental Cuckoo
Brown Wood-Owl
Fork-tailed Swift
Himalayan Swiftlet
Hoopoe
Himalayan Honeyguide
Darjeeling Pied Woodpecker
Rufous-bellied Woodpecker
Scaly-bellied Woodpecker
Horned Lark
Nepal Martin
Tibetan Shrike
Yellow-billed Blue Magpie
Large-billed Crow
Northern Raven   c
Long-tailed Minivet
Northern Wren
Scaly-breasted Wren-Babbler
White-throated Laughing-thrush
Streaked Laughing-thrush
Black-faced Laughing-thrush
Chestnut-crowned Laughing-thrush
Stripe-throated Yuhina
Rufous-vented Yuhina
White-browed Fulvetta
Black-capped Sibia
Dark-sided Flycatcher
Rufous-gorgeted Flycatcher
Slaty-blue Flycatcher
Yellow-bellied Fantail
Orange-barred Leaf-Warbler
Gray-faced Leaf-Warbler
Tickell's Leaf-Warbler
Dull Green Leaf-Warbler
Black-browed Warbler

Himalayan Rubythroat   c
Orange-flanked Bush-Robin
Golden Bush-Robin
Black Redstart
Blue-fronted Redstart   c
Gouldenstadt's Redstart
Stonechat
Gray Bushchat
White-throated Redstart
White-capped River Chat
Blue Whistling-Thrush
White-collared Blackbird
Black-throated Thrush   c
Grandala
Brown Dipper
Rufous-breasted Accentor   c
Robin Accentor   c
Alpine Accentor
Sikkim Black Tit   c
Coal Tit
Yellow-browed Tit
Crested Brown Tit
White-tailed Nuthatch
Wallcreeper   r
Northern Treecreeper
Olive-backed Pipit
Rose-breasted Pipit
Yellow Wagtail
Gray Wagtail
White Wagtail
Fire-tailed Sunbird
Spot-winged Grosbeak
White-winged Grosbeak
Himalayan Greenfinch
Scarlet Rosefinch
Nepal Rosefinch
Pink-browed Rosefinch
Beautiful Rosefinch
Spot-winged Rosefinch
White-browed Rosefinch
Red-faced Rosefinch
Streaked Rosefinch
Hodgson's Rosy-Finch
Brandt's Rosy-Finch
Little Bunting

85

Royal Chitwan National Park, Nepal

THE ROYAL CHITWAN NATIONAL PARK in southcentral Nepal encompasses 210 square miles (546 km²) of low-altitude forest, streams, and grassland in the *terai,* plus an even larger recent extension. The park, once the hunting ground of the King of Nepal, was created to preserve the one-horned rhinoceros and also protects a host of other mammals (tiger, leopard, bear, and gaur, to name a few), as well as birds. We estimate that nearly 400 species of bird will eventually be recorded in the park.

The Chitwan habitat varies from still water (in small lakes), to moving water (in the Narayani and Rapti Rivers), to tall tiger grassland, to subtropical forest with *Terminalia, Bombax,* and *Sal* as conspicuous genera. The park is generally closed during the summer monsoons and reopens in September. Winter is a good time to see Palearctic migrants, while spring (February to April) is best for observing nesting activities. By late May, temperatures here are bearable but not comfortable.

In a 24-hour visit to the park one may see about 100 species of birds. Try to include a variety of habitats: tall grass, forest edge, and dense forest, as well as a trip to the confluence of the Narayani and Rapti Rivers for water and shorebirds. En route to the confluence stop at a small lake or two for still-water and marsh birds.

The rivers are home to the narrow-snouted gavial (a crocodile), and to such birds as Black Ibis, Lesser Adjutant Stork, Black-necked Stork, Red-wattled Lapwing, Great Thick-knee, and Stork-billed, Pied, and White-breasted Kingfishers. The Gray-headed Fishing-Eagle, vultures, and Crested Treeswift soar over the grasslands. The marshy pools may have Bronze-winged and Pheasant-tailed Jacanas. The forests are (at times) alive with Great Indian Hornbill, Indian Peacock, parakeets, orioles, fantails, babblers, bulbuls, and woodpeckers.

Birding from elephant back is a novel experience, but we urge you to take advantage of every opportunity to walk the tracks. Guides are necessary for protection. As in most tropical forests there will be many quiet hours with occasional flurries of activities.

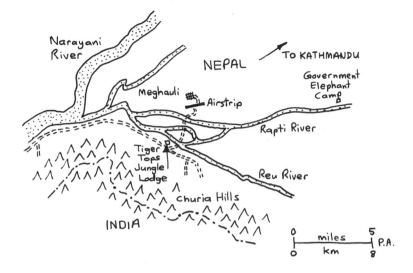

This park can be explored from the romantic comfort of Tiger Tops Jungle Lodge, which is wildlife oriented and features elephant rides and possible tiger viewing. Bird watchers are always welcome, and special arrangements are made to suit their particular needs. Contact Tiger Tops, PO Box 242, Kathmandu, Nepal, or your travel agent. The prices quoted you will include round-trip flights to and from Kathmandu.

CHECKLIST

Little Dabchick	Black Ibis c
Great Cormorant	Bar-headed Goose W
Little Cormorant	Lesser Whistling-Duck
Darter c	Ruddy Shelduck c
Purple Heron	Spot-billed Duck c
Gray Heron c	Cotton Pygmy-Goose r
Green Heron	Goosander r W
Indian Pond-Heron c	Black-shouldered Kite
Cattle Heron c	Black Kite c
Great Egret	Shikra
Little Egret c	Changeable Hawk-Eagle
Short-billed Egret c	Gray-headed Fishing-Eagle
Black-crowned Night-Heron	Long-billed Vulture c
Painted Stork	Indian White-backed Vulture c
White Open-billed Stork	Egyptian Vulture
White-necked Stork c	Marsh Harrier
Black-necked Stork c	Crested Serpent-Eagle

Osprey W
Red-legged Falconet
Black Francolin c
Kalij Pheasant
Red Junglefowl c
Indian Peafowl c
Common Gallinule
Bengal Bustard
Pheasant-tailed Jacana
Bronze-winged Jacana
Greater Painted-snipe r
Red-wattled Lapwing c
Spur-winged Lapwing
Little Ringed Plover c
Snowy Plover
Common Greenshank W
Green Sandpiper W
Common Sandpiper W
Stonecurlew
Great Thick-knee
Little Pratincole
Great Black-headed Gull W
River Tern c
Black-bellied Tern c
Pompadour Green-Pigeon c
Orange-breasted Green-Pigeon
Red Turtle-Dove c
Spotted Turtle-Dove c
Green-winged Pigeon
Great Parakeet
Rose-ringed Parakeet c
Rose-breasted Parakeet
Blossom-headed Parakeet
Chestnut-winged Cuckoo
Common Hawk-Cuckoo
Indian Cuckoo
Green-billed Malkoha
Greater Coucal
Black Coucal
Grass Owl
Eurasian Scops-Owl
Brown Fish-Owl
Jungle Owlet
Brown Hawk-Owl
Spotted Owlet c
Long-tailed Nightjar
Franklin's Nightjar

Crested Treeswift c S
Pied Kingfisher c
Eurasian Kingfisher c
Blue-eared Kingfisher
Stork-billed Kingfisher
White-breasted Kingfisher c
Chestnut-headed Bee-eater
Blue-tailed Bee-eater
Green Bee-eater c
Blue-bearded Bee-eater
Indian Roller
Dollar Roller r
Hoopoe c
Malabar Pied Hornbill c
Great Hornbill
Lineated Barbet
Blue-throated Barbet
Rufous Piculet
Lesser Yellow-naped Woodpecker
  c
Three-toed Golden-backed
  Woodpecker c
Fulvous-breasted Pied Woodpecker
  c
Gray-capped Woodpecker
Greater Golden-backed
  Woodpecker
Blue-winged Pitta r S
Green-breasted Pitta r
Sand Lark c
Plain Martin c
Barn Swallow c W
Red-rumped Swallow
Black-hooded Oriole c
Black Drongo c
White-bellied Drongo
Crow-billed Drongo
Spangled Drongo
Ashy Woodswallow c W
Chestnut-tailed Starling
Pied Myna
Indian Myna c
Jungle Myna
Bank Myna
Hill Myna r
Red-billed Blue Magpie
Rufous Treepie

Large-billed Crow
Pied Woodshrike   c
Black-faced Cuckoo-shrike
Scarlet Minivet   c
Small Minivet
Rosy Minivet
Common Iora
Golden-fronted Leafbird
Black-crested Yellow Bulbul
Red-whiskered Bulbul
Red-vented Bulbul   c
Puff-throated Babbler
Striated Tit-Babbler
Chestnut-capped Babbler
Yellow-eyed Babbler
Striated Babbler
Jungle Babbler   c
Lesser Necklaced Laughing-thrush
Rufous-necked Laughing-thrush
White-bellied Yuhina
Red-breasted Flycatcher   c   W
Brook's Niltava
Gray-headed Flycatcher   c
White-browed Fantail   c
White-throated Fantail
Asian Paradise-Flycatcher
Clamorous Reed-Warbler
Pallas's Leaf-Warbler   r   W
Greenish Warbler   c   W
Hodgson's Prinia
Jungle Prinia
Yellow-bellied Prinia

Common Tailorbird
Bluethroat   W
Himalayan Rubythroat   r   W
Asian Magpie-Robin
White-rumped Shama
Black Redstart
Black-backed Forktail
Stonechat
Pied Bushchat   c
White-tailed Bushchat
Orange-headed Thrush
Great Tit
Chestnut-bellied Nuthatch   c
Velvet-fronted Nuthatch
Richard's Pipit
Yellow Wagtail   c   W
Citrine Wagtail   c   W
Gray Wagtail   W
White Wagtail   W
Large Pied Wagtail
Pale-billed Flowerpecker
Purple Sunbird
Scarlet Sunbird
Streaked Spiderhunter
Oriental White-eye
House Sparrow
Baya Weaver
Strawberry Finch
Spotted Munia
Scarlet Rosefinch   W
Yellow-breasted Bunting   W
Gray-hooded Bunting

86
Sri Lanka (Ceylon)

THE ISLAND OF SRI LANKA, formerly known as Ceylon, is pear-shaped, tropical, and located off the south coast of India. It is a fascinating land for tourists, and birders will be happy to note that there is a fine field guide in English. Colombo, the chief city, is clean, has many fine hotels, and its streets are lined with flowering trees. The Deliwala Zoo is worth a visit.

The flatter north and east portions of the island are drier with rainfalls as low as 40 inches (1016 mm). The south and west are hillier and wetter with up to 200 inches (5080 mm) of rain (chiefly during the southwest monsoons from May through September). The highlands are considerably cooler than the tropical lowlands.

Wilpattu National Park is just west of Anuradhapura (a famed ancient city), about 112 miles (180 km) north of Colombo. Leopard, chital, sambar, wild boar, sloth bear, and monkeys live in the forests, grasslands, lagoons, and streamsides of the park. Birds include many waterbirds, storks, Pheasant-tailed Jacana, Great Thick-knee, parakeets, eagles, owls, junglefowl, and hornbills. The Hotel Wilpattu is the headquarters for rooms, boats, and game drives.

Ruhuna-Yala National Park in the southeast is covered with park-like plains, scrub jungle with rocky outcrops, and water-holes. The dry season in this part of the island is July through September, a time when many birds and mammals (including Indian elephant, leopard and sloth bear) concentrate along the two rivers. Birds are plentiful and feature Black-necked, Painted, and Lesser Adjutant Storks, Ceylon Junglefowl, Malabar Pied Hornbill, and many migrant shorebirds. Brown's Safari Beach Hotel at Amaduwa-Yala is located on a fine beach adjacent to the reserve.

There are twenty endemic birds on Sri Lanka. Occurring in all life zones are the Ceylon Spurfowl, Ceylon Junglefowl, Emerald-collared Parakeet, Ceylon Hanging-Parrot, Red-faced Malkoha, Brown-capped Babbler, and Spot-winged Ground-Thrush. The Ceylon Coucal lives only in the wet, low southwest. Found there and in the higher hill country are the White-headed Starling, Ceylon Myna, Ceylon Magpie, Ceylon Laughing-thrush, and Legge's Flowerpecker. Re-

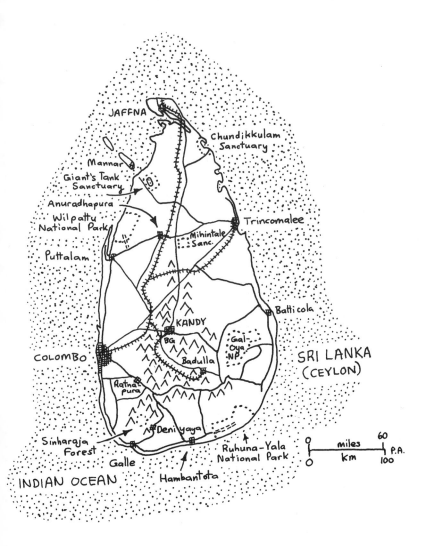

stricted to the hills are Ceylon Pigeon, Yellow-eared Bulbul, Ceylon Blue Flycatcher, Ceylon Warbler, Ceylon Whistling-Thrush, and Ceylon White-eye.

The Sinharaja forest, south of Ratnapura, is the last primary lowland wet forest left, and it is rapidly being destroyed.

Kandy, 72 miles (115 km) east of Colombo in the beautiful high country at 1600 feet (488 m), is surrounded by tea plantations and forest. Kandy has many inns. Most visitors will go to the famous Buddhist Temple of the Sacred Tooth and watch the daily elephant dip in the river at Katugastota 3 miles (5 km) away. Birders should visit the Royal Botanical Gardens at Peradeniya, 4 miles (6.4 km) south. There the birdlife includes Blossom-headed and Emerald-collared Parakeets, Ceylon Hanging-Parrot, Brown-headed and Yellow-fronted Barbets, Scarlet Minivet, Asian Paradise-Flycatcher, Ceylon Myna, three sunbirds, and Ceylon White-eye.

To see the high-country endemics travel to Horton Plains, 120 miles (192 km) east of Colombo. Near the Farr Inn (7 rooms) there is a trail through rhododendron forests (at 6000 feet [1830 m], home to such birds as Ceylon Warbler, Black-headed Babbler, Indian Scimitar-Babbler, Yellow-eared Bulbul, Ceylon White-eye, and Ceylon Blue Flycatcher.

CHECKLIST

Little Dabchick   c
Wilson's Storm-Petrel   r M
Wedge-tailed Shearwater   r M
White-tailed Tropicbird   r M
Spot-billed Pelican   c
Brown Booby   M
Great Cormorant
Indian Cormorant   c
Little Cormorant   c
Darter   c
Lesser Frigatebird   r M
Gray Heron   c
Purple Heron   c
Great Egret   c
Short-billed Egret   c
Little Egret   c
Western Reef-Heron   r
Cattle Heron   c
Indian Pond-Heron   c
Green Heron
Black-crowned Night-Heron   c
Malay Night-Heron   r W
Yellow Bittern
Cinnamon Bittern
Black Bittern
White-necked Stork
Black-necked Stork
Asian Open-billed Stork
Painted Stork   c
Lesser Adjutant Stork

Sacred Ibis
Glossy Ibis   r
Eurasian Spoonbill
Greater Flamingo
Lesser Whistling-Duck   c
Cotton Pygmy-Goose   c
Spot-billed Duck   r
Northern Pintail   c W
Garganey   c W
Green-winged Teal   r W
Northern Shoveler   r W
Osprey   W
Jerdon's Baza
Eurasian Honey-Kite
White-bellied Sea-Eagle
Gray-headed Fishing-Eagle
Brahminy Kite   c
Black Kite
Black-shouldered Kite
Shikra   c
Besra Sparrowhawk
Crested Goshawk
Common Buzzard   r W
Rufous-bellied Hawk-Eagle   r
Black Eagle
Changeable Hawk-Eagle
Mountain Hawk-Eagle   r
Crested Serpent-Eagle   c
Pallid Harrier   c W
Montagu's Harrier   W

Pied Harrier   r W
Marsh Harrier   W
Common Kestrel
Peregrine Falcon
Indian Peafowl
Ceylon Junglefowl
Ceylon Spurfowl
Rain Quail
Jungle Bush-Quail
Painted Francolin
Gray Francolin
Common Buttonquail
Slaty-breasted Rail   r
Slaty-legged Crake   r W
Ruddy-breasted Crake   r
White-breasted Waterhen   c
Common Gallinule
Watercock
Purple Swamphen   c
Common Coot   r
Pheasant-tailed Jacana   c
Greater Painted-snipe
Common Oystercatcher   r W
Red-wattled Lapwing   c
Yellow-wattled Lapwing   c
Gray Plover   W
Lesser Golden Plover   c W
Great Sand Plover   W
Mongolian Plover   c W
Little Ringed Plover
Snowy Plover   c
Ruddy Turnstone   c W
Eastern Curlew   c W
Whimbrel   c W
Black-tailed Godwit   r W
Bar-tailed Godwit   r W
Terek Sandpiper   r W
Green Sandpiper   W
Wood Sandpiper   c W
Marsh Sandpiper   c W
Common Greenshank   c W
Common Redshank   c W
Common Sandpiper   c W
Ruff   W
Sanderling   r W
Curlew Sandpiper   c W
Broad-billed Sandpiper   r W

Little Stint   c W
Temminck's Stint   r W
Long-toed Stint   W
Common Snipe   r W
Pintail Snipe   c W
Jack Snipe   r W
Black-winged Stilt   c
Black-capped Avocet   r W
Crab Plover   r
Great Thick-knee
Stonecurlew
Indian Courser
Collared Pratincole
Little Pratincole
Great Skua   r M
Great Black-headed Gull   W
Brown-headed Gull   c W
Whiskered Tern   c W
White-winged Black Tern   r W
Gull-billed Tern   c W
Caspian Tern
Lesser Crested Tern   c W
Greater Crested Tern   c
Common Tern   W
Roseate Tern
Least Tern   c
Bridled Tern   M
Yellow-legged Green-Pigeon   r
Pompadour Green-Pigeon   c
Orange-breasted Green-Pigeon   c
Green Fruit-Pigeon
Rock Pigeon
Ceylon Pigeon
Spotted Turtle-Dove   c
Collared Turtle-Dove
Green-winged Pigeon   c
Great Parakeet   c
Rose-ringed Parakeet   c
Blossom-headed Parakeet   c
Emerald-collared Lorikeet
Ceylon Hanging-Parrot
Indian Cuckoo
Lesser Cuckoo   r W
Common Hawk-Cuckoo
Plaintive Cuckoo   c W
Banded Bay Cuckoo   r
Drongo Cuckoo

437

Jacobin Cuckoo
Chestnut-winged Cuckoo   r W
Common Koel   c
Blue-faced Malcoha
Red-faced Malcoha   r
Sirkeer Cuckoo   r
Greater Coucal   c
Ceylon Coucal
Barn Owl   r
Bay Owl   r
Short-eared Owl   r W
Brown Wood-Owl
Brown Fish-Owl
Forest Eagle-Owl   r
Eurasian Scops-Owl   r
Collared Scops-Owl
Jungle Owlet
Brown Hawk-Owl
Ceylon Frogmouth   r
Gray Nightjar
Large-tailed Nightjar
Indian Nightjar
Alpine Swift
House Swift   c
Asian Palm-Swift   c
Brown Needletail
Edible-nest Swiftlet   c
Crested Treeswift   c
Indian Trogon
Pied Kingfisher   c
Eurasian Kingfisher   c
Blue-eared Kingfisher   r
Black-backed Kingfisher   r
Stork-billed Kingfisher
White-breasted Kingfisher   c
Black-capped Kingfisher   r W
Green Bee-eater   c
Blue-tailed Bee-eater   c W, r S
Chestnut-headed Bee-eater
Indian Roller   c
Dollar Roller   r
Hoopoe
Malabar Pied Hornbill
Malabar Gray Hornbill   c
Brown-headed Barbet   c
Yellow-fronted Barbet   c
Coppersmith Barbet   c

Crimson-throated Barbet   c
Little Scaly-bellied Green
   Woodpecker
Lesser Yellow-naped Woodpecker
Yellow-fronted Pied Woodpecker
Brown-capped Pygmy Woodpecker
Rufous Woodpecker
Lesser Golden-backed Woodpecker
   c
Greater Golden-backed
   Woodpecker   c
Black-backed Woodpecker
Blue-winged Pitta   W
Oriental Skylark
Rufous-winged Bush-Lark   c
Ashy-crowned Finch-Lark   c
Barn Swallow   c W
Pacific Swallow   c
Red-rumped Swallow   c
Black Drongo
Ashy Drongo   W
White-bellied Drongo   c
Greater Racquet-tailed Drongo
Eurasian Golden-Oriole   r W
Asian Black-headed Oriole   c
Hill Myna
Ceylon Myna
Ceylon Magpie
Large-billed Crow   c
House Crow   c
Great Tit   c
Velvet-fronted Nuthatch
Jungle Babbler   c
Striated Jungle Babbler
Ashy-headed Laughing-thrush   r
Indian Scimitar-Babbler
White-throated Babbler
Yellow-eyed Babbler   c
Brown-capped Babbler
Black-headed Babbler
Scarlet Minivet   c
Small Minivet
Pied Woodshrike   c
White-browed Woodshrike   c
Black-headed Cuckoo-shrike
Black-faced Cuckoo-shrike
Black Bulbul   c

Red-vented Bulbul   c
Yellow-browed Bulbul
Black-crested Yellow Bulbul   c
White-browed Bulbul   c
Yellow-eared Bulbul
Common Iora
Golden-fronted Leafbird
Gold-mantled Leafbird   c
Indian Blue Robin   W
Pied Bushchat   c
Indian Robin   c
Asian Magpie-Robin   c
White-rumped Shama
Eurasian Blackbird
Pied Thrush   W
Orange-headed Thrush   r W
Scaly Thrush   r
Spot-winged Thrush
Blue Rock-Thrush   r W
Ceylon Whistling-Thrush
Clamorous Reed-Warbler   c
Blyth's Reed-Warbler   c W
Booted Warbler   r W
Hume's Whitethroat   W
Greenish Warbler   c W
Large-billed Leaf-Warbler   W
Common Tailorbird   c
Zitting Cisticola   c
Gray-breasted Prinia
Ashy Prinia   c
Jungle Prinia
Tawny-flanked Prinia   c
Ceylon Warbler
Red-breasted Flycatcher   c W

Tickell's Niltava
Ceylon Blue Flycatcher
Asian Brown Flycatcher   c W
Brown-breasted Flycatcher   r W
Gray-headed Flycatcher   c
Asian Paradise-Flycatcher
Black-naped Monarch
White-browed Fantail
Richard's Pipit   c
Gray Wagtail   c W
Yellow Wagtail   c W
White Wagtail   r W
Forest Wagtail   W
Ashy Woodswallow
Schach Shrike
Brown Shrike   c W
Pale-billed Flowerpecker   c
Thick-billed Flowerpecker
Legge's Flowerpecker
Loten's Sunbird   c
Purple Sunbird   c
Purple-rumped Sunbird
Oriental White-eye   c
Ceylon White-eye
Baya Weaver   c
Streaked Weaver
Java Sparrow   r
Black-headed Munia
White-backed Munia   c
Black-throated Munia
Spotted Munia   c
White-throated Munia
House Sparrow   c

439

87

Hokkaido, Japan

THE NORTHERNMOST OF JAPAN'S MAIN ISLANDS, Hokkaido, has a severe but dry winter, a sudden efflorescence in April and May, warm, dry summers, and wet autumns marked by colorful foliage.

Most visitors will fly to Sapporo via frequent jets from Tokyo. The island is connected with Honshu via the Hakodate–Aomari ferry, a four-and-a-half-hour trip. Railway passengers and those with cars will find it a relatively inexpensive excursion for pelagic birds.

A number of Siberian birds have their southern limit here, including Blakiston's Fish-Owl, Hazel Grouse, several woodpeckers, Marsh Tit, and Pine Grosbeak. Hokkaido is the southern breeding limit of White-tailed Sea-Eagle, Japanese Crane, Siberian Rubythroat, several grasshopper warblers, Long-tailed Rosy-Finch, and Yellow-breasted Bunting.

About 12.5 miles (20 km) west of Sapporo is the Hotel Haseyawa Garden in a farming and woodland area. Summer birds include White-bellied Green-Pigeon, cuckoos, Gray Nightjar, starlings, Narcissus Flycatcher, Siberian, Gray, and Brown Thrushes, Siberian Blue-Robin, Oriental Greenfinch, Gray-headed, Japanese Yellow, and Meadow Buntings.

Akan National Park in eastern Hokkaido has vast forests, hot springs, lakes, and lofty mountains. It is located several hours by road north of Kushiro (airport and hotels), and visitors can stay in Akan Kohan Spa adjacent to Lake Akan at the Akankosa, Ichikawa, or New Akan Hotels. Around Lake Akan summer birds include White-tailed Sea-Eagle, swifts, tits, dipper, Japanese Bush-Warbler, and Black-faced Bunting. In the Teshikaga region, on the east side of the park, look for Mandarin Duck, Hazel Grouse, Streaked and Gray's Grasshopper-Warblers, and Yellow-breasted Bunting.

Along the Kushiro–Lake Akan road, just 10 miles (16 km) from Kushiro, is the Tancho-Zuru Crane Sanctuary. This is the home of the Japanese Crane, which winters here on cultivated fields. Most of these birds withdraw to interior marshes in the summer although some birds are kept captive. In Japan's mad rush to industrialize much of the Japanese Cranes' former feeding area has been destroyed.

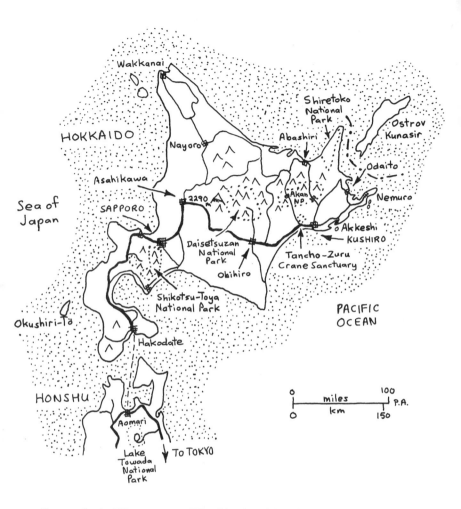

One and a half hours east of Kushiro is Akkeshi, a little port with several small inns. Fishing boats can be hired to reach Daikoku Island, a seabird colony. Among the breeders are Leach's Storm-Petrel, Temminck's Cormorant, Slaty-backed Gull, Sooty Guillemot, Tufted Puffin, Pallas's Grasshopper-Warbler, and Siberian Ruby-throat.

Nemuro is the easternmost town in Japan, practically touching the Kurile Islands (controlled by the USSR). Lying offshore are two small Japanese controlled islands named Yuriri and Meyururi, on which three cormorants nest (Temminck's, Pelagic, and Bare-faced). Other birds to look for in the vicinity are Harlequin Duck, snipe, Rhinoceros Auklet, Tufted Puffin, and shorebirds.

441

In winter the hardy birder who leaves behind the snow fields and comforts of Sapporo will find much of interest in eastern Hokkaido. Visiting the ocean shores, ponds, and fields one may find loons, Whooper Swans (at Odaito), sea ducks, Steller's Sea-Eagle, gulls, Marbled and Ancient Murrelets, and flocks of Japanese Cranes.

CHECKLIST

Red-throated Loon   M
Black-throated Loon   c M
Yellow-billed Loon   r W
Little Dabchick   c S
Horned Grebe   r W
Black-necked Grebe   M
Red-necked Grebe   S
Black-footed Albatross   M
Laysan Albatross   M
Northern Fulmar   r W
Streaked Shearwater   c S
Pale-footed Shearwater   r M
Leach's Storm-Petrel   S
Temminck's Cormorant   c
Pelagic Cormorant   c
Gray Heron   c S
Yellow Bittern   S
Schrenck's Bittern   S
Eurasian Bittern
Whooper Swan   c W
Bewick's Swan   r W
Swan Goose   r W
Bean Goose   W
White-fronted Goose   W
Lesser White-fronted Goose   r W
Snow Goose   r W
Brent Goose   r W
Northern Pintail   M
Green-winged Teal   c
Baikal Teal   W
Spot-billed Duck   c S
Mallard   c
Gadwall   W
Falcated Teal   c
Eurasian Wigeon   c M
Garganey   r M
Northern Shoveler   W
Northern Pochard   M

Baer's Pochard   r W
Tufted Duck   c M
Greater Scaup   c W
Mandarin Duck   S
Common Goldeneye   c W
Long-tailed Duck   c W
Harlequin Duck   c W
Black Scoter   c W
White-winged Scoter   c W
Smew   W
Red-breasted Merganser   c
Goosander   W
Osprey   S
Eurasian Honey-Buzzard   S
Black Kite   c
White-tailed Sea-Eagle   W
Steller's Sea-Eagle   r W
Marsh Harrier   S
Northern Harrier   r W
Northern Goshawk
Japanese Sparrowhawk   S
Eurasian Sparrowhawk   S
Common Buzzard   S
Rough-legged Buzzard   W
Golden Eagle   c
Mountain Hawk-Eagle
Common Kestrel   r S
Merlin   W
European Hobby   r S
Gyrfalcon   r W
Peregrine Falcon
Hazel Grouse
Japanese Quail   S
Japanese Crane
Water Rail   S
Baillon's Crake   r S
Ruddy-breasted Crake   S
Common Gallinule   c S

Common Coot   c S
Northern Lapwing   M
Gray Plover   c M
Lesser Golden Plover   c M
Little Ringed Plover   c S
Snowy Plover   c S
Long-billed Plover   c
Mongolian Plover   c M
Eurasian Curlew   M
Whimbrel   c M
Eastern Curlew   M
Bar-tailed Godwit   c M
Spotted Redshank   M
Common Redshank   M
Common Greenshank   c M
Nordmann's Greenshank   r M
Green Sandpiper   M
Wood Sandpiper   M
Terek Sandpiper   M
Common Sandpiper   c S
Gray-tailed Tattler   c M
Ruddy Turnstone   c M
Solitary Snipe   W
Pintail Snipe   r M
Swinhoe's Snipe   r M
Japanese Snipe   S
Common Snipe   c
Eurasian Woodcock   S
Great Knot   M
Rufous-necked Stint   c M
Sharp-tailed Sandpiper   M
Dunlin   c M
Sanderling   M
Spoon-billed Sandpiper   r M
Red Phalarope   r M
Little Phalarope   M
Pomarine Jaeger   M
Long-tailed Jaeger   r M
Great Skua   r M
Black-tailed Gull   c S
Mew Gull   W
Herring Gull   c W
Slaty-backed Gull   c
Glaucous Gull   c W
Black-headed Gull   c M
Black-legged Kittiwake   c M
Common Tern   c M

Thick-billed Murre   W
Common Murre   c
Sooty Guillemot   c S
Marbled Murrelet   W
Ancient Murrelet
Crested Auklet   c W
Least Auklet   c W
Rhinoceros Auklet
Horned Puffin   W
Tufted Puffin
White-bellied Green-Pigeon   S
Oriental Turtle-Dove   r S
Hodgdon's Hawk-Cuckoo   r S
Eurasian Cuckoo   c S
Oriental Cuckoo   S
Lesser Cuckoo   S
Eurasian Scops-Owl   S
Collared Scops-Owl
Northern Eagle-Owl   r
Blakiston's Fish-Owl   r
Snowy Owl   r W
Brown Hawk-Owl   S
Ural Owl
Long-eared Owl   r
Short-eared Owl   W
Gray Nightjar   S
Fork-tailed Swift   c S
Crested Kingfisher   r
Eurasian Kingfisher   c S
Ruddy Kingfisher   S
Eurasian Wryneck   S
Gray-headed Woodpecker
Black Woodpecker   r
Great Spotted Woodpecker
White-backed Woodpecker   c
Lesser Spotted Woodpecker   r
Japanese Pygmy Woodpecker   c
Northern Three-toed Woodpecker
   r
Northern Skylark   c S
Sand Martin   c S
Barn Swallow   S
Asian Martin   c S
Brown-eared Bulbul   c S
Eurasian Jay   c
Eurasian Nutcracker
Eurasian Crow   c

Large-billed Crow   c
Northern Raven   W
Long-tailed Tit   c
Great Tit   c
Varied Tit   c
Marsh Tit   c
Willow Tit
Coal Tit   c
Eurasian Nuthatch
Northern Treecreeper
Brown Dipper
Northern Wren
Japanese Robin   S
Siberian Rubythroat   S
Siberian Blue-Robin   S
Orange-flanked Bush-Robin   S
Daurian Redstart   M
Stonechat   c S
Siberian Thrush   r S
Blue Rock-Thrush   c
Scaly Thrush   S
Japanese Thrush   S
Pale Thrush   M
Eye-browed Thrush   r S
Dusky Thrush   W
Brown-headed Thrush   c S
Arctic Warbler   S
Pale-legged Leaf-Warbler   S
Eastern Crowned Warbler   c S
Great Reed-Warbler   c S
Black-browed Reed-Warbler   c S
Pallas's Grasshopper-Warbler   r S
Lanceolated Warbler   S
Gray's Grasshopper-Warbler
Stub-tailed Bush-Warbler   S
Japanese Bush-Warbler   c S
Goldcrest
Dark-sided Flycatcher   S
Gray-streaked Flycatcher   r M
Asian Brown Flycatcher   c S
Narcissus Flycatcher   c S
Mugimaki Flycatcher   r M

Blue-and-white Flycatcher   c S
Japanese Accentor
White Wagtail   c S
Japanese Wagtail   c
Gray Wagtail   c S
Olive-backed Pipit   c S
Water Pipit   c M
Bohemian Waxwing   W
Japanese Waxwing   W
Brown Shrike   S
Bull-headed Shrike   c S
Tiger Shrike   r S
Great Gray Shrike   W
Purple-backed Starling   c S
White-cheeked Starling   c S
Japanese White-eye
Tree Sparrow   c
Cinnamon Sparrow
Brambling   c M
Oriental Greenfinch   c
Eurasian Siskin
Common Redpoll   W
Pallas's Rosefinch   W
Long-tailed Rosy-Finch   c S
Arctic Rosy-Finch   W
Pine Grosbeak
Red Crossbill
White-winged Crossbill   r W
Eurasian Bullfinch
Hawfinch   S
Yellow-billed Grosbeak   c S
Gray-hooded Bunting   c S
Yellow-breasted Bunting   S
Rustic Bunting   c M
Gray Bunting   r S
Japanese Yellow Bunting   r S
Meadow Bunting   c S
Black-faced Bunting   c S
Marsh Bunting   r S
Reed Bunting   c S
Lapland Longspur   r W

88

Honshu and Kyushu, Japan

JAPAN IS A STRING OF MANY ISLANDS with four major ones: Hokkaido, Honshu, Shikoku, and Kyushu. This section deals with two of the three warmer islands, Honshu and Kyushu. Most visitors come only to Honshu, the largest island, where Tokyo, Kyoto, Osaka, Mt. Fuji, and the Japanese Alps are located.

The climate is of the "four seasons" variety, with warm wet summers and cold snowy winters. Due to the north-south alignment, the southwest of Kyushu is nearly subtropical, while northern Honshu and Hokkaido tend toward subarctic conditions. Japan is very mountainous, with high ranges forming the backbone of most islands. The vertical distribution of vegetation and climates in the mountains greatly affects bird distribution. In general it would be best to visit the mountains from May through August, and spend most of the winter in the plains.

Tokyo has some parks of interest for viewing woodland birds and wintering waterfowl. Meiji Shrine Park at Yoyogi, the National Garden for Nature Study at Meguro, Ueno Park and Zoo, and Hama Park near Shinbashi are all recommended. In the summer the commoner birds are Black Kite, Rufous Turtle-Dove, Barn Swallow, crows, Azure-winged Magpie, White-cheeked Starling, Great Tit, Bull-headed Shrike, and Tree Sparrow. In winter one should look for Mandarin Duck, Brown-eared Bulbul, Japanese Bush-Warbler, Brown and Dusky Thrushes, and Daurian Redstart. The best birding spot on Tokyo Bay is Shinhama Waterfowl Preserve, near the mouth of the Edo River, good for seeing shorebirds and waders on migration and ducks and geese in winter.

Mt. Fuji at 12,388 feet (3776 m) dominates a vast area, much of which is excellent for birds. Lake Yamanaka, a half day west of Tokyo, is one of many lakes on the north side of Mt. Fuji with adjacent hotels. Climbs up Fuji are often undertaken, and birders can find Mountain Hawk-Eagle, Copper Pheasant, many woodpeckers, Orange-flanked Bush-Robin, Japanese Robin, and several buntings and tits.

Those unable to hike are fortunate in that a number of places in central Honshu have roads and hotels. Nikko National Park can be reached by road, or via a special two-hour express electric train. There are many Japanese-style hotels and three Western-style (Nikko Kanaya, Nikko Lakeside, and Chuzenji Kanaya Hotels). While crowds visit Toshugu Temple, birders will find the rich mountain forests very rewarding.

The Karuizawa Plateau, 90 miles (144 km) west of Tokyo (4 hours by train), is another summer paradise 3049 feet (930 m) above sea level, with many hotels (for example, Green, Kajima-no-mori, Mampei, Seizan, and Hoshiro Hot Springs Hotels). The smoking volcano Asama, the rich conifer woodlands, and the high mountains of Joshinetsu National Park all add up to a fine area with an abundance of summer birds.

In northern Honshu visitors can fly to Aomori on Toa Airlines. The great bay there is a haven for wintering waterfowl. In the summer visitors should visit Towada National Park. The road up the east side from Furumaki follows the Oirase River, a beautiful drive below cliffs and waterfalls. In the river and nearby woods one should look for Brown Dipper, Ruddy Kingfisher, warblers, jays, tits, and flycatchers. On the west side of Lake Towada, a huge crater lake, is the Towada Hotel at Namariyama. Alpine forests and tall peaks abound.

Matsushima Bay near Sendai is one of Japan's finest, with many pine-clad islands. Boat trips are available, including one to Kinkazan Island with its cherry blossoms, a shrine, and herds of deer. Marine birding is good, and early spring brings masses of ducks, including many Falcated Teal. Visitors can stay at the Matsushima Park Hotel, with fine views of the island.

In western Honshu near Osaka is the fascinating city of Kyoto. On its west side, about 23 minutes by train, is the beautiful spot known as Arashiyama, on the Oi River. The varied vegetation and hot springs are good for birds and an excellent spot to see Japanese monkeys.

Kyushu, the southernmost of the major islands, is characterized by warm-zone evergreens. The "crane resort" near the little village of Arasaki (near Kagoshima) is a Natural Monument, with protection and a feeding program. From November to March hundreds of Hooded and the rare White-naped Cranes winter in the fallow rice paddies. There are many hotels in the city of Kagoshima and flights to Osaka and Tokyo by Toa and All Nippon Airlines. The subtropical coasts, the masses of camellias, the active volcanoes, and the mountainous interior with several national parks are enticing. Copper Pheasants are common near Miyaji in Aso National Park.

446

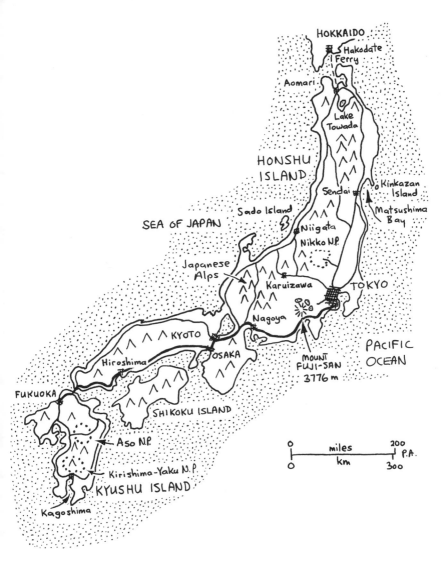

CHECKLIST

Red-throated Loon   W
Black-throated Loon   c W
Yellow-billed Loon   r W
Little Dabchick   c
Horned Grebe   r W
Black-necked Grebe   W

Red-necked Grebe   W
Great Crested Grebe   r W
Black-footed Albatross   M
Laysan Albatross   M
Northern Fulmar   r W
Streaked Shearwater   c

447

Pale-footed Shearwater   r M
Sooty Shearwater   r M
Short-tailed Shearwater   r M
Band-rumped Storm-Petrel   S
Leach's Storm-Petrel   S
Swinhoe's Storm-Petrel   S
Great Cormorant   c
Temminck's Cormorant   c W
Pelagic Cormorant   c W
Gray Heron   c
Cattle Heron   S
Eastern Reef-Heron   r
Great Egret   S
Short-billed Egret
Little Egret   c
Japanese Night-Heron   S
Black-crowned Night-Heron   c
Yellow Bittern   S
Schrenck's Bittern   S
Eurasian Bittern   r W
White Stork   r
Black Stork   r W
Japanese Crested Ibis   r
Eurasian Spoonbill   r W
Black-faced Spoonbill   r W
Whooper Swan   W
Bewick's Swan   r W
Swan Goose   r W
Bean Goose   W
White-fronted Goose   W
Lesser White-fronted Goose   r W
Snow Goose   r W
Brent Goose   r W
Ruddy Shelduck   r W
Northern Pintail   c W
Green-winged Teal   c W
Baikal Teal   c W
Spot-billed Duck   c
Mallard   c W
Gadwall   W
Falcated Teal   c W
Eurasian Wigeon   c W
Garganey   r M
Northern Shoveler
Northern Pochard   r W
Tufted Duck   c W
Greater Scaup   c W

Mandarin Duck
Common Goldeneye   c W
Long-tailed Duck   r W
Harlequin Duck   W
Black Scoter   c W
White-winged Scoter   c W
Smew   W
Red-breasted Merganser   c W
Goosander   W
Osprey
Eurasian Honey-Buzzard   S
Black Kite   c
White-tailed Sea-Eagle   r W
Marsh Harrier   W
Northern Harrier   r W
Northern Goshawk
Japanese Sparrowhawk   S
Eurasian Sparrowhawk
Gray-faced Buzzard   S
Common Buzzard   c
Golden Eagle   r
Mountain Hawk-Eagle   S
Common Kestrel
Merlin   W
European Hobby   r W
Peregrine Falcon   W
Rock Ptarmigan   r
Japanese Quail
Chinese Bamboo-Partridge   c
Green Pheasant   c
Copper Pheasant
Hooded Crane   r W
White-naped Crane   r W
Water Rail   W
Baillon's Crake   r
Ruddy-breasted Crake   S
Watercock   r S
Common Gallinule   c
Common Coot   c
Greater Painted-snipe
Common Oystercatcher   r W
Northern Lapwing   W
Gray-headed Lapwing   r
Gray Plover   c M
Lesser Golden Plover   c M
Little Ringed Plover
Snowy Plover   c S

Long-billed Plover   S
Mongolian Plover   M
Great Sand Plover   r M
Eurasian Curlew   c M
Whimbrel   c M
Little Curlew   r M
Eastern Curlew   c M
Bar-tailed Godwit   c M
Spotted Redshank   c M
Common Redshank   r M
Marsh Sandpiper   r M
Common Greenshank   c M
Nordmann's Greenshank   r M
Green Sandpiper   M
Wood Sandpiper   M
Terek Sandpiper   M
Common Sandpiper
Gray-tailed Tattler   c M
Ruddy Turnstone   c M
Solitary Snipe   W
Pintail Snipe   r M
Swinhoe's Snipe   M
Japanese Snipe   S
Common Snipe   W
Jack Snipe   r W
Eurasian Woodcock
Red Knot   r M
Great Knot   M
Red-necked Stint   c M
Temminck's Stint   r M
Long-toed Stint   r M
Sharp-tailed Sandpiper   M
Pectoral Sandpiper   r M
Dunlin   c W
Curlew Sandpiper   r M
Sanderling   M
Spoon-billed Sandpiper   r M
Broad-billed Sandpiper   r M
Ruff   r M
Red Phalarope   r M
Little Phalarope   M
Great Thick-Knee
Oriental Pratincole   r M
Pomarine Jaeger   M
Parasitic Jaeger   r M
Long-tailed Jaeger   r M
Great Skua   r M

Black-tailed Gull   c
Mew Gull   W
Herring Gull   c W
Slaty-backed Gull   c W
Glaucous Gull   r W
Black-headed Gull   c W
Black-legged Kittiwake   c W
Common Tern   c M
Little Tern   c S
Thick-billed Murre   r W
Common Murre   c W
Sooty Guillemot   W
Marbled Murrelet   W
Ancient Murrelet   c W
Japanese Murrelet
Crested Auklet   W
Least Auklet   r W
Rhinoceros Auklet   c S
Horned Puffin   r W
Tufted Puffin   r W
White-bellied Green-Pigeon
Oriental Turtle-Dove   c
Collared Turtle-Dove   r
Hodgson's Hawk-Cuckoo   S
Eurasian Cuckoo   c W
Oriental Cuckoo   S
Lesser Cuckoo   S
Eurasian Scops-Owl   S
Collared Scops-Owl
Brown Hawk-Owl   S
Ural Owl
Long-eared Owl   r
Short-eared Owl   r W
Gray Nightjar   S
Fork-tailed Swift   c S
Crested Kingfisher   c
Eurasian Kingfisher   c
Ruddy Kingfisher   S
Eurasian Wryneck   W
Japanese Green Woodpecker
Black Woodpecker   r
Great Spotted Woodpecker
White-backed Woodpecker
Japanese Pygmy Woodpecker   c
Blue-winged Pitta   r S
Northern Skylark   c
Sand Martin   M

Barn Swallow   c S
Red-rumped Swallow   c S
Asian Martin   c S
Ashy Minivet   S
Brown-eared Bulbul   c
Eurasian Jay   c
Black-billed Magpie
Azure-winged Magpie   c
Eurasian Nutcracker
Rook   W
Eurasian Crow   c
Large-billed Crow   c
Long-tailed Tit   c
Great Tit   c
Varied Tit   c
Willow Tit
Coal Tit   c
Eurasian Nuthatch
Northern Treecreeper
Brown Dipper
Northern Wren
Japanese Robin   S
Siberian Rubythroat   M
Siberian Blue-Robin   S
Orange-flanked Bush-Robin
Daurian Redstart   c W
Stonechat   S
Siberian Thrush   r S
Blue Rock-Thrush   c
Scaly Thrush
Japanese Thrush   S
Pale Thrush   W
Eye-browed Thrush   c M
Dusky Thrush   c W
Brown-headed Thrush
Arctic Warbler   S
Pale-legged Leaf-Warbler   c S
Eastern Crowned Warbler   c S
Great Reed-Warbler   c S
Black-browed Reed-Warbler   S
Pallas's Grasshopper-Warbler   r S
Lanceolated Warbler   S
Gray's Grasshopper-Warbler   M
Zitting Cisticola   c S
Stub-tailed Bush-Warbler   S
Japanese Bush-Warbler   c

Japanese Grass-Warbler   r S
Goldcrest
Dark-sided Flycatcher   S
Gray-streaked Flycatcher   r M
Asian Brown Flycatcher   c S
Narcissus Flycatcher   c S
Mugimaki Flycatcher   r M
Blue-and-white Flycatcher   c S
Black Paradise-Flycatcher   S
Alpine Accentor   r
Japanese Accentor
White Wagtail   c W
Japanese Wagtail   c
Gray Wagtail   c
Olive-backed Pipit   c
Water Pipit   c W
Bohemian Waxwing   W
Brown Shrike   S
Bull-headed Shrike   c
Tiger Shrike   S
Purple-backed Starling   S
White-cheeked Starling   c
Japanese White-eye   c
Tree Sparrow   c
Cinnamon Sparrow   c W
Brambling   c W
Oriental Greenfinch   c
Eurasian Siskin   c W
Common Redpoll   W
Pallas's Rosefinch   W
Long-tailed Rosy-Finch   W
Arctic Rosy-Finch   r W
Red Crossbill
Hawfinch   c W
Yellow-billed Grosbeak   c
Gray-hooded Bunting
Yellow-throated Bunting   W
Pine Bunting   r W
Rustic Bunting   c W
Gray Bunting
Japanese Yellow Bunting
Meadow Bunting
Black-faced Bunting   c
Marsh Bunting   r
Reed Bunting   c W

89
Beijing (Peking), China

BEIJING, THE POLITICAL AND CULTURAL CAPITAL OF CHINA, with over 7 million inhabitants, is now the most often visited Chinese city for westerners and many are encouraged to see some of the sights outside the city. The most recent published report on Beijing's birdlife dates from World War I. Since this area is now becoming a popular destination for tourists, we feel these "ancient" records will be of use and interest (even if only historical interest) to visiting birders.

The four-seasons climate has long cold winters, warm and rainy summers, and pleasant months in between. The annual rainfall is about 25 inches (635 mm).

The Great Plain of China stretches to the south and east of Beijing. In agricultural areas, along canals, ponds, and fallow fields waterfowl, hawks, shorebirds, pipits, thrushes, and buntings are often in evidence. About 6.2 miles (10 km) northwest of Beijing, both the Summer Palace, situated on a large lake, and adjacent Jade Spring Hill should have some of the foothill forest birds and waterfowl.

The Ming Tombs and the Great Wall lie about 31.3 miles (50 km) northwest and are often visited on day trips from Beijing. Both are in mountainous country with birdlife somewhat different from that of the plains. If forests can be visited in the mountains, look for Forest Wagtail, Chinese Bush-Warbler, tits, Rock Bunting, and Oriental Greenfinch. Along rivers look for the rare Ibisbill and Brown Dipper.

Any existing protected forest area on the plains would be of great interest. Oak forests in the lowlands hold a number of woodpeckers, nuthatches, and tits not found in the hills.

Note: This is one of a very few localities not visited by either author or our collaborators. The material was gathered from sources researched over 50 years ago and is presented with the hope that it will aid birders caught up in the recent surge in tourism to the area. As anywhere, many changes in the birdlife will have occurred over such a period of time.

CHECKLIST

Little Dabchick	Garganey M
Great Cormorant M	Northern Shoveler M
Gray Heron	Northern Pochard M
Black-crowned Night-Heron c S	Baer's Pochard r W
Yellow Bittern c S	Tufted Duck c M
Whooper Swan M	Mandarin Duck S H
Bewick's Swan M	Smew c M
Bean Goose c W	Goosander W
Ruddy Shelduck W	Osprey M
Northern Pintail M	Black Kite c
Green-winged Teal c M	Marsh Harrier M
Baikal Teal M	Northern Harrier M
Spot-billed Duck M	Pied Harrier M
Mallard c	Eurasian Sparrowhawk
Falcated Teal M	Upland Hawk r H

Greater Spotted Eagle   M
Common Kestrel
Amur Falcon   c M L, r S H
Merlin   c M
Japanese Quail
Chukar Partridge   c H
Green Pheasant   H
Reeve's Pheasant   r H
Yellow-legged Buttonquail   r L
Great Bustard   W
Northern Lapwing   c M
Gray-headed Lapwing   M
Lesser Golden Plover   M
Little Ringed Plover   M
Great Sand Plover   M
Common Redshank   c M
Common Greenshank   M
Green Sandpiper   M
Wood Sandpiper   M
Common Sandpiper   M
Solitary Snipe   W
Common Snipe   W
Eurasian Woodcock   M
Red-necked Stint   M
Long-toed Stint   M
Ibisbill   H
Herring Gull   M
Black-headed Gull   M
White-winged Black Tern   M
Oriental Turtle-Dove
Collared Turtle-Dove
Red Turtle-Dove   S H
Spotted Turtle-Dove
Eurasian Cuckoo   c S
Northern Eagle-Owl   r W
Little Owl   M
Eurasian Swift   c S
Fork-tailed Swift   M L, S H
Common Kingfisher   r
Black-capped Kingfisher   S
Hoopoe   S
Gray-headed Woodpecker
Great Spotted Woodpecker
Crested Lark   c S H
Northern Skylark   c W
Sand Martin   M
Northern Crag-Martin   S H

Barn Swallow   c S
Red-rumped Swallow   c S
Asian Martin   S
Black Drongo   c S
Spangled Drongo   S H
Black-naped Oriole   c S
Eurasian Jay   H
Black-billed Magpie   c
Azure-winged Magpie
Red-billed Chough   c H
Daurian Jackdaw   W L, M H
Rook   c
Large-billed Crow   c
Collared Crow   c
Long-tailed Tit   W L, S H
Great Tit
Coal Tit   c W L, c H
Eurasian Nuthatch   H
Chinese Nuthatch   L
Wallcreeper   r M H
Brown Dipper   H
Northern Wren
Pere David's Laughing-thrush   c
   H
Vinous-throated Parrotbill   W L,
   c H
Siberian Rubythroat   c M
Bluethroat   M
Siberian Blue-Robin   M
Orange-flanked Bush-Robin   M
Daurian Redstart   c M
Plumbeous Water-Redstart   S H
Pied Wheatear   M L, r S H
Blue Rock-Thrush   S H
Red-throated Thrush   r W
Dusky Thrush   c W
Yellow-browed Warbler   c M
Pallas's Leaf-Warbler   c M
Arctic Warbler   c M
Eastern Crowned Warbler   M
Clamorous Reed-Warbler   c M
Great Reed-Warbler   c S
Black-browed Reed-Warbler   c S
   L
Paddyfield Warbler   r S L
Chinese Bush-Warbler   c H
Asian Brown Flycatcher   c M

453

Narcissus Flycatcher   r S H
Red-breasted Flycatcher   c M
Asian Paradise-Flycatcher   r M
   L, r S H
Siberian Accentor   c W
White Wagtail
Yellow Wagtail   c M
Citrine Wagtail   r M
Forest Wagtail   c S H
Tree Pipit   c M
Richard's Pipit   r M
Water Pipit   c W H
Brown Shrike   S H
Bull-headed Shrike   S H
White-cheeked Starling   c W L
Tree Sparrow   c
Brambling   c W H
Oriental Greenfinch   c H

Eurasian Siskin   r W
Common Redpoll   r W
Scarlet Rosefinch   c M H
Pallas's Rosefinch   W
Hawfinch   W
Rock Bunting   c H
Little Bunting   W
Yellow-browed Bunting   M
Yellow-throated Bunting   W
Yellow-breasted Bunting   c M
Pine Bunting   c W
Rustic Bunting   W
Chestnut Bunting   r M H
Meadow Bunting
Black-faced Bunting   c M
Pallas's Bunting   c W L
Lapland Longspur   c W

90

Shanghai, China

ONE OF THE WORLD'S LARGEST CITIES, Shanghai is located near the mouth of the Yangtze River near the East China Sea. It is actually on the Huang-p'u River, a tributary of the Yangtze. The trickle of businessmen and tourists visiting Shanghai will probably increase and include birders. What changes have occurred in the last decades and which areas have been preserved or are open to birding tourists is of much interest. This account draws upon pre-1945 material.

In the city, including the People's Park, which has many trees, look for Black Kite, Spotted Dove, Barn Swallow, Chinese Bulbul, Tree Sparrow, Crested Myna, Rook, and Large-billed Crow.

Many birds live in the suburban areas where trees, shrubs, and ponds remain. On the fringes and farther out in the wheat and rice areas some of the following might be seen in season: Yellow Bittern, Chinese Pond-Heron, Indian Cuckoo, Vinous-throated Parrotbill, Long-tailed Tit, Black-billed Magpie, Azure-winged Magpie, Eurasian Blackbird, Pale Thrush, Japanese Bush-Warbler, White-cheeked Starling, Hawfinch, and Gray-headed Bunting.

Migration and winter birding can be exciting. Many Korean, Japanese, and Siberian migrants funnel down the coast or fly across the sea to this area of easternmost China. An island at the mouth of the Yangtze, previously known as Shaweishan Island, has an impressive list of birds, including thrushes and Japanese Robin. At Woosung, north of Shanghai on the Yangtze estuary, there may be large wintering rafts of ducks as well as Whooper and Bewick's Swans.

CHECKLIST

Great Crested Grebe   W
Spot-billed Pelican
Dalmatian Pelican   W
Great Cormorant
Gray Heron   c
Green Heron   c S
Chinese Pond-Heron   c

Cattle Heron   S
Yellow Bittern   r S
Schrenck's Bittern   r S
Cinnamon Bittern   r S
Eurasian Bittern   c S
Whooper Swan   c W
Bewick's Swan   W

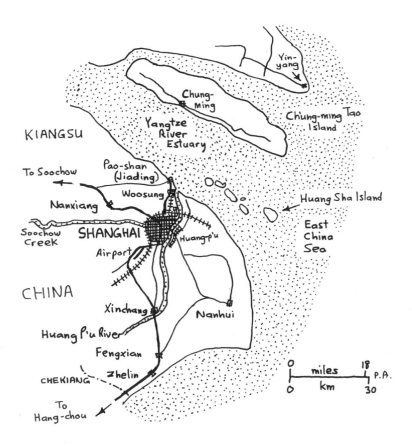

Swan Goose   r W
Bean Goose   W
White-fronted Goose   r W
Graylag Goose   r W
Common Shelduck   c W
Northern Pintail   c W
Green-winged Teal   c W
Baikal Teal   r W
Spot-billed Duck   c W
Mallard   c W
Falcated Teal   c W
Garganey
Northern Shoveler   r W
Northern Pochard   W
Baer's Pochard   W
Tufted Duck   c W

Greater Scaup   W
Mandarin Duck   c W
White-winged Scoter   W
Smew   c W
Red-breasted Merganser   W
Goosander   W
Osprey
Northern Harrier   W
Eurasian Sparrowhawk   c W
Common Buzzard   r W
Upland Buzzard   c W
Common Kestrel
Peregrine Falcon   W
Japanese Quail   W
Chinese Bamboo-Partridge   r
Green Pheasant   r

456

Yellow-legged Buttonquail   S
Water Rail   W
White-breasted Waterhen   S
Watercock
Common Gallinule
Common Coot   c W
Greater Painted-snipe   r M
Northern Lapwing   c W
Lesser Golden Plover   M
Little Ringed Plover   S
Snowy Plover   M
Long-billed Plover   r
Mongolian Plover   M
Great Sand Plover   M
Whimbrel   M
Little Curlew   M
Eastern Curlew   c M
Common Redshank   M
Common Greenshank   W
Green Sandpiper   M
Wood Sandpiper   r M
Terek Sandpiper   M
Ruddy Turnstone   r W
Solitary Snipe   M
Pintail Snipe   c M
Swinhoe's Snipe   M
Common Snipe   c W
Eurasian Woodcock   W
Red Knot   r M
Great Knot   r M
Red-necked Stint   M
Temminck's Stint   r M
Long-toed Stint   r M
Sharp-tailed Sandpiper   M
Dunlin   r W
Curlew Sandpiper   W
Spoon-billed Sandpiper   r M
Mew Gull   W
Herring Gull   r W
Black-headed Gull   c W
Little Tern   c S
Oriental Turtle-Dove
Red Turtle-Dove   S
Spotted Turtle-Dove   c
Large Hawk-Cuckoo   r M
Indian Cuckoo   c S
Eurasian Cuckoo   S

Asian Barred Owlet
Short-eared Owl   W
Fork-tailed Swift   r M
Eurasian Kingfisher
Black-capped Kingfisher   r M
Hoopoe   r M
Eurasian Wryneck   M
Gray-headed Woodpecker
Great Spotted Woodpecker   c
Blue-winged Pitta   r M
Northern Skylark   W
Sand Martin   c M
Barn Swallow   c S
Dark Cuckoo-shrike   r M
Chinese Bulbul   c
Black-naped Oriole   S
Black-billed Magpie   c
Azure-winged Magpie   c
Daurian Jackdaw   W
Rook   c
Large-billed Crow
Collared Crow
Long-tailed Tit   c
Great Tit   c
Masked Laughing-thrush   c
Hwamei Laughing-thrush
Vinous-throated Parrotbill   c
Siberian Rubythroat   M
Siberian Blue-Robin   M
Asian Magpie Robin   r
Daurian Redstart   W
Siberian Thrush   W
Blue Rock-Thrush   M
Scaly Thrush   W
Gray-backed Thrush   W
Eurasian Blackbird   c
Pale Thrush   c W
Dusky Thrush   c W
Yellow-browed Warbler   c M
Arctic Warbler   M
Eastern Crowned Warbler   r M
Great Reed-Warbler   S
Black-browed Reed-Warbler   S
Pallas's Grasshopper-Warbler   M
Middendorf's Warbler   M
Zitting Cisticola   c S
Japanese Bush-Warbler   c S

Asian Brown Flycatcher   M
Yellow-rumped Flycatcher   c M
Narcissus Flycatcher   S
Red-breasted Flycatcher   M
Asian Paradise-Flycatcher   S
White Wagtail   c W
Gray Wagtail   c M
Yellow Wagtail   M
Olive-backed Pipit   r W
Richard's Pipit   r M
Red-throated Pipit   W
Water Pipit   W
Brown Shrike   S
Bull-headed Shrike   r W
Tiger Shrike   S
Schach Shrike   r W

White-cheeked Starling   c W
Crested Myna   c
Tree Sparrow   c
White-rumped Munia   c
Brambling   W
Eurasian Siskin   r W
Hawfinch   r W
Yellow-billed Grosbeak   c
Little Bunting   W
Yellow-throated Bunting   r W
Yellow-breasted Bunting   M
Rustic Bunting   c W
Chestnut Bunting   M
Black-faced Bunting   c W
Pallas's Bunting   c W
Marsh Bunting   c W

91
Taiwan

A BIRDING TOUR TO THE FAR EAST should not overlook Taiwan, the island Republic of China. Here is a land of contrasts, from bustling crowded cities to sparsely populated areas in majestic mountainous regions with much original habitat still intact.

Modern facilities and efficient transportation systems provide ready access from the northern capital Taipei to most places. However, parts of the island are restricted, and permits would be required in advance. While it is not necessary to visit these areas for birding, you may encounter signs marking restricted areas. To overcome language difficulties that could cause problems outside of Taipei, consult a local tourist-information office when planning an itinerary.

One-day trips out of Taipei can be arranged by bus to several places where birding opportunities are good. The Wulai area has an amusement park complex that provides access to forested areas; Yangming-shaw Park, overlooking Taipei, offers gardens and adjacent forest areas with good birding in the early morning; a trip to the coastal harbor towns of Keelung and Yehliu may provide some new birds. Other areas near Taipei that are worth visiting include Chinshan (paddy fields and open areas) and Kuantu (marshlands and mudflats).

Kenting Botanical Park, near the extreme south of Taiwan, has nature trails and a large variety of birds can be found. A stopover on the way at Kaohsiung for a visit to Cheng Ching Lake could provide an opportunity to see migratory waterfowl. For mountain birds, a visit to the village of Alishan is recommended. Access is by narrow-gauge railway from Chiayi. A 5–7-hour trip by a switchback system takes you over 7000 feet (2133 m). Many hotels are available here and numerous trails wind around the area, which is set up as a Chinese tourist resort.

Two other popular attractions that can be good for birding are Taroko Gorge and Sun Moon Lake. Flights are available to the gorge, making it a comfortable day trip from Taipei. Landslides, which can close roads, make the west-east bus services undependable for tight schedules. Sun Moon Lake is Taiwan's Niagara Falls, offering hotels and recreation facilities, with many birds easily found along walkways.

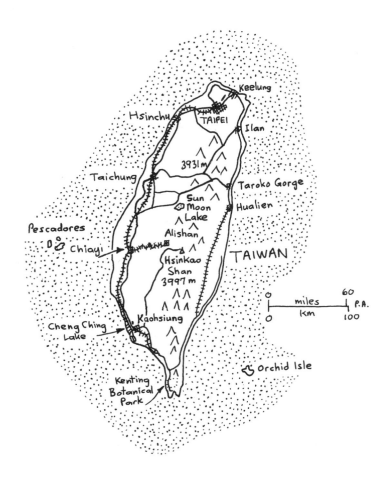

CHECKLIST

Little Dabchick
Great Cormorant   c W
Lesser Frigatebird   r S
Gray Heron   W
Great Egret   W
Little Egret   c
Eastern Reef-Heron
Cattle Heron   c
Green Heron
Cinnamon Bittern
Yellow Bittern   c
Black-crowned Night-Heron

Northern Pintail   c W
Northern Shoveler   c W
Green-winged Teal   c W
Eurasian Wigeon   W
Mallard   W
Spot-billed Duck   c W
Garganey   c W
Tufted Duck   c W
Chinese Goshawk   M
Crested Goshawk
Asiatic Sparrowhawk   M
Gray-faced Buzzard   M

Marsh Harrier   W
Northern Harrier   W
Black Kite   c
Crested Serpent-Eagle
Osprey
Common Kestrel   c   W
Formosan Hill Partridge   c
Chinese Bamboo Partridge   c
Swinhoe's Pheasant   r
Ring-necked Pheasant
Mikado Pheasant   r   H
Barred Buttonquail
White-breasted Waterhen   c
Common Coot   W
Watercock   r   S
Common Gallinule   c
Ruddy-breasted Crake
Slaty-breasted Rail
Greater Painted-snipe
Snowy Plover
Lesser Golden Plover   W
Little Ringed Plover   c   W
Gray Plover   W
Northern Lapwing   W
Common Sandpiper   c
Dunlin   c   W
Red-necked Stint   W
Long-toed Stint   W
Temminck's Stint   W
Common Snipe   c   W
Swinhoe's Snipe   c   W
Pintail Snipe   c   W
Wandering Tattler   M
Ruddy Turnstone   W
Black-tailed Godwit   W
Eurasian Curlew   W
Whimbrel   W
Wood Sandpiper   W
Common Greenshank   c   W
Green Sandpiper   W
Oriental Pratincole
Black-headed Gull   c   W
Whiskered Tern   W
Gull-billed Tern   M
Caspian Tern   W
Little Tern   W
Greater Crested Tern   S

Green-winged Pigeon
Spotted Turtle-Dove   c
Oriental Turtle-Dove
Red Turtle-Dove   c   S
Ashy Pigeon
White-bellied Green-Pigeon   c
Lesser Coucal   c
Oriental Cuckoo   S
Large Hawk-Cuckoo   S
Collared Scops-Owl
Mountain Scops-Owl   H
Brown Wood-Owl   H
Savanna Nightjar
House Swift   c
Fork-tailed Swift
White-throated Needletail   H
Eurasian Kingfisher   c
Black-browed Barbet   c
Gray-capped Woodpecker
White-backed Woodpecker   H
Gray-headed Woodpecker   H
Blue-winged Pitta   r   H
Oriental Skylark   c
Asian Martin   c
Barn Swallow   c
Red-rumped Swallow   c
Pacific Swallow   c (south)
Plain Martin
Dark Cuckoo-shrike
Black Drongo   c
Bronzed Drongo   H
Black-naped Oriole
Maroon Oriole
Large-billed Crow
Gray Treepie   c
Eurasian Jay
Eurasian Nutcracker   H
Black-billed Magpie
Formosan Blue Magpie
Red-headed Tit   c
Coal Tit   c
Yellow Tit   r   H
Green-backed Tit   H
Varied Tit
Eurasian Nuthatch   c   H
Black-throated Parrotbill   H
Vinous-throated Parrotbill   c

Formosan Barwing   c H
Brown-eared Fulvetta   c H
Streak-throated Fulvetta   H
Gray-cheeked Fulvetta   c
White-throated Laughing-thrush
Gray-sided Laughing-thrush
Hwamei Laughing-thrush
Formosan Laughing-thrush   H
White-eared Sibia   c
Steere's Babbler   c
Pygmy Wren-Babbler   H
Spot-breasted Scimitar-Babbler   M
Rufous-necked Scimitar-Babbler   c
Rufous-capped Babbler   c
Formosan Yuhina   c
White-bellied Yuhina
Ashy Minivet
Gray-throated Minivet   c H
Brown-eared Bulbul
Black Bulbul   c
Chinese Bulbul   c
Styan's Bulbul
Collared Finch-billed Bulbul   c
Brown Dipper
Northern Wren   c
Little Forktail   H
Siberian Rubythroat   c W
Blue Rock-Thrush
White-tailed Robin   H
Formosan Whistling-Thrush   c H
Daurian Redstart   W
Plumbeous Water-Redstart   c H
Orange-flanked Bush-Robin
White-browed Bush-Robin   H
Johnstone's Bush-Robin   c H
Brown-headed Thrush   c W
Dusky Thrush   W
Pale Thrush   W
Island Thrush   r H
Scaly Thrush
Great Reed-Warbler   c W

Yellow-bellied Bush-Warbler   H
Chinese Bush-Warbler
Strong-footed Bush-Warbler   H
Golden-headed Cisticola
Zitting Cisticola   c
Arctic Warbler   W
Yellow-bellied Prinia   c
Brown Prinia
Tawny-flanked Prinia   c
Formosan Firecrest   H
White-throated Warbler   c
Black-naped Blue Flycatcher   c
Gray-spotted Flycatcher   W
Snowy-browed Flycatcher   H
Ferruginous Flycatcher   c H
Dark-sided Flycatcher   r M
Vivid Niltava   H
Alpine Accentor   H
Red-throated Pipit   c W
Olive-backed Pipit   c W
White Wagtail   c
Gray Wagtail
Yellow Wagtail   c W
Brown Shrike   c M
Schach Shrike   c
Crested Myna
Purple-backed Starling   W
White-shouldered Starling   W
Fire-breasted Flowerpecker   c H
Japanese White-eye   c
Black-headed Munia   r
Spotted Munia   c
White-rumped Munia   c
Tree Sparrow   c
Cinnamon Sparrow   H
Eurasian Siskin   W H
Vinaceous Rosefinch   c H
Black-faced Bunting   c W
Beavan's Bullfinch   H
Brown Bullfinch   c H

92
Hong Kong

HONG KONG IS A THRIVING AND BUSTLING CITY, a British Crown Colony, and represents the only place in the great region of China where bird watchers can go about their business without let or hindrance. Nevertheless several of the better areas are adjacent to the Chinese border and caution should be exercised in such a delicate situation.

Because of its geographical position, rather than any particularly attractive areas, Hong Kong offers birds that are rare or impossible to see elsewhere. Chinese Egret, for example, is not only very rare, but very local in range. There are good marshes that attract a variety of eastern Palearctic waders in April and September–October. Here it is possible to see the elusive Asiatic Dowitcher, Nordmann's Greenshank, and Spoon-billed Sandpiper. During the breeding season the egretries are a major attraction and altogether 350 species have been recorded, though only 67 breed regularly.

Stopover visitors should take the Peak Tram to the top of Hong Kong Island and explore the many paths for typical birds. Those with more time in the months of May through July should visit the egretry at Yim Tso Ha near Sha Tau Kok at the eastern end of the land border with China. Take a car via Shatin, Taipo, and Plover Cove Reservoir. The egretry is next to the road and has a few pairs of Chinese Egrets.

Best area at any season are the Mai Po Marshes at the west end of the land border with China. This is a regular 50-plus species spot and excellent for migrant waders. A permit, required to wander into prohibited areas near the border, is obtainable from the Agriculture and Fisheries Department, 393 Canton Road, Kowloon.

For woodland birds try the Tai Po Kau Forestry Reserve, reached by train from Kowloon Station. Take the road from the station at Tai Po Kau to the main road, turn left, and continue to a small park on the right. The Forest Reserve lies through the park. There are well-signposted paths. Try to get a very early start as it gets crowded here, particularly on weekends. Additional spots for woodland birding include the woods around Jubilee Reservoir (east of Tsuen Wan), the top of the road to Tai Mo Shan Mountain, and the area of Shek Kong

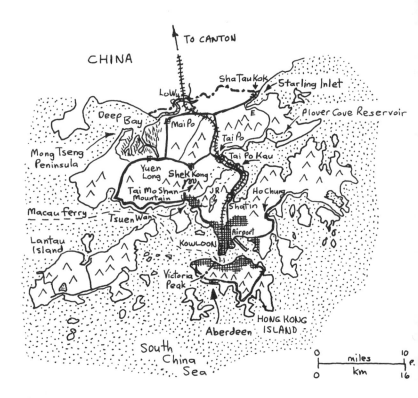

To CANTON

CHINA

ShaTauKok
Starling Inlet
LoWu
Plover Cove Reservoir
Deep Bay
Mai Po
E
Tai Po
Mong Tseng Peninsula
Tai Po Kau
Yuen Long
Shek Kong
Ho Chung
Tai Mo Shan Mountain
JR
Macau Ferry
Tsuen Wan
Shatin
Lantau Island
Airport
Kowloon
Victoria Peak
HONG KONG ISLAND
Aberdeen
South China Sea
miles
km

village, along with the Lam Tsuen Valley, which runs northeastward from Shek Kong. The Mong Tseng Peninsula in the northwest has large areas of scrubland and marsh overlooking Deep Bay.

Visitors may wish to contact the Hong Kong Bird Watching Society, c/o Zoology Department, University of Hong Kong, Hong Kong.

CHECKLIST

Great Crested Grebe   c W
Spot-billed Pelican   W
Great Cormorant   W
Gray Heron   c W
Purple Heron   r M
Green Heron   r S
Chinese Pond-Heron   c
Cattle Heron   c S
Eastern Reef-Heron
Chinese Egret   S

Great Egret   W
Little Egret
Black-crowned Night-Heron   M
Yellow Bittern   c S
Cinnamon Bittern   S
Eurasian Bittern   r W
Green-winged Teal   c W
Spot-billed Duck   c W
Falcated Teal   W
Red-breasted Merganser   r W

Goosander   W
Osprey   r   W
Black Kite   c
White-bellied Sea-Eagle   c
Marsh Harrier   W
Pied Harrier   r   W
Eurasian Sparrowhawk   W
Common Buzzard   W
Greater Spotted Eagle   W
Common Kestrel   c   W
European Hobby   W
Peregrine Falcon
Chinese Francolin   c
Japanese Quail   M
Slaty-breasted Rail
White-breasted Waterhen   c
Common Gallinule
Common Coot   r   W
Greater Painted-snipe   r   W
Little Ringed Plover   M
Snowy Plover   c   W
Mongolian Plover   r   M
Great Sand Plover   M
Eurasian Curlew   W
Whimbrel   M
Spotted Redshank   W
Common Redshank   M
Marsh Sandpiper   r   M
Asiatic Dowitcher   r   M
Nordmann's Greenshank   r   M
Common Greenshank   r   M
Green Sandpiper   W
Wood Sandpiper   M
Terek Sandpiper   M
Common Sandpiper   c
Gray-tailed Tattler   r   M
Ruddy Turnstone   M
Pintail Snipe   W
Swinhoe's Snipe   W
Eurasian Woodcock   W
Red-necked Stint   M
Temminck's Stint   r   W
Dunlin   W
Curlew Sandpiper   M
Sanderling   M
Spoon-billed Sandpiper   r   M
Broad-billed Sandpiper   M

Little Phalarope   M
Oriental Pratincole   r   M
Black-tailed Gull   W
Herring Gull   W
Black-headed Gull   c   W
Gull-billed Tern   r   M
Caspian Tern   W
Oriental Turtle-Dove   W
Red Turtle-Dove   c   M
Spotted Turtle-Dove   c
Rose-ringed Parakeet
Indian Cuckoo   S
Eurasian Cuckoo   S
Plaintive Cuckoo   S
Common Koel
Greater Coucal
Lesser Coucal   r
Collared Scops-Owl
Gray Nightjar   r   M
Savanna Nightjar   r   M
Fork-tailed Swift   M
House Swift   r   S
Pied Kingfisher   c
Eurasian Kingfisher
White-breasted Kingfisher
Black-capped Kingfisher
Great Himalayan Barbet
Eurasian Wryneck   W
Oriental Skylark   W
Sand Martin   M
Barn Swallow   S
Red-rumped Swallow   M
Dark Cuckoo-shrike   W
Red-whiskered Bulbul   c
Chinese Bulbul   c
Red-vented Bulbul
Chestnut Bulbul   M
Black Drongo   c   S
Spangled Drongo   S
Black-naped Oriole   S
Eurasian Jay   M
Red-billed Blue Magpie   c
Black-billed Magpie   c
Large-billed Crow   r
Collared Crow
Great Tit
Masked Laughing-thrush   c

Black-throated Laughing-thrush r
Hwamei Laughing-thrush
Orange-flanked Bush-Robin W
Asian Magpie-Robin c
Daurian Redstart c W
Stonechat W
Chestnut-bellied Rock-Thrush W
Blue Rock-Thrush W
Blue Whistling-Thrush
Gray-backed Thrush W
Japanese Thrush M
Eurasian Blackbird W
Dusky Warbler c W
Yellow-browed Warbler W
Pallas's Leaf-Warbler W
Pale-legged Leaf-Warbler M
Great Reed-Warbler M
Black-browed Reed-Warbler r W
Common Tailorbird c
Tawny-flanked Prinia
Yellow-bellied Prinia
Brown Prinia
Zitting Cisticola
Stub-tailed Bush Warbler r W
Japanese Bush-Warbler W
Gray-streaked Flycatcher r M
Asian Brown Flycatcher W
Red-breasted Flycatcher W
Blue-and-white Flycatcher M

Asian Paradise-Flycatcher M
White Wagtail W
Gray Wagtail c W
Yellow Wagtail W
Forest Wagtail M
Olive-backed Pipit W
Richard's Pipit
Red-throated Pipit W
Upland Pipit r
Brown Shrike W
Schach Shrike c
Silky Starling W
White-shouldered Starling S
White-cheeked Starling r W
Black-collared Starling
Indian Myna r
Crested Myna
Fork-tailed Sunbird
Fire-breasted Flowerpecker r
Japanese White-eye
Tree Sparrow c
Spotted Munia c
Oriental Greenfinch
Yellow-billed Grosbeak r W
Gray-hooded Bunting W
Little Bunting W
Black-faced Bunting c W
Crested Bunting

93

Khao Yai National Park, Thailand

KHAO YAI COVERS forest-clad hills some 103 miles (205 km) north-east of Bangkok. Formerly a wild area beloved of outlaws, the park is now something of a playground for the more affluent inhabitants of the capital who flock out in their cars to enjoy the scenery, water falls, and golf. But this should not deter the bird watcher. There are plenty of wilderness areas and the arrival of tourism has resulted in excellent accommodation and facilities. It is perhaps the best tropical-forest birding in southeast Asia that is easily accessible.

Around the park headquarters and Khao Yai Motor Lodge the forest has been cleared, but it is only a short journey to pristine forest. There are plenty of birds and the lodge organizes nocturnal game-viewing trips that might produce a bird or two. There is also a wildlife watch tower, but special permission must be obtained from the Royal Forest Department.

Birds are plentiful and varied. Wetland species include Darter, Cinnamon Bittern, Pied Harrier, Gray-headed Fishing-Eagle, and White-breasted Waterhen, but raptors are varied and there are hosts of pigeons and doves to be found. There are seven cuckoos, six kingfishers, four bee-eaters, twelve woodpeckers, three broadbills, the Lesser Blue Pitta, hosts of warblers including no less than nine species of *Phylloscopus,* seven species of sunbirds, and so on. With such a wealth it is difficult to pick out individual species. Without a doubt the most impressive bird is the fantastic Great Hornbill, which can be seen even near the lodge.

The drive to Khao Yai takes three to four hours, all on paved roads. Leave the city on Paholythin Highway, pass the Don Muang Airport, and continue to Saraburi. Continue on the Friendship Highway and start bird watching among the forests. Turn right before Pak Chong and take the winding road through the hills to Nong Khing on the high grassy plateau. For bookings for bungalows and motel write to Khao Yai Motor Lodge, PO Box 11, Pak Chong, Nakhou Ratchasima. A dormitory and camp ground are also available.

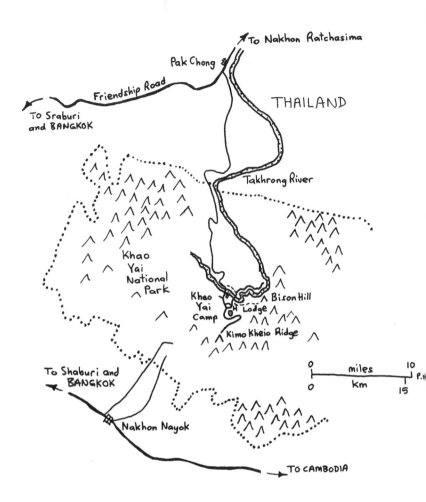

CHECKLIST

Darter c
Green Heron
Chinese Pond-Heron c
Cattle Heron c
Little Egret c
Cinnamon Bittern
Eurasian Honey-Buzzard
Black-shouldered Kite
Gray-headed Fishing-Eagle r
Crested Serpent-Eagle c

Marsh Harrier M
Pied Harrier r W
Japanese Sparrowhawk W
Crested Goshawk
Shikra
Rufous-winged Buzzard r
Black Eagle
Mountain Hawk-Eagle W
Collared (Red-thighed) Falconet
Oriental Hobby

468

Peregrine Falcon   r W
Chinese Francolin
Kalij Pheasant
Silver Pheasant   r
Red Junglefowl   c
Ruddy-breasted Crake
White-breasted Waterhen   c
Marsh Sandpiper   r M
Wedge-tailed Green-Pigeon
Thick-billed Green-Pigeon
Pompadour Green-Pigeon
Yellow-legged Green-Pigeon
Mountain Fruit-Pigeon
Barred Cuckoo-Dove
Red Turtle-Dove   c
Spotted Turtle-Dove   c
Green-winged Pigeon
Rose-breasted Parakeet
Vernal Hanging-Parrot
Chestnut-winged Cuckoo
Plaintive Cuckoo
Drongo Cuckoo
Green-billed Malkoha
Coral-billed Ground-Cuckoo   r
Brown Fish-Owl
Brown Hawk-Owl
Great Eared Nightjar   c
Large-tailed Nightjar
Savanna Nightjar
Himalayan Swiftlet
White-throated Needletail
Brown Needletail
Fork-tailed Swift
House Swift   c
Asian Palm-Swift
Orange-breasted Trogon
Red-headed Trogon
Blue-eared Kingfisher
Stork-billed Kingfisher
Banded Kingfisher
White-breasted Kingfisher   c
Black-capped Kingfisher
Chestnut-headed Bee-eater
Blue-tailed Bee-eater
Blue-throated Bee-eater
Blue-bearded Bee-eater
Dollar Roller

Wreathed Hornbill
Indian Pied Hornbill
Great Hornbill   c
Lineated Barbet   r
Green-eared Barbet
Moustached Barbet   c
Blue-eared Barbet   r
Coppersmith Barbet   r
Rufous Woodpecker   r
Laced Woodpecker
Black-headed Woodpecker
Greater Yellow-naped Woodpecker
Lesser Yellow-naped Woodpecker
Common Golden-backed
   Woodpecker
Bamboo Woodpecker
Black-and-buff Woodpecker
Great Slaty Woodpecker   r
White-bellied Woodpecker
Gray-headed Woodpecker   r
Heart-spotted Woodpecker
Greater Golden-backed
   Woodpecker
Banded Broadbill
Silver-breasted Broadbill
Long-tailed Broadbill
Blue Pitta
Red-winged Flycatcher-shrike
Dark Cuckoo-shrike
Lesser Cuckoo-shrike
Ashy Minivet
Rosy Minivet
Small Minivet   c
Scarlet Minivet   c
Common Iora   c
Great Iora
Golden-fronted Leafbird
Blue-winged Leafbird
Black-crested Yellow Bulbul   c
Red-whiskered Bulbul
Gray-cheeked Bulbul
Gray-eyed Bulbul
Ashy Bulbul
Ashy Drongo
Greater Racquet-tailed Drongo
Black-naped Oriole   c
Slender-billed Oriole

Maroon Oriole
Asian Fairy-Bluebird
Green Magpie
Large-billed Crow
Sultan Tit
Velvet-fronted Nuthatch   c
Puff-throated Babbler
Scaly-crowned Babbler
White-browed Scimitar-Babbler
Striped Tit-Babbler
White-crested Laughing-thrush
Lesser Necklaced Laughing-thrush
Black-throated Laughing-thrush
White-bellied Yuhina
Siberian Rubythroat   W
Siberian Blue-Robin   W
White-rumped Shama   c
White-throated Rock-Thrush
Blue Whistling-Thrush
Dusky Warbler   M
Radde's Warbler   W
Yellow-browed Warbler   c W
Greenish Warbler   W
Blyth's Leaf-Warbler   W
Sulfur-breasted Warbler   W
Thick-billed Warbler   W
Common Tailorbird
Dark-necked Tailorbird
Mountain Tailorbird

Golden-headed Cisticola
Stub-tailed Bush-Warbler   W
Asian Brown Flycatcher   W
Verditer Flycatcher
Red-breasted Flycatcher   W
Little Pied Flycatcher
Rufous-bellied Niltava
Pale Blue Niltava
Hill Niltava
Gray-headed Flycatcher
Black-naped Monarch
Asian Paradise-Flycatcher
Ashy Woodswallow
Brown Shrike   c W
Tibetan Shrike   r W
Golden-crested Myna
Hill Myna
Ruby-cheeked Sunbird
Purple-naped Sunbird
Olive-backed Sunbird
Purple Sunbird
Black-throated Sunbird
Crimson Sunbird
Little Spiderhunter
Thick-billed Flowerpecker
Yellow-vented Flowerpecker
Oriental White-eye
Pin-tailed Parrot-Finch   r
Spotted Munia

94
Taman Negara
National Park, Malaysia

TAMAN NEGARA IS MALAYSIA'S PRIMARY NATIONAL PARK and covers 1677 square miles (4360 km²) of forested hill country some 100 miles (161 km) northeast of Kuala Lipis. Its remote jungles hold a wealth of birds set to advantage midst beautiful and rugged landscapes. Access is from Kuala Lumpur by car to Kuala Lipis, then by train to Tembeling, and by boat along the Tembeling River to the park. Accommodation is in a fine lodge and adjacent bungalows perched on a cliff top with outstanding views.

The river trip up to the park is usually good for kingfishers, Crested Treeswift, and Blue-bearded Bee-eater. Bird-like screams of the gibbons can sometimes be heard. The surroundings of the headquarters are alive with birds; and Pied Hornbill, Brown-throated Sunbird, green-pigeons, and various bulbuls should prove no difficulty. At night various rare mammals can sometimes be seen from a roofed tower at the edge of a clearing.

Leeches can be a pest, and visitors have found that boat trips are often more rewarding and relaxing than lengthy walks. Broadbills, malkohas, drongos, leafbirds, woodpeckers, and piculets can all be picked up by this means. The greatest thrill, perhaps, is the huge Rhinoceros Hornbill, which can sometimes be seen from the lodge and from boat trips.

Make your arrangements well in advance through Chief Game Warden, Federation of Malaya, 202 Temiang Road, Seremban, Malaysia. An agency, Malaysian Wildlife Tours and Safaris, PO Box 84, Petaling Jaya, Malaysia, also organizes complete trips with guides from Kuala Lumpur.

Another fifty or so species are possible in the remote highlands of the park. However, it requires a complicated and arduous journey not recommended for most casual visitors. Many of these birds can be seen at the Malayan hill station resorts of Cameron Highlands and Fraser's Hill. These species have been left off the checklist, which covers the lowlands of the park only.

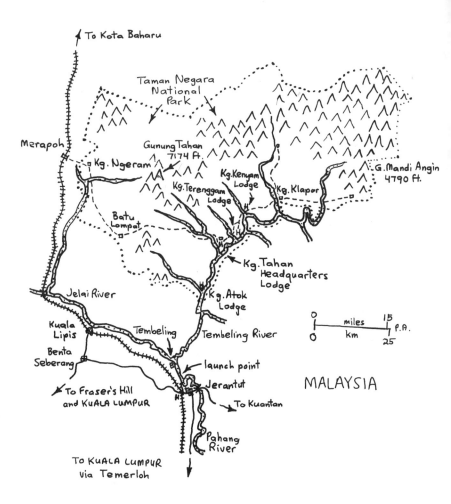

MALAYSIA

CHECKLIST

Cotton Pygmy-Goose
Lesser Fish-Eagle   c
Crested Serpent-Eagle
Crested Goshawk
Rufous-bellied Hawk-Eagle   r
Changeable Hawk-Eagle
Wallace's Hawk-Eagle
Black-thighed Falconet
Long-billed Partridge   r
Roul-roul Wood-Partridge   r

Crestless Fireback   r
Crested Fireback   r
Malaysian Peacock-Pheasant   r
Great Argus Pheasant   r
Little Green-Pigeon
Large Green-Pigeon
Jambu Fruit-Dove
Green-winged Pigeon
Blue-rumped Parrot
Blue-crowned Hanging-Parrot

Rufous-bellied Malkoha
Raffle's Malkoha
Red-billed Malkoha
Chestnut-breasted Malkoha
Short-toed Coucal
Bay Owl
Reddish Scops-Owl
Collared Scops-Owl
Gould's Frogmouth
Malaysian Eared Nightjar
Brown Needletail
Fork-tailed Swift
Whiskered Treeswift
Red-naped Trogon
Daird's Trogon
Cinnamon-rumped Trogon
Orange-breasted Trogon
Blue-eared Kingfisher
Black-backed Kingfisher
Rufous-backed Kingfisher
Stork-billed Kingfisher
Banded Kingfisher
Black-capped Kingfisher
Rufous-collared Kingfisher
Red-bearded Bee-eater
Bushy-crested Hornbill
Wreathed Hornbill
Black Hornbill
Rhinoceros Hornbill   c
Helmeted Hornbill
Gold-whiskered Barbet
Red-crowned Barbet
Red-throated Barbet
Yellow-crowned Barbet
Blue-eared Barbet
Brown Barbet
Malaysian Honeyguide
Rufous Woodpecker
Crimson-winged Woodpecker
Checker-throated Woodpecker
Banded Woodpecker
Olive-backed Woodpecker
Buff-rumped Woodpecker
Buff-necked Woodpecker
Great Slaty Woodpecker
Gray-headed Woodpecker
Orange-backed Woodpecker

Black-and-yellow Broadbill
Green Broadbill
Giant Pitta
Garnet Pitta
Banded Pitta
Large Woodshrike
Black-faced Cuckoo-shrike
Bar-bellied Cuckoo-shrike
Lesser Cuckoo-shrike
Scarlet Minivet
Green Iora
Lesser Green Leafbird
Greater Green Leafbird
Black-and-white Bulbul
Black-headed Bulbul
Scaly-breasted Bulbul
Gray-bellied Bulbul
Puff-backed Bulbul
Cream-vented Bulbul
Red-eyed Bulbul
Spectacled Bulbul
Finsch's Bulbul
Ochraceous Bulbul
Gray-cheeked Bulbul
Yellow-bellied Bulbul
Hairy-backed Bulbul
Buff-vented Bulbul
Streaked Bulbul
Ashy Bulbul
Bronzed Drongo
Greater Racquet-tailed Drongo
Dark-throated Oriole
Asian Fairy-Bluebird
Malayan Crested Jay
Green Magpie
Black Magpie
Slender-billed Crow
Sultan Tit
Velvet-fronted Nuthatch
Black-capped Babbler
Short-tailed Babbler
White-chested Babbler
Ferruginous Babbler
Horsfield's Babbler
Moustached Babbler
Scaly-crowned Babbler
Rufous-crowned Babbler

Gray-breasted Babbler
Chestnut-backed Scimitar-Babbler
Striped Wren-Babbler
Gray-headed Babbler
Fluffy-backed Tit-Babbler
Brown Fulvetta
Malaysian Rail-Babbler
White-rumped Shama
Rufous-tailed Shama   r
White-crowned Forktail
Blue Whistling-Thrush
Yellow-breasted Gerygone
Pale-legged Leaf-Warbler
Eastern Crowned Warbler   W
Dark-necked Tailorbird
Gray-chested Jungle-Flycatcher
Verditer Flycatcher
Rufous-chested Flycatcher
White-tailed Niltava
Pale Blue Niltava
Malaysian Niltava

Tickell's Niltava
Gray-headed Flycatcher
Pearled Fantail
Black-naped Monarch
Maroon-breasted Flycatcher
Rufous-winged Flycatcher
Asian Paradise-Flycatcher
Hill Myna
Plain Sunbird
Red-throated Sunbird
Ruby-cheeked Sunbird
Purple-naped Sunbird
Scarlet Sunbird
Long-billed Spiderhunter
Spectacled Spiderhunter
Gray-breasted Spiderhunter
Scarlet-breasted Flowerpecker
Yellow-vented Flowerpecker
Orange-bellied Flowerpecker
White-bellied Munia

95

Singapore

THIS ISLAND NATION of 225 square miles (585 km²) is only 26 miles (42 km) long at most and 14 miles (22.5 km) wide at its widest point. It is connected with West Malaysia by a rail-and-road bridge. Although little of its original vegetation is intact, it is a major business and tourist center with an important harbor and airport. It is one of the healthiest and cleanest cities in Asia, with excellent hotels and duty-free shops.

Most visitors stay along Orchard Road, a mile or so from the Botanical Gardens on Holland Road. The rich plantings here are good for Blue-throated Bee-eater, Yellow-vented Bulbul, Black-naped Oriole, Asian Magpie-Robin, and Philippine Starling. Commoner garden birds in suburban Singapore also include Pink-necked Green-Pigeon, Spotted Dove, Lesser Coucal, Crested Treeswift, Pacific Swallow, Pied Triller, Common Iora, Long-tailed Tailorbird, Brown Shrike, Brown-throated and Olive-backed Sunbirds, and Spotted Munia.

In central Singapore and along the waterfront, visitors may see Brahminy Kite, various shorebirds, Gray-rumped Swiftlet, House Swift, Indian Myna, and Tree Swallow.

The Bukit Timah Nature Reserve is located on the island's highest hill (581 feet [176 m]) on the southwest side of the large uninhabited forest known as the Water Catchment Area. There is a small steep road up into the forests. Flying lemur, monkeys, pangolin, and chevrotain still occur in this dense forest. Much of Singapore's bird list is rain-forest species now restricted to the central forest. Among the rarer birds to look for in this reserve are Little Barbet, Checker-throated and Banded Woodpeckers, Large Woodshrike, Greater Racquet-tailed Drongo, Short-tailed Babbler, Lesser Green Leafbird, Asian Fairy-Bluebird, Black-headed Bulbul, Hill Myna, and Raffle's Sunbird.

In the Pandan, a small mangrove reserve on the east side of the expanding Jurong Industrial Park, look for Brahminy Kite, Slate-breasted Rail, many migrant shorebirds, White-collared and Black-capped Kingfisher, and mangrove landbirds. The Kranji Reserve near Mandai is harder to find, and has similar mangrove habitat.

CHECKLIST

Brown Booby	Barred Buttonquail
Green Heron c	Slaty-breasted Rail c
Cattle Heron W	Red-legged Crake
Eastern Reef-Heron	White-breasted Waterhen
Great Egret W	Common Gallinule
Little Egret r W	Greater Painted-snipe
Yellow Bittern	Lesser Golden Plover c W
Cinnamon Bittern	Little Ringed Plover W
Lesser Whistling-Duck	Mongolian Plover c W
Black Baza W	Great Sand Plover W
Eurasian Honey-Buzzard r W	Eurasian Curlew W
Brahminy Kite c	Whimbrel c W
White-bellied Sea-Eagle	Black-tailed Godwit W
Crested Serpent-Eagle	Common Redshank c W
Japanese Sparrowhawk W	Common Greenshank W
Besra Sparrowhawk r	Wood Sandpiper c W
Crested Goshawk r	Terek Sandpiper r W
Changeable Hawk-Eagle	Common Sandpiper c W
Black-thighed Falconet	Pintail Snipe W
King Quail r	Red-necked Stint W

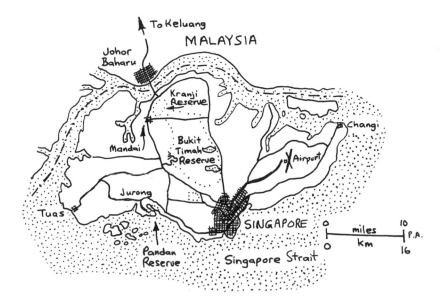

Long-toed Stint   c W
Oriental Pratincole   W
Black-naped Tern
Greater Crested Tern   W
Lesser Crested Tern
Thick-billed Green-Pigeon
Little Green-Pigeon   r
Pink-necked Green-Pigeon   c
Jambu Fruit-Dove   r W
Green Fruit-Pigeon
Spotted Turtle-Dove   c
Peaceful Dove
Green-winged Pigeon
Long-tailed Parakeet
Blue-rumped Parrot   r
Blue-crowned Hanging-Parrot   r
Chestnut-winged Cuckoo   r W
Common Hawk-Cuckoo   r W
Plaintive Cuckoo
Brush Cuckoo   r
Drongo Cuckoo   r
Common Koel   W
Black-bellied Malkoha   r
Rufous-bellied Malkoha   r
Greater Coucal   c
Lesser Coucal
Collared Scops-Owl
Malay Fish-Owl
Malaysian Eared Nightjar
Large-tailed Nightjar
Edible-nest Swiftlet   c
White-bellied Swiftlet
Brown Needletail
Gray-rumped Swiftlet
House Swift   c
Asian Palm-Swift
Crested Treeswift
Whiskered Treeswift
Eurasian Kingfisher
Blue-eared Kingfisher   r
Rufous-backed Kingfisher   r
Stork-billed Kingfisher   r W
Ruddy Kingfisher
White-breasted Kingfisher
Black-capped Kingfisher   W
White-collared Kingfisher   c
Blue-tailed Bee-eater

Blue-throated Bee-eater
Dollar Roller
Red-crowned Barbet
Blue-eared Barbet
Brown Barbet
Rufous Woodpecker
Crimson-winged Woodpecker
Banded Woodpecker   r
Common Golden-backed
   Woodpecker   c
Olive-backed Woodpecker
Bamboo Woodpecker
Buff-rumped Woodpecker
Buff-necked Woodpecker
Great Slaty Woodpecker
White-bellied Woodpecker
Gray-headed Woodpecker
Gray-capped Woodpecker   r
Brown-capped Woodpecker
Gray-and-buff Woodpecker   r
Orange-backed Woodpecker   r
Black-and-red Broadbill   r
Banded Broadbill   r
Blue-winged Pitta   r
Garnet Pitta
Barn Swallow   c M
Pacific Swallow   c
Large Woodshrike
Bar-bellied Cuckoo-shrike
Pied Triller   c
Ashy Minivet   W
Fiery Minivet
Scarlet Minivet
Common Iora   c
Great Iora   r
Lesser Green Leafbird   r
Greater Green Leafbird
Blue-winged Leafbird
Straw-headed Bulbul   r
Black-headed Bulbul
Gray-bellied Bulbul   r
Sooty-headed Bulbul   r
Yellow-vented Bulbul   c
Olive-winged Bulbul   c
Cream-vented Bulbul
Red-eyed Bulbul
Spectacled Bulbul   r

Buff-vented Bulbul
Crow-billed Drongo   W
Bronzed Drongo
Greater Racquet-tailed Drongo
Black-naped Oriole   c
Asian Fairy-Bluebird
House Crow   c
Large-billed Crow   c
Short-tailed Babbler
White-chested Babbler
Abbott's Babbler
Large Wren-Babbler
Chestnut-winged Babbler
Striped Tit-Babbler
Asian Magpie-Robin
White-rumped Shama
Arctic Warbler   W
Great Reed-Warbler   W
Common Tailorbird   c
Dark-necked Tailorbird
Ashy Tailorbird
Rufous-tailed Tailorbird
Yellow-bellied Prinia   c
Zitting Cisticola
Asian Brown Flycatcher   W
Mangrove Niltava
Pied Fantail   c
Black-naped Monarch
Rufous-winged Flycatcher
Mangrove Whistler
Gray Wagtail   W
Yellow Wagtail   W

Forest Wagtail
Richard's Pipit
Brown Shrike   W
Tiger Shrike   W
Philippine Starling   c
White-shouldered Starling   W
Purple-backed Starling   W
Indian Myna   c
Jungle Myna
White-vented Myna   c
Hill Myna
Brown-throated Sunbird
Purple-naped Sunbird
Purple-throated Sunbird
Copper-throated Sunbird
Olive-backed Sunbird   c
Crimson Sunbird   c
Little Spiderhunter
Gray-breasted Spiderhunter
Yellow-breasted Flowerpecker   r
Yellow-vented Flowerpecker   r
Orange-bellied Flowerpecker   c
Oriental White-eye   c
Tree Sparrow   c
Baya Weaver
Java Sparrow   r
White-rumped Munia   c
Javan Munia   c
Spotted Munia   c
Black-headed Munia
White-headed Munia

96
Kinabalu National Park, (Borneo), Malaysia

MOUNT KINABALU IS THE HIGHEST PEAK between the Himalayas and New Guinea, reaching 13,455 feet (4100 m). Located near the northern tip of the island of Borneo, it is celebrated by botanists and ornithologists alike for its links with distant areas as well as for a high degree of endemism.

The lower elevations are covered with dense tropical forests, although these have been extensively cut by the native Busans near villages and along roads. Above 5000 feet (1524 m) (as at Tenompok) the forest gradually becomes less tall, and moss and tree ferns become common. The amazing mixture of trees includes sixty species of oaks, eighty species of figs, fir-like conifers, podocarpus, tulip trees, chestnuts, and myrtles. Orchids are legion, and at the higher elevations rhododendrons dominate. At the treeline and above, there are many small plants similar to those of New Zealand and Europe.

Birdlife is rich, with a great diversity occurring along the road in surviving forests such as around Tenompok Pass at 4800 feet (1463 m). Although fewer species occur above 5000 feet (1524 m) many of them are Bornean endemics, and there are even some found only on Mt. Kinabalu. Among the birds found at moderate elevations are the trogons, Wreathed Hornbill, woodpeckers, broadbills, Black-and-crimson Oriole, Ashy Drongo, Black-breasted Triller, Temminck's Babbler, Rufous-winged Fulvetta, Chestnut-capped Laughing-thrush, and Pygmy White-eye.

Tourists can find many of Kinabalu's birds in the vicinity of the pass, located 5 hours by Land Rover from Kota Kinabalu, Sabah's chief city, with a variety of hotels and an airport. An airstrip on the mountain can also be used, if arrangements are made for Land Rovers to meet the plane. A tourist complex has been established in Ranau with cabins, a youth hostel, a small lodge, electricity, fireplaces, cooking facilities, and a simple bar-restaurant. Hire of camping equipment, guides, and porters can be undertaken there. For reservations write to Kinabalu National Park, PO Box 626, Kota Kinabalu, Sabah, Malaysia.

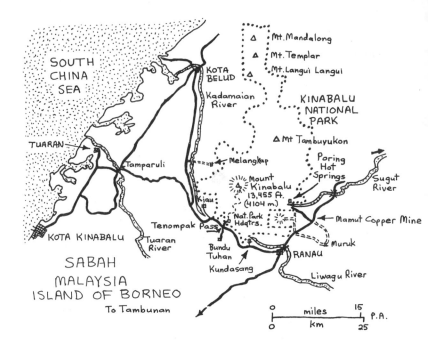

A long day's trip can be made to the summit via the trail from Tenompok to Kambaranga and Paka Cave, preferable with guides. Above 10,000 feet (3048 m) look for such specialties as Mountain Black-eye, Island Thrush, White-browed Shortwing, and Kinabalu Friendly Warbler. If time can be spent in the woodland in between look for barbets, Green Magpie, Mountain Minivet, Pale-faced Bulbul, Bornean Mountain-Whistler, and Black-capped White-eye.

Many lowland species can be found in the vicinity of Poring Hot Spring, located at 1700 feet (520 meters). It can be reached via road north of Ranau to the east of the mountain.

CHECKLIST

Green Heron	Red-breasted Tree-Partridge
Eurasian Honey-Kite	Roulroul Wood-Partridge L
Crested Serpent-Eagle	Crimson-headed Wood-Partridge
Besra Sparrowhawk	Great Argus Pheasant r L
Gray-faced Buzzard W	Red-legged Crake r L
Changeable Hawk-Eagle	Common Sandpiper W
Black Eagle	Pintail Snipe W L
Peregrine Falcon r	Pink-necked Green-Pigeon
King Quail	Thick-billed Green-Pigeon L

480

Green Fruit-Pigeon   r L
Mountain Fruit-Pigeon   c
Slender-billed Cuckoo-Dove
Little Cuckoo-Dove   c
Green-winged Pigeon
Blue-crowned Hanging-Parrot   L
Large Hawk-Cuckoo   c .
Hodgson's Hawk-Cuckoo
Indian Cuckoo   c
Oriental Cuckoo   W
Lesser Cuckoo   c
Banded Bay Cuckoo
Plaintive Cuckoo   L
Violet Cuckoo
Red-eyed Bronze-Cuckoo
Drongo-Cuckoo
Raffle's Malkoha   r
Rufous-bellied Malkoha   r L
Black-bellied Malkoha   L
Chestnut-breasted Malkoha
Red-billed Malkoha   L
Lesser Coucal
Greater Coucal   L
Mountain Scops-Owl   r
Reddish Scops-Owl   r
Collared Owlet   r
Brown Hawk-Owl   r
Malaysian Eared Nightjar
Large-tailed Nightjar   L
Edible-nest Swiftlet   L
White-bellied Swiftlet   c
Brown Needletail
Crested Treeswift
Whitehead's Trogon
Cinnamon-rumped Trogon   r
Orange-breasted Trogon   L
Black-backed Kingfisher   L
Banded Kingfisher
Rufous-collared Kingfisher
Red-bearded Bee-eater   L
Wreathed Hornbill
Bushy-crested Hornbill   L
Rhinoceros Hornbill
Helmeted Hornbill   r L
Gold-whiskered Barbet   L
Brown Barbet   L
Red-throated Barbet   L

Yellow-crowned Barbet   r
Golden-naped Barbet   c
Mountain Barbet   c
Black-throated Barbet   c
Little Barbet   L
Coppersmith Barbet   c
Rufous Piculet   L
Rufous Woodpecker
Crimson-winged Woodpecker   c
Checker-throated Woodpecker
Banded Woodpecker
Gray-capped Woodpecker
Brown-capped Woodpecker   c
Olive-backed Woodpecker   L
Maroon Woodpecker   c
Orange-backed Woodpecker
Black-and-yellow Broadbill
Black-and-red Broadbill   L
Long-tailed Broadbill
Whitehead's Broadbill
Dusky Broadbill   r
Green Broadbill   L
Blue-banded Pitta   r
Banded Pitta   r
Pacific Swallow   c L
Barn Swallow   W
Pied Woodshrike
Black-winged Woodshrike   L
Bar-bellied Cuckoo-shrike
Black-faced Cuckoo-shrike   c
Black-breasted Triller
Mountain Minivet   c
Scarlet Minivet
Common Iora   L
Greater Green Leafbird
Blue-winged Leafbird   c
Asian Fairy-Bluebird   L
Straw-headed Bulbul   L
Black-headed Bulbul   c L
Black-crested Yellow Bulbul
Scale-breasted Bulbul   r
Sooty-headed Bulbul   c
Flavescent Bulbul
Yellow-vented Bulbul
Olive-winged Bulbul   L
Cream-vented Bulbul   L
Ochraceous Bulbul   c

Spectacled Bulbul   L
Gray-cheeked Bulbul   L
Yellow-bellied Bulbul   L
Ashy Bulbul
Ashy Drongo   c
Spangled Drongo
Black-and-crimson Oriole   c
Gray Treepie   c
Short-tailed Magpie   r
Green Magpie
Velvet-fronted Nuthatch
Black-capped Babbler   r L
Temminck's Babbler
Ferruginous Babbler   L
Rufous-crowned Babbler   L
Scaly-crowned Babbler   L
Moustached Babbler
Plain Babbler   L
Chestnut-backed Scimitar-Babbler
Mountain Wren-Babbler
Small Wren-Babbler
Gray-throated Babbler
Gray-headed Babbler
Chestnut-winged Babbler   r L
Black Laughing-thrush
Gray-and-brown Laughing-thrush
Chestnut-capped Laughing-thrush
   c
White-browed Shrike-Babbler
Rufous-winged Fulvetta   c
White-bellied Yuhina
Brown Fulvetta
Siberian Blue Robin   r W
White-browed Shortwing
Chestnut-naped Forktail   r
White-crowned Forktail   c
Sunda Whistling-Thrush
Chestnut-capped Thrush   r L
Everett's Thrush   r
Orange-headed Thrush   r
Island Thrush   c
Eye-browed Thrush   c W
Yellow-breasted Warbler   c
Yellow-bellied Warbler
Arctic Warbler   W
Mountain Leaf-Warbler   c
Mountain Tailorbird   c

Yellow-bellied Prinia   L
Stub-tailed Bush-Warbler
Strong-footed Bush-Warbler
Kinabalu Friendly Warbler
Gray-chested Jungle-Flycatcher   r
Olive-backed Jungle-Flycatcher   r
Rufous-tailed Jungle-Flycatcher   r
Asian Brown Flycatcher   W
White-throated Jungle-Flycatcher
Dark-sided Flycatcher   W
Ferruginous Flycatcher   r W
Indigo Flycatcher   c
Verditer Flycatcher   r L
Snowy-browed Flycatcher
Little Pied Flycatcher
Blue-and-white Flycatcher   W
White-tailed Niltava
Bornean Niltava   r
Pygmy Blue Flycatcher   r
Gray-headed Flycatcher
White-throated Fantail   c
Pearled Fantail
Pied Fantail   r
Black-naped Monarch   L
Asian Paradise-Flycatcher   L
Bornean Mountain-Whistler
Gray Wagtail   W
White-breasted Woodswallow
Brown Shrike   W
Brown-throated Sunbird   L
Purple-naped Sunbird   L
Olive-backed Sunbird
Crimson Sunbird   L
Scarlet Sunbird   c
Little Spiderhunter
Gray-breasted Spiderhunter
Whitehead's Spiderhunter   c
Orange-bellied Flowerpecker   L
Plain Flowerpecker   r
Black-sided Flowerpecker   c
Everett's White-eye
Black-capped White-eye
Pygmy White-eye
Mountain Black-eye   c
Tawny-breasted Parrot-Finch   r
Dusky Munia   L
Black-headed Munia

97

Philippines

WITH MORE THAN 7000 ISLANDS, birders visiting the Philippines should concentrate on southern Luzon, eastern Mindanao, and Palawan. Compared to the islands of Micronesia, Polynesia, and even Melanesia, the Philippines have a huge avifauna with dozens of highly interesting unique forms. While it is true that some islands are totally denuded of original vegetation, there are still vast tracts of mature hill forest on the larger islands. The next decade will be pivotal in the battle against the short-sighted, quick-profit timber industries, which are cancers on the landscape. There are some national parks, but their integrity is violated by both timber and subsistence agricultural pressure.

Manila is well-connected with the rest of the world and boasts many relatively inexpensive hotels of superb quality. Commonest birds in town are Barn Swallow, Tree Sparrow, and Crested Myna. The best freshwater marsh in the islands is located near Calaman, an hour's drive north of Manila.

Quezon National Park is located east of Lucena, a town with a hotel on Tayabas Bay, a four-hour drive southeast of Manila. The park, situated on an isthmus between Lamon Bay and Tayabas Bay, preserves lush forests that flank rivers, waterfalls, and gorges. There are miles of cleared paths and scenic viewpoints, as well as a natural swimming pool. In addition to crab-eating macaque and Philippine deer, birders may find Philippine Falconet, Bleeding-heart Pigeon, Scale-feathered Cuckoo, Red-crested Malkohas, Philippine Trogon, Rufous and Taristic Hornbills, Philippine Fairy-Bluebird, and the Coleto.

Other spots in southern Luzon closer to Manila are also worth visiting. The Lakeview Resort Hotel in Los Banos on beautiful volcano-ringed Laguna de Bay is a good base for inspecting a variety of habitats, including the dense mountain forests of Mt. Makiling National Park. In these areas visitors may find Green-headed Racquet-tailed Parrot, Guaiabero, Philippine Eared Nightjar, Blue-tailed and Chestnut-headed Bee-eaters, Balicassio, Black-naped Oriole, Black-crowned Tree-Babbler, Blue-headed Fantail, Yellow-bellied Whistler,

Schach Shrike, Purple-throated, Mountain, and Flaming Sunbirds, and Orange-breasted Flowerpecker.

Mindanao is best visited by flying to Davao City (there are several scheduled jets a day from Manila) and basing at one of several hotels, such as the Davao Insular Hotel. Mindanao, the southernmost major island in the Philippines, is the major stronghold of the Philippine Monkey-eating Eagle, nearly as large as the neotropical Harpy Eagle, and down to a few hundred survivors. Mt. Apo National Park, 19 miles (30 km) west of Davao, preserves rugged mountains (reaching 9540 feet [2907 m]), waterfalls, hot mineral springs, and great forests. There are no hotel facilities in the park, although it is possible at times to arrange to stay overnight in private homes in such places as Tudaya. Major efforts in the late 1970s by a team from Films and Research of an Endangered Environment (201 N. Wells St., Suite 1735, Chicago, Illinois 60606) have resulted in the discovery and filming of several nests of this great eagle. Local inquiry may find guides to help you see a current nest from a safe distance.

Although the climb up Mt. Apo is exceedingly difficult, visitors to the park will find access to good forest in several areas. Do try to get as high in elevation as is safe and comfortable to insure a sampling of the distinctive montane avifauna. Birds of interest here include Rufous-bellied Hawk-Eagle, Philippine Hanging Parakeet, Black-faced Coucal, Lesser Treeswift, Writhed-billed, Rufous, and Wattled Hornbills, White-bellied Woodpecker, Scarlet Minivet, Stripe-headed and Plain-headed Creepers, Blue Fantail, Celestial Blue Monarch, Naked-faced Spiderhunter, Bicolored, Philippine, and Fire-breasted Flowerpeckers, and Everett's and Cinnamon White-eye.

Whether you are lucky enough to see the Monkey-eating Eagle or not in the wild, you may wish to see and to support the captive breeding project in Baracatan near Davao City.

The third major island for birders to visit is long, mountainous, and narrow Palawan. It is in the southwest and is faunistically and geographically close to Borneo. There are daily flights to Puerto Princesa, its main city, from Manila, and some overnight facilities, like the Rafols Hotel. The top tourist attraction is St. Paul's Subterranean National Park with its underground river, beaches, and forested hills. It is located on the west side of the island, with access via a four-hour jeep and boat ride. The Palawan Peacock Pheasant lives in the park's woodland.

The road north from Puerto Princesa leads to a number of interesting places. Boats are available on the Langogan River for cruising and drifting through the jungle where mynas, cockatoo, malcohas, and parrots live. At another point there is a one-hour trail to a Batac tribal

PHILIPPINES

LUZON

PACIFIC
OCEAN

Laguna de Bay
Quezon National Park

South
China
Sea

MANILA

Lucena

Mindoro

Samar

PALAWAN

Negros

Leyte

Puerto
Princesa

MINDANAO

Sulu Sea

DAVAO CITY

miles
km

P.A.

MOUNT APO
NATIONAL PARK

Celebes Sea

village with an American mission. Opposite the town of Roxas one can take a half-hour boat trip out to Tabon Island with its flourishing megapode colony. There is tented accommodation on the island. Birds of Palawan that can be noted at these areas include White-bellied Sea-Eagle, Green and Nutmeg Imperial-Pigeons, Nicobar Pigeon, Philippine Cockatoo, Palawan Malkoha, Stork-billed Kingfisher, Palawan Hornbill, Fiery Minivet, Palawan Tit, Black-headed and Olive-winged Bulbul, Palawan Leafbird, Asian Fairy-Bluebird, Blue Paradise-Flycatcher, Hill Myna, and Palawan Flowerpecker.

CHECKLIST

(LU = Luzon, MI = Mindanao, PA = Palawan)

Little Dabchick
Darter   r

Lesser Frigatebird   PA, MI
Black Bittern   r, LU

485

Yellow Bittern   c
Cinnamon Bittern   c
Green Heron   c
Cattle Heron
Eastern Reef-Heron
Little Egret
Great Egret
Short-billed Egret
Great-billed Heron   r
Gray Heron   W, LU
Purple Heron   c
Nankeen Night-Heron
Water Whistling-Duck   c
Spotted Whistling-Duck   MI
Common Shelduck   r W, LU
Northern Pintail   c W, LU
Philippine Duck   c LU, r MI
Mallard   c LU, r MI
Eurasian Wigeon   W LU
Garganey   c W
Northern Shoveler   r W, LU
Northern Pochard   r W, LU
Tufted Duck   r W, LU
Cotton Pygmy-Goose   r LU
Osprey
Jerdon's Baza   r MI, PA
Barred Honey-Buzzard   r LU, MI
Eurasian Honey-Buzzard   c LU,
   MI, r PA
Black-shouldered Kite
Brahminy Kite   c
White-bellied Sea-Eagle
Gray-headed Fishing-Eagle   r
Marsh Harrier   W
Pied Harrier   r W
Japanese Sparrowhawk   W
Besra Sparrowhawk   LU, MI
Crested Goshawk   r MI, PA
Chinese Goshawk   W LU, PA
Gray-faced Buzzard   W c LU; r
   MI, PA
Monkey-eating Eagle   r LU, c
   MI
Rufous Hawk-Eagle
Changeable Hawk-Eagle   r MI,
   PA
Philippine Hawk-Eagle   r PA, LU

Philippine Falconet   c LU, MI
Oriental Hobby   r MI
Peregrine Falcon
Orange-footed Scrubfowl
King Quail
Red Junglefowl   c
Palawan Peacock Pheasant   PA
Common Buttonquail   r LU, MI
Worcester's Buttonquail   r LU
Barred Buttonquail   c PA, r LU
Spotted Buttonquail   LU
Banded Rail   c LU
Barred Rail
Slaty-legged Crake   r LU, MI
Ruddy-breasted Crake   r LU, MI
White-browed Crake   c
Bush-hen   r LU, MI
White-breasted Waterhen   c
Common Gallinule   c
Watercock
Purple Swamphen   LU, MI
Common Coot   LU
Pheasant-tailed Jacana   c LU, MI
Greater Painted-snipe   r
Gray Plover   W
Lesser Golden Plover   c W
Little Ringed Plover   c
Snowy Plover   r W
Malay Plover
Mongolian Plover   W
Great Sand Plover   W
Whimbrel   W
Eurasian Curlew   W
Black-tailed Godwit   r W
Bar-tailed Godwit   r W
Common Redshank   c W
Marsh Sandpiper   r W
Common Greenshank   r W
Wood Sandpiper   c W
Common Sandpiper   c W
Gray-tailed Tattler   r W
Terek Sandpiper   W
Ruddy Turnstone   W
Snipe, species   W
Sanderling   W
Red-necked Stint   W
Long-toed Stint   W

Curlew Sandpiper   r W
Black-winged Stilt   r
Little Phalarope   r W
Oriental Pratincole
Black-headed Gull   r W
Whiskered Tern
Little Tern   r
Common Tern
Crested Tern
Brown Noddy   r
Thick-billed Green-Pigeon   PA
Pompadour Green-Pigeon   LU,
   MI
Pink-necked Green-Pigeon
White-eared Brown Fruit-Dove
   LU, MI
Amethyst Brown Fruit-Dove   LU,
   MI
Southern Brown Fruit-Dove   MI
Yellow-breasted Fruit-Dove   H
   LU, MI
Merrill's Fruit-Dove   r LU
Black-chinned Fruit-Dove   LU,
   MI
Green Fruit-Pigeon   c PA, r LU,
   MI
Pink-bellied Fruit-Pigeon   r LU, c
   MI
Nutmeg Fruit-Pigeon   c PA
Slender-billed Cuckoo-Dove   c
Island Turtle-Dove   PA
Red Turtle-Dove   LU
Spotted Turtle-Dove   c LU, MI
Peaceful Dove   c LU, MI
Green-winged Pigeon
Bleeding-heart Pigeon   r LU,
   MI
Nicobar Pigeon   PA, small islands
Mindanao Lorikeet   H MI
Philippine Cockatoo   r LU, MI, c
   PA
Blue-headed Racquet-tailed Parrot
   r MI
Crimson-spotted Racquet-tailed
   Parrot   r H LU, MI
Green-headed Racquet-tailed
   Parrot   r LU

Palawan Racquet-tailed Parrot   c
   PA
Blue-naped Parrot   c PA, r MI,
   LU
Blue-backed Parrot   r LU, MI
Guaiabero   LU, MI
Philippine Hanging-Parrot   c LU,
   MI
Large Hawk-Cuckoo
Cuckoo (*Cuculus*), sp.   W
Plaintive Cuckoo   c
Brush Cuckoo   r
Violet Cuckoo
Drongo Cuckoo   LU, PA
Common Koel   LU, PA
Palawan Malkoha
Chestnut-breasted Malkoha   PA
Red-crested Malkoha   LU
Rough-crested Cuckoo   c LU
Scale-feathered Cuckoo   c LU
Greater Coucal   r LU, PA
Philippine Coucal   c
Black-faced Coucal   MI
Rufous Coucal   LU
Lesser Coucal
Grass Owl   r LU, MI
Eurasian Scops-Owl   LU, MI
Collared Scops-Owl
Giant Scops-Owl   c H MI
Philippine Hawk-Owl   LU, MI
Spotted Wood-Owl   PA
Philippine Frogmouth   r LU, MI
Great Eared Nightjar   LU, MI
Large-tailed Nightjar
Savanna Nightjar   LU, MI
Himalayan Swiftlet
Edible-nest Swiftlet   PA
Uniform Swiftlet
Pygmy Swiftlet
White-bellied Swiftlet
Brown Needletail
Philippine Needletail   MI
House Swift   LU
Asian Palm-Swift   LU, MI
Whiskered Treeswift   LU, MI
Philippine Trogon   LU, MI
Eurasian Kingfisher   W

Blue-eared Kingfisher   W
Dwarf River Kingfisher   r LU
Silvery Kingfisher   r MI
Black-backed Kingfisher   c PA
Stork-billed Kingfisher   c PA, r
  LU, MI
White-collared Kingfisher   c
Ruddy Kingfisher   r PA; LU, MI
White-breasted Kingfisher   c
Black-capped Kingfisher   r PA
Spotted Wood Kingfisher   r PA
Blue-tailed Bee-eater   c LU, MI,
  r PA
Chestnut-headed Bee-eater   c LU,
  MI, r PA
Dollar Roller   c LU, MI, PA
Tarictic Hornbill   LU, MI
Writhed-billed Hornbill   c MI
Palawan Hornbill   PA
Rufous Hornbill   c LU, MI
Coppersmith Barbet   c LU, MI
Common Golden-backed
  Woodpecker   c PA
Great Slaty Woodpecker   PA
Sooty Woodpecker   LU, MI
White-bellied Woodpecker
Philippine Pygmy Woodpecker   c
  LU, MI
Greater Golden-backed
  Woodpecker   c
Wattled Broadbill   r MI
Blue-breasted Pitta
Koch's Pitta   r H LU
Hooded Pitta
Steere's Pitta   r MI
Singing Bush-Lark   c LU, r MI
Oriental Skylark   c LU MI
Plain Martin   LU
Barn Swallow   c W
Pacific Swallow
Red-rumped Swallow   r LU,
  PA
Bar-bellied Cuckoo-shrike   c
Philippine Black Cuckoo-shrike   r
  LU
Muller's Cuckoo-shrike   r LU,
  MI

Sharp-tailed Cuckoo-shrike   r LU,
  MI
Black-and-white Triller   LU, MI
Pied Triller   c
Fiery Minivet   PA
Scarlet Minivet   c LU, MI
Ashy Drongo   c PA
Balicassiao Drongo   c LU
Spangled Drongo   c MI, PA
Dark-throated Oriole   LU, MI,
  PA
Isabella Oriole   LU
Black-naped Oriole   c
Slender-billed Crow   r LU, MI; c
  PA
Large-billed Crow   c LU, MI
Elegant Tit   c LU, MI
Palawan Tit   PA
White-fronted Tit   r LU
Velvet-fronted Nuthatch   c LU,
  MI
Stripe-headed Creeper   LU, MI
Plain-headed Creeper   r LU, MI
Ashy-headed Babbler   PA
Streaked Wren-Babbler   r MI
Falcated Wren-Babbler   r PA
Pygmy Tree-Babbler   r MI
Black-crowned Tree-Babbler   LU,
  MI
Whitehead's Tree-Babbler   LU
Palawan Tit-Babbler   r PA
Gray-faced Tit-Babbler   c PA
Brown Tit-Babbler   c MI
Black-headed Bulbul   PA
Yellow-wattled Bulbul   LU, MI
Olive-winged Bulbul   PA
Yellow-vented Bulbul   c LU, MI
Gray-cheeked Bulbul   PA
Olive Bulbul   PA
Philippine Bulbul   c LU, MI
Plain-throated Bulbul   MI
Common Iora   PA
Yellow-billed Leafbird   MI
Palawan Leafbird   c PA
Asian Fairy-Bluebird   PA
Philippine Fairy-Bluebird   LU,
  MI

White-browed Shortwing   H LU,
  MI
Philippine Water-Redstart   H LU
Asian Magpie-Robin   LU, MI
White-browed Shama   LU
Palawan Shama   c PA
Pied Bushchat   LU, MI
Blue Rock-Thrush   W
Scaly Thrush   W LU, PA
Island Thrush   H LU, MI
Dusky Thrush   W LU, MI
Yellow-breasted Gerygone   r LU,
  MI
Striated Grass-Warbler   c LU,
  MI
Tawny Grass-Warbler   H LU,
  MI
Zitting Cisticola   c
Golden-headed Cisticola   LU, MI
Great Reed-Warbler   M
Mountain Leaf-Warbler   H
Philippine Leaf-Warbler   MI
DuBois's Leaf-Warbler   LU
Arctic Warbler   W
Mountain Tailorbird   H
Luzon Tailorbird   LU
Common Tailorbird   c LU, r
  MI
Black-headed Tailorbird   r MI
White-eared Tailorbird   r MI
Red-tailed Tailorbird   c PA
Blue Fantail   MI
Blue-headed Fantail   c LU
Black-and-cinnamon Fantail   c H,
  MI
Pied Fantail   c
Rufous-tailed Jungle Flycatcher
  MI
Snowy-browed Flycatcher   H LU,
  MI
Little Slaty Flycatcher   MI
Little Pied Flycatcher   H
Hill Niltava   PA
Mangrove Niltava   c
Gray-streaked Flycatcher   W
Verditer Flycatcher   H
Canary Flycatcher   H

Black-naped Monarch   c
Celestial Blue Monarch   r LU,
  MI
Rufous Paradise-Flycatcher   r
  LU, MI
Blue Paradise-Flycatcher   PA
Mangrove Whistler   LU, PA
Yellow-bellied Whistler   LU, MI
Yellow Wagtail   W
Gray Wagtail   W
White Wagtail   M LU, PA
Richard's Pipit   c
Petchora Pipit   r W
Red-throated Pipit   r W
White-breasted Woodswallow   c
Brown Shrike   c W
Schach Shrike
Strong-billed Shrike   H LU
Lesser Starling   H MI
Philippine Starling   c
Purple-backed Starling   W
Crested Myna   c LU
Mount Apo Myna   r H MI
Coleto   c LU, MI
Hill Myna   PA
Brown-throated Sunbird
Purple-throated Sunbird   c
Copper-throated Sunbird   PA
Olive-backed Sunbird   c
Hachisuka's Sunbird   H MI
Flaming Sunbird   LU
Mountain Sunbird   LU, MI
Lovely Sunbird   LU, MI, PA
Little Spiderhunter   c
Naked-faced Spiderhunter   c MI;
  LU
Olive-backed Flowerpecker   LU,
  MI
Palawan Flowerpecker   c PA
Striped Flowerpecker   r LU, MI,
  PA
Gray-breasted Flowerpecker   H
  MI
Olive-capped Flowerpecker   r H
  MI
Yellow-crowned Flowerpecker   r
  H LU, MI

Bicolored Flowerpecker   c LU, MI

Philippine Flowerpecker   c LU, MI

Orange-bellied Flowerpecker   r LU, MI

White-bellied Flowerpecker   c H LU, MI

Pygmy Flowerpecker

Fire-breasted Flowerpecker   r H LU, MI

Philippine White-eye   LU

Mountain White-eye   c H

Everett's White-eye   c MI

Yellow White-eye   LU

Goodfellow's White-eye   H MI

Cinnamon White-eye   H MI

Tree Sparrow   c LU, MI

Spotted Munia   c LU

White-bellied Munia

Black-headed Munia   c

Java Sparrow   c LU

Red Crossbill   H LU

98
Bali, Indonesia

BALI LIES JUST TO THE EAST OF JAVA in the center of Indonesia. Famous for its colorful arts, music, and theater, Bali's image is further enhanced by its natural scenic grace, its beautiful people, and distinctive Hindu-Balinese religious traditions. Hardly remote these days, Bali has international jet connections with Australia, Asia, Europe, and North America.

There is a wide choice of lodging in the vicinity of Denpasar, the chief city of the island. Many hotels are on or near the beaches. The Hotel Bali Oberoi is located at Kuta, near the airport and 6 miles (9.6 km) south of Denpasar. Five miles (8 km) to the east of Denpasar is the top resort area of Sanur Beach, home of the posh Hotel Bali Beach and the Bali Hyatt, plus a variety of others. Cars with or without drivers are easy to arrange.

The southern half of the island is heavily populated, and visitors will note miles of terraced rice paddies, tea, coffee, cocoa, and citrus. For a glimpse of birding possibilities visitors can take 4-hour package tours to the monkey forest at Sangeh from major hotels.

The northern half of Bali consists of a long wall of tall volcanic peaks with heavy tropical and subtropical forest on steeper slopes. Many fine birds occur in these forests. Do consider spending a few nights at the town of Ubud, which is 14 miles (22.4 km) closer to the mountains than Denpasar. Balinese-style bungalows are available at the Tjampuan Motel and the Puri Palais.

The northwest corner of Bali features the Bali Barat Nature Reserve, where most of the surviving thousand or so Rothschild's (White or Bali) Mynas live. The reserve covers 77 square miles (200 km^2) and is also home to several rare mammals. The Myna also survives on nearby Penida Island.

Bali is located just west of Wallace's Line, a zoogeographical dividing line that separates many Asian species from those of New Guinea and Australia. Bali is home to four of the five species, not found in Java, that are closely related to forms found east of the line: Black-naped Fruit-Dove, Rainbow Lorikeet, Lesser Sulfur-crested Cockatoo, and Brown Honeyeater.

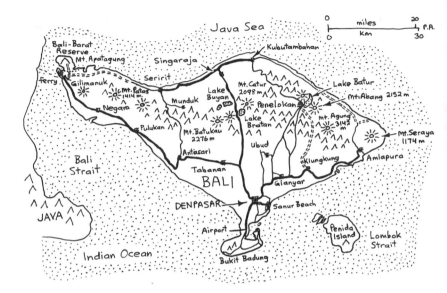

There are occasional cruises to the little-known islands to the east, such as Komodo and Lombolk, which would be highly interesting for both "dragons" and birds.

CHECKLIST

Little Dabchick	Common Gallinule
Little Pied Cormorant	Gray Plover c W
Lesser Frigatebird	Lesser Golden Plover W
Javan Pond-Heron c	Malay Plover
Cattle Heron c	Great Sand Plover W
Eastern Reef-Heron	Whimbrel c W
Osprey	Wood Sandpiper c W
Eurasian Honey-Buzzard W	Common Sandpiper c W
Black-shouldered Kite	Ruddy Turnstone c W
Brahminy Kite	Red-necked Stint c W
White-bellied Sea-Eagle	Great Thick-knee
Crested Serpent-Eagle	White-winged Black Tern W
Black Eagle	Black-naped Tern
Black-thighed Falconet	Little Tern
Moluccan Kestrel	Crested Tern
Green Junglefowl	Thick-billed Green-Pigeon
Barred Buttonquail	Little Green-Pigeon
White-breasted Waterhen	Pink-necked Green-Pigeon

492

Pink-necked Fruit-Dove   c
Black-naped Fruit-Dove   c
Dark-backed Fruit-Pigeon
Slender-billed Cuckoo-Dove
Little Cuckoo-Dove
Island Turtle-Dove   c
Spotted Turtle-Dove   c
Peaceful Dove   c
Green-winged Pigeon
Rainbow Lorikeet
Lesser Sulfur-crested Cockatoo
Rose-breasted Parakeet
Long-tailed Parakeet
Vernal Hanging-Parakeet
Lesser Cuckoo
Brush Cuckoo
Drongo-Cuckoo
Common Koel
Chestnut-breasted Malkoha
Greater Coucal
Lesser Coucal
Barn Owl
Bay Owl
Collared Scops-Owl
Malay Eagle-Owl
Malay Fish-Owl
Asian Barred Owlet
Gould's Frogmouth
Blyth's Frogmouth
Large-tailed Nightjar
Savanna Nightjar
Edible-nest Swiftlet   c
White-bellied Swiftlet   c
Asian Palm-Swift
Crested Treeswift
Whiskered Treeswift
Eurasian Kingfisher
Rufous-backed Kingfisher
Java Kingfisher   c
White-collared Kingfisher   c
Rainbow Bee-eater   M
Chestnut-headed Bee-eater
Blue-throated Bee-eater
Wreathed Hornbill
Southern Pied Hornbill
Lineated Barbet
Blue-crowned Barbet

Blue-eared Barbet
Coppersmith Barbet   c
Rufous Piculet
Laced Woodpecker
Common Golden-backed
  Woodpecker   c
Great Slaty Woodpecker
White-bellied Woodpecker
Gray-headed Woodpecker
Banded Pitta
Singing Bush-Lark   c
Pacific Swallow
Black-winged Cuckoo-shrike   c
Lesser Cuckoo-shrike
White-winged Triller
Small Minivet
Scarlet Minivet   c
Orange-spotted Bulbul   c
Black-headed Bulbul
Sooty-headed Bulbul   c
Spectacled Bulbul   c
Gray-cheeked Bulbul
Black Drongo   c
Ashy Drongo   c
Spangled Drongo
Dark-throated Oriole
Black-naped Oriole   c
Gray Treepie   c
Racquet-tailed Treepie
Slender-billed Crow   c
Large-billed Crow
Great Tit
Horsfield's Babbler
Gray-breasted Babbler
Chestnut-backed Scimitar-Babbler
Pearly-cheeked Babbler
Asian Magpie-Robin
White-crowned Forktail
Pied Bushchat
Chestnut-capped Thrush
Orange-headed Thrush
Yellow-breasted Gerygone
Sunda Warbler
Mountain Leaf-Warbler   c
Striated Grass-Warbler
Ashy Tailorbird   c
Mountain Tailorbird   c

Bar-winged Prinia   c
Zitting Cisticola
Golden-headed Cisticola
Strong-footed Bush-Warbler   c
Olive-backed Jungle-Flycatcher
Snowy-browed Flycatcher
Little Pied Flycatcher
Pale Blue Niltava
Gray-headed Flycatcher
Pied Fantail   c
Mangrove Whistler
Golden Whistler
Richard's Pipit   c
White-breasted Woodswallow   c
Brown Shrike   c W
Tiger Shrike   c W
Schach Shrike   c
Lesser Glossy-Starling
Philippine Starling   c
Pied Myna   c
Black-winged Starling   c
Rothschild's Myna   r

Hill Myna   c
Brown Honeyeater   c
Brown-throated Sunbird   c
Purple-throated Sunbird
Copper-throated Sunbird
Olive-backed Sunbird   c
Gray-breasted Spiderhunter
Yellow-vented Flowerpecker
Orange-bellied Flowerpecker   c
Scarlet-headed Flowerpecker   c
Scarlet-backed Flowerpecker   c
Fire-breasted Flowerpecker   c
Mountain White-eye   c
Mangrove White-eye
Javan Gray-throated White-eye   r
Tree Sparrow   c
Streaked Weaver
Strawberry Finch
Java Sparrow   c
Javan Munia   c
Spotted Munia   c
Black-headed Munia   c

99

Wau, Papua New Guinea

WAU IS A RELATIVELY NEW DESTINATION for vagabonding birders intent on seeing mountain-forest birds in New Guinea, especially birds-of-paradise. As there is no road connection with Port Moresby, visitors must fly into Wau on light aircraft. Alternatively, visitors can fly in larger aircraft to Lae and arrange for vehicles to drive them up from Lae, a four-hour trip over dirt roads via Bulolo, which, in turn, is a 40-minute drive north of Wau and has a hotel and airstrip. The road from Bulolo to Wau runs alongside the new McAdam National Park, which has some tall forest but has not yet been developed for access.

The Hotel Wau in "downtown" Wau is rustic and has a restaurant and bar with local color. The McAdam Memorial Park, southeast of Wau, has some native forest in addition to imported conifer forests, which unfortunately are sterile for indigenous wildlife.

The Wau Ecology Institute, located ten minutes above Wau on the Edie Creek Road, was incorporated in 1971 and is affiliated with the Bishop Museum of Honolulu. Serving native biologists and teachers, it is also a base for visiting scientists, particularly insect and plant specialists. There is a laboratory and library, plus a "motel" unit with a kitchen for visiting groups. Larger parties can arrange for cooks, and all booking requests should go to: Manager, Wau Ecology Institute, Box 77, Wau, Papua New Guinea. Raggiana Bird-of-Paradise gather in a treetop lek on the grounds in the latter half of the year.

Four-wheel-drive Land Cruisers and a truck with guides and drivers can be hired for several trips to various elevations on nearby Mt. Kaindi. A large percentage of New Guinea montane-forest birds can be seen along various stretches of the dirt road up Mt. Kaindi. Cloudy, misty days are better for activity than hot, dry, sunny ones, and there are altitudinal preferences for many species. The road passes through magnificent forest, and dozens of exciting birds can be seen right from the road, including the Brown Sicklebill Bird-of-Paradise and Princess Stephanie's Astrapia, both with impressive long tails. The last five miles (8 km) are the richest, and there are two trails to attempt. A small gravity canal crosses the road at one point, and there

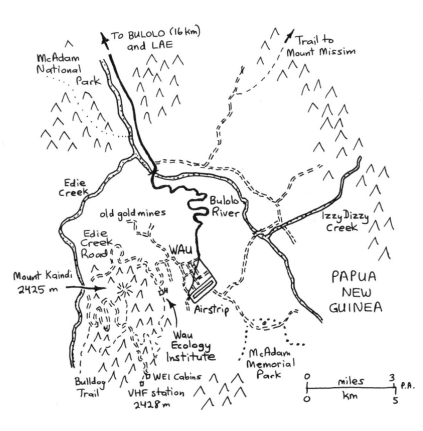

is a fine level trail on the canal bank for miles through good forest.
Also, there is a moss-forest trail to the top of Mt. Kaindi. The latter
often has fallen tree trunks in the way, but the rough walk does get
one into exciting niches. Birds regularly seen along the road include
Brehm's Parrot, Musschenbroek's Lorikeet, Friendly Fantail, Canary
Flycatcher, Blue Flyrobin, Regent Whistler, Torrentlark (lower down
at stream crossings), Smoky Melipotes, Belford's Melidictes, Fan-
tailed Berrypecker, and Tit-Berrypecker.

Those willing to camp might be able to organize (through the
institute) an overnight trek to Mt. Mission, which is to the north. A
four-mile (6.4 km) hike from the end of the dirt road to superb
forest is necessary. In addition to unique birds-of-paradise, visitors
on such an outing may also find spiny anteater, sugar glider, and
tree kangaroo.

496

CHECKLIST

Great Egret   r
Short-billed Egret   r
Pacific Black Duck
Australian Black-shouldered Kite
Crested Baza
Long-tailed Honey-Buzzard
Black Kite   c
Brahminy Kite   c
Whistling Kite
Gray Goshawk
Brown Goshawk   c
Black-mantled Goshawk
Gray-headed Goshawk   r
Collared Sparrowhawk   r
eagle, sp.
Little Eagle   r
Spotted Harrier
Oriental Hobby
Brown Falcon   c
Orange-footed Scrubfowl
Brown Quail   c
Banded Rail   c
Forbes's Rail
Bush-hen
Lesser Golden Plover   M
Little Ringed Plover
Common Sandpiper   M
Superb Fruit-Dove
Diadem Fruit-Dove
White-breasted Fruit-Dove   c
Ornate Fruit-Dove   c
Pink-spotted Fruit-Dove   c
Wompoo Fruit-Dove
Rufous-breasted Fruit-Pigeon   r
Black-belted Fruit-Pigeon
Bare-eyed Mountain-Pigeon   c
Slender-billed Cuckoo-Dove   c
Black-billed Cuckoo-Dove   c
Giant Cuckoo-Dove
White-throated Pigeon   r
Cinnamon Ground-Dove   r
Pheasant Pigeon   r
Dusk-orange Lorikeet   c

Rainbow Lorikeet   c
Goldie's Lorikeet   c
Black-capped Lorikeet
Red-flanked Lorikeet
Little Red Lorikeet   c
Papuan Lory
Whiskered Lorikeet
Musschenbroek's Lorikeet   c
Emerald Lorikeet
Sulfur-crested Cockatoo   r
Red-breasted Pygmy-Parrot   c
Double-eyed Fig-Parrot   r
Brehm's Parrot   c
Madarasz's Parrot
Blue-collared Parrot
Eclectus Parrot
Papuan King-Parrot   c
Oriental Cuckoo   M
Brush Cuckoo   c
Chestnut-breasted Cuckoo
Fan-tailed Cuckoo   r
Rufous-throated Bronze-Cuckoo
White-eared Bronze-Cuckoo
White-crowned Koel
Common Koel   M
Black Jungle Coucal
Black Scrub Coucal
Barn Owl
Hawk-Owl, sp.
Papuan Frogmouth
Moustached Treeswift
White-bellied Swiftlet   c
Mountain Swiftlet   c
Whitehead's Swiftlet
Azure Kingfisher
Mountain Yellow-billed Kingfisher
Sacred Kingfisher   W
Rainbow Bee-eater   W
Dollar Roller   W
Singing Bush-Lark
Pacific Swallow
Varied Triller
Slaty Cuckoo-shrike   r

497

Cicada Cuckoo-shrike   r
Muller's Cuckoo-shrike   c
Black-bellied Cuckoo-shrike
Yellow-eyed Cuckoo-shrike
Rufous-underwing Cuckoo-shrike
Stout-billed Cuckoo-shrike
Hooded Cuckoo-shrike
White-bellied Cuckoo-shrike   c
Richard's Pipit
Gray Wagtail
Pied Bushchat   c
Chestnut-backed Jewel-Babbler
Spotted Jewel-Babbler
Blue-capped Babbler
Orange-crowned Fairywren   r
White-shouldered Fairywren
Golden-headed Cisticola
Mountain Leaf-Warbler   c
New Guinea Thornbill   r
Gray Gerygone   c
Black-throated Gerygone
Large-billed Gerygone
Treefern Gerygone
Pale-billed Scrubwren
Noisy Scrubwren
Buffy-faced Scrubwren
Gray-green Scrubwren   r
Chanting Scrubwren
White-throated Scrubwren
Mountain Peltops   c
Black-throated Thicket-Fantail
Rufous-backed Fantail   r
Dimorphic Fantail   c
Black Fantail   c
Chestnut-bellied Fantail
Friendly Fantail   c
Willie Wagtail   c
Northern Fantail   c
Fantail Monarch
Black-faced Monarch
Black-winged Monarch   c
White-bellied Monarch
Spot-winged Monarch
Frilled Monarch
Satin Monarch
Black-breasted Flatbill
Yellow-footed Flycatcher

Canary Flycatcher
Torrent Flycatcher
Red-backed Robin
White-faced Robin
Black-throated Flyrobin
Black Flyrobin
Blue Flyrobin
White-browed Flyrobin
Golden-faced Whistler
Mottled Whistler
Sclater's Whistler
Regent Whistler   c
Gray-headed Whistler
Modest Whistler   c
Black-headed Whistler
White-bellied Whistler
Rufous-naped Whistler
Rufous Shrike-thrush
Gray Shrike-thrush
Hooded Pitohui
Dusky Pitohui
Wattled Ploughbill
Schach Shrike
White-breasted Woodswallow
Black-breasted (Greater)
   Woodswallow   c
Metallic Starling
Golden-breasted Myna
Brown Oriole   c
Torrentlark
Hooded Butcherbird   c
Spangled Drongo   c
Pygmy Drongo   r
Loria's Bird-of-Paradise   r
Crinkle-collared Manucode
Trumpet Manucode   r
Magnificent Riflebird   c
Brown Sicklebill Bird-of-Paradise
   r
Princess Stephanie's Astrapia   c
Superb Bird-of-Paradise
Lawes's Parotia
King Bird-of-Paradise
Magnificent Bird-of-Paradise
Blue Bird-of-Paradise   r
Raggiana Bird-of-Paradise   c
White-throated Catbird

MacGregor's Gardenerbird
Fawn-breasted Bowerbird   c
Black Sittella
Mountain Sittela
New Guinea Treecreeper
Olive-backed Sunbird
Gray-winged Bowbill
Mountain Red-headed Myzomela
   c
Black-and-red Myzomela   c
Black Myzomela
Smoky Melipotes   c
Sooty Melidectes
Cinnamon-browed Melidectes
Belford's Melidectes   c
Cinnamon-breasted Melidectes   c
Long-billed Honeyeater
Obscure Honeyeater
Black-throated Honeyeater
Brown Honeyeater   c
Many-spotted Honeyeater

Puff-backed Honeyeater
Diamond Honeyeater
Red-backed Honeyeater   c
Meyer's Friarbird   c
Helmeted (Papuan) Friarbird   c
Red-capped Flowerpecker   c
Black Berrypecker   c
Yellow-bellied Berrypecker   r
Fan-tailed Berrypecker   c
Spotted Berrypecker   c
Tit-Berrypecker   c
Crested Berrypecker   r
Black-fronted White-eye
New Guinea Mountain White-eye
   c
Blue-faced Parrot-Finch
Streak-headed Munia   c
Grand Munia
Chestnut-breasted Munia
New Britain Munia

100
Port Moresby, Papua New Guinea

PORT MORESBY, THE CAPITAL OF PAPUA NEW GUINEA, is served by jets from Honolulu, Tokyo, Manila, Sydney, Brisbane, Cairns, and Fiji. It is much more westernized than visitors expect, with paved roads, many air-conditioned hotels, and even a bird club. The old Port Moresby Bird Club is now the New Guinea Bird Society, PO Box 1598, Boroko (Port Moresby), Papua New Guinea.

Common birds around town and the hotels are Peaceful Dove, Papuan Frogmouth, Willie Wagtail, Green Figbird, and Rufous-banded, Tawny-breasted, and Yellow-tinted Honeyeaters. Crested and Bridled Terns, Eastern Reef-Heron, and Lesser Frigatebirds can be seen over the ocean. The airport's fields have Australian Pratincole, Little Curlew, Singing Bush-Lark, and Pacific Swallow.

The Moitaka (Waigani) sewerage ponds and neighboring marshes are very rich in birds, particularly in the morning. Many rarities show up, and among the birds commonly seen are cormorants, herons (including Pied), whistling-ducks, Whistling Kite, rails, Purple Swamphen, Comb-crested Jacana, Masked Lapwing, sandpipers, stilt, and many savanna birds.

The climate of the coast is quite dry, with only 45 inches (1143 mm) of rain, mostly falling between December and March. The hills are considerably wetter, however. From May to November the land is dry and parched, and the dirt roads become dust bowls. Thus most of the countryside (except the river valleys and higher mountains) supports a savanna grassland with scattered eucalyptus and scrub. In these ubiquitous savannas look for Bar-shouldered Dove, Pheasant Coucal, Blue-winged Kookaburra, White-shouldered Fairywren, White-throated Gerygone, Mimic Honeyeater, Papuan Friarbird, and mannikins.

There is some wet forest along the Brown River, an hour's ride north of town. Trucks make birding difficult by midmorning since there is a scarcity of wide trails away from the road. This and the Vanapa River area should be birded for several days because of their

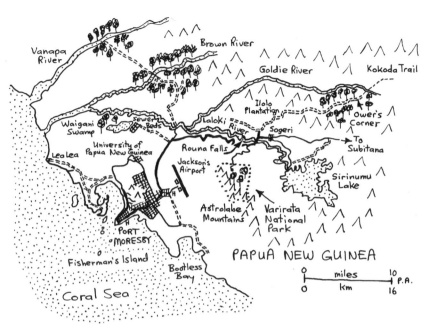

rich avifauna. Watch for Orange-bellied Fruit-Dove, Black-belted Fruit-Pigeon, parrots (including Red-cheeked), Rufous-bellied Kookaburra, Lowland Yellow-billed Kingfisher, Green-backed Gerygone, Lowland Peltops, fantails, Frilled Monarch, Yellow-faced and Golden-breasted Mynas, Magnificent Riflebird, King Bird-of-Paradise, Raggiana Bird-of-Paradise, sunbirds, and honeyeaters.

A pretty area in the foothills is around Rouna Falls, where there are trails and some woodland. Brahminy Kite, White-bellied Swiftlet, Moustached Treeswift, and savanna birds predominate. The Varirata National Park, which has some trails and a few good birds, can be reached via a spur road south.

The best birding for foothill wet-forest birds is along the last few miles of the new road to Ower's Corner. A dawn trip in that area can be immensely rewarding, even from the road, which, being a dead end, has very little traffic. In these forested hills look for Gray-headed Goshawk, Dusk-orange Lorikeet, Black-capped Lorikeet, White-crowned Koel, Golden Triller, Stout-billed Cuckoo-shrike, Raggiana Bird-of-Paradise, and Red Myzomela.

CHECKLIST

Australian Dabchick c
Brown Booby
Little Pied Cormorant c
Little Black Cormorant c
Darter
Greater Frigatebird
Lesser Frigatebird c
White-faced Heron r
Pied Heron c
Cattle Heron r
Great Egret c
Little Egret c
Short-billed Egret c
Eastern Reef-Heron
Green Heron
Nankeen Night-Heron
Sacred Ibis r
Royal Spoonbill r
Water Whistling-Duck
Spotted Whistling-Duck c
Pacific Black Duck
Gray Teal
Green Pygmy-Goose r
Crested Baza
Long-tailed Honey-Buzzard r
Black Kite
Brahminy Kite c
Whistling Kite c
Gray Goshawk r
Brown Goshawk
Gray-headed Goshawk
Collared Sparrowhawk
Little Eagle
White-bellied Sea-Eagle r
Marsh Harrier
Peregrine Falcon r
Brown Falcon r
Orange-footed Scrubfowl r
King Quail
Brown Quail
Lewin's Rail
White-browed Crake
Bush-hen r

Dusky Gallinule c
Purple Swamphen c
Comb-crested Jacana c
Masked Plover c
Lesser Golden Plover c M
Mongolian Plover M
Great Sand Plover M
Little Ringed Plover
Whimbrel M
Little Curlew M
Wandering Tattler M
Common Sandpiper c M
Terek Sandpiper r M
Japanese Snipe c M
Black-tailed Godwit M
Sharp-tailed Sandpiper c M
Curlew Sandpiper M
Red-necked Stint M
Black-winged Stilt c M
Australian Pratincole W
White-winged Black Tern M
Gull-billed Tern
Common Tern M
Black-naped Tern
Bridled Tern
Greater Crested Tern c
Lesser Crested Tern
Superb Fruit-Dove
Beautiful Fruit-Dove
Diadem Fruit-Dove
Orange-bellied Fruit-Dove c
Dwarf Fruit-Dove r
Orange-fronted Fruit-Dove c
Ornate Fruit-Dove
Pink-spotted Fruit-Dove
Wompoo Fruit-Dove c
Torres Strait Fruit-Pigeon
Pinon Fruit-Pigeon
Black-belted Fruit-Pigeon c
Bare-eyed Mountain-Pigeon c
Slender-billed Cuckoo-Dove c
Black-billed Cuckoo-Dove
Bar-shouldered Dove

Peaceful Dove   c
Green-winged Pigeon
Cinnamon Ground-Dove
Yellow-streaked Lorikeet   r
Dusk-orange Lorikeet
Rainbow Lorikeet   c
Black-capped Lorikeet
Red-flanked Lorikeet
Sulfur-crested Cockatoo   r
Buff-faced Pygmy-Parrot   r
Orange-breasted Fig-Parrot
Double-eyed Fig-Parrot
Red-cheeked Parrot   c
Eclectus Parrot
Papuan King-Parrot
Oriental Cuckoo   r M
Brush Cuckoo   c
Red-eyed Bronze-Cuckoo   r
White-crowned Koel
Common Koel   M
Channel-billed Cuckoo
Black Jungle Coucal
Pheasant Coucal   c
Barn Owl
Papuan Frogmouth
Large-tailed Nightjar
Moustached Treeswift
White-bellied Swiftlet   c
Uniform Swiftlet   c
White-throated Needletail   M
Papuan Needletail   r
Azure Kingfisher
Little Kingfisher   r
Rufous-bellied Kookaburra   c
Blue-winged Kookaburra   c
Macleay's Kingfisher
Lowland Yellow-billed Kingfisher
Mountain Yellow-billed Kingfisher
Sacred Kingfisher   c W
Common Paradise-Kingfisher
Rainbow Bee-eater   c
Dollar Roller   c
Singing Bush-Lark   c
Pacific Swallow   c
Tree Martin
Golden Triller   r
White-winged Triller

Varied Triller
Black Cuckoo-shrike
Muller's Cuckoo-shrike   r
Yellow-eyed Cuckoo-shrike
Rufous-underwing Cuckoo-shrike
   c
Stout-billed Cuckoo-shrike
Black-faced Cuckoo-shrike   c
White-bellied Cuckoo-shrike   c
Pied Bushchat
Lowland Jewel-babbler   r
Papuan Babbler
Cobalt Fairywren
White-shouldered Fairywren
Clamorous Reed-Warbler   c
Golden-headed Cisticola   c
Yellow-bellied Gerygone   c
Green-backed Gerygone   c
Black-throated Gerygone
Large-billed Gerygone
Mangrove Gerygone
White-throated Gerygone
Chanting Scrubwren
Lowland Peltops
Mountain Peltops
Sooty Thicket-Fantail
Black-throated Thicket-Fantail
Willie Wagtail   c
Banded Fantail
Black-faced Monarch
Black-winged Monarch
Spot-winged Monarch
Golden Monarch   r
Frilled Monarch   c
Shining Monarch
Leaden Monarch
Lemon-breasted Flycatcher   c
Black-tailed Whistler   r
Gray-headed Whistler
Rufous Shrike-thrush
Gray Shrike-thrush   c
Hooded Pitohui
Rusty Pitohui
White-breasted Woodswallow   c
Singing Starling   c
Metallic Starling   c
Yellow-faced Myna   c

Golden-breasted Myna
Brown Oriole   c
Green Figbird
Hooded Butcherbird
Black-backed Butcherbird   c
Black Butcherbird
Spangled Drongo   c
Torresian Crow   c
Bare-faced Crow
Glossy-mantled Manucode
Jobi Manucode   r
Trumpet Manucode   r
Magnificent Riflebird
King Bird-of-Paradise
Raggiana Bird-of-Paradise
Fawn-breasted Bowerbird
Black Sunbird   c
Olive-backed Sunbird
Gray-winged Bowbill   r
Rufous-banded Honeyeater   c
Modest Honeyeater   c
Freckled Honeyeater
Pale-eyed Honeyeater   r

Pygmy Honeyeater   r
Dwarf Honeyeater
Dusky Myzomela   c
White-throated Myzomela
Red Myzomela
Black Myzomela
White-throated Honeyeater
Long-billed Honeyeater
Brown Honeyeater
Singing Honeyeater
Yellow-tinted Honeyeater   c
Mimic Honeyeater   c
White-marked Honeyeater
Graceful Honeyeater
Helmeted Friarbird
Red-capped Flowerpecker
Black Berrypecker
Black-fronted White-eye
Streak-headed Munia   r
Gray-headed Mannikin   c
Grand Mannikin
Chestnut-breasted Mannikin

101
Darwin, Northern Territory

DARWIN, A SMALL, MODERN CITY at the northern tip of Australia
on the Timor Sea, has an important airport with good connections to
all of Australia but only a few flights a week to Bali and Singapore.
There are hotels and motels, rental cars, and a road system that allows
access to most of the better bird habitats.

The birdlife is rich, abundant, and varied, perhaps the most exciting
birding spot in Australia. Darwin averages 65 inches (1651 mm) of rain
a year, most of it from December to March. Thus from January
through April all but the paved roads are impassable, and most tourists visit between May and late November. In the wet season wildlife
is scattered, but in the dry season birds are attracted to the numerous
lagoons in often spectacular numbers.

Visitors with only one full day will do well to go to Fogg and
Humpty-Doo Dams. Go south on the Stuart Highway for about 22
miles (35.2 km) through eucalyptus forest and turn left on the Arnhem (Marrakai) Highway, a paved road. About 12 miles (19.2 km) out
there is a fork. Take the left for 2 miles (3 km), until you see the signs
indicating Fogg Dam to the left. A dirt road goes over the low earthen
dam, where you should see many waterbirds including thousands of
Magpie Geese and numbers of White-headed Shelduck, jacana, stork,
ibis, spoonbills, whistling-duck, and shorebirds. The surrounding eucalyptus woodlands have many passerines. Fortunately no permit is
needed here or for other areas mentioned. Returning to the fork and
taking a left turn you cross Humpty-Doo Dam, a good spot for Brolga
Crane and home to many waterbirds when water levels are good.
Continuing eastward, the road crosses the Adelaide River and a section of the Marrakai Plains, which by October have thousands of
Little Curlew. It then enters more woodland from which the safari
trips leave the road northward out onto unmarked tracks that are not
recommended for rented cars. This entire road is fine for birds of the
plains, ponds, and edge, with the added attraction of Red-tailed Black
Cockatoo, Galah, and Blue-winged Kookaburra. Agile wallaby and
the introduced Asian water buffalo are commonly seen among the
magnetic anthills and billibongs.

For wet-forest birds you should visit Howard Springs, located 15 miles (24 km) east of Darwin and reached by a four-mile paved road running east from the Stuart Highway. Howard Springs is a swimming spot surrounded by a riparian "rain" forest and features the elusive Rainbow Pitta. The Howard River to the east (reached via a good gravel road going right before the entrance to the springs) is flanked by even more wet forest and can be excellent just after dawn.

The mangrove habitat has some special birds, for example, some of the robins, whistlers, and shrike-thrushes. Berry Springs to the southwest of Noonamah is a good spot.

An excellent shorebird roost at high tide near Darwin can be visited by going to the rocks on the ocean at the west end of the suburb of Nightcliff (on Casuarina Drive). It is a superb place for Oriental, Mongolian, and Great Sand Plover, Gray-tailed Tattler, and many other shorebirds.

Those with more time should consider going much farther east to one of the lodges along the rivers near the rugged western escarpment

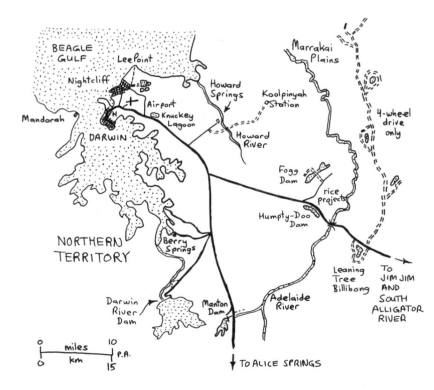

of western Arnhemland. The Nourlangie Camp and the Patonga Safari Lodge on Jim Jim Creek serve as good bases to see aboriginal cave paintings, giant anthills, many mammals, and masses of birds. This area has four unique birds as well: the Black-banded Fruit-Dove, Chestnut-quilled Pigeon, Partridge Pigeon, and White-lined Honeyeater. The area can be reached by road in five hours or by small plane from Darwin, using local vehicles and guides upon arriving.

CHECKLIST

Australian Dabchick   c
Australian Pelican   c
Australian Darter   c
Little Black Cormorant
Little Pied Cormorant   c
Darter
White-necked Heron
White-faced Heron
Pied Heron   c
Green Heron
Cattle Heron   c
Great Egret   c
Little Egret   c
Short-billed Egret   c
Eastern Reef-Heron
Nankeen Night-Heron
Black Bittern   r
Black-necked Stork   c
Sacred Ibis
Straw-necked Ibis   c
Glossy Ibis   c
Royal Spoonbill   c
Magpie Goose   c
Water Whistling-Duck   c
Plumed Whistling-Duck   c
White-headed Shelduck   c
Pacific Black Duck   c
Gray Teal   c
Green Pygmy-Goose   c
Australian Black-shouldered Kite
Black Kite   c
Black-breasted Kite   r
Brahminy Kite
Whistling Kite   c
Gray Goshawk   r

Brown Goshawk   r
Collared Sparrowhawk   r
White-bellied Sea-Eagle
Marsh Harrier
Osprey
Australian Hobby
Nankeen Kestrel
Brown Falcon   c
Orange-footed Scrubfowl
Brown Quail   r
Brolga Crane
Chestnut Rail   r
Banded Rail
White-browed Crake   W
Purple Swamphen   W
Comb-crested Jacana   c
Australian Bustard   r
Common Oystercatcher
Masked Lapwing   c
Red-kneed Plover   W
Black-fronted Plover
Red-capped Plover   c
Mongolian Plover   c M
Great Sand Plover   c M
Oriental Plover   M
Lesser Golden Plover   c M
Gray Plover   M
Ruddy Turnstone   M
Little Curlew   c M
Eastern Curlew   M
Whimbrel   M
Marsh Sandpiper   M
Common Greenshank   c M
Wood Sandpiper   M
Common Sandpiper   c M

Gray-tailed Tattler   c M
Terek Sandpiper M
Red Knot   M
Great Knot   c M
Sharp-tailed Sandpiper   c M
Red-necked Stint   c M
Curlew Sandpiper   M
Broad-billed Sandpiper   M
Sanderling   M
Bar-tailed Godwit   M
Black-tailed Godwit   M
Swinhoe's Snipe   M
Black-winged Stilt   c
Bushcurlew   r
Great Thick-knee   r
Australian Pratincole   W
Silver Gull   r
Whiskered Tern   c W
White-winged Black Tern   M
Caspian Tern
Gull-billed Tern   W
Little Tern   W
Greater Crested Tern   c
Lesser Crested Tern
Red-crowned Fruit-Dove
Torres Strait Fruit-Pigeon   c S
Bar-shouldered Dove
Peaceful Dove   c
Diamond Dove   r W
Green-winged Pigeon   r
Rainbow Lorikeet   c
Varied Lorikeet
Red-tailed Black-Cockatoo   c
Sulfur-crested Cockatoo
Little Corella   c
Galah   c
Cockatiel   W
Red-winged Parrot   c
Northern Rosella
Oriental Cuckoo   r M
Pallid Cuckoo   r
Brush Cuckoo
Horsfield's Bronze-Cuckoo   r W
Red-eyed Bronze-Cuckoo
Common Koel   S
Channel-billed Cuckoo   r
Pheasant Coucal

Barn Owl
Boobook Hawk-Owl
Barking Hawk-Owl
Australian Frogmouth
Spotted Nightjar   r S
Large-tailed Nightjar
Fork-tailed Swift   M
Little Kingfisher   r
Azure Kingfisher
Blue-winged Kookaburra   c
Macleay's Kingfisher   c
Sacred Kingfisher
Red-backed Kingfisher
White-collared Kingfisher
Rainbow Bee-eater   c
Dollar Roller   c S
Rainbow Pitta
Singing Bush-Lark   r
Tree Martin
Fairy Martin   W
Richard's Pipit
Black-faced Cuckoo-shrike   c
White-bellied Cuckoo-shrike   c
White-winged Triller   c
Varied Triller
Gray-crowned Babbler
Clamorous Reed-Warbler   r
Golden-headed Cisticola
Zitting Cisticola
Rufous Songlark   r W
Red-backed Fairywren   r
White-throated Gerygone   r S
Large-billed Gerygone   r
Green-backed Gerygone
Mangrove Gerygone
Lemon-breasted Flycatcher   c
Weebill
Mangrove Robin
White-browed Flyrobin   r
Banded Fantail
Willie Wagtail   c
Leaden Monarch
Mangrove Monarch   r
Shining Monarch
Restless Flycatcher
Rufous Whistler
White-breasted Whistler

Gray Whistler
Rufous Shrike-thrush   r
Mistletoebird
Striated Pardalote   W
Mangrove Silvereye
Black-tailed Treecreeper
Brown Honeyeater   c
Dusky Myzomela
Mangrove Red-headed Myzomela
White-gaped Honeyeater   c
Black-chinned Honeyeater
White-throated Honeyeater
Blue-faced Honeyeater   c
Helmeted Friarbird   r W
Little Friarbird   c
Silver-crowned Friarbird   c
White-rumped Miner
Bar-breasted Honeyeater
Rufous-banded Honeyeater
Rufous-throated Honeyeater
Banded Honeyeater
Crimson Finch   c

Chestnut-breasted Munia   r
Masked Finch
Pictorella Finch   r
Long-tailed Finch   c
Double-barred Finch   c
Gouldian Finch   r
Olive-backed Oriole   S
Yellow Oriole   c
Green Figbird   c
Spangled Drongo
Magpielark   c
White-breasted Woodswallow   W
Masked Woodswallow   r W
White-browed Woodswallow   r W
Black-faced Woodswallow   c
Little Woodswallow   W
Pied Butcherbird   c
Gray Butcherbird
Black Butcherbird
Great Bowerbird
Torresian Crow   c

102
Alice Springs, Northern Territory

ALICE SPRINGS IS A SMALL CITY in the very heart of Australia's "Center." It is surprisingly well-known around the world, and today has miles of paved streets, a small business district, several fine hotels and motels, an airport serviced by jets from the capital cities, and a network of paved roads in several directions. There are such extremely wet and dry years in the interior that many birds have learned to be opportunistic nomads and the bird watcher will note great variation from one visit to the next.

The city lies in a valley among the MacDonnel Ranges, which run east to west with several gaps. Plenty of trees around town ensure a variety of birdlife at the motels and along the river beds. Some town birds are kites, falcons, Diamond Dove, Port Lincoln Parrot, Black-faced Cuckoo-shrike, honeyeaters, and Magpielark.

Around the airport watch for Australian Pratincole and Richard's Pipit. Between the airport and town, just before reaching the gap where the railroad, highway, and river squeeze through, take a dirt road west to a dump and sewage ponds, often known as the "water works." These can be very good for waders and ducks. During the day, when the gates are open, visitors can drive around the dykes. Since they allow duck hunting in Alice Springs, birds straying away from the ponds are shot and as a result are alert and shy. Hoary-headed Grebe, Plumed Whistling-Duck, Pink-eared Duck, and a number of herons, spoonbills, other ducks, plovers, and sandpipers may be found. The road beyond crosses a creek bed about three miles (5 km) farther on. This area is good for parrots, White-backed Swallow, babblers, and honeyeaters.

In the vicinity of town are several small national parks. Simpson's Gap, the most accessible, is just 10 miles (16 km) west via a paved road. It has a large number of ghost gums *(Eucalyptus papuana)* and good cover for wildlife. The gap itself is a water gap, out through the MacDonnel Ranges, reached via a marked dirt road to the right. This passes a pond, a riverbed, and some good fields, and is flanked by stunted open woodland. Birds seen in a good year include Crested Pigeon, Galah, Budgerygar, Red-backed Kingfisher, Rufous Songlark, Black-faced Woodswallow, White-winged Triller, White-plumed Honeyeater, and many others. The park is open from eight to eight, and a small fee is charged.

Ayer's Rock–Mount Olga National Park, an hour's flight to the southwest, is on a number of itineraries. A night at one of the small hotels, both for photographing the huge "rock" and for dawn and dusk desert birding, can be rewarding. The road to the Olgas and the scrub north of the airport can both be worthwhile if it is not overly hot and windy. A touring bus meets the daily flight from Alice Springs.

CHECKLIST

Australian Dabchick c	White-faced Heron
Hoary-headed Grebe c	Great Egret r
Australian Pelican r	Short-billed Egret r
Little Red Cormorant	Glossy Ibis r
Great Cormorant r	Sacred Ibis r
Darter r	Straw-necked Ibis
White-necked Heron	Royal Spoonbill r

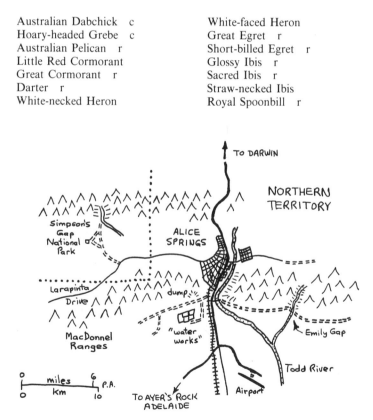

Yellow-billed Spoonbill
Plumed Whistling-Duck
Pacific Black Duck   c
Gray Teal   c
Pink-eared Duck
White-eyed Pochard   r
Maned Duck   r
Australian Black-shouldered Kite
   c
Letter-winged Kite   r
Black Kite   c
Whistling Kite   c
Brown Goshawk   r
Collared Sparrowhawk
Little Eagle
Wedge-tailed Eagle
Spotted Harrier   r
Peregrine Falcon
Australian Hobby
Nankeen Kestrel   c
Brown Falcon   c
Little Buttonquail   r
Black-tailed Gallinule   r
Purple Swamphen
Common Coot
Australian Bustard   r
Masked Lapwing   c
Red-kneed Plover   c
Black-fronted Plover
Common Sandpiper   c M
Common Greenshank   M
Wood Sandpiper   M
Black-winged Stilt   c
Red-necked Avocet   c
Australian Pratincole
Whiskered Tern
Gull-billed Tern
Diamond Dove   c
Common Bronzewing
Crested Pigeon   c
Plumed Pigeon
Red-tailed Black-Cockatoo   r
Major Mitchell's Cockatoo   r
Galah   c
Cockatiel   r
Port Lincoln Parrot   c
Mulga Parrot

Bourke Parrot
Budgerygar   c
Pallid Cuckoo   r
Black-eared Cuckoo   r
Horsfield's Bronze-Cuckoo   r
Barn Owl   r
Boobook Hawk-Owl   r
Australian Frogmouth   r
Australian Owlet-Nightjar
Spotted Nightjar
Red-backed Kingfisher   c
Rainbow Bee-eater   c
White-backed Swallow   c
Tree Martin   c
Fairy Martin
Richard's Pipit   c
Black-faced Cuckoo-shrike
Ground Cuckoo-shrike
White-winged Triller   S
Chestnut Quail-thrush   r
Cinnamon Quail-thrush   r
Gray-crowned Babbler
White-browed Babbler
Brown Songlark
Rufous Songlark   c
Turquoise Wren
Blue-and-white Wren
Variegated Wren
Rufous-crowned Emu-wren   r
Clamorous Reed-Warbler
Western Gerygone
Weebill
Broad-tailed Thornbill   r
Slate-backed Thornbill   r
Chestnut-rumped Thornbill
Yellow-rumped Thornbill
Red-throated Scrubwren   r
Southern Whiteface   c
Banded Whiteface
Dusky Grasswren   r
Striated Grasswren   r
Crimson Chat   r
Orange Chat   r
Red-capped Robin
Hooded Robin   c
Willie Wagtail   c
Rufous Whistler   r

Gray Shrike-thrush
Crested Bellbird
Chiming Wedgebill   r
White-browed Treecreeper
Varied Sittela   r
Mistletoebird
Striated Pardalote   W
Red-browed Pardalote
Black Honeyeater   r
Pied Honeyeater   r
Singing Honeyeater   r
Yellow-fronted Honeyeater
Gray-headed Honeyeater
White-plumed Honeyeater   c
White-rumped Miner   c

White-fronted Honeyeater   r
Spiny-cheeked Honeyeater   c
White-rumped Miner
Painted Finch   r
Zebra Finch   c
Magpielark   c
Masked Woodswallow   r
Black-faced Woodswallow   c
Little Woodswallow   r
Gray Butcherbird
Pied Butcherbird
Australian Magpie   c
Spotted Bowerbird   r
Little Crow   c
Torresian Crow

103
Perth–Albany,
Western Australia

PERTH, WITH INTERNATIONAL AIR CONNECTIONS from Africa, Asia, and Europe, is a beautiful city isolated in the southwestern corner of Australia. The climate is Mediterranean, with winter rains followed by superb wildflowers in the spring. King's Park and nearby Pelican Point on the Swan River host many species of local birds. Look for Whistling Kite, Red-necked Avocet, Silver Gull, Purple-crowned Lorikeet, White-tailed Black-Cockatoo (autumn and winter), Australian Frogmouth, Singing Honeyeater, Red Wattlebird, Western Spinebill, thornbills, Western Warbler, and Gray Butcherbird.

Red-capped Parrots, members of a genus endemic to this area, occur commonly to the south, particularly in the forests of marri *(Eucalyptus calophylla).* Birds are plentiful in the wet forests of the Darling Ranges, such as at Yanchep and John Forrest National Park.

The Dryandra Forest Reserve is located 100 miles (160 km) southeast of Perth, about 12.5 miles (20 km) northwest of Narrogin, where there is accommodation. This area is drier than those to the west, being open forest and heath. In the wandoo forests *(Eucalyptus wandoo)* look for Shrike-tit, Rufous Treecreeper, Blue-breasted Fairywren, Western Yellow-Robin, Gray Shrike-thrush, Chestnut Quailthrush, Western Rosella, Port Lincoln Parrot, and White-tailed Black-Cockatoo. In the higher areas flowers of the genus *Dryandra* attract wattlebirds, spinebills, and numerous other honeyeaters, including White-eared, Yellow-plumed, Brown-headed, White-naped, Brown, White-cheeked, and New Holland. Two special attractions are the rare numbat (banded anteater), and the mound-building Malleefowl.

Albany is a small city located at the western end of the Great Australian Bight, 252 miles (406 km) southeast of Perth. Winters here are wet (30 inches [762 mm] of rain) and windy (May–August). Visitors may be able to arrange a boat to visit Eclipse Island, south of Albany. In the winter it is possible to see large rafts of up to five species of albatrosses, shearwaters, skuas, and other pelagics. In the

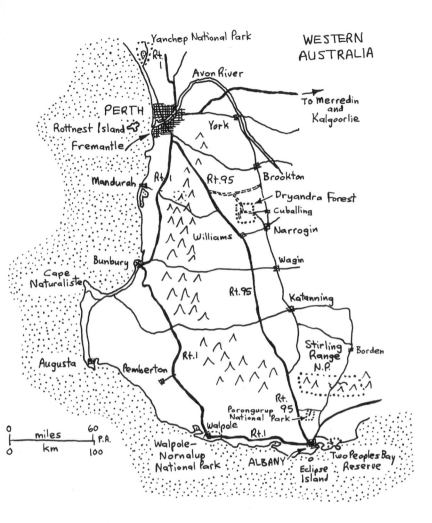

summer the island is a nesting site for Great-winged Petrel, Pale-footed Shearwater, and Little Shearwater. Yellow-nosed Albatross can often be seen close to shore from a cliff-walk called "the Gap" 7 miles (11.2 km) south of Albany.

The Two Peoples Bay reserve, located about 22 miles (35 km) east of Albany, via Kalgan Lower, is dominated by Mount Gardner, which offers fine views of ocean, lakes, and swamps. This new reserve replaced an announced townsite when the presumedly extinct Noisy Scrub-bird was rediscovered living in the area. It is as elusive as two other extreme rarities also living in the park: Western Bristlebird and

Western Whipbird. It would not be unusual to miss seeing all three in a full day's work. There is a resident warden here who should be contacted and who will instruct you on closed areas and give you tips. Other species of interest in the area are Brush Bronzewing, Rock Parrot (also check the Albany railway yards where they eat spilled grain), Swamp Parrot, Red-capped Parrot, Southern Emu-wren, Red-winged Fairywren, White-breasted Robin, Tawny-crowned Honeyeater, and the beautiful Red-eared Firetail.

CHECKLIST

Emu   r
Great Crested Grebe
Australian Dabchick
Hoary-headed Grebe
Little Penguin
Wandering Albatross   r W
Black-browed Albatross   c W
Gray-headed Albatross   W
Yellow-nosed Albatross   c W
Shy Albatross   W
Giant Petrel   W
Great-winged Petrel
Cape Petrel   W
White-headed Petrel   W
Medium-billed Prion   W
Pale-footed Shearwater
Little Shearwater
Sooty Shearwater   r S
Wedge-tailed Shearwater
Wilson's Storm-Petrel   M
White-faced Storm-Petrel
Australian Pelican
Tasman Gannet
Red-tailed Tropicbird   r
Darter
Little Pied Cormorant   c
Black-faced Cormorant   r
Yellow-faced Cormorant
Great Cormorant   c
Little Black Cormorant   c
White-necked Heron   r
White-faced Heron   c
Cattle Heron
Great Egret

Eastern Reef-Heron
Nankeen Night-Heron
Little Bittern   r
Black Bittern
Brown Bittern
Straw-necked Ibis   c
Black Swan   c
Mute Swan
Freckled Duck   r
Cape Barren Goose   r
Chestnut-breasted Shelduck   c
Pacific Black Duck   c
Gray Teal   c
Chestnut Teal   c
White-faced Shoveler   r
Pink-eared Duck
White-eyed Pochard
Maned Duck   c
Blue-billed Duck
Musk Duck   c
Osprey
Australian Black-shouldered Kite
Whistling Kite   c
Square-tailed Kite   r
Collared Sparrowhawk
Brown Goshawk
Little Eagle
White-bellied Sea-Eagle   r
Wedge-tailed Eagle
Spotted Harrier   r
Marsh Harrier
Australian Hobby
Peregrine Falcon   r
Brown Falcon   c

Nankeen Kestrel   c
Malleefowl
Stubble Quail
Brown Quail
King Quail
Banded Rail
Lewin's Rail   r
Australian Crake   r
Spotless Crake
Baillon's Crake   r
Black-tailed Gallinule   r
Dusky Gallinule
Common Coot   c
Bushcurlew
Common Oystercatcher
Tasman Oystercatcher
Banded Lapwing   c
Lesser Golden Plover   r M
Gray Plover   M
Red-kneed Plover
Hooded Plover
Double-banded Plover   r W
Great Sand Plover   M
Red-capped Plover   c
Black-fronted Plover
Black-winged Stilt
Red-necked Avocet
Banded Stilt   r
Ruddy Turnstone   M
Eastern Curlew   r M
Wood Sandpiper   M
Common Greenshank   M
Common Sandpiper   M
Terek Sandpiper   r M
Bar-tailed Godwit   M
Red Knot   r M
Great Knot   r M
Sharp-tailed Sandpiper   c M
Red-necked Stint   c M
Curlew Sandpiper   c M
Sanderling   M
Great Skua   c W
Parasitic Jaeger   M
Silver Gull   c
Pacific Gull
Kelp Gull   r
Caspian Tern

Whiskered Tern
Bridled Tern
Crested Tern   c
White-lored Tern
Spotted Turtle-Dove   c
Laughing Turtle-Dove
Common Bronzewing   c
Brush Bronzewing   r
Red-tailed Black-Cockatoo   r
White-tailed Black-Cockatoo   c
Little Corella   r
Long-billed Corella
Galah
Purple-crowned Lorikeet   c
Regent Parrot
Swamp Parrot   r
Red-capped Parrot   c
Western Rosella
Port Lincoln Parrot   c
Mulga Parrot
Elegant Parrot
Rock Parrot
Pallid Cuckoo   c S
Fan-tailed Cuckoo   c S
Black-eared Cuckoo   S
Horsfield's Bronze-Cuckoo   S
Shining Bronze-Cuckoo   S
Barn Owl
Masked Owl   r
Boobook Hawk-Owl
Barking Hawk-Owl   r
Australian Frogmouth
Australian Owlet-Nightjar
Spotted Nightjar   r
Fork-tailed Swift   M
Laughing Kookaburra
Sacred Kingfisher   c S
Rainbow Bee-eater   S
Noisy Scrub-bird   r
Welcome Swallow   c
Tree Martin   c
Fairy Martin   r
Richard's Pipit
Black-faced Cuckoo-shrike   c
White-winged Triller   S
Southern Scrub-Robin   r
Chestnut Quail-thrush   r

Scarlet Robin   c
Red-capped Robin
Hooded Robin
White-breasted Robin   c
Western Yellow-Robin   c
Jacky Winter
Shrike-tit
Rufous Whistler   c
Golden Whistler   c
Gray Shrike-thrush   c
Crested Bellbird   r
Restless Monarch   r
Gray Fantail   c
Willie Wagtail   c
Western Whipbird   r
White-browed Babbler
Clamorous Reed-Warbler
Little Grass-Warbler
Rufous Songlark   S
Brown Songlark   S
Splendid Fairywren   c
Blue-crested Fairywren
Red-winged Fairywren
Southern Emu-wren   r
Western Bristlebird   r
Rufous Bristlebird   r
White-browed Scrubwren   c
Fieldwren
Broad-tailed Thornbill   c
Yellow-rumped Thornbill   c
Western Thornbill   c
Western Gerygone   c
Weebill   c
White-fronted Chat

Varied Sittela   c
Rufous Treecreeper
Red Wattlebird   c
Little Wattlebird
Spiny-cheeked Honeyeater
White-rumped Miner
Singing Honeyeater   c
White-eared Honeyeater
Purple-gaped Honeyeater
White-plumed Honeyeater
Yellow-plumed Honeyeater
Brown-headed Honeyeater
White-naped Honeyeater
Brown Honeyeater   c
New Holland Honeyeater   c
White-cheeked Honeyeater
Tawny-crowned Honeyeater
Western Spinebill   c
Mistletoebird
Spotted Pardalote
Striated Pardalote
Silvereye   c
Eurasian Goldfinch
Zebra Finch
Red-browed Firetail   r
Red-eared Firetail   r
Magpielark   c
Black-faced Woodswallow   c
Dusky Woodswallow
Gray Butcherbird   c
Australian Magpie   c
Gray Currawong   c
Australian Raven   c
Little Crow

104
National Parks of the "Mallee," Victoria

IN THE DRY COUNTRY OF NORTHWESTERN VICTORIA are three outstanding national parks boasting some of Australia's best wildlife. Many parrots and kangaroos can be seen while searching for Emu and Malleefowl. The area has rain between May and October, but with great seasonal variation, and is subject to droughts. It can be dry and windy in summer.

Mallee is a term used to describe the dense, dwarf, many-trunked eucalyptus scrub woodland that blankets much of the area. Other habitats include patches of pines on sand dunes, tall gums on riparian bottoms, and dry heaths. The wheat farms of the area have taken much of the water that used to flood into these parks periodically, and many plants and animals have suffered. Wyperfeld National Park, for instance, is one of the few protected places in Australia where visitors can easily see many Emu and large kangaroos in the wild. Unfortunately there is no lodge, and visitors must camp or commute from motels in Dimboola, Jeparit, Hopetown, and Mildura.

Little Desert National Park, 15 miles (24 km) west of Dimboola, is a fine place to see Malleefowl. The sandy road-and-trail leading to a well-known mound of this "incubator-bird" turns right shortly after entering the park. The area is good for Gilbert Whistler, Southern Scrub-Robin, many thornbills, and honeyeaters. The nature trail near the south side of the park (where one finds water and toilets) goes through Mallee eucalypts and is good for Tawny Frogmouth, parrots, and honeyeaters.

Wyperfeld is Victoria's largest national park, with an area of 218 square miles (566 km²). In addition to the kangaroos and Emu, the park is good for Wedge-tailed Eagle, Major Mitchell Cockatoo, and White-winged Chough. In the scrub of the sand ridges, fifteen minutes' walk west of the camping area, look for the exquisite Splendid Fairywren, Red-throated Scrubwren, and Red-capped Robin.

There is permanent water in the Hattah Lakes National Park, 50 miles (80 km) south of Mildura, and most of the waterbirds on the

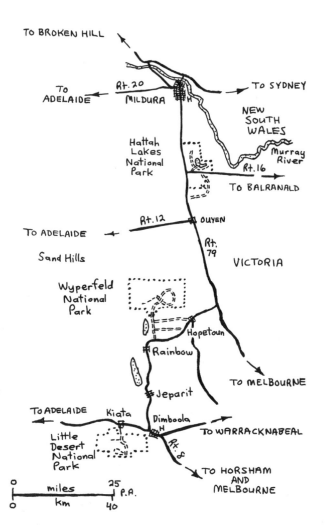

checklist occur only here. Parrots are a specialty, featuring Yellow Rosella and Regent Parrot in the tall red gums that line the lake; Bluebonnet, Mulga, and Red-backed Parrots near the ranger's house, and Major Mitchell Cockatoo elsewhere.

The dirt road along the southeastern boundary has a little spur road into the park where a water tray and neighboring areas of porcupine grass provide habitat for many fine birds. Specialties include Rufous-crowned Emu-wren, Splendid Fairywren, Striated Grass-wren, and Chestnut Quail-thrush.

Enroute to western Victoria visitors may wish to check the marsh on the west side of Lake Wendouree in Ballarat, which is 63 miles (101 km) west of Melbourne. Musk and Blue-billed Duck, Purple Swamphen, Clamorous Reed-Warblers, and dozens of Black Swan may be found.

CHECKLIST

Emu c	Brown Falcon c
Great Crested Grebe	Peregrine Falcon r
Australian Dabchick	Australian Hobby
Hoary-headed Grebe	Malleefowl
Australian Pelican	Stubble Quail r
Great Cormorant	Painted Buttonquail r
Little Black Cormorant	Little Buttonquail r
Little Pied Cormorant	Dusky Gallinule
Great Egret	Purple Swamphen
White-necked Heron r S	Common Coot c
White-faced Heron	Masked Lapwing c
Nankeen Night-Heron r	Banded Lapwing r
Sacred Ibis	Red-kneed Plover
Glossy Ibis r S	Black-fronted Plover r
Straw-necked Ibis	Sharp-tailed Sandpiper
Royal Spoonbill	Black-winged Stilt
Yellow-billed Spoonbill	Bushcurlew r
Black Swan	Silver Gull
Chestnut-breasted Shelduck	Peaceful Dove
Pacific Black Duck c	Common Bronzewing
Gray Teal	Crested Pigeon c
White-faced Shoveler r	Rainbow Lorikeet
Pink-eared Duck r	Musk Lorikeet
Maned Duck	Purple-crowned Lorikeet
White-eyed Pochard	Little Lorikeet
Blue-billed Duck r	Swift Parrot
Musk Duck	Yellow-tailed Black-Cockatoo
Australian Black-shouldered Kite	Red-tailed Black-Cockatoo c
Whistling Kite	Sulfur-crested Cockatoo c
Collared Sparrowhawk r	Major Mitchell's Cockatoo c
Brown Goshawk	Little Corella r
Little Eagle	Long-billed Corella r
Wedge-tailed Eagle	Galah c
White-bellied Sea-Eagle	Cockatiel c
Spotted Harrier r	Regent Parrot
Marsh Harrier	Crimson Rosella
Nankeen Kestrel c	Eastern Rosella
Gray Falcon r	Yellow Rosella c

Ring-necked Parrot   c
Bluebonnet Parrot
Red-rumped Parrot   c
Mulga Parrot   c
Elegant Parrot   r
Blue-winged Parrot   r
Budgerygar
Pallid Cuckoo   r
Fan-tailed Cuckoo
Black-eared Cuckoo
Horsfield's Bronze-Cuckoo
Barn Owl
Barking Hawk-Owl   r
Boobook Hawk-Owl
Australian Frogmouth
Australian Owlet-Nightjar
Spotted Nightjar
Laughing Kookaburra
Red-backed Kingfisher
Sacred Kingfisher
Rainbow Bee-eater   c
Singing Bush-Lark
White-backed Swallow
Welcome Swallow   c
Tree Martin   c
Fairy Martin   r
Richard's Pipit   c
Ground Cuckoo-shrike   r
Black-faced Cuckoo-shrike
White-winged Triller
Southern Scrub-Robin
Chestnut Quail-Thrush   r
Gray-crowned Babbler   c
Chestnut-crowned Babbler
White-browed Babbler
Clamorous Reed-Warbler
Little Grass-Warbler
Brown Songlark   S
Rufous Songlark   S
Superb Blue Fairywren
Variegated Wren   c
Splendid Fairywren   c
Rufous-crowned Emu-wren   r
Weebill   c
Striated Thornbill
Yellow Thornbill
Brown Thornbill

Broad-tailed Thornbill
Chestnut-rumped Thornbill
Samphire Thornbill
Yellow-rumped Thornbill   c
Buff-rumped Thornbill
Red-throated Scrubwren
Chestnut-rumped Scrubwren
Shy Scrubwren   r
Fieldwren   r
Striated Grasswren   r
Southern Whiteface
White-fronted Chat
Crimson Chat   r
Red-capped Robin
Hooded Robin   r
Flame Robin   r
Jacky Winter
Restless Monarch
Satin Monarch
Willie Wagtail   c
Gray Fantail   c
Golden Whistler
Rufous Whistler
Red-lored Whistler   r
Gilbert Whistler
Gray Shrike-thrush
Shrike-tit   r
Crested Bellbird
Varied Sitella
Brown Treecreeper   c
White-throated Treecreeper
Mistletoebird
Spotted Pardalote
Yellow-rumped Pardalote
Striated Pardalote   c
Silvereye   c
Striped Honeyeater
Black Honeyeater   r
White-fronted Honeyeater   r
Singing Honeyeater
Fuscous Honeyeater
White-eared Honeyeater   c
Purple-gaped Honeyeater
Yellow-plumed Honeyeater
White-plumed Honeyeater   c
Brown-headed Honeyeater   c
White-naped Honeyeater

Black-chinned Honeyeater
New Holland Honeyeater   c
Tawny-crowned Honeyeater
Eastern Spinebill   r
Noisy Miner   c
White-rumped Miner   c
Black-eared Miner
Spiny-cheeked Honeyeater   c
Little Wattlebird
Red Wattlebird   c
Blue-faced Honeyeater   c
Little Friarbird
Diamond Firetail
Zebra Finch
House Sparrow
Eurasian Goldfinch

European Starling   c
Magpielark   c
White-winged Chough   c
Apostlebird   r
White-breasted Woodswallow
Masked Woodswallow
White-browed Woodswallow
Black-faced Woodswallow
Dusky Woodswallow   c
Gray Currawong
Pied Butcherbird   r
Gray Butcherbird
Australian Magpie
Australian Raven   c
Little Raven
Little Crow

105
Melbourne, Victoria

MELBOURNE is a large, pleasant city on Port Philip Bay. There are a major airport and plentiful hotels, except during the time of the Melbourne Cup in early November. The Botanical Gardens, near the city center, are very beautiful and a fine place to see many birds. The waterfowl are rather tame, and many passerines live on the lawns, flowering eucalypts, and in the palm gully. Look for cormorants, Australian Dabchick, Nanken Night-Heron, Black Swan, White-eyed Pochard, Dusky Gallinule, Common Coot, Silver Gull, Spotted Turtle-Dove, White-plumed Honeyeater, Eastern Spinebill, Little Wattlebird, Magpielark, and Little Raven. Introduced species are seen to advantage.

Although many species can be found along rivers, in patches of woodland, and in the greener suburbs, birders should visit three superb areas further afield.

The Dandenong Hills, 25 miles (40 km) to the east, with its Sherbrooke Forest, is well-known for Superb Lyrebirds. Take the Burwood Highway east to Fern Tree Gully National Park and turn left toward Olinda; look for Sherbrooke Road to the right, and take another right before the post office. There is a maze of trails in dense forest of tree ferns and towering mountain ash. Listen for a fantastic mimic, or for scratching in the leaves on the forest floor. The Superb Lyrebirds are often seen with Pilotbirds. Also look on the ground for Scaly Thrush, Eastern Whipbird, and White-browed Scrub-Robin, while in the trees you may see Pink and Rose Robins, treecreepers, and Olive Whistler.

To the south of Woori Yallock, just west of Yellingbo, is the Yellingbo Wildlife Reserve. Park just west of the bridge over Woori Yallock Creek. Victoria's only endemic, the endangered Helmeted Honeyeater, can be seen here. In the trees and in the reedy areas near the creek, birds are plentiful. Look for Laughing Kookaburra, Azure Kingfisher, Little Grass-Warbler, Golden-headed Cisticola, Southern Emu-wren, and Bell Miner.

Phillip Island, located several hours to the south of Melbourne, can be reached by road and across the causeway at San Remo (a good spot

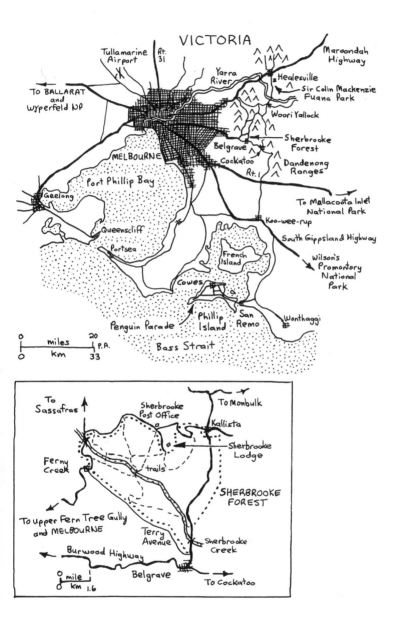

for Black-faced Cormorant and Pacific Gull). Several woodlands protected as koala sanctuaries are in the northeast part of the island. At Rhyll, also in the northeast, look for swans, oystercatchers, and shorebirds.

The Nobbies at the west tip, high above the sea, is a good spot to scan for such pelagics as albatross, gannet, and Giant Petrel. During the day, young penguins can be found in burrows below the parking lot and lunch room. Hooded Dotterel occur on nearby beaches. The biggest attraction (seen by up to 100,000 people a year) is the "Penguin Parade." Summerland Beach is well signposted and full of visitors for several hours from dusk on, as the many hundreds of Little (Fairy Blue) Penguins come ashore under floodlights. The best time is October through January. An equally exciting show is provided by the hundreds of thousands of Short-tailed Shearwaters that begin massing toward dusk and then wing en masse to their burrows along the south coast of Phillip Island (300,000 birds in one colony at Cape Woolamai).

There are several nice hotels in Cowes at the north tip of the island. Plan on a midnight return to Melbourne if you are not staying in Cowes after the penguin show.

Those driving west of Melbourne toward Ballarat should look for flocks of white Sulfur-crested Cockatoo and Long-billed Corellas feeding on the ground in sheep country.

CHECKLIST

(M = Melbourne Urban areas; D = Dandenongs; Y = Yellingbo Helmeted Honeyeater Sanctuary; PI = Philip Island, coastal. If a bird occurs in three or four of these areas the distributional symbols are omitted.)

Little Penguin   c PI
Wandering Albatross   PI
Black-browed Albatross   PI
Shy Albatross   PI
Yellow-nosed Albatross   PI
Giant Petrel   c PI
Short-tailed Shearwater   c PI
Fluttering Shearwater   PI
Tasman Gannet   PI
Great Cormorant   PI, c M
Little Pied Cormorant
Little Black Cormorant   PI, c M
Yellow-faced Cormorant   M, PI
Black-faced Cormorant   PI

Australian Dabchick   PI, D, c M
Hoary-headed Grebe   PI
Great Crested Grebe   r M
White-necked Heron   r M
White-faced Heron   c
Great Egret   M, PI
Nankeen Night-Heron   c M
Brown Bittern   r M
Sacred Ibis   M, PI
Straw-necked Ibis   M, PI
Royal Spoonbill   M, PI
Yellow-billed Spoonbill   M, PI
Black Swan   M, c PI

Chestnut-breasted Shelduck   M, PI
Pacific Black Duck   c M, PI
Mallard
Gray Teal   c M, PI
Chestnut Teal   PI
White-eyed Pochard   M, PI
Maned Duck
Blue-billed Duck   PI
Musk Duck   M, PI
Australian Black-shouldered Kite
Whistling Kite
Brown Goshawk
Wedge-tailed Eagle   r D, Y
Spotted Harrier   r Y
Marsh Harrier   Y, c PI
Peregrine Falcon
Australian Hobby
Nankeen Kestrel
Brown Falcon
Stubble Quail   PI
Painted Buttonquail   r D
Lewin's Rail   r Y
Banded Rail   PI, r Y
Baillon's Crake   r M
Australian Crake   r M
Dusky Gallinule   c M, PI
Purple Swamphen   M, PI
Common Coot   c M, PI
Common Oystercatcher   PI
Tasman Oystercatcher   PI
Masked Lapwing   c
Banded Lapwing   PI
Hooded Plover   PI
Red-capped Plover   c PI
Black-fronted Plover   M PI
Whimbrel   c M PI
Eastern Curlew   c M PI
Common Greenshank   M PI
Sharp-tailed Sandpiper   M PI
Red-necked Stint   M PI
Bar-tailed Godwit   c PI
Japanese Snipe   W PI
Great Skua   r PI
Pacific Gull   c PI
Silver Gull   c PI
White-lored Tern   r S

Crested Tern   c PI
Spotted Turtle-Dove   c M
Common Bronzewing   r D, Y
Brush Bronzewing
Musk Lorikeet   D, PI
Swift Parrot   W
Sulfur-crested Cockatoo
Yellow-tailed Black-Cockatoo   r D, Y
Long-billed Corella
Gang-gang Cockatoo   D, Y
Australian King-Parrot   D, Y
Crimson Rosella   c D, Y
Eastern Rosella   c
Blue-winged Parrot   r PI
Pallid Cuckoo
Brush Cuckoo   r D
Fan-tailed Cuckoo
Horsfield's Bronze-Cuckoo
Shining Bronze-Cuckoo
Powerful Hawk-Owl   r D
Boobook Hawk-Owl
Australian Frogmouth   r
White-throated Needletail   M
Fork-tailed Swift   r M
Laughing Kookaburra   c
Sacred Kingfisher
Azure Kingfisher   r Y
Superb Lyrebird   c D
Northern Skylark   c PI
Welcome Swallow   c
Tree Martin   M, D
Fairy Martin   M, D
Black-faced Cuckoo-shrike   c
Red-whiskered Bulbul   r M
Scaly Thrush   r D, Y
Eurasian Blackbird   c M, D
Song Thrush   D, c M
Golden-headed Cisticola   r Y
Little Grass-Warbler   PI, r Y
Superb Blue Fairywren   c
Southern Emu-wren   r Y
Straited Thornbill   c
Yellow Thornbill   M, D
Brown Thornbill   c
Buff-rumped Thornbill   D
Yellow-rumped Thornbill

White-browed Scrubwren
Large-billed Scrubwren   r D
Pilotbird   r D
White-fronted Chat   PI
Jacky Winter   D, PI
Scarlet Robin   D, PI
Flame Robin   D, PI
Pink Robin   r D
Rose Robin   D, Y
Eastern Yellow Robin   c
Gray Fantail   c
Rufous Fantail   D, Y
Willie Wagtail   c
Satin Monarch   r D
Restless Monarch   D
Golden Whistler   c
Rufous Whistler
Olive Whistler   r D
Gray Shrike-thrush   c
Shrike-tit
Eastern Whipbird   c D, Y
Varied Sittela   D, Y
White-throated Treecreeper   c, D,Y
Red-browed Treecreeper   r D, Y
Mistletoebird   D, PI
Spotted Pardalote   c
Eastern Striated Pardalote   c
Silvereye   c
Yellow-faced Honeyeater   c D,Y

White-plumed Honeyeater   c M, PI
White-eared Honeyeater
Helmeted Honeyeater   Y
White-naped Honeyeater   c
Crescent Honeyeater   D
New Holland Honeyeater
Eastern Spinebill   c
Noisy Miner
Bell Miner   c D, Y
Little Wattlebird   c M, PI
Red Wattlebird   c PI, M, D
Beautiful Firetail   r D, Y
Red-browed Firetail   c D, Y
House Sparrow   c
Tree Sparrow   c M
Eurasian Goldfinch   c
Eurasian Greenfinch   c M, PI
European Starling   c
Indian Myna   c M, D
Olive-backed Oriole   D, Y
Magpielark   c
Dusky Woodswallow
Pied Currawong   c D
Gray Currawong   D
Gray Butcherbird   c PI
Australian Magpie   c
Australian Raven   c M, D
Little Raven   c M, PI

106
Sydney, New South Wales

SYDNEY IS THE CAPITAL OF NEW SOUTH WALES and the largest city in Australia. Most visitors arrive in Sydney by air or sea and from there venture into other areas. Nearly 400 species of birds have been noted in the environs. There is plenty of accommodation around the city but none in the national parks.

In the Botanical Gardens on Sydney Harbour near the opera house and within walking distance of hotels, such birds as Silver Gull, Greater Crested Tern, Black-faced Cuckoo-shrike, Magpielark, Jacky Winter, Superb Blue Fairywren, White-plumed Honeyeater, Noisy Miner, and Laughing Kookaburra are found. The inexpensive ferry trip to Taronga Zoo is well worthwhile. At Centennial Park there are ponds with Australian Dabchick, Musk Duck, Purple Swamphen, and Dusky Gallinule.

Until just recently the Malabar Cliffs were renowned for the albatrosses attracted to huge offal pipes. Since the closing of the "beach-fouler," birds such as Wandering and Black-browed Albatross, Giant Fulmar, shearwaters, gannets, and skuas are less concentrated. The many headlands along the coast are still worth visiting for pelagics, particularly in the winter months.

In the Botany Bay area near the airport there are ponds and mud-flats that are good for cormorants, Black Swan, ducks, moorhens, shorebirds, gulls, and terns.

Royal National Park (dedicated in 1879) is about an hour's drive to the south. It is predominantly a heath-covered sandstone plateau adjacent to the ocean and has many heath species, such as Chestnut-rumped Scrubwren, Southern Emu-wren (shy), and various heath honeyeaters, including Tawny-crowned. Lady Carrington Drive is a one-way dirt road extending from Audley south to McKell Avenue.

This drive allows access to dense rain forest, flanked by tall eucalyptus woodland. The many exciting birds that can be found here include Laughing Kookaburra, Azure Kingfisher, Crimson Rosella, Superb Lyrebird, fantails, Golden Whistler, Eastern Whipbird, Rose Robin, Variegated Fairywren, Green Catbird, and Satin Bowerbird. Sydney's only endemic, the Rock Warbler, can be found near waterfalls along

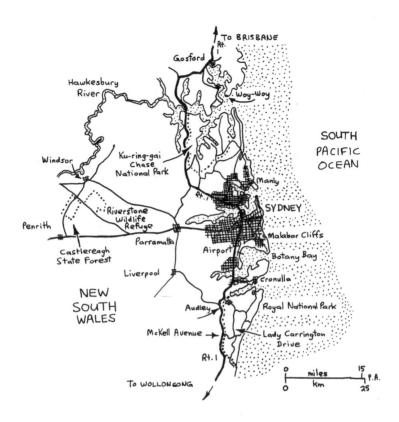

McKell Avenue. Beware of leeches in the rain forest.

Ku-ring-gai Chase National Park on the north side is also good for many birds and has excellent trails. The eucalyptus forests around Woy-Woy are good for Rainbow and Musk Lorikeets and Eastern Rosella. There are still some marshes and ponds in the Hawkesbury River District near Windsor that are good for waterbirds. A good variety of inland birds typical of forests growing on the undulating shale lands can be found in Castlereagh State Forest south of Windsor. Many of these do not occur in the sandstone formations of the coastal parks.

CHECKLIST

Little Penguin	Black-browed Albatross c W
Wandering Albatross c W	Shy Albatross r W

Yellow-nosed Albatross   r W
Giant Petrel   c W
Pale-footed Shearwater   M
Wedge-tailed Shearwater   S
Sooty Shearwater   r S
Short-tailed Shearwater   M
Fluttering Shearwater   M
Wilson's Storm-Petrel   r M
White-faced Storm-Petrel   r S
Australian Pelican
Tasman Gannet   c
Great Cormorant   c
Little Black Cormorant
Yellow-faced Cormorant
Little Pied Cormorant
Australian Dabchick   c
Hoary-headed Grebe   r
White-necked Heron
White-faced Heron   c
Green Heron
Little Egret   r
Great Egret   c
Cattle Heron   r
Eastern Reef-Heron
Nankeen Night-Heron
Black-necked Stork   r
Sacred Ibis   S
Straw-necked Ibis
Royal Spoonbill   r S
Yellow-billed Spoonbill   r S
Black Swan   c
Pacific Black Duck   c
Mallard
Gray Teal   c
Chestnut Teal   r
White-eyed Pochard
Maned Duck
Musk Duck
Australian Black-shouldered Kite
Brown Goshawk   r
White-bellied Sea-Eagle
Marsh Harrier
Nankeen Kestrel
Brown Falcon
Stubble Quail   r
King Quail   r
Painted Buttonquail   r

Little Buttonquail   r
Banded Rail   r
Baillon's Crake   r
Dusky Gallinule   c
Purple Swamphen   c
Common Coot   c
Tasman Oystercatcher   r
Masked Lapwing   c
Red-capped Plover   c
Double-banded Plover   W
Mongolian Plover   M
Black-fronted Plover
Lesser Golden Plover   r M
Ruddy Turnstone   M
Japanese Snipe   M
Eastern Curlew   M
Gray-tailed Tattler   M
Red Knot   M
Sharp-tailed Sandpiper   c M
Red-necked Stint   c M
Curlew Sandpiper   M
Bar-tailed Godwit   c M
Great Skua   r W
Pomarine Jaeger   M
Parasitic Jaeger   M
Silver Gull   c
Whiskered Tern   r S
Caspian Tern   r
White-fronted Tern   W
Little Tern   S
Greater Crested Tern   c
Top-knot Pigeon   r S
Rock Pigeon   c
Spotted Turtle-Dove   c
Peaceful Dove
Brush Bronzewing
Wonga Pigeon
Rainbow Lorikeet
Scaly-breasted Lorikeet
Musk Lorikeet
Little Lorikeet
Swift Parrot   r W
Yellow-tailed Black-Cockatoo   r
Sulfur-crested Cockatoo
Galah   r
Australian King-Parrot
Crimson Rosella   c

Eastern Rosella
Red-rumped Parrot
Turquoise Parrot   r
Pallid Cuckoo   c S
Brush Cuckoo   S
Fan-tailed Cuckoo
Black-eared Cuckoo   r
Horsfield's Bronze-Cuckoo
Shining Bronze-Cuckoo
Common Koel   S
Pheasant Coucal
Boobook Hawk-Owl
Australian Frogmouth
White-throated Needletail   M
Azure Kingfisher
Laughing Kookaburra   c
Sacred Kingfisher   S
Rainbow Bee-eater   S
Dollar Roller   S
Superb Lyrebird
Singing Bush-Lark
Northern Skylark
Welcome Swallow   c
Tree Martin   c S
Fairy Martin   c W
Richard's Pipit
Black-faced Cuckoo-shrike   c
Cicada Cuckoo-shrike   S
White-winged Triller
Red-whiskered Bulbul
Scaly Thrush
Eurasian Blackbird
Spotted Quail-thrush   r
Golden-headed Cisticola
Little Grass-Warbler
Clamorous Reed-Warbler
Brown Songlark   r S
Rufous Songlark   r S
Superb Blue Fairywren
Variegated Fairywren
Southern Emu-wren
White-throated Gerygone
Brown Gerygone   c
Weebill
Striated Thornbill   c
Yellow Thornbill   c
Brown Thornbill   c

Buff-rumped Thornbill
Yellow-rumped Thornbill
White-browed Scrubwren
Yellow-throated Scrubwren   c
Large-billed Scrubwren
Chestnut-rumped Scrubwren
Southern Whiteface
Speckled Warbler
Rock-Warbler
Pilotbird
White-fronted Chat
Jacky Winter   c
Scarlet Robin
Red-capped Robin
Rose Robin
Hooded Robin
Eastern Yellow-Robin   c
Gray Fantail   c
Rufous Fantail   c W
Willie Wagtail   c
Leaden Monarch   S
Restless Monarch
Black-faced Monarch   S
Golden Whistler
Rufous Whistler   S
Gray Shrike-thrush   c
Shrike-tit
Eastern Whipbird
Varied Sittella
Brown Treecreeper
White-throated Treecreeper
Red-browed Treecreeper
Mistletoebird
Spotted Pardalote   c
Yellow-tipped Pardalote   r
Eastern Striated Pardalote
Silvereye   c
Brown Honeyeater
Scarlet Honeyeater
Lewin Honeyeater   c
Fuscous Honeyeater
Yellow-faced Honeyeater
White-plumed Honeyeater
White-eared Honeyeater
Yellow-tufted Honeyeater
Brown-headed Honeyeater
White-naped Honeyeater

Black-chinned Honeyeater
Noisy Friarbird
Crescent Honeyeater   r
New Holland Honeyeater   c
White-cheeked Honeyeater
Tawny-crowned Honeyeater
Painted Honeyeater   r S
Regent Honeyeater   r W
Eastern Spinebill   c
Bell Miner   r
Noisy Miner
Little Wattlebird   c
Red Wattlebird   c
House Sparrow
Diamond Firetail
Red-browed Firetail   c
Double-barred Finch
Zebra Finch
Spotted Munia

Chestnut-breasted Munia
Eurasian Goldfinch
Eurasian Greenfinch
European Starling   c
Indian Myna   c
Olive-backed Oriole
Green Figbird
Spangled Drongo   r
Magpielark   c
White-winged Chough
White-browed Woodswallow   S
Dusky Woodswallow
Pied Currawong   c
Gray Currawong   r
Gray Butcherbird
Australian Magpie   c
Green Catbird
Satin Bowerbird
Australian Raven

Brisbane, Queensland

SOUTHEASTERN QUEENSLAND IS OF EXCEPTIONAL INTEREST to birders because of the forest lodges in Lamington National Park, both of which are located only a few hours south of Brisbane on scenic paved highways. They are nearly unique in Australia where, unlike Africa, North America, and Europe, there are next to no facilities located in natural settings.

Brisbane, Queensland's capital, is intersected by the meandering Brisbane River, along which lie the botanical gardens. In common with most Australian cities the gardens are the best place to see some of the local birds. Visitors there should see Pacific Black Duck, Dusky Gallinule, Pale-headed Rosella, Rainbow Lorikeet, Sacred Kingfisher, Tree Martin, Black-faced Cuckoo-shrike, Gray Shrikethrush, Silvereye, and Green Figbird.

On the west side of the city, birders should check the trees lining the river beside Queensland University, the scrub adjacent to the Indooroopilly Golf Links, and the eucalyptus woodlands on Mt. Cootha.

Moreton Bay, to the east of the city, has many Black Swans, cormorants, shorebirds, and terns. Suggested localities would be Sandgate and Redcliffe to the northeast, and Wellington Point and Cleveland to the southeast.

Many roads wind southward toward the Gold Coast and Lamington. These are flanked with attractive woodland, farms, and many marshes that are home to cormorants, herons, egrets, ibis, and spoonbills.

Tamborine Mountain National Park, 45 miles (72 km) south of Brisbane, has a rain forest spiced with palms, macrosamias, and waterfalls. Albert Lyrebird, Australian Scrubturkey, and Eastern Whipbird occur there.

The Gold Coast is a long row of small beach cities with many hotels stretching from Southport to Coolangatta. The Currumbin Bird Sanctuary is world famous for the hundreds of Rainbow and Scaly-

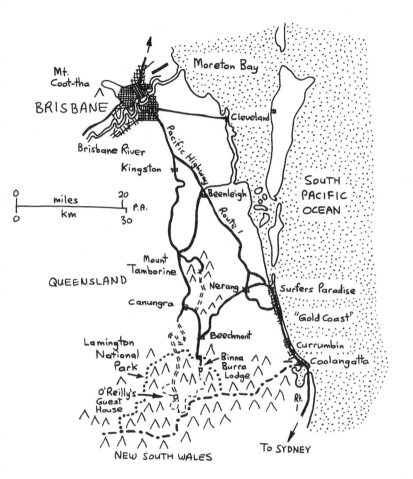

breasted Lorikeets that come to take handouts, even perching on visitors' heads. These beautiful birds, along with Laughing Kookaburra and Noisy Miners, are a spectacle worth seeing. Unfortunately, the operation is so commercialized now that one's enjoyment has to transcend screaming children, piped music, and shoddy ground ripe with the stench of spilled honey.

Thirty miles (48 km) inland from the Gold Coast and 70 miles (112 km) south of Brisbane, the Lamington National Park straddles the McPherson Range on the New South Wales border. Forests blanket most of the park's 76 square miles (198 km^2), which has peaks of close to 4000-foot (1220-m) elevation. Several distinct types of forest are represented, which have very different aspects and birdlife. The subtropical rain forest contains dozens of species of trees including hoop pine, rose mahogany, camphorwood, tulipwood, red carabeen, and silky beech, all drenched with epiphytes, including staghorn ferns. In the higher elevations there are forests of the ancient antarctic beech *(Nothofagus moori)*. In the better drained and poorer soils at lower elevations there is an open eucalyptus forest with an understory of grasses and grass trees.

There are two unpretentious, friendly lodges within the park, each with adjacent rain forest, an excellent bird feeding program, and people who understand birders. Both have regular minibus service from Brisbane.

Binna Burra Lodge (Beechmont, via Nerang, Queensland 4211) is reached via a paved road. Australian Scrubturkey and Pied Currawongs come to its grounds to feed. Albert Lyrebirds and many other fine birds appear along the excellent rain-forest trails nearby.

O'Reilly's Guest House (Lamington National Park, via Canungra, Queensland 4275), at 3100 feet (945 m), is reached via a long dirt road. There is room for several dozen guests, all of whom enjoy feeding various marsupials at night and some of the most gorgeous birds in the world in the early morning. Brilliant gold-and-black Regent Bowerbirds, Satin Bowerbirds, and Crimson Rosellas will come to feed from your hand. Superb Blue Fairywren are common nearby. The trails in the adjacent forests have many Australian Scrubturkey, Wonga Pigeon, and Spine-tailed Logrunners. The trail to Moran's Falls is good for Noisy Pitta. By walking the road through the rain forest for several miles downhill you should find many whistlers and fantails, and there is a good chance of seeing Paradise Riflebird.

The trails, administered by the Queensland Forest Service here, are among the finest in the world, many being passable for wheelchairs.

CHECKLIST

(RF = Rain forest areas.)

Australian Dabchick c	White-faced Heron c
Wedge-tailed Shearwater	White-necked Heron c
Australian Pelican	Great Egret c
Tasman Gannet	Little Egret c
Great Cormorant	Short-billed Egret c
Little Black Cormorant c	Cattle Heron c
Yellow-faced Cormorant c	Brown Bittern r
Little Pied Cormorant c	Black Bittern r
Darter	Sacred Ibis c

Straw-necked Ibis   c
Yellow-billed Spoonbill
Royal Spoonbill   c
Black Swan   c
Chestnut Teal
Gray Teal
Pacific Black Duck   c
White-eyed Pochard
Maned Duck
Australian Black-shouldered Kite
   c
Crested Baza   r   S
Brahminy Kite
Whistling Kite   c
Brown Goshawk
Collared Sparrowhawk   r
Gray Goshawk   r
Red Goshawk   r
White-bellied Sea-Eagle
Wedge-tailed Eagle
Peregrine Falcon   r
Nankeen Kestrel   c
Australian Brushturkey   c   RF
Brown Quail   r
King Quail   r
Black-breasted Buttonquail   r
Dusky Gallinule   c
Purple Swamphen   c
Common Coot
Banded Rail
Comb-crested Jacana
Common Oystercatcher   c
Red-capped Plover
Black-fronted Plover
Lesser Golden Plover   M
Masked Lapwing   c
Ruddy Turnstone   M
Red-necked Stint   c   M
Sharp-tailed Sandpiper   c   M
Curlew Sandpiper   M
Common Sandpiper   M
Common Greenshank   M
Japanese Snipe   M
Bar-tailed Godwit   c   M
Eastern Curlew   c   M
Whimbrel   c   M
Black-winged Stilt

Bushcurlew   r
Silver Gull   c
Gull-billed Tern
Caspian Tern   r
Little Tern   c
Crested Tern   c
Rock Pigeon   c
Red-crowned Fruit-Dove   r   RF
Wompoo Fruit-Dove   RF
Topknot Pigeon   c   RF
Slender-billed Cuckoo-Dove   RF
White-headed Pigeon   RF
Green-winged Pigeon   RF
Wonga Pigeon   RF
Bar-shouldered Dove
Peaceful Dove
Spotted Turtle-Dove   c
Crested Pigeon   c
Rainbow Lorikeet   c
Scaly-breasted Lorikeet   c
Musk Lorikeet   r
Little Lorikeet
Galah
Yellow-tailed Black-Cockatoo   r
   RF
Glossy Black-Cockatoo   r   RF
Sulfur-crested Cockatoo
Pale-headed Rosella   c
Crimson Rosella   c   RF
Australian King-Parrot   RF
Pallid Cuckoo   S
Brush Cuckoo   c   RF   S
Fan-tailed Cuckoo   c   RF   S
Horsfield's Bronze-Cuckoo   c   RF
   S
Shining Bronze-Cuckoo   c   S
Channel-billed Cuckoo   r   S
Common Koel   S
Pheasant Coucal   c
Barn Owl   r
Boobook Hawk-Owl
Powerful Hawk-Owl   r   RF
Barking Hawk-Owl   r
Australian Frogmouth
Fork-tailed Swift   r   M
White-throated Needletail   M
Azure Kingfisher   r

Laughing Kookaburra   c
Sacred Kingfisher   c
Macleay's Kingfisher
Rainbow Bee-eater   S
Dollar Roller   S
Noisy Pitta   RF S
Rufous Scrub-bird   r RF
Albert Lyrebird   RF
Spangled Drongo
Welcome Swallow   c
Fairy Martin   c
Tree Martin   c
Richard's Pipit
Black-faced Cuckoo-shrike   c
White-bellied Cuckoo-shrike   r
Yellow-eyed Cuckoo-shrike   r RF
  S
Cicada Cuckoo-shrike   r S
Varied Triller   r RF
White-winged Triller   r
Gray-crowned Babbler
Spine-tailed Logrunner   c RF
Scaly Thrush   RF
Golden-headed Cisticola
Tawny Grass-Warbler   r
Clamorous Reed-Warbler
Superb Blue Fairywren   c
Variegated Fairywren
Red-backed Fairywren
White-throated Gerygone
Brown Gerygone   c RF
Weebill
Yellow Thornbill   r
Brown Thornbill   c
Buff-rumped Thornbill
Yellow-rumped Thornbill   c
White-browed Scrubwren   c
Yellow-throated Scrubwren   c RF
Large-billed Scrubwren   c RF
Eastern Bristlebird   r
Jacky Winter
Rose Robin
Eastern Yellow Robin   c RF
Pale Yellow Robin   r RF
Gray Fantail   c
Rufous Fantail   c
Willie Wagtail   c

Leaden Monarch
Satin Monarch   r
Restless Monarch
Black-faced Monarch   c RF
Spectacled Monarch   r
White-eared Monarch   r
Gray Shrike-thrush
Rufous Shrike-thrush   r RF
Golden Whistler
Rufous Whistler
Olive Whistler   r RF
Shrike-tit
Eastern Whipbird   c RF
Varied Sittela   r
White-throated Treecreeper   c
Mistletoebird
Striated Pardalote
Spotted Pardalote   c
Silvereye   c
Brown Honeyeater   c
Scarlet Myzomela
Varied Honeyeater
Lewin Honeyeater   c RF
Yellow-tufted Honeyeater
Yellow-faced Honeyeater   c
White-throated Honeyeater
Black-chinned Honeyeater
White-naped Honeyeater
Eastern Spinebill   c
White-cheeked Honeyeater
Blue-faced Honeyeater
Bell Miner
Noisy Miner   c
Red Wattlebird   r
Noisy Friarbird   c
Little Friarbird   c
Red-browed Firetail   c
Chestnut-breasted Munia   r
Spotted Munia   c
Double-barred Finch
Zebra Finch   r
Eurasian Goldfinch
House Sparrow   c
European Starling   c
Olive-backed Oriole   S
Green Figbird   c S
Dusky Woodswallow

White-breasted Woodswallow   S
Magpielark   c
Pied Currawong   c
Pied Butcherbird   c
Gray Butcherbird   c
Australian Magpie   c

Green Catbird   c RF
Regent Bowerbird   RF
Satin Bowerbird   c RF
Paradise Riflebird
Torresian Crow   c

108
Cairns, Queensland

CAIRNS, THE NORTHERNMOST CITY IN QUEENSLAND, is the jumping-off point for the lush mountain jungles of the Atherton tablelands and offers good access to several islands in the Great Barrier Reef as well. There are a number of motels, rental cars, and an airport with flights to Brisbane and Sydney, with several flights a week to Darwin, Alice Springs, and Port Moresby (Papua New Guinea).

The Cairns waterfront (Esplanade) is only a block or two from the various motels. Its mudflats provide one of the richest shorebird and wader feeding grounds in the world (now threatened with beautification) and are only a stone's throw from the business district. Just before and after high tide is best for visibility, though telescopes are as necessary here as anywhere else. Numbers build up from August to November, when the flats are alive with interesting Asian shorebirds. Pelicans, herons, spoonbills, and ibis stand out, but even more exciting birds are the frequent good numbers of Broad-billed and Terek Sandpipers, Great Knots, and other rarely seen birds.

The daily morning ferry out to Green Island, with a late afternoon return, allows you to taste the Great Barrier Reef, as do the walk-in underwater observatory, the glass-bottom boats, snorkeling, and fishing. The Coral Cay Hotel is worth a night free from the midday influx. The island is forested in the middle and lined with nice beaches and fringing reef. Birds of interest include Eastern Reef-Heron, Great Thick-knee, Green-winged Pigeon, Torres Straits Fruit-Pigeon (the huge white pigeons stream across the ocean daily from their nests on the island to feed on the mainland), Red-crowned Fruit-Dove, Olive-backed Sunbird, and Silver-eye.

From October into the summer, Michaelmas Cay (two hours north of Green Island by boat) is home to thousands of breeding terns, chiefly Bridled, Sooty, and Brown Noddy. There are usually Black-naped, both Crested Terns, and White-capped Noddy as well, with occasional frigatebirds overhead. Chartering a boat can be expensive, costing hundreds of dollars. Even if not on a birding tour do not give up; ask around Cairns to see if you can join an excursion or fishing boat going out.

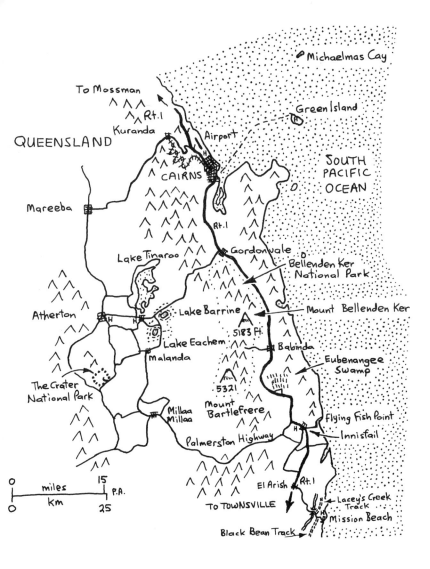

The rain forests of the Atherton Tableland, exceptionally rich in localized birds, can be reached via several paved roads within two or three hours from Cairns. Much of this verdant countryside has been cleared for crops and dairying; yet representative areas have been preserved in national parks. Lodging is the only handicap, with only a small lodge that has a few primitive rooms at Lake Barrine and

541

several small motels in Atherton, an hour away from the birds.

Lake Barrine and Lake Eachem National Parks are small and adjacent to each other. Each has a large ring of gorgeous forest around placid crater lakes, marred only by the motorboats, chiefly at weekends. There are a number of easy walking trails into dense forest where many of the finest birds live. Among the specialties of renown here, look for Orange-footed Scrubfowl, Australian Brushturkey, Wompoo Fruit-Dove, Topknot and White-headed Pigeons, Australian King-Parrot, Stripe-breasted Shrike-thrush, Macleay's Honeyeater, Tooth-billed Catbird, and Queen Victoria's Riflebird. Both parks are well signposted, east of Yungburra, just south of the Atherton–Gordonvale–Cairns highway.

Crater National Park is 15 miles (24 km) southwest of Atherton, via a fine paved highway. The trails near the parking lot there are good for Golden Bowerbird, Satin Bowerbird, and Gray-headed Flyrobin.

The best place for seeing Great Cassowary is in the vicinity of Mission Beach, about three hours' south of Cairns. Take the Bruce Highway south through Innisfail to El Arish, 76 miles (121 km) south of Cairns, and turn left (east) to Mission Beach (7 miles or 11 km), where visitors can base at the Moonglow Motel. There are wide dirt roads through fine forest a few miles west of the ocean along the El Arish road, known as the Black Bean Track and Lacey's Creek Track. Go early and go quietly to see Great Cassowary. This area is also good for White-tailed Paradise-Kingfisher, White-eared Monarch, and Noisy Pitta.

CHECKLIST

Great Cassowary	Green Heron
Wilson's Storm-Petrel r M	Cattle Heron
Australian Dabchick	Great Egret c
Great Crested Grebe	Little Egret c
Australian Pelican c	Short-billed Egret c
Brown Booby	Eastern Reef-Heron c
Darter	Nankeen Night-Heron
Great Cormorant	Black-necked Stork r
Little Black Cormorant	Sacred Ibis c
Yellow-faced Cormorant	Straw-necked Ibis c
Little Pied Cormorant c	Royal Spoonbill c
Great Frigatebird r	Magpie Goose
Lesser Frigatebird '	Water Whistling-Duck
Great-billed Heron r	Plumed Whistling-Duck
White-faced Heron c	Black Swan
White-necked Heron	Pacific Black Duck

Gray Teal   c
White-eyed Pochard
Maned Duck
Green Pygmy-Goose
Cotton Pygmy-Goose
Australian Black-shouldered Kite
   c
Crested Baza
Black Kite   c
Square-tailed Kite   r
Brahminy Kite
Whistling Kite   c
Gray Goshawk
Brown Goshawk
Collared Sparrowhawk
White-bellied Sea-Eagle   r
Marsh Harrier
Osprey
Peregrine Falcon   r
Austrailian Hobby   r
Nankeen Kestrel
Orange-footed Scrubfowl
Australian Brushturkey   c
Brown Quail
King Quail
Brolga Crane   c
Sarus Crane   c
Banded Rail
Dusky Gallinule   c
Purple Swamphen
Common Coot
Comb-crested Jacana
Tasman Oystercatcher   r
Masked Lapwing   c
Red-capped Plover
Mongolian Plover   M
Great Sand Plover   M
Black-fronted Plover
Lesser Golden Plover   M
Gray Plover   r M
Ruddy Turnstone   c M
Japanese Snipe   M
Whimbrel   c M
Eastern Curlew   c M
Marsh Sandpiper   r M
Common Greenshank   c M
Asiatic Dowitcher   r M

Common Sandpiper   M
Gray-tailed Tattler   c M
Terek Sandpiper   M
Red Knot   M
Great Knot   c M
Sharp-tailed Sandpiper   c M
Red-necked Stint   c M
Curlew Sandpiper   c M
Broad-billed Sandpiper   r M
Black-tailed Godwit   c M
Bar-tailed Godwit   c M
Black-winged Stilt   c
Bushcurlew
Great Thick-knee
Silver Gull   c
Caspian Tern
Gull-billed Tern   c
Common Tern   r M
Roseate Tern   r M
Black-naped Tern   S
Sooty Tern   S
Bridled Tern   S
Little Tern   S
Greater Crested Tern   c
Lesser Crested Tern   S
Brown Noddy   S
White-capped Noddy   r
Red-crowned Fruit-Dove
Superb Fruit-Dove
Wompoo Fruit-Dove   c
Torres Straits Fruit-Pigeon
Topknot Pigeon
White-headed Pigeon
Slender-billed Cuckoo-Dove   c
Spotted Turtle-Dove   c
Bar-shouldered Dove
Peaceful Dove
Green-winged Pigeon   c
Rainbow Lorikeet
Scaly-breasted Lorikeet
Little Lorikeet
Sulfur-crested Cockatoo
Double-eyed Fig-Parrot
Australian King-Parrot   c
Crimson Rosella   c
Pale-headed Rosella
Brush Cuckoo

Fan-tailed Cuckoo
Shining Bronze-Cuckoo S
Common Koel
Pheasant Coucal c
Channel-billed Cuckoo r S
Barn Owl
Boobook Hawk-Owl
Australian Frogmouth
Papuan Frogmouth r
White-throated Nightjar r
Large-tailed Nightjar c
White-throated Needletail c M
Fork-tailed Swift c M
Gray Swiftlet c
Azure Kingfisher
Laughing Kookaburra c
Blue-winged Kookaburra
Macleay's Kingfisher c
Sacred Kingfisher c
White-collared Kingfisher r
White-tailed Paradise-Kingfisher
  S
Rainbow Bee-eater c S
Dollar Roller S
Noisy Pitta
Singing Bush-Lark
Welcome Swallow c
Tree Martin c
Fairy Martin c
Richard's Pipit
Black-faced Cuckoo-shrike c
Yellow-eyed Cuckoo-shrike
White-bellied Cuckoo-shrike c
Cicada Cuckoo-shrike
White-winged Triller
Varied Triller r
Scaly Thrush r
Eastern Yellow-Robin
Pale Yellow-Robin
Gray-headed Flyrobin c
Golden Whistler c
Gray Whistler
Rufous Whistler
Rufous Shrike-thrush
Stripe-breasted Shrike-thrush
Gray Shrike-thrush
Yellow-breasted Boatbill

Black-faced Monarch
Spectacled Monarch c
White-eared Monarch r
Pied Monarch
Leaden Monarch
Satin Monarch
Rufous Fantail
Gray Fantail c
Willie Wagtail c
Black-headed Logrunner
Eastern Whipbird c
Clamorous Reed-Warbler
Tawny Grass-Warbler
Golden-headed Cisticola c
Variegated Fairywren
Red-backed Fairywren
Fernwren r
Atherton Scrubwren
Large-billed Scrubwren c
Yellow-throated Scrubwren c
White-browed Scrubwren
Brown Gerygone c
Large-billed Gerygone
Black-throated Gerygone
White-throated Gerygone
Mountain Thornbill c
Varied Sittella
Little Treecreeper c
Brown Treecreeper r
Helmeted Friarbird c
Noisy Friarbird c
Little Friarbird
Noisy Miner
Macleay's Honeyeater c
Graceful Honeyeater
Lewin's Honeyeater c
Yellow-faced Honeyeater
White-gaped Honeyeater
Bridled Honeyeater
Mangrove Honeyeater
Yellow Honeyeater
White-throated Honeyeater r
White-naped Honeyeater r
Brown Honeyeater
Modest Honeyeater
Blue-faced Honeyeater
Eastern Spinebill

Dusky Myzomela   c
Scarlet Myzomela
Olive-backed Sunbird   c
Mistletoebird
Spotted Pardalote
Silvereye   c
House Sparrow   c
Red-browed Firetail   c
Crimson Finch
Double-barred Finch
Chestnut-breasted Munia
Spotted Munia   c
Metallic Starling   c
Indian Myna   c
Yellow Oriole
Olive-backed Oriole

Green Figbird   c
Spangled Drongo
Golden Bowerbird   r
Satin Bowerbird
Tooth-billed Catbird   c
Black-eared Catbird   c
Queen Victoria's Riflebird
Magpielark   c
White-breasted Woodswallow   c
Dusky Woodswallow
Black Butcherbird
Gray Butcherbird   r
Pied Butcherbird   c
Australian Magpie
Pied Currawong   c
Australian Raven

109
New Caledonia

THIS RICH FRENCH ISLAND, lying halfway between Brisbane and Fiji, is 250 miles (400 km) long and about 30 miles (48 km) wide. It makes an expensive yet rewarding stopover for birders. Most of the hotels are located in Noumea, a good base from which to reach the two best birding areas. Rental cars can be arranged, and there is a supermarket in central Noumea — take picnics with you as often as possible since meal prices are astronomical here.

In the high hills behind Noumea there is still some native forest left. Take the main road to the airport for about 9 miles (14 kilometers) until a sign marking Mt. Koghis is seen. Leaving the airport road take the somewhat bumpy dirt road that winds about 3 miles (5 kilometers) uphill to the L'Auberge des Monts Koghis. The wooded areas along the road uphill are good for Long-tailed Triller, Rufous Whistler, Collared Fantail, New Caledonian Monarch, Scarlet Myzomela, and Silver-eared and Barred Honeyeaters.

The small hotel at Mt. Koghis is also expensive but well worth the cost, for it is right at the center of action. Behind the hotel is the botanical preserve of Mt. Koghis with a number of trails fanning out into dense, wet, montane forest with giant tree ferns. Birds of note include White-bellied Sparrowhawk, Cloven-feathered Dove, White-throated Pigeon, Red-crowned Parakeet, both cuckoo-shrikes, New Caledonian Whistler, both fantails, Western Shrikebill, Yellow-bellied Robin, and Crow Honeyeater. Kagus were heard and seen here in 1968 by one of the authors, and may still survive.

An entirely different forest, at a lower elevation with many palms and a different birdlife, can be seen in the Haute-Yaté Reserve, 53 miles (85 km) from Noumea. The necessary permit, obtainable from the Service des Eaux et Forets in Noumea, must be produced for the guard at the entry gate. Proceed southeast from Noumea to the Yaté road, which crosses the island. The hilly, dusty, and desolate two-hour drive toward Yaté over ruined country is followed by an unmarked left turn onto another dirt road, just before a lake on the left. Once past the guardhouse, the road eventually skirts another lake. In the scrub country the New Caledonian Crow and New Caledonian Friar-

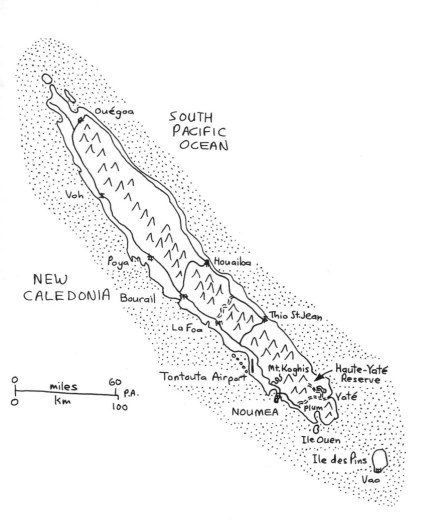

SOUTH PACIFIC OCEAN

Ouégoa

Voh

Poya

NEW CALEDONIA Bourail

Houailou

La Foa

Thio St.Jean

Tontouta Airport

Mt.Koghis

Haute-Yaté Reserve

Yaté

Plum

NOUMEA

Ile Ouen

Ile des Pins

Vao

miles 60
Km 100
P.A.

bird are both specialties. When one reaches the forest, the New Caledonian Fruit-Pigeon and rare Crested Parakeet may be seen, as well as some other forest birds. This is an all-day trip by car, with few facilities of any kind.

Captive Kagus can be seen in the zoo at the Parc Forestier de Noumea high on a barren hill behind Montravel, a few miles north of town and open weekend afternoons.

The Loyalty Islands and the Isle of Pines, with a few small hotels and light aircraft service, have some birds of interest. Visits can be arranged in Noumea.

CHECKLIST

Wedge-tailed Shearwater
Audubon's Shearwater
Fluttering Shearwater
White-tailed Tropicbird
Brown Booby
Red-footed Booby
Masked Booby
Lesser Frigatebird
Little Pied Cormorant
White-faced Heron   c
Green Heron   r
Eastern Reef-Heron
Nankeen Night-Heron
Brown Bittern   r
Pacific Black Duck
Gray Teal
White-eyed Pochard   r
Whistling Kite   c
Brown Goshawk
White-bellied Sparrowhawk
Marsh Harrier
Osprey
Peregrine Falcon
Red Junglefowl
Painted Buttonquail   r
Banded Rail
New Caledonian Wood-Rail   r
Spotless Crake
White-browed Crake
Purple Swamphen
Kagu
Lesser Golden Plover   c M
Ruddy Turnstone   M
Whimbrel   M
Bar-tailed Godwit   r M
Gray-tailed Tattler   M
Sharp-tailed Sandpiper   M
Sanderling   M
Great Thick-knee   r
Silver Gull
White-lored Tern
Roseate Tern
Sooty Tern

Greater Crested Tern
White-capped Noddy
Brown Noddy
Fairy Tern
Red-bellied Fruit-Dove
Cloven-feathered Dove
Pacific Fruit-Pigeon
New Caledonian Fruit-Pigeon
White-throated Pigeon   c F
Green-winged Pigeon
Spotted Turtle-Dove
Rainbow Lorikeet
New Caledonian Lorikeet   r
Crested Parakeet   r
Red-crowned Parakeet
Fan-tailed Cuckoo
Shining Bronze-Cuckoo
Long-tailed Cuckoo   W
Barn Owl   c
Grass Owl   r
White-throated Nightjar   r
Uniform Swiftlet   c
White-bellied Swiftlet
Sacred Kingfisher   c
New Caledonian Mountain
    Cuckoo-shrike
Melanesian Cuckoo-shrike
Long-tailed Triller   c
New Caledonian Whistler   c F
Rufous Whistler
New Caledonian Grass-Warbler
Fantail Gerygone   c
Spotted Fantail   c
Gray Fantail   c
Melanesian Monarch   c
Western Shrikebill
Yellow-bellied Robin
Island Thrush
Green-backed White-eye   c F
Silvereye   c
Scarlet Myzomela   c
Silver-eared Honeyeater   c
Barred Honeyeater   c

Crow Honeyeater
New Caledonian Friarbird
House Sparrow   c
Red-throated Parrot-Finch
Chestnut-breasted Munia
Common Waxbill   c

Red-browed Firetail
White-breasted Woodswallow   c
Striated Starling   c
Indian Myna   c
New Caledonian Crow   r

110
Fiji

FIJI, A MAJOR STOPOVER on transoceanic air and sea routes, offers some of the best birding in the Pacific. The main islands are surprisingly large; Viti Levu is 90 miles by 60 miles (145 km by 96 km), and Vanua Levu is 105 miles by 30 miles (168 km by 48 km).

Most birders will arrive by air at Nadi (pronounced Nan-dee), on the drier west side of Viti Levu. There are a number of hotels around the airport (such as the Nadi Travelodge) and the excellent Regency on the ocean. Rental cars are easily available.

The best and simplest way to see many of Fiji's endemics is by renting a car or hiring a taxi to go to Nausori Highlands. From the airport follow the main paved road toward Nadi town for about 2 miles (3.2 km), and turn left on a dirt road, opposite Public School 3013. After 2 more miles (3.2 km), turn left on Mulo Mulo Road, which climbs up through farms and grasslands to a lumber mill. The main dirt road veers right and continues for 13 miles (21 km) through fine tropical forest to a small settlement.

There is still a good amount of forest left where Many-colored Fruit-Dove, Golden Fruit-Dove, Peale's Fruit-Pigeon, Collared Lorikeet, Yellow-breasted Musk-Parrot, Island Thrush, Fiji Warbler, Spotted Fantail, shrikebills, Vanikoro and Blue-crested Monarchs, Scarlet Robin, Polynesian Starling, and Wattled and Giant Forest Honeyeaters live. There are no food or lodging facilities in the mountains.

At resorts on the coast of Viti Levu visitors should find on the grounds such birds as Eastern Reef-Heron, Many-colored Fruit-Dove, White-collared Kingfisher, Polynesian Triller, Fiji Slaty Flycatcher, Vanikoro Monarch, Orange-breasted Myzomela, Wattled Honeyeaters, and Red-headed Parrot-Finch.

Suva, the capital, at the southeastern tip of Viti Levu, is the main port, connected by frequent flights from Nadi and increasing overseas flights. The botanical gardens and parks feature many introduced species, as well as native species common to the lowlands of Viti Levu. Shorebirds are best seen at Suva Point and Vatuwanga at low tide.

Joske's Thumb is a conspicuous volcanic plug about 10 miles (16 km) west of Suva. Near an adjacent dairy farm and in the flanking forests many of Fiji's birds can be seen. The Pink-billed Parrot-Finch has been rediscovered here.

Some of the finest birds occur only on the other islands. Vanua Levu, the second largest island, is well known for the beautiful Orange Dove and the exotic Silktail. There are several daily flights from Nadi and Suva to Savusavu airport on Vanua Levu. Guests can stay at the Savusavu Travelodge and the small Namale Plantation. Taveuni, a smaller island about 25 miles (40 km) long, is mongoose-free and also has Orange Fruit-Dove and Silktail. It is a diver's paradise, with one hotel, the Travelodge at Waiyevo. There are flights from Suva and Vanua Levu island, plus a ferry to Taveuni from Buca Bay on Vanua Levu. Much of Taveuni has good birding since rainfall is over 200 inches (5080 mm) a year, and much of the island is dense forest.

Several one-day (and longer) boat trips are available from Lautoka and the Regency Hotel that offer pelagic birding, swimming on picture-perfect isles, and return. Terns and occasional frigatebird and tubenoses are quite possible.

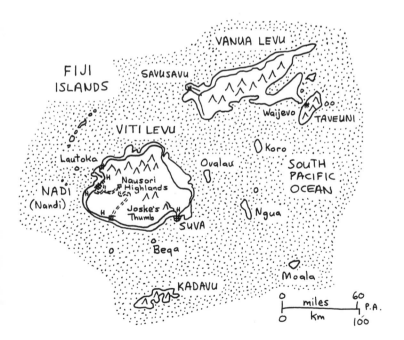

Kadavu Island, due to its remoteness, is not considered on the checklist, although it is home to the Velvet Fruit-Dove, Kadavu Fantail, and Kadavu Honeyeater. A few other very localized birds occur on equally remote isles to the east of the large islands.

CHECKLIST

(VI = Viti Levu, VA = Vanua Levu, TA = Taveuni)

Pterodroma, species S
Wedge-tailed Shearwater
Buller's Shearwater   r M
Sooty Shearwater   r M
Short-tailed Shearwater   M
White-throated Storm-Petrel   r
White-tailed Tropicbird
Red-tailed Tropicbird   r
Brown Booby   c
Red-footed Booby
Masked Booby   r
Lesser Frigatebird   c
Eastern Reef-Heron   c
Green Heron
Pacific Black Duck   c
Fiji Goshawk   c
Marsh Harrier   c
Peregrine Falcon
Red Junglefowl   TA
Brown Quail
Purple Swamphen   TA
Barred-winged Rail   r VI
Banded Rail   TA
White-browed Crake   VI
Spotless Crake   r VI; TA
Lesser Golden Plover   c M
Ruddy Turnstone   c M
Eastern Curlew   M
Whimbrel   c M
Bristle-thighed Curlew   r M
Bar-tailed Godwit   c M
Wandering Tattler   c M
Gray-tailed Tattler   r M
Sanderling   r M
Black-naped Tern
Crested Tern   c
Sooty Tern

Spectacled Tern
Fairy Tern
White-capped Noddy
Brown Noddy
Many-colored Fruit-Dove   c
Orange Fruit-Dove   VA, TA
Golden Fruit-Dove   VI
Spotted Turtle-Dove
Friendly Ground-Dove
Peale's Fruit-Pigeon   c
White-throated Pigeon
Red-throated Lorikeet   VI, TA
Collared Lory
Red-breasted Musk-Parrot   TA
Yellow-breasted Musk-Parrot   VI
Fan-tailed Cuckoo
Long-tailed Cuckoo   r W
Barn Owl
White-rumped Swiftlet   c
White-collared Kingfisher   c
Pacific Swallow   c
Polynesian Triller   c
Red-vented Bulbul   c VI
Island Thrush
Silktail   VA, TA
Fiji Warbler
Long-legged Warbler   r VA, VI
Spotted Fantail   c
Fiji Slaty Flycatcher   c
Fiji Shrikebill
Black-faced Shrikebill
Vanikoro Monarch   c
Blue-crested Monarch
Scarlet Robin
Golden Whistler
Orange-breasted Myzomela   c
Wattled Honeyeater   c

Giant Forest Honeyeater
Layard's White-eye
Silvereye   c
Red-headed Parrot-Finch   c
Pink-billed Parrot-Finch   r VI
Strawberry Finch   c

Java Sparrow   VA, VI
Polynesian Starling   c
Indian Myna   c
Jungle Myna   c VI, VA
White-breasted Woodswallow   c
Australian Magpie   TA

111
New Zealand

THIS BEAUTIFUL COUNTRY combines excellent birding, superb facilities, many resident birders, a healthy climate, good field guides, and diversified habitats; and English is spoken. The islands deserve many chapters, but an excellent bird-finding book has recently been published, and thus a general run-down of highlights and a fairly complete list of birds found on and around the major islands will be more useful.

From Auckland the best day trip is to Miranda, about 50 miles (80 km) southeast on the Firth of Thames. At high tide huge numbers of shorebirds roost on the shell-banks, including Red Knot, Bar-tailed Godwit, and oystercatchers. Wrybill are seen at all tides, and Red-breasted Plover nest here. The coastal drive back, via Clevedon and Papakura, is pretty and has Eastern Reef-Heron, Tui, Honeyeater, and Sacred Kingfisher.

Little Barrier Island is a forested volcanic island 50 miles (80 km) north of Auckland and can be reached via chartered boat or seaplane. Permission for day trips can be obtained from The Secretary, Hauraki Gulf Maritime Park, PO Box 2206, Auckland. It is now the only place in the world for Stitchbird, and has tuataras — an earthworm that grows to 55 inches (1397 mm) (there are no snakes in New Zealand) — and a good native bird fauna including Brown Kiwi, Brown Teal, Kaka, Rifleman, Pied Robin, New Zealand Robin, and Whitehead. This and many other islands up and down the coast have nesting seabirds.

The Rotorua area has many lakes, Maori villages, and volcanic geysers. It is a good area for New Zealand Grebe, cormorants, ducks, and Fernbird.

At Wellington, the capital, pelagic enthusiasts can crisscross Cook Strait back and forth to the South Island. Kapiti Island is an hour's ride north of Wellington and three miles (4.8 km) by boat arranged by Mr. D. Benett, 11 Douglas St., Paraparaumu. A permit is needed from the District Office, Department of Lands and Survey, Wellington. Kapiti has forest, bush, open areas, and lagoons; the best birds are Brown Kiwi, Little Spotted Kiwi, Weka, parakeets, cuckoos, Whitehead, and many seabirds.

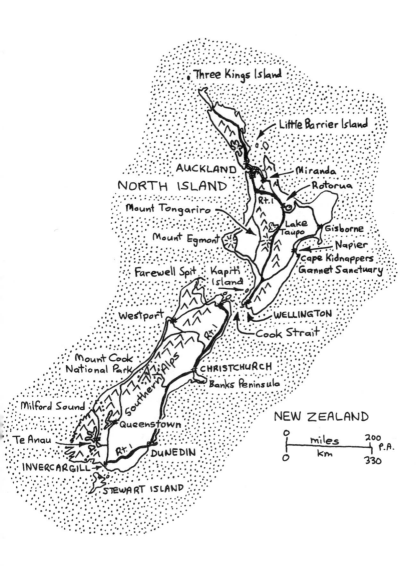

NEW ZEALAND

miles 0 — 200 P.A.

km 0 — 330

Christchurch, the most "English" city in the world outside of England, has good maritime access, Spotted Cormorant at Redcliff, and New Zealand Pigeon in the botanical gardens. Mount Cook National Park has Kea at the Hermitage Hotel. Dunedin is close to the Taiaroa Head Royal Albatross colony, and visitors can book a visit from mid-February to mid-September at any office of the Government Tourist Bureau.

Lake Te Anau is a good base for visiting the Southern Alps. At Cascade Creek there are Paradise Shelduck, New Zealand Robin, Rifleman, and Yellowhead. Boulderwren and Kea live near the Homer Tunnel. Milford Sound is spectacular: boat trips there often produce views of Fiordland Crested Penguin.

Invercargill is the stepping-off place for Stewart Island. There is a ferry boat from Bluff some days and daily amphibian air service (except during gales). It is best to stay overnight, for bush birds are common, there are good pelagic boat trips, and the natives are the nicest anywhere. Penguins, albatrosses, shearwaters, diving-petrels, cormorants, skuas, gulls, and terns can all be seen on halfday boat trips and some from shore.

CHECKLIST

(NI = North Island, SI = South Island [not Summer])

Brown Kiwi   r
Little Spotted Kiwi   r SI
Great Spotted Kiwi   r SI
Yellow-eyed Penguin   SI
Little Penguin   c
White-flippered Penguin   SI
Fiordland Crested Penguin   SI
Great Crested Grebe   SI
New Zealand Grebe   NI; r SI
Wandering Albatross   W
Royal Albatross
Black-browed Albatross   c W
Gray-headed Albatross   W
Yellow-nosed Albatross   W
Buller's Albatross   W
Shy Albatross
Light-mantled Albatross   r W
Giant Petrel   c W
Southern Fulmar   r W
Cape Petrel   c W
Great-winged Petrel   NI
White-headed Petrel   r W
Scaled Petrel   S
Pycroft's Petrel   NI
Blue-footed Petrel   S NI
Black-winged Petrel   NI
Broad-billed Prion
Medium-billed Prion   W

Fairy Prion
Parkinson's Petrel   S NI
Westland Petrel   S SI
Pale-footed Shearwater
Buller's Shearwater   NI
Sooty Shearwater   c
Short-tailed Shearwater   S
Fluttering Shearwater   NI
Hutton's Shearwater
Little Shearwater   NI
White-faced Storm-Petrel
Common Diving-Petrel
Tasman Gannet
Brown Booby   r S NI
Great Cormorant   c
Yellow-faced Cormorant   c
Little Black Cormorant   NI
Little Pied Cormorant   c
King Cormorant   SI
Spotted Cormorant   c
White-faced Heron
Great Egret   r
Eastern Reef-Heron
Brown Bittern
Royal Spoonbill   r
Mute Swan   c
Black Swan   c
Canada Goose   SI

Paradise Shelduck   c
Mallard   c
Pacific Black Duck   c
Gray Teal
Brown Teal   r
White-faced Shoveler
Blue Duck   r
New Zealand Scaup
Marsh Harrier   c
New Zealand Falcon   r
Chukar
Brown Quail   c
California Quail
Common Pheasant
Indian Peacock   NI
Banded Rail
Weka
Baillon's Crake
Spotless Crake
Purple Swamphen
Takahe   r SI
Common Coot
Common Oystercatcher   c
Tasman Oystercatcher
Masked Lapwing   c
Lesser Golden Plover   M
Red-breasted Plover
Double-banded Plover
Great Sand Plover   r M NI
Black-fronted Plover
Wrybill Plover
Eastern Curlew   r M
Whimbrel   r M
Bar-tailed Godwit   c M
Wandering Tattler   r M
Gray-tailed Tattler   r M
Terek Sandpiper   r M
Ruddy Turnstone   M
Red Knot   c M
Sharp-tailed Sandpiper   M
Curlew Sandpiper   r M
Black-winged Stilt   c
Black Stilt   r
Great Skua
Parasitic Jaeger   M
Kelp Gull   c
Silver Gull   c

Black-billed Gull
Whiskered Tern
White-winged Black Tern   r M
Caspian Tern
Antarctic Tern
White-lored Tern   r NI
Little Tern   r M
White-fronted Tern   c
New Zealand Pigeon   c
Rock Pigeon   c
Spotted Turtle-Dove   NI
Kakapo Parrot   r SI
Sulfur-crested Cockatoo   NI
Kaka Parrot
Kea Parrot   c SI
Crimson Rosella   NI
Eastern Rosella
Red-crowned Parakeet
Yellow-crowned Parakeet
South Island Parakeet   r SI
Shining Bronze-Cuckoo
Long-tailed Cuckoo   S
Boobook Hawk-Owl
Little Owl   SI
Sacred Kingfisher   c
Laughing Kookaburra   NI
Rifleman
Bushwren   r SI
Boulderwren   SI
Northern Skylark   c
Welcome Swallow
Richard's Pipit
Dunnock   c
Fernbird
Brown Creeper-Warbler   SI
Whitehead   NI
Yellowhead   SI
Gray Gerygone   c
Gray Fantail   c
Pied Robin
New Zealand Robin
Song Thrush   c
Eurasian Blackbird   c
Silvereye   c
Stitchbird
Bell Honeyeater   c
Tui Honeyeater   c

Yellowhammer   c
Cirl Bunting
Chaffinch   c
Eurasian Greenfinch   c
Eurasian Goldfinch   c
Common Redpoll   c
House Sparrow   c

European Starling   c
Indian Myna   c NI
Saddleback   r
Kokako   r
Australian Magpie
Rook

Bibliography
Taxonomic Index
Alphabetical Key to the
 Taxonomic Index

Bibliography

The following works will be of interest to prospective travelers around the world. For your convenience these references are listed in geographical groupings. There is a mix of field guides, travel guides, checklists, and scientific papers.

There is rarely a totally adequate field guide to the birds of any area in the tropics in print at any given time. Guides to neighboring lands are often very useful, and you would be wise to anticipate future travels and purchase guides when they are published, as most have skyrocketed in value in recent years, and become unavailable.

Other editions of some of these titles have appeared or may appear in other countries under a different publisher and date. The edition consulted in preparing this work is the one listed.

GENERAL INTEREST WORLDWIDE

Austin, Oliver L., Jr. 1961. *Birds of the World.* New York: Golden Press.
Brown, Leslie, and Dean Amadon. 1968. *Eagles, Hawks and Falcons of the World.* 2 vols. New York: McGraw-Hill.
Burton, John A., ed. 1973. *Owls of the World.* New York: E. P. Dutton.
Campbell, Bruce. 1974. *The Dictionary of Birds in Color.* New York: Viking.
Clements, James F. 1978. *Birds of the World: A Checklist.* 2nd ed. New York: Two Continents.
Curry-Lindahl, Kai, and Jean-Paul Harroy. 1972. *National Parks of the World.* New York: Golden Press for the I.U.C.N.
Devillers, Pierre. 1976–1978. "Projet de Nomenclature Française des Oiseaux du Monde." *Le Gerfaut — De Giervalk* 66: 153–168, 391–421; 67: 171–200, 337–365, 469–489; 68: 129–136, 233–240, 703–720.
Edwards, Ernest P. 1974. *A Coded List of Birds of the World.* Sweet Briar, Va.: E. P. Edwards.
Fisher, James, and Roger T. Peterson. 1964. *The World of Birds.* London: Macdonald.
Forshaw, Joseph M. 1973. *Parrots of the World.* Garden City, N.Y.: Doubleday.
Gooders, John. 1969–1971. *Birds of the World.* London: I P C Magazines.

————. 1975. *The World's Wildlife Paradises.* London: London Editions Limited.

————. 1975. *The Great Book of Birds.* New York: Dial.

Goodwin, Derek. 1970. *Pigeons and Doves of the World.* London: British Museum (Natural History).

Grossman, Mary Louise, Shelley Grossman, and John Hamlet. 1964. *Birds of Prey of the World.* New York: Clarkson N. Potter.

Gruson, Edward S., and Richard A. Forster. 1976. *Checklist of the Birds of the World.* London: Collins.

Hancock, James, and Hugh Elliott. 1978. *The Herons of the World.* New York: Harper and Row.

Harroy, Jean-Paul, ed. 1971. *United Nations List of National Parks and Equivalent Reserves.* 2nd ed. Brussels: Hayez for I.U.C.N.

Heintzelman, Donald S. 1979. *A Manual for Bird Watching in the Americas.* New York: Universe.

Morony, John J., Jr., Walter J. Bock, and John Farrand, Jr. 1975. *Reference List of the Birds of the World.* New York: Am. Mus. Nat. Hist., Dept. of Ornithology.

Ogilvie, M. A. 1976. *The Winter Birds [Arctic].* New York: Praeger.

Parkes, Kenneth C. 1978. "A Guide to forming and capitalizing compound names of Birds in English." *Auk* 95: 324–326.

Pasquier, Roger F. 1980. *Watching Birds: An Introduction to Ornithology.* Boston: Houghton Mifflin.

Peters, James L. 1931–1979. *Checklist of Birds of the World.* 13 vols. (of 15). Cambridge, Mass.: Harvard Univ. Press.

Peterson, Roger Tory. 1979. *Penguins.* Boston: Houghton Mifflin.

Ripley, S. Dillon. 1977. *Rails of the World.* Boston: Godine.

Scott, Peter. 1957. *A Coloured Key to the Waterfowl of the World.* Slimbridge, England: Wildfowl Trust.

Thomson, A. Landsborough, ed. 1964. *A New Dictionary of Birds.* London: Nelson.

Todd, Frank S. 1979. *Waterfowl: Ducks, Geese, and Swans of the World.* San Diego: Sea World Press.

Tuck, Gerald, and Hermann Heinzel. 1978. *A Field Guide to the Seabirds of Britain and the World.* London: Collins.

Walkinshaw, Lawrence. 1973. *Cranes of the World.* New York: Winchester.

NORTH AMERICA (UNITED STATES AND CANADA)

American Ornithologists' Union. 1957. *Check-List of North American Birds.* 5th ed. and supplements. Baltimore: A.O.U.

Arbib, Robert S., Jr., Olin S. Pettingill, Jr., and Sally H. Spofford. 1966. *Enjoying Birds around New York City.* Boston: Houghton Mifflin.

Behle, William H. 1958. *The Bird Life of Great Salt Lake.* Salt Lake City: Univ. of Utah Press.

Berger, Andrew J. 1972. *Hawaiian Birdlife.* Honolulu: Univ. Press of Hawaii.

Boyle, William J., Jr. 1979. *New Jersey Field Trip Guide.* Summit, N.J.: Summit Nature Club

Brandt, Herbert. 1951. *Arizona and Its Bird Life.* Cleveland: The Bird Research Foundation.

Bull, John, and John Farrand, Jr. 1977. *The Audubon Society Field Guide to North American Birds: Eastern Region.* New York: Knopf.

Cruickshank, Helen G. 1968. *A Paradise of Birds: When Spring Comes to Texas.* New York: Dodd, Mead.

Davis, William A., and Stephen M. Russell. 1979. *Birds in Southeastern Arizona.* Tucson: Tucson Audubon Soc.

Gabrielson, Ira N., and Frederick C. Lincoln. 1959. *The Birds of Alaska.* Washington: Wildlife Management Inst.

Godfrey, W. Earl. 1966. *The Birds of Canada.* Ottawa: Nat. Mus. of Canada.

Hill, Norman P. 1965. *The Birds of Cape Cod, Massachusetts.* New York: William Morrow.

Jehl, Joseph R., Jr., and Blanche A. Smith. 1970. *Birds of the Churchill Region, Manitoba.* Winnipeg: Manitoba Mus. of Man and Nature.

Judd, W. W., and J. Murray Speirs, eds. 1964. *A Naturalist's Guide to Ontario.* Toronto: Univ. of Toronto Press.

Kelly, Alice H. 1978. *Birds of Southeastern Michigan and Southwestern Ontario.* Bloomfield Hills, Mich.: Cranbrook Inst. Sci.

Kenyon, Karl W., and Richard E. Phillips. 1965. "Birds from the Pribilof Islands and Vicinity." *Auk* 82: 624–635.

Kessel, Brina, and Danial D. Gibson. 1978. *Status and Distribution of Alaska Birds.* Cooper Orn. Soc., Studies in Avian Biol. No. 1.

———, Robert B. Weeden, and George C. West. 1967. *Bird-Finding in Interior and South Central Alaska.* Anchorage: Alaska Orn. Soc.

Kitching, Jessie. 1976. *Birdwatcher's Guide to Wildlife Sanctuaries [North America].* New York: Arco.

Lane, James A. 1979. *A Birder's Guide to Southeastern Arizona.* Denver: L and P Press.

———. 1979. *A Birder's Guide to Southern California.* Denver: L and P Press.

———. 1979. *A Birder's Guide to the Rio Grande Valley of Texas.* Denver: L and P Press.

———. 1980. *A Birder's Guide to Florida.* Denver: L and P Press.

——— and John L. Tveten. 1980. *A Birder's Guide to the Texas Coast.* Denver: L and P Press.

Laycock, George. 1976. *The Bird Watcher's Bible.* Garden City, N.Y.: Doubleday.

McCaskie, Guy, Paul De Benedictis, Richard Erickson, and Joseph Morlan. 1979. *Birds of Northern California: Annotated Field List.* Berkeley: Golden Gate Audubon Soc.

Montague, Richard W., and Susan H. Johnson. 1976. *Exploring Alaska's Mount McKinley National Park.* Anchorage: Alaska Travel Publications.

Murie, Adolph. 1963. *Birds of Mount McKinley, Alaska.* Mount McKinley Nat. Hist. Ass.

Oberholser, Harry C., and Edgar B. Kincaid, Jr. 1974. *The Bird Life of Texas.* 2 vols. Austin: Univ. of Texas Press.

Ogden, John C. 1969. *Checklist of Birds, Everglades National Park.* Everglades Nat. Hist. Ass.

Peterson, Roger T. 1960. *A Field Guide to the Birds of Texas.* Boston: Houghton Mifflin.

————. 1961. *A Field Guide to Western Birds.* Cambridge, Mass.: Houghton Mifflin.

————. 1980. *A Field Guide to the Birds [Eastern North America].* Boston: Houghton Mifflin.

Pettingill, Olin S., Jr. 1953. *A Guide to Bird Finding West of the Mississippi.* New York: Oxford Univ. Press.

————, ed. 1974. *The Bird Watcher's America.* New York: Thomas Y. Crowell.

————. 1980. *A Guide to Bird Finding East of the Mississippi.* Boston: Houghton Mifflin.

Phillips, Allen, Joe Marshall, and Gale Monson. 1964. *The Birds of Arizona.* Tucson: Univ. of Arizona Press.

Pough, Richard H. 1953. *Audubon Guides: All the Birds of Eastern and Central North America.* Garden City, N. Y.: Doubleday.

Preble, Edward A., and W. L. McAtee. 1923. *Birds and Mammals of the Pribilof Islands, Alaska.* Washington: Bureau of Biological Survey, North American Fauna No. 46.

Rickert, Jon E. 1978. *A Guide to North American Bird Clubs.* Elizabethtown, Ky.: Avian Publications.

Riley, Laura and William. 1979. *Guide to the National Wildlife Refuges [U.S.A.].* Garden City, N.Y.: Doubleday.

Robbins, Chandler S. 1975. *A.B.A. Checklist: Birds of Continental United States and Canada.* Austin: American Birding Association.

————, Bertel Bruun, and Herbert S. Zim. 1966. *Birds of North America.* New York: Golden Press.

Robinson, Leif J., and Robert H. Stymiest. 1978. *Where to Find Birds in Eastern Massachusetts.* Belmont, Mass.: Bird Observer of Eastern Mass.

Scharff, Robert, ed. 1966. *Yellowstone and Grand Teton National Parks.* New York: David McKay.

Scofield, Michael. 1978. *The Complete Outfitting and Source Book for Bird Watching [N. Am.].* Marshall, Calif.: Great Outdoors Trading Co.

Smith, Mike, and Virginia Matusek. 1975. *Guide to the Everglades.* Tampa: Trend House.

Snyder, L. L., and T. M. Shortt. 1957. *Arctic Birds of Canada.* Toronto: Univ. of Toronto Press.

Steffee, Nina D., and C. Russell Mason. 1971. *Where to Find Birds and Enjoy Natural History in Florida.* Maitland: Fla. Audubon Soc.

Stewart, Darryl. 1977. *Point Pelee.* Detroit: Wayne Univ. Press.

Stirling, David. 1972. *Birds of Vancouver Island.* Victoria: David Stirling.

————, and Jim Woodford. 1975. *Where to Go Bird Watching in Canada.* Saanichton, B.C.: Hancock House.

Udvardy, Miklos D. F. 1977. *The Audubon Society Field Guide to North American Birds: Western Region.* New York: Knopf.

MIDDLE AMERICAS (MEXICO, CENTRAL AMERICA, AND WEST INDIES)

Alden, Peter. 1968. *Checklist for the Birds of Mexico.* Tucson: P. Alden.

————. 1969. *Finding the Birds in Western Mexico: A guide to the states of Sonora, Sinaloa, and Nayarit.* Tucson: Univ. of Arizona Press.

Bacon, P. R., and R. P. ffrench. 1972. *The Wildlife Sanctuaries of Trinidad and Tobago.* Port-of-Spain: Wildlife Conservation Committee.

Barbour, Thomas. 1945. *A Naturalist in Cuba.* Boston: Little, Brown.

Biaggi, Virgilio. 1970. *Los Aves de Puerto Rico.* San Juan: Univ. of Puerto Rico Press.

Birnbaum, Stephen, ed. 1979. *The Caribbean, Bermuda, and the Bahamas 1980.* Boston: Houghton Mifflin.

Blake, Emmet R. 1953. *Birds of Mexico: A Guide for Field Identification.* Chicago: Univ. of Chicago Press.

Bond, James. 1970. *Native and Winter Resident Birds of Tobago.* Philadelphia: Acad. of Nat. Sci.

————. 1971. *Birds of the West Indies.* Boston: Houghton Mifflin.

Brudenell-Bruce, Piers. 1975. *The Birds of the Bahamas.* New York: Taplinger.

Cox, Thorton. 1974. *Travellers' Guide to the Caribbean.* London: Thorton Cox.

Cross, Cliff. 1971. *Yucatan Peninsula.* Tucson: H. P. Books.

————. 1974. *Central America Guide.* Tucson: H. P. Books.

————. 1974. *Mexico Guide.* Tucson: H. P. Books.

Davis, L. Irby. 1972. *A Field Guide to the Birds of Mexico and Central America.* Austin: Univ. of Texas Press.

DiPerna, Paula. 1979. *The Complete Travel Guide to Cuba.* New York: St. Martins Press.

Edwards, Ernest P. 1968. *Finding Birds in Mexico.* 2nd ed. Sweet Briar, Va.: E. P. Edwards.

————. 1972. *A Field Guide to the Birds of Mexico.* Sweet Briar, Va.: E. P. Edwards.

————. 1976. *Supplement to Finding Birds in Mexico.* Sweet Briar, Va.: E. P. Edwards.

Eisenmann, Eugene. 1955. "The Species of Middle American Birds." *Trans. Linnaean Soc. New York* 7: 1–128.

———— and Horace Loftin. 1968. "Birds of the Panama Canal Zone area." *Florida Naturalist* 41: 57–60, 95.

Franz, Carl. 1974. *The People's Guide to Mexico.* Sante Fe, N. Mex.: John Muir Publications.

Garrido, Orlando H., and Florentino Garcia Montaña. 1975. *Catálogo de las Aves de Cuba.* Havana: Academia de Ciencias de Cuba.

Johnston, D. W., C. H. Blake, and D. W. Buden. 1971. "Avifauna of the Cayman Islands." *Q. Jl. Fla. Acad. Sci.* 34: 141–156.

Land, Hugh C. 1970. *Birds of Guatemala.* Wynnewood, Pa.: Livingston.

Lundberg, Donald E. 1968. *Costa Rica.* San Jose: Juan Mora.

Paynter, Raymond A., Jr. 1955. "The Ornithogeography of the Yucatán Peninsula." *Bull. Peabody Mus. Nat. Hist* 9: 1–347.

Peterson, Roger T., and Edward L. Chalif. 1973. *A Field Guide to Mexican Birds and Adjacent Central America.* Boston: Houghton Mifflin.

Ridgely, Robert S. 1976. *A Guide to the Birds of Panama.* Princeton, N.J.: Princeton Univ. Press.

Russell, Stephen M. 1964. "A Distributional Study of the Birds of British Honduras (Belize)." *Am. Orn. Un. Orn. Monogr.* 1: 1–95.

Skutch, Alexander F. 1977. *A Bird Watcher's Adventures in Tropical America.* Austin: Univ. of Texas Press.

Slud, Paul. 1964. "The Birds of Costa Rica: Distribution and Ecology." *Bull. Am. Mus. Nat. Hist.* 128: 1–430.

Smithe, Frank B. 1966. *The Birds of Tikal.* New York: Natural History Press.

Wetmore, Alexander, and Bradshaw H. Swales. 1931. "The Birds of Haiti and the Dominican Republic." *Bull. U. S. Nat. Mus.* 155.

Wright, Philip, and Paul F. Wright. 1969. *Exploring Jamaica.* London: Andre Deutsch.

SOUTH AMERICA
(INCLUDING TRINIDAD AND TOBAGO)

Alden, Peter. 1977. *A Checklist of the Birds of Venezuela.* Lincoln, Mass.: Mass. Audubon Soc.

Blake, Emmet R. 1977. *Manual of Neotropical Birds.* Vol. 1. Chicago: Univ. of Chicago Press.

Brooks, John, ed. 1979. *South American Handbook.* Bath, England: Trade and Travel Publications.

Butler, Thomas Y. 1979. *The Birds of Ecuador and the Galápagos Archipelago.* Portsmouth, N. H.: Ramphastos Agency.

Chapman, Frank M. 1921. "The distribution of bird-life in the Urubamba Valley of Peru." *Bull. U. S. Nat. Mus.* 117: 1–138.

———. 1926. "The Distribution of Bird-Life in Ecuador." New York: *Bull. Am. Mus. Nat. Hist.* Vol. LV.

Delacour, Jean, and Dean Amadon. 1973. *Curassows and related birds.* New York: Am. Mus. of Nat. Hist.

Dorst, Jean. 1967. *South America and Central America: A Natural History.* New York: Random House.

Dunning, John S. 1970. *Portraits of Tropical Birds.* Wynnewood, Pa.: Livingston.

Epler, Bruce, and Alan White. 1972. *Galápagos* Guide. Quito: Imprenta Mariscal.

ffrench, Richard. 1973. *A Guide to the Birds of Trinidad and Tobago.* Wynnewood, Pa.: Livingston.

Harris, Michael. 1974. *A Field Guide to the Birds of Galápagos.* New York: Taplinger.

Haverschmidt, F. 1968. *Birds of Surinam.* Edinburgh: Oliver and Boyd.

Heintzelman, Donald S. 1973. *Finding Birds in Trinidad and Tobago.* Allentown, Pa.: Donald S. Heintzelman.

Hilty, Steven. 1977. *Field Checklist of the Birds of Colombia.* Tucson: S. Hilty.

Humphrey, P. S., D. Bridge, P. W. Reynolds, and R. T. Peterson. 1970. *Birds of Isla Grande (Tierra del Fuego).* Lawrence, Kansas: Univ. of Kansas Mus. of Nat. Hist. for Smithsonian Inst.

Jacobs, Charles and Bobette. 1979. *South American Travel Digest.* Palm Desert, Calif.: Travel Digests.

Johnson, A. W. 1967 and 1972. *The Birds of Chile.* 2 vols. and supplement. Buenos Aires: Platt Establecimientos Graficos S. A.

Koepcke, Maria. 1970. *The Birds of the Department of Lima, Peru.* Rev. English ed. Wynnewood, Pa.: Livingston.

Meisch, Lynn. 1977. *A Traveler's Guide to El Dorado and the Inca Empire: Colombia, Ecuador, Peru, Bolivia.* New York: Penguin.

Meyer de Schauensee, Rodolphe. 1964. *The Birds of Colombia.* Narbeth, Pa.: Livingston.

———. 1966. *The Species of Birds of South America and Their Distribution.* Narbeth, Pa.: Livingston.

———. 1970. *A Guide to the Birds of South America.* Wynnewood, Pa.: Livingston.

———, William H. Phelps, Jr., and Guy Tudor. 1978. *A Guide to the Birds of Venezuela.* Princeton, N. J.: Princeton Univ. Press.

Mitchell, M. H. 1957. *Observations on Birds of Southeastern Brazil.* Toronto: Univ. of Toronto Press.

Morrison, Tony. 1974. *Land Above the Clouds* [*Andes*]. London: Andre Deutsch.

Olrog, Claus C. 1959. *Los Aves Argentinas: Una Guia de Campo.* Buenos Aires: Instituto Migual Lillo.

———. 1968. *Las Aves Sudamericanas: Una Guia de Campo.* Vol. 1. Buenos Aires: Instituto Miguel Lillo.

Parker, Theodore A., III. 1978. *Birds of the Tambopata Nature Reserve, Madre de Dios, Peru.* Tucson: T. Parker.

———, Susan Allen Parker, and Manuel A. Plenge. 1978. *A Checklist of Peruvian Birds.* Tucson: T. Parker.

Paynter, Raymond A., Jr., and Alastair M. G. Caperton. 1977. *Ornithological Gazetteer of Paraguay.* Cambridge, Mass.: Harvard Mus. Comp. Zool., Bird Dept.

——— and Melvin A. Traylor, Jr. 1977. *Ornithological Gazetteer of Ecuador.* Cambridge, Mass.: Harvard Mus. of Comp. Zool. Bird Dept.

Schafer, E., and William H. Phelps. 1954. "Los Aves del Parque Nacional Henri Pittier (Rancho Grande) y sus funciones ecologicas." *Boln. Soc. Venez. Cienc. Nat.* 16 (83): 3–167.

Schulz, J. P. 1971. *Nature Preservation in Surinam.* Paramaribo: STINASU.

Sick, Helmut, and L. F. Pabst. 1968. "As Aves do Rio de Janeiro (Guanabara)." *Arg. Mus. Nac. Rio de Janeiro* 53: 99–1960.

Snyder, Dorothy E. 1966. *The Birds of Guyana.* Salem, Mass.: Peabody Mus.

Thorton, Ian. 1971. *Darwin's Islands, A Natural History of the Galápagos.* Garden City, N.Y.: Natural History Press.

Todd, W.E.C., and M. A. Carriker, Jr. 1922. "The Birds of the Santa Marta region of Colombia: a study in altitudinal distribution." *Ann. Carnegie Mus.* 10: 146–296.

Woods, Robin W. 1975. *The Birds of the Falkland Islands.* Oswestry, Shropshire: Anthony Nelson.

Worth, C. Brooke. 1967. *A Naturalist in Trinidad.* Philadelphia: J. B. Lippincott.

WESTERN PALEARCTIC (EUROPE, NORTH AFRICA AND MIDDLE EAST)

Alden, Peter C., and Dorothy S. Long. 1978. *Checklist of European Birds with Rationale for the selection of English Names.* Lincoln, Mass.: Mass. Audubon Soc.

Antonio Fernandez, Juan. 1975. *Doñana, Spain's Wildlife Wilderness.* New York: Taplinger.

Bannerman, David A. 1963. *Birds of the Atlantic Islands,* Vol. 1.: A History of the Birds of the Canary Islands and of the Salvages. Edinburgh: Oliver and Boyd.

Benson, S. Vere. 1970. *Birds of Lebanon and the Jordan Area.* London: I.C.P.B. and Frederick Warne.

British Ornithologists' Union. 1971. *The Status of Birds in Britain and Ireland.* Oxford: Blackwell.

Bruun, Bertel. 1978. *Birds of Britain and Europe.* New York: Larousse.

Cramp, Stanley, and K. E. L. Simmons, eds. 1977. *The Birds of the Western Palearctic,* Vol. 1: Ostrich to Ducks. Oxford: Oxford Univ. Press.

Curry-Lindahl, Kai. 1964. *Europe: A Natural History.* New York: Random House.

Etchécopar, R. D., and F. Hüe. 1967. *The Birds of North Africa from the Canary Islands to the Red Sea.* London: Oliver and Boyd.

Ferguson-Lees, Quentin Hockliffe, and Ko Zweeres. 1975. *A Guide to Birdwatching in Europe.* London: Bodley Head.

Gooders, John. 1967. *Where to Watch Birds [Britain].* London: Andre Deutsch.

———. 1970. *Where to Watch Birds in Europe.* London: Andre Deutsch.

Heinzel, Hermann, Richard Fitter, and John Parslow. 1972. *The Birds of Britain and Europe with North Africa and the Middle East.* London: Collins.

Hollom, P. A. D., A. Vittery, R. F. Porter, and J. E. Squire. 1971. *Checklist of the Birds of Turkey.* Orn. Soc. of Turkey.

Hüe, F., and R. D. Etchécopar. 1970. *Les Oiseaux du Proche et du Moyen Orient.* Paris: N. Boubée et Cie.

Hundley, Margaret H. 1965. "Iceland—Land of Glacier and Geyser." *Florida Naturalist* 38(2): 35–39.

Jespersen, Paul. 1946. *The Breeding Birds of Denmark.* Copenhagen: Munksgaard.

Keating, Leslie. 1971. *Morocco by car: A guide for tourists.* Havant, Hants, UK: Kenneth Mason.

Kidson, Peter. 1974. *Iceland in a nutshell: Complete Reference Guide.* Reykjavik: Iceland Travel Books.

Mountfort, Guy. 1958. *Wild Paradise: The Story of the Coto Doñana Expeditions.* Boston: Houghton Mifflin.

———. 1962. *Portrait of a River: The Wildlife of the Danube from the Black Sea to Budapest.* London: Hutchinson.

Nelson, Bryan. 1974. *Azraq: Desert Oasis.* Athens, Ohio: Ohio Univ. Press.

Peterson, Roger T., Guy Mountfort, and P. A. D. Hollom. 1966. *A Field Guide to the Birds of Britain and Europe.* Boston: Houghton Mifflin.

Pink, Annette, and Paul Watkins. 1976. *See Madeira and the Canaries.* London: Format.

Sanders, Jeremy, and Karin Berg. No date (1970s). *A Guide to Birdwatching in Denmark.* Stockholm: Fack.

Smith, K. D. 1965. "On the birds of Morocco." *Ibis* 107: 493–526.

Strickland, M. J., and M. D. Gallagher. 1969. *A Guide to the Birds of Bahrain.* Muharraq, Bahrain: ROAC Press.

Taylor, R.J.F. 1953. *Notes on the Birds of Finnmark.* Stavanger Museum Sterna No. 10.

Venables, L.S.V. and U. M. Venables. 1955. *Birds and Mammals of Shetland.* Edinburgh: Oliver and Boyd.

Vittery, A., ed. 1972. *Bird Report 1968–1969.* Orn. Soc. of Turkey.

Voous, K. H. 1960. *Atlas of European Birds.* London: Nelson.

Weber, Karl, and Lukas Hoffmann. 1970. *Camargue: The Soul of a Wilderness.* London: George G. Harrap.

Williamson, Kenneth, and Geoffrey Schomberg, eds. 1976. *Wildlife in Britain: Guide to Natural Habitats, Safari Parks and Zoos.* Basingstoke, Hampshire: The [British] Automobile Association.

Yeatman, Laurent. 1976. *Atlas des Oiseaux nicheurs de France de 1970 à 1975.* Paris: Societe Ornithologique de France.

SUBSAHARAN AFRICA
(INCLUDING INDIAN OCEAN ISLANDS)

Alexander, Douglas. 1972. *Holiday in Seychelles.* Cape Town: Purnell

———. 1973. *Holiday in Mauritius.* London: Macdonald.

Automobile Association of South Africa. 1974. *Road Atlas and Touring Guide of Southern Africa.* Johannesburg: A.A.S.A.

Bannerman, David A. 1953. *The Birds of West and Equatorial Africa.* 2 vols. London: Oliver and Boyd.

Benson, C. W. 1953. *A Checklist of the Birds of Nyasaland.* Blantyre and Lusaka: Nyasaland Soc.

———, R. K. Brooke, R. J. Dowsett, and M.P.S. Irwin. 1971. *The Birds of Zambia.* London: Collins.

Berlioz, Jacques. 1946. *Oiseaux de la Réunion.* Paris: Librairie Larose.

Berry, P. S. M. 1976. "Some Further Luangwa Valley Observations." *Bulletin of the Zambian Ornithological Soc.* 8(2): 41–44.

Bolles, Edmund Blair. 1979. *Fodor's Animal Parks of Africa.* New York: David McKay.

Bourquin, O., John Vincent, and P. M. Hitchins. 1971. "The Vertebrates of the Hluhluwe Game Reserve–Corridor–Umfolozi Game Reserve Complex." *Lammergeyer* 14 (Natal Parks Bd.).

Brown, Leslie. 1965. *Africa, a Natural History.* New York: Random House.

Cave, F. O., and J. D. Macdonald. 1955. *Birds of the Sudan: Their Identification and Distribution.* Edinburgh: Oliver and Boyd.

Clancey, P. A. 1964. *The Birds of Natal and Zululand.* Edinburgh: Oliver and Boyd.

Clark, John, and Ian Loe. 1974. *A Guide to the National Parks of Zambia.* Lusaka: Anglo American Corp.

Cox, Thorton. 1975. *Travellers Guide to Southern Africa.* New York: Hastings.

Dekeyser, P. L. 1956 and 1961. "Le Parc National du Niokolo-Koba." Oiseaux.1^e fasc. 4, and 2^e fasc. 36. *Mem. Inst. fr. Afr. noire* 48: 79–141, and 62: 363–375.

——— and J. H. Derivot. 1966. *Les Oiseaux de L'Ouest Africain.* 3 vols. Dakar: Institut Fondamental d'Afrique Noire.

Diallo, Siradiou. 1977. *Zaïre Today.* Paris: Editions Jeune Afrique.

Dowsett, R. J. 1969. "List of the Birds of the Luangwa Valley Game Reserves." *Bulletin of the Zambian Ornithological Society* 1(1): 5–19.

Elgood, J. H., and F. C. Sibley. 1964. "The Tropical Forest Edge Avifauna of Ibadan, Nigeria." *Ibis* 106(2): 221–248.

Forbes-Watson, Alec D. 1971. *Skeleton Checklist of East African Birds.* Nairobi: National Museum.

Hall, B. P., and R. E. Moreau. 1970. *An Atlas of Speciation in African Passerine Birds.* London: British Mus. Nat. Hist.

Hopkins, Brian. 1969, 1970. "The Olokemeji Forest Reserve." *Nigerian Field* 34: 115–147; 35: 54–77, 123–141.

Jackson, Frederick J. 1938. *The Birds of Kenya Colony and the Uganda Protectorate.* London: Gurney and Jackson.

Janicot, Claude, and Flavien Ranaivo. 1968. *Les Guides Bleus: Madagascar.* Paris: Hachette.

Jensen, R. A. C. 1966. *The Birds of the Victoria Falls National Park, Rhodesia.* Cape Town: Percy Fitzpatrick Inst. of Afr. Orn., South African Avifauna Series No. 33.

Johnson, Peter. 1977. *As Free as a Bird* [*South Africa*]. New York: Two Continents.

Kemp, A. C. 1974. *The Distribution and Status of the Birds of the Kruger National Park.* Pretoria: The National Parks Board of Trustees (Koedoe Monograph No. 2).

Lagraulet, Jean. 1970. *Animaux et Reserves d'Afrique.* Paris: Fernand Nathan.

Lariviére, J., and A. R. Dupuy. 1978. *Senegal: ses parcs, ses animaux.* Paris: Fernand Nathan.

Lippens, Leon, and Henri Wille. 1976. *Les Oiseaux du Zaïre.* Belgium: Lannoo Tielt.

Mackworth-Praed, C. W., and C. H. B. Grant. 1957, 1960. *Birds of Eastern and North Eastern Africa.* 2 vols. London: Longmans.

———. 1962, 1963. *Birds of the Southern Third of Africa.* 2 vols. London: Longmans.

———. 1970, 1973. *Birds of West Central and Western Africa.* 2 vols. London: Longmans.

McLachlan, G. R., and R. Liversidge. 1978. *Roberts Birds of South Africa.* Cape Town: John Voelcker Bird Book Fund.

Milon, Philippe, Jean-Jacques Petter, and Georges Randrianasolo. 1973. *Faune de Madagascar:* XXXV : Oiseaux. Paris and Tananarive: Office de la Recherche Scientifique et Technique Outre-Mer and Central National de la Recherche Scientifique.

Moreau, R. E. 1966. *The Bird Faunas of Africa and Its Islands.* New York and London: Academic Press.

Morel, Gerard J. 1972. *Liste Commentée des Oiseaux du Senegal et de la Gambie.* Dakar: Office de la Recherche Scientifique et Technique Outre-Mer.

Natal Parks, Game and Fish Preservation Board. No date. *Mkuzi Game Reserve.* Pietermaritzburg.

Newman, Kenneth. 1971. *Birdlife in Southern Africa.* Cape Town: Purnell.

Penny, Malcolm. 1974. *The Birds of Seychelles and the Outlying Islands.* New York: Taplinger.

Pooley, A. C. and J. E. W. Dixon. 1966. *A Checklist of the Birds occurring in the Ndumu Game Reserve in northern Zululand.* Cape Town: Percy Fitzpatrick Inst. of Afr. Orn., South African Avifauna Series No. 39.

Rand, Austin L. 1936. "The Distribution and Habits of Madagascar Birds." *Bull. Am. Mus. Nat. Hist.* 72: 143–499.

Rémy, Myléne. 1974. *Senegal Today.* Paris: Editions Jeune Afrique.

Ripley, S. Dillon, and Gorman M. Bond. 1971. *Systematic Notes on a Collection of Birds from Kenya.* Smithsonian Contributions to Zoology III.

Rountree, F. R., R. Guerin, S. Pelte, and J. Vinson. 1952. "Catalogue of the Birds of Mauritius." *Bull. Mauritius Inst.* 3: 155–217.

Sander, F. 1956, 1957. "A List of Birds of Lagos and its Environs, with brief notes on their status." *Nigerian Field* 21(4): 147–162; 22(1): 5–17; 22(2): 55–69.

Smithers, Reay H. N. 1957. "The Excursions and Congress Environment." *Bokmakierie* 9(1): 3–16.

———, ed. 1969. *Check List of the Birds of South Africa.* Cape Town: South African Orn. Soc.

Staub, France. 1976. *Birds of the Mascarenes and Saint Brandon.* Port Louis, Mauritius: Organisation Normale des Entreprises Ltee.

Steele, David. 1973. *Game Sanctuaries of Southern Africa.* London: Robert Hale.

Wallace, D.I.M. 1973. "Sea-birds at Lagos and in the Gulf of Guinea." *Ibis* 115(4): 559–571.

Watson, George E., Richard L. Zusi, and Robert E. Storer. 1963. *Preliminary Field Guide to the Birds of the Indian Ocean.* Washington: Smithsonian Inst.

Williams, John G. 1964. *A Field Guide to the Birds of East and Central Africa.* Boston: Houghton Mifflin.

——— . 1968. *A Field Guide to the National Parks of East Africa.* Boston: Houghton Mifflin.

——— . 1968. *Safari Journal.* London: Collins.

White, C.M.N. 1965. *A Revised Check List of African Non-Passerine Birds.* Lusaka: Dept. of Game and Fisheries.

Winterbottom, J. M. No date. *A Guide to Bird Watching near Cape Town.* Cape Town: Percy Fitzpatrick Inst. of Afr. Orn.

——— . 1967. "A Revised List of the Birds of the Bontebok National Park, Swellendam." *Koedoe* 10: 122–131.

Zimmerman, Dale A. 1972. "The Avifauna of the Kakamega Forest, Western Kenya, including a bird population study." *Bull. of the Am. Mus. Nat. Hist.* 149(3).

——— . 1978. "Birding Kenya's Kakamega Forest." *Birding* 10(5): 241–249.

SOUTH AND EAST ASIA

Ali, Salim. 1949. *Indian Hill Birds.* London: Oxford Univ. Press.

——— . 1968. *The Book of Indian Birds.* Bombay: Bombay Nat. Hist. Soc. Press.

——— . 1977. *Field Guide to the Birds of the Eastern Himalayas.* Delhi: Oxford Univ. Press.

——— and S. Dillon Ripley. 1968–1974. *Handbook of the Birds of India and Pakistan.* 10 vols. Bombay: Oxford Univ. Press.

Anon. 1967. *Birds of Delhi and District: Field Check List.* New Delhi.

Austin, Oliver L., Jr. 1948. "The Birds of Korea." *Bull. Mus. Comp. Zool.* 101(1): 1–301.

——— and N. Kuroda. 1953. "The Birds of Japan; their status and distribution." *Bull. Mus. Comp. Zool.* 109(4): 277–637.

Bates, R. S. P., and E. H. N. Lowther. 1952. *Breeding Birds of Kashmir.* London: Oxford Univ. Press.

Cheng, Tso-Hsin. 1955, 1958. *A Distribution List of Chinese Birds.* 2 vols. (In Chinese.) Beijing: Science Publishing House.

Covarrubias, Miguel. 1947. *Island of Bali.* New York: Knopf.

Dalton, Bill. 1977. *Indonesia Handbook.* Franklin Village, Mich.: Moon.

Darnton, Iris. 1975. *Jungle Journeys to Ceylon.* Lavenham, Suffolk: Galaxy.

Delacour, Jean. 1947. *Birds of Malaysia.* New York: Macmillan.

——— and Ernst Mayr. 1946. *Birds of the Philippines.* New York: Macmillan.

Dickinson, E. C. 1963. "A Preliminary List of the Birds of Khao Yai National Park." *Nat. Hist. Bull. of the Siam Soc.* 20(3): 183–204.

───── and J. A. Tubb. 1964. "Some additions and corrections to the Preliminary List of the Birds of Khao Yai National Park." *Nat. Hist. Bull. of the Siam Soc.* 20(4): 269–277.

Dresser, H. E. 1902 and 1903. *A Manual of Palaearctic Birds.* London.

duPont, John E. 1971. *Philippine Birds.* Greenville, Del.: Del. Mus. Nat. Hist.

Etchécopar, R. D., and F. Hüe. 1978. Diseaux de Chine, de Mongolie et de Corée, non passereaux. Paris: Pacifique

Fleming, Robert L., Sr., and Robert L. Fleming, Jr. 1970. *Birds of Kathmandu Valley and Surrounding Hills: A Check List.* Kathmandu: R. Fleming.

───── , and Lain Singh Bangdel. 1976. *Birds of Nepal.* Kathmandu: R. Fleming.

Frome, N. F. 1947. "The Birds of Delhi and district." *J. Bombay Nat. Hist. Soc.* 47: 277–300.

Gibson-Hill, C. A. 1949. "A Checklist of the Birds of Singapore Island." *Bull. Raffles Mus.* 21: 132–183.

Glenister, A. C. 1951. *The Birds of the Malay Peninsula, Singapore, and Penang.* London: Oxford Univ. Press.

Gore, M. E. J. 1968. "A Checklist of the Birds of Sabah, Borneo." *Ibis* 110: 165–196.

───── and Pyong-oh Won. 1971. *The Birds of Korea.* Seoul: Royal Asiatic Soc.

Henry, G. M. 1971. *A Guide to the Birds of Ceylon.* 2nd ed. London: Oxford Univ. Press.

Herklots, G. A. C. 1967. *Hong Kong Birds.* 2nd ed. Hong Kong: South China Morning Post Ltd.

Hutson, H. P. W. 1954. *The Birds About Delhi.* Delhi: Delhi Bird Watching Soc.

King, Ben F., and Edward C. Dickinson. 1975. *A Field Guide to the Birds of South-East Asia.* Boston: Houghton Mifflin.

Kobayashi, Keisuke. 1963. *Birds of Japan in Natural Colours.* (In Japanese.) Osaka: Hoikusha.

Lekagul, Boonsong, and Edward W. Cronin, Jr. 1974. *Bird Guide of Thailand.* 2nd (revised) ed. Bangkok: Ass'n. for the Cons. of Wildlife.

La Touche, J. D. D. 1925–1934. *A Handbook of the Birds of Eastern China.* 9 vols. London: Taylor and Francis.

Lynch, Michael, ed. 1978. *All-Asia Guide.* Hong Kong: South China Morning Post.

Medway, Lord, and David R. Wells. 1976. *The Birds of the Malay Peninsula.* Vol. V. Conclusion and survey of every species. London: Witherby.

Ornithological Soc. of Japan. 1974. *Check-list of Japanese Birds.* Tokyo: Gakken.

Pfeffer, Pierre. 1968. *Asia, a Natural History.* New York: Random House.

Phillips, W. W. A. 1975. *A 1975 Annotated Checklist of the Birds of Ceylon (Sri Lanka).* Colombo: Wildlife and Nature Prot. Soc. of Ceylon.

Ripley, S. Dillon. 1961. *A Synopsis of the Birds of India and Pakistan: together with those of Nepal, Sikkim, Bhutan and Ceylon.* Bombay: Bombay Nat. Hist. Soc.

Robinson, H. C., and F. N. Chasen. 1927–1939. *The Birds of the Malay Peninsula.* 4 vols. London: Witherby.

The Sabah Society. 1978. *Kinabalu: Summit of Borneo.* Kota Kinabalu, The Sabah Society.

Saxena, V. S. 1970(?). *Birds of Bharatpur Sanctuary: Field Check List.* Jappur: Rajasthan Forest Department.

Severinghaus, Sheldon R., and Kenneth T. Blackshaw. 1976. *A New Guide to the Birds of Taiwan.* Taipei: Mei Ya Publications.

Smythies, B. E. 1953. *The Birds of Burma.* London: Oliver and Boyd.

————. 1968. *The Birds of Borneo.* London: Oliver and Boyd.

Sowerby, Arthur deC. 1943. *Birds recorded from or known to occur in the Shanghai area.* Musee Heude Notes d'Ornithologie: Shanghai.

Vaurie, Charles. 1959, 1965. *The Birds of the Palearctic Fauna: A Systematic Reference.* 2 vols. London: Witherby.

Webster, Michael, and Karen Phillipps. 1976. *A New Guide to the Birds of Hong Kong.* Hong Kong: Sino-American Publishing Co.

Wilder, G. D., and H. W. Hubbard. 1924. "List of the Birds of Chihli Province (Beijing)." *Journal of the North China Branch of the Royal Asiatic Soc.,* Vol. LV.

Whistler, H. 1949. *Popular Handbook of Indian Birds.* London: Gurney and Jackson.

Yamashina, Yoshimoro. 1961. *Birds in Japan: A Field Guide.* Tokyo: Tokyo News Service Ltd.

AUSTRALIA AND OCEANIA

Beehler, Bruce McP. 1978. *Upland Birds of Northeastern New Guinea.* Wau Ecology Institute Handbook No. 4.

Belcher, W. J., and R. B. Sibson. 1972. *Birds of Fiji in Colour.* Auckland: Collins.

Blackburn, A. 1971. "Some notes on Fijian Birds." *Notornis* 18 (3): 147–174.

Condon, H. T. 1975. *Checklist of the Birds of Australia.* 1. Non-Passerines. Melbourne: R.A.O.U.

Cooper, William T., and Joseph M. Forshaw. 1977. *The Birds of Paradise and Bowerbirds.* Sydney: Collins.

Crawford, D. N. 1972. "Birds of Darwin Area, with some records from other parts of Northern Territory." *Emu* 72: 131–148.

C.S.I.R.O. 1969. *An Index of Australian Bird Names.* Canberra: C.S.I.R.O.

Dalton, Bill, and David Stanley. 1979. *South Pacific Handbook.* Rutland, Vt.: Moon.

Darken, Robert C. deC. 1971. *Simpson's Gap National Park.* Darwin: Northern Territory Reserves Board.

Delacour, Jean. 1966. *Guide des Oiseaux de la Nouvelle Caledonie et de ses Dependances.* Neuchatel, Switz.: Delachaux and Niestle.

Diamond, Jared M. 1972. *Avifauna of the Eastern Highlands of New Guinea.* Cambridge, Mass.: Pub. Nuttall Orn. Club 12.

duPont, John E. 1976. *South Pacific Birds.* Greenville, Del.: Del. Mus. Nat. Hist.

Falla, R. A., R. B. Sibson, and E. G. Turbott. 1979. *The New Guide to the Birds of New Zealand.* Auckland: Collins.

Frith, H. J., ed. 1979. *Complete Book of Australian Birds.* Sydney: Reader's Digest.

Gill, H. B. 1970. "Birds of Innisfail and hinterland." *Emu* 70: 105–116.

Gillham, Mary. 1966. *A Naturalist in New Zealand.* London: Museum Press.

Harper, Peter C., and F. C. Kinsky. 1978. *Southern Albatrosses and Petrels: An Identification Guide.* Wellington: Price Milburn.

Holyoak, D. T. 1979. "Notes on the birds of Viti Levu and Taveuni, Fiji." *Emu* 79: 7–18.

King, Warren B. 1967. *Seabirds of the Tropical Pacific Ocean.* Washington: Smithsonian Inst.

Kinsky, F. C., ed. 1970. *Annotated Checklist of the Birds of New Zealand.* Wellington: Reed and Orn. Soc. of N.Z.

MacDonald, J. D. 1973. *Birds of Australia.* Sydney: Reed.

Mackay, Roy D. 1970. *Handlist of the Birds of Port Moresby and District, Papua.* Melbourne: Nelson.

Mayr, Ernst. 1945. *Birds of the Southwest Pacific.* New York: Macmillan.

McKenzie, H. Ross. 1972. *In Search of Birds in New Zealand.* Wellington: Reed.

Mercer, Robin. 1967. "A Field Guide to Fiji Birds." *Fiji Mus. Spec. Publs.* 1: 1–39.

Moon, Geoff. 1979. *The Birds Around Us: New Zealand Birds, their Habits and Habitats.* Auckland: Heinemann.

Morcombe, Michael. 1969. *Australia's National Parks.* Melbourne: Lansdowne Press.

Peckover, William S., and L.W.C. Filewood. 1976. *Birds of New Guinea and tropical Australia.* Sydney: Reed.

Rand, Austin L., and E. Thomas Gilliard. 1968. *Handbook of New Guinea Birds.* Garden City, N.Y.: Natural History Press.

Roff, A. Derek. 1976. *Preliminary Checklist of the Birds of Ayer's Rock–Mt. Olga National Park.* Darwin: Northern Territory Reserves Board.

Schodde, Richard. 1975. *Interim List of Australian Songbirds* (Passerines). Melbourne: R.A.O.U.

Serventy, Dominic, Vincent Serventy, and John Warham. 1971. *The Handbook of Australian Sea-birds.* Sydney: Reed.

Serventy, Dominic L., and H. M. Whittell. 1976. *Birds of Western Australia.* 5th ed. Perth: Univ. of West. Australia Press.

Slater, Peter. 1971. *A Field Guide to Australian Birds:* Vol. 1, Non-Passerines. Wynnewood, Pa.: Livingston.

———. 1974. *A Field Guide to Australian Birds:* Vol. 2, Passerines. Adelaide: Rigby.

Smith, L. H. 1971. *The Birds of Wyperfeld National Park*. Melbourne: National Parks Service.

Storr, G. M. 1967. "List of Northern Territory Birds." *Spec. Publs. W. Aust. Mus.* 4: 1–90.

Vuilleumier, Francois, and Michael Gochfeld. 1976. "Notes sur l'Avifaune de Nouvelle-Caledonie." *Alauda* 44(3): 237–273.

Wade, Peter, ed. 1975. *Every Australian Bird Illustrated*. Adelaide: Rigby.

Warner, D. W. 1947. "The Ornithology of New Caledonia and the Loyalty Islands." Ph.D. Thesis (unpublished). Ithaca, N.Y.: Cornell Univ.

Wheeler, W. Roy. 1967. "The Birds of Cairns, Cooktown and the Atherton Tablelands." *Australian Bird Watcher,* Dec. 67.

———. 1967. *A Handlist of the Birds of Victoria*. Melbourne: Melbourne Univ. Press for Vic. Orn. Res. Group.

———. 1973. *O'Reilly's–Green Mountains Bird List*. Brisbane: W. R. Smith and Paterson.

———. 1974. *Birds and where to find them: New South Wales*. Milton, Queensland: Jacaranda Press.

Taxonomic Index

The following index is arranged in a sequence according to modern evolutionary phylogeny. There has long been heated debate over which families evolved when, and from what line. There will be continual reshuffling in the future as our knowledge of such matters increases. Modern biochemical research, such as radioactive DNA hybridization experiments, is altering our understanding of relationships at the genus and family level. At the species level we are finding that there are vast numbers of birds involved in complicated clines, superspecies, subgenera, and clusters of subspecies. These gray zones are infuriating to bird tickers who grew up believing that everything was black and white.

Interpreting a vast array of technical literature, all the field guides, and the existing world and regional avifaunal checklists has been no easy task. The opinions, conclusions, names, and sequences remind one of the usual state of world politics. There is no unanimously accepted, regularly appearing compendium of our latest understanding in bird evolution along with English and scientific names. Imagine chemistry being taught without an organized chart of the elements!

Alternate English names have been given (of necessity) in the index, as we have attempted to use only one name throughout the book. As you travel the world you will find more than one name for the same bird, and equally absurd, you will find the same name in use for two entirely unrelated birds of different families! We have taken the liberty of coining some more logical and correctly applied names when neither existing name was suitable as well as of selecting the name we feel most appropriate and accurate when two or more names are in use. Those "discarded" names will usually be given in the index in parentheses to aid use of field guides.

Prefixes have had to be invented for a number of birds (particularly European) whose names have become "generic" names for other related birds worldwide, such as Jay, Wren, Waxwing, Oystercatcher, Lapwing, etc. These proposed prefixes have often been kept generalized by utilizing such words as Northern, Eastern, Greater, Lesser, Common, and the like.

In several cases a new prefix has been invented, after considerable thought, where identical names were in use. Thus, the White-necked Raven of Africa, with its huge white collar, retains its name. In North America, a bird called White-necked Raven (which has no visible white neck feathers) here is called Chihuahuan Raven after the high desert (yucca grassland), which is the core of its habitat preference. The Old World Thrushes called Redstarts were so named after the Anglo-Saxon word *steort,* meaning tail. As English settlers opened new lands many bird names were transferred to vaguely similar, though unrelated, birds. Thus, we have an American wood-warbler with red on the tail that became known as the American Redstart. Although we can't do much about that, we do feel strongly that we should not add insult to injury by saddling the dozen or so members of the genus *Myioborus* with that name. All members of *Myioborus* have extensive and conspicuous white outer tail feathers, none has red on the tail, and the genus is not closely related to *Setophaga.* Thus, we have judiciously coined the term "Whitestart," while the older name of Redstart is listed in parentheses in the Taxonomic Index.

The designation of English names is a matter under consideration by an international ad hoc committee chaired by Peter Alden. The committee would be pleased to hear of your views and philosophy.

HOW TO USE THE INDEX

Please note that all numbers given after each species refer to the *section (or chapter) number* (I–III), not to any page number. Each species will be listed in that area's checklist with any given abundance, seasonal, or elevational tips. It may also be mentioned in the text of the given chapter.

The "generic" names, such as Apalis, Becard, or Bittern, used when two or more related species appear together, are listed as headings for quick reference. The prefixes for each species listed are given after the initial entry and are indented. Thus, under Bittern you will see just Least, Little, American, etc., along with the scientific name(s) without repeating Bittern.

The binomial scientific names are fully spelled out, except when we list two or more members of the same genus. In such cases the second, third, etc., listings carry only the capitalized initial of each genus. In species undergoing proposed taxonomic changes there may be an alternative genus listed, and in many cases alternative (lumped, or split) populations listed as well. This is for your convenience, as these other names will be in use somewhere in various pertinent books and papers you will also be using. Taxonomy is not so cut and dried as you may believe.

A simple example:

Turnstone
Ruddy *Arenaria interpres* 1, 3–9, etc.
Black *A. melanocephala* 3, 13–14, etc.

translates to: Ruddy Turnstone, *Arenaria interpres,* is listed in areas
1 (Pribilofs), 3 (Vancouver Island), 4 (Bathurst Inlet), etc.; and the
Black Turnstone, *Arenaria melanocephala,* is found in areas 3 (Vancouver Island), 13 (Los Angeles), 14 (San Francisco), etc.

Note: Ruddy is the prefix for *A. interpres* in most of the world,
although in much of the Old World where it does not overlap with
A. melanocephala it goes unprefixed. We have chosen to use Ruddy
worldwide to avoid confusion, and as a matter of principle.

A complicated example:

Flicker
Northern (Common, Yellow (Red)-shafted, Gilded)
Colaptes auratus (cafer, chrysoides) 2, 3, 5–14, etc.

This superspecies, which we call Northern Flicker, will also be called
Common Flicker. Its three component parts consist of birds known
in many field guides and lists under the names of Yellow-shafted
Flicker, *Colaptes auratus* (the nominate, or original [first described],
name), along with forms once considered good species — the Red-
shafted Flicker, *Colaptes cafer,* and the Gilded Flicker, *Colaptes
chrysoides.* Due to widespread hybridization and other factors they
have been "lumped" into one species. We abhor the name "Common"
when any reasonable alternative is available. As Flickers are strictly
New World (and thus not "common" to the Old World as well), and
as this species is totally absent in most of Latin America and is the
only one found in North America (other than a local species in Cuba),
it is called Northern.

The Use of "Quotes" and (Parentheses):

Plover (Dotterel)
Long-billed *Charadrius placidus* 87, 88, 90
"Killdeer" *C. vociferus* 3, 5–14, etc.
Hooded *C. cucullatus* 103, 105

The use of the parentheses around Dotterel serves to provide readers
with names which (though not in use in this book) may appear as a
last name in some species of that grouping in certain regional field
guides.

579

The first bird listed above is the Long-billed Plover. The second bird is not called the Killdeer Plover (yet), since the quote marks mean that you do not add the word "Plover" from the head.

In Australia all plovers of the genus *Charadrius* are called Dotterels, the local field guides showing Hooded Dotterel. In our attempt to provide some standards of usage within groups, we have used Hooded Plover.

> Martin
> Sand (Bank "Swallow") *R. riparia* 1, 2, 4–12 . . .

Quotes around Swallow indicate that this bird is also known as Bank Swallow, not Bank Martin.

If in an area checklist you see a name that is not found in your field guide, you can find the alternate names in the index. Many scientists and persons of foreign tongues will use the scientific names extensively in their travels. You can also communicate with foreign ornithologists you happen to meet by using those names, as well. Zones of overlap for studies can also be ferreted out in many species pairs. Some alternate scientific names which may appear in older works are listed in parentheses for your convenience.

The sequence of families and species in the index is adapted from the most recent Peters's *Check-list of the Birds of the World* volumes (including the 1979 second edition of Volume I), Deviller's *Projet de Nomenclature Française des Oiseaux du Monde* (for the rest of the non-passerines), Clements' *Birds of the World: A Checklist* (for most passerines except for those covered in the new Volume 8 of Peters's), and other sources. This taxonomic index is more futuristic in names and sequence than most local field guides. The sequence of species used for the III local lists tends to follow somewhat outdated lines used in those field guides. The field guides and local avifaunal checklists you will be using employ a wide variety of sequences.

CAPITALIZATION AND PUNCTUATION OF ENGLISH BIRD NAMES

We have attempted to follow (in most cases) the rules laid out in an article by Kenneth C. Parkes in *The Auk* 95:324–326 (April 1978) entitled "A Guide to Forming and Capitalizing Compound Names of Birds in English."

As you use various field guides and local checklists you will note many variations in the orthography of the English names. Variations could include for *Ptilinopus iozonus* 1) Orange-bellied Fruitdove, 2) Orangebellied Fruitdove, 3) Orange-bellied Fruit-dove, 4) Orange-bellied Fruit-Dove, and 5) Orange-Bellied Fruit-Dove, etc.

It should be stressed that the following "rules" are still open to reasoned debate, may change in due time, and do not deal with all problems.

The "Rules"

I. Compound bird names should be spelled as a *single word, unhyphenated,* if
   - A. The second component is the word *bird,* e.g., Secretarybird, Indigobird.
   - B. The second component is a part of the body, e.g., Crescentchest, Longclaw, Violetear.
   - C. The name describes an activity of the bird (even if inaccurate), e.g., Kingfisher, Logrunner.
   - D. The second component is a misnomer, such as a fanciful nonornithological noun, e.g., Hillstar, Woodnymph; or the second component is a generic or family name that is incorrect or distantly related, e.g., Honeycreeper, Meadowlark.
   - E. The second component is a broadly categorical bird name, not applying to any one particular kind of bird, e.g. Orangequit, Peafowl.
   - F. The name is onomatapoeic, e.g., Bobwhite, Chiffchaff.

   Exceptions: Names should be hyphenated with only the first letter capitalized under the above rules if
   - (1) Spelling as a single word would result in a double or triple letter between words, e.g., Bush-hen, Thick-knee, Bee-eater.
   - (2) An unhyphenated word would be excessively long or clumsy or would imply an incorrect pronunciation, e.g., Firewoodgatherer, Chuck-will's-widow, Silky-flycatcher, Foliagegleaner.

II. Compound bird names should be spelled as two capitalized, hyphenated words if the second component correctly implies relationship to a specific group of birds taxonomically, e.g., Night-Heron, Ground-Dove, Rock-Thrush, Fruit-Pigeon, Scrub-Robin.

   Exceptions: Some bird names of this nature have become sufficiently ensconced in the English language as single nouns in their own right, e.g., Skylark, Stonechat, Goshawk.

   Note: Use of the hyphen implies a taxonomic grouping.

OSTRICH:*STRUTHIONIDAE*
Ostrich *Struthio camelus* 66, 71
RHEAS:*RHEIDAE*
Rhea
Greater *Rhea americana* 42, 43
Darwin's (Lesser) *Pterocnemia pennata*
38, 41
CASSOWARIES:*CASUARIIDAE*
Great (Double-wattled) Cassowary
Casuarius casuarius 108
EMU:*DROMAIIDAE*
Emu *Dromaius novaehollandiae* 103, 104
KIWIS:*APTERYGIDAE*
Kiwi
Brown *Apteryx australis* III
Little Spotted *A. owenii* III
Great Spotted *A. haastii* III
TINAMOUS:*TINAMIDAE*
Tinamou
Gray *Tinamus tao* 28, 37
Solitary *T. solitarius* 44
Great *T. major* 20, 24, 31, 33, 37,
48
White-throated *T. guttatus* 47
Highland *Nothocercus bonapartei* 22
Tawny-breasted *N. julius* 31
Cinereous *Crypturellus cinereus* 37,
47
Little *C. soui* 19, 24, 27, 28, 30, 31, 33,
37, 47, 48
Brown *C. obsoletus* 44, 45
Undulated *C. undulatus* 33, 37
Brazilian *C. strigulosus* 47
Red-legged *C. atrocapillus* 28, 29
Thicket (Rufescent) *C. cinnamomeus*
16, 18
Slaty-breasted *C. boucardi* 19, 20
Variegated *C. variegatus* 33, 47, 48
Bartlett's *C. bartletti* 37
Small-billed *C. parvirostris* 44
Tataupa *C. tataupa* 43, 44
Red-winged *Rhynchotus rufescens* 42,
43
Ornate *Nothoprocta ornata* 38
Chilean *N. perdicaria* 39
Andean *N. pentlandii* 38
Curve-billed *N. curvirostris* 32
Nothura
Darwin's *Nothura darwinii* 38
Spotted *N. maculosa* 42, 43
Elegant Crested-Tinamou *Eudromia ele-*
gans 41

ALBATROSSES:*DIOMEDEIDAE*
Albatross
Wandering *Diomedea exulans* 39, 40,
71, 103, 105, 106, III
Royal *D. epomophora* 39, III
Galapagos (Waved) *D. irrorata* 34
Black-footed *D. nigripes* 3, 13–15, 87, 88
Laysan *D. immutabilis* 15, 87–8
Black-browed *D. melanophrys* 39–41,
46, 71, 103, 105, 106, III
Shy (White-capped) *D. cauta* 39, 71,
103, 105, 106, III
Gray-headed *D. chrysostoma* 39, 40,
103, III
Yellow-nosed *D. chlororhynchos* 39, 75,
103, 105, 106, III
Buller's *D. bulleri* III
Sooty *Phoebetria fusca* 40
Light-mantled *P. palpebrata* III
SHEARWATERS:*PROCELLARIIDAE*
Giant Petrel *Macronectes giganteus* (and
halli) 35, 39–41, 71, 74, 75, 103, 105,
106, III
Fulmar
Southern (Antarctic) *Fulmarus glacial-*
oides 39, 40, III
Northern (The) *F. glacialis* 1, 3, 13, 14,
49, 50, 51, 87, 88
Petrel
Cape (Pintado,"Pigeon") *Daption ca-*
pense 35, 39, 40, 71, 75, 103, III
Great-winged (Gray-faced) *Ptero-*
droma macroptera 71, 103, III
White-headed *P. lessonii* 103, III
Mascarene (Reunion) *P. aterrima (ros-*
trata) 75
Herald (South Trinidad) *P. armin-*
joniana (heraldica) 75
Soft-plumaged *P. mollis* 61
Scaled *P. inexpectata* 1, III
Black-capped *P. hasitata* 25, 26
Barau's *P. baraui* 75
Dark-rumped (Hawaiian) *P. phae-*
opygia 15, 34
Black-winged *P. nigripennis* III
Blue-footed (Cook's) *P. cookii* 39, III
Pycroft's Petrel *P. longirostris (pycrofti)*
III
Prion (Whalebird)
Broad-billed *Pachyptila vittata* 74, III
Medium-billed *P. salvini* (*vittata*) 103,
III

Dove *P. desolata* 39, 40
Slender-billed *P. belcheri* 39, 40
Fairy *P. turtur* III
Petrel
  Bulwer's *Bulweria bulwerii* 15, 61
  White-chinned ("Cape Hen") *Procellaria aequinoctialis* 39, 40, 71
  Westland *P. westlandica* III
  Parkinson's (Black) *P. parkinsoni* 34, III
Shearwater
  Cory's *Calonectris diomedea* 7, 55, 59–61
  Streaked *C. leucomelas* 87, 88
  Wedge-tailed *Puffinus pacificus* 15, 74–76, 86, 103, 106, 107, 109, 110
  Buller's (New Zealand) *P. bulleri* 3, 14, 110, III
  Pale (Flesh)-footed *P. carneipes* 87, 88, 103, 106, III
  Pink-footed *P. creatopus* 3, 13, 14, 39
  Greater (Great) *P. gravis* 7, 40
  Sooty *P. griseus* 3, 7, 13–15, 35, 39, 40, 61, 71, 88, 103, 106, 110, III
  Short-tailed (Slender-billed) *P. tenuirostris* 1, 3, 14, 88, 105, 106, 110
  Christmas *P. nativitatus* 15
  Manx (Levantine, Balearic, Black-vented) *P. puffinus* 7, 13, 15, 49, 50, 55, 59–61
  Fluttering *P. gavia (puffinus)* 105, 106, 109, III
  Hutton's *P. huttoni (puffinus)* III
  Audubon's (Dusky-backed) *P. lherminieri* 25–27, 34, 75, 76, 109
  Little *P. assimilis* 61, 103, III
STORM-PETRELS:*HYDROBATIDAE*
Storm-Petrel
  Wilson's *Oceanites oceanicus* 7, 35, 39, 40, 71, 74, 75, 86, 103, 106, 108
  White-vented *O. gracilis* 34, 35
  Gray-backed *Garrodia nereis* 40
  White-faced *Pelagodroma marina* 103, 106, III
  Black-bellied *Fregetta tropica* 74
  White-throated *Nesofregetta albigularis* 110
  European (The) *Hydrobates pelagicus* 49, 50, 61
  Wedge-rumped (Galapagos) *Oceanodroma tethys* 34, 35

  Band-rumped (Harcourt's, Madeiran) *O. castro* 15, 34, 88
  Swinhoe's *O. monorhis* 88
  Leach's *O. leucorhoa* 3, 7, 13, 27, 49, 61, 87, 88
  Markham's (Sooty) *O. markhami* 35
  Tristram's (Sooty) *O. tristami* 15
  Black *O. melania* 13, 14
  Ashy *O. homochroa* 13, 14
  Ringed *O. hornbyi* 35
  Fork-tailed *O. furcata* 1, 3
DIVING-PETRELS: PELECANOIDIDAE
Diving-Petrel
  Peruvian (Humboldt) *Pelecanoides garnotii* 35, 39
  Common (Subantarctic) *P. urinator (urinatrix)* 40, III
PENGUINS:*SPHENISCIDAE*
Penguin
  King *Aptenodytes patagonicus* 40
  Gentoo *Pygoscelis papua* 40
  Rockhopper *Eudyptes chrysocome (crestatus)* 40
  Fiordland Crested *E. pachyrhynchus* III
  Macaroni *E. chrysolophus* 40
  Yellow-eyed *Megadyptes antipodes* III
  Little (Blue, Fairy) *Eudyptula minor* 103, 105, 106, III
  Jackass *Spheniscus demersus* 71
  Humboldt *S. humboldti* 35, 39
  Magellanic *S. magellanicus* 40, 41
  Galapagos *S. mendiculus* 34
LOONS (DIVERS):*GAVIIDAE*
Loon (Diver)
  Red-throated *Gavia stellata* 1, 3, 5, 7, 13, 14, 49–52, 54, 58, 87, 88
  Black-throated (Arctic) *G. arctica (pacifica)* 1, 3–5, 13, 14, 16, 51–55, 87–88
  Common (Great Northern) *G. immer* 3–10, 13, 14, 49, 50
  Yellow (White)-billed *G. adamsii* 1, 3, 4, 54, 87
GREBES:*PODICIPEDIDAE*
Grebe
  White-tufted *Rollandia (Podiceps) rolland* 35, 36, 38–42
  Titicaca (Short-winged) *R. (Centropelma) microptera* 38

Dabchick (Grebe)
 Australian *Tachybaptus novaeholland-iae* 100–18
 Little (The) *T. ruficollis* 51–53, 55–62, 66–68, 71–74, 81–83, 85–89, 91, 97, 98
 Aloatra *T. rufolavatus* 74
 Madagascar *T. pelzelni* 74
 American (Least) *T. dominicus* 9, 16, 19–21, 24, 25, 27, 29–31, 43, 44, 46, 47
Grebe
 Pied-billed *Podilymbus podiceps* 3, 6–14, 16, 17, 19–21, 25–27, 30–32, 34, 35, 39, 51–54, 46, 47
 Atitlán (Giant) *P. gigas* 21
 Hoary-headed *Poliocephalus (Podiceps) poliocephalus* 102–106
 New Zealand *P. (P.) rufopectus* III
 Great *Podiceps major* 35, 39, 41, 42
 Horned (Slavonian) *P. auritus* 1–3, 5–8, 13, 14, 49, 51, 87, 88
 Red-necked *P. grisegena* 1–3, 7, 51, 52, 55–58, 87, 88
 Great Crested *P. cristatus* 51–53, 55–60, 66, 88, 90, 92, 103–105, 108, III
 Black-necked (Eared) *P. nigricollis* 3, 9–14, 16, 17, 21, 51–53, 55–59
 Silvery *P. occipitalis* 32, 36, 38–41
 Western *Aechmophorus occidentalis* 3, II, 13, 14, 16
TROPICBIRDS:*PHAETHONTIDAE*
Tropicbird
 Red-billed *Phaethon aethereus* 16, 25–27, 34, 62, 74
 Red-tailed *P. rubricauda* 15, 74–76, 103, IIO
 White-tailed *P. lepturus* 15, 25, 26, 74–76, 86, 109, IIO
FRIGATEBIRDS:*FREGATIDAE*
Frigatebird
 Magnificent *Fregata magnificens* 8, 16, 18, 19, 24–28, 30, 31, 46, 48
 Great *F. minor* 15, 34, 74, 76, 108
 Lesser *F. ariel* 74–76, 86, 97, 98, 108–110
CORMORANTS:
PHALACROCORACIDAE
Cormorant (Shag)
 Great (Black, White-breasted, Large, The) *Phalacrocorax carbo (lucidus)* 7, 49–56, 58, 59, 62, 64, 66–68, 70, 71, 78, 82, 85–92, 103–108, III
 Temminck's (Japanese) *P. capillatus* 87, 88

Socotra *P. nigrogularis* 78
 Yellow-faced (Pied) *P. varius* 103, 105–108, III
 Flightless *P. harrisi* 34
 Double-crested *P. auritus* 3, 6–9, 11–14, 16, 25
 Neotropic (Olivaceous) *P. olivaceus* 9, 16, 18, 19, 24, 26, 27, 29–31, 33, 35, 37–39, 42–44, 46, 48
 Indian *P. fuscicollis* 79, 82, 86
 Little Black *P. sulcirostris* 103–108, III
 Brandt's *P. penicillatus* 3, 13, 14, 16
 Cape *P. capensis* 71
 Bank *P. neglectus* 71
 Spotted *P. punctatus* III
 "Shag" *P. aristotelis* 49–51, 54, 60
 Red-faced *P. urile* 1
 Pelagic *P. pelagicus* 1, 3, 13, 14, 87, 88
 Red-legged *P. gaimardi* 35, 39
 Rock *P. magellanicus* 40, 41
 Guanay *P. bougainvillii* 35, 39, 41
 King (Blue-eyed) *P. atriceps (albiventer carunculatus)* 40, 41, III
 Black-faced *P. fuscescens* 103–105
 Little Pied (Short-billed) *P. melanoleucos* 98, 103–109, III
 Little *P. niger* 79, 82, 85
 Pygmy *P. pygmeus* 55, 56
 Long-tailed (Reed) *P. africanus* 60, 62–64, 66, 70–74
 Crowned *P. coronatus (africanus)* 71
Anhinga *Anhinga anhinga* 8, 9, 16, 19, 24, 25, 27, 29–31, 33, 37, 46–48
 Darter *A. melanogaster (rufa)* 62, 63, 66–74, 79, 82, 85, 86, 93, 97, 103, 107, 108
BOOBIES:*SULIDAE*
Gannet
 Northern (North Atlantic, The) *Sula (Morus) bassana* 7, 8, 49–52, 58–62
 Cape *S. (M.) capensis (bassana)* 71
 Tasman (Australian) *S. (M.) serrator (bassana)* 103, 105–107, III
Booby (Gannet)
 Blue-footed *Sula nebouxii* 16, 34
 Peruvian *S. variegata* 35, 39
 Masked (Blue-faced) *S. dactylatra* 15, 25, 26, 34, 75, 76, 109, IIO
 Red-footed *S. sula* 15, 25–27, 34, 74, 76, 109, IIO
 Brown *S. leucogaster* 15, 16, 24–28, 46, 86, 95, 108–III

PELICANS:*PELECANIDAE*
Pelican
Eastern (African) White *Pelecanus onocrotalus* 55, 56, 62, 64, 66, 68, 71, 72, 82
Pink-backed *P. rufescens* 62–68, 72, 74
Spot-billed *P. philippensis* 86, 90, 92
Dalmatian *P. crispus* 55, 56, 90
Australian *P. conspicillatus* 103, 104, 106–108
American White *P. erythrorhynchos* 8–11, 13, 14, 16, 18
Brown *P. occidentalis* 8, 9, 13, 14, 16, 18, 19, 21, 24–28, 30, 31, 34
Peruvian *P. thagus (occidentalis)* 35, 39
HERONS:*ARDEIDAE*
Bittern
Eurasian (Great, The) *Botaurus stellaris* 51–53, 55–59, 81, 87, 88, 90, 92
Brown (Australian) *B. poiciloptilus* 103, 105, 107, 109, 111
American *B. lentiginosus* 5–9, 11, 13, 16, 25
Pinnated (Savanna) *B. pinnatus* 27, 31
Least *Ixobrychus exilis* 6–9, 13, 16, 21, 25, 27, 31, 35, 43, 48
Little *I. minutus* 52, 55–60, 62, 63, 66, 68, 70, 74, 77, 81, 103
Yellow *I. sinensis* 76, 79, 86–89, 91, 92, 95, 97
Stripe-backed *I. involucris* 27, 39, 42, 43
Schrenck's *I. eurhythmus* 87, 88, 90
Cinnamon (Chestnut) *I. cinnamomeus* 79, 83, 86, 90–93, 95, 97
Dwarf *I. sturmii* 68, 69
Black *I. (Dupetor) flavicollis* 79, 86, 97, 101, 103, 107
Tiger-Heron (Tiger-Bittern)
White-crested (African) *Tigriornis leucolophus* 63
Rufescent *Tigrisoma lineatum* 27, 29, 30, 33, 37, 43, 44, 47, 48
Fasciated *T. fasciatum* 36
Bare-throated *T. mexicanum* 16, 19
Zigzag Heron *Zebrilus undulatus* 37
Night-Heron
Japanese *Gorsachius goisagi* 88
Malay ("Bittern") *G. melanolophus* 86
White-backed *G. leuconotus* 69, 70, 72
Black-crowned (The) *Nycticorax nycticorax* 6–9, 11, 13–16, 19, 24–27, 29–32, 35, 36, 38–43, 46, 47, 55–60, 77, 79, 81–83, 85, 86, 88, 89, 91, 92
Rufous (Nankeen) *N. caledonicus* 97, 100, 101, 103–106, 108, 109
Yellow-crowned *N. (Nyctanassa) violaceus* 7–9, 16, 18–20, 24–27, 29, 30, 34
Heron
Boat-billed *Cochlearius cochlearius* 16, 19, 20, 27, 29, 30, 37
Capped *Pilherodius pileatus* 29, 30, 33, 37, 48
Whistling *Syrigma sibilatrix* 29, 42–44
Pond-Heron
Squacco "Heron" *Ardeola ralloides* 55–60, 62, 64, 66, 68–70, 72, 74, 77, 78
Indian *A. grayii* 79, 81–83, 85, 86
Chinese *A. bacchus* 90, 92, 93
Javan *A. speciosa* 98
Madagascar *A. idae* 64, 66, 74
Rufous-bellied *A. rufiventris* 68–70
Heron
Cattle (Buff-backed, "Egret") *Bubulcus (A., Egretta) ibis* 7–9, 11, 15–20, 23–27, 29–35, 42, 47, 48, 59, 60, 62–64, 66, 68–76, 81–83, 85, 86, 88, 90–93, 95, 97, 98, 100, 101, 103, 106–108
Green (Little, Striated, Green-backed, Lava, Mangrove) *Butorides (A.) striatus (virescens, sundevalli)* 3, 6–9, 12–14, 16, 18–21, 24–27, 29–31, 33–37, 42–44, 46–48, 62–64, 66–70, 72, 74, 85, 86, 90–93, 95–97, 100, 101, 106, 108–110
Pied *Egretta (Notophoyx) picata* 100, 101
Black *E. (Melanophoyx) ardesiaca* 62, 64, 66–70, 72, 74
Little Blue *E. (Florida) caerulea* 7–9, 16, 18–20, 24–27, 29–33, 46, 48
Louisiana (Tricolored) *E. (Hydranassa) tricolor* 7–9, 16, 18, 19, 24–27, 30, 31, 48
Egret
Reddish *E. (Dichromanassa) rufescens* 8, 9, 16, 18, 25, 30
Eastern "Reef-Heron" *E. sacra* 88, 91, 92, 95, 97, 98, 100, 101, 103, 106, 108–111

Western "Reef-Heron" (Dimorphic Mascarene) *E. gularis (dimorpha)* 62, 74, 78, 86

Chinese (Swinhoe's) *E. eulophotes* 92

Snowy *E. thula* 7–9, 11, 13, 14, 16, 18, 19, 24–29, 31–36, 39, 42, 43, 46–48

Little *E. garzetta* 55–64, 66–73, 77–79, 81–83, 85, 86, 88, 91–93, 95, 97, 100, 101, 106–108

Short-billed (Intermediate, Plumed, Yellow-billed, Median) *E. intermedia* 62, 64, 66, 68, 69, 71–73, 79, 82, 85, 86, 88, 97, 99–102, 107, 108

Great (Common, White, Large) *Egretta (Ardea) alba* 6–9, 13, 14, 16, 18, 19, 24–27, 29–35, 37, 39, 41–43, 46–48, 55–57, 62–64, 67–70, 72–74, 77, 79, 82, 85, 86, 88, 91, 92, 95, 97, 99–108, 111

Heron

Purple *Ardea purpurea* 52, 55–60, 62–64, 66–68, 70, 72, 74, 77–79, 82, 85, 86, 92, 97

White-faced *A. (Egretta) novaehollandiae* 100–109, 111

White-necked (Pacific) *A. pacifica* 101–108

Gray (The) *A. cinerea* 49, 50, 52, 53, 55–63, 66–74, 76, 78, 81, 82, 85–92, 97

Great Blue *A. herodias (occidentalis)* 3, 6–14, 16–19, 21, 24–27, 30, 31, 34

Cocoi (White-necked) *A. cocoi* 27, 29–31, 33, 37, 42, 43, 46–48

Black-headed (-necked) *A. melanocephala* 62–69, 71, 72

Madagascar *A. humbolti* 74

Goliath *A. goliath* 62, 64, 66–70, 72–74

Great-billed (Giant) *Ardea sumatrana* 97, 108

HAMMERKOP:*SCOPIDAE*

Hammerkop (Hammerhead) *Scopus umbretta* 62–66, 68–74

STORKS:*CICONIIDAE*

Stork

Wood (American "Wood Ibis") *Mycteria americana* 8, 9, 16, 19, 24, 25, 29, 30, 37, 43

Yellow-billed (African "Wood Ibis") *M. ibis* 62, 64, 66–70, 73, 74

Painted *M. leucocephala* 82, 85, 86

White (Asian) Open-billed *Anastomus oscitans* 82, 85, 86

Black (African) Open-billed *A. lamelligerus* 64, 66, 68–70, 72–74

Black *Ciconia nigra* 55–58, 62, 66, 69, 72, 73, 77, 88

Abdim's (White-bellied) *C. abdimii* 62, 64–66, 68–70, 72, 73

White (Woolly)-necked *C. episcopus (stormi)* 62, 66–69, 72, 73

Maguari *C. maguari* 29, 42, 43

White *C. ciconia (boyciana)* 52, 53, 55–60, 62, 65, 66, 68, 69, 72, 73, 77, 82, 88

Black-necked (Australian "Jabiru") *Ephippiorhynchus asiaticus* 82, 85, 86, 101, 106, 108

Saddle-billed *E. senegalensis* 62, 64, 66, 68–70, 72, 73

Jabiru *Jabiru mycteria* 19, 29, 37, 43

Lesser Adjutant *Leptoptilos javanicus* 86

Greater Adjutant *L. dubius* 82

Marabou *L. crumeniferus* 62, 64–66, 68–70, 72, 73

SHOEBILL:*BALAENICIPITIDAE*

Shoebill (Whale-headed Stork) *Balaeniceps rex* 64

IBISES:*THRESKIORNITHIDAE*

Ibis

White *Eudocimus albus* 8, 9, 16, 18, 19, 24, 25, 29, 30

Scarlet *E. ruber* 27, 29, 47, 48

Bare-faced (Whispering) *Phimosus infuscatus* 29–31, 43

Glossy *Plegadis falcinellus* 7, 8, 25, 27, 29, 55, 56, 59, 60, 62, 64, 66–68, 72, 74, 77, 82, 86, 101, 102, 104

White-faced *P. chihi* 9, 11, 12, 16, 39, 42, 43

Puna *P. ridgwayi* 36, 38

Sharp-tailed *Cercibis oxycerca* 29

Plumbeous *Theristicus caerulescens* 43, 44

Buff-necked (Black-faced) *T. caudatus (melanopis)* 29, 31, 36, 38, 39, 41–43

Green *Mesembrinibis cayennensis* 29, 30, 33, 37, 44, 47

Hadada *Bostrychia (Hagedashia) hagedash* 62, 64–70, 72, 73

Olive (Green) *B. (Lampribis) olivacea* 65, 66

Madagascar Crested *Lophotibis cristata* 74

Sacred (Black-headed, Australian White) *Threskiornis aethiopicus (melanocephalus, moluccas)* 62–64, 66, 68–72, 74, 82, 86, 100–102, 104–108

Straw-necked *T. spinicollis* 101, 103–108

Hermit (Bald, Waldrapp) *Geronticus eremita* 60

Black *Pseudibus papillosa (davisoni)* 82, 85

Japanese Crested *Nipponia nippon* 88

Spoonbill

Eurasian (The) *Platalea leucorodia* 52, 55–57, 59, 60, 62, 82, 86, 88

Royal *P. regia (leucorodia)* 100–102, 104–108, 111

Black-faced *P. minor* 88

African *P. alba* 62, 64, 66, 68–72, 74

Yellow-billed *P. flavipes* 102, 104–107

Roseate *P. (Ajaia) ajaja* 8, 9, 16, 18, 19, 25, 27, 29, 42, 43, 46

FLAMINGOS:*PHOENICOPTERIDAE*

Flamingo

American (Greater) *Phoenicopterus ruber* 18, 25, 30, 34

Greater *P. (ruber) roseus* 58–60, 62, 66, 68, 71, 74, 78, 82, 86

Chilean *P. chilensis* 35, 38, 41, 42

Lesser *Phoeniconaias minor* 64, 66, 71, 74

Andean *Phoenicoparrus andinus* 38

James's (Puna) *P. jamesi* 38

AMERICAN VULTURES: *CATHARTIDAE*

Vulture

Black *Coragyps atratus* 7–9, 12, 16–24, 27–33, 35, 37, 39, 41–48

Turkey *Cathartes aura* 3, 6–9, 11–13, 16–25, 27–33, 35, 39, 41–48

Marsh (Lesser Yellow-headed) *C. burrovianus* 19, 29, 30, 43, 44, 48

Jungle (Greater Yellow-headed) *C. melambrotus* 33, 37, 47, 48

Condor

California *Gymnogyps californianus* 13

Andean *Vultur gryphus* 30, 32, 35, 36, 39, 41

King Vulture *Sarcoramphus papa* 19, 20, 29, 33, 37

HAWKS AND EAGLES: *ACCIPITRIDAE*

Osprey *Pandion haliaetus* 3, 5, 7–10, 16, 18, 19, 24–27, 29–35, 37, 39, 46, 48, 53, 54, 56–58, 60–64, 66, 68, 72, 77, 78, 85–92, 97, 98, 101, 103, 108, 109

Baza (Cuckoo-falcon, Hawk)

African *Aviceda cuculoides* 63, 65, 66, 72

Madagascar *A. madagascariensis* 74

Jerdon's (Brown) *A. jerdoni* 86, 97

Crested *A. subcristata* 99, 100, 107, 108

Black *A. leuphotes* 95

Kite

Gray-headed (Cayenne) *Leptodon cayanensis* 19, 20, 27–30, 33, 37, 47, 48

Hook-billed (Tree-snail) *Chondrohierax uncinatus* 18, 20, 24, 26, 48

Cuban *C. wilsonii (uncinatus)* 25

Honey-Buzzard (Honey-Kite)

Long-tailed *Henicopernis longicauda* 99, 100

Eurasian (Crested) *Pernis apivorus (ptilorhynchus)* 53, 55–60, 62, 65, 67, 68, 72, 77, 79, 82, 87, 88, 93, 95–98

Barred *P. celebensis* 97

Kite

Swallow-tailed *Elanoides forficatus* 8, 19, 20, 22–25, 27, 31–33, 37, 44, 47, 48

Bat ("Hawk") *Machaerhamphus alcinus* 62, 65, 66, 68–70, 74

Pearl *Gampsonyx swainsonii* 27, 29, 30, 37

White-tailed *Elanus leucurus (caeruleus)* 9, 13, 16, 19, 23, 24, 27, 29, 30, 39, 42, 44, 46, 48

Black-shouldered (Black-winged) *E. caeruleus* 59, 60, 62–73, 82, 85, 86, 93, 97, 98

Australian Black-shouldered *E. notatus* 99, 101–108

Letter-winged *E. scriptus* 102

Scissor (Swallow)-tailed *Chelictinia riocourii* 62

Everglade (Snail, Marsh-snail) *Rostrhamus sociabilis* 8, 19, 25, 29–31, 33, 42–44, 47, 48

Slender-billed *R. hamatus* 29, 33, 47, 48

Double-toothed *Harpagus bidentatus* 19, 20, 22, 24, 27, 30, 31, 37, 47, 48

Rufous-thighed *H. diodon* 44, 45

Plumbeous *Ictinia plumbea* 19, 20, 24, 27, 29, 31, 33, 37, 44, 47, 48

Mississippi *I. mississippiensis* 9

Square-tailed *Lophoictinia isura* 103, 108

Black-breasted ("Buzzard") *Hamirostra melanosternon* 101

Red *Milvus milvus* 56–61

Black (Yellow-billed, Black-eared, Fork-tailed, Pariah, Brown) *M. migrans* 55–60, 62–70, 72–74, 77, 79, 81–83, 85–89, 91, 92, 99–101, 108

Whistling *Haliastur sphenurus* 99–105, 107–109

Brahminy (Red-backed "Sea-Eagle") *H. indus* 79, 86, 95, 97–101, 107

Sea-Eagle (Fish-Eagle, Eagle)

White-bellied (-breasted) *Haliaeetus leucogaster* 86, 92, 95, 97, 98, 100, 101, 103, 104, 106–108

African *H. vocifer* 62, 64, 66–73

Madagascar *H. vociferoides* 74

Pallas's *H. leucoryphus* 82

White-tailed *H. albicilla* 49, 53–56, 87, 88

Bald ("Eagle") *H. leucocephalus* 1–3, 6–11

Steller's *H. pelagicus* 1, 87

Fishing-Eagle

Lesser (Himalayan Gray-headed) *Ichthyophaga humilis (nana)* 94

Gray-headed *I. ichthyaetus* 81, 82, 85, 86, 93, 97

Vulture

Palm-nut *Gypohierax angolensis* 62–64, 67

"Lammergeier" (Bearded) *Gypaetus barbatus* 55, 60, 66, 81, 84

Egyptian *Neophron percnopterus* 55, 56, 58–61, 66, 77, 82, 85

Hooded *Necrosyrtes monachus* 62, 64–66, 68–70, 73

Indian White-backed *Gyps bengalensis* 79, 82, 83, 85

African White-backed *G. africanus* 62, 64, 65, 69, 72, 73

Long-billed *G. indicus* 82, 83, 85

Ruppell's (Griffon) *G. rueppellii* 62, 66

Himalayan (Griffon) *G. himalayensis* 80, 81, 84

Griffon *G. fulvus* 55, 56, 59, 60, 77, 82, 83

Cape *G. coprotheres (fulvus)* 72, 73

Cinereous (Eurasian Black) *Aegypius monachus* 59, 60

Lappet-faced *A. (Torgos) tracheliotus* 60, 62, 64, 66, 69

White-headed *A. (Trigonoceps) occipitalis* 62, 64, 66, 69, 72, 73

Pondicherry (Indian Black, King) *A. (Sarcogyps) calvus* 82

Snake-Eagle (Harrier-Eagle, Eagle)

Short-toed *Circaetus gallicus* 55–60, 62, 77, 81

Beaudouin's *C. beaudouini (gallicus)* 62

Black-breasted *C. pectoralis (gallicus)* 64, 66, 68–70

Brown *C. cinereus* 62, 64, 66, 68, 69, 72, 73

Southern (Banded) *C. fasciolatus* 67, 72

Banded (Smaller) *C. cinerascens* 62, 65, 68, 69

Bateleur *Terathopius ecaudatus* 62, 64–70, 72, 73

Serpent-Eagle

Crested *Spilornis cheela* 82, 83, 85, 86, 91, 93–96, 98

Madagascar *Eutriorchis astur* 74

Harrier-Hawk

African ("Gymnogene") *Polyboroides typus* 62, 63, 65–69, 71–73

Madagascar *P. radiatus* 74

Harrier

Spotted *Circus assimilis* 99, 102–105

Northern (Hen, Marsh "Hawk") *C. cyaneus (hudsonius)* 2, 5–14, 25, 26, 51–59, 77, 83, 84, 87–90

Cinereous *C. cinereus* 32, 36, 38–42

Pallid *C. macrourus* 56, 64–66, 68, 77, 78, 82, 86

Pied *C. melanoleucus* 86, 89, 92, 93, 97

Montagu's *C. pygargus* 51–53, 55–59, 62, 64, 66, 68, 82, 86

African (African Marsh) *C. ranivorus* 64, 66, 68, 71, 72, 82

Marsh (Swamp, Eastern, Mascarene) *C. aeruginosus (spilonotus, approximans, maillardi)* 51–53, 55–60, 62–64, 66, 74–79, 85–89, 91–93, 97, 100, 101, 103–106, 108–111

Long-winged *C. buffoni* 27, 31, 42, 43, 48

Chanting-Goshawk
  Gabar "Goshawk" *Melierax (Micronisus) gabar* 62, 66, 68–70, 73
  Dark *M. metabates* 62, 66, 68–70, 73
  Pale *M. canorus* 66, 71
Goshawk (Sparrowhawk)
  Gray-bellied *Accipiter poliogaster* 33
  Crested *A. trivirgatus* 86, 91, 93–95, 97
  African *A. tachiro* 62, 63, 65–70, 72
  "Shikra" (Little Banded) *A. badius* 62, 63, 65, 66, 68–70, 72, 73, 79, 82, 85, 86, 93
  Chinese *A. soloensis* 91, 97
  Gray-headed *A. poliocephalus* 99, 100
  Brown (Australian) *A. fasciatus* 99–109
  Gray (White) *A. novaehollandiae* 99–101, 107, 108
  Black-mantled *A. melanochlamys* 99
  Fiji *A. rufitorques* 110
Sparrowhawk (Hawk)
  White-bellied *A. haplochrous* 109
  Tiny *A. superciliosus* 24, 31, 47
  Little *A. minullus* 65–69, 72, 73
  Besra (Asiatic) *A. virgatus* 83, 86, 91, 95–97
  Japanese (Asiatic) *A. gularis* 87, 88, 93, 95, 97
  Levant *A. brevipes* 55, 56, 77
  Frances's *A. francesii* 74
  Collared *A. cirrhocephalus* 99–104, 107, 108
  Ovampo *A. ovampensis* 66, 69
  Madagascar *A. madagascariensis* 74
  Eurasian (Northern, European) *A. nisus* 51–58, 60, 61, 77, 79, 81, 83, 84, 87–90, 92
  Rufous-breasted *A. rufiventris* 64, 66
  Sharp-shinned *A. striatus* 2, 3, 6–10, 12–14, 16, 17, 21, 22, 25, 30, 32, 45
  Bicolored *A. bicolor* 20, 22, 33, 37, 44, 47
  Cooper's *A. cooperii* 3, 6, 7, 9, 10, 12–14, 16, 17, 22
  Gundlach's *A. gundlachi* 25
Goshawk
  Great (Black "Sparrowhawk") *A. melanoleucus* 62, 64–68, 72
  Henst's *A. henstii* 74
  Northern *A. gentilis* 2, 3, 7, 10, 12, 52–54, 56–58, 60, 80, 84, 87, 88
  Red *A. (Erythrotriorchis) radiatus* 107

Buzzard-Eagle (Buzzard, Eagle)
  Grasshopper *Butastur rufipennis* 62, 66
  Rufous-winged *B. liventer* 93
  White-eyed *B. teesa* 79, 82
  Gray-faced *B. indicus* 88, 91, 96, 97
Lizard Buzzard *Kaupifalco monogrammicus* 62–70, 72
Crane Hawk *Geranospiza caerulescens* 16, 20, 29, 31, 43, 47
Hawk
  Slate-colored *Leucopternis schistacea* 33, 37, 47
  Plumbeous *L. plumbea* 24
  Barred (Black-chested Prince) *L. princeps* 22, 31
  Black-faced *L. melanops* 48
  White-browed *L. kuhli* 47
  Semiplumbeous *L. semiplumbea* 24, 31
  White *L. albicollis* 18–20, 22, 24, 27, 28, 31, 48
  Mantled *L. polionota* 44, 45
  Gray *Asturina (Buteo) nitida* 12, 16, 18, 19, 24, 27–30, 47, 48
  Rufous Crab *Buteogallus aequinoctialis* 48
  Lesser Black (Common, Mangrove) *B. anthracinus (subtilis)* 12, 16, 19, 24–28, 30, 31
  Great Black *B. urubitinga (ridgwayi)* 16, 19, 27, 29, 30, 37, 43, 48
  Savanna *B. (Heterospizias) meridionalis* 27, 29, 31, 43, 47, 48
  Harris's (Bay-winged) *Parabuteo unicinctus* 9, 12, 16, 29, 30, 35, 39, 46
  Black-collared *Busarellus nigricollis* 19, 27, 29, 43, 48
Black-chested Buzzard-Eagle *Geranoaetus melanoleucus* 32, 36, 39, 41
Solitary Eagle *Harpyhaliaetus solitarius* 28
Hawk (Buzzard)
  Roadside *B. magnirostris* 18–20, 23, 24, 28–31, 33, 36, 37, 42–48
  White-rumped *B. leucorrhous* 30, 45
  Ridgway's *B. ridgwayi* 25
  Red-shouldered *B. lineatus* 6–9, 13, 14
  Broad-winged *B. platypterus* 6–9, 21–28, 30, 37
  Short-tailed *B. brachyurus* 8, 16, 19, 20, 24, 27–30, 33, 37, 45, 46, 48
  White-throated *B. albigula* 36, 39

Swainson's *B. swainsoni* 2, 8–10, 12–14, 16, 20–24, 29, 42, 43

Galapagos *B. galapagoensis* 34

White-tailed *B. albicaudatus* 9, 16, 19, 23, 27, 29, 30, 45, 46–48

Red-backed *B. polyosoma* 32, 35, 38–41

Puna (Variable) *B. poecilochrous* 32, 36, 38

Zone-tailed *B. albonotatus* 12, 16, 21, 24, 29, 30, 43

Hawaiian *B. solitarius* 15

Buzzard (Hawk)

Red-tailed *B. jamaicensis* 2–4, 6–10, 12–14, 16, 17, 21–23, 25

Common (Eurasian, Steppe), *B. buteo (vulpinus)* 51–53, 55–61, 64–66, 68, 69, 71, 72, 77, 83, 86–88, 90–92

Mountain *B. oreophilus* 65, 66

Madagascar *B. brachypterus* 74

Long-legged *B. rufinus* 60, 62, 66, 77, 81–83

Upland *B. hemilasius* 89, 90

Ferruginous *B. regalis* 11, 12

Rough-legged *B. lagopus* 1–5, 7, 10–12, 53, 54, 57, 87

Jackal *B. rufofuscus* 72

Augur *B. augur (rufofuscus)* 64–66, 68, 70, 71

Eagle

Harpy *Harpia harpyja* 37, 45, 48

Philippine Monkey-eating *Pithecophaga jefferyi* 97

Black (Indian) *Ictinaetus malayensis* 83, 86, 93, 96, 98

Lesser Spotted *Aquila pomarina* 55–57, 66, 68, 69, 73, 77, 82

Greater Spotted *A. clanga* 53, 55–57, 77, 82, 89, 92

Tawny (Steppe) *A. rapax (nipalensis)* 60, 64, 66, 68–70, 72, 73, 77, 79, 82–84

Imperial *A. heliaca* 55–57, 59, 60

Wahlberg's *A. wahlbergi* 62, 65–70, 72, 73

Golden *A. chrysaetos* 2–4, 10–13, 53, 55, 56, 59, 60, 81, 84, 87, 88

Wedge-tailed *A. audax* 102–105, 107

Verreaux's (Black) *A. verreauxii* 66, 68, 71

Bonelli's *Hieraaetus fasciatus* 58–60, 82

African "Hawk-Eagle" *H. spilogaster* 62, 64–70, 72, 73

Booted *H. pennatus* 55, 56, 59, 60, 62, 71, 77

Little *H. morphnoides* 99, 100–104

Hawk-Eagle

Ayre's *H. dubius* 65, 66, 68

Rufous-bellied *H. kienerii* 86, 94, 97

Black-and-white *Spizastur melanoleucus* 28, 48

Long-crested "Eagle" *Lophaetus occipitalis* 62, 64–70, 72

Changeable *Spizaetus cirrhatus* 83, 85, 86, 94, 95, 97

Mountain *S. nipalensis* 83, 86–88, 93

Philippine *S. philippensis* 97

Wallace's *S. nanus* 94

Black *S. tyrannus* 18–20, 24, 28, 30, 33, 37, 45, 47, 48

Ornate *S. ornatus* 20, 22, 24, 27, 28, 31, 33, 37, 48

Crowned *Stephanoaetus coronatus* 62, 65–68, 72

Eagle

Black-and-chestnut (Isidor's) *Oroaetus isidori* 30

Martial *Polemaetus bellicosus* 62, 64, 66, 68–70, 72, 73

SECRETARYBIRD:*SAGITTARIIDAE*

Secretarybird *Sagittarius serpentarius* 66, 69, 71–73

FALCONS:*FALCONIDAE*

Caracara

Black *Daptrius ater* 33, 37, 48

Red-throated (Noisy) *D. americanus* 24, 33, 37, 47, 48

Carunculated *Phalcoboenus carunculatus* 32

Mountain *P. megalopterus* 36, 38, 39

Striated (Forster's) *P. australis* 40

Crested *Polyborus plancus (cheriway)* 8, 9, 12, 16, 18, 25, 29, 30, 31, 39–47

Chimango *Milvago chimango* 39, 41–43

Yellow-headed (Buffy) *M. chimachima* 24, 27–31, 33, 43–48

Laughing Falcon *Herpetotheres cachinnans* 16, 18, 19, 29–31, 33, 37, 43, 47, 48

Forest-Falcon (Micrastur)

Barred *Micrastur ruficollis* 19, 20, 22, 24, 30, 31, 37

Lined *M. gilvicollis* 47, 48

Slaty-backed *M. mirandollei* 24

Collared *M. semitorquatus* 16, 19, 20, 24, 30

Pygmy Falcon *Polihierax semitorquatus* 66

Falconet
  Red-legged *Microhierax caerulescens* 85, 93
  Black-thighed (-legged) *M. fringillarius* 94, 95, 98
  Philippine *M. erythrogenys* 97

Brown Falcon *Falco berigora* 99–106

Kestrel
  Lesser *Falco naumanni* 55, 56, 58–60, 62, 64, 66, 68, 73, 77, 78
  American (Sparrow "Hawk") *F. sparverius* 2, 3, 5–14, 16, 17, 19, 20–22, 24–26, 29–32, 35, 36, 38–41, 43–45
  Common (Rock, Eurasian) *F. tinnunculus* 51–66, 68, 71, 72, 77, 78, 81–84, 86–92
  Madagascar *F. newtoni* 74
  Mauritius *F. punctatus* 75
  Seychelles *F. araea* 76
  Moluccan *F. moluccensis* 98
  Nankeen (Australian) *F. cenchroides* 101–108
  Greater (White-eyed) *F. rupicoloides* 66, 72
  Gray *F. ardosiaecus* 62, 64, 65
  Dickinson's *F. dickinsoni* 68–70
  Barred *F. zoniventris* 74

Falcon
  Red-necked (-headed) *F. chicquera* 62, 68, 69, 82
  Red-footed *F. vespertinus* 55–57, 73, 77
  Amur (Red-footed) *F. amurensis* 66, 68, 73, 89
  Eleanora's *F. eleanorae* 60, 61, 74
  Sooty *F. concolor* 74
  Aplomado *F. femoralis* 27, 29, 32, 36, 38, 39, 43, 46
  "Merlin" (Pigeon "Hawk") *F. columbarius* 2, 3, 5, 7, 8, 12, 25–27, 29, 32, 49–51, 53, 54, 56, 58, 77, 87–89
  Bat *F. rufigularis* 20, 27, 28, 30, 31, 33, 37, 47, 48

Hobby
  European *F. subbuteo* 52, 53, 55–62, 65, 66, 68, 70, 78, 83, 87, 88, 92
  African *F. cuvieri* 62, 64, 65
  Oriental *F. severus* 83, 93, 97, 99

Australian (Little "Falcon") *F. longipennis* 101–105, 108

Falcon
  New Zealand *F. novaeseelandiae* 111
  Gray *F. hypoleucos* 104
  Prairie *F. mexicanus* 11, 12
  Lanner *F. biarmicus* 60, 64, 66, 68–70, 72, 73, 82
  Saker *F. cherrug* 56, 57
  "Gyrfalcon" *F. rusticolus* 1, 2, 4, 49, 54, 87
  Peregrine *F. peregrinus* 1, 4, 5, 7, 8, 10, 12, 14, 16, 19, 24–27, 30, 32, 34–36, 39–41, 44, 48, 50, 53–60, 62, 66–68, 74, 77, 78, 86–88, 90, 92, 93, 96, 97, 100, 102–105, 107–110
  Barbary *F. peregrinoides (peregrinus)* 60, 61
  Orange-breasted *F. deiroleucus* 20, 33
  Taita *F. fasciinucha* 66, 70

DUCKS, GEESE AND SWANS:
  ANATIDAE

Magpie Goose *Anseranas semipalmata* 101, 108

Whistling-Duck (Tree-Duck)
  Spotted *Dendrocygna guttata* 97, 100
  Plumed *D. eytoni* 101, 102, 108
  Fulvous *D. bicolor* 9, 16, 25, 27, 29–31, 42, 62, 66, 68, 72, 74
  Water (Wandering) *D. arcuata* 97, 100, 101, 108
  Lesser (Indian) *D. javanica* 79, 85, 86, 95
  White-faced *D. viduata* 29, 30, 43, 46, 62–64, 66–70, 72, 74
  West Indian *D. arborea* 25, 26
  Black-bellied *D. autumnalis* 9, 12, 16, 19, 26, 27, 29, 30, 43

White-backed Duck *Thalassornis leuconotos* 62, 66–68, 70, 74

Swan
  Mute *Cygnus olor* 3, 7, 51–53, 55, 56, 103, 111
  Black *C. atratus* 103–108, 111
  Black-necked *C. melanocoryphus* 39–42
  Trumpeter *C. buccinator* 3, 10
  Whooper *C. cygnus* 1, 49, 50, 52–54, 87–90
  Bewick's *C. bewicki (columbianus)* 52, 53, 87–90
  Whistling *C. columbianus* 11, 3–7, 10–11

Coscoroba *Coscoroba coscoroba* 40–42

Goose
Swan (Chinese) *Anser cygoides* 87, 88, 90
Pink-footed *A. brachyrhynchus (fabalis)* 49, 52, 53
Bean *A. fabalis* 52–54, 57, 58, 87–90
(Greater) White-fronted *A. albifrons* 3–5, 9, 14, 49, 52, 53, 55, 57, 87, 88, 90
Lesser White-fronted *A. erythropus* 54, 87, 88
Greylag *A. anser* 49, 52–60, 82, 90
Bar-headed *A. indicus* 82, 85
Snow *A. caerulescens (hyperborea)* 3–5, 7, 9, 11, 14, 87, 88
Emperor *A. canagicus* 1
Nene (Hawaiian) *Branta sandvicensis* 15
Canada *B. canadensis* 1, 3–7, 9–11, 13, 14, 51, 53, 111
Barnacle *B. leucopsis* 52, 53
Brent ("Brant") *B. bernicla (nigricans)* 1, 3, 4, 7, 13, 14, 49, 51–53, 87, 88
Red-breasted *B. ruficollis* 56
Cape Barren *Cereopsis novaehollandiae* 103

Freckled Duck *Stictonetta naevosa* 103

Goose
Andean *Chloephaga melanoptera* 36, 38, 39
Upland *C. picta* 40, 41
Kelp *C. hybrida* 40
Ashy-headed *C. poliocephala* 40, 41
Ruddy-headed *C. rubidiceps* 40
Orinoco *Neochen jubata* 37
Egyptian *Alopochen aegyptiaca* 51, 62, 64, 66, 68–72

Shelduck (Duck)
Ruddy *Tadorna ferruginea* 55, 56, 60, 77, 82, 85, 88, 89
Cape *T. cana* 71
Paradise *T. variegata* 111
Chestnut-breasted (Mountain) *T. tadornoides* 103–105
Common (Red-billed, The) *T. tadorna* 50–53, 55, 56, 58, 60, 77, 90, 97
White-headed (Burdekin) *T. radjah* 101

Steamer-Duck
Flightless *Tachyeres pteneres* 40
Falkland *T. brachypterus* 40, 41

Spur-winged Goose *Plectropterus gambensis* 62, 66, 68, 69, 71–73

Duck
Muscovy *Cairina moschata* 16, 19, 29, 30, 37, 43, 44, 48
Hartlaub's *Pteronetta hartlaubi* 63
Knob-billed Goose (Comb "Duck") *Sarkidiornis melanotos (sylvicola)* 29, 43, 62, 64, 66–70, 72–74, 82

Pygmy-Goose
Green *Nettapus pulchellus* 100, 101, 108
Cotton (White) ("Teal") *N. coromandelianus* 79, 82, 85, 86, 94, 97, 108
African *N. auritus* 62, 63, 66, 68–70, 72–74

Duck
Wood (Carolina) *Aix sponsa* 3, 6–9, 25
Mandarin *A. galericulata* 51, 87–90
Maned (Wood, "Goose") *Chenonetta jubata* 102, 103, 105–108
Brazilian *Amazonetta brasiliensis* 29, 43, 44, 46
Torrent *Merganetta armata* 32, 36, 38, 39, 41
Blue *Hymenolaimus malacorhynchos* 111

Wigeon
Eurasian (European, The) *Anas penelope* 1, 3, 49–61, 66, 77, 82, 87, 88, 91, 97
American *A. americana* 1–19, 21, 25–27, 30, 31, 49
Chiloe (Southern) *A. sibilatrix* 39–42

Teal
Falcated *A. falcata* 1, 87–90, 92
Baikal *A. formosa* 1, 87–90
Green-winged (Common, European, The) *A. crecca (carolinensis)* 1–14, 16, 17, 25, 49–61, 66, 77, 82, 86–92
Speckled *A. flavirostris* 32, 36, 38–42
Cape ("Wigeon") *A. capensis* 64, 66, 71
Gray *A. gibberifrons* 100–109, 111
Madagascar *A. bernieri* 74
Chestnut *A. castanea* 103, 105–107
Brown *A. aucklandica* 111

Duck
"Gadwall" *A. strepera* 1, 3, 6–14, 16–18, 25, 49, 51–53, 56–60, 77, 82, 87, 88
"Mallard" *A. platyrhynchos (diazi)* 1–3, 5–7, 9–14, 40, 49, 51–61, 77, 78, 87–91, 97, 105, 106, 111

Mottled *A. fulvigula (platyrhynchos)* 8, 9

Hawaiian *A. wyvilliana (platyrhynchos)* 15

American Black *A. rubripes (platyrhynchos)* 5–7

Yellow-billed *A. undulata* 64, 66, 68, 71, 72

Meller's *A. melleri* 74, 75

Spot-billed *A. poecilorhyncha* 82, 85–92

Pacific Black (Gray) *A. superciliosa* 99

Philippine *A. luzonica* 97

African Black *A. sparsa* 66, 68, 72, 73

Crested *A. (Lophonetta) specularioides* 36, 38–41

Bronze-winged (Spectacled) *A. specularis* 39, 41

Pintail
 Northern (The) *A. acuta* 1–17, 21, 25, 49–60, 62, 66, 77, 79, 82, 86–91, 97

 Yellow-billed (Brown) *A. georgica* 32, 36, 38–42

 White-cheeked (Bahama) *A. bahamensis* 25–27, 30, 34, 35, 46

 Red-billed "Duck" *A. erythrorhyncha* 64, 66, 68, 70, 71, 74

Teal
 Puna *A. puna (versicolor)* 36, 38

 Silver *A. versicolor* 39–42

 Hottentot *A. hottentota (punctata)* 64, 66, 68, 72, 74

 "Garganey" *A. querquedula* 51–53, 55–60, 62, 66, 77, 79, 82, 83

 Blue-winged *A. discors* 3, 5, 7–9, 11, 12, 16–19, 21, 22, 24–27, 29–36

 Cinnamon *A. cyanoptera* 3, 9, 11–14, 16, 31, 35, 36, 38–42

Shoveler
 Red *A. platalea* 39, 41, 42

 Cape *A. smithii* 71

 White-faced (Australian, Blue-winged) *A. rhynchotis* 103, 104, 111

 Northern (The) *A. clypeata* 1, 3, 5–19, 21, 25, 26, 30, 49–53, 55–62, 66, 77, 79, 82, 86–91, 97

Duck
 Pink-eared *Malacorhynchus membranaceus* 102, 103

 Marbled "Teal" *Marmaronetta (Anas) angustirostris,* 59, 60, 79

Pochard
 Red-crested *Netta rufina* 52, 55, 56, 58–60, 82

 Rosy-billed *N. peposaca* 39, 42

 Southern (African) *N. erythrophthalma* 66, 68, 71, 72

 "Canvasback" *Aythya valisineria* 3, 6, 7, 9–14, 16, 17

 Northern (Common, The) *A. ferina* 1, 49–53, 55–60, 62, 77, 82, 87–90, 97

 "Redhead" *A. americana* 1, 3, 6, 7, 9–14, 16, 17, 21, 25

 Ring-necked "Duck" *A. collaris* 3, 6–10, 12–14, 16–18, 21, 25, 26

 White-eyed (Australian) *A. australis* 102–109

 Baer's *A. baeri* 87, 89, 90

 Ferruginous "Duck" (White-eyed) *A. nyroca* 55–60, 77, 79, 82

 Madagascar *A. innotata* 74

 Tufted "Duck" *A. fuligula* 1, 49–53, 55–60, 62, 77, 82, 87–91, 97

Scaup
 New Zealand *A. novaeseelandiae* 111

 Greater (Northern, The) *A. marila* 1–7, 10, 14, 49–52, 54–56, 58, 87, 88, 90

 Lesser (American) *A. affinis* 2–14, 16–19, 21, 25, 26, 30

Eider
 Common (The) *Somateria mollissima* 1, 4, 5, 7, 49–54, 58

 King *S. spectabilis* 1, 4, 5, 7, 54

 Steller's *Polysticta stelleri* 1, 54

Duck
 Harlequin *Histrionicus histrionicus* 1–3, 5, 7, 10, 14, 49, 87, 88

 Long-tailed ("Oldsquaw") *Clangula hyemalis* 1–5, 7, 49, 51, 53, 54, 87, 88

Scoter
 Black (Common, American) *Melanitta nigra* 1, 3–5, 7, 14, 49–53, 58–60, 87, 88

 Surf *M. perspicillata* 2–7, 13, 14, 50

 White-winged (Velvet) *M. fusca (deglandi)* 1, 3–7, 13, 14, 50–54, 58, 87, 88, 90

Goldeneye
 Common (The) *Bucephala clangula* 1, 3, 5–7, 10, 11, 13, 14, 50–58, 87, 88

 Barrow's *B. islandica* 1–3, 7, 10, 11, 49

 "Bufflehead" *B. albeola* 1–3, 5–7, 9–14

Merganser
  "Smew" *Mergus albellus* 1, 51–57, 77,
    87–90
  Hooded *M. (Lophodytes) cucullatus* 3,
    6–9, 25
  Red-breasted *M. serrator* 1, 3–9, 11, 13,
    14, 25, 49–54, 56–58, 60, 77, 87, 88,
    90, 92
  "Goosander" (Great, Common) *M.
    merganser* 1, 3, 5–7, 10, 11, 49, 51–54,
    56, 57, 85, 87–90, 92
Duck
  Black-headed *Heteronetta atricapilla*
    39, 42
  Masked *Oxyura dominica* 9, 16, 25–27,
    29, 31, 33
  Ruddy (Andean) *O. jamaicensis (fer-
    ruginea)* 3, 6–14, 16, 17, 21, 25, 32, 36,
    38, 39, 41
  White-headed *O. leucocephala* 56, 59,
    60
  Maccoa *O. maccoa* 66, 71, 72
  Lake *O. vittata* 39, 42
  Blue-billed *O. australis* 103–105
  Musk *Biziura lobata* 103–106
    SCREAMERS:*ANHIMIDAE*
Screamer
  Horned *Anhima cornuta* 29, 31, 33, 37
  Black-necked (Northern) *Chauna cha-
    varia* 30
  Southern *C. torquata* 42, 43
    MEGAPODES:*MEGAPODIIDAE*
Orange-footed Scrubfowl *Megapodius
    freycinet* 97, 99–101, 108
Malleefowl *Leipoa ocellata* 103, 104
Australian Brushturkey *Alectura lathami*
    107, 108
    GUANS:*CRACIDAE*
Chachalaca
  Plain *Ortalis vetula* 9, 18–20
  Gray-headed *O. cinereiceps* 24
  Chestnut-winged *O. garrula* 30
  Rufous-vented *O. ruficauda* 26–29
  West Mexican (Rufous-bellied) *O. poli-
    ocephala (wagleri)* 16
  Chaco *O. canicollis* 43
  Little *O. motmot* 48
  Buff-browed *O. superciliaris* 47
  Speckled *O. guttata* 31, 33, 36, 37
Guan
  Band-tailed *Penelope argyrotis* 28, 30
  Andean *P. montagnii* 32

Marail *P. marail* 48
  Rusty-margined *P. superciliaris* 46
  Dusky-legged *P. obscura* 44, 45
  Spix's *P. jacquacu* 33, 37
  Crested *P. purpurascens* 20, 24, 30
Piping-Guan
  Blue-throated (White-crested) *Aburria
    pipile (cujubi)* 27, 33, 37, 48
  Black-fronted *A. jacutinga* 44
Guan
  Black *Chamaepetes unicolor* 22, 23
  Sickle-winged *C. goudotii* 30, 31
Curassow
  Razor-billed *Crax mitu* 37
  Helmeted *C. pauxi* 28
  Great *C. rubra* 19, 20, 24
  Yellow-knobbed *C. daubentoni* 29
  Black *C. alector* 48
    TURKEYS:*MELEAGRIDIDAE*
Turkey
  Wild (Common, The) *Meleagris gal-
    lopavo* 7–9, 12, 15
  Ocellated *Agriocharis ocellata* 20
    GROUSE:*TETRAONIDAE*
Grouse
  Spruce *Dendragapus (Canachites)
    canadensis* 2, 5
  Blue *D. obscurus* 3, 10
Ptarmigan
  Willow (Red "Grouse") *Lagopus lago-
    pus (scoticus)* 2, 4, 5, 50, 54
  Rock (The) *L. mutus* 2, 4, 5, 49, 54, 88
  White-tailed *L. leucurus* 2
Grouse
  Black *Tetrao (Lyurus) tetrix* 53, 57
  "Capercaillie" *T. urogallus* 53, 54, 57
  Hazel ("Hazelhen") *Bonasa (Tetrastes)
    bonasia* 53, 87
  Ruffed *B. umbellus* 2, 3, 7, 10
Greater Prairie Chicken *Tympanuchus
    cupido* 9
    PARTRIDGES:*PHASIANIDAE*
Long-tailed Wood-Partridge *Dendrortyx
    macroura* 17
Quail
  Banded *Philortyx fasciatus* 17
  Mountain *Oreortyx picta* 3, 13
  Scaled *Callipepla squamata* 9, 12
  Elegant *C. (Lophortyx) douglasii* 16
  Gambel's *C.(L.) gambelii* 12
  California *C.(L.) californica* 3, 13–15,
    39, 41, 111

Bobwhite
Northern (Virginian) *Colinus vir-giniaus* 6–9, 25
Black-throated (Yucatan) *C. ni-grogularis* 18, 19
Spot-bellied *C. leucopogon* 22
Crested *C. cristatus* 29–31, 48
Wood-Quail
Marbled *Odontophorus gujanensis* 33, 48
Spot-winged *O. capueira* 45, 46
Rufous-fronted *O. erythrops* 31
Black-fronted *O. atrifrons* 30
White-throated *O. leucolaemus* 22
Starred *O. stellatus* 37
Spotted *O. guttatus* 20, 23
Quail
Singing *Dactylortyx thoracicus* 21
Montezuma (Harlequin) *Cyrtonyx montezumae* 12, 16
Ocellated *C. ocellatus* 21
Quail
Common (European, African, Migratory, The) *Coturnix coturnix* 15, 51–53, 55–60, 65, 66, 68, 71–75, 77, 82
Japanese *C. japonica* 87–90, 92
Rain (Black-breasted) *C. coromandelica* 86
Harlequin *C. delegorguei* 64–66, 68, 69, 73, 74
Stubble *C. pectoralis* 103–106
Brown *C. (Synoicus) ypsilophorus (australis)* 99–101, 103, 107, 108, 110–111
Blue *C. (Excalfactoria) adansonii* 63, 68, 72
King (Painted, Blue-breasted) *C. (E.) chinensis* 95–97, 100, 103, 106, 107
Partridge
Madagascar *Margaroperdix madagarensis* 74, 75
Stone *Ptilopachus petrosus* 62
Jungle Bush-Quail *Perdicula asiatica* 82, 86
Partridge
Sand *Ammoperdix heyi* 77
Gray (Common, The) *Perdix perdix* 51, 53, 56, 57
"Chukar" *Alectoris chukar* 15, 55, 77, 81, 89, 111
Barbary *A. barbara* 60, 61
Red-legged *A. rufa* 51, 58, 59, 61
Snow *Lerwa lerwa* 84

Tibetan Snowcock *Tetraogallus tibetanus* 84
Hill-Partridge
Common *Arborophila torqueola* 83
Formosan *A. crudigularis* 91
Red-breasted (Tree-Partridge) *A. hyperythra* 96
Wood-Partridge
Crimson-headed *Haematortyx sanguiniceps* 96
Roulroul (Crested) *Rollulus roulroul* 94, 96
Long-billed Partridge *Rhizothera longirostris* 94
Francolin (Partridge)
Black *Francolinus francolinus* 79, 82, 83, 85
Painted *F. pictus* 86
Chinese *F. pintadeanus* 75, 92, 93
Spurfowl (Francolin)
Red-necked (Gray-winged) *F. afer (cranchii)* 64, 66, 68, 69
Swainson's *F. swainsonii* 69, 70, 73
Gray-breasted *F. rufopictus* 66
Yellow-necked *F. leucoscepus* 66
Francolin
Jackson's *F. jacksoni* 66
Handsome *F. nobilis* 64
Scaly *F. squamatus* 65, 66
Double-spurred *F. bicalcaratus* 60, 62, 63
Hildebrandt's *F. hildebrandti* 66, 68, 69
Natal *F. natalensis* 69, 70, 72, 73
Cape *F. capensis* 71
Crested *F. sephaena* 66–68, 70, 72, 73
Kirk's (Crested) *F. rovuma (sephaena)* 68
Shelley's *F. shelleyi* 66, 68, 72
Gray-winged *F. africanus* 71
Coqui *F. coqui* 66, 68, 70, 73
Gray *F. pondicerianus* 75, 79, 82, 86
Chinese Bamboo Partridge *Bambusicola thoracica* 88, 90, 91
Ceylon Spurfowl *Galloperdix bicalcarata* 86
Blood Pheasant *Ithaginis cruentus* 84
Western Tragopan *Tragopan melanocephalus* 79
Impeyan (Himalayan Monal) Pheasant *Lophophorus impejanus* 84

Junglefowl (Chicken)
  Red *Gallus gallus* 15, 75, 85, 93, 97, 109, 110
  Ceylon *G. lafayettei* 86
Pheasant
  Kalij *Lophura leucomelana* 83, 85, 93
  Silver *L. nycthemera* 97
  Crestless Fireback *L. erythropthalma* 94
  Crested Fireback *L. ignita (rufa)* 94
  Mikado *Syrmaticus mikado* 91
  Copper *S. soemmerringi* 88
  Common (Ring-necked, The) *Phasianus colchicus* 3, 6, 7, 11, 13, 15, 51, 53, 56–58, 91, 111
  Green *P. versicolor* 88–90
Peacock-Pheasant
  Malaysian *Polyplectron malacense* 94
  Palawan *P. emphanum* 97
Great Argus Pheasant *Argusianus argus* 94, 96
Indian Peafowl (Peacock) *Pavo cristatus* 15, 83, 85, 86, 111
  GUINEAFOWL:*NUMIDIDAE*
Guineafowl
  Helmeted (Tufted) *Numida meleagris (mitrata)* 25, 60, 62, 64, 66, 68–75
  Crested *Guttera edouardi* 64, 65, 68, 69, 72
  Kenya (Coastal, Crested) *G. pucherani* 67
  Vulturine *Acryllium vulturinum* 66
  MESITES:*MESITORNITHIDAE*
Mesite
  White-breasted *Mesitornis variegata* 74
  Brown *M. unicolor* 74
Bensch's Monia *Monias benschi* 74
  BUTTONQUAIL:*TURNICIDAE*
Buttonquail (Bustardquail, Quail)
  Common (Andalusian "Hemipode") *Turnix sylvatica* 60, 62, 66, 68, 70, 72, 73, 86, 97
  Yellow-legged *T. tanki* 89, 90
  Barred *T. suscitator* 82, 91, 95, 97, 98
  Madagascar *T. nigricollis* 74, 75
  Spotted *T. ocellata* 97
  Black-breasted *T. melanogaster* 107
  Painted *T. varia* 103–106, 109
  Worcester's *T. worcesteri* 97
  Little *T. velox* 102, 104, 106

CRANES:GRUIDAE
Crane
  European (Common, Gray, The) *Grus grus* 53–57, 60, 77
  Hooded *G. monacha* 88
  Sandhill *G. canadensis* 1, 2, 4, 5, 8–10, 12, 25
  Japanese *G. japonensis* 87
  Whooping *G. americana* 5, 9
  White-naped *G. vipio* 88
  Sarus *G. antigone* 82, 108
  Brolga *G. rubicunda* 101, 108
  Siberian (White) *G. leucogeranus* 82
  Wattled *Bugeranus carunculatus* 69
  Demoiselle *Anthropoides virgo* 60, 79
  Blue (Paradise, Stanley) *A. paradisea* 71
Crowned Crane
  Western *Balearica pavonina* 62
  Eastern *B. regulorum* 64–66, 69
  LIMPKIN:*ARAMIDAE*
Limpkin *Aramus guarauna* 8, 19, 20, 25, 27, 29, 30, 33, 42–44, 48
  TRUMPETERS:*PSOPHIIDAE*
Trumpeter
  Gray-winged *Psophia crepitans* 33, 48
  Pale-winged *P. leucoptera* 31
  RAILS:*RALLIDAE*
Rail
  Madagascar Gray-throated *Canirallus kioloides* 74
  Forbes's (Chestnut) *C. (Rallicula) forbesi* 99
Flufftail (Crake)
  White-spotted *Sarothura pulchra* 65
  Buff-spotted *S. elegans* 65, 66, 72
  Red-chested *S. rufa* 65, 71
  Chestnut-tailed (headed) *S. lugens* 68
  Madagascar *S. insularis* 74
  Water's *S. watersi* 74
Crake (Rail)
  Yellow *Coturnicops noveboracensis* 5, 9
  Red-legged (Malay Banded) *Rallina fasciata* 95, 96
  Slaty-legged (Philippine Banded) *R. eurizonoides* 86, 97
  Russet-crowned *Anurolimnas (Laterallus) viridus* 46
  American Black *Laterallus jamaicensis* 9, 14, 25, 39
  Galapagos *L. spilonotus* 34
  Gray-breasted *L. exilis* 27, 31, 33, 47, 48

Rufous-sided *L. melanophaius* 31, 37, 43, 47

White-throated *L. albigularis* 23, 24

Ruddy (Red) *L. ruber* 18, 19

Barred-winged Rail *Nesoclopeus poecilopterus* 110

Rail

Banded (Buff-banded) *Gallirallus philippensis* 97, 99, 101, 103, 105–111

"Weka" *G. australis* 111

Barred *G. torquatus* 97

Slaty-breasted *G. striatus* 86, 91, 92, 95

New Caledonian Wood-Rail *Tricholimnas lafresnayanus* 109

Corn Crake (Corncrake) *Crex crex* 50, 53, 56, 57, 66, 69, 77

Rail

Lewin's (Water) *Dryolimnas (Rallus) pectoralis* 100, 103, 105

White-throated *D. cuvieri* 74

King *Rallus elegans* 7–9, 25

Clapper *R. longirostris* 7–9, 13, 16, 19, 25–27, 47

Virginia *R. limicola* 3, 6, 7, 9, 13, 14, 32

Water *R. aquaticus* 49–53, 55–60, 77, 79, 87, 88, 96

Kaffir *R. caerulescens* 66, 68

Madagascar *R. madagascariensis* 74

Wood-Rail

Rufous-necked *Aramides axillaris* 16, 27

Gray-necked *A. cajanea* 18–20, 24, 27, 29, 30, 37, 43, 46–48

Giant *A. ypecaha* 42, 43

Slate-breasted *A. saracura* 45

Waterhen

White-breasted *Amaurornis phoenicurus* 82, 83, 86, 90–93, 95, 97, 98

Brown "Crake" *A. akool* 79, 82

"Bush-hen" (Plain "Swamphen") *A. olivacea* 97, 99, 100

Olivier's "Rail" *A. (Porzana) olivieri* 74

Crake

African Black *A. (Limnocorax) flavirostris* 62–64, 66, 68–70, 72, 73

Spotless (Sooty "Rail") *Porzana tabuensis* 103, 109–111

Ruddy-breasted (Ruddy) *P. fusca* 79, 82, 83, 86–88, 91, 93, 97

Ash-throated *P. albicollis* 27, 43, 46, 48

Sora (Rail) *P. carolina* 3, 5–10, 12–14, 16, 21, 25–27, 31, 32, 35

Spotted *P. porzana* 52, 53, 56–60, 68, 77, 79

Little *P. parva* 53, 56–58, 77

Australian (Spotted) *P. fluminea* 103, 104

Baillon's (Marsh) *P. pusilla* 53, 56, 58, 59, 74, 77, 79, 82, 87, 88, 103, 105, 106, 111

Yellow-breasted *Poliolimnas (P.) flaviventris* 25, 27, 48

Zapata Rail *Cyanolimnas cerverai* 25

Paint-billed Crake *Neocrex erythrops* 43

Rail

Plumbeous *Pardirallus (Rallus) sanguinolentus* 35, 36, 38, 39, 41–43

Blackish *P. (R.) nigricans* 31, 43, 45, 46

Spotted *P. (R.) maculatus* 25, 27, 43

Chestnut *Eulabeornis castaneoventris* 101

Watercock *Gallicrex cinerea* 82, 86, 88, 90, 91, 97

Gallinule (Moorhen)

Black-tailed ("Native Hen") *Gallinula (Tribonyx) ventralis* 102, 103

Dusky *G. tenebrosa* 100, 103–108

Common (The) *G. chloropus* 6–9, 12, 13, 15–17, 19–21, 24–27, 29, 31, 34–36, 38, 42, 46, 50–53, 55–62, 64, 66, 68, 71, 72, 74–77, 81, 82, 85–88, 90–92, 95, 97, 98

Lesser *G. angulata* 63, 68, 69, 72, 73

Spot-flanked *G. (Porphyriops) melanops* 39, 42

Azure (Little) *G. (Porphyrula) flavirostris* 29, 33, 37, 48

Purple *G. (P.) martinica* 8, 9, 16, 19, 24–27, 29, 33, 37, 43, 46, 48

Allen's *G. (Porphyrio) alleni* 62, 68, 74

Swamphen (Gallinule)

Purple *Porphyrio porphyrio* 59, 60, 62, 64, 66, 68, 70–72, 79, 81, 82, 86, 97, 100–102, 104–111

"Takahe" *P. (Notornis) mantelli* 111

Coot

Common (Black) *Fulica atra* 49–53, 55–61, 77, 82, 86–88, 90–92, 97, 102–108, 111

Red-knobbed (Crested) *F. cristata* 59, 60, 64, 66, 68, 70, 72, 74

American *F. americana* 3, 6–19, 21, 24, 25, 30–32, 35, 36, 38

Slate-colored *F. ardesiaca* 32, 38
 Caribbean *F. caribaea* 25–27
 Red-gartered *F. armillata* 39–43
 White-winged *F. leucoptera* 39, 41, 42
 Red-fronted *F. rufifrons* 39, 42
 Giant *F. gigantea* 38
 FINFOOTS:*HELIORNITHIDAE*
African (Peter's) Finfoot *Podica senega-
 lensis* 63, 66, 68, 70, 72, 73
Sungrebe *Heliornis fulica* 19, 24, 33, 37, 47
 KAGU:*RHYNOCHETIDAE*
Kagu *Rhynochetos jubatus* 109
 SUNBITTERN:*EURYPYGIDAE*
Sunbittern *Eurypyga helias* 29, 33, 37, 47
 SERIEMAS:*CARIAMIDAE*
Red-legged Seriema *Caraima cristata* 43
 BUSTARDS:*OTIDIDAE*
Bustard
 Little *Otis tetrax* 58–60
 Great *O. tarda* 57, 59, 60, 89
 Denham's (Stanley, Jackson's) *O.
 (Neotis) denhami (cafra)* 66, 71
 Ludwig's *O. (N.) ludwigii* 71
 Arabian (Sudan) *Ardeotis (Choriotis)
 arabs* 60, 62
 Kori *A.(C.) kori* 66, 73
 Australian *A.(C.) australis* 102
 Houbara *Chlamydotis undulata* 60, 61,
 77–79
 Buff-crested ("Korhaan") *Eupodotis
 (Lophotis) ruficrista* 66, 73
 Black ("Korhaan") *E. (Afrotis) atra
 (afra)* 71
 White-bellied *E. senegalensis (cafra)*
 66
 Black-bellied ("Korhaan") *E. (Lissotis)
 melanogaster* 62, 64, 66, 68–70
 Hartlaub's *E.(L.) hartlaubii* 66
 Bengal ("Florican") *E. bengalensis* 85
 JACANAS:*JACANIDAE*
Jacana (Lily-trotter)
 Lesser *Microparra capensis* 66, 68, 69,
 72
 African *Actophilornis africana* 62–64,
 66–70, 72, 73
 Madagascar *A. albinucha* 74
 Comb-crested ("Lily-trotter") *Iredi-
 parra gallinacea* 100, 101
 Pheasant-tailed *Hydrophasianus chi-
 rurgus* 79, 81, 82, 85, 86, 97
 Bronze-winged *Metopidius indicus* 82,
 85

Northern (Middle American) *Jacana
 spinosa* 9, 16, 18–21, 25
Wattled *J. jacana* 24, 27, 29–31, 33, 37,
 42–44, 46–48
PAINTED-SNIPE:*ROSTRATULIDAE*
Painted-snipe
 Greater (The) *Rostratula benghalensis*
 62–64, 66, 68, 69, 71–74, 79, 82, 85,
 86, 88, 90–92, 95, 97
 Argentine (South American) *Nycti-
 cryphes semicollaris* 39, 42, 43
 CRABPLOVER:*DROMADIDAE*
Crabplover *Dromas ardeola* 67, 74, 76, 86
 OYSTERCATCHERS:
 HAEMATOPODIDAE
Oystercatcher
 Magellanic *Haematopus leucopodus* 40
 Blackish (Humboldt Black) *H. ater* 35,
 39–41
 American *H. palliatus* 7–9, 16, 25, 30,
 34, 35, 39, 41, 42
 (North American) Black *H. bachmani*
 3, 13, 14
 Common (Pied) *H. ostralegus* 49–54,
 56, 58–60, 62, 78, 86, 88, 101, 103, 105,
 107, 111
 African (Black) *H. moquini* 61, 71
 Tasman (Sooty, Variable) *H. fuligino-
 sus (unicolor)* 103, 105, 106, 108, 111
 IBISBILL:*IBIDORHYNCHIDAE*
Ibisbill *Ibidorhyncha struthersii* 83, 84, 89
 STILTS:*RECURVIROSTRIDAE*
Stilt
 Black-winged (Common, Pied)
 Himantopus himantopus 55, 56, 58–
 60, 62, 64, 66–72, 74, 78, 79, 82, 86,
 97, 100–104, 107, 108, 111
 Black-necked (Common, American)
 H. mexicanus (himantopus) 8, 9, 11–
 16, 18, 19, 25–27, 29–31, 34–36, 38, 39,
 41–43
 Black *H. novaezelandiae* 111
 Banded *Cladorhynchus leucocephalus*
 103
Avocet
 Black-capped (Old World, The) *Recur-
 virostra avosetta* 51–53, 55–60, 62, 66,
 67, 71, 74, 78, 82, 86
 American *R. americana* 8–14, 16
 Red-necked *R. novaehollandiae* 102,
 103
 Andean *R. andina* 35

THICK-KNEES:*BURHINIDAE*
"Stonecurlew" *Burhinus oedicnemus* 55–
61, 77–79, 82, 85, 86
Senegal "Dikkop" *B. senegalensis* 62
Water "Dikkop" *B. vermiculatus* 64, 66–
70, 72, 73
Spotted "Dikkop" *B. capensis* 62, 64, 66,
68–70, 72, 73
Double-striped *B. bistriatus* 25, 29
Peruvian *B. superciliaris* 35
"Bushcurlew" *B. magnirostris* 101, 103,
104, 107, 108
Great (Beach "Stonecurlew") *Esacus
recurvirostris (magnirostris)* 82, 85,
86, 88, 98, 101, 108, 109
PRATINCOLES:*GLAREOLIDAE*
Courser
Egyptian ("Plover", "Crocodilebird")
Pluvianus aegyptius 62, 63
Two-banded *Rhinoptilus africanus* 66
Heuglin's *R. cinctus* 66, 69
Bronze-winged (Violet-tipped) *R. chal-
copterus* 68, 69, 72, 73
Cream-colored *Cursorius cursor* 60–62,
66, 77, 78
Indian (Small) *C. coromandelicus* 82,
86
Temminck's *C. temminckii (rufus)* 62,
64, 66, 68, 69, 72
Pratincole
Australian *Stiltia isabella* 100–102
Collared (Common, The) *Glareola pra-
tincola* 55, 56, 58–61, 64, 67, 68, 77,
82, 86
Oriental (Eastern) *G. maldivarum* 88,
91, 92, 95, 97
Black-winged (Russian) *G. nordmanni*
56, 64
Madagascar *G. ocularis* 74
Rock (White-collared) *G. nuchalis* 70
Little *G. lactea* 79, 82, 85, 86
Gray *G. cinerea* 63
PLOVERS:*CHARADRIIDAE*
Lapwing (Plover)
Northern (Crested, The) *Vanellus
vanellus* 50–53, 55–61, 77, 87–91
Long-toed *V. crassirostris* 64, 66, 68
Blacksmith *V. armatus* 66, 68–73
Spur-winged *V. spinosus* 55, 62, 64, 66,
77, 85
Black-headed *V. tectus* 62, 66
Yellow-wattled *V. malabaricus* 82, 86

White-crowned (headed) *V. albiceps*
62, 63, 69, 70
Senegal (Lesser Black-winged) *V. lugu-
bris* 62–64, 66–69, 72, 73
Black-winged *V. melanopterus* 66
Crowned *V. coronatus* 64, 66, 71–73
Wattled *V. senegallus* 62, 64, 66, 68, 69,
70, 72
Sociable *V. gregarius* 77, 82
White-tailed *V. leucurus* 77, 79, 82
Pied *V. (Hoploxypterus) cayanus* 29,
33, 37, 47
Southern *V. chilensis* 27, 29–31, 39, 41–
44, 47
Andean *V. resplendens* 32, 36, 38
Gray-headed *V. cinereus* 83, 88, 89
Red-wattled *V. indicus* 79, 82, 83, 85,
86
Banded *V. tricolor* 103–105
Masked(Spur-winged)*V. miles (novae-
hollandiae)* 101, 102, 104–108, 111
Plover (Dotterel)
Greater Ringed *Charadrius hiaticula*
49–55, 57–64, 66–68, 71, 72, 74–78
Semipalmated *C. semipalmatus* 1–9, 11,
13, 14, 16, 19, 24–27, 30, 31, 34, 35, 39,
42, 46, 48
Long-billed *C. placidus* 87, 88, 90
Little Ringed *C. dubius* 51–53, 55–63,
66, 76–78, 82, 83, 85–92, 95, 97, 99,
100
Wilson's *C. wilsonia* 8, 9, 16, 19, 24–27,
30, 31
Killdeer *C. vociferus* 3, 5–14, 16, 18, 19,
24–27, 35
Piping *C. melodus* 7–9, 25
Black-banded *C. thoracicus* 74
Kittlitz's *C. pecuarius* 62, 64, 66, 69,
72, 74
Three-banded *C. tricollaris* 64, 66, 69,
70, 72–74
Forbes's *C. forbesi* 63
Snowy (Kentish, Salt) *C. alexandrinus
(nivosus)* 8, 9, 11–14, 16, 25, 26, 35, 39,
52, 53, 55–62, 77, 78, 82, 85–88, 90–
92, 97
White-fronted *C. marginatus (alexandrinus)* 63, 66, 67, 69–71, 73,
74
Red-capped *C. ruficapillus (alexandrinus)* 101, 103–108
Malay *C. peronii* 97, 98

Chestnut-banded *C. venustus (pallidus)* 66

Collared *C. collaris* 16, 24, 26, 27, 29–31, 33, 37, 39, 43, 46, 48

Double-banded *C. bicinctus* 103, 106, 111

Two-banded *C. falklandicus* 40, 42

Puna *C. alticola* 35, 36, 38

Mongolian (Lesser Sand) *C. mongolus* 1, 66, 67, 76, 78, 86–88, 90, 92, 95, 97, 100, 101, 106, 108

Great Sand (Large) *C. leschenaultii* 67, 74–78, 86, 88–90, 92, 95, 97, 98, 101, 103, 108, 111

Caspian *C. asiaticus* 66, 68, 69, 77, 78

Oriental *C. veredus* 101

Rufous-chested (New Zealand) *C. (Zonibyx) modestus* 40

Mountain *C. montanus* 13

Black-fronted *C. melanops* 101–108, 111

Red-kneed *C. cinctus* 101–104

Hooded *C. rubricollis* 103, 105

Red-breasted (New Zealand) *C. obscurus* 111

Wrybill *Anarhynchus frontalis* 111

Diademed Sandpiper-Plover *Phegornis mitchellii* 38, 39

Plover

European Golden (Greater, The) *Pluvialis apricaria* 49–55, 58–61, 78

Lesser Golden (American, The) *P. dominica* 1–5, 7, 9, 15, 24–27, 29, 39, 42, 43, 74, 86–91, 95, 97–99, 101, 103, 106–111

Gray (Black-bellied) *P. squatarola* 3–9, 13–16, 18, 19, 24–27, 30, 31, 34, 35, 39, 41, 42, 48, 51–53, 55, 57–63, 67, 71, 74–76, 78, 86–88, 91, 97, 98, 101, 103, 108

Dotterel

European (The) *Eudromias morinellus* 52, 54, 57, 60

Tawny-throated *Oreopholus (E.) ruficollis* 35, 38, 39, 41

SANDPIPERS:*SCOLOPACIDAE*

Godwit

Black-tailed *Limosa limosa* 49–62, 66, 74, 77, 82, 86, 91, 95, 97, 100, 101, 108

Hudsonian *L. haemastica* 5, 7, 9, 25–27, 35, 41, 42

Bar-tailed *L. lapponica* 1, 51–54, 58–62, 71, 74–76, 78, 86–88, 97, 101, 103, 105–111

Marbled *L. fedoa* 8, 9, 11, 13, 14, 16, 24, 25

Curlew

Little ("Whimbrel") *Numenius minutus* 88, 90, 100, 101

"Whimbrel" *N. phaeopus* 1–3, 5, 7–9, 13, 14, 16, 19, 24–27, 30, 31, 34, 35, 39, 42, 48–54, 57–63, 67, 71, 74–76, 78, 86–92, 95, 97, 98, 100, 101, 105, 107–111

Bristle-thighed *N. tahitiensis* 1, 15, 110

Slender-billed *N. tenuirostris* 60

Eurasian (Northern, The) *N. arquata* 50–62, 66, 67, 71, 74–78, 82, 88, 91, 92, 95, 97

Eastern *N. madagascariensis* 86–88, 90, 101, 103, 105–108, 110, 111

Long-billed *N. americanus* 8–11, 13, 14, 16, 19

Upland Sandpiper (Plover) *Bartramia longicauda* 2, 7–9, 24–27, 42

Redshank

Spotted (Greater) *Tringa erythropus* 1, 51–60, 62, 66, 77, 78, 82, 87, 88, 92

Common (Lesser, The) *T. totanus* 49–63, 66, 67, 77, 78, 82, 86–90, 92, 95, 97

Greenshank

Marsh Sandpiper *T. stagnatilis* 56, 58, 59, 62–64, 66–69, 71, 72, 74, 75, 77, 78, 82, 86, 88, 92, 93, 97, 101, 108

Common (The) *T. nebularia* 1, 51–53, 55–64, 66–78, 82, 83, 85–92, 95, 97, 101–103, 105, 107, 108

Nordmann's (Spotted) *T. guttifer* 87, 88, 92

Yellowlegs (Yellowshank)

Greater *T. melanoleuca* 1, 3, 5–14, 16, 18, 19, 24–27, 29–33, 35, 36, 38, 39, 42, 46, 48

Lesser *T. flavipes* 1–11, 13, 16, 18, 19, 24–27, 29–33, 35, 38, 39, 41–44, 46, 48

Sandpiper

Solitary *T. solitaria* 2, 5–10, 16, 17, 19, 20, 24–27, 29–31, 33, 35, 37, 43, 44, 47, 48

Green *T. ochropus* 51–53, 55–62, 65, 66, 68, 69, 74, 77, 78, 82, 83, 85–92

Wood *T. glareola* 1, 51–66, 68–70, 72–74, 76–79, 82, 86–92, 95, 97, 98, 101–103

Willet *Catoptrophorus semipalmatus* 7–11, 13, 14, 16, 18, 19, 24–26, 34

Sandpiper
 Terek *Xenus cinereus* 67, 74–76, 78, 86–
  88, 90, 92, 95, 97, 100, 101, 103, 108,
  111
 Common *Actitis hypoleucos* 1, 50–78,
  81–83, 85–89, 91, 92, 95–103, 107, 108
 Spotted *A. macularia* 2–4, 6–14, 16–19,
  21, 24–27, 29–35, 37, 39, 44, 46–48
Tattler
 Gray-tailed (Polynesian) *Heteroscelus
  brevipes (incanus)* 1, 87, 88, 92, 97,
  101, 106, 108–111
 Wandering *H. incanus* 1–3, 13–16, 34,
  91, 100, 110, 111
Turnstone
 Ruddy (The) *Arenaria interpres* 1, 3–9,
  11, 13–16, 18, 19, 24–27, 30, 31, 34, 35,
  39, 41, 42, 48–54, 57–62, 67, 71, 74–
  76, 78, 86–88, 90–92, 97, 98, 101, 103,
  106–111
 Black *A. melanocephala* 3, 13, 14, 16
Phalarope
 Wilson's *Phalaropus tricolor* 5, 7, 9–13,
  16, 34, 35, 38, 42
 Little (Red-necked, Northern) *P. loba-
  tus* 1–5, 7, 11, 13, 14, 34, 35, 49, 50, 54,
  87, 88, 92, 97
 Red (Gray) *P. fulicarius* 1, 3, 5, 7, 13–15,
  34, 39, 49, 61, 87, 88
Woodcock
 Eurasian *Scolopax rusticola* 50–53, 55–
  59, 61, 77, 83, 87–90, 92
 American *S. minor* 6, 7
Snipe
 Solitary *Gallinago solitaria* 87–90
 Japanese (Latham's) *G. hardwickii* 87,
  88, 100, 105–108
 Pintail *G. stenura* 82, 83, 86–88, 90–92,
  95, 96
 Swinhoe's (Chinese) *G. megala* 87, 88,
  90–92, 101
 Great *G. media* 52, 62, 63, 66, 69
 Madagascar *G. macrodactyla* 74
 Ethiopian (African) *G. nigripennis* 63,
  66, 68, 71
 Common (Fantail, Paraguayan, The)
  G. gallinago 1–14, 16, 19, 23–27, 29–
  31, 39, 40, 42, 43, 46, 48–64, 66, 77,
  78, 82, 83, 86–91
 Puna *G. andina* 38
 Andean *G. jamesoni* 32
 Cordilleran *G. stricklandii* 40

Jack *Lymnocryptes minimus* 50–52, 54,
  56, 58, 60, 61, 77, 82, 86, 88
Dowitcher
 Short-billed *Limnodromus griseus* 1, 3,
  5–9, 13, 14, 16, 24–27, 29, 30, 31, 34,
  35, 48
 Long-billed *L. scolopaceus* 1, 3, 7–9, 12–
  14, 16, 30
 Asiatic *L. semipalmatus* 92, 108
Surfbird *Aphriza virgata* 2, 3, 13, 14, 16, 24,
  35, 39
Knot
 Great *Calidris tenuirostris* 87, 88, 90,
  101, 103, 108
 Red (The) *C. canutus* 1, 5, 7–9, 13, 16,
  24–27, 30, 35, 41
Sanderling *C. (Crocethia) alba* 1, 3–9, 13–
  16, 18, 24–27, 30, 34, 35, 39, 41, 42,
  46, 49–54, 57–63, 67, 71, 74–76,
  78, 86–88, 92, 97, 101, 103, 109,
  110
Sandpiper
 Semipalmated *Calidris pusilla* 1, 4–9,
  24–27, 35, 41, 46, 48
 Western *C. mauri* 1, 3, 7–14, 16, 18, 19,
  24–27, 30, 31, 35
 Red (Rufous)-necked "Stint" *C. ruficollis* 1, 87–92, 95, 97, 98, 100, 101, 103,
  105–108
 Little "Stint" *C. minuta* 51–60, 62–64,
  66–69, 71, 72, 74, 76–78, 86
 Long-toed "Stint" *C. subminuta* 1, 86,
  88–91, 95, 97
 Least *C. minutilla* 1, 3–14, 16–19, 24–27,
  29–31, 35, 48
 Temminck's "Stint" *C. temminckii* 1,
  51–54, 56–60, 64, 66, 77, 79, 82, 83,
  86, 88, 90–92
 White-rumped *C. fuscicollis* 4, 5, 7–9,
  19, 25–27, 37, 39–42, 44, 46
 Baird's *C. bairdii* 1, 2, 4, 5, 7, 9, 11, 24,
  32, 35
 Pectoral *C. melanotos* 1, 4–9, 19, 24–27,
  30, 32, 33, 35–39, 42–43, 88
 Sharp-tailed *C. acuminata* 1, 15, 87, 88,
  90, 100, 101, 103–109, 111
 Purple *C. maritima* 7, 49, 50, 53,
  54
 Rock *C. ptilocnemis* 1, 3
 "Dunlin" *C. alpina* 1, 3, 5–9, 13, 14, 16,
  49–62, 64, 74, 77, 78, 82, 87, 88,
  90–92

Curlew *C. ferruginea* 51–53, 55–64, 66–
68, 71, 72, 74–78, 82, 86, 88, 90, 92,
97, 100, 101, 103, 106–108, 111
Stilt *C. (Micropalama) himantopus* 1, 4,
5, 7–9, 16, 19, 24–27, 29, 42
Spoon-billed *Eurynorhynchus pygmeus*
87, 88, 90, 92
Broad-billed *Limicola falcinellus* 53,
59, 67, 78, 86, 88, 92, 101, 108
Buff-breasted *Tryngites subruficollis* 1,
5, 7, 9, 24–26, 42
Ruff *Philomachus pugnax* 1, 7, 26, 51–62,
64, 66, 68, 69, 71–74, 77–79, 82, 83,
86, 88
SEEDSNIPE:*THINOCORIDAE*
Seedsnipe
Rufous-bellied *Attagis gayi* 32, 38, 39
Gray-breasted *Thinocorus orbig-*
nyianus 36, 38, 39
Least *T. rumicivorus* 35, 38, 39, 41
SHEATHBILLS:*CHIONIDIDAE*
Snowy Sheathbill *Chionis alba* 40, 41
SKUAS:*STERCORARIIDAE*
Skua
Great (Chilean, The) *Stercorarius*
(Catharacta) skua (chilensis) 35, 39–
41, 49, 50, 60, 71, 74–76, 86–88, 103,
105, 106, 111
Jaeger (Skua)
Pomarine *S. pomarinus* 1, 4, 5, 7, 13–15,
24, 34, 35, 87, 88, 106
Parasitic (Arctic) *S. parasiticus* 1, 3–5,
7, 13, 14, 24–26, 35, 39, 41, 42, 49–51,
54, 58–61, 71, 88, 103, 106, 111
Long-tailed *S. longicaudus* 1, 2, 4, 5, 35,
54, 87, 88
GULLS AND TERNS:*LARIDAE*
Gull
Dolphin *Larus (Leucophaeus) scoresbii*
40, 41
Pacific *L. (Gabianus) pacificus* 103, 105
Band-tailed *L. belcheri (atlanticus)* 35,
41, 42
Gray *L. modestus* 35, 39
Heermann's *L. heermanni* 3, 13, 14, 16
Laughing *L. atricilla* 7–9, 16, 18, 21, 24–
27, 30, 31, 34, 35, 48
Lava *L. fuliginosus* 34
Sooty *L. hemprichii* 67
Black-tailed *L. crassirostris* 87, 88, 92
Mew (Common) *L. canus* 2, 3, 5, 13, 14,
49, 50–59, 87, 88, 90

Audouin's *L. audouinii* 55, 59, 60
Ring-billed *L. delawarensis* 5–14, 16, 25,
31
California *L. californicus* 3, 10, 11
Great Black-backed *L. marinus* 5–7,
49–54, 59, 60, 78
Kelp (Southern Black-backed) *L.*
dominicanus 35, 39–42, 46, 71, 74,
103, 111
Western *L. occidentalis (livens)* 3, 13,
14
Glaucous-winged *L. glaucescens* 1, 3,
13, 14
Glaucous *L. hyperboreus* 1, 4, 5, 7, 49–
51, 53, 54, 87
Iceland *L. glaucoides* 5, 7, 49, 50
Thayer's *L. thayeri* 3–5, 13
Herring *L. argentatus (cachinnans)*
2–9, 11, 13, 14, 16, 18, 25, 49–61, 78,
87–90, 92
Lesser Black-backed *L. fuscus* 5, 7, 49–
55, 57–64, 66, 67, 78
Slaty-backed *L. schistisagus* 1, 87, 88
Great Black-headed *L. ichthyaetus* 85,
86
Brown-headed *L. brunnicephalus* 82,
86
Gray-headed *L. cirrocephalus* 35, 42,
62, 64, 66, 69–71, 74
Silver(Red-billed,Hartlaub's)*L. novae-*
hollandiae 71, 101, 103–109, 111
Black-billed *L. bulleri* 111
Brown-hooded (Pampas) *L. maculi-*
pennis 39–42
Black-headed *L. ridibundus* 1, 7, 49–62,
66, 67, 77, 78, 87–92, 97
Slender-billed *L. genei* 55, 56, 58–60,
62, 78
Bonaparte's *L. philadelphia* 3, 5–9, 12–
14, 16, 25
Andean *L. serranus* 32, 35, 36, 38, 39
Franklin's *L. pipixcan* 9–11, 16, 21, 24,
31, 34, 35, 39
Little *L. minutus* 7, 51, 53, 55–60
Ross's *L. (Rhodostethia) roseus* 1, 5
Mediterranean *L. melanocephalus*
55–60
Sabine's *L. (Xema) sabini* 1, 3–5, 13, 14,
34, 35, 39
Black-legged "Kittiwake" *L. (Rissa)*
tridactylus 1, 3, 7, 13, 14, 49–52, 54,
59–60, 87, 88

Red-legged "Kittiwake" *L.* *(R.) brevirostris* 1

Ivory *L. (Pagophila) eburneus* 1, 50

Swallow-tailed *L. (Creagrus) furcatus* 34, 35

Tern

Whiskered (Marsh) *Chlidonias hybrida* 55, 56, 58–60, 62, 66, 74, 77, 81, 82, 86, 91, 97, 101–103, 106

Black-fronted (Whiskered) *C. albostriatus (hybrida)* 111

White-winged Black *C. leucopterus* 55–57, 59, 62, 66, 68–72, 74, 77, 86, 89, 98, 100, 101, 111

Black *C. niger (nigra)* 6–13, 16, 18, 24–26, 30, 31, 51–53, 55–60, 62, 63

Large-billed *Phaetusa simplex* 29–31, 33, 37, 48

Gull-billed *Sterna (Gelochelidon) nilotica* 8, 9, 16, 24, 25, 27, 30, 31, 48, 52, 53, 56, 58–60, 62, 64, 66, 67, 77, 78, 82, 86, 91, 92, 100–102, 107, 108

Caspian *S. (Hydroprogne) caspia* 3, 5–11, 13, 14, 16, 19, 25, 30, 52, 53, 55, 56, 58–60, 62, 67, 71, 74, 86, 91, 92, 101, 103, 106–108, 111

Royal *S. maxima* 7–9, 13, 16, 18, 19, 24–28, 30, 31, 34, 35, 41, 42, 46, 48, 60, 62, 63

Greater Crested *S. bergii* 71, 74, 76, 86, 91, 95, 97, 98, 100, 101, 103, 105–110

Lesser Crested *S. bengalensis* 60, 67, 74, 78, 86, 95, 100, 101, 108

Sandwich (Cayenne) *S. sandvicensis (eurygnatha)* 8, 9, 24–27, 30, 31, 41, 42, 46, 48, 51–53, 55, 56, 58–63, 71

Elegant *S. elegans* 13, 14, 16, 35, 39

Roseate *S. dougallii* 7, 8, 18, 25–27, 58, 59, 63, 67, 74–76, 86, 108, 109

White-fronted *S. striata* 106, 111

Black-naped *S. sumatrana* 76, 95, 98, 100, 108, 110

South American *S. hirundinacea* 35, 39–42, 46

Common *S. hirundo* 1, 3, 6–9, 13, 14, 16, 24–27, 30, 34, 35, 41, 42, 48, 50–53, 55–63, 67, 71, 74, 75, 86–88, 97, 100, 108

Arctic *S. paradisaea* 1–5, 7, 13, 35, 39, 41, 49–54, 60, 63, 71

Antarctic *S. vittata* 111

Forster's *S. forsteri* 7–9, 11, 13, 14, 16, 25

Trudeau's *S. trudeaui* 39, 42

White-cheeked *S. repressa* 78

Damara *S. balaenarum* 63, 71, 76

Spectacled (Gray-backed) *S. lunata* 15, 110

Bridled *S. anaethetus* 18, 25–28, 63, 74, 76, 86, 100, 103, 108

Sooty *S. fuscata* 15, 25–27, 34, 74–76, 108–110

Black-bellied *S. melanogaster* 79, 82, 85

River *S. aurantia* 79, 82, 85

Little (Least) *S. albifrons* 7–9, 13, 16, 18, 24–27, 30, 48, 51–53, 55, 56, 58–60, 62, 63, 74–76, 78, 86, 88, 90, 91, 97, 98, 101, 106–108, 111

Yellow-billed (Amazonian) *S. superciliaris* 27, 29, 33, 37, 48

Peruvian *S. lorata* 35

White-lored (Fairy) *S. nereis* 103, 109, 111

Inca *Larosterna inca* 35, 39

Noddy

Blue-gray *Procelsterna cerulea* 15

Brown (Common) *Anous stolidus* 15, 25–27, 34, 74–76, 97, 108–110

Lesser (White-capped) *A. tenuirostris* 74–76

Black (White-capped) *A. minutus* 8, 15, 108–110

Fairy (White) Tern *Gygis alba* 15, 74, 76, 109, 110

Skimmer

Black *Rynchops niger (nigra)* 7–9, 16, 25, 27, 29, 35, 37, 39, 42, 43, 48

African *R. flavirostris* 62, 64, 66–70

AUKS:*ALCIDAE*

Murre (Guillemot)

Common (Thin-billed, The) *Uria aalge* 1, 3, 14, 49, 50, 52–54, 87, 88

Thick-billed (Brunnich's) *U. lomvia* 1, 7, 49, 54, 87, 88

Razorbill *Alca torda* 7, 50, 52–54, 58–61

Guillemot

Black *Cepphus grylle* 7, 49, 50, 53, 54

Pigeon *C. columba* 1, 3, 14

Sooty (Spectacled) *C. carbo* 87, 88

Murrelet

Marbled *Brachyramphus marmoratus* 1, 3, 14, 87, 88

Xantus's *Endomychura (B.) hypoleuca* 13

Ancient *Synthliboramphus antiquus* 1, 3, 13, 14, 87, 88

Japanese *S. wumizusume* 88

Auklet

Arctic (Dovekie, Little "Auk") *Alle alle* 7, 50, 54

Cassin's *Ptychoramphus aleuticus* 3, 13, 14

Crested *Aethia cristatella* 1, 87, 88

Least *A. pusilla* 1, 87, 88

Parakeet *Cyclorrhynchus psittacula* 1

Rhinoceros *Cerorhinca monocerata* 3, 14, 87, 88

Puffin

Atlantic (The) *Fratercula arctica* 49, 50, 54, 59–61

Horned *F. corniculata* 1, 87, 88

Tufted *Lunda cirrhata* 1, 3, 14, 87, 88

SANDGROUSE:*PTEROCLIDAE*

Sandgrouse

Pin-tailed *Pterocles alchata* 58–60, 77

Namaqua *P. namaqua* 71

Chestnut-bellied *P. exustus* 62, 66, 79, 82

Spotted *P. senegallus* 60, 77

Black-bellied *P. orientalis* 59–61, 77, 79

Crowned *P. coronatus* 60

Yellow-throated *P. gutturalis* 66

Masked *P. personatus* 74

Black-faced *P. decoratus* 66

Lichtenstein's *P. lichtensteinii* 66

Double-banded *P. bicinctus* 69, 73

Four-banded *P. quadricinctus* 62

PIGEONS AND DOVES:
COLUMBIDAE

Pigeon (Wood-Pigeon)

Rock (Common) ("Dove") *Columba livia* 3, 6–9, 12–15, 50, 51, 59–61, 75, 77, 81–83, 86, 106, 107, 111 (incomplete listings)

Snow *C. leuconota* 81

Speckled *C. guinea* 62, 66, 71

Stock ("Dove") *C. oenas* 50–53, 55–60

Wood *C. palumbus* 50–53, 55–60

Long-toed *C. bollii* 61

Laurel *C. junoniae* 61

Olive (Rameron) *C. arquatrix* 64–66, 68, 71

Ashy *C. pulchricollis* 83, 91

Ceylon *C. torringtoni* 86

White-throated *C. vitiensis* 99, 109, 110

White-headed *C. leucomela* 107, 108

White-crowned *C. leucocephala* 8, 18, 25, 26

Red-necked *C. squamosa* 25, 26

Scaled *C. speciosa* 19, 20, 24, 27, 30, 31, 47, 48

Picazuro *C. picazuro* 42–44

Bare-eyed *C. corensis* 29, 30

Spot-winged *C. maculosa* 36, 43

Band-tailed *C. fasciata* 3, 12–14, 16, 21–23, 27, 30–32, 36

Chilean *C. araucana* 39

Ring-tailed *C. caribaea* 25

Pale-vented *C. cayennensis* 19, 24, 27, 29–31, 37, 44, 47, 48

Red-billed *C. flavirostris* 9, 16, 19, 22

Plain *C. inornata* 25

Plumbeous *C. plumbea* 31, 33, 37, 45, 47, 48

Ruddy *C. subvinacea* 22, 23, 28, 37

Short-billed *C. nigrirostris* 19, 20, 22, 24

Dusky *C. goodsoni* 31

Delegorgue's *C. delegorguei* 72

Bronze-naped *C. iriditorques* 65, 66, 68

Turtle-Dove (Dove)

Pink-breasted (Dusky) *Streptopelia lugens* 64

European (The) *S. turtur* 51, 52, 55–62, 77, 78

Oriental (Rufous) *S. orientalis* 81, 83, 88–92

Laughing (Palm) *S. senegalensis* 55, 62, 63, 66–73, 79, 81, 82, 103

Madagascar *S. picturata* 74–76

Spotted *S. chinensis* 13, 15, 75, 79, 83, 85, 86, 89–93, 95, 97, 98, 103, 105–111

Island (Javan, Philippine) *S. bitorquata* 97, 98

Mourning *S. decipiens* 62, 66–69, 73

Cape (Ring-necked) *S. capicola* 64–73

Vinaceous *S. vinacea* 62, 63

Red (Dwarf) *S. tranquebarica* 79, 82, 83, 85, 89–93, 97

Red-eyed *S. semitorquata* 62–73

Pink-headed *S. roseogrisea* 62

Collared *S. decaocto* 50–53, 55–57, 78, 79, 81, 82, 86, 88, 89

Lemon (Cinnamon) Dove *Aplopelia larvata (simplex)* 65, 66, 68, 72

Cuckoo-Dove

Barred *Macropygia unchall* 93

Slender-billed (Pink-breasted, Brown "Pigeon") *M. amboinensis (phasianella)* 96–100, 107, 108
Black-billed (Rusty) *M. nigrirostris* 99, 100
Little *M. ruficeps* 96, 98
Great *Reinwardtoena reinwardtsi* 99
Wood-Dove
  Emerald-spotted *Turtur chalcospilos* 64, 66–70, 72, 73
  Black-billed *T. abyssinicus* 62
  Blue-spotted (Red-billed) *T. afer* 62–65, 68
  Tambourine "Dove" *T. tympanistria* 63–69, 72
Namaqua (Long-tailed) Dove *Oena capensis* 62, 66–74
Green-winged Pigeon (Emerald Dove) *Chalcophaps indica* 85, 86, 91, 93–98, 100, 101, 107–109
Bronzewing
  Common (Forest) *Phaps chalcoptera* 102–105
  Brush *P. elegans* 103, 105, 106
Pigeon
  Crested *Ocyphaps lophotes* 102, 104, 107
  Plumed *Petrophassa plumifera* 102
  Partridge *P. (Geophaps) smithii* 101
  Chestnut-quilled *P. rufipennis (albipennis)* 101
Dove
  Diamond *Geopelia cuneata* 101, 102
  Peaceful (Barred, Zebra) *G. striata (placida)* 15, 75, 76, 95, 97, 98, 100, 101, 104, 106–108
  Bar-shouldered *G. humeralis* 100, 101, 107, 108
Wonga Pigeon *Leucosarcia melanoleuca* 106, 107
Dove
  Mourning *Zenaida macroura* 3, 6–14, 16, 17, 21, 25
  Spot-eared (Eared) *Z. auriculata* 26, 27, 29–32, 35, 36, 38, 39, 41–44
  Zenaida *Z. aurita* 18, 25, 26
  Galapagos *Z. galapagoensis* 34
  White-winged *Z. asiatica* 8, 9, 12, 16, 18, 21, 25, 35
Ground-Dove
  Common (Scaly-breasted, The) *Columbina passerina* 8, 9, 12, 16, 18, 21, 25–32, 47, 48

Plain-breasted (Least) *C. minuta* 19, 27, 29, 35, 46, 48
Ruddy *C. talpacoti* 16, 18–20, 23, 24, 27–31, 37, 43–48
Picui *C. picui* 39, 42, 43
Croaking *C. cruziana* 35, 38
Blue *Claravis pretiosa* 19, 20, 24, 27–30, 33, 44, 47, 48
Maroon-chested *C. mondetoura* 23
Bare-faced *Metropelia ceciliae* 35, 36, 38
Black-winged *M. melanoptera* 32, 36, 38, 39
Golden-spotted *M. aymara* 38
Dove
  Inca *Scardafella inca* 9, 12, 16, 17, 21
  Scaled *S. squammata* 29, 30
  White-tipped (-fronted) *Leptotila verreauxi* 9, 16, 18, 19, 21–24, 27–32, 35, 37, 42–44, 48
  Gray-fronted *L. rufaxilla* 27, 33, 36, 37, 45, 47, 48
  Gray-headed *L. plumbeiceps* 19, 20, 31
  Pallid *L. pallida* 31
  Grenada *L. wellsi* 26
  White-bellied *L. jamaicensis* 18, 25
  Gray-chested *L. cassinii* 19, 24
Quail-Dove
  Costa Rican *Geotrygon costaricensis* 22, 23
  Sapphire *G. saphirina* 31, 33
  Gray-headed *G. caniceps* 25
  Crested *G. versicolor* 25
  Lined *G. linearis* 27, 28, 30
  Rufous-breasted *G. chiriquensis* 23
  White-throated *G. frenata* 31
  Key West *G. chrysia* 25
  Bridled *G. mystacea* 25, 26
  Ruddy *G. montana* 16, 20, 22, 24–28, 30, 33, 37, 46–48
  Blue-headed *Starnoenas cyanocephala* 25
Pigeon
  Nicobar *Caloenas nicobarica* 97
  Bleeding-heart *Gallicolumba luzonica* 97
Ground-Dove
  Cinnamon (Red-throated) *G. rufigula* 99, 100
  Friendly *G. stairi* 110
Pheasant Pigeon *Otidiphaps nobilis* 99

Brown Fruit-Dove
  Lesser (White-eared) *Phapitreron leucotis* 97
  Greater (Amethyst) *P. amethystina* 91
  Southern *P. cinereiceps (amethystina)* 97
Green-Pigeon
  Little *Treron olax* 94, 95, 98
  Pink-necked *T. vernans* 95–98
  Orange-breasted *T. bicincta* 85, 86
  Pompadour *T. pompadora* 85, 86, 93, 97
  Thick-billed *T. curvirostra* 93, 95–98
  Large *T. capellei* 94
  Yellow-legged *T. phoenicoptera* 79, 82, 86, 93
  Yellow-bellied *T. waalia* 62
  Madagascar *T. australis* 74
  African (The) *T. calva* 62–66, 68–70, 72, 73
  Wedge-tailed *T. sphenura* 83, 93
  White-bellied (Japanese) *T. sieboldii* 87, 88, 91
Fruit-Dove
  Black-banded (backed) *Ptilinopus cinctus* 101
  Pink-necked *P. porphyrea* 98
  Merrill's *P. merrilli* 97
  Yellow-breasted *P. occipitalis* 97
  Jambu *P. jambu* 94, 95
  Black-chinned *P. leclancheri* 97
  Wompoo (Magnificent) ("Pigeon") *P. magnificus* 99, 100
  Pink-spotted (Collared) *P. perlatus* 99, 100
  Ornate *P. ornatus* 99, 100
  Orange-fronted *P. aurantiifrons* 100
  Superb (Purple-crowned) *P. superbus* 99, 100, 108
  Many-colored *P. perousii* 110
  Red-crowned (Pink-capped) *P. regina (ewingi)* 101, 107, 108
  Red-bellied (Grey's) *P. greyii* 109
  Diadem (Coroneted) *P. coronulatus* 99, 100
  Beautiful (Crimson-capped) *P. pulchellus* 100
  White-breasted *P. rivoli* 99
  Orange-bellied *P. iozonus* 100
  Black-naped *P. melanospila* 98
  Dwarf *P. naina (nanus)* 99
  Orange *P. victor* 110

Golden *P. luteovirens* 110
  Velvet *P. layardi* 110
Cloven-feathered Dove *Drepanoptila holosericea* 109
Blue Pigeon
  Madagascar *Alectroenas madagascariensis* 74
  Mauritius *A. nitidissima* 75
  Seychelles *A. pulcherrima* 76
Fruit-Pigeon (Imperial-Pigeon)
  Pink-bellied *Ducula poliocephala* 97
  Green *D. aenea* 86, 95–97
  Pacific *D. pacifica* 109
  Rufous-breasted *D. chalconota* 99
  Peale's *D. latrans* 110
  New Caledonian (Giant) *D. goliath* 109
  Pinon (Black-shouldered) *D. pinon* 100
  Black-belted (Zoe) *D. zoeae* 99, 100
  Mountain *D. badia* 93, 96
  Dark-backed *D. lacernulata* 98
  Nutmeg (Pied) *D. bicolor (melanura)* 97
  Torres Strait (Nutmeg) *D. spilorrhoa* 100, 101, 108
Topknot Pigeon *Lopholaimus antarcticus* 106–108
New Zealand Pigeon *Hemiphaga novaeseelandiae* 111
Bare-eyed Mountain-Pigeon *Gymnophaps albertisii* 99, 100
    PARROTS:PSITTACIDAE
Cockatiel *Nymphicus hollandicus* 101, 102, 104
Cockatoo
  Gang-gang *Callocephalon fimbriatum* 105
  "Galah" *Eolophus roseicapillus* 101–107
  Major Mitchell's *Cacatua leadbeateri* 102, 104
  Lesser Sulfur-crested *C. sulphurea* 98
  Sulfur-crested (White) *C. galerita* 99–101, 104–108, 111
  Philippine (Red-vented) *C. haematuropygia* 97
  Little "Corella" *C. sanguinea* 101, 103–106
  Long-billed "Corella" *C. tenuirostris* 103–106
Black-Cockatoo (Cockatoo)
  White-tailed *Calyptorhynchus baudinii* 103
  Yellow-tailed *C. funereus* 104–107

Red-tailed *C. magnificus* 101–104
Glossy *C. lathami* 107
Kea *Nestor notabilis* 111
Kaka *N. meridionalis* 111
Kakapo *Strigops habroptilus* 111
Swamp (Ground) Parrot *Pezoporus wallicus* 103
Budgerygah *Melopsittacus undulatus* 102, 104
Parrot (Parakeet)
Bourke *Neophema bourkii* 102
Blue-winged *N. chrysostoma* 104, 105
Elegant *N. elegans* 103, 104
Rock *N. petrophila* 103
Turquoise *N. pulchella* 106
Swift *Lathamus discolor* 103, 105, 106
Parakeet
Crested (Horned) *Eunymphicus cornutus* 110
Red-crowned (-fronted) *Cyanoramphus novaezelandiae* 109, 111
Yellow-crowned (-fronted) *C. auriceps* 111
South Island (Orange-fronted) *C. malherbi* 111
Parrot (Parakeet)
Red-capped *Purpureicephalus spurius* 103
Red-rumped (-backed) *Psephotus haematonotus* 104
Mulga *P. varius* 102–104
Bluebonnet *P. haematogaster* 104
(Mallee) Ring-necked *Barnardius barnardi* 104
Port Lincoln (Twenty-eight) *B. zonarius* 102, 103
Rosella
Crimson *Platycercus elegans* 104–108, 111
Yellow *P. flaveolus* 104
Eastern *P. eximius* 104–106, 111
Pale-headed *P. adscitus* 107, 108
Northern *P. venustus* 101
Western *P. icterotis* 102
Hanging-Parrot
Vernal *Loriculus vernalis* 93, 97
Ceylon ("Lorikeet") *L. beryllinus* 86
Philippine *L. philippensis* 97
Blue-crowned *L. galgulus* 94, 95
Lovebird
Gray-headed *Agapornis cana* 74–76
Fischer's *A. fischeri* 66

Masked (Yellow-collared) *A. personata* 66
Lillian's *A. lilianae* 69
Black-cheeked *A. nigrigenis* 70
Red-winged Parrot *Aprosmictus erythropterus* 101
King-Parrot
Australian *Alisterus scapularis* 105–108
Papuan (Green-winged) *A. chloropterus* 99, 100
Regent Parrot *Polytelis anthopeplus* 55
Musk-Parrot
Red-breasted *Prosopeia tabuensis* 110
Yellow-breasted *P. personata* 110
Parrot
Red-cheeked *Geoffroyus geoffroyi* 100
Blue-collared *G. simplex* 99
Eclectus (Red-sided) *Eclectus roratus* 99, 100
Brehm's *Psittacella brehmii* 99
Madarasz's *P. madaraszi* 99
"Guaiabero" *Bolbopsittacus lunulatus* 97
Blue-rumped *Psittinus cyanurus* 94, 95
Racquet-tailed Parrot
Blue-headed (crowned) *Prioniturus discurus* 97
Green-headed *P. luconensis* 97
Crimson-spotted *P. montanus* 97
Palawan *P. platenae* 97
Parrot
Blue-naped *Tanygnathus lucionensis* 97
Blue-backed (Muller's) *T. sumatranus* 97
Parakeet
Great (Alexandrine, Large Indian) *Psittacula eupatria* 85, 86
Rose-ringed (Ring-necked) *P. krameri* 62, 75, 78, 79, 82, 85, 86, 92
Slaty-headed *P. himalayana (finschi)* 80, 81, 83
Blossom (Plum)-headed *P. cyanocephala (roseata)*, 80, 85, 86
Emerald-collared *P. calthorpae* 86
Rose-breasted (Moustached) *P. alexandri* 85, 93, 97
Long-tailed *P. longicauda* 95, 97
Fig-Parrot
Orange-breasted *Opopsitta gulielmiterti* 100

Double-eyed *O. diophthalma* 99, 100, 108

Pygmy-Parrot
Buff-faced *Micropsitta pusio* 100
Red-breasted *M. bruijnii* 99

Lorikeet
Musschenbroek's *Neopsittacus musschenbroekii* 99
Emerald *N. pullicauda* 99
Whiskered *Oreopsittacus arfaki* 99
New Caledonian *Charmosyna diadema* 109
Red-flanked *C. placentis* 99, 100
Red-throated *C. amabilis* 110
Little Red (Fairy) *C. pulchella* 99
Papuan (Fairy) *C. papou* 99
Musk *Glossopsitta concinna* 104–107
Little *G. pusilla* 104, 106–108
Purple-crowned *G. porphyrocephala* 103, 104
Collared ("Lory") *Phigys solitarius* 110
Black-capped ("Lory") *Lorius lory* 99, 100
Yellow-streaked *Chalcopsitta sintillata* 100
Dusk-orange *Pseudeos fuscata* 99, 100
Rainbow *Trichoglossus haematodus* 98–101, 104, 106–109
Mindanao *T. johnstoniae* 97
Scaly-breasted *T. chlorolepidotus* 106–108
Varied *T. versicolor* 101
Goldie's *T. goldiei* 99

Vasa Parrot
Greater *Coracopsis vasa* 74
Lesser (Black) *C. nigra* 74, 76

Parrot
Gray *Psittacus erithacus* 63–65
Brown-necked (Cape) *Poicephalus robustus* 62, 68–70
Red-headed (Jardine's) *P. gulielmi* 66
African Brown-headed *P. cryptoxanthus* 67, 68, 72, 73
Senegal *P. senegalus* 62
Orange (Red)-bellied *P. rufiventris* 66
Brown (Meyer's) *P. meyeri* 65, 66, 67, 70

Parakeet
Mountain *Bolborhynchus aurifrons* 38, 39
Barred *B. lineola* 22, 23, 31
Andean *B. orbygnesius* 36

Parrotlet
Blue-rumped (Mexican) *Forpus cyanopygius* 16
Green-rumped *F. passerinus* 25–30, 47, 48
Blue-winged *F. xanthopterygius* 30, 33, 44–46
Spectacled *F. conspicillatus* 31
Dusky-billed (Sclater's) *F. sclateri* 33, 37

Parakeet
Plain *Brotogeris tirica* 45, 46
Canary (White)-winged *B. versicolurus (chiriri)* 43
Orange-chinned (Brown-shouldered) *B. jugularis* 24, 29, 30
Cobalt-winged *B. cyanoptera* 33, 37
Golden-winged *B. chrysopterus* 47, 48

Parrotlet (Touit)
Lilac-tailed *Touit batavica* 27, 28, 48
Scarlet-shouldered *T. huetii* 47
Red-winged *T. dilectissima* 31

Parrot
Red-capped *Pionopsitta pileata* 44, 45
Brown-hooded (Beautiful) *P. haematotis (pulchra)* 19, 20, 22, 24, 31
Orange-cheeked *P. barrabandi* 37
Caica *P. caica* 48
Vulturine *Gypopsitta vulturina* 47
Blue-headed *Pionus menstruus* 23, 24, 27, 28, 30, 31, 33, 37, 47, 48
Red-billed *P. sordidus* 28, 30
Scaly-headed *P. maximiliani* 43–46
White-crowned *P. senilis* 19, 20, 23
Dusky *P. fuscus* 47, 48

Parrot (Amazon)
Yellow-billed *Amazona collaria* 25
Cuban *A. leucocephala* 25
Hispaniolan *A. ventralis* 25
White-fronted *A. albifrons* 16, 18–20, 22
Yellow-lored *A. xantholora* 18, 19
Black-billed *A. agilis* 25
Puerto Rican *A. vittata* 25
Lilac-crowned *A. finschi* 16
Red-lored *A. autumnalis* 19, 20, 22, 24
Turquoise-fronted *A. aestiva* 43, 44
Yellow-headed *A. oratrix* 19
Yellow-crowned *A. ochrocephala* 29, 33, 37
Orange Winged *A. amazonica* 27, 28, 30, 33, 47, 48

Mealy *A. farinosa* 19, 20, 24, 33, 37, 47, 48
St. Lucia *A. versicolor* 26
Red-necked *A. arausiaca* 26
St. Vincent *A. guildingii* 26
Imperial *A. imperialis* 26
Parrot (Caique)
Black-headed *Pionites melanocephala* 33, 48
White-bellied *P. leucogaster* 37, 47
Red-fan (Hawk-headed) Parrot *Deroptyus accipitrinus* 48
Parakeet
Monk *Myiopsitta monachus* 42, 43
Slender-billed *Enicognathus leptorhynchus* 39
Burrowing Parrot *Cyanoliseus patagonus* 41
Parakeet
Reddish-bellied *Pyrrhura frontalis* 43–45
Pearly *P. perlata* 47
Painted *P. picta* 48
Santa Marta *P. viridicata* 30
Maroon-tailed *P. melanura* 33
Rock (Black-capped) *P. rupicola* 37
Blood-eared *P. hoematotis* 28
Sulfur-winged *P. hoffmanni* 22, 23
Thick-billed Parrot *Rhynchopsitta pachyrhyncha* 16
Parakeet (Conure)
Black-hooded (Nanday) *Nandayus nenday* 43
Blue-crowned *Aratinga acuticaudata* 43
Green *A. holochlora* 21
Crimson-fronted *A. finschi* 22, 23
Scarlet-fronted *A. wagleri* 28, 30, 31, 36
Mitred *A. mitrata* 36
White-eyed (Amazonian) *A. leucophthalmus* 33, 37, 44
Hispaniolan *A. chloroptera* 25
Cuban *A. euops* 25
Dusky-headed *A. weddellii* 33, 37
Olive-throated (Aztec) *A. nana* 16, 18–20, 25
Orange-fronted *A. canicularis* 16
Brown-throated *A. pertinax* 25, 28–30, 48
Peach-fronted *A. aurea* 47

Macaw
Blue-and-yellow (-gold) *Ara ararauna* 27, 33, 37, 48
Military *A. militaris* 16, 30
Great Green *A. ambigua* 22
Scarlet *A. macao* 19, 29, 33, 37, 48
Red-and-green *A. chloroptera* 33, 37, 48
Chestnut-fronted *A. severa* 33, 37, 48
Red-bellied *A. manilata* 27, 37, 47
Blue-headed *A. couloni* 37
Red-shouldered *A. nobilis* 48
TURACOS:*MUSOPHAGIDAE*
Turaco (Touraco)
Guinea *Touraco persa* 62
Black-billed *T. schuttii* 64, 65
Knysna *T. corythaix* 68, 70
Fischer's *T. fischeri* 67
Hartlaub's *T. hartlaubi* 65, 66
Purple-crested *T. porphyreolophus* 68, 69, 72, 73
Ruwenzori *T. johnstoni* 64
Violet *Musophaga violacea* 62
Ross's *M. rossae* 64–66
Go-away-bird (Loerie)
Gray (Southern, The) *Corythaixoides concolor* 68–70, 72, 73
Bare-faced *C. personata* 63, 66
White-bellied *C. leucogaster* 64, 66
Western Grey Plaintain-eater *Crinifer piscator* 62, 63
Great Blue Turaco *Corythaeola cristata* 64, 65
CUCKOOS:*CUCULIDAE*
Cuckoo
Jacobin (Pied Crested) *Clamator jacobinus (serratus)* 64, 66, 67, 72, 82, 83, 86
Levaillant's *C. levaillantii* 62–68, 70
Chestnut (Red)-winged *C. coromandus* 85, 86, 93, 95
Great Spotted *C. glandarius* 55, 58, 60, 62–64, 66, 68, 69, 72, 73
Thick-billed *Pachycoccyx audeberti* 67–69, 74
Hawk-Cuckoo
Large *Cuculus sparverioides* 83, 90, 91, 96, 97
Common *C. varius* 82, 85, 86, 95
Hodgson's (Malayan) *C. fugax* 87, 88, 96
Cuckoo
Red-chested *C. solitarius* 63–66, 68–73

Black *C. (Clamator) clamosus (cafer)* 65, 66, 68–70, 72

Indian *C. micropterus* 83, 86, 90, 92, 96

Eurasian (Common, Clock, The) *C. canorus* 50–60, 64, 67, 68, 73, 81, 83, 84, 87–90, 92

African *C. gularis (canorus)* 66, 69

Oriental (Himalayan, Blyth's) *C. saturatus* 80, 83, 84, 87, 88, 91, 96, 98

Lesser *C. poliocephalus* 67, 74, 83, 86–88, 96, 98

Pallid *C. pallidus* 101–107

Barred Long-tailed *Cercococcyx montanus* 68

Banded Bay *Cacomantis sonneratii* 86, 96

Plaintive *C. merulinus* 81, 83, 86, 92, 93, 95–97

Brush *C. variolosus* 95, 97–101, 105–108

Chestnut-breasted *C. castaneiventris* 99

Fan-tailed *C. pyrrhophanus* 99, 103–110

Bronze-Cuckoo
    Red-eyed (Little, Malayan) *Chrysococcyx (Chalcites) malayanus (minutillus)* 96, 100, 101
    Shining (Golden) *C.(C.) lucidus (plagosus)* 103, 104, 106–109, 111
    Horsfield's *C.(C.) basalis* 101–107
    Rufous-throated *C.(C.) ruficollis* 99
    White-eared (Meyer's) *C.(C.) meyeri* 99

Cuckoo
    Black-eared *C. osculans* 102–104, 106
    Violet *C.(C.) xanthorhynchus* 96, 97
    Klaas's *C. klaas* 62, 63, 65–68, 70–72
    Emerald *C. cupreus* 63–66, 68–70, 72
    Didric *C. caprius* 63–70, 72, 73
    Drongo *Surniculus lugubris* 83, 86, 93, 95–98

Koel
    White-crowned *Caliechthrus leucolophus* 99, 100
    Common (Indian, The) *Eudynamys scolopacea* 79, 82, 83, 86, 92, 95, 98–101, 106–108
    Long-tailed "Cuckoo" *E. (Urodynamis) taitensis* 109–111

Cuckoo
    Channel-billed *Scythrops novaehollandiae* 100, 101, 107, 108
    Black-billed *Coccyzus erythropthalmus* 6, 7, 26

Yellow-billed *C. americanus* 6–9, 12, 24–26

Mangrove *C. minor* 8, 16, 19, 25, 26

Dark-billed *C. melacoryphus* 34

Bay-breasted *Piaya (Hyetornis) rufigularis* 25

Chestnut-bellied *P. (H.) pluvialis* 25

Squirrel *P. cayana* 16, 18–20, 22–24, 27–31, 33, 37, 43–45, 47, 48

Black-bellied (Red-billed) *P. melanogaster* 37, 48

Little Squirrel *P. minuta* 24, 27, 31, 33, 47, 48

Lizard-Cuckoo
    Great *Saurothera merlini* 25
    Hispaniolan *S. longirostris* 25
    Jamaican *S. vetula* 25
    Puerto Rican *S. vielloti* 25

Green Cuckoo ("Yellowbill") *Ceuthmochares aereus* 62, 63, 65, 67, 68, 72

Malkoha (Malcoha)
    Black-bellied *Phaenicophaeus (Rhopodytes) diardi* 95
    Rufous (Chestnut)-bellied *P. (R.) sumatranus* 94–96
    Green-billed *P. (R.) tristis* 83, 85, 93
    Blue-faced *P. (R.) viridirostris* 86
    Sirkeer "Cuckoo" *P. (Taccocua) leschenaultii* 86
    Raffle's *P. (Rhinortha) chlorophaea* 94, 96
    Red-billed *P. (Zanclostamus) javanicus* 94
    Chestnut-breasted *P. (Rhamphococcyx) curvirostris* 94, 96–98
    Red-faced *P. pyrrhocephalus* 86
    Rough (Red)-crested "Cuckoo" *P. (Dasylophus) superciliosus* 97
    Scale-feathered "Cuckoo" *P. (Lepidogrammus) cumingi* 97

Ani
    Greater *Crotophaga major* 24, 27, 29–31, 33, 37, 43, 44, 47, 48
    Smooth-billed *C. ani* 8, 24–31, 33, 37, 43–48
    Groove-billed *C. sulcirostris* 9, 16, 18–20, 22, 24, 28–30, 35

Cuckoo
    Guira *Guira guira* 42–46
    Striped *Tapera naevia* 24, 27, 29–31, 37, 43, 44, 46–48

Lesser Ground-Cuckoo *Morococcyx ery-
thropygus* 16
Cuckoo
  Pheasant *Dromococcyx phasianellus* 20
  Pavonine *D. pavoninus* 28
Roadrunner
  Greater (The) *Geococcyx californianus*
    9, 12, 13
  Lesser *G. velox* 16, 18
Coral-billed Ground-Cuckoo *Carpococ-
cyx renauldi* 93
Coua
  Delalande's *Coua delalandei* 74
  Giant *C. gigas* 74
  Coquerel's *C. coquereli* 74
  Red-breasted *C. serriana* 74
  Red-fronted *C. reynaudii* 74
  Running *C. cursor* 74
  Red-capped *C. ruficeps* 74
  Crested *C. cristata* 74
  Verreaux's *C. verreauxi* 74
  Blue *C. caerulea* 74
Coucal
  New Guinea (Black Jungle) *Centropus
    menbeki* 99, 100
  Pheasant *C. phasianinus* 100, 101, 106–
    108
  Black Scrub (Bernstein's) *C. bernsteini*
    99
  Ceylon (Green-billed) *C. chlororhyn-
    chus* 86
  Short-toed *C. rectunguis* 94
  Greater *C. sinensis* 79, 82, 85, 86, 92,
    95, 96
  Philippine *C. viridis* 97
  Black *C. toulou* 65, 67–69, 74, 85
  Lesser *C. bengalensis* 91, 92, 95–98
  Black-throated *C. leucogaster* 63
  Blue-headed *C. monachus* 63, 65
  Senegal *C. senegalensis* 62, 63, 68–70
  Rufous-bellied *C. epomidis (senegalen-
    sis, grillii)* 63
  White-browed *C. superciliosus* 64–69,
    71–73
  Black-faced *C. melanops* 97
  Rufous *C. unirufus* 97
HOATZIN:*OPISTHOCOMIDAE*
Hoatzin *Opisthocomus hoazin* 29, 33, 37
  BARN OWLS:*TYTONIDAE*
Owl
  Madagascar Red *Tyto soumagnei* 74
  Barn *T. alba* 7–9, 12–16, 21, 24–27, 32,

  34, 35, 39, 42, 51–53, 56–61, 68, 72–74,
    76, 86, 98–104, 107–110
  Masked *T. novaehollandiae* 103
  Grass *T. capensis* 65, 66, 72, 85, 97, 109
  Bay *Phodilus badius* 86, 94, 98
    OWLS:*STRIGIDAE*
Screech-Owl
  Cuban *Otus lawrencii* 25
  Vermiculated *O. guatemalae* 20, 28
  Puerto Rican *O. nudipes* 25
  Tawny-bellied *O. watsonii* 33, 37
  Bare-shanked *O. clarkii* 22
  Tropical *O. choliba* 24, 27, 30, 31, 33,
    37, 44, 46, 47
  Whiskered *O. trichopsis* 12, 16, 21
  Northern (Common) *O. asio (ken-
    nicotti)* 3, 6–9, 12–14
Scops-Owl
  White-faced *O. leucotis* 62, 63, 65, 66,
    68, 69
  Madagascar *O. rutilus* 74
  Bare-legged *O. insularis (rutilus)* 76
  Eurasian (Common, The) *O. scops* 55,
    56, 58–60, 85–88, 97
  African *O. senegalensis* 62, 66–68,
    73
  Flammulated ("Screech-Owl") *O.
    flammeolus* 12, 13
  Collared *O. bakkamoena* 86–88, 91, 92,
    94, 95, 97, 98
  Reddish *O. rufescens* 94, 96
  Sokoke (Morden's "Owlet") *O. ireneae*
    67
  Mountain *O. spilocephalus* 83, 91, 96
  Giant *O. gurneyi* 97
Eagle-Owl
  Great Horned "Owl" *Bubo virginianus*
    2, 6–10, 12–14, 29, 32, 39
  Eurasian (Northern) *B. bubo* 56, 57,
    60, 82, 83, 87, 89
  Spotted *B. africanus* 66, 68, 71, 72
  Forest *B. nipalensis* 86
  Malay *B. sumatrana* 98
  Verreaux's (Milky) *B. lacteus* 62, 64–
    69, 73
  Dusky *B. coromandus* 79, 82
Fish-Owl
  Blakiston's *Ketupa blakistoni* 87
  Brown *K. zeylonensis* 82, 85, 86, 93
  Malay (Buffy) *K. ketupa* 95, 98
Pel's Fishing-Owl *Scotopelia peli* 62, 66,
  68–70, 72

Snowy Owl *Nyctea scandiaca* 1, 2, 4, 5, 7, 49, 50, 54, 87

Northern Hawk-Owl (Day Owl) *Surnia ulula* 2, 5, 54

Pygmy-Owl

Eurasian *Glaucidium passerinum* 53, 54, 57

Northern *G. gnoma* 3, 12–14, 17, 21

Cuban *G. siju* 25

Least *G. minutissimum* 16, 37

Andean *G. jardinii* 23, 32

Ferruginous *G. brasilianum* 12, 16, 18, 27–30, 33, 35, 37, 44, 45

Austral *G. nanum* 39

Owlet (Pygmy-Owl)

Pearl-spotted *G. perlatum* 62, 65, 66, 68, 69, 73

Red-chested *G. tephronotum* 65

African Barred *G. capense* 68, 69

Collared (Pygmy) *G. brodiei* 83, 96

(Barred) Jungle *G. radiatum* 85, 86

Asian Barred (Cuckoo) *G. cuculoides* 90, 98

Elf Owl *Micrathene whitneyi* 9, 12

Hawk-Owl (Owl)

Powerful *Ninox strenua* 105, 107

Barking (Winking) *N. connivens* 101, 103, 104, 107

Boobook ("Morepork") *N. novae-seelandiae* 101–104, 106–108, 111

Brown (Oriental) *N. scutulata* 83, 85–88, 93, 96

Madagascar *N. superciliaris* 74

Philippine *N. philippensis* 97

Owl

Little *Athene noctua* 51, 52, 55–60, 77, 89, 111

Spotted "Owlet" *A. brama* 79, 82, 83, 85

Burrowing *A. (Speotyto) cunicularia* 8, 11–13, 25, 29, 32, 35, 36, 38, 39, 41–43, 45

Mottled *Ciccaba virgata* 16, 20, 23, 24, 27, 28, 31, 37, 47

Black-banded *C. huhula* 33, 47

Wood-Owl

African *Strix (C.) woodfordii* 65–70, 72

Spotted *S. seloputo* 97

Brown *S. leptogrammica* 84, 86, 91

Owl

Tawny *S. aluco* 51–53, 55–60

Spotted (Western) *S. occidentalis* 12, 14

Barred *S. varia* 7–9

Rusty-barred *S. hylophila* 45

Rufous-legged *S. rufipes* 39

Ural *S. uralensis* 54, 87, 88

Great Gray *S. nebulosa* 2, 10, 54

Spectacled *Pulsatrix perspicillata* 22, 24, 27, 28, 30, 33, 37, 47, 48

Tawny-browed (White-chinned) *P. koeniswaldiana* 45

Striped *Asio (Rhinoptynx) clamator* 24, 27, 30, 47

Long-eared (Northern) *A. otus* 6, 7, 11, 50, 52, 53, 55, 57, 58, 60, 61, 87, 88

Abyssinian Long-eared *A. abyssinicus (otus)* 66, 71

Stygian *A. stygius* 25

Madagascar Long-eared *A. madagascariensis* 74

Short-eared *A. flammeus* 1, 2, 4, 5, 7, 10, 11, 13, 15, 25, 32, 34, 35, 39–42, 49–57, 60, 86–88, 90

Marsh *A. capensis (helvola)* 60, 66, 68, 74

Jamaican *Pseudoscops grammicus* 25

Tengmalm's (Boreal) *Aegolius funereus* 2, 53, 54, 57

Saw-whet *A. acadicus* 7, 10, 14

OILBIRD:*STEATORNITHIDAE*

Oilbird *Steatornis caripensis* 27

FROGMOUTHS:*PODARGIDAE*

Frogmouth

Australian (Tawny) *Podargus strigoides (plumiferus)* 101–108

Papuan (Giant) *P. papuensis* 99, 100, 108

Philippine *Batrachostomus septimus* 97

Gould's *B. stellatus* 94, 98

Ceylon *B. moniliger* 86

Blyth's (Javan) *B. javensis (affinis)* 98

POTOOS:*NYCTIBIIDAE*

Potoo

Great *Nyctibius grandis* 29, 33, 37

Common *N. griseus (jamaicensis)* 16, 19, 20, 24, 25, 27–29, 31, 33, 37, 48

Rufous *N. bracteatus* 37

OWLET-NIGHTJARS: *AEGOTHELIDAE*

Australian Owlet-Nightjar *Aegotheles cristatus* 102–104

NIGHTJARS:*CAPRIMULGIDAE*

Nighthawk

Short-tailed (Semicollared) *Lurocalis semitorquatus* 27, 28, 45, 58

Sand-colored *Chordeiles rupestris* 37

Lesser *C. acutipennis* 9, 12, 13, 16, 18, 19, 24, 27, 30, 31, 35, 46, 48

Common (Antillean) *C. minor (gundlachi)* 3, 6–10, 12, 13, 19–21, 24, 25, 37

Nacunda *Podager nacunda* 27, 29, 43, 44, 47

Nightjar

Spotted *Eurostopodus guttatus* 101–104

White-throated *E. mystacalis (albogularis)* 108, 109

Malaysian Eared *E. temminckii* 94–96

Great *E. macrotis* 93, 97

Pauraque

Common *Nyctidromus albicollis* 9, 16, 18–20, 23, 24, 27–31, 33, 37, 46–48

Least *Siphonorhis brewsteri* 25

Poor-will

Western (Common) *Phalaenoptilus nuttallii* 12–14

Yucatan *Nyctiphrynus (Otophanes) yucatanicus* 18–20

Ocellated *N. ocellatus* 37

Nightjar

"Chuck-will's-widow" *Caprimulgus carolinensis* 7–9, 25

Rufous *C. rufus* 24, 26, 27

Greater Antillean *C. cubanensis* 25

Buff-collared *C. ridgwayi* 16

"Whip-poor-will" *C. vociferus (noctitherus)* 6–9, 12, 16, 21, 25

"Cheer-for-will" (Sooty, Dusky) *C. saturatus* 22, 23

Band-winged *C. longirostris* 28, 30, 32, 35, 38, 39, 46

White-tailed *C. cayennensis* 26, 27, 29, 30, 48

Little *C. parvulus* 47

Blackish *C. nigrescens* 47, 48

Red-necked *C. ruficollis* 59, 60

Gray (Jungle) *C. indicus* 83, 86–88, 92

Eurasian (European) *C. europaeus* 53, 55–60, 65, 66, 68, 77

Egyptian *C. aegyptius* 62

Syke's (Sind) *C. mahrattensis* 79

Madagascar *C. madagascariensis* 74

Large (Long, White)-tailed *C. macrurus* 85, 86, 93, 95, 97, 98, 100, 101, 108

Dusky (South African, Black-shouldered) *C. pectoralis (fraenatus)* 62, 63, 66–68, 70, 72

Rufous-cheeked *C. rufigena* 70

Donaldson-Smith's *C. donaldsoni* 66

Abyssinian *C. poliocephalus* 66

Indian *C. asiaticus* 82, 86

Natal *C. natalensis* 63

Plain *C. inornatus* 63, 67

Franklin's *C. monticolus (affinis)* 82, 85

Savanna *C. affinis* 91–93, 97, 98

Freckled *C. tristigma* 66, 68

Collared *C. enarratus* 74

Gabon (Mozambique) *C. (Scotornis) fossii* 64, 66–69, 72

Long-tailed *C.(S.) climacurus* 62

Standard-wing *Macrodipteryx longipennis* 62, 63

Pennant-winged *M. (Semeiophorus) vexillarius* 68–70

Ladder-tailed *Hydropsalis climacocerca* 33, 37, 48

Scissor-tailed *H. brasiliana* 43, 46

Long-trained *Macropsalis creagra* 45

SWIFTS:*APODIDAE*

Swiftlet

White-rumped *Collocalia (Aerodramus) spodiopygia* 110

Mascarene Cave *C.(A.) francica* 75, 76

Uniform (Gray) *C.(A.) vanikorensis* 97, 100, 101, 109

Mountain *C.(A.) hirundinacea* 99

Himalayan *C.(A.) brevirostris* 84, 93, 97

Whitehead's *C.(A.) whiteheadi* 97

Edible-nest (Thunberg's, Brown-rumped) *C.(A.) fuciphaga* 95, 97, 98

White-bellied (Glossy) *C. esculenta* 95–100, 109

Pygmy (Philippine) *C. troglodytes (marginata)* 97

Swift

Chestnut-collared *Cypseloides rutilus* 16, 27, 28, 30, 31, 36

American (The) Black *C. (Nephoecetes) niger* 3, 25, 26

Great Dusky *C. (Aerornis) senex* 44

White-collared *Streptoprocne zonaris* 19–28, 30–33, 35, 37, 44–46

Biscutate *S. biscutata* 46

White-naped *S. semicollaris* 16, 17

Needletail (Spine-tailed Swift)
  White-throated (Asiatic) *Hirundapus (Chaetura) caudacutus* 91, 93, 100, 105–108
  Brown (-throated, Malaysian) *H. (C.) giganteus* 86, 93–95, 97
  Philippine *Mearnsia (C.) picina* 97
  Papuan *M. (C.) novaeguineae* 100
  Boehm's *M. (C.) (Neafrapus) boehmi* 67, 69
  Madagascar *Zoonavena (C.) grandidieri* 74
  Mottle-throated ("Swift") *Chaetura (Telacanthura) ussheri* 62, 67
Swift
  Silver-rumped *C. (Rhaphidura) leucopygialis* 95
  Sabine's *C.(R.) sabini* 65
  Band-rumped *C. spinicauda* 24, 27, 30, 31, 47, 48
  Lesser Antillean *C. martinica* 26
  Gray-rumped *C. cinereiventris* 26–28, 31, 33, 45, 46
  Chimney *C. pelagica* 6, 7, 9, 25, 31, 35
  Vaux's *C. vauxi* 3, 12–14, 16–20, 22, 23, 28
  Chapman's *C. chapmani* 27, 47
  Short-tailed *C. brachyura* 24, 26–28, 33, 37, 47, 48
  Ashy-tailed *C. andrei* 30, 44, 46
  Scarce *Apus (Schoutedenapus) myoptilus* 65, 68
  Alpine *A. melba* 55, 58–60, 64, 65, 71–74, 86
  Mottled *A. aequatorialis* 64–66, 68
  African Black *A. barbatus (sladeniae)* 66, 70–72
  Nyanza *A. niansae* 65, 66
  Pallid *A. pallidus* 59, 60, 62, 78
  Plain *A. unicolor* 60, 61
  Common (Eurasian, The) *A. apus* 1, 50–62, 65–69, 74, 77, 78, 89
  Pacific (Fork-tailed, Large White-rumped) *A. pacificus* 1, 84, 87–94, 101, 103, 105, 107, 108
  House (Little) *A. affinis (nipalensis)* 60, 62–68, 71–73, 79, 82, 83, 86, 91–93, 95, 97
  Horus *A. horus* 66, 68–70, 73
  White-rumped (Long-tailed) *A. caffer* 59, 60, 64–66, 68, 71–73

White-throated *Aeronautes saxatalis* 10, 12–14, 16, 17, 21
White-tipped *A. montivagus* 28, 30, 32, 36
Andean *A. andecolus* 36, 38
Swallow-tailed Swift
  Great (Barranca) *Panyptila sanctihieronymi* 16
  Lesser (Jungle) *P. cayennensis* 19, 20, 24, 27, 28, 31, 33, 47, 48
Palm-Swift
  Antillean *Tachornis phoenicobia* 25
  Amazonian (Fork-tailed) *T. (Reinarda) squamata* 27, 29, 33, 37, 47, 48
  Asian *Cypsiurus balasiensis* 82, 86, 93, 95, 97, 98
  African *C. parvus* 62, 63, 67–70, 73, 74
  TREESWIFTS:*HEMIPROCNIDAE*
Treeswift
  Crested *Hemiprocne coronata* 85, 95, 98
  Moustached *H. mystacea* 94, 100
  Whiskered *H. comata* 94, 95, 97, 98
  HUMMINGBIRDS:*TROCHILIDAE*
Green-fronted Lancebill *Doryfera ludovicae* 22, 23, 31
Tooth-billed Hummingbird *Androdon aequatorialis* 31
Hermit
  Saw-billed *Ramphodon naevius* 46
  Rufous-breasted *Glaucis hirsuta* 24, 26–28, 30, 33, 37, 47, 48
  Pale-tailed Barbthroat *Threnetes leucurus* 33, 37, 47
  Band-tailed Barbthroat *T. ruckeri* 24, 30, 31
  White-whiskered *Phaethornis yaruqui* 31
  Green *P. guy* 22, 23, 27, 31
  Tawny-bellied *P. syrmatophorus* 31
  Long-tailed *P. superciliosus* 16, 19, 20, 24, 30, 33, 37, 47, 48
  Scale-throated *P. eurynome* 44, 45
  White-bearded *P. hispidus* 33, 37
  Pale-bellied *P. anthophilus* 28, 30
  Straight-billed *P. bourcieri* 33, 48
  Needle-billed *P. philippii* 37
  Dusky-throated *P. squalidus* 46
  Sooty-capped *P. augusti* 28
  Planalto *P. pretrei* 46
  Reddish *P. ruber* 37, 46–48

Little *P. longuemareus (adolphi)* 19, 20, 22, 24, 27, 28, 30, 31, 33, 48
Sicklebill
  White-tipped *Eutoxeres aquila* 31
  Buff-tailed *E. condamini* 36
Scaly-breasted Hummingbird *Phaeochroa cuvierii* 20, 74
Sabrewing
  Wedge-tailed *Campylopterus curvipennis* 18–20
  Gray-breasted *C. largipennis* 33, 37, 47, 48
  Rufous *C. rufus* 21
  Violet *C. hemileucurus* 22, 23
  White-tailed *C. ensipennis* 27
  Lazuline *C. falcatus* 28
Swallow-tailed Hummingbird *Eupetomena macroura* 46
Jacobin
  White-necked *Florisuga mellivora* 19, 20, 24, 27, 28, 30, 31, 37, 47, 48
  Black *Melanotrochilus fuscus* 45, 46
Violetear
  Brown *Colibri delphinae* 22, 27, 28, 30, 31
  Green *C. thalassinus* 17, 21–23, 28, 30–32, 36
  Sparkling *C. coruscans* 30–32, 36
  White-vented *C. serrirostris* 45, 46
Mango
  Green-throated *Anthracothorax viridigula* 27, 47, 48
  Green-breasted *A. prevostii* 18–20
  Black-throated *A. nigricollis* 24, 27–31, 44, 47, 48
  Jamaican *A. mango* 25
  Antillean *A. dominicus* 25
  Green *A. viridus* 25
Carib
  Purple-throated *Eulampis jugularis* 26
  Green-throated *Sericotes holosericeus* 25, 26
Hummingbird
  Ruby-topaz *Chrysolampis mosquitus* 27, 29, 30, 48
  Crested *Orthorhynchus cristatus* 25, 26
  Violet-headed *Klais guimeti* 28
Purple (Black)-breasted Plovercrest *Stephanoxis lalandi* 45
Coquette
  Tufted *Lophornis ornata* 27, 48
  Dot-eared *L. gouldii* 47

Spangled *L. stictolopha* 28
Black-crested *Paphosia helenae* 18, 20
Racquet-tailed *Discosura longicauda* 48
Thorntail
  Black-bellied *Popelairia langsdorffi* 46
  Green *P. conversii* 31
Blue-chinned Sapphire *Chlorestes notatus* 27, 47
Emerald
  Blue-tailed *Chlorostilbon mellisugus* 24, 27–33, 48
  Fork-tailed *C. canivetii (assimilis)* 16–20
  Glittering-bellied *C. aureoventris* 42–46
  Puerto Rican *C. maugaeus* 25
  Hispaniolan *C. swainsonii* 25
  Cuban *C. ricordii* 25
  Red-billed *C. gibsoni* 30
  Coppery *C. russatus* 30
Hummingbird
  Dusky *Cyanthus sordidus* 17
  Broad-billed *C. latirostris* 12, 16, 17
  Blue-headed *Cyanophaia bicolor* 26
Woodnymph
  Common (Fork-tailed, Green (Blue)-crowned) *Thalurania furcata (ridgwayi)* 16, 24, 30–31, 33, 37, 47, 48
  Violet-capped *T. glaucopis* 44–46
Hummingbird
  Fiery-throated *Panterpe insignis* 22, 23
  Violet-bellied *Damophila julie (panamensis)* 24
  Sapphire-throated *Lepidopyga coeruleogularis* 24
  Sapphire-bellied *L. lilliae* 30
  White-eared *Hylocharis leucotis* 12, 16, 17, 21
  Gilded *H. chrysura* 46
Sapphire
  Rufous-throated *H. sapphirina* 47, 48
  White-chinned *H. cyanus* 30, 37, 48
  Blue-headed *H. grayi* 31
  Golden-tailed *Chrysuronia oenone* 28, 33, 37
Streamertail *Trochilus polytmus* 25
White-throated Hummingbird *Leucochloris albicollis* 45
Goldenthroat
  White-tailed *Polytmus guainumbi* 27, 29, 48

Green-tailed *P. theresiae* 47, 48
Hummingbird
  Buffy *Leucippus fallax* 30
  White-bellied *Amazilia chionogaster* 19, 20
  Green-and-white *A. viridicauda* 36
  White-chested "Emerald" *A. chionopectus* 27
  Versicolored "Emerald" *A. versicolor* 46
  Glittering-throated "Emerald" *A. fimbriata* 28, 29, 33, 46, 48
  Sapphire-spangled "Emerald" *A. lactea* 37
  Blue-chested *A. amabilis (decora)* 24, 31
  Purple-chested *A. rosenbergi* 31
  Andean "Emerald" *A. franciae* 31
  Plain-bellied "Emerald" *A. leucogaster* 47, 48
  Red-billed "Azurecrown" *A. cyanocephala* 19, 21
  Berylline *A. beryllina* 16, 17
  Steely-vented *A. saucerrottei* 22, 30, 31
  Copper-rumped *A. tobaci* 27–29
  Snowy-breasted *A. edward* 23, 24
  Cinnamon *A. rutila* 16, 18, 19
  Buff-bellied *A. yucatanensis* 9, 18–20
  Rufous-tailed *A. tzacatl* 20, 22–24, 30, 31
  Amazilia *A. amazilia* 35
  Violet-crowned *A. violiceps* 12, 16, 17
  Stripe-tailed *Eupherusa eximia* 18, 22, 23
  White-tailed "Emerald" *Elvira chionura* 23
  Coppery-headed "Emerald" *E. cupreiceps* 22
White-vented Plumeleteer *Chalybura buffonii* 24, 28, 30
Mountaingem (Hummingbird)
  Blue-throated ("Hummingbird") *Lampornis clemenciae* 12, 16, 17
  Amethyst-throated *L. amethystinus* 21
  Green-throated *L. viridipallens* 21
  Variable (White-throated) *L. castaneoventris (calolaema)* 22, 23
  Garnet-throated *Lamprolaima rhami* 21
Speckled Hummingbird *Adelomyia melanogenys* 28, 31–33, 36
Blossomcrown *Anthocephala floriceps* 30

Whitetip *Urosticte benjamini* 31
Brazilian Ruby *Clytolaema rubricauda* 45
Gould's Jewelfront *Polyplancta aurescens* 33, 37
Brilliant
  Fawn-breasted *Heliodoxa rubinoides* 31
  Violet-fronted *H. leadbeateri* 28
  Green-crowned *H. jacula* 22, 23
  Empress *H. imperatrix* 31
Hummingbird
  Rivoli's (Magnificent) *Eugenes fulgens* 12, 16, 17, 21–23
  Violet-chested *Sternoclyta cyanopectus* 28
Topaz
  Crimson *Topaza pella* 47, 48
  Fiery *T. pyra* 33
Hillstar
  Andean *Oreotrochilus estella* 32, 36, 38
  White-sided *O. leucopleurus* 39
  Black-breasted *O. melanogaster* 36
  White-tailed *Urochroa bougueri* 31
Giant Hummingbird *Patagona gigas* 32, 35–39
Sunbeam
  Shining *Aglaeactis cupripennis* 32, 36
  White-tufted *A. castelnaudii* 36
Mountain Velvetbreast *Lafresnaya lafresnayi* 30, 32
Great Sapphirewing *Pterophanes cyanopterus* 32, 36
Inca
  Bronzy *Coeligena coeligena* 28
  Brown *C. wilsoni* 31
  Collared *C. torquata* 31, 32
Starfrontlet
  White-tailed *C. phalerata* 30
  Buff-winged *C. lutetiae* 32
  Violet-throated *C. violifer* 36
Sword-billed Hummingbird *Ensifera ensifera* 32, 36
Green-backed Firecrown *Sephanoides sephanoides* 39, 41
Coronet
  Buff-tailed *Boissonneaua flavescens* 31, 32
  Chestnut-breasted *B. matthewsii* 36
  Velvet-purple *B. jardini* 31
Sunangel
  Amethyst-throated *Heliangelus amethysticollis* 36

Purple-throated *H. viola* 32
Puffleg
  Sapphire-vented *Eriocnemis luciani* 32, 36
  Greenish *Haplophaedia aureliae* 31
Booted Racquet-tail *Ocreatus under-
    woodii* 28, 31
Trainbearer
  Black-tailed *Lesbia victoriae* 32, 36
  Green-tailed *L. nuna* 32, 36
Bronze-tailed Comet *Polyonymus caroli*
    38
Thornbill
  Purple-backed *Ramphomicron micro-
    rhynchum* 31, 32, 36
  Black-backed *R. dorsale* 30
Metaltail
  Black *Metallura phoebe* 38
  Scaled *M. aeneocauda* 36
  Tyrian *M. tyrianthina* 30, 32, 36
Blue-mantled Thornbill *Chalcostigma
    stanleyi* 32, 36
Sylph
  Long-tailed *Aglaiocercus kingi
    (emmae)* 28
  Violet-tailed *A. coelestis* 31
Bearded Mountaineer *Oreonympha nobi-
    lis* 36
Wedge-billed Hummingbird *Schistes
    geoffroyi* 31
Fairy
  Purple-crowned *Heliothryx barroti* 18,
    20, 23, 24, 31
  Black-eared *H. aurita* 33, 37, 47, 48
Starthroat
  Plain-capped *Heliomaster constantii* 16
  Long-billed *H. longirostris* 24, 27, 28,
    30, 31
Oasis Hummingbird *Rhodopis vesper* 35,
    38
Sheartail
  Peruvian *Thaumastura cora* 35, 38
  Slender *Doricha enicura* 21
  Mexican *D. eliza* 18
Woodstar
  Costa Rican *Philodice bryantae* 22, 23
  Purple-throated *P. mitchellii* 31
Hummingbird
  Sparkling-tailed *Tilmatura dupontii* 21
  Ruby-throated *Archilochus colubris*
    6–9, 16, 18, 21, 22, 25
  Black-chinned *A. alexandri* 9, 12, 13

Anna's *A. (Calypte) anna* 12–14
Costa's *A. (C.) costae* 12
Woodstar
  Bahama *Calliphlox (Philodice) eve-
    lynae* 25
  Amethyst *C. amethystina* 29, 45
Hummingbird
  Bee *Mellisuga (Calypte) helenae* 25
  Vervain *M. minima* 25
  Calliope *Stellula calliope* 10, 13, 16
  Bumblebee *Atthis heliosa* 17
  Wine-throated *A. ellioti* 21
Woodstar
  Purple-collared *Myrtis fanny* 35, 38
  White-bellied *Acestrura mulsant* 32, 36
  Gorgeted *A. heliodor* 30
Hummingbird
  Broad-tailed *Selasphorus platycercus*
    12, 17
  Rufous *S. rufus* 3, 9, 10, 12–14, 16, 17
  Allen's *S. sasin* 13, 14
  Volcano *S. flammula* 22, 23
  Scintillant *S. scintilla* 22, 23
    MOUSEBIRDS:*COLIIDAE*
Mousebird
  Speckled *Colius striatus* 64–68, 71–73
  White-backed *C. colius* 71
  White-headed *C. leucocephalus* 66
  Red-faced *C. indicus* 68–73
  Blue-naped *C. macrourus* 62, 64, 66,
    67
    TROGONS:*TROGONIDAE*
Quetzal
  Resplendent (The) *Pharomachrus mo-
    cinno* 22, 23
  Crested *P. antisianus* 31
  White-tipped *P. fulgidus* 28, 30
  Pavonine *P. pavoninus* 37
Trogon
  Cuban *Priotelus temnurus* 25
  Hispaniolan *Temnotrogon roseigaster*
    25
  Slaty-tailed (Massena) *Trogon massena*
    18–20, 24, 31
  Black-tailed *T. melanurus* 24, 33, 37,
    47, 48
  Blue-tailed *T. comptus* 31
  White-tailed *T. viridis* 24, 27, 31, 33, 37,
    47, 48
  Citreoline (White-eyed) *T. citreolus
    (melanocephalus)* 16, 18–20
  Mountain (Mexican) *T. mexicanus* 16

Elegant (Coppery-tailed) *T. elegans* 12, 16, 17, 21

Collared (Bar-tailed) *T. collaris* 20, 22, 23, 27, 28, 31, 37, 48

Orange-bellied *T. aurantiiventris* 23

Masked *T. personatus* 30, 31

Black-throated *T. rufus* 24, 44, 45, 47, 48

Surucua *T. surrucura* 44, 45

Blue-crowned *T. curucui* 33, 37, 43

Violaceous *T. violaceus* 18–20, 24, 27, 30, 31, 33, 37, 47, 48

Narina *Apaloderma narina* 64–68, 72

Bar-tailed *A. (Heterotrogon) vittatum* 65, 66, 68

Indian (Malabar) *Harpactes fasciatus* 86

Red-naped *H. kasumba* 94

Diard's *H. diardii* 94

Philippine *H. ardens* 97

Whitehead's *H. whiteheadi* 96

Cinnamon-rumped *H. orrhophaeus* 94, 96

Orange-breasted *H. oreskios* 93, 94, 96

Red-headed *H. erythrocephalus* 93

KINGFISHERS:*ALCEDINIDAE*

Kingfisher

Crested *Ceryle lugubris* 87, 88

Giant *C. maxima* 62–66, 68–73

Ringed *C. torquata* 9, 16, 19, 24, 26, 29–31, 33, 37, 42–44, 46–48

Belted *C. alcyon* 2, 3, 6–10, 12–14, 16–20, 24–27, 30

Pied *C. rudis* 62–64, 66–70, 72, 73, 77–79, 81, 82, 85, 86, 92

Amazon *Chloroceryle amazona* 19, 24, 28–31, 33, 37, 43, 44, 48

Green-and-rufous *C. inda* 33, 37, 47, 48

Green *C. americana* 9, 12, 16–19, 24, 27–31, 33, 37, 42, 43, 47, 48

American Pygmy *C. aenea* 19, 27, 29, 30, 33, 37, 47, 48

Eurasian (Common, River, The) *Alcedo atthis* 51–53, 55–60, 77, 78, 81, 82, 85–92, 95, 97, 98

Half-collared *A. semitorquata* 68–70

Blue-eared *A. meninting* 85, 86, 93–95, 97

Shining Blue *A. quadribrachys* 63, 64

Dwarf River *A. (Ceyx) cyanopectus* 97

Silvery *A. (C.) argentatus* 97

Malachite *Corythornis (Alcedo) cristata* 62–64, 66–70, 72–74

African Pygmy *C. (Ispidina) picta* 62–69, 72

Madagascar Pygmy *C.(I.) madagascariensis* 74

Dwarf *C. (Myioceyx) lecontei* 64

Azure *Alcyone (Ceyx) azureus* 99–101, 105–108

Little *A.(C.) pusillus* 100, 101

Black-backed (Three-toed) *Ceyx erithacus* 86, 94, 96, 97

Rufous-backed *C. rufidorsum* 94, 95, 98

Stork-billed *Pelargopsis capensis* 85, 86, 93–95, 97

Banded *Lacedo pulchella* 93, 94, 96

Kookaburra

Laughing *Dacelo novaeguineae (gigas)* 103–108, 111

Blue-winged *D. leachii* 100, 101, 108

Rufous-bellied *D. gaudichaud* 100

Kingfisher

Ruddy *Halcyon coromanda* 87, 88, 95, 97

Chocolate-backed *H. badia* 64

White-breasted (throated) *H. smyrnensis* 79, 81–83, 85, 86, 92, 93, 95, 97

Black-capped *H. pileata* 86, 89, 90, 92, 93, 95, 97

Java *H. cyanoventris* 98

Gray-headed *H. leucocephala* 62–64, 66–70

Woodland *H. senegalensis (cyanoleuca)* 62–66, 68, 69, 72, 73

Mangrove (Coastal) *H. senegaloides* 67

Blue-breasted *H. malimbica* 62–64

Brown-hooded *H. albiventris* 67–70, 72, 73

Striped *H. chelicuti* 62, 64–70, 72, 73

Macleay's (Forest) *H. macleayii* 100, 101, 107, 108

Red-backed *H. pyrrhopygia* 101, 102, 104

Lowland Yellow-billed *H. torotoro* 100

Mountain Yellow-billed *H. megarhyncha* 99, 100

Sacred *H. sancta* 99–101, 103–109, 111

White-collared (Collared, Mangrove) *H. chloris* 95, 97, 98, 101, 108, 110

Rufous (Chestnut)-collared *H. concreta* 94, 96

Paradise-Kingfisher
  Common *Tanysiptera galatea* 100
  White-tailed (Buff-breasted) *T. sylvia*
    108
        TODIES:*TODIDAE*
Tody
  Cuban *Todus multicolor* 25
  Narrow-billed *T. angustirostris* 25
  Puerto Rican *T. mexicanus* 25
  Jamaican *T. todus* 25
  Broad-billed *T. subulatus* 25
        MOTMOTS:*MOMOTIDAE*
Motmot
  Tody *Hylomanes momotula* 20
  Blue-throated *Aspatha gularis* 21
  Broad-billed *Electron platyrhynchum*
    24, 31, 33, 37
  Keel-billed *E. carinatum* 19
  Turquoise-browed *Eumomota super-
    ciliosa* 18
  Rufous *Baryphthengus ruficapillus* 24,
    31, 33, 37, 44–46
  Russet-crowned *Momotus mexicanus*
    16
  Blue-crowned *M. momota* 18–20, 22,
    24, 27, 30, 31, 33, 36, 37, 47
        BEE-EATERS:*MEROPIDAE*
Bee-eater
  Red-bearded *Nyctyornis amicta* 94, 96
  Blue-bearded *N. athertoni* 85, 93
  Black *Merops gularis* 63, 64
  Blue-headed *M. muelleri* 65
  Red-throated *M. bulocki* 62
  White-fronted *M. bullockoides* 66, 68–
    70, 72, 73
  Little *M. pusillus* 62–70, 72, 73
  Blue-breasted *M. variegatus* 64
  Cinnamon-chested *M. oreobates* 64–66
  Swallow-tailed *M. hirundinaceus* 62,
    68–70
  Somali *M. revoilii* 66
  White-throated *M. albicollis* 62–67
  Green *M. orientalis* 62, 78, 82, 85, 86
  Boehm's *M. boehmi* 68
  Blue-throated *M. viridis (bicolor)* 93,
    95, 98
  Blue-cheeked (Madagascar) *M. super-
    ciliosus (persicus)* 62, 64–67, 69, 74,
    77, 78, 82
  Blue-tailed *M. philippinus* 82, 85, 86,
    93, 95, 97
  Rainbow *M. ornatus* 98–104, 106–108

Eurasian (European, The) *M. apiaster*
    51–53, 55–60, 62, 65–68, 70–73, 77,
    78, 81
Chestnut-headed *M. leschenaulti* 85,
    86, 93, 97, 98
Rosy *M. malimbicus* 63
Northern Carmine *M. nubicus* 62, 66,
    67
Southern Carmine *M. nubicoides* 68,
    69, 73
        ROLLERS:*CORACIIDAE*
Roller
  Eurasian (European, The) *Coracias
    garrulus* 55–61, 63, 64, 66–69, 72, 73,
    76–78, 81
  Abyssinian *C. abyssinica* 62
  Lilac-breasted *C. caudata* 66–70, 73
  Racquet-tailed *C. spatulata* 68, 69
  Rufous-crowned *C. naevia* 62, 66–68,
    72, 73
  Indian *C. benghalensis* 79, 82, 85,
    86
  Blue-bellied *C. cyanogaster* 62
  Cinnamon (Broad-billed) *Eurystomus
    glaucurus* 62–70, 72, 74
  Blue-throated *E. gularis* 63, 64
  Dollar ("Dollarbird," Eastern Broad-
    billed) *E. orientalis (pacificus)* 85, 86,
    93, 95, 97, 99–101, 106–108
        GROUND-ROLLERS:
        BRACHYPTERACIIDAE
Ground-Roller
  Short-legged   *Brachypteracias lep-
    tosomus* 74
  Scaled *B. squamigera* 74
  Pitta-like *B. pittoides* 74
  Crossley's *Atelornis crossleyi* 74
  Long-tailed *Uratelornis chimaera* 74
        CUCKOO-ROLLER:
        LEPTOSOMATIDAE
Cuckoo-Roller (Kirombo Courol) *Lep-
    tosomus discolor* 74
        HOOPOE:*UPUPIDAE*
Hoopoe (Northern, African) *Upupa epops
    (africana)* 55–62, 64, 66, 68–74, 77–
    79, 81–86, 89, 90
WOOD-HOOPOES:*PHOENICULIDAE*
Wood-Hoopoe
  Green (Red-billed) *Phoeniculus pur-
    pureus* 62, 64, 66–70, 72, 73
  White-headed *P. bollei* 65, 66
  Black *P. aterrimus* 62, 63

Scimitarbill
   Abyssinian *P. (Rhinopomastus) Minor*
      66
   Southern (The) *P. (R.) cyanomelas* 64,
      66–70, 62, 63
      HORNBILLS:*BUCEROTIDAE*
Hornbill
   African Gray *Tockus nasutus* 62–64,
      66, 68–70, 63
   Red-billed *T. erythrorhynchus* 62, 66,
      69, 70, 72, 73
   Von der Decken's *T. deckeni* 66
   Yellow-billed *T. flavirostris* 66, 68, 70,
      72, 73
   Hemprich's *T. hemprichii* 66
   Pale-billed *T. pallidirostris* 68
   Dwarf *T. camurus* 63
   African Pied *T. fasciatus* 62, 63
   Crowned *T. alboterminatus* 64–69, 72,
      73
   Malabar Gray *T. griseus (gingalensis)*
      86
   Indian Gray *T. birostris* 79, 82
   White-crested *Tropicranus (Berenicor-
      nis) albocristatus* 63
   Yellow-casqued *Ceratogymna elata* 62
   Piping *Bycanistes fistulator* 62
   Trumpeter *B. bucinator* 67–70, 72
   Gray-cheeked   (Black-and-white
      Casqued) *B. subcylindricus* 64–67
   Silvery-cheeked *B. brevis* 66–68
   Malabar Pied *Anthracoceros coronatus*
      85, 86
   Indian Pied *A. albirostris malabaricus*
      93
   Southern Pied *A. convexus (albirostris)*
      98
   Black *A. malayanus* 94
   Palawan *A. marchei* 97
   Bushy-crested *Anorrhinus galeritus*
      94
   Writhed-billed   *Rhyticeros   (Aceros)
      leucocephalus* 97
   Wreathed *R. (A.) undulatus* 93, 94, 96,
      98
   Rhinoceros *Buceros rhinoceros* 94, 96
   Great *B. bicornis* 97
   Helmeted *Rhinoplax vigil* 94, 96
   Abyssinian Ground *Bucorvus abys-
      sinicus* 62
   Southern Ground *B. cafer (leadbeateri)*
      66, 68, 69, 72, 73

      JACAMARS:*GALBULIDAE*
Jacamar
   Chestnut (White-eared) *Galbalcyrhyn-
      chus leucotis (purusianus)* 33
   Brown *Brachygalba lugubris* 33, 48
   Pale-headed *B. goeringi* 29
   Yellow-billed   *Galbula   albirostris
      (cyanicollis)* 47, 48
   Green-tailed *G. galbula* 48
   Rufous-tailed   *G.   ruficauda* 19, 20,
      27–31
   White-chinned *G. tombacea* 33
   Bluish-fronted *G. cyanescens* 37
   Bronzy *G. leucogastra* 33
   Paradise *G. dea* 37, 47, 48
   Great *Jacamerops aurea* 37, 48
      PUFFBIRDS:*BUCCONIDAE*
Puffbird
   White-necked *Notharchus macrorhyn-
      chus* 19, 20, 24, 28, 30, 33, 37, 44, 47,
      48
   Black-breasted *N. pectoralis* 24, 31
   Pied *N. tectus* 24, 30, 31, 47, 48
   Chestnut-capped *Bucco macrodactylus*
      33
   Spotted *B. tamatia* 48
   Collared *B. capensis* 33, 47, 48
   Barred *Nystalus radiatus* 31
   White-eared *N. chacuru* 44, 45
   Striolated *N. striolatus* 37, 47
   Russet-throated   *Hypnelus   ruficollis*
      28–30
   Crescent-chested   *Malacoptila   striata*
      46
   White-chested *M. fusca* 33, 48
   Semicollared *M. semicincta* 37
   Rufous-necked *M. rufa* 47
   White-whiskered *M. panamensis* 19,
      20, 24, 31
   Moustached *M. mystacalis* 28, 31
   Lanceolated Monklet *Micromonacha
      lanceolata* 31, 33
Nunlet
   Rusty-breasted *Nonnula rubecula* 44
   Brown *N. brunnea* 33
Nunbird
   Black (White-winged) *Monasa atra* 48
   Black-fronted (Uniform) *M. nigrifrons*
      33, 37
   White-fronted *M. morphoeus* 33, 37,
      47
   Yellow-billed *M. flavirostris* 33

Aerial Puffbird ("Swallow-wing") *Cheli-doptera tenebrosa* 29, 33, 37, 47, 48
BARBETS:*CAPITONIDAE*
Barbet
Scarlet-crowned *Capito aurovirens* 33
Spot-crowned *C. maculicoronatus* 24, 31
Black-spotted *C. niger* 33, 37, 48
Lemon-throated *Eubucco richardsoni* 33, 37
Red-headed *E. bourcierii* 22, 23, 31
Prong-billed *Semnornis frantzii* 22, 23
Toucan *S. ramphastinus* 31
Great Himalayan *Megalaima virens* 79, 83, 92
Brown-headed (Green) *M. zeylanica* 82, 86
Lineated *M. lineata* 85, 93, 98
Green-eared *M. faiostricta* 93
Gold-whiskered *M. chrysopogon* 94, 96
Red-crowned *M. rafflesii* 94, 95
Red-throated (Gaudy) *M. mystacophanos* 94, 96
Yellow-fronted *M. flavifrons* 86
Golden-throated *M. franklinii* 83
Black-browed (Muller's) *M. oorti* 91
Mountain *M. monticola* 96
Blue-throated *M. asiatica* 83, 85
Moustached *M. incognita* 93
Yellow-crowned *M. henricii* 94, 96
Blue-crowned *M. armillaris* 98
Golden-naped *M. pulcherrima* 96
Blue-eared (Little) *M. australis* 93–96, 98
Black-throated *M. eximia* 96
Crimson-throated *M. rubricapilla* 86
Coppersmith *M. haemacephala* 79, 82, 83, 86, 93, 96–98
Brown *Calorhamphus fuliginosus* 94, 95
Naked-faced *Gymnobucco calvus* 63
Bristle-nosed *G. peli* 63
Gray-throated *G. bonapartei* 64, 65
White-eared *Stactolaema (Buccanodon) leucotis* 68, 72
Green *Pogoniulus (B.) olivaceus* 67, 68
Yellow-spotted *P. duchaillui* 63, 65
Tinkerbird
Speckled *P. scolopaceus* 63–65
Green *P. simplex* 67
Red-fronted *P. pusillus* 66, 67, 72

Yellow-fronted *P. chrysoconus* 62, 64, 68–70
Lemon-rumped *P. leucolaima* 62–64
Golden-rumped *P. bilineatus* 65–68, 72
Yellow-throated *P. subsulphureus* 64
Red-rumped *P. atroflavus* 62
Barbet
Spot-flanked *Lybius (Tricholaema) lacrymosus* 64, 66
Pied *L. (T.) leucomelas* 70, 72, 73
Red-fronted *L. (T.) diadematus* 66
Hairy-breasted *L. (T.) flavipunctatus (hirsutus)* 63–65
Vieillot's *L. vieilloti* 62
Black-collared *L. torquatus* 66–70, 72, 73
White-headed *L. leucocephalus* 64, 66
Brown-breasted *L. melanopterus* 66
Double-toothed *L. bidentatus* 63, 64, 66
Bearded *L. dubius* 62
Yellow-billed *Trachyphonus purpuratus* 63–65
Crested (Levaillant's) *T. vaillantii* 68, 69, 72, 73
Red-and-yellow *T. erythrocephalus* 66
D'Arnaud's (Black-billed Ground, Pale-billed Ground) *T. darnaudii (usambiro)* 66
HONEYGUIDES:*INDICATORIDAE*
Honeyguide
Scaly (-throated) *Indicator variegatus* 65–68, 72
Spotted *I. maculatus* 62
Black-throated (Greater) *I. indicator* 62, 64–70, 72
Lesser *I. minor* 63–69, 72
Thick-billed *I. conirostris (minor)* 64, 65
Least *I. exilis* 63, 65, 68
Chapin's (C. Least, Dwarf) *I. pumilio* 65
Himalayan (Yellow-rumped) *I. xanthonotus* 84
Cassin's *Prodotiscus insignis* 64–68
TOUCANS:*RAMPHASTIDAE*
Toucanet
Emerald (Blue-throated) *Aulacorhynchus prasinus (caeruleogularis)* 20, 22, 23, 30, 31, 37
Groove (Yellow)-billed *A. sulcatus (calorhynchus)* 28, 30

Crimson-rumped *A. haematopygus* 31

Aracari

Green *Pteroglossus viridis* 48

Lettered *P. inscriptus* 33, 37, 47

Red-necked *P. bitorquatus* 47

Ivory-billed *P. flavirostris* 33

Brown-mandibled *P. mariae (flavirostris)* 37

Black-necked *P. aracari* 47, 48

Chestnut-eared *P. castanotis* 33, 37, 44

Many-banded *P. pluricinctus* 33

Collared *P. torquatus* 19, 20, 24, 30

Fiery-billed *P. frantzii* 23

Stripe-billed *P. sanguineus* 31

Curl-crested *P. beauharnaesii* 37

Toucanet

Spot-billed *Selenidera maculirostris (gouldii)* 45, 47

Golden-collared *S. reinwardtii* 33, 37

Guianan *S. culik* 48

Yellow-eared *S. spectabilis* 24

Saffron *Baillonius bailloni* 44, 45

Plate-billed Mountain-Toucan *Andigena laminirostris* 32

Toucan

Red-breasted *Ramphastos dicolorus* 44, 45

Channel-billed *R. vitellinus* 27, 47, 48

Yellow-ridged *R. culminatus (vitellinus)* 33, 37

Keel-billed *R. sulfuratus* 19, 20, 24, 30

Toco *R. toco* 43, 44

Red-billed *R. tucanus* 47, 48

Cuvier's *R. cuvieri (tucanus)* 33, 37

Yellow-throated (Chestnut (Black)-mandibled) *R. ambiguus (swainsoni)* 24, 31

WOODPECKERS:*PICIDAE*

Wryneck

Eurasian (Northern, The) *Jynx torquilla* 50, 51, 53, 55–58, 60, 66, 77, 79, 87, 88, 90, 91

Red-breasted (African) *J. ruficollis* 64, 66, 72

Piculet

Speckled (Spotted) *Picumnus innominatus* 83

Gold-fronted *P. aurifrons* 33, 37

Golden-spangled *P. exilis* 48

Scaled *P. squamulatus* 28, 29

Arrowhead *P. minutissimus* 48

White-barred *P. cirratus* 43, 45, 46

Rufous-breasted *P. rufiventris* 33

Olivaceous *P. olivaceus* 31

Grayish *P. granadensis* 31

Chestnut *P. cinnamomeus* 30

Rufous *Sasia abnormis* 96, 98

White-browed (Rufous) *S. ochracea* 85

Antillean *Nesoctites micromegas* 25

Woodpecker

White *Melanerpes (Leuconerpes) candidus* 43

Lewis's *M. (Asyndesmus) lewis* 12

Guadeloupe *M. herminieri* 26

Puerto Rican *M. portoricensis* 25

Red-headed *M. erythrocephalus* 6–9

Acorn *M. formicivorus* 12–14, 16, 17, 19, 21–23, 31

Yellow-tufted *M. cruentatus* 33, 37, 47, 48

Yellow-fronted *M. flavifrons* 44–46

Black-cheeked *M. (Centrurus) pucherani* 19, 20, 24, 31

Hispaniolan *M. striatus* 25

Jamaican *M. radiolatus* 25

Golden-cheeked (Orange-naped) *M. (Centrurus) chrysogenys* 16

Red-crowned *M. rubricapillus* 24, 27–30

Yucatan (Red-vented) *M. (Centrurus) pygmaeus* 18, 19

Gila *M. (C.) uropygialis* 12, 16

Golden-fronted (Hoffmann's) *M. (C.) aurifrons* 9, 18–22

Red-bellied (Southeastern) *M. (C.) carolinus* 7–9

Sapsucker

Yellow-bellied (Red-breasted, Red-naped) *Sphyrapicus varius (nuchalis, ruber)*, 3, 6–10, 12–14, 16, 17, 21, 22, 25

Williamson's *S. thyroideus* 10, 12, 13

Woodpecker

Cuban Green *Xiphidiopicus percussus* 25

Fine-spotted *Campethera punctuligera* 62

Bennett's *C. bennettii* 68, 69, 73

Nubian *C. nubica* 64, 66

Golden-tailed *C. abingoni* 67, 68, 70, 72, 73

African (Little) Spotted *C. cailliauti* 64, 68

Fine-banded *C. tullbergi (taeniolaema)* 65, 66

Buff-spotted *C. nivosa* 63, 65
Brown-eared *C. caroli* 64, 65
Ground *Geocolaptes olivaceus* 71
Cardinal *Dendropicos fuscescens (lafresneyi)* 62, 65–70, 72, 73
Melancholy *D. lugubris (gabonensis)* 63
Stierling's *D. stierlingi* 68
Bearded *D. (Thripias) namaquus* 66, 68–70, 73
Yellow-crested *D. (T., Mesopicos) xantholophus* 65
Fire-bellied *D. (M.) pyrrhogaster* 63
Gray *D. (M.) goertae* 62, 63, 66
Olive *D. (M.) griseocephalus* 72
Philippine Pygmy *Picoides (Dendrocopos) maculatus* 97
Brown-capped (Indian Pygmy) *P. (D.) moluccensis* 86, 95, 96
Japanese Pygmy *P. (D.) kizuki* 97, 98
Gray-capped (-headed, Pygmy) *P. (D.) canicapillus (hardwickii)* 82, 85, 91, 95, 96
Lesser Spotted *P. (D.) minor* 51–58, 87
Fulvous-breasted Pied *P. (D.) macei (analis)* 80, 83, 85
Brown-fronted Pied *P. (D.) auriceps* 80, 81, 83
Yellow-fronted Pied *P. (D.) mahrattensis* 79, 82, 86
Rufous-bellied ("Sapsucker") *P. (D.) hyperythrus* 83, 84
Darjeeling Pied *P. (D.) darjellensis* 83, 84
Middle Spotted *P. (D.) medius* 53, 55–57
White-backed *P. (D.) leucotos* 87, 88, 91
Himalayan Pied *P. (D.) himalayensis* 80
Sind Pied *P. (D.) assimilis* 79
Syrian *P. (D.) syriacus* 55–57
Great Spotted *P. (D.) major* 50–61, 87–90
Checkered *P. (D.) mixtus* 43
Striped *P. (D.) lignarius* 39
Ladder-backed *P. (D.) scalaris* 9, 12, 16–18
Nuttall's *P. (D.) nuttallii* 13, 14
Downy *P. (D.) pubescens* 2, 3, 6–10, 13, 14
Red-cockaded *P. (D.) borealis* 8, 9
Brown-barred *P. (D.) stricklandi* 17

Arizona *P. (D.) arizonae (stricklandi)* 12, 16
Hairy *P. (D.) villosus* 2, 3, 6–8, 10, 12–14, 17, 21–23, 25
White-headed *P. (D.) albolarvatus* 13
Northern Three-toed *P. tridactylus* 2, 3, 5, 10, 13, 14
Black-backed (American) Three-toed *P. arcticus* 2, 10
Yellow-vented *Venilornis dignus* 31
Bar-bellied *V. nigriceps* 36
Smoky-brown *V. fumigatus* 19, 20, 22, 23, 28, 30, 31
Little *V. passerinus* 37, 43
White-spotted *V. spilogaster* 44, 45
Blood-colored *V. sanguineus* 48
Yellow-eared *V. maculifrons* 46
Red-stained *V. affinis* 33, 37, 47
Golden-collared *V. cassini* 48
Red-rumped *V. kirkii* 27–30
White-throated *Piculus leucolaemus* 31, 33, 37, 48
Yellow-throated *P. flavigula* 37, 46, 47
Golden-green *P. chrysochloros* 47, 48
White-browed *P. aurulentus* 44, 45
Golden-olive *P. rubiginosus* 19, 21–23, 27, 28, 30, 31, 48
Gray-crowned *P. auricularis* 16
Crimson-mantled *P. rivolii* 32, 36
Flicker
   Spot-breasted *Colaptes (Chrysoptilus) punctigula* 29–31, 33, 48
   Green-barred *C. (C.) melanochloros* 43–45
   Golden-breasted *C. (C.) melanolaimus (melanochloros)* 42
   Northern (Common, Yellow-[Red-] shafted, Gilded) *Colaptes auratus (cafer, chrysoides)* 2, 3, 5–14, 16, 17, 21, 25
   Fernandina's *C. fernandinae* 25
   Chilean *C. pitius* 39, 41
   Andean *C. rupicola* 36, 38
   Campo (Field) *C. campestris (campestroides)* 42, 43, 45, 46
Woodpecker
   Rufous *Celeus (Micropternus) brachyurus* 86, 94–96
   Cinnamon *C. loricatus* 24, 31
   Waved *C. undatus* 47, 48
   Scale-breasted *C. grammicus* 33, 37
   Chestnut-colored *C. castaneus* 20

Chestnut (Elegant) *C. elegans* 27, 33, 37, 47, 48
Pale-crested *C. lugubris* 43
Blond-crested *C. flavescens* 44
Cream-colored *C. flavus* 33, 37, 47, 48
Rufous-headed *C. spectabilis* 37
Ringed *C. torquatus* 47
Lineated *Dryocopus lineatus* 16, 18–20, 24, 27–31, 33, 37, 44, 47, 48
Pileated *D. pileatus* 3, 7–9
White-bellied *D. javensis* 95, 97, 98
Black *D. martius* 52, 53, 55, 57, 87, 88
Crimson-bellied *Campephilus (Phloeoceastes) haematogaster* 31
Red-necked *C. (P.) rubricollis* 37, 47, 48
Robust *C. (P.) robustus* 44, 45
Pale-billed *C. (P.) guatemalensis* 16, 18–20
Crimson-crested *C. (P.) melanoleucos* 24, 27–31, 33, 37, 43, 47, 48
Cream-backed *C. (P.) leucopogon* 43, 44
Magellanic *C. magellanicus* 41
Ivory-billed *C. principalis* 25
Banded *Picus miniaceus* 94–96
Crimson-winged *P. puniceus* 94–96
Lesser Yellow-naped *P. chlorolophus* 83, 84, 86
Checker-throated *P. mentalis* 94, 96
Laced *P. vittatus* 98
Little Scaly-bellied Green (Streak-throated) *P. xanthopygaeus* 86
Scaly-bellied (Large) *P. squamatus* 80, 84
Japanese Green *P. awokera* 88
Gray-headed (Black-naped Green) *P. canus* 56, 57, 83, 87, 89–91, 94, 98
European (The) Green *P. viridis* 51–53, 57–60
Olive-backed *Dinopium rafflesii* 94, 95, 96
Golden-backed Woodpecker
    Himalayan *D. shorii* 85
    Common *D. javanense* 79, 95, 97, 98
    Lesser (Black-rumped) *D. benghalense* 82, 86
    Greater *Chrysocolaptes lucidus* 85, 97
Woodpecker
    Black-backed *C. festivus* 86
    Bamboo *Gecinulus viridis* 95
    Maroon *Blythipicus rubiginosus* 96

Orange-backed *Reinwardtipicus (Chrysocolaptes) validus* 94–96
Buff-rumped *Meiglyptes tristis* 94, 95
Buff-necked *M. tukki* 94, 95
Gray-and-buff *Hemicircus concretus* 95
Sooty *Mulleripicus funebris* 97
Great Slaty *M. pulverulentus* 94, 95, 97, 98
BROADBILLS:*EURYLAIMIDAE*
Broadbill
    African *Smithornis capensis* 65, 68, 69, 72
    Black-and-red *Cymbirhynchus macrorhynchus* 95, 96
    Banded *Eurylaimus javanicus* 93, 95
    Black-and-yellow *E. steerii* 97
    Silver-breasted *Serilophus lunatus* 93
    Long-tailed *Psarisomus dalhousiae* 93, 96
    Green *Calyptomena viridis* 94, 96
    Whitehead's *C. whiteheadi* 96
    Dusky *Corydon sumatranus* 96
    WOODCREEPERS: *DENDROCOLAPTIDAE*
Woodcreeper (Woodhewer)
    Plain-brown *Dendrocincla fuliginosa* 24, 27, 28, 30, 31, 33, 37, 44–48
    Tawny-winged *D. anabatina* 19, 20
    Ruddy *D. homochroa* 19, 20, 22
    Long-tailed *Deconychura longicauda* 24, 37
    Olivaceous *Sittasomus griseicapillus* 19, 20, 22, 27–28, 33, 37, 43–46
    Wedge-billed *Glyphorhynchus spirurus* 19, 20, 22, 24, 31, 33, 36, 37, 47, 48
    Long-billed *Nasica longirostris* 33, 47
    Cinnamon-throated *Dendrexetastes rufigula* 33, 37, 47
    Bar-bellied *Hylexetastes stresemanni* 31
    Strong-billed *Xiphocolaptes promeropirhynchus* 20, 28, 30
    White-throated *X. albicollis* 44, 45
    Great Rufous *X. major* 43
    Barred *Dencrocolaptes certhia* 20, 31, 33, 37, 47, 48
    Black-banded *D. picumnus* 28, 37, 48
    Straight-billed *Xiphorhynchus picus* 27–30, 33, 37, 47, 48
    Striped *X. obsoletus* 47
    Ocellated *X. ocellatus* 33, 37
    Spix's *X. spixii* 37, 47
    Chestnut-rumped *X. pardalotus* 48

Buff-throated *X. guttatus* 27

Ivory-billed *X. flavigaster* 16, 18–20

Black-striped *X. lachrymosus* 24

Spotted *X. erythropygius* 22, 31

Olive-backed *X. triangularis* 28, 31

White-striped *Lepidocolaptes leucogaster* 16, 17

Streak-headed *L. souleyetii* 19, 24, 27–29

Narrow-billed *L. angustirostris* 42, 43

Spot-crowned *L. affinis* 21, 23, 30, 31

Scaled *L. squamatus* 45

Lesser *L. fuscus* 46

Lineated *L. albolineatus* 37, 48

Scythebill

Red-billed *Campylorhamphus trochilirostris* 28, 31, 37, 43

Brown-billed *C. pusillus* 31

Curve-billed *C. procurvoides* 33

OVENBIRDS:*FURNARIIDAE*

Miner

Common *Geositta cunicularia* 36, 38, 39, 41, 42

Grayish *G. maritima* 35

Coastal *G. peruviana* 35

Puna *G. punensis* 38

Creamy-rumped *G. isabellina* 39

Rufous-banded *G. rufipennis* 39

Thick-billed *G. crassirostris* 38

Stout-billed ("Cinclodes") *G. (Cinclodes) excelsior* 32

Slender-billed *G. tenuirostris* 38

Earthcreeper

Straight-billed *Upucerthia ruficauda* 38, 39

White-throated *U. albigula* 38

Scale-throated *U. dumetaria* 38, 39, 41

Buff-breasted *U. validirostris* 38

Cinclodes

Bar-winged (Common) *Cinclodes fuscus* 32, 36, 38, 39, 41

White-winged *C. atacamensis* 36, 38, 39

Gray-flanked *C. oustaleti* 39

Dark-bellied *C. patagonicus* 39, 41

Seaside (Surf) *C. nigrofumosus* 35, 39

Blackish *C. antarcticus* 40

Crag Chilia *Chilia melanura* 39

Hornero

Pale-legged *Furnarius leucopus* 30, 37

Rufous *F. rufus* 42, 43, 45, 46

Des Mur's Wiretail *Sylviorthorhynchus desmursii* 39, 41

Thorn-tailed Rayadito *Aphrastura spinicauda* 39, 41

Tit-Spinetail

Tufted *Leptasthenura platensis* 42

Plain-mantled *L. aegithaloides* 38, 39, 41, 42

Streaked *L. striata* 38

Andean *L. andicola* 32, 38

Thistletail

White-chinned *Schizoeaca fuliginosa* 32

Puna *S. helleri (fuliginosa)* 36

Spinetail

Itatiaia *S. (Oreophylax) moreirae* 45

Chotoy *Synallaxis (Schoeniphylax) phryganophila* 42, 43

Rufous-capped *S. ruficapilla* 44, 45

Sooty-fronted *S. frontalis* 43

Azara's *S. azarae* 31, 32, 36

Dark-breasted *S. albigularis* 33

Pale-breasted *S. albescens* 27–31, 43, 48

Chicli *S. spixi* 45

Slaty *S. brachyura* 23, 31

Cabanis's *S. cabanisi* 48

Gray-bellied *S. cinerascens* 44

Plain-crowned *S. gujanensis* 37, 47, 48

Rufous *S. unirufa* 31, 32

Rusty (Coastal Range) *S. castanea (unirufa)* 28

Rusty-headed *S. fuscorufa* 30

Rufous-breasted *S. erythrothorax* 19

Stripe-breasted *S. cinnamomea* 27, 28

White-browed *S. gularis* 32

White-whiskered *S. (Poecilurus) candei* 30

Red-faced *Certhiaxis (Cranioleuca) erythrops* 22, 23, 31

Pallid *C. (C.) pallida* 45

Olive *C. (C.) obsoleta* 44

Streak-capped *C. (C.) hellmayri* 30

Crested (Venezuelan Tree) *C. (C.) subcristata* 28

Stripe-crowned *C. (C.) pyrrhophia* 43

Marcapata *C. (C.) marcapatae* 36

Creamy-crested *C. (C.) albicapilla* 36

Speckled *C. (C.) gutturata* 33, 37

Yellow-throated (Marsh) *C. cinnamomea* 27, 29, 30, 43, 44, 46, 48

Canastero
  Lesser *Tripophaga (Asthenes) pyrr-holeuca* 39, 41
  Canyon *T. (A.) pudibunda* 38
  Rusty-fronted *T. (A.) ottonis* 36
  Cordilleran *T. (A.) modesta* 38, 39
  Cactus *T. (A.) cactorum* 35, 38
  Creamy-breasted *T. (A.) dorbignyi* 38
  Dusky-tailed *T. (A.) humicola* 39
  Patagonian *T. (A.) patagonica* 41
  Streak-throated *T. (A.) humilis* 36, 38
  Streak-backed *T. (A.) wyatti* 36
  Line-fronted *T. (A.) urubambensis* 36
  Many-striped *T. (A.) flammulata* 32, 36
  Hudson's *T. (A.) hudsoni* 42
Thornbird
  Rufous (Plain)-fronted *Phacellodomus rufifrons* 29, 43
  Little *P. sibilatrix* 42, 43
  Freckle-breasted *P. striaticollis* 42
  Greater *P. ruber* 43
Bay-capped Wren-Spinetail *Spartonoica maluroides* 42
Wren-like Rushbird *Phleocryptes melanops* 35, 36, 38, 39, 42
Curve-billed Reedhaunter *Limnornis curvirostris* 42
Firewood-gatherer *Anumbius annumbi* 42, 45
Band-tailed Earthcreeper *Eremobius phoenicurus* 41
Orange-fronted Plushcrown *Metopothrix aurantiacus* 33
Spotted Barbtail *Margarornis (Premnoplex) brunnescens* 22, 23, 28, 30, 31
Treerunner
  Ruddy *M. rubiginosus* 22, 23
  Fulvous-dotted *M. stellatus* 31
  Pearled *M. squamiger* 32, 36
Sharp-tailed Streamcreeper *Lochmias nematura* 45, 46
White-throated Cacholote *Pseudoseisura gutturalis* 41
Tuftedcheek
  Buffy *Pseudocolaptes lawrencii* 22, 23
  Streaked *P. boissonneautii* 28, 32, 36
Point-tailed Palmcreeper *Berlepschia rikeri* 47
Foliage-gleaner
  Chestnut-winged "Hookbill" *Philydor (Ancistrops) strigilatus* 33, 37

Striped "Woodhaunter" *P. (Hyloctistes) subulatus* 37
Guttulated *P. (Syndactyla) guttulatus* 28
Lineated *P. (S.) subalaris* 23, 31
Buff-browed *P. (S.) rufosuperciliatus* 45
Montane *P. (Anabacerthia) striaticollis* 28, 30, 31
White-browed *P. (A.) amaurotis* 45
Scaly-throated *P. (A.) variegaticeps* 23, 31
Rufous-tailed *P. ruficaudatus* 47
Rufous-rumped *P. erythrocercus* 33, 37, 47, 48
Chestnut-winged *P. erythropterus* 33
Ochre-breasted *P. lichtensteini* 44, 46
Black-capped *P. atricapillus* 46
Buff-fronted *P. rufus* 23, 28, 31, 44–46
Cinnamon-rumped *P. pyrrhodes* 33, 37, 47
White-collared *P. (Anabazenops) fuscus* 45
Peruvian Recurvebill *P. (Simoxenops) ucayalae* 37
Treehunter
  Uniform *Thripadectes ignobilis* 31
  Streak-breasted *T. rufobrunneus* 22, 23
  Streak-capped *T. virgaticeps* 28, 31
  Flammulated *T. flammulatus* 32
Foliage-gleaner
  Buff-throated *Automolus ochrolaemus* 24, 48
  Olive-backed *A. infuscatus* 33, 37, 47
  White-eyed *A. leucophthalmus* 46
  Brown-rumped *A. melanopezus* 33
  Ruddy *A. rubiginosus* 31, 33, 48
  Chestnut-crowned *A. rufipileatus* 33, 37, 47
Leaftosser (Leafscraper)
  Tawny-throated *Sclerurus mexicanus* 31
  Short-billed *S. rufigularis* 47
  Black-tailed *S. caudacutus* 33, 37, 47
  Gray-throated *S. albigularis* 22, 27
  Scaly-throated *S. guatemalensis* 20
Sharp-billed Treehunter *Xenops (Heliobletus) contaminatus* 45
Xenops (Zenops)
  Rufous-tailed *Xenops milleri* 37, 48
  Plain *X. minutus* 20, 24, 28, 30, 31, 33, 46–48

Streaked *X. rutilans* 27, 28, 30, 31, 36, 44–46

White-throated Treehunter *Pygarrhichas albogularis* 39, 41

ANTBIRDS:*FORMICARIIDAE*

Antshrike

Fasciated *Cymbilaimus lineatus* 24, 33, 37, 48

Spot-backed *Hypoedaleus guttatus* 44

Giant *Batara cinerea* 45

Tufted *Mackenziaena severa* 44, 45

Undulated *Frederickena unduligera* 33

Great *Taraba major* 24, 27, 29, 31, 33, 37, 43, 47, 48

Black-crested *Sakesphorus canadensis* 27–30, 48

Black-backed (Coastal) *S. melanonotus* 28, 30

Barred *Thamnophilus doliatus* 18–20, 24, 27–30, 37, 43, 48

Bar-crested *T. multistriatus* 31

Lined *T. palliatus* 46, 47

White-shouldered *T. aethiops* 37, 47

Uniform *T. unicolor* 31

Black-capped *T. schistaceus* 33, 37

Mouse-colored *T. murinus* 48

Slaty *T. punctatus* 24, 30, 31, 46, 48

Amazonian *T. amazonicus* 47, 48

Variable *T. caerulescens* 36, 43–45

Rufous-capped *T. ruficapillus* 45

Spot-winged *Pygiptila stellaris* 33, 37, 47, 48

Russet *Thamnistes anabatinus* 20, 31

Antvireo

Spot-breasted *Dysithamnus stictothorax* 46

Plain *D. mentalis* 19, 20, 22, 27, 28, 31, 44–47

Spot-crowned *D. puncticeps* 24, 31

Antshrike

Dusky-throated *Thamnomanes ardesiacus* 33, 37, 48

Plumbeous *T. plumbeus* 28

Cinereous *T. caesius* 33, 46–48

Bluish-slate *T. schistogynus* 37

Antwren

Pygmy *Myrmotherula brachyura (ignota)* 24, 33, 37, 48

Sclater's *M. sclateri* 37

Streaked *M. surinamensis* 24, 31, 33, 37, 47, 48

Rufous-bellied *M. guttata* 48

Plain-throated *M. hauxwelli* 33, 37, 47

Star-throated *M. gularis* 45

Brown-bellied *M. gutturalis* 48

Checker-throated *M. fulviventris* 24

White-eyed *M. leucophthalma* 37

Ornate *M. ornata* 33, 37

Rufous-tailed *M. erythrura* 33

White-flanked *M. axillaris* 24, 27, 33, 37, 46–48

Slaty *M. schisticolor* 22, 28, 30, 31

Long-winged *M. longipennis* 37, 47, 48

Unicolored *M. unicolor* 46

Gray *M. menetriesii* 33, 37, 47, 48

Banded Antbird *Dichrozona cincta* 37

Antwren

Black-capped *Herpsilochmus pileatus* 43

Spot-tailed *H. sticturus* 48

Rufous-winged *H. rufimarginatus* 28, 44, 46, 47

Dot-winged *Microrhopias quixensis* 20, 24, 31, 48

White-fringed *Formicivora grisea* 27–30, 48

Rusty-backed *F. rufa* 43

Antbird

Ferruginous *Drymophila ferruginea* 44, 45

Rufous-tailed *D. genei* 45

Ochre-rumped *D. ochropyga* 45

Striated *D. devillei* 37

Long-tailed *D. caudata* 28, 30

Dusky-tailed *D. malura* 44

Scaled *D. squamata* 46

Antwren

Streak-capped *Terenura maculata* 44

Rufous-rumped *T. callinota* 31

Chestnut-shouldered *T. humeralis* 37

Antbird

Gray *Cercomacra cinerascens* 33, 37, 47, 48

Dusky *C. tyrannina* 19, 20, 24, 31, 47, 48

Jet *C. nigricans* 30, 31

Stub-tailed *Sipia berlepschi* 31

Esmeraldas *S. rosenbergi* 31

Fire-eye

White-backed *Pyriglena leuconota* 47

White-shouldered *P. leucoptera* 44, 45

Antbird

White-browed *Myrmoborus leucophrys* 37, 48

Ash-breasted *M. lugubris* 47

Black-faced *M. myotherinus* 33, 37, 47
Warbling *Hypocnemis cantator* 33, 37, 48
Black-chinned *H. melanopogon* 48
Band-tailed *H. maculicauda* 37, 47
Bare-crowned *Gymnocichla nudiceps* 24
Black-headed *Percnostola rufifrons* 48
White-lined *P. macrolopha* 37
Spot-winged *P. leucostigma* 33
Silvered *Sclateria naevia* 27, 33, 37, 47, 48
White-bellied *Myrmeciza longipes* 24, 27, 28, 30
Chestnut-backed *M. exsul* 24, 31
Ferruginous-backed *M. ferruginea* 48
White-bibbed *M. loricata* 45, 46
Dull-mantled *M. laemosticta* 24, 31
Chestnut-tailed *M. hemimelaena* 37
Plumbeous *M. hyperythra* 33, 37
Goeldi's *M. goeldii* 37
White-shouldered *M. melanoceps* 33
Sooty *M. fortis* 33
Immaculate *M. immaculata* 22, 31
Black-throated *M. atrothorax* 37
White-plumed *Pithys albifrons* 48
White-throated *Gymnopithys salvini* 37
Bicolored *G. leucaspis (bicolor)* 24, 31, 33
Spotted *Hylophylax naevioides* 24
Spot-backed *H. naevia* 33, 48
Scale-backed *H. poecilonota* 33, 37, 47, 48
Ocellated *Phaenostictus mcleannani* 24
Bare-eye
    Black-spotted *Phlegopsis nigromaculata* 33, 37, 47
    Reddish-winged *P. erythroptera* 33
Ant-thrush
    Short-tailed *Chaemaeza campanisona* 28, 44, 45
    Striated *C. nobilis* 33
    Rufous-tailed *C. ruficauda* 28, 45
    Rufous-capped *Formicarius colma* 33, 37, 47, 48
    Black-faced *F. analis* 19, 20, 22, 24, 27, 28, 30, 33, 37, 47, 48
Wing-banded Antbird *Myrmornis torquata* 47, 48
Antpitta
    Undulated *Grallaria squamigera* 31, 32
    Variegated *G. varia* 44, 45

Scaled *G. guatimalensis* 22, 23, 27
Plain-backed *G. haplonota* 28
Chestnut-crowned *G. ruficapilla* 31
Santa Marta *G. bangsi* 30
Tawny *G. quitensis* 32
Streak-chested *Hylopezus (G.) perspicillatus* 24
Spotted *H. macularius* 48
Fulvous-bellied *H. fulviventris* 31
Thrush-like *Myrmothera campanisoma* 33, 37, 48
Ochre-breasted *Grallaricula flavirostris* 31
Gnateater (usually separate family: *CONOPOPHAGIDAE*)
Hooded *Conopophaga roberti* 47
Ash-throated *C. peruviana* 37
Chestnut-crowned *C. castaneiceps* 31
Chestnut-belted *C. aurita* 33
Rufous *C. lineata* 44, 45
TAPACULOS:*RHINOCRYPTIDAE*
Black-throated Huet-huet *Pteroptochos tarnii* 41
Moustached Turca *P. megapodius* 39
Tapaculo
    White-throated *Scelorchilus albicollis* 39
    Rusty-belted *Liosceles thoracicus* 33
Olive-crowned Crescentchest *Melanopareia maximiliani* 43
Slaty Bristlefront *Merulaxis ater* 45
Tapaculo
    Unicolored *Scytalopus unicolor* 31, 32
    Mouse-colored *S. speluncae* 45
    Rufous-vented *S. femoralis* 31
    Silver(y)-fronted *S. argentifrons* 22, 23
    Brown-rumped *S. latebricola* 30
    Andean *S. magellanicus* 36
TYRANT FLYCATCHERS: *TYRANNIDAE*
Tyrannulet
    Greenish *Phyllomyias (Xanthomyias) virescens* 45
    Planalto *P. fasciatus* 45
    Sooty-headed *P. grisceiceps* 31
    Black-capped *P. (Tyranniscus) nigrocapillus* 30
    Gray-capped *P. (Oreotriccus) griseocapillus* 45
    Rough-legged *P. (Acrochordopus) burmeisteri* 44
    White-fronted *P. (A.) zeledoni* 22, 23

Paltry *Zimmerius (Tyranniscus) vilis-simus* 20–24, 28, 30

Slender-footed *Z. (T.) gracilipes* 47, 48

Golden-faced *Z. (T.) viridiflavus* 31

White-lored *Ornithion inerme* 47, 48

Yellow-bellied *O. semiflavum* 20

Brown-capped *O. brunneicapillum* 24, 28, 30, 31

Northern Beardless ("Flycatcher") *Camptostoma imberbe* 12, 16

Southern Beardless *C. obsoletum* 24, 27–31, 33, 35, 43, 46–48

Mouse-colored *Phaeomyias murina* 27–31, 43, 47, 48

Flycatcher

Scrub *Sublegatus modestus (arenarum, glaber)* 24, 27–30

Suiriri *Suiriri suiriri (affinis)* 44

Yellow-crowned Tyrannulet *Tyrannulus elatus* 24, 30, 33, 37, 47, 48

Elaenia (Flycatcher)

Forest *Myiopagis gaimardii* 27, 28, 30, 37, 47, 48

Yellow-crowned *M. flavivertix* 47

Jamaican *M. cotta* 25

Greenish *M. viridicata* 16–20, 24, 30, 44

Elaenia

Yellow-bellied *Elaenia flavogaster* 18, 19, 21, 23, 24, 26–31, 44, 46–48

Caribbean *E. martinica* 18, 25, 26

Greater Antillean *E. fallax* 25

White-crested (Peruvian) *E. albiceps (modesta)* 32, 35, 36, 39, 41

Small-billed *E. parvirostris* 42, 43

Olivaceous *E. mesoleuca* 45

Mottle-backed *E. gigas* 33

Plain-crested *E. cristata* 47, 48

Lesser *E. chiriquensis* 23, 24, 27, 29–31

Rufous-crowned *E. ruficeps* 48

Mountain *E. frantzii* 22, 23, 30

Tyrannulet

White-throated *Mecocerculus leuco-phrys* 28, 30, 32, 36

White-tailed *M. poecilocercus* 36

White-banded *M. stictopterus* 32

Torrent *Serpophaga cinerea* 23, 31, 32, 36

White-crested *S. subcristata* 42, 43

Sooty *S. nigricans* 42–45

Pale-tipped *Inezia subflava* 29, 30, 48

Slender-billed *I. tenuirostris* 30

Tit-Tyrant

Tufted *Anairetes parulus* 32, 36, 39, 41

Yellow-billed *A. flavirostris* 36, 38

Pied Crested *A. reguloides* 35

Ash-breasted *A. alpinus* 36

Unstreaked *A. (Uromyias) agraphia* 36

Many-colored Rush-Tyrant *Tachuris ru-brigastra* 35, 36, 38, 39, 41, 42

Sharp-tailed Tyrant *Culicivora caudacuta* 43

Bearded Tachuri *Polystictus pectoralis* 43

Doradito

Crested *Pseudocolopteryx sclateri* 27

Warbling *P. flaviventris* 39, 42, 43

Tawny-crowned Pygmy-Tyrant *Eus-carthmus meloryphus* 35, 43, 46

Flycatcher

Streak-necked *Mionectes striaticollis* 36

Olive-striped *M. olivaceus* 22, 24, 27, 28, 30, 31

Ochre-bellied *M. (Pipromorpha) oleagi-neus* 19, 20, 24, 27, 30, 33, 37, 47, 48

McConnell's *M. (P.) macconnelli* 37, 47, 48

Gray-hooded *M. (P.) rufiventris* 44, 45

Slaty-capped *Leptopogon superciliaris* 27, 28, 31

Sepia-capped *L. amaurocephalus* 20, 30, 33, 37, 44–46

Bristle-Tyrant

Marble-faced *Phylloscartes (Pogono-triccus) ophthalmicus* 28, 31

Variegated *P. (P.) poecilotis* 31

Venezuelan *P. (P.) venezuelanus* 28

Yellow-bellied *P. (P.) flaviventris* 28

Tyrannulet

Bay-ringed *P. (Leptotriccus) sylviolus* 44

Mottle-cheeked *P. ventralis* 36, 44, 45

Serra do Mar *P. difficilis* 45

Sao Paulo *P. paulistus* 44

Yellow *Capsiempis flaveola* 24, 28–30, 44–46

Bronze-olive Pygmy-Tyrant *Pseudotric-cus pelzelni* 31

Antpipit (Gnatpipit)

Ringed *Corythopis torquata* 37, 47, 48

Southern *C. delalandi* 44

Pygmy-Tyrant

Eared *Myiornis auricularis* 44–46

Short-tailed (Black-capped) *M. ecau-datus (atricapillus)* 27, 31, 47, 48

Scale-crested *Lophotriccus pileatus* 22, 28, 31

Double-banded *L. vitiosus* 48

Helmeted *L. (Colopteryx) galeatus* 47, 48

Pale-eyed *Atalotriccus pilaris* 24, 28–30

Black-chested Tyrant *Poecilotriccus (Taeniotriccus) andrei* 47

Bentbill

Northern *Oncostoma cinereigulare* 20

Southern *O. olivaceum* 24, 30

Tody-Tyrant

Black-throated *Hemitriccus (Idioptilon) granadensis* 30

Hangnest *H. (I.) nidipendulus* 45

White-eyed *H. (I.) zosterops* 37

Pearly-vented *H. (I.) margaritaceiventer* 28, 30, 43

Eye-ringed *H. (I.) orbitatus* 46

Pygmy-Tyrant

Drab-breasted *H. diops* 44, 45

Brown-breasted *H. obsoletus* 45

Flammulated *H. flammulatus* 37

Tody-Flycatcher

Golden-winged *Todirostrum calopterum* 33

Black-headed *T. nigriceps* 24, 30, 31

Painted *T. chrysocrotaphum* 33, 37, 47, 48

Common *T. cinereum* 19, 22–24, 28–31, 36, 37, 46, 48

Spotted *T. maculatum* 47, 48

Slate-headed *T. sylvia* 20, 28–31

Rusty-fronted *T. latirostre* 33, 37

Ochre-faced *T. plumbeiceps* 45

Brownish Flycatcher *Cnipodectes subbrunneus* 24, 33

Flatbill

Rufous-tailed *Ramphotrigon ruficauda* 37, 47

Large-headed *R. megacephala* 37, 44, 45

Olivaceous *Rhynchocyclus olivaceus* 24, 30, 37, 47

Eye-ringed *R. brevirostris* 20, 22, 23, 31

Fulvous-breasted *R. fulvipectus* 31

Flycatcher (Flatbill)

Yellow-olive *Tolmomyias sulphurescens* 18–20, 24, 27–31, 43–48

Yellow-margined *T. assimilis* 24, 33, 37

Gray-crowned *T. poliocephalus* 33, 37, 47, 48

Yellow-breasted *T. flaviventris* 27–30, 33, 37, 46–48

Spadebill

White-crested *Platyrinchus platyrhynchos* 47, 48

White-throated *P. mystaceus* 20, 22, 23, 27, 31, 45

Golden-crowned *P. coronatus* 24, 31, 37

Cinnamon-crested *P. saturatus* 47, 48

Royal Flycatcher

Northern *Onychorhynchus mexicanus* 18–20, 24

Amazonian *O. coronatus* 33, 37, 47

Flycatcher

Ornate *Myiotriccus ornatus* 31

Ruddy-tailed *Terenotriccus erythrurus* 20, 24, 30, 33, 37, 47

Tawny-breasted *Myiobius villosus* 31

Whiskered *M. barbatus* 33, 47, 48

Sulfur-rumped *M. sulphureipygius* 19, 20, 24, 31

Black-tailed *M. atricaudus* 24

Flavescent *Myiophobus flavicans* 28

Handsome *M. pulcher* 31

Bran-colored *M. fasciatus* 27–29, 31, 33, 35, 37, 46–48

Belted *Xenotriccus callizonus* 21

Cinnamon *Pyrrhomyias cinnamomea* 28, 30–32, 36

Tufted *Mitrephanes phaeocercus (olivaceus)* 16, 17, 21–23, 31

Pewee

Olive-sided ("Flycatcher") *Contopus (Nuttallornis) borealis* 2, 3, 7, 10, 12–14, 21–24, 27, 28, 30, 31, 33

Wood (Eastern) *C. virens* 6–9, 18–20, 22, 24, 25, 30, 31, 33, 37

Western (Wood) *C. sordidulus (richardsoni)* 3, 10, 12–14, 21, 22

Tropical *C. cinereus* 18–20, 24, 27, 28, 30, 35, 44, 45, 48

White-throated *C. albogularis* 48

Dark (Greater) *C. lugubris (fumigatus)* 22, 23

Greater (Smoke-colored) *C. fumigatus* 28, 31, 32, 36

Coues's ("Flycatcher," Greater) *C. pertinax (fumigatus)* 12, 16, 17, 21

Ochraceous *C. ochraceus* 22

Lesser Antillean *C. latirostris* 25, 26

Greater Antillean *C. caribaeus* 25

Flycatcher
  Yellow-bellied *Empidonax flaviventris* 5–9, 23
  Acadian *E. virescens* 7, 9, 24, 30, 31
  Willow, Alder (Traill's) *E. trailli* and *alnorum* 2, 3, 6, 7, 9, 10, 12, 13, 16, 24, 37 (Note: recently split, ranges not final)
  Least *E. minimus* 7, 9, 16, 22
  Hammond's *E. hammondii* 3, 10, 12
  Dusky *E. oberholseri (wrightii)* 10, 12, 13
  Western *E. difficilis* 3, 10, 12–14, 16, 17
  Euler's *E. euleri* 27, 42, 44–46
  Black-capped *E. atriceps* 22, 23
  Buff-breasted *E. fulvifrons* 12, 17, 21
  Fuscous *Cnemotriccus fuscatus* 27
Phoebe
  Eastern *Sayornis phoebe* 7–9, 17
  Black *S. nigricans (latirostris)* 12–14, 16, 17, 19, 21, 23, 28, 30–32, 36
  Say's *S. saya* 2, 10, 12–14, 17
Vermilion Flycatcher *Pyrocephalus rubinus (nanus)* 9, 12, 16–19, 29–32, 34, 35, 37, 42, 43
Chat-Tyrant
  Rufous-breasted *Ochthoeca rufipectoralis* 32, 36
  Yellow-bellied *O. diadema* 30
  Crowned *O. frontalis* 32
  D'Orbigny's *O. oenanthoides* 38
  Brown-backed *O. fumicolor* 32, 36
  White-browed *O. leucophrys* 35, 36, 38
  Drab "Water-Tyrant" *O. (Ochthornis) littoralis* 33, 37
Bush-Tyrant
  Streak-throated *Myiotheretes striaticollis* 30, 32, 36
  Santa Marta *M. pernix* 30
  Smoky *M. fumigatus* 32, 36
  Red-rumped *M. erythropygius* 32
Fire-eyed Diucon *Xolmis (Pyrope) pyrope* 39, 41
Monjita
  Gray *X. cinerea* 43
  White-rumped *X. velata* 45, 46
  Black-and-white *X. dominicana* 43
  White *X. irupero* 42, 43
  Rusty-backed *Neoxolmis (X.) rubetra* 41
Shrike-Tyrant
  Black-billed *Agriornis montana* 32, 38, 39

White-tailed *A. albicauda* 36, 38
Great *A. livida* 39
Mouse-brown "Monjita" *A. (Xolmis) murina* 41
Ground-Tyrant
  Spot-billed *Muscisaxicola maculirostris* 32, 36, 38, 39
  Little *M. fluviatilis* 36
  Dark-faced *M. macloviana* 39–41
  Cinnamon-bellied *M. capistrata* 39
  Rufous-naped *M. rufivertex* 36, 38, 39
  Puna *M. juninensis* 38
  White-browed *M. albilora* 36, 39, 41
  Plain-capped *M. alpina* 32, 36, 38, 39
  White-fronted *M. albifrons* 36, 38
  Ochre-naped *M. flavinucha* 38, 39
  Black-fronted *M. frontalis* 39
Rufous-backed Negrito *Lessonia rufa (oreas)* 36, 38, 39, 41
Black-Tyrant
  Crested *Knipolegus lophotes* 45
  Velvety *K. nigerrimus* 45, 46
  White-winged *K. aterrimus* 36
  Rufous-tailed "Tyrant" *K. poecilurus* 31
  Blue-billed *K. cyanirostris* 45
  Hudson's *K. (Phaeotriccus) hudsoni* 43
Spectacled Tyrant *Hymenops perspicillata* 39, 41–43
Water-Tyrant
  Pied *Fluvicola pica* 27, 29–31, 43, 48
  Masked *F. nengeta* 46
White-headed Marsh-Tyrant *Arundinicola leucocephala* 27, 29–31, 43, 48
Tyrant
  Long-tailed *Colonia colonus* 24, 31, 44, 45, 48
  Strange-tailed *Alectrurus (Yetapa) risoria* 43
  Streamer-tailed *Gubernetes yetapa* 43, 45, 46
  Yellow-browed *Satrapa icterophrys* 42, 43, 45, 46
Short-tailed Field-Tyrant *Muscigralla brevicauda* 35
Cliff Flycatcher *Hirundinea ferruginea* 45, 46, 48
Cattle Tyrant *Machetornis rixosus* 28–30, 42–46
Attila
  Bright-rumped *Attila spadiceus* 16, 19,

20, 22–24, 27, 28, 30, 31, 33, 37, 47
Dull-capped *A. bolivianus* 37
Gray-hooded *A. rufus* 45
Cinnamon *A. cinnamomeus* 33, 47, 48
Rufous Casiornis *Casiornis rufa* 43
Mourner
  Grayish *Rhytipterna simplex* 33, 37, 47, 48
  Rufous *R. holerythra* 20, 24, 31
  Cinereous *Laniocera hypopyrrha* 37, 47
  Speckled *L. rufescens* 24
Sirystes *Sirystes sibilator* 24, 33, 37, 44, 45, 48
Flycatcher
  Jamaican (Rufous-tailed) *Myiarchus validus* 25
  Short-crested *M. ferox* 29, 33, 37, 46, 47
  Venezuelan *M. venezuelensis (ferox)* 27, 28
  Panama *M. panamensis (ferox)* 24, 30, 31
  Apical *M. apicalis* 31
  Pale-edged *M. cephalotes* 28
  Brown-crested (Wied's) *M. tyrannulus* 9, 12, 16, 18–21, 26–30, 43, 48
  Nutting's *M. nuttingi* 16
  Yucatan *M. yucatanensis* 18
  Dark (Dusky)-capped *M. barbirostris* 25
  Stolid *M. stolidus (antillarum)* 25, 26
  Swainson's *M. swainsoni* 27, 37, 43, 45, 48
  Great Crested *M. crinitus* 7–9, 20, 24, 25, 30
  Ash-throated *M. cinerascens* 12–14, 16
  Dusky-capped (Olivaceous) *M. tuberculifer* 12, 16, 18–24, 27, 28, 30, 31, 33, 36, 47, 48
  Galapagos (Large-billed) *M. magnirostris* 34
  Flammulated *Deltarhynchus flammulatus* 16
Kiskadee
  Great *Pitangus sulphuratus* 9, 16, 18–22, 24, 27–31, 33, 37, 41–48
  Lesser *P. lictor* 24, 29, 30, 33, 37, 47, 48
Flycatcher (Kiskadee)
  Boat-billed *Megarhynchus pitangua* 16, 18–20, 23, 24, 27–30, 33, 37, 44, 45, 47, 48
  Dusky-chested *Myiozetetes (Tyrannopsis) luteiventris* 37

Rusty-margined *M. cayanensis* 24, 28–31, 37, 47, 48
Gray-capped *M. granadensis* 23, 31, 33, 37
Social *M. similis* 16, 18–24, 28–31, 33, 37, 41–48
Three-striped *Conopias trivirgata* 44
Lemon-browed *C. cinchoneti* 31
White-ringed *C. parva* 24, 48
White-bearded *C. (Myiozetetes) inornata* 29
Sulfur-bellied *Myiodynastes luteiventris* 12, 16, 19, 20, 22, 33, 37
Streaked (Solitary) *M. maculatus* 19, 20, 23, 24, 27–31, 33, 37, 43–47
Golden-bellied *M. hemichrysus* 22, 23
Golden-crowned *M. chrysocephalus* 28, 30, 31, 36
Piratic *Legatus leucophaius* 19, 20, 24, 27, 28, 30, 31, 33, 37, 44, 45, 48
Variegated *Empidonomus varius* 29, 33, 37, 44, 45, 47, 48
Crowned Slaty *E. aurantioatrocristatus* 33, 37, 43
Sulfury *Tyrannopsis sulphurea* 27, 47, 48
Flycatcher (Kingbird)
  Scissor-tailed *Tyrannus (Muscivora) forficatus* 8, 9, 21
  Fork-tailed *T. (M.) savana (tyrannus)* 19, 24, 26, 27, 29–31, 33, 42–45, 47, 48
Kingbird
  Eastern *T. tyrannus* 3, 6–11, 18–20, 22, 24, 25, 30, 33, 37, 44
  Cassin's *T. vociferans* 12, 13, 16, 17
  Western *T. verticalis* 8–13, 16, 17, 21
  Tropical (Couch's) *T. melancholicus (couchii)* 9, 12, 16, 18–20, 22–24, 26–31, 35–37, 42–48
  Gray *T. dominicensis* 8, 24–27, 29–31, 48
  Giant *T. cubensis* 25
  Loggerhead *T. caudifasciatus* 25
  Thick-billed *T. crassirostris* 12, 16, 17
White-naped Xenopsaris *Xenopsaris albinucha* 43
Becard
  Green-backed *Pachyramphus viridis* 43, 44
  Barred *P. versicolor* 22–23, 30, 31
  Cinereous *P. rufus* 28, 30, 47, 48

Chestnut-crowned *P. castaneus* 28, 44, 45

Cinnamon *P. cinnamomeus* 19, 20, 24, 30, 31

White-winged *P. polychopterus* 24, 27, 30, 31, 33, 36, 37, 43, 48

Black-capped *P. marginatus* 33, 37, 47

Black-and-white *P. albogriseus* 23, 28

Gray-collared *P. major* 16, 20

Rose-throated *P. (Platypsaris) aglaiae* 12, 16–21

Pink-throated *P. (P.) minor* 33, 37, 47, 48

Crested (Southern, Rufous) *P. (P.) validus (rufus)* 43, 45

Jamaican *P. (P.) niger* 25

Tityra

Black-tailed *Tityra cayana* 27, 33, 37, 44, 45, 47, 48

Masked *T. semifasciata* 16, 18–20, 22–24, 28, 30–31, 37

Black-crowned *T. inquisitor* 19, 20, 24, 29, 33, 37, 44, 48

MANAKINS:*PIPRIDAE*

Manakin

Greater *Schiffornis major* 37

Thrush-like *S. turdinus* 20, 24, 30, 31, 37, 47, 48

Greenish *S. virescens* 46

Wing-barred *Piprites chloris* 28, 33, 37, 44, 47, 48

Cinnamon *Neopipo cinnamomea* 37

Green *Chloropipo holochlora* 33

Yellow-headed *C. flavicapilla* 31

Tyrant-Manakin

Tiny *Tyranneutes virescens* 48

Dwarf *T. stolzmanni* 33, 37, 47

Manakin

Fiery-capped *Machaeropterus pyrocephalus* 37

Club-winged *M. (Allocotopterus) deliciosus* 31

White-bearded *Manacus manacus* 27, 30, 33, 46–48

Golden-collared *M. vitellinus (manacus)* 24, 31

White-collared *M. candei (manacus)* 19, 20

White-throated *Corapipo gutturalis* 48

Pin-tailed *Ilicura militaris* 45, 46

Golden-winged *Masius chrysopterus* 31

Long-tailed *Chiroxiphia linearis* 22

Lance-tailed *C. lanceolata* 24, 28–30

Blue-backed *C. pareola* 27, 47

Swallow-tailed *C. caudata* 44–46

White-crowned *Pipra pipra* 31, 47, 48

Blue-crowned *P. coronata* 24, 31, 33, 37

Opal-crowned *P. iris* 47

White-fronted *P. serena* 48

Crimson-hooded *P. aureola* 48

Band-tailed *P. fasciicauda* 37, 47

Wire-tailed *P. (Teleonema) filicauda* 28, 33

Red-capped *P. mentalis* 19, 20, 24, 31

Golden-headed *P. erythrocephala* 27, 28, 30, 33, 48

Red-headed *P. rubrocapilla* 37, 47

Round-tailed *P. chloromeros* 37

COTINGAS:*COTINGIDAE*

Cotinga

Guianan Red *Phoenicircus carnifex* 48

Swallow-tailed *Phibalura flavirostris* 45

Black-and-gold *Tijuca atra* 45

Red-crested *Ampelion rubrocristata* 30, 32, 36

Fruiteater

Green-and-black *P. riefferii* 31

Barred *P. arcuata* 32

Golden-breasted *P. aureopectus* 28, 30

Orange-breasted *Pipreola jucunda (aureopectus)* 31

Handsome *P. formosa* 28

Scaled *Ampelioides tschudii* 31

White-browed Purpletuft *Iodopleura isabellae* 33, 47

Piha

Screaming *Lipaugus vociferans* 37, 47, 48

Rufous *L. unirufus* 18, 20, 24

Cotinga

Purple-throated *Porphyrolaema porphyrolaema* 33

Lovely *Cotinga amabilis* 18

Blue *C. nattererii* 24, 31

Plum-throated *C. maynana* 33, 37

Purple-breasted *C. cotinga* 47

Spangled *C. cayana* 37, 47, 48

Pompadour *Xipholena punicea* 48

White-tailed *X. lamellipennis* 47

White *Carpodectes hopkei* 31

Fruitcrow

Bare-necked *Gymnoderus foetidus* 33, 37, 48

Crimson *Haematoderus militaris* 48

Purple-throated *Querula purpurata* 24, 31, 33, 37, 47, 48

Red-ruffed *Pyroderus scutatus* 31, 44

Umbrellabird

Bare-necked *Cephalopterus glabricollis* 22, 23

Amazonian *C. ornatus* 33

Long-wattled *C. penduliger* 31

Capuchinbird (Calfbird) *Perissocephalus tricolor* 48

Bellbird

Three-wattled *Procnias tricarunculata* 22, 23

White *P. alba* 27, 48

Bearded *P. averano* 27, 28

Bare-throated *P. nudicollis* 46

Cock-of-the-Rock (usually separate family: *RUPICOLIIDAE*)

Guianan (Orange) *Rupicola rupicola* 48

Andean (Red) *R. peruviana* 31, 32, 36

SHARPBILL:*OXYRUNCIDAE*

Sharpbill *Oxyruncus cristatus* 45, 46, 48

PLANTCUTTERS:*PHYTOTOMIDAE)*

Plantcutter

White-tipped *Phytotoma rutila* 43

Rufous-tailed *P. rara* 39, 41

PITTAS:*PITTIDAE*

Pitta

Giant *P. caerulea* 94

Koch's *P. kochi* 97

Blue-breasted *P. erythrogaster* 97

Blue-banded *P. arcuata* 96

Garnet *P. granatina* 94

Blue *P. cyanea* 93

Banded *P. guajana* 94, 95, 98

Hooded (Black-headed) *P. sordida* 85, 97

Indian (Fairy, Blue-winged) *P. brachyura (nympha)* 85, 86, 88, 90, 91, 95

African *P. angolensis* 67, 68

Steere's *P. steerii* 97

Rainbow (Black-breasted) *P. iris* 101

Noisy (Buff-breasted) *P. versicolor* 107, 108

ASITIES:*PHILEPITTIDAE*

Asity

Velvety *Philepitta castanea* 74

Schlegel's *P. schlegeli* 74

Wattled *Neodrepanis coruscans* 74

NEW ZEALAND WRENS: *ACANTHISITTIDAE*

Rifleman *Acanthisitta chloris* 111

Bushwren *Xenicus longipes* 111

Boulderwren (Rockwren) *X. gilviventris* 111

LYREBIRDS:*MENURIDAE*

Lyrebird

Superb *Menura novaehollandiae (superba)* 105, 106

Albert's *M. alberti* 107

SCRUB-BIRDS: *ATRICHORNITHIDAE*

Scrub-bird

Noisy *Atrichornis clamosus* 103

Rufous *A. rufescens* 107

LARKS:*ALAUDIDAE*

Bush-Lark (Bushlark)

Singing *Mirafra javanica* 66, 97–101, 104, 106, 108

Madagascar *M. hova* 74

Monotonous *M. passerina* 70

Clapper *M. apiata (damarensis)* 71

Red-winged *M. hypermetra* 66

Rufous-naped *M. africana* 64–66, 70, 72

Flappet *M. rufocinnamomea* 64, 66–70, 72

Fawn-colored *M. africanoides* 66

Pink-breasted *M. poecilosterna* 66

Sabota *M. sabota* 72, 73

Rufous (Red)-winged *M. erythroptera* 82, 86

Dusky *M. nigricans* 69, 70

Karoo *M. (Certhilauda) albescens* 71

Finch-Lark (Sparrow-Lark)

Chestnut-backed *Eremopterix leucotis* 62, 68, 69, 73

Chestnut-headed *E. signata* 66

Gray-backed *E. verticalis* 71

Black-crowned (White-fronted) *E. nigriceps* 62, 78, 79

Ashy-crowned *E. grisea* 82, 86

Fischer's *E. leucopareia* 66

Lark

Bar-tailed *Ammomanes cincturus* 60, 77

Rufous-tailed ("Finch-Lark") *A. phoenicurus* 82

Desert *A. deserti* 60, 77, 78

Dunn's *A. dunni* 77

Bifasciated (Hoopoe) *Alaemon alaudipes* 60, 77, 78

Thick-billed (Clotbey) *Rhamphocorys clotbey* 60, 77

Calandra *Melanocorypha calandra* 55, 56, 58–60

Short-toed (Red-capped) *Calendrella cinerea (brachydactyla)* 55, 56, 58–60, 64, 66, 68, 71, 77, 78, 82

Sand *C. raytal* 79, 82, 85

Lesser Short-toed (Dark) *C. rufescens (cheleensis)* 59–61, 77, 78

Stark's *C. starki* 71

Dupont's *Chersophilus duponti* 60

Short-tailed *Pseudalaemon fremantlii* 66

Crested *Galerida cristata* 52, 53, 55–60, 62, 77, 78, 82, 89

Thekla *G. theklae* 59, 60

Sun *G. modesta* 62

Cape Thick-billed *G. magnirostris* 71

Wood *Lullula arborea* 51–53, 57–60

Skylark

    Northern (European, The) *Alauda arvensis* 1, 3, 15, 50–61, 78, 87–90, 105, 106, 111

    Oriental (Eastern, Small) *A. gulgula* 79, 82, 83, 86, 91, 92 97

Lark

    Horned (Shore) *Eremophila alpestris* 2–7, 9–14, 17, 51, 53–55, 60, 84

    Temminck's (Horned) *E. bilopha* 60, 77

SWALLOWS:*HIRUNDINIDAE*

Swallow

    Tree *Tachycineta bicolor* 1, 3–14, 16, 19, 25, 30

    Mangrove *T. albilinea* 16, 18, 19, 24

    White-winged *T. albiventer* 27, 29, 30, 33, 37, 44, 47, 48

    White-rumped *T. leucorrhoa* 42–46

    Violet-green *T. thalassina* 1–3, 10–14, 16, 17, 21

    Bahama *Callichelidon cyaneoviridis* 25

    Golden *Kalochelidon euchrysea* 25

Martin (Glider)

    Brown-chested *Progne tapera* 24, 30, 33, 37, 42, 44, 46, 48

    Purple (Snowy-bellied) *P. subis (dominicensis)* 3, 6–9, 12–14, 16, 18–20, 24–27

Gray-breasted *P. chalybea* 16, 18–20, 23, 24, 27–31, 33, 37,

Southern (Galapagos) *P. modesta* 34, 41

Swallow

    Brown-bellied *Notiochelidon murina* 30, 32, 36, 38

    Blue-and-white *N. cyanoleuca* 22, 23, 27, 28, 30–33, 35, 36, 38, 39, 41, 42, 44–46

    Pale-footed *N. flavipes* 36

    Black-capped *N. pileata* 21

    White-banded *Atticora fasciata* 33, 37, 48

    Black-collared *A. melanoleuca* 48

    White-thighed *Neochelidon tibialis* 24, 31, 45

    Tawny-headed *Alopochelidon fucata* 43

    Rough-winged *Stelgidopteryx ruficollis* 3, 6–9, 11–14, 16–23, 27–31, 33, 37, 44–48

    White-backed *Cheramoeca leucosternum* 102, 104

    Gray-rumped *Pseudhirundo griseopyga* 65, 66, 68, 70, 72

Martin

    Plain (Brown-throated Sand) *Riparia paludicola* 60, 64–66, 68, 69, 71, 72, 74, 82, 83, 85, 91, 95

    Sand (Bank "Swallow") *R. riparia* 1, 2, 4–12, 16, 24–27, 29–31, 33, 34, 44, 51–62, 64–66, 68, 69, 74, 77, 78, 82, 87–90, 92

    Banded *R. cincta* 64, 66

Crag-Martin

    Mascarene *Phedina borbonica* 74, 75

    Northern *Ptyonoprogne rupestris* 55, 59–61, 78, 89

    Pale (Rock) *P. obsoleta* 60

    Rock "Martin" *P. fuligula* 64, 66, 68, 70–72

    Dusky *P. concolor* 82

Swallow

    Barn (Field, European, The) *Hirundo rustica* 2, 3, 5–14, 16–19, 24–27, 29–31, 33, 35, 37, 39, 41, 42, 44, 46–64, 66–74, 77, 78, 81–83, 85–92, 95–97

    Angola *H. angolensis* 64–5

    Pacific *H. tahitica* 86, 91, 95–97, 99, 100, 110

    White-throated *H. albigularis* 71, 72

    Ethiopian *H. aethiopica* 63, 67

Wire-tailed *H. smithii* 62, 64–66, 68–70, 72, 73, 79, 82
Blue *H. atrocaerulea* 68
West African (White-throated Blue) *H. nigrita* 63
Pied-winged *H. leucosoma* 62
Greater Striped *H. cucullata* 71
Lesser Striped *H. abyssinica* 64–70, 72, 73
Rufous-chested (Red-breasted) *H. semirufa* 63–66, 73
Mosque *H. senegalensis* 62–69
Red-rumped (Striated) *H. daurica* 55, 59, 60, 62, 64–66, 68, 77, 78, 80–83, 85, 86, 88, 89, 91, 92, 97
Welcome *H. neoxena* 103–108, III
Martin (Swallow)
Andean *Petrochelidon andecola* 36, 38
Tree *P. nigricans* 99, 101–108
Cliff *P. pyrrhonota* 1, 3–14, 16, 17, 24–26, 33
Cave *P. fulva* 18, 25, 35
Indian (Cliff) *P. (Hirundo) fluvicola* 82
Fairy *P. ariel* 101–108
House *Delichon urbica* 50–62, 66, 68, 77, 78, 81
Asian (House) *D. dasypus* 87–89, 91
Nepal (House) *D. nipalensis* 80, 84
Saw-wing (Rough-winged Swallow)
White-headed *Psalidoprocne albiceps* 64, 65
Fanti (Black) *P. obscura (holomelaena)* 65–68, 72
Square-tailed *P. nitens* 64
CUCKOO-SHRIKES: *CAMPEPHAGIDAE*
Cuckoo-shrike (Graybird)
Ground *Pteropodocys maxima* 102, 104
Black-faced (Large) *Coracina novaehollandiae (gularis, javensis)* 83, 85, 86, 94, 96, 100–108
Melanesian *C. caledonica* 109
Stout-billed *C. caeruleogrisea* 99, 100
Bar-bellied *C. striata* 94–97
Yellow-eyed (Barred) *C. lineata* 99, 100, 107, 108
Rufous-underwing (Boyer's) *C. boyeri* 99, 100
White-bellied (Little, Papuan) *C. papuensis* 99–101, 107, 108
Hooded (Black-hooded) *C. longicauda* 99

New Caledonian (Mountain) *C. analis* 109
Gray *C. caesia* 64–66, 68
White-breasted *C. pectoralis* 62, 65, 66, 68
Ashy (Madagascar) *C. cinerea* 74
Mauritius *C. typica* 75
Reunion *C. newtoni* 75
Philippine Black *C. coerulescens* 97
Cicada (Long-billed, Slaty) *C. tenuirostris* 99, 106–108
Muller's (Black-shouldered, Moluccan) *C. morio* 97, 99, 100
Slaty (Gray's) *C. schisticeps* 99
New Guinea Black *C. meleana* 100
Black-bellied *C. montana* 99
Sharp-tailed *C. mcgregori* 97
Dark (Black-winged) *C. melaschistos* 81, 83, 90–93
Lesser *C. fimbriata* 93, 94
Black-headed *C. melanoptera* 86
Orange (Golden "Triller") *Campochaera sloetii* 100
Triller
Black-breasted *Chlamydochaera jefferyi* 96
Black-and-white *Lalage melanoleuca* 97
Pied *L. nigra* 95, 97
White-winged *L. sueurii* 100–104, 106–108
Varied *L. leucomela* 99–101, 107, 108
Polynesian *L. maculosa* 110
Long-tailed *L. leucopyga* 109
Cuckoo-shrike (Minivet)
Black *Campephaga flava* 64–66, 68, 70, 72, 73
Red-shouldered *C. phoenicea (sulphurata)* 63, 65, 67
Purple-throated *C. quiscalina* 65, 66
Minivet
Rosy *Pericrocotus roseus* 85, 93
Ashy *P. divaricatus* 88, 93, 95
Fiery *P. igneus* 95, 97
Small *P. cinnamomeus* 79, 82, 85, 86, 93
Mountain (Yellow-throated (Gray-chinned)) *P. solaris (montanus)* 83, 96
Long-tailed *P. ethologus* 79, 81, 83, 84
Short-billed *P. brevirostris* 83
Scarlet *P. flammeus* 83, 85, 86, 93–97

Woodshrike (Flycatcher-shrike)
Pied (Bar-winged) *Hemipus picatus* 83,
85, 86, 96
Black-winged *H. hirundinaceus* 96
Large *Tephrodornis gularis (virgatus)*
94, 95
White-browed (Common) *T. pon-
dicerianus* 82, 86
DRONGOS:*DICRURIDAE*
Drongo
Pygmy (Papuan) *Chaetorhynchus
papuensis* 99
Square-tailed *Dicrurus ludwigii (shar-
pei)* 63–65, 68, 72
African (Fork-tailed) *D. adsimilis* 62–
70, 72, 73
Crested *D. forficatus* 74
Black *D. macrocercus* 79, 81–83, 85, 86,
89, 91, 92, 98
Ashy (Gray) *D. leucophaeus* 80, 81, 83,
86, 93, 96–98
White-bellied *D. caerulescens* 83, 85, 86
Crow-billed *D. annectans* 85, 95
Bronzed *D. aeneus* 91, 94, 95
Lesser Racquet-tailed *D. remifer* 83
Balicassiao *D. balicassius* 97
Spangled (Hair-crested) *D. hottentottus
(bracteatus)* 85, 89, 92, 96–101, 106–
108
Greater Racquet-tailed *D. paradiseus*
86, 94, 95
ORIOLES:*ORIOLIDAE*
Oriole
Brown *Oriolus szalayi* 99, 100
Olive-backed *O. sagittatus* 101, 105–108
Yellow *O. flavocinctus* 101, 108
Dark-throated *O. xanthonotus* 94, 97,
98
Isabella *O. isabellae* 97
Eurasian (The) Golden *O. oriolus* 52,
55–60, 62, 65–68, 73, 77, 79, 81, 82, 86
African Golden *O. auratus* 62, 65–67,
69, 70, 72
Slender-billed *O. tenuirostris (chinen-
sis)* 93
Black-naped *O. chinensis* 89–93, 95, 97,
98
Green-headed *O. chlorocephalus* 68
Western Black-headed *O. brachyrhyn-
chus* 65
African Black-headed *O. larvatus* 65–
70, 72, 73

Black-winged *O. nigripennis* 63–66
Black-hooded (Asian Black-headed) *O.
xanthornus* 85, 86
Black-and-crimson *O. cruentus* 96
Maroon *O. traillii* 83, 91, 93
Green (Southern, Yellow) Figbird
Sphecotheres vieilloti (flaviventris)
100, 101, 106–108
CROWS AND JAYS: *CORVIDAE*
Malay Crested Jay *Platylophus
galericulatus* 94
Black Magpie *Platysmurus leucopterus* 94
Jay
Pinyon *Gymnorhinus cyanocephala* 13
Blue *Cyanocitta cristata* 6–9
Steller's *C. stelleri* 3, 10, 12–14, 16, 17, 21
Scrub *Aphelocoma coerulescens* 8, 12–14
Mexican (Arizona, Gray-breasted) *A.
ultramarina* 12, 17
Unicolored *A. unicolor* 21
Azure-hooded *Cyanolyca cucullata* 22
Silver-throated *C. argentigula* 22, 23
Turquoise *C. turcosa* 32
Bushy-crested *Cissilopha melanocya-
nea* 21
San Blas (Black-and-blue) *C. san-
blasiana* 16
Yucatan *C. yucatanica* 18, 19
Purplish-backed *C. beecheii* 16
Purplish *Cyanocorax cyanomelas* 43
Violaceous *C. violaceus* 37
Cayenne *C. cayanus* 48
Black-chested *C. affinis* 24, 30, 31
Plush-crested *C. chrysops* 43, 44
Tufted *C. dickeyi* 16
Green *C. yncas* 9, 16, 19, 20, 27
Brown *Psilorhinus morio* 18–20, 22
Magpie *Calocitta formosa* 16
Eurasian (The) *Garrulus glandarius*
51–53, 55, 57–60, 83, 87–89, 91, 92
Gray (Canada) *Perisoreus canadensis*
2, 3, 5, 10
Siberian *P. infaustus* 54
Magpie
Ceylon *Urocissa ornata* 86
Formosan Blue *U. caerulea* 91
Yellow-billed Blue *U. flavirostris* 80, 81,
84
Red-billed Blue *U. erythrorhyncha* 83,
85, 92
Green *Cissa chinensis* 93, 94, 96
Short-tailed *C. thalassina* 96

Azure-winged *Cyanopica cyana* 59, 88–90

Treepie

Rufous (Indian) *Dendrocitta vagabunda (rufa)* 79, 82, 85

Gray *D. formosae (occipitalis)* 83, 91, 96, 98

Racquet-tailed *Crypsirina temia* 98

Magpie

Black-billed (The) *Pica pica* 2, 10, 11, 51–60, 88–92

Yellow-billed *P. nuttalli* 14

Nutcracker

Clark's *Nucifraga columbiana* 3, 10, 13

Eurasian (Spotted, The) *N. caryocatactes* 53, 57, 81, 87, 88, 91

Chough

Red-billed (The) *Pyrrhocorax pyrrhocorax* 59–61, 81, 89

Alpine (Yellow-billed) *P. graculus* 55, 57, 60

Piapiac *Ptilostomus afer* 62

Jackdaw

Western (Common, The) *Corvus monedula* 51–53, 55–60, 81

Daurian *C. dauuricus* 89, 90

Crow

House *C. splendens* 67, 75, 79, 81–83, 86, 95

New Caledonian *C. moneduloides* 109

Slender-billed *C. enca* 94, 97, 98

Bare-faced *C. tristis* 100

Cape ("Rook") *C. capensis* 65, 66, 71

"Rook" *C. frugilegus* 51–58, 88–90, 111

American (Common) *C. brachyrhynchos* 5–10, 13, 14

Northwestern *C. caurinus* 3

Mexican *C. imparatus* 9

Sinaloan (Mexican) *C. sinaloae* 16

Fish *C. ossifragus* 7, 8

Palm *C. palmarum* 25

Jamaican *C. jamaicensis* 25

Cuban *C. nasicus* 25

White-necked *C. leucognaphalus* 25

Eurasian (Carrion, Hooded) *C. corone (cornix)* 50–58, 87, 88

Large-billed (Jungle) *C. macrorhynchos* 81–93, 95, 97, 98

Torresian (Australian, Papuan) *C. orru (cecilae)* 100–102, 107

Little *C. bennetti* 102–104

Collared *C. torquatus* 89, 90, 92

Pied *C. albus* 62–68, 71, 72, 74

Hawaiian *C. tropicus* 15

Raven

Australian *C. coronoides* 103–106, 108

Little *C. mellori* 104, 105

Chihuahuan (White-necked) *C. cryptoleucus* 9, 12

Brown-necked "Crow" *C. ruficollis* 60, 77

Northern (Common, The) *C. corax* 1–5, 10–13, 16, 17, 49, 50, 53–57, 59

Fan-tailed *C. rhipidurus* 66

White-necked (naped) *C. albicollis* 64, 66, 68, 71, 72

BUTCHERBIRDS:*CRACTICIDAE*

Butcherbird

Black-backed *Cracticus mentalis* 100

Gray *C. torquatus* 101–108

Pied *C. nigrogularis* 101, 102, 104, 107, 108

Black *C. quoyi* 100, 101, 108

Hooded (Black-headed) *C. cassicus* 99, 100

Australian (Black-backed, Western, White-backed) Magpie *Gymnorhina tibicen (dorsalis, hypoleuca)* 102, 104–108, 110

Currawong

Pied *Strepera graculina* 105–108

Gray *S. versicolor (arguta)* 103–106

MAGPIELARKS:*GRALLINIDAE*

Magpielark (Mudlark) *Grallina cyanoleuca* 101–108

Torrentlark *G. bruijni* 99

White-winged "Chough" *Corcorax melanorhamphos* 104, 106

Apostlebird *Struthidea cinerea* 104

BOWERBIRDS:
PTILONORHYNCHIDAE

Catbird

White-throated (-eared) *Ailuroedus buccoides* 99

Green *A. crassirostris* 106, 107

Black-eared (Spotted) *A. melanotis* 108

"Stage-maker" (Tooth-billed "Bowerbird") *Scenopoeetes dentirostris* 108

MacGregor's Gardenerbird ("Bowerbird") *Amblyornis macgregoriae* 99

Bowerbird

Golden ("Regentbird") *Sericulus aureus* 108

Regent (Australian "Regentbird") *S. chrysocephalus* 107
Satin *Ptilonorhynchus violaceus* 106–108
Spotted (Western) *Chlamydera maculata* 102
Great *C. nuchalis* 101, 108
Fawn-breasted *C. cerviniventris* 99, 100
BIRDS-OF-PARADISE: *PARADISAEIDAE*
Loria's Bird-of-Paradise *Loria loriae* 99
Manucode
Glossy-mantled *Manucodia ater* 100
Jobi *M. jobiensis* 100
Crinkle-collared *M. chalybatus* 99
Trumpet ("Trumpetbird") *Phonygammus keraudrenii* 99, 100
Riflebird
Paradise *Ptiloris paradiseus* 107
Queen Victoria's *P. victoriae* 108
Magnificent *P. magnificus* 99, 100
Sicklebill Bird-of-Paradise
Short-tailed ("Paradigalla") *Paradigalla brevicauda* 99
Brown (Meyer's) *Epimachus meyeri* 99
Princess Stephanie's Astrapia *Astrapia stephaniae* 99
Superb Bird-of-Paradise *Lophorina superba* 99
Lawes's Parotia *Parotia lawesii* 99
Bird-of-Paradise
King (Red) *Cicinnurus regius* 99, 100
Magnificent *Diphyllodes magnificus* 99
Greater *Paradisaea apoda* 27
Raggiana *P. raggiana* 99, 100
Blue *P. rudolphi* 99
TITS:PARIDAE
Tit
Marsh *Parus palustris* 51–53, 57, 87
Sombre *P. lugubris* 55
Willow *P. montanus* 51–54, 57, 87, 88
Chickadee
Black-capped *P. atricapillus* 2, 6, 7, 10
Carolina *P. carolinensis* 7, 9
Mexican (Gray-sided) *P. sclateri* 12, 16, 17
Mountain (White-browed) *P. gambeli* 10, 12, 13
Gray-headed (Siberian "Tit") *P. cinctus* 54
Boreal (Brown-capped) *P. hudsonicus* 2, 5
Chestnut-backed *P. rufescens* 3, 14

Bridled Titmouse *P. wollweberi* 12, 16, 17
Tit
Sikkim Black (Rufous-bellied) *P. rubidiventris (beavani)* 84
Simla Black *P. rufonuchalis* 80, 81
Spot-winged Black *P. melanolophus* 80
Coal *P. ater* 51–53, 55, 57, 59, 60, 83, 87–89, 91
Elegant *P. elegans* 97
Palawan *P. amabilis* 97
Crested *P. cristatus* 52, 53, 57, 59
Crested Brown (Gray-crested) *P. dichrous* 84
African Gray *P. afer* 66
Southern Black *P. niger* 68–70, 72, 73
White-shouldered Black *P. leucomelas* 62
White-bellied (breasted) *P. albiventris* 65, 66
Dusky *P. funereus* 65
Red-throated *P. fringillinus* 66
Rufous (Cinnamon)-breasted *P. rufiventris* 68
Great (Gray) *P. major* 51–60, 80–83, 85–90, 92
Green-backed *P. monticolus* 80, 81, 83, 91
Yellow-cheeked *P. spilonotus* 83
Yellow *P. holsti* 91
Blue *P. caeruleus* 51–53, 55–61
Varied *P. varius* 15, 87, 88, 91
White-fronted *P. semilarvatus* 97
Titmouse
Plain *P. inornatus* 12–14
Tufted (Black-crested) *P. bicolor (atricristatus)* 7–9
Tit
Sultan *Melanochlora sultanea* 93, 94
Yellow-browed *Sylviparus modestus* 83, 84
Long-tailed *Aegithalos caudatus* 51, 53, 55–59, 87–90
Red-headed (Black-throated) *A. concinnus* 80, 83, 91
Bushtit *Psaltriparus minimus (melanotis)* 3, 12–14, 16, 17, 21
Penduline-Tit
Eurasian (The) *Remiz pendulinus* 55–58
Sudan *Anthoscopus punctifrons* 62
Mouse-colored *A. musculus* 66
Gray (African) *A. caroli* 66, 68, 72

Verdin *Auriparus flaviceps* 9, 12
  NUTHATCHES:*SITTIDAE*
Nuthatch
  Eurasian *Sitta europaea* 51–53, 55, 57,
    59, 60, 81, 87–89, 91
  Chestnut-bellied *S. castanea* 80, 82, 83,
    85
  White-tailed *S. himalayensis* 83, 84
  Pygmy *S. pygmaea* 12–14, 17
  Brown-headed *S. pusilla* 8, 9, 25
  Red-breasted *S. canadensis* 3, 6, 7, 10,
    12–14
  Chinese *S. villosa* 89
  White-cheeked *S. leucopsis* 80, 81
  White-breasted *S. carolinensis* 6, 7, 10,
    12–14, 17
  Kruper's *S. krueperi* 55
  Rock *S. neumayer* 55
  Velvet-fronted *S. frontalis* 85, 86, 93,
    94, 96, 97
  SITTELLAS:*NEOSITTIDAE*
  (including DAPHOENOSITTIDAE,
    RHABDORNITHIDAE, and
    CLIMACTERIDAE)
Sittella (Nuthatch)
  Varied (Orange-winged, Black-capped,
    Striated, White-headed) *Neositta
    chrysoptera (pileata, striata, leuco-
    cephala, leucoptera)* 102–108
  Mountain (Papuan) *N. papuensis* 99
  Black (Pink-faced) *Daphoenositta
    miranda* 99
Creeper (Barkrunner)
  Stripe-headed *Rhabdornis mysticalis*
    99
  Plain-headed *R. inornatus* 97
Treecreeper (Barkrunner)
  Little *Climacteris minor* 108
  Red-browed *C. erythrops* 105, 106
  White-browed *C. affinis* 102
  Brown *C. picumnus* 104, 106, 108
  Rufous *C. rufa* 103
  Black-tailed *C. melanura* 101
  White-throated *C. leucophaea* 104–
    107
  New Guinea *C. platens* 99
  TREECREEPERS:*CERTHIIDAE*
Treecreeper
  Northern (Brown "Creeper") *Certhia
    familiaris (americana)* 3, 6, 7, 9, 10,
    12–14, 16, 17, 21, 51, 53, 57, 81, 84, 87,
    88

Short-toed *C. brachydactyla* 52, 55,
  57–60
Himalayan *C. himalayana* 79–81
Nepal *C. nipalensis* 83
Sikkim *C. discolor* 85
Spotted Creeper *Salpornis spilonotus* 66,
  68
  BABBLERS:*TIMALIIDAE*
Babbler
  Puff-throated (Spotted) *Pellorneum
    ruficeps* 83, 84, 93
  Brown-capped *P. fuscocapillum* 86
  Black-capped *P. capistratum* 94, 96
  Temminck's (Jungle) *Trichastoma pyr-
    rogenys* 96
  Short-tailed *T. malaccense* 94, 95
  Ashy-headed *T. cinereiceps* 97
  White-chested *T. rostratum* 94, 95
  Ferruginous *T. bicolor* 94, 96
  Horsfield's *T. sepiarium* 94, 98
  Abbot's *T. abbotti* 95
Akalat (Illadopsis, Babbler)
  Mountain *T. pyrrhopterum* 64, 65
  Scaly-breasted *T. albipectus* 65
  Rufous-winged *T. rufescens* 62
  Pale-breasted *T. rufipennis* 64, 65
  Brown *T. fulvescens* 65
  Gray-chested *T. poliothorax* 65
Babbler
  Moustached *Malacopteron magnirostre*
    94, 96
  Scaly-crowned *M. cinereum* 93, 94, 96
  Rufous-crowned *M. magnum* 94, 96
  Gray-breasted *M. albogulare* 94, 98
  Plain *M. affine* 96
Scimitar-Babbler
  Rusty-cheeked *Pomatorhinus ery-
    throgenys* 83
  Spot-breasted *P. erythrocnemis* 91
  Slaty-headed (Indian) *P. horsfieldii* 86
  White-browed *P. schisticeps* 93
  Chestnut-backed *P. montanus* 94, 96,
    98
  Rufous-necked (Lesser) *P. ruficollis* 83,
    91
Babbler
  Papuan (Rufous) *Pomatostomus isido-
    rei* 100
  Gray-crowned *P. temporalis (rubecu-
    lus)* 101, 102, 104, 107
  White-browed *P. superciliosus* 102–104
  Chestnut-crowned *P. ruficeps* 104

Wren-Babbler
  Streaked *Ptilocichla mindanensis* 97
  Falcated *P. falcata* 97
  Striped *Kenopia striata* 94
  Large *Napothera macrodactyla* 95
  Mountain *N. crassa* 96
  Small *N. epilepidotus* 96
  Scaly-breasted (Large) *Pnoepyga albiventer* 83, 84
  Pygmy (Lesser Scaly-breasted) *P. pusilla* 83, 91
Jery
  Common *Neomixis tenella* 74
  Green *N. viridis* 74
  Stripe-throated *N. striatigula* 74
  Wedge-tailed *N. flavoviridis* 74
Babbler
  Rufous-capped (Red-headed) *Stachyris ruficeps* 91
  Black-chinned *S. pyrrhops* 83
Tree-Babbler
  Pygmy *S. plateni* 97
  Black-crowned *S. capitalis* 97
  Whitehead's *S. whiteheadi* 97
  Palawan *S. hypogrammica* 97
Babbler
  Gray (Black)-throated *S. nigriceps* 83, 96
  Gray-headed *S. poliocephala* 94, 96
  Chestnut-winged *S. erythroptera* 95, 96
  Pearly-cheeked *S. melanothorax* 98
  White-throated (Rufous-bellied) *Dumetia hyperythra* 86
  Black-headed *Rhopocichla atriceps* 86
Tit-Babbler
  Striped (Yellow-breasted "Babbler") *Macronous gularis* 85, 93, 95
  Gray-faced *M. kelleyi* 97
  Brown *M. striaticeps* 97
  Fluffy-backed *M. ptilosus* 94
Babbler
  Chestnut (Red)-capped *Timalia pileata* 85
  Yellow-eyed *Chrysomma sinense* 79, 85, 86
  Spiny *Turdoides nipalensis* 83
  Common *T. caudatus* 79, 82
  Striated (Rufous) *T. earlei* 79, 85, 86
  Large Gray *T. malcolmi* 82
  Fulvous *T. fulvus* 60
  Rufous "Chatterer" *T. rubiginosus* 66, 67

Jungle (Seven Sisters) *T. striatus* 79, 82, 85, 86
  Black-lored *T. melanops* 64, 66
  Blackcap *T. reinwardtii* 62
  Sudan (Brown) *T. plebejus* 62, 66
  Arrow-marked *T. jardineii* 64, 66, 68–70, 72, 73
  Squamulated *T. squamulatus* 67
  White-rumped *T. leucopygius* 64, 70
  Northern Pied *T. hypoleucus* 66
Laughing-thrush
  Ashy-headed *Garrulax cinereifrons* 86
  Gray-and-brown *G. palliatus* 96
  Masked *G. perspicillatus* 90, 92
  White-throated *G. albogularis* 83, 84, 91
  White-crested *G. leucolophus* 83, 93
  Lesser Necklaced *G. monileger* 85, 93
  Black *G. lugubris* 96
  Striated *G. striatus* 83
  Formosan *G. morrisonianus* 91
  Black-throated *G. chinensis* 92, 93
  Variegated *G. variegatus* 80, 81
  Pere David's *G. davidi* 89
  Gray-sided *G. caerulatus* 83, 91
  Chestnut-capped *G. mitratus* 96
  Rufous-necked *G. ruficollis* 85
  Hwamei *G. canorus* 15, 90–92
  Streaked *G. lineatus* 80, 81, 84
  Black-faced *G. affinis* 84
  Chestnut-crowned (Red-headed) *G. erythrocephalus* 83, 84
Steere's Babbler *Liocichla steerii* 91
Red-billed Leiothrix *Leiothrix lutea* 15, 83
Nepal Cutia *Cutia nipalensis* 83
Shrike-Babbler
  White-browed (Red-winged) *Pteruthius flaviscapis (erythropterus)* 83, 96
  Green *P. xanthochlorus* 83
Barwing
  Hoary *Actinodura nipalensis* 83
  Formosan *A. morrisoniana* 91
Minla
  Blue-winged *Minla cyanouroptera* 83
  Bar-throated (Chestnut-tailed) *M. strigula* 83
  Red-tailed *M. ignotincta* 83
Fulvetta (Nun-Babbler, Tit-Babbler)
  Rufous-winged (Chestnut-headed) *Alcippe castaneceps* 83, 96
  White-browed *A. vinipectus* 83, 84

Streak-throated (Brown-headed) *A. cinereiceps* 91

Brown-eared (Gould's) *A. brunnea* 91

Brown *A. brunneicauda* 94, 96

Gray-cheeked (-eyed) *A. morrisonia* 91

Nepal *A. nipalensis* 83

Abyssinian "Hill-Babbler" *A. abyssinica* 64, 65

Capuchin Babbler *Phyllanthus atripennis* 62, 63

Sibia

Black-capped *Heterophasia capistrata* 83, 84

White-eared *H. auricularis* 91

Yuhina

Yellow-naped (whiskered) *Yuhina flavicollis* 83

Stripe-throated *Y. gularis* 83, 84

Rufous-vented *Y. occipitalis* 83, 84

Formosan *Y. brunneiceps* 91

White-bellied *Y. zantholeuca* 83, 85, 91, 93, 96

White-throated Oxylabes *Oxylabes madagascariensis* 74

Crossley's Babbler *Mystacornis crossleyi* 74

LOGRUNNERS:
ORTHONYCHINIDAE

Logrunner (Chowchilla)

Spine-tailed *Orthonyx temminckii* 107

Black-headed (Northern) *O. spaldingii* 108

Whipbird

Eastern *Psophodes olivaceus* 105–108

Western *P. nigrogularis* 103

Chiming Wedgebill *P. (Sphenostoma) occidentalis* 102

Quail-thrush

Spotted *Cinclosoma punctatum* 106

Chestnut *C. castanotum* 102–104

Cinnamon *C. cinnamomeum (castaneothorax)* 102

Jewel-Babbler (Eupetes)

Spotted (High Mountain) *Eupetes (Ptilorrhoa) leucostictus* 99

Lowland *E. (P.) caerulescens* 100

Mid-mountain (Chestnut-backed) *E. (P.) castanonotus* 99

Malaysian Rail-Babbler *E. macrocerus* 94

Blue-capped Babbler *Ifrita kowaldi* 99

BULBULS:*PYCNONOTIDAE*

Bulbul

Collared Finch-billed *Spizixos semitorques* 97

Straw-headed (Yellow-crowned) *Pycnonotus zeylanicus* 95, 96

Striated *P. striatus* 83

Black-and-white *P. melanoleucos* 94

Black-headed *P. atriceps* 94–98

Black-crested Yellow *P. melanicterus (dispar)* 85, 86, 93, 96

Scaly-breasted *P. squamatus* 94, 96

Gray-bellied *P. cyaniventris* 94, 95

Red-whiskered *P. jocosus* 75, 82, 83, 92, 93, 105, 106

Chinese (Light-vented) *P. sinensis* 90–92

Stayn's (Formosan) *P. taivanus* 91

White-cheeked *P. leucogenys* 78–83

Red-vented *P. cafer* 15, 79, 81–83, 85, 86, 92, 110

Sooty-headed *P. aurigaster* 95, 96, 98

Cape *P. capensis* 71

Garden (White (Yellow)-vented, Black-capped) *P. barbatus (dodsoni, xanthopygos, tricolor)* 60, 62–70, 72, 73

Puff-backed *P. eutilotis* 94

Yellow-wattled *P. urostictus* 97

Orange-spotted *P. bimaculatus* 98

Yellow-eared *P. penicillatus* 86

Flavescent (Pale-faced) *P. flavescens* 96

Yellow-vented *P. goiavier* 95–97

White-browed *P. luteolus* 86

Olive-winged (Olive-brown, Large Olive) *P. plumosus* 95–97

Cream-vented (White-eyed Brown) *P. simplex* 94–96

Red-eyed *P. brunneus* 94, 95

Spectacled *P. erythropthalmos* 94, 95, 96, 98

Shelley's *P. masukuensis* 65

Greenbul

Little *P. (Andropadus) virens* 62, 63, 65, 67, 68

Little Gray *P. (A.) gracilis* 65

Ansorge's *P. (A.) ansorgei* 65

Cameroun Sombre *P. (A.) curvirostris* 64, 65, 68

Eastern (Zanzibar) Sombre *P. (A.) importunus (insularis)* 67, 71, 72

Yellow-whiskered *P. (A.) latirostris* 63–66

Slender-billed *P. (A.) gracilirostris* 63, 65, 66

Mountain (Olive-breasted) *P. (A.) tephrolaemus* 64, 66, 68

Stripe-cheeked *P. (A.) milanjensis* 68

Honeyguide *Baeopogon indicator* 63–65

Spotted *Ixonotus guttatus* 63

Leaf-love (Greenbul)

Simple *Chlorocichla simplex* 63

Yellow-throated *C. flavicollis* 62, 63

Yellow-bellied *C. flaviventris* 66–70, 72

Joyful *C. laetissima* 64

Swamp Palm Bulbul (White-tailed Greenbul) *Thescelocichla leucopleura* 62, 63

Leaf-love Greenbul (African Leaf-love) *Phyllastrephus scandens* 62

Terrestrial Brownbul (Bulbul) *P. terrestris* 67–70, 72

Greenbul

Gray-olive *P. cerviniventris* 68

Toro Olive *P. baumanni* 65

Yellow-streaked *P. flavostriatus (alfredi)* 68

White-throated *P. albigularis* 63

Fischer's *P. fischeri* 65–68

Greenbul (Tetraka)

Long-billed (Common) *P. madagascariensis* 74

Spectacled (Short-billed) *P. zosterops* 74

Appert's *P. apperti* 74

Dusky *P. tenebrosus* 74

Yellow-browed *P. xanthophrys* 74

Gray-crowned *P. cinereiceps* 74

Bristlebill

Chestnut-tailed (Common, The) *Bleda syndactyla* 65

Gray-headed *B. canicapilla* 62, 63

Yellow-spotted Nicator *Nicator chloris* 62–64, 68–70, 72

Bulbul

Finsch's *Criniger finschii* 94

Ochraceous *C. ochraceus* 94, 96

Gray-cheeked (Olive White-throated) *C. bres* 93, 94, 96–98

Yellow-bellied (Crestless White-throated) *C. phaeocephalus* 94, 96

Gray-eyed *Hypsipetes propinquus* 93

Buff-vented *H. charlottae* 94, 95

Palawan (Golden-eyed) *H. palawanensis* 97

Hairy-backed *H. criniger* 94

Philippine *H. philippinus* 97

Plain-throated *H. everetti* 97

Yellow-browed *H. indicus* 86

Streaked *H. malaccensis* 94

Rufous-bellied *H. virescens* 83

Ashy *H. flavala* 93, 96

Chestnut *H. castanotus* 92

Brown (Chestnut)-eared *H. amaurotis* 87, 88, 91

Thick-billed *H. crassirostris* 76

Mascarene (Olivaceous) *H. borbonicus* 75

Black *H. madagascariensis* 74, 80, 81, 83, 86, 91

PARROTBILLS:
PARADOXORNITHIDAE

Bearded Reedling ("Tit") *Panurus biarmicus* 52, 53, 56–58

Parrotbill

Vinous-throated *Paradoxornis webbianus* 89–91

Black-throated (Orange, Nepal) *P. nipalensis (verreauxi)* 83, 91

WRENTIT:*CHAMAEIDAE*

Wrentit *Chamaea fasciata* 13, 14

LEAFBIRDS:*IRENIDAE*

Iora

Common *Aegithina tiphia* 82, 85, 86, 93, 95–97

Green *A. viridissima* 94

Great *A. lafresnayei* 93, 95

Leafbird (Chloropsis)

Yellow-billed *Chloropsis flavipennis* 97

Palawan *C. palawanensis* 97

Greater Green *C. sonnerati* 94–96

Lesser Green *C. cyanopogon* 94, 95

Blue-winged (Gold-mantled) *C. cochinchinensis* 86, 93, 95, 96

Golden-fronted *C. aurifrons* 85, 86, 93

Orange-bellied *C. hardwickei* 83

Fairy Bluebird

Asian (The) *Irena puella* 93–97

Philippine *I. cyanogaster* 97

DIPPERS:*CINCLIDAE*

Dipper

Eurasian (White-bellied, Water "Ouzel," The) *Cinclus cinclus* 53–55, 57, 59, 60

Brown *C. pallasii* 83, 84, 87–89, 91
North American *C. mexicanus* 2, 3, 10, 12–13, 17, 23
White-capped *C. leucocephalus* 31, 32, 35, 36, 38
   WRENS:*TROGLODYTIDAE*
Wren (Tree-Wren)
  Boucard's (Spotted) *Campylorhynchus jocosus* 17
  Spotted *C. gularis* 16
  Yucatan *C. yucatanicus* 18
  Cactus *C. brunneicapillus* 9, 12
  Bicolored *C. griseus* 29, 30
  White-headed *C. albobrunneus* 24, 31
  Thrush-like (Amazon) *C. turdinus* 33, 37
  Stripe-backed *C. nuchalis* 29, 30
  Band-backed *C. zonatus* 19, 21
  Gray-barred *C. megalopterus* 17
Wren
  Rock *Salpinctes obsoletus* 10, 12, 13, 21
  Canyon *Catherpes mexicanus* 12, 13, 16, 17
  Rufous *Cinnycerthia unirufa* 32
  Sedge (Short-billed Marsh) *Cistothorus platensis* 6–9, 17, 39, 40, 42
  Marsh (Long-billed) *Telmatodytes palustris* 3, 6–9, 11, 13, 14, 16
  Bewick's *Thryomanes bewickii* 3, 9, 12–14, 17
  Zapata *Ferminia cerverai* 25
  Black-bellied *Thryothorus fasciatoventris* 24, 31
  Sooty-headed *T. spadix* 31
  Plain-tailed *T. euophrys* 32, 36
  Moustached *T. genibarbis* 28, 31, 37, 47
  Coraya *T. coraya* 33, 47, 48
  Happy *T. felix* 16
  Spot-breasted *T. maculipectus* 18–20
  Rufous-breasted *T. rutilus* 24, 27, 28, 30
  Bay (Black-capped) *T. nigricapillus* 24, 31
  Stripe-throated *T. thoracicus* 31
  Banded *T. pleurostictus* 17
  Carolina *T. ludovicianus (albinucha)* 6–9, 18, 20
  Rufous-and-white *T. rufalbus* 22, 24, 28, 30
  Sinaloa (Bar-vented) *T. sinaloa* 16
  Plain *T. modestus* 21–24

Buff-breasted *T. leucotis* 24, 28–30, 33, 48
Long-billed *T. longirostris* 46
Northern (Winter, Common, The) *Troglodytes troglodytes* 1, 3, 6, 7, 14, 49–53, 55–60, 81, 84, 87, 88, 91
House (Northern, Southern) *T. aedon (musculus)* 3, 6–10, 12–14, 16–19, 21–24, 26–31, 33, 35–48
Brown-throated *T. brunneicollis (aedon)* 12, 16, 17
Rufous-browed *T. ruficiliatus (solstitialis)* 21
Ochraceous *T. ochraceus (solstitialis)* 22, 23
Mountain *T. solstitialis* 32, 36
Timberline *Thryorchilus browni* 22
White-bellied *Uropsila leucogastra* 18
Wood-Wren
  White-breasted *Henicorhina leucosticta* 19, 20, 24, 31, 33, 48
  Gray-breasted *H. leucophrys* 21–23, 28, 30, 31
Wren
  Nightingale *Microcerculus marginatus (philomela)* 24, 28, 30, 31, 33, 37, 47
  Wing-banded *M. bambla* 48
  Chestnut-breasted *Cyphorhinus thoracicus* 31
  Musician *C. aradus* 33, 37, 48
  Song *C. phaeocephalus (aradus)* 24
   MOCKINGBIRDS:*MIMIDAE*
Catbird (Mockingbird)
  Gray (The) *Dumetella carolinensis* 6–10, 18–20, 24, 25
  Black *Melanoptila glabrirostris* 18
Mockingbird
  Blue *Melanotis caerulescens* 16, 17
  Blue-and-white *M. hypoleucus (caerulescens)* 21
  Northern (The) *Mimus polyglottos* 6–9, 12–17, 27
  Tropical *M. gilvus* 18, 19, 21, 24, 26, 27, 29, 30, 46, 48
  Bahama *M. gundlachii* 25
  Chilean *M. thenca* 39
  Long-tailed *M. longicaudatus* 35
  Chalk-browed *M. saturninus* 42, 43, 45
  Patagonian *M. patagonicus* 41
  White-banded *M. triurus* 41–43
  Charles *Nesomimus trifasciatus* 34
  Galapagos *N. parvulus (trifasciatus)* 34

Hood *N. macdonaldi (trifasciatus)* 34
San Cristobal (Chatham) *N. melanotis (trifasciatus)* 34
Thrasher
Sage ("Mockingbird") *Oreoscoptes montanus* 11, 12
Brown *Toxostoma rufum* 6–9
Long-billed *T. longirostre* 9
Cozumel *T. guttatum* 18
Bendire's *T. bendirei* 12
Curve-billed *T. curvirostre* 9, 12, 16, 17
California *T. redivivum* 13, 14
Crissal *T. dorsale* 12
Trembler
Brown (The) *Cinclocerthia ruficauda* 26
White-breasted ("Thrasher") *Ramphocinclus brachyurus* 26
Black-capped Mockingthrush (Marsh Mockingbird) *Donacobius atricapillus* [possibly a wren] 33, 37, 46–48
Thrasher
Pearly-eyed *Margarops fuscatus* 25, 26
Scaly-breasted *M. fuscus* 26
THRUSHES:*TURDIDAE*
Blue (White-browed) Shortwing *Brachypteryx montana (cruralis)* 96, 97
Scrub-Robin
Karoo *Cercotrichas (Erythropygia) coryphaeus* 71
Red-backed (White-browed (-winged)) *C. (E.) leucophrys (zambesiana)* 64, 66, 68, 70, 72, 73
Rufous ("Chat," "Bushchat," "Warbler") *C. (E.) galactotes* 55, 59, 60, 62, 66, 77, 78
Eastern Bearded *C. (E.) quadrivirgata* 67, 68, 72
Black *C. podobe* 62
"Rock Jumper" *Chaetops frenatus* 71
Southern *Drymodes brunneopygia* 103, 104
Robin
Starred (White-starred Bush) *Pogonocichla stellata* 66, 68
Whiskered ("Akalat") *Erithacus cyornithopsis* 64, 65
Equatorial ("Akalat") *E. aequatorialis* 65
Forest *E. erythrothorax* 65
European *E. rubecula* 50–53, 55–61
Japanese *E. akahige* 87, 88

Thrush-Nightingale *Luscinia (E.) luscinia* 53, 56, 66–68, 77
Nightingale *L. (E.) megarhynchos* 51, 52, 55, 57–60, 63, 77, 78
Siberian Rubythroat *L. (E.) calliope* 1, 82, 87–91, 93
Bluethroat *L. (E.) svecicus* 51, 53, 54, 56–58, 60–62, 77, 79, 83, 85, 89
Himalayan Rubythroat *L. (E.) pectoralis* 81, 84, 85
Blue Robin
Indian (Blue "Chat") *L. (E.) brunneus* 80, 83, 86
Siberian *L. (E.) cyane* 87–90, 93, 96
Bush-Robin
Orange-flanked (Red-flanked "Bluetail") *Tarsiger (E.) cyanurus* 80, 81, 83, 84, 87–89, 91, 92
Golden *T. (E.) chrysaeus* 83, 84
White-browed *T. (E.) indicus* 91
Johnstone's (Collared) *T. (E.) johnstoniae* 91
Robin-Chat
Gray-winged *Cossypha polioptera (insulana)* 65
Natal (Red-capped) *C. natalensis* 67–69, 72, 73
Chorister *C. dichroa* 72
Ruppell's *C. semirufa* 66
Heuglin's (White-browed) *C. heuglini* 64, 66–70, 72, 73
Blue-shouldered *C. cyanocampter* 65
Cape *C. caffra* 64–66, 68, 71, 72
White-throated *C. humeralis* 72, 73
Snowy-crowned (-headed) *C. niveicapilla* 62–65
White-crowned *C. albicapilla* 62
Olive-flanked *C. (Dessonornis) anomola* 68
Morning-Thrush (Warbler)
Spotted *Cichladusa guttata* 67, 69, 70
Scrub *C. arquata* 66, 67
Alethe
Brown-chested *Alethe poliocephala* 65, 66
Fire-crested *A. castanea* 62
Cholo (Mountain) *A. choloensis* 68
Magpie-Robin
Asian (Robin "Dayal") *Copsychus saularis* 79, 82, 83, 85, 86, 90, 92, 95, 97, 98
Seychelles *C. sechellarum* 76

Madagascar *C. albospecularis* 74

Shama

White-rumped *C. malabaricus* 15, 85, 86, 93–95

White-browed *C. luzoniensis* 97

Palawan *C. niger* 97

Rufous-tailed *C. pyrropygus* 94

Persian (White-throated) Robin *Irania gutturalis* 77

Redstart

Blue-headed *Phoenicurus caeruleocephalus* 83

Black *P. ochruros* 51, 52, 55, 57–61, 77, 79, 81, 82, 84, 85

Eurasian (White-fronted, The) *P. phoenicurus* 50–51, 53–62, 77, 78

Hodgson's *P. hodgsoni* 83

Blue-fronted *P. frontalis* 81, 83, 84

White-throated *P. schisticeps* 84

Daurian *P. auroreus* 87–92

Moussier's *P. moussieri* 60

Guldenstadt's *P. erythrogaster* 84

Philippine Water *P. (Rhyacornis) bicolor* 97

Plumbeous Water *P. (R.) fuliginosus* 81, 83, 89, 91

White-tailed (Blue-) Robin *Cinclidium leucurum* 83, 91

Grandala *Grandala coelicolor* 84

Bluebird

Eastern *Sialia sialis* 6–9, 12, 17, 21

Western *S. mexicana* 3, 12–14, 17

Mountain *S. currocoides* 10, 12, 13

Forktail

Little *Enicurus scouleri* 81, 91

Chestnut-naped *E. ruficapillus* 96

Black-backed *E. immaculatus* 85

Slaty-backed *E. schistaceus* 83

White-crowned *E. leschenaulti (frontalis)* 94, 96, 98

Spotted *E. maculatus* 81, 83

Solitaire

Townsend's *Myadestes townsendi* 2, 3, 10, 12, 13

Brown-backed *M. obscurus* 16, 17, 21

Cuban *M. elisabeth* 25

Rufous-throated *M. genibarbis* 25

Andean *M. ralloides* 28, 31, 36

Black-faced *M. melanops (ralloides)* 22, 23

Black *Entomodestes coracinus* 31

Rusty-Thrush (Ant-Thrush)

Red-tailed *Neocossyphus rufus* 65, 67

White-tailed *N. peonsis* 65

Chat

Familiar (Red-tailed) *Cercomela familiaris* 66, 68–72

Brown Rock *C. fusca* 82

Hill *C. sordida* 66

"Whinchat" *Saxicola rubetra* 51–53, 55–63, 66, 77, 78

Canary Islands *S. dacotiae* 61

"Stonechat" *S. torquata* 51, 52, 55–62, 64–66, 68, 71–72, 74, 77–78, 81–85, 87, 88, 92

Reunion *S. borbonensis (torquata)* 75

White-tailed "Bushchat" *S. leucura* 79, 85

Pied "Bushchat" *S. caprata (delacouri)* 79, 81–83, 85, 86, 97–100

Gray "Bushchat" *S. ferrea* 80, 83, 84

Northern "Ant-Chat" (Anteater) *Myrmecocichla aethiops* 62, 65, 66

Southern "Ant-Chat" (Anteater) *M. formicivora* 71

Sooty *M. nigra* 64, 66

Arnott's *M. arnotti* 66, 69

Mocking Cliff *Thamnolaea cinnamomeiventris* 66, 68, 70

Wheatear

Isabelline *Oenanthe isabellina* 66, 77, 78

Northern (The) *O. oenanthe* 1, 2, 49–62, 66, 67, 77, 78

Desert *O. deserti* 60, 77, 78

Black-eared *O. hispanica* 55, 58–60, 62, 77, 78

Variable *O. picata* 77

Mourning *O. lugens (lugubris)* 60, 66, 77, 78

Hooded *O. monacha* 78

Pied *O. pleschanka* 56, 66, 77, 78, 79

White-crowned (Black) *O. leucopyga* 60

Black *O. leucura* 59, 60

Mountain ("Chat") *O. monticola* 71

Greater Red-rumped *O. moesta* 60, 77

Capped *O. pileata* 66, 71

White-capped River Chat *Chaimarrornis leucocephalus* 81, 83, 84

Indian Robin *Saxicoloides fulicata* 79, 82, 86

Rock-Thrush
 Madagascar *Monticola imerinus* 74
 Cape *M. rupestris* 71
 Sentinel *M. explorator* 72
 Little *M. rufocinerea* 66
 Angola *M. angolensis* 68
 (White-backed, The) *M. saxatilis* 55, 57–60, 66, 67, 78
 Blue-headed (capped) *M. cinclorhynchus* 80, 81, 83
 Chestnut-bellied *M. rufiventris* 83, 92
 Blue *M. solitarius* 55, 59, 60, 81, 82, 86–92, 97
 White-throated *M. gularis* 93
Whistling-Thrush
 Ceylon *Myiophoneus blighi* 86
 Sunda *M. glaucinus* 96
 Formosan *M. insularis* 91
 Blue (Himalayan) *M. caeruleus (flavirostris)* 81, 83, 84, 92–94
Thrush (Ground-Thrush)
 Chestnut-capped *Zoothera interpres* 96, 98
 Pied *Z. wardii* 86
 Orange-headed *Z. citrina* 85, 86, 96, 98
 Everett's *Z. everetti* 96
 Siberian *Z. sibirica* 87, 88, 90
 Abyssinian *Z. piaggiae* 66
 Orange *Z. gurneyi* 68
 Spotted (Natal) *Z. guttata* 67, 68
 Spot-winged *Z. spiloptera* 86
 Plain-backed *Z. mollissima (griseiceps)* 83
 Scaly (Tiger, White's, Speckled Mountain, Australian, Ground, Golden) *Z. dauma* 83, 86–88, 90, 91, 97, 105–108
Thrush
 Varied *Ixoreus (Z.) naevius* 2, 3, 14
 Aztec *Ridgwayia (Z.) pinicola* 17
 Forest *Cichlherminia lherminieri* 26
 Hawaiian *Phaeornis obscurus* 15
 Small Kauai *P. palmeri* 15
Nightingale-Thrush
 Black-billed *Catharus gracilirostris* 22, 23
 Orange-billed *C. aurantiirostris* 16, 17, 21, 23, 27–28, 30, 31
 Slaty-backed *C. fuscater* 22, 30
 Russet *C. occidentalis* 16, 17
 Ruddy-capped *C. frantzii* 21–23

Thrush
 "Veery" *C. fuscescens* 6–10, 20, 25
 Gray-cheeked *C. minimus* 2, 4–9, 25, 30
 Swainson's *C. ustulatus* 2, 3, 6–10, 12–14, 16, 17, 20, 22–25, 30, 31, 33, 37
 Hermit *C. guttatus* 2, 3, 6–10, 12–14, 16, 17, 21
 Wood *Hylocichla mustelina* 6–9, 18–20, 22
 Yellow-legged *Platycichla flavipes* 27, 28, 30, 45, 46
 Pale-eyed *P. leucops* 31, 36
 African *Turdus pelios (olivaceus)* 62, 63, 65
 Olive *T. olivaceus* 64, 66, 68, 71
 Kurrichane *T. libonyanus* 68–70, 72, 73
 African Bare-eyed *T. tephronotus* 67
 Groundscraper *T. litsipsirupa* 70, 73
 Tickell's *T. unicolor* 81
 Japanese *T. cardis* 87, 88, 92
 White-collared "Blackbird" *T. albocinctus* 83, 84
 Ring ("Ouzel") *T. torquatus* 52, 54, 55, 57–60
 Gray-winged "Blackbird" *T. boulboul* 83
 Eurasian (Common) "Blackbird" *T. merula* 49–53, 55–61, 77, 81, 86, 90, 92, 104–106, 111
 Gray-backed *T. hortulorum* 90, 92
 Island (Mountain "Blackbird") *T. poliocephalus* 91, 96, 97 109, 110
 Brown-headed *T. chrysolaus* 87, 88, 91
 Gray-headed (Chestnut) *T. rubrocanus* 80, 81
 Pale (Pallid) *T. pallidus* 87, 88, 90, 91
 Eye-browed (Gray-headed) *T. obscurus* 1, 87, 88, 96
 Black (Red)-throated *T. ruficollis* 78–80, 82–84, 89
 Dusky *T. naumanni (eunomus)* 87, 89–91, 97
 "Fieldfare" *T. pilaris* 49–59, 61
 "Redwing" *T. iliacus (musicus)* 49–54, 56–61
 Song *T. philomelos* 50–61, 77, 78, 105, 106, 111
 Mistle *T. viscivorus* 51–53, 55–60, 81
 White-chinned *T. aurantius* 25
 Red-legged *T. (Mimocichla) plumbeus* 25, 26

Chiguanco *T. chiguanco* 35, 36, 38

Sooty ("Robin") *T. nigrescens* 22, 23

Great *T. fuscater* 30, 32, 36

Glossy-black *T. serranus* 28, 31

Black-hooded *T. olivater* 28, 30

Rufous-bellied *T. rufiventris* 42–46

Austral *T. falcklandii* 39–41

Pale-breasted *T. leucomelas* 28–30, 44, 46–48

Creamy-bellied *T. amaurochalinus* 37, 42–46

Mountain ("Robin") *T. plebejus* 22, 23

Black-billed *T. ignobilis* 31, 33, 37

Lawrence's *T. lawrencii* 33, 37

Cocoa (Hauxwell's) *T. fumigatus (hauxwelli)* 26–28, 37, 47, 48

Pale-vented *T. obsoletus* 31, 33

Clay-colored ("Robin") *T. grayi* 18–24, 30

Bare-eyed (Eye-ringed) *T. nudigenis* 26–29, 47, 48

White-eyed *T. jamaicensis* 25

White-throated ("Robin") *T. assimilis* 16, 17, 19, 20, 22, 31

White-necked *T. albicollis* 27, 28, 33, 37, 44, 46–48

Rufous-backed ("Robin") *T. rufopalliatus* 12, 16, 17

La Selle *T. swalesi* 25

Rufous-collared ("Robin") *T. rufitorques* 21

Black ("Robin") *T. infuscatus* 21

American "Robin" (Lawn) *T. migratorius* 1–14, 16, 17, 25

  OLD WORLD WARBLERS: *SYLVIIDAE*

Gnatwren

Collared *Microbates collaris* 48

Long-billed *Ramphocaenus melanurus (rufiventris)* 19, 20, 24, 27, 28, 30, 33, 47, 48

Gnatcatcher

Blue-gray *Polioptila caerulea* 6–9, 12, 13, 16–19, 21, 25

Black-tailed *P. melanura* 12

Cuban *P. lembeyei* 25

White-lored *P. albiloris* 18

Tropical *P. plumbea* 19, 20, 24, 28–30, 47, 48

Cream-bellied *P. lactea* 44

Guianan *P. guianensis* 48

Slate-throated *P. schistaceigula* 31

Masked *P. dumicola* 42, 43

Chestnut-headed Tesia *Tesia castaneocoronata* 83

Bush-Warbler

Stub(Short)-tailed *Cettia squameiceps* 87, 88, 92, 93, 96

Japanese (Manchurian) *C. diphone (canturians, cantans)* 15, 87, 88, 90, 92

Strong-footed (Brownish-flanked, Mountain) *C. fortipes (montanus)* 80, 91, 96, 98

Yellow-bellied *C. acanthizoides* 91

Cetti's ("Warbler") *C. cetti* 55, 56, 58–60, 79

Rush "Warbler" *Bradypterus baboecala* 68, 69, 72

Cinnamon Bracken "Warbler" *B. cinnamomeus* 68

Victorin's Scrub "Warbler" *B. victorini* 71

Barratt's (Scrub) *B. barratti* 68

Chinese *B. tacsanowskius* 89, 91

Kinabalu Friendly "Warbler" *B. accentor* 96

Ceylon (Palliser's) *B. palliseri* 86

Grasshopper-Warbler

Gray's *Locustella fasciolata* 87, 88

Savi's "Warbler" *L. luscinioides* 52, 55–59, 77

River "Warbler" *L. fluviatilis* 56, 57

Pallas's *L. certhiola* 87, 88, 90

Middendorf's *L. ochotensis* 90

Western (Pale, The) *L. naevia* 52, 53, 57, 58, 60

Lanceolated "Warbler" *L. lanceolata* 87, 88

Reed-Warbler

Moustached "Warbler" *Acrocephalus (Lusciniola) melanopogon* 55–59, 77, 79

Aquatic "Warbler" *A. paludicola* 57, 58

Sedge "Warbler" *A. schoenobaenus* 51–60, 62, 64, 66, 68–70, 77

Paddyfield "Warbler" *A. agricola* 79, 82, 89

Black-browed *A. bistrigiceps* 87–90, 92

Blyth's *A. dumetorum* 79, 82, 86

European *A. scirpaceus* 51–53, 55–60, 62, 64, 66, 67

Marsh "Warbler" *A. palustris* 52, 53, 56, 57, 64, 68, 69, 77

Clamorous *A. stentoreus* 77, 79, 81, 82, 85, 86, 89, 100–103, 106–108

Great *A. arundinaceus* 52, 53, 55–60, 64, 66, 68, 69, 72, 77, 87–92, 95, 97

Thick-billed "Warbler" *A. aedon* 93

Cape (Greater Swamp) *A. gracilirostris* 66, 71, 72

Madagascar (Swamp "Warbler") *A. newtoni* 74

Brush-Warbler

Seychelles *Bebrornis sechellensis* 76

Madagascar *Nesillas typica* 74

Kiritika Warbler *Thamnornis chloropetoides* 74

Chloropeta (Yellow-Warbler)

Natal *Chloropeta natalensis (batesi)* 65, 66

Mountain *C. similis* 66, 68

Warbler

Icterine *Hippolais icterina* 51–53, 55–58, 66

Melodious *H. polyglotta* 58–60, 62

Olive-tree *H. olivetorum* 64, 66

Olivaceous *H. pallida* 55, 56, 59, 60, 62, 66, 77, 78

Booted *H. caligata* 77, 82, 86

Barred *Sylvia nisoria* 50, 51, 53, 56, 57, 66, 77

Orphean *S. hortensis* 58–60, 62, 82

Garden *S. borin* 51–62, 65, 66, 68, 69, 72, 77

"Blackcap" *S. atricapilla* 50–53, 55–61, 65, 66, 77

Whitethroat

Greater *S. communis* 50–53, 55–62, 66, 69, 77, 78

Lesser *S. curruca* 50–53, 55–57, 77–79, 82

Hume's *S. althaea* 86

Warbler

Desert *S. nana* 60, 78, 79

Sardinian *S. melanocephala* 55, 58–62, 77, 78

Subalpine *S. cantillans* 58–60, 62

Spectacled *S. conspicillata* 58–61

Tristam's *S. deserticola* 60

Dartford *S. undata* 58–60

Leaf-Warbler

Willow "Warbler" *Phylloscopus trochilus* 50–66, 69, 70, 72, 77, 78

"Chiffchaff" *P. collybita* 50–53, 55–62, 65, 77–79, 82, 83

Plain (Sind) *P. neglectus* 79

Bonelli's "Warbler" *P. bonelli* 57–60, 62

Tytler's *P. tytleri* 81

Wood "Warbler" *P. sibilatrix* 51–53, 55–58, 61–63, 65

Tickell's *P. affinis* 81, 84

Dusky "Warbler" *P. fuscatus* 92, 93

Radde's "Warbler" *P. schwarzi* 93

Orange-barred *P. pulcher* 83, 84

Yellow-browed "Warbler" (Plain) *P. inornatus* 50, 51, 81–83, 89, 90, 92, 93

Pallas's (Lemon-rumped) *P. proregulus* 80, 81, 83, 85, 89, 92

Gray-faced *P. maculipennis* 83, 84

Arctic "Warbler" *P. borealis* 2, 54, 87–91, 95–97

Large-billed *P. magnirostris* 86

Greenish "Warbler" (Dull-green) *P. trochiloides* 82–86, 93

Pale-legged *P. tenellipes* 87, 88, 92, 94

Large Crowned *P. occipitalis* 80, 81

Eastern Crowned *P. coronatus* 83, 87–90, 94

Blyth's (Crowned) *P. reguloides* 83, 93

Black-browed (Yellow-throated, Small Crowned) "Warbler" *P. cantator* 83, 84

Sulfur-breasted "Warbler" *P. ricketti (cantator, trivirgatus)* 93

Mountain (Island) *P. (Seicercus) trivirgatus* 96–99

Philippine *P. olivaceus* 97

DuBois's *P. cebuensis* 97

Leaf-Warbler (Woodland-Warbler)

Yellow-throated *P. ruficapillus* 68

Uganda *P. budongoensis* 65

Brown *P. umbrovirens* 65, 66

Warbler

Yellow-breasted *Seicercus montis* 96

Golden-spectacled (Yellow-eyed) *S. burkii* 83

Gray-headed "Flycatcher-Warbler" *S. xanthoschistos* 81, 83

Sunda *S. grammiceps* 98

White-throated (Fulvous-faced "Flycatcher-Warbler") *S. (Abroscopus) albogularis* 91

Yellow-bellied *S. (A.) superciliaris* 96

Black-faced *S. (A.) schisticeps* 83

Kinglet
Ruby-crowned *Regulus calendula* 2, 3,
5–10, 12–14, 16, 17
"Goldcrest" *R. regulus* 50–55, 57, 58,
81, 87, 88
"Firecrest" *R. ignicapillus* 52, 55,
57–61
Formosan "Firecrest" *R. goodfellowi*
91
Golden-crowned *R. satrapa* 3, 6, 7, 9,
12, 14, 17
Streaked Scrub Warbler *Scotocerca in-
quieta* 60, 77
Cisticola
Pectoral-patch *Cisticola brunnescens*
66
Wing-snapping (Ayre's Cloud) *C. ayre-
sii* 66
Golden-headed *C. exilis* 91, 93, 97–101,
105–108
Zitting (Streaked, Fan-tailed "War-
bler") *C. juncidis* 58–60, 62–64, 66,
68–70, 72, 73, 77, 82, 83, 86, 88, 90–
92, 95, 97, 98, 101
Madagascar *C. cherina* 67
Desert *C. aridula* 66, 72
Croaking *C. natalensis* 63, 65, 66, 68,
70, 72
Stout *C. robusta* 64–66
Gray-backed *C. subruficapilla* 71
Wailing *C. lais* 66, 68
Levaillant's (Tinkling) *C. rufilata* 71
Ashy *C. cinereola* 66
Rattling *C. chiniana* 65–70, 72, 73
Lyne's *C. distincta* 66
Tiny *C. nana* 66
Short-winged *C. brachyptera* 63, 68, 69
Neddicky (Piping) *C. fulvicapilla*
68–73
Lazy *C. aberrans* 68
Whistling *C. lateralis* 63, 65
Chattering *C. anonyma* 63
Red-faced *C. erythrops* 63, 65, 66, 68–
70, 72
Singing *C. cantans* 63, 66, 68
Hunter's *C. hunteri* 66
Chubb's *C. chubbi* 64, 65
Winding *C. galactotes* 63–68, 72
Prinia
Tawny-flanked *Prinia subflava (inor-
nata)* 62, 65–70, 72, 73, 82, 86, 91, 92
Karoo *P. maculosa* 71

Pale *P. somalica* 66
White-chinned *P. leucopogon* 65
Banded *P. bairdii* 65
Graceful *P. gracilis* 77, 78
Ashy (Long-tailed) *P. socialis* 79, 86
Gray-breasted (Franklin's) *P. hodgsoni*
82, 86
Yellow-bellied *P. flaviventris* 79, 85, 91,
92, 95, 96
Bar-winged *P. familiaris* 98
Brown *P. polychroa* 91, 92
Striated (Brown Hill) *P. criniger* 80, 83
Jungle *P. sylvatica* 85, 86
Rufous-fronted *P. buchanani* 82
Hodgson's *P. cinereocapilla* 85
Apalis
Yellow (Black)-breasted *Apalis flavida*
66, 68, 70, 72
Rudd's *A. ruddi* 72
Black-throated *A. jacksoni* 65
White-winged *A. chariessa* 68
Bar-throated *A. thoracica (murina)* 66,
68, 71, 72
Gray *A. cinerea* 65, 66
Buff-throated *A. rufogularis* 65
Chestnut-throated *A. porphyrolaema*
65, 66
Black-headed *A. melanocephala* 66–
68
Black-collared *A. pulchra* 65, 66
Collared *A. ruwenzori* 64
Grassbird
Moustached ("Warbler") *Melocichla
mentalis* 63, 65, 66, 68, 69
Cape *Sphenoeacus afer* 71
Emu-tail
Brown *Dromaeocercus brunneus* 74
Gray *D. seebohmi* 74
Tailorbird
Common (Kipling's) *Orthotomus
sutorius (longicaudus)* 79, 82, 83, 85,
86, 92, 93, 95, 97
Dark-necked *O. atrogularis* 93–95
Luzon *O. derbianus* 97
Ashy *O. ruficeps (sepium)* 95, 98
Rufous-tailed (-crowned) (Red-
headed) *O. sericeus* 95, 97
Mountain *O. cucullatus* 93, 96–98
White-eared *O. cinereiceps* 97
Black-headed *O. nigriceps* 97
Black-faced Rufous Warbler *Bathmocer-
cus cerviniventris (rufus)* 65

Camaroptera
Bleating (Green-backed) *Camaroptera brachyura* 65, 67–69, 72
Gray-backed *C. brevicaudata (harterti)* 62–64, 66, 68, 70
Stierling's *C. stierlingi* 68, 72
Olive-green *C. chloronota* 65
Moho (Oriole Warbler) *Hypergerus atriceps* 62, 63
Gray-capped Warbler *Eminia lepida* 64, 66
Eremomela
Yellow-bellied *Eremomela icteropygialis* 66, 68, 70, 73
Green-capped *E. scotops* 68, 72, 73
Green-backed *E. canescens* 62, 66
Turner's *E. turneri* 65
Burnt-necked *E. usticollis* 68, 69, 72
Crombec
White-browed *Sylvietta leucophrys (chapini)* 64–66
Green *S. virens* 63, 64
Red-faced *S. whytii* 66, 68
Senegal *S. brachyura* 62, 66
Cape (Long-billed) *S. rufescens* 68, 70, 71, 73
Tit-Warbler
Brown *Parisoma lugens* 66
Banded *P. boehmi* 66
Rand's Warbler *Randia pseudozosterops* 74
Grass-Warbler (Grassbird, Marsh-Warbler)
Fan-tailed (African) *Schoenicola platyura (brevirostris)* 65
Japanese *Megalurus pryeri* 88
Tawny (Rufous-capped) *M. timoriensis* 97, 107, 108
Striated *M. palustris* 97, 98
Little *M. gramineus* 103–106
New Caledonian *Megalurulus mariei* 109
Fernbird *Bowdleria punctata* 111
Songlark
Rufous *Cinclorhamphus mathewsi* 101–104, 106
Brown *C. cruralis* 102–104, 106
Warbler
Long-legged *Trichocichla rufa* 110
Fiji *Vitia ruficapilla* 110

Hyliota (Yellow-bellied Warbler)
Yellow-bellied (African) *Hyliota flavigaster* 62, 68
Southern *H. australis* 65
FAIRYWRENS:*MALURIDAE*
Fairywren (Wren)
Orange-crowned (Rufous) *Clytomyias insignis* 99
Cobalt (Blue) *Todopsis cyanocephalus* 100
Superb Blue *Malurus cyaneus* 104–107
Splendid (Black-backed, Turquoise, Banded) *M. splendens (melanotus, callianus)* 102–104
White-winged (Blue(Black)-and-white) *M. leucopterus (cyanotus)* 102
Variegated (Purple-backed, Lovely) *M. lamberti (assimilis, amabilis)* 102, 104, 106–108
Red-winged *M. elegans* 103
Blue-breasted *M. pulcherrimus* 103
Red-backed *M. melanocephalus* 101, 107, 108
White-shouldered *M. alboscapulatus* 99, 100
Grasswren
Dusky *Amytornis purnelli* 102
Striated *A. striatus (whitei)* 102, 104
Emu-wren
Southern *Stipiturus malachurus* 103, 105, 106
Rufous-crowned (Mallee) *S. ruficeps (mallee)* 102, 104
AUSTRALIAN WARBLERS: *ACANTHIZIDAE*
Bristlebird
Eastern *Dasyornis brachypterus* 107
Western *D. longirostris* 103
Rufous *D. broadbenti* 103
Gerygone (Warbler)
White-throated *Gerygone olivacea* 100, 101, 106–108
Brown (Northern) *G. mouki (richmondi)* 106–108
Fairy (Black-throated) *G. palpebrosa (flavida)* 99, 100, 108
Large-billed (Swamp) *G. magnirostris* 99–101, 108
Green-backed *G. chloronota* 100, 101
Mangrove (Buff-breasted) *G. levigaster (cantator)* 100, 101
Western (White-tailed) *G. fusca* 101, 103

New Guinea Gray (Mountain) *G. cinerea* 99

Yellow-bellied *C. chrysogaster* 100

Treefern (Brown-breasted) *G. ruficollis* 99

Fantail *G. flavolateralis* 109

New Zealand Gray *G. igata* 111

Yellow-breasted ("Flyeater") *G. sulphurea* 94, 97, 98

Weebill *Smicrornis brevirostris (flavescens)* 101–104, 106, 107

Whiteface

Southern *Aphelocephala leucopsis* 102, 104, 106

Banded *A. nigricincta* 102

Thornbill

Yellow (Little) *Acanthiza nana* 104–107

Striated *A. lineata* 104–106

Brown *A. pusilla* 104–107

Broad-tailed *A. apicalis* 102–104

Mountain *A. katherina* 108

New Guinea *A. murina* 99

Slate-backed *A. robustirostris* 102

Western *A. inornata* 103

Samphire *A. iredalei* 104

Buff-rumped (-tailed) *A. reguloides* 104–107

Yellow-rumped (-tailed) *A. chrysorrhoa* 102, 103, 105–107

Chestnut-rumped (-tailed) *A. uropygialis* 102, 104

Scrubwren

Pale-billed *Sericornis spilodera* 99

Noisy (Large Mountain) *S. nouhuysi* 99

White-browed (Spotted) *S. frontalis (maculatus)* 103, 105–108

Buff-faced *S. perspicillatus* 99

Large-billed *S. magnirostris* 105–108

Gray-green (Dusky) *S. arfakianus* 99

Yellow-throated *S. citreogularis (lathami)* 106–108

Atherton *S. keri* 108

Red-throat *S. Pyrrholaemus brunneus* 102, 104

Chestnut-rumped ("Heathwren") *Hylacola (S.) pyrrhopygia* 104, 106

Shy ("Heathwren") *H. (S.) cauta* 104

Fernwren *Crateroscelis (Oreoscopus) gutturalis* 108

Scrubwren (Mouse-babbler)

Chanting (Lowland) *C. murina* 99, 100

Mountain (White-throated) *C. robusta* 99

Fieldwren *Calamanthus fuliginosus* 103, 104

Speckled Warbler *Chthonicola sagittata* 106

Pilotbird *Pycnoptilus floccosus* 105, 106

Whitehead *Mohoua albicilla* 111

Yellowhead *M. ochrocephala* 111

Brown Creeper-Warbler *Finschia novaeseelandiae* 111

Silktail *Lamprolia victoriae* 110

AUSTRALIAN CHATS:
    EPHTHIANURIDAE

Chat (Honeychat)

White-fronted *Epthianura albifrons* 103–106

Crimson *E. tricolor* 102, 104

Orange *E. aurifrons* 102

OLD WORLD FLYCATCHERS:
    MUSCICAPIDAE

Flycatcher

Little Gray *Bradornis microrhynchus (pumilus)* 66

Pallid (Pale) *B. pallidus* 62–64, 66–68, 70, 72

"Silverbird" *Empidornis semipartitus* 66

White-eyed Slaty *Melaenornis chocolatina* 64–66

Northern Black *M. edolioides* 62, 63, 66

Southern Black *M. pammelaina* 66, 68–70, 72, 73

Fiscal *M. silens* 71, 72

White-browed Forest *Fraseria cinerascens* 62, 63

Common *F. ocreata* 63

Jungle-Flycatcher

Olive-backed *Rhinomyias olivacea* 96, 98

Gray-chested *R. umbratilis* 94, 96

Rufous-tailed *R. ruficauda* 96, 97

White-throated *R. gularis* 97

Flycatcher

Pied *Ficedula (Muscicapa) hypoleuca* 51–55, 57–61, 63, 65, 77

Collared *F. (M.) albicollis* 55–57, 77, 78

Yellow-rumped *F. (M.) zanthopygia* 90

Narcissus *F. (M.) narcissina* 87, 89, 90

Mugimaki *F. (M.) mugimaki* 87, 88

Red-breasted (-throated) *F.(M.)parva* 55–7, 79, 82–84, 86, 89, 90, 92, 93

Rufous-gorgeted (Kashmir Red-breasted) *F.(M.)subrubra (strophiata, hyperythra)* 81, 83, 84

Snowy-browed (Thicket, Red-breasted Blue) *F.(M.)hyperythra* 83, 91, 96–98

Rufous-chested *F.(M.)dumetoria* 94

Little Slaty *F.(M.)basilanica* 97

Slaty-backed (Rusty-breasted) Blue *F.(M.)hodgsonii (amabilis)* 83

Westermann's (Little Pied) *F.(M.)westermanni* 83, 93, 96–98

Ultramarine (White-browed Blue) *F.(M.)superciliaris* 80, 83

Slaty-blue *F.(M.)tricolor (leucomelanura)* 79, 80, 84

Blue-and-white *Cyanoptila cyanomelana* 87, 88, 92, 96

Niltava (Flycatcher) (includes *Cyornis* and *Muscicapa* in part)

Small *Niltava macgrigoriae* 83

Rufous-bellied *N. sundara* 80, 83, 93

Vivid *N. vivida* 91

White-tailed *N. concreta* 94, 96

Brook's (Pale-chinned) *N. poliogenys* 84

Pale Blue *N. unicolor* 93, 94, 98

Blue-throated *N. rubeculoides* 83

Hill *N. banyumas (whitei)* 93, 97

Bornean *N. superba (venusta)* 96

Malaysian *N. turcosa* 94

Tickell's *N. tickelliae* 86, 94

Mangrove *N. rufigastra* 95, 97

Flycatcher

Pygmy Blue *Muscicapella hodgsoni* 97

Spotted (Stripped) *Muscicapa striata* 50–61, 63, 64, 66–70, 73, 77

Dark-sided (Siberian, Asian Sooty) *M. sibirica* 81, 83, 84, 87, 88, 91, 95, 96

Gray-streaked (-spotted) *M. griseisticta* 87, 88, 92, 97

Asian Brown *M. latirostris* 86–90, 92, 93, 95, 96

Brown-breasted *M. muttui* 86

Rusty (Rufous)-tailed *M. ruficauda* 81

Ferruginous *M. ferruginea (rufilata)* 91, 96

African Dusky (Pygmy) *M. adusta* 66, 68, 72

Swamp *M. aquatica* 62, 64

Cassin's Gray *M. cassini* 63

Ashy (Little Blue, Blue-gray) *M. caerulescens* 65–70, 72

Sooty (Dusky) *M. infuscata (fuliginosa)* 65

Ceylon Blue *M. sordida* 86

Verditer *M. thalassina* 80, 81, 83, 93, 94, 96, 97

Indigo *M. indigo* 96

Gray Tit-Flycatcher *Myioparus plumbeus* 62, 68, 70, 72

Newtonia

Dark *Newtonia amphichroa* 74

Common *N. brunneicauda* 74

Archbold's *N. archboldi* 74

Fanovana *N. fanovanae* 74

Flycatcher

"Jacky Winter" (Australian Brown, White-tailed) *Microeca leucophaea* 103–105, 107

Lemon-breasted *M. flavigaster* 100–101

Yellow-footed (Little Yellow, Gray-headed) *M. griseoceps* 99

Papuan (Canary) *M. papuana* 99

Gray-headed *Culicapa ceylonensis* 81, 83, 85, 86, 93, 94, 96, 98

Canary *C. helianthea* 97

Peltops (Shieldbill)

Mountain (Singing) *Peltops montanus* 99, 100

Lowland (Clicking) *P. blainvillii* 100

Torrent (River) Flycatcher *Monachella muelleriana* 99

Robin

Red-backed (Garnet) *Eugerygone rubra* 99

Scarlet *Petroica multicolor* 103, 105, 106, 110

Red-capped *P. goodenovii* 102–104, 106

Flame *P. phoenicea* 104, 105

Pink *P. rodinogaster* 105

Rose *P. rosea* 105–107

Hooded *P. cucullata* 102–104, 106

Pied ("Tomtit") *P. macrocephala* 111

New Zealand (Friendly) *P. australis* 111

White-faced *Eopsaltria leucops* 99

Pale Yellow *E. capito* 107, 108

Eastern (Northern, Southern) Yellow *E. australis (chrysorrhoa)* 103, 105–108

Western Yellow *E. griseogularis* 103

White-breasted *E. georgiana* 103

Yellow-bellied *E. flaviventris* 109

Mangrove *Peneoenanthe pulverulenta*
101

Flycatcher
Rufous-winged *Philentoma pyrhop-terum* 94, 95
Maroon-breasted *P. velatum* 94

Flyrobin (Robin, Flycatcher, Thicket-Flycatcher)
White-browed *Poecilodryas superciliosa* 99, 101
Black-throated *P. albonotata* 99
Black (White-winged) *Peneothello sigillatus* 99
Blue (Slaty) *P. cyanus* 99
Gray-headed *Heteromyias (Poecilodryas) cinereifrons* 108

Shrike-Flycatcher *Megabyas flammulatus* 65

Flycatcher
Black-and-white *Bias musicus* 63, 68
Ward's *Pseudobias wardi* 76
Fairy ("Warbler") *Stenostira scita* 71

Batis (Puff-back)
Cape *Batis capensis* 67, 68, 71
Zululand *B. fratrum* 68, 72
Chin-spot *B. molitor* 64–70, 72, 73
Senegal *B. senegalensis* 62
Pygmy *B. perkeo* 66
Black-headed *B. minor* 64, 66

Wattle-eye
Northern (Common) *Platysteira cyanea* 62–64, 66
Black-throated *P. peltata (laticincta)* 66, 68, 72
Blisset's (Red-cheeked) *P. blissetti (chalybea)* 63, 65
Chestnut *P. castanea* 63, 65

Flycatcher
Little Yellow *Erythrocercus holochlorus* 67
Chestnut-capped *E. mccallii* 63
Livingstone's *E. livingstonei* 68
Northern Fairy (Blue) *E. longicauda* 62, 63, 66

Crested-Flycatcher
White-tailed *Trochocercus albonotatus* 64, 65, 68
Dusky *T. nigromitratus* 65
Blue-mantled (African) *T. cyanomelas* 67, 68, 72
Blue-headed *T. nitens* 63

Paradise-Flycatcher
African *Tersiphone viridis* 62–67
Madagascar *T. mutata* 74
Seychelles *T. corvina* 76
Mascarene ("Coq de Bois") *T. bourbonnensis* 75
Asian *T. paradisi* 79, 81, 85, 86, 89, 90, 92–94, 96
Black (Japanese) *T. atrocaudata* 88
Black-headed (Red-bellied) *T. rufiventer (nigriceps)* 62, 63, 65
Rufous *T. cinnamomea* 97
Blue *T. cyanescens* 97

Monarch
Celestial Blue *Hypothymis coelestis* 97
Black-naped *H. azurea* 86, 93–97
Restless (Paperbark) ("Flycatcher") *Seisura inquieta* 101, 103–107

Boatbill (Flatbill)
Yellow-breasted (Boat-billed "Flycatcher") *Machaerirhynchus flaviventer* 108
Black-breasted *M. nigripectus* 99

Elepaio *Chasiempis sandwichensis* 15

Fiji Slaty (Cinereous) Flycatcher *Mayrornis lessoni* 110

Shrikebill
Western (Southern) *Clytorhynchus pachycephaloides* 109
Fiji (Polynesian) *C. vitiensis* 110
Black-faced *C. nigrogularis* 110

Monarch (Flycatcher, Broadbill)
Fantail (Black) *Monarcha axillaris* 99
Shining *M. alecto* 100, 101
Black-faced (Gray-winged) *M. melanopsis* 99, 100, 106–108
Black-winged (Pearly) *M. frater (canescens)* 99, 100
White-eared *M. leucotis* 107, 108
Spot-winged *M. guttula* 99, 100
Spectacled *M. trivirgata* 107, 108
White-bellied (Black-and-white) *M. manadensis* 99
Golden (Black-and-yellow) *M. chrysomela* 100
Pied *Arses kaupi* 108
Frilled *A. telescophthalmus* 99, 100
Leaden *Myiagra rubecula* 100, 101, 106–108
Melanesian (Broad-billed "Flycatcher") *M. caledonica* 109
Vanikoro *M. vanikorensis* 110

Satin *M. cyanoleuca* 99, 104, 105, 107, 108

Mangrove (Broad-billed "Flycatcher") *M. ruficollis* 101

Blue-crested *M. azureocapilla* 110

Fantail

Yellow-bellied *Rhipidura hypoxantha* 83, 84

Black-throated (White-breasted Thicket-) *R. leucothorax* 99, 100

Blue *R. superciliaris* 97

Blue-headed *R. cyaniceps* 97

Black-and-cinnamon *R. nigrocinnamomea* 97

Rufous-backed *R. rufidorsa* 99

Rufous (-fronted) *R. rufifrons* 105–108

Kadavu *R. personata* 110

Dimorphic *R. brachyrhyncha* 99

Spotted *R. spilodera* 109, 110

Gray (Collared) *R. fuliginosa* 103–109, 111

Black *R. atra* 99

Chestnut-bellied *R. hyperythra* 99

Friendly *R. albolimbata* 99

White-throated *R. albicollis* 85, 96

White-browed (-breasted) *R. aureola* 79, 85, 86

Pied *R. javanica* 95–98

Banded (Northern, White-throated) *R. rufiventris (setosa)* 99–101

Pearled (Spotted) *R. perlata* 94, 96

Willie "Wagtail" *R. leucophrys* 99–108

WHISTLERS:*PACHYCEPHALIDAE*

Ploughbill (Wattled "Shrike-tit") *Eulacestoma nigropectus* 99

Shrike-tit (Crested, Australian, Eastern, Western) *Falcunculus frontatus* 103–107

Crested Bellbird (Bell "Whistler") *Oreoica gutturalis* 102–104

Whistler

Golden-faced *Pachycare flavogrisea* 99

Mottled *Rhagologus leucostigma* 99

Rufous-naped *Pachycephala rufinucha* 99

Olive *P. olivacea* 105, 107

Red-lored *P. rufogularis* 104

Gilbert's *P. inornata* 104

Bornean Mountain *P. hypoxantha* 96

Mangrove (White-bellied) *P. cinerea* 95, 97, 98

Modest (Brown-backed) *P. modesta* 99

Yellow-bellied *P. philippinensis* 97

Black-headed *P. monarcha* 99

Sclater's *P. soror* 99

Gray (Brown) *P. simplex (griseiceps)* 99–101, 108

Golden *P. pectoralis* 98, 103–108, 110

Black-tailed (Mangrove Golden) *P. melanura (pectoralis)* 100

New Caledonian *P. caledonica* 109

White-bellied *P. leucogaster* 99

Regent (Schlegel's) *P. schlegelii* 99

Rufous *P. rufiventris (monarcha)* 101–109

White-breasted *P. lanioides* 101

Shrike-thrush (Thrush-Whistler)

Rufous (Brown, Little) *Colluricincla megarhyncha* 99–101, 107, 108

Stripe-breasted (Bower's) *C. boweri* 108

Gray (Western) *C. harmonica (rufiventris)* 99, 100, 102–108

Pitohui

Hooded (Black-headed) *Pitohui dichrous* 99, 100

Rusty *P. ferrugineus* 100

Dusky (Black) *P. nigrescens* 99

ACCENTORS:*PRUNELLIDAE*

Accentor

Alpine *Prunella collaris* 55, 57, 59, 60, 81, 84, 88, 91

Robin *P. rubeculoides* 84

Rufous-breasted *P. strophiata* 81, 83, 84

Siberian *P. montanella* 89

"Dunnock" *P. modularis* 51–55, 57–60, 111

Japanese *P. rubida* 87, 88

Maroon-backed *P. immaculata* 83

PIPITS:*MOTACILLIDAE*

Wagtail

Forest *Dendronanthus indicus* 86, 89, 92, 95

Yellow (Blue-headed, etc.) *Motacilla flava* 1, 51–64, 66–68, 76–78, 82–86, 89–92, 95

Citrine (Yellow-hooded) *M. citreola* 79, 82, 83, 89

Gray *M. cinerea* 1, 51, 53, 55, 57–61, 77, 78, 82–88, 90–92, 95–97, 99

White (Pied) *M. alba* 1, 49–62, 77, 78, 81–92, 97

Japanese *M. grandis* 87, 88

Indian Pied (Large) *M. madaraspatensis* 79, 82, 83, 85

African Pied *M. aguimp* 62–64, 66–70, 72, 73

Mountain *M. clara* 64, 66, 68, 70

Cape (Wells's) *M. capensis* 66, 70–72

Madagascar *M. flaviventris* 74

Golden Pipit *Tmetothylacus tenellus* 64, 66, 67

Longclaw

Cape *Macronyx capensis* 71, 72

Yellow-throated *M. croceus* 62–66, 68, 72

Sharpe's *M. sharpei* 66

Pangani *M. aurantiigula* 66

Rosy-breasted (Pink-throated) *M. ameliae* 65, 66

Pipit

Richard's (Paddyfield, Australian, New Zealand) *Anthus novaeseelandiae (richardii, australis)* 51, 64–66, 68–73, 79, 81–83, 85, 86, 89, 90, 92, 95, 97, 99, 101–104, 106–108, 111

Tawny *A. campestris* 55–60, 77, 78

Long-billed *A. similis* 66, 68, 72

Plain-backed *A. leucophrys* 62, 63, 65, 66, 72

Meadow *A. pratensis* 50–57, 59, 60, 77

Tree *A. trivialis* 50–55, 57–62, 65, 66, 68, 76–78, 82, 86

Olive-backed (Indian Tree) *A. hodgsoni* 79, 81–84, 87, 88, 90–92

Rose-breasted (Rosy) *A. roseatus* 84

Red-throated *A. cervinus* 53–55, 57, 60, 62, 66, 67, 77, 90–92, 97

Petchora *A. gustavi* 97

Water (Rock) *A. spinoletta* 1–7, 9–14, 16, 17, 50, 52, 53, 55–60, 77–79, 87–90

Upland *A. sylvanus* 83, 92

Berthelot's *A. berthelotii* 61

Striped *A. lineiventris* 66, 68

Bushveld (Little Tawny) *A. caffer* 72

Sokoke *A. sokokensis* 67

Malindi *A. melindae* 67

Sprague's *A. spragueii* 9, 10, 12

Short-billed *A. furcatus* 42

Yellowish (Chaco) *A. lutescens (chacoensis)* 29, 35, 43, 46, 47

Correndera *A. correndera* 39–42

Hellmayr's *A. hellmayri* 45

Paramo *A. bogotensis* 32

WAXWINGS:*BOMBYCILLIDAE*

Waxwing

Bohemian *Bombycilla garrulus* 1, 2, 5, 10, 51, 53, 54, 57, 87, 88

Japanese *B. japonica* 87

Cedar *B. cedrorum* 3, 6–9, 12–14, 17, 21, 25

SILKY-FLYCATCHERS: *PTILOGONATIDAE*

Silky-flycatcher

Gray *Ptilogonys cinereus* 16, 17, 21

Long-tailed *P. caudatus* 22, 23

"Phainopepla" *Phainopepla nitens* 12, 13

"Phainoptila" (Black-and-yellow)*Phainoptila melanoxantha* 22, 23

PALMCHAT:*DULIDAE*

Palmchat *Dulus dominicus* 25

WOODSWALLOW:*ARTAMIDAE*

Woodswallow

Ashy *Artamus fuscus* 85, 86, 93

White-breasted *A. leucorhynchus* 96–101, 104, 107–110

Black-breasted (Greater) *A. maximus* 99

Masked *A. personatus* 101, 102, 104

White-browed *A. superciliosus* 101, 104, 106

Black-faced *A. cinereus* 101–104

Dusky *A. cyanopterus* 103–108

Little *A. minor* 101, 102

VANGAS:*VANGIDAE*

Vanga

Red-tailed *Calicalicus madagascariensis* 74

Rufous *Schetba rufa* 74

Hook-billed *Vanga curvirostris* 74

Southwestern (LaFresnaye's) *Xenopirostris xenopirostris* 74

Van Dam's *X. damii* 74

Pollen's *X. polleni* 74

Sickle-billed *Falculea palliata* 74

White-headed *Leptopterus viridis* 74

Bare-eyed *L. chabert* 74

Blue *L. madagascarinus* 74

Bernier's *Oriolia bernieri* 74

Helmeted ("Helmetbird") *Euryceros prevostii* 74

Kinkimavo *Tylas eduardi* 74

Nuthatch (Coral-billed "Nuthatch") *Hypositta corallirostris* 74

SHRIKES:*LANIIDAE*
Brubru Shrike *Nilaus afer (nigritemporalis)* 62, 66, 68–70, 72, 74
Puffback-Shrike
  Pringle's *Dryoscopus pringlii* 66
  Gambian *D. gambensis* 62–65
  Black-backed *D. cubla* 66–70, 72, 73
  Pink-footed *D. angolensis* 65
Tchagra (Bush-Shrike)
  Black-capped *Tchagra minuta* 63, 65, 68
  Black-crowned (headed) *T. senegala* 60, 62–69, 72
  Cape *T. tchagra* 72
  Brown-crowned (headed) *T. australis* 65–68, 70, 72, 73
  Three-streaked *T. jamesi* 66
  Rosy-patched Shrike *T. cruenta* 66
Gonolek
  Red-bellied (Barbary "Shrike") *Laniarius barbarus* 62
  Black-headed *L. erythrogaster* 63, 64
Boubou (Bush-Shrike)
  Luhder's *L. luhderi* 65
  Cape (Southern) *L. ferrugineus* 63, 69–72
  Tropical *L. aethiopicus* 64–68
  Slate-colored *L. funebris* 66
Bush-Shrike
  Gray-green *Telophorus bocagei* 65
  Sulfur-breasted *T. sulfureopectus* 62, 63, 66, 68–70, 72, 73
  Olive *T. olivaceus* 68
  Black-fronted *T. nigrifrons* 66, 68
  "Bokmakierie" *T. zeylonus* 71
  Gorgeous (Four-colored) *T. quadricolor* 67, 72
  Doherty's *T. dohertyi* 64, 66
  Fiery-breasted (Rosy-patched) *Malaconotus cruentus* 63, 65
  Gray-headed *M. blanchoti (hypopyrrhus)* 62, 68–70, 72, 73
Shrike
  Yellow-billed *Corvinella corvina* 62, 63
  Magpie *C. melanoleuca* 68, 73
  Tiger (Thick-billed) *Lanius tigrinus* 87, 88, 90, 95, 98
  Souza's *L. souzae* 68
  Bull-headed *L. bucephalus* 87–90
  Brown *L. cristatus* 66, 67, 82, 83, 86–93, 95–98

Red-backed *L. collurio* 51–53, 55–58, 66–70, 72, 73, 77, 78
Red-tailed *L. isabellinus (collurio)* 66, 67, 77, 78
Bay-backed *L. vittatus* 79, 82
Schach (Rufous-backed, Black-headed) *L. schach* 79, 82, 83, 86, 90–92, 97–99
Tibetan (Gray-backed) *L. tephronotus* 83, 84, 93
Strong-billed *L. validirostris* 97
MacKinnon's *L. mackinnoni* 64, 65
Lesser Gray *L. minor* 55–58, 64, 66, 69, 72, 77, 78
Loggerhead *L. ludovicianus* 6–9, 11–14, 16, 17
Great Gray (Northern) *L. excubitor* 2, 3, 5, 7, 10, 51–61, 77–79, 82, 87
Fiscal-Shrike (Shrike)
  Gray-backed *L. excubitoroides* 65, 66
  Long-tailed *L. cabanisi* 66, 67
  Taita *L. dorsalis* 66
  Common *L. collaris* 63–66, 68, 71, 72
Shrike
  Woodchat *L. senator* 55, 57–60, 62, 63, 78
  Masked *L. nubicus* 55, 77, 78
HELMET-SHRIKES:*PRIONOPIDAE*
White-crowned Shrike
  Northern *Eurocephalus rueppelli* 66
  Southern *E. anguitimens* 73
Helmet-Shrike
  White (Crested, Straight-crested) *Prionops plumata (cristata)* 62, 66, 68–70, 72
  Gray-crested *P. poliolopha* 66
  Red-billed *P. caniceps* 63, 69, 70
  Retz's (Red-billed) *P. retzii* 66–68
  Chestnut-fronted *P. scopifrons* 67
NEW ZEALAND WATTLEBIRDS: *CALLAEIDAE*
Kokako (Wattled Crow) *Callaeas cinerea* III
Saddleback *Creadion carunculatus* III
STARLINGS:*STURNIDAE*
Starling (Fruit-Starling)
  Polynesian *Aplonis tabuensis* 110
  Striated *A. striatus* 109
  Singing *A. cantoroides* 100
  Lesser (Glossy) *A. minor* 97, 98
  Philippine (Glossy) *A. panayensis* 95, 97, 98

Metallic (Shining) *A. metallicus* 99, 100, 108
Stuhlmann's *Poeoptera stuhlmanni* 65
Starling (Chestnut-wing, Sharptail)
  Waller's *Onychognathus walleri* 65, 66
  Pale-winged *O. nabouroup* 71
  Red-winged *O. morio* 66, 68, 70–72
  Chestnut-winged *O. fulgidus* 63, 64
  Slender-billed *O. tenuirostris* 66
  Bristle-crowned *O. salvadorii* 66
Glossy-Starling (Starling)
  Purple-headed *Lamprotornis purpureiceps* 63
  Black-bellied (-breasted) *L. corruscus* 67, 72
  Purple *L. purpureus* 62, 63
  Cape (Red-shouldered) *L. nitens* 72, 73
  Bronze (Short)-tailed *L. chalcurus* 62
  Blue-eared *L. chalybaeus* 62, 66–69, 73
  Lesser Blue-eared (Little) *L. chloropterus* 62, 66, 68, 69
  Splendid *L. splendidus* 62, 63, 65
  Burchell's *L. australis* 73
  Southern Long-tailed *L. mevesii* 69
  Ruppell's Long-tailed *L. purpuropterus* 64, 66
  Northern Long-tailed *L. caudatus* 62
Starling
  Abbott's *Cinnyricinclus femoralis* 66
  Sharpe's *C. sharpii* 65, 66
  Amethyst (Violet-backed) *C. leucogaster* 62–70, 72, 73
  Magpie *Speculipastor bicolor* 66
  African Pied *Spreo bicolor* 71
  Superb *S. superbus* 66, 67
  Chestnut-bellied *S. pulcher* 62
  Hildebrandt's *S. hildebrandti* 66
  Golden-breasted (Regal) *Cosmopsarus regius* 66
  Madagascar *Saroglossa (Martlaubius) aurata* 74
  Wattled *Creatophora cinerea* 64, 66, 68–73
Starling (Myna)
  Chestnut-tailed (Gray-headed "Myna") *Sturnus malabaricus* 83, 85
  Brahminy "Myna" *S. pagodarum* 82
  Silky (Red-billed) *S. sericeus* 92
  Purple (Violet)-backed (Red-cheeked) *S. philippensis* 87, 88, 95, 97
  Rose-colored (Rosy "Pastor") *S. roseus* 55, 56, 79, 82

European (Common, Northern, The) *S. vulgaris* 3, 5–14, 25, 49–58, 60, 61, 71, 77, 78, 82, 83, 104–107, 111
Spotless *S. unicolor* 59, 60
White-cheeked *S. cineraceus* 87–90, 92
Pied "Myna" (Asian Pied) *S. contra* 82, 84, 98
Black-collared *S. nigricollis* 92
Black-winged *S. melanopterus* 98
White-shouldered *S. sinensis* 91
Myna
  Rothschild's (Bali) *Leucopsar rothschildi* 98
  Indian (Common) *Acridotheres tristis* 15, 74–76, 79, 82, 83, 85, 92, 95, 105, 106, 108–111
  Bank *A. ginginianus* 82, 85
  Jungle *A. fuscus* 83, 85, 95, 110
  White-vented *A. grandis (javanicus)* 95
  Crested *A. cristatellus* 3, 90–92, 97
  Golden-crested *Ampeliceps coronatus* 93
  Golden-breasted *Mino anais* 99, 100
  Yellow-faced *M. dumontii* 100
  Mount Apo *Basilornis miranda* 97
  Ceylon *Gracula ptilogenys* 86
  Hill (Talking, "Grackle") *G. religiosa* 85, 86, 93–95, 97, 98
Oxpecker
  Yellow-billed *Buphagus africanus* 62, 64, 66, 68, 69
  Red-billed *B. erythrorhynchus* 65, 66, 69, 70, 72, 73
Coleto *Sarcops calvus* 97
HONEYEATERS:*MELIPHAGIDAE*
Honeyeater
  Long-billed *Melilestes megarhynchus* 99, 100
  Dwarf (Gray-bellied "Longbill") *Oedistoma iliolophum* 100
  Pygmy ("Longbill") *O. pygmaeum* 100
  Pale-eyed (Green-backed) *Glycichaera fallax (claudi)* 100
  Brown (Tawny-breasted) *Lichmera indistincta* 98–101, 103, 106–108
  Silver-eared *L. incana* 109
  Freckled (White-eared) *L. alboauricularis* 100
Myzomela (Honeyeater, Curvebill)
  White-throated (-chinned) *Myzomela albigula* 100
  Dusky *M. obscura* 100, 101, 108

Red *M. cruentata* 100

Black *M. nigrita* 99, 100

Mangrove Red-headed *M. erythrocephala* 101

Mountain Red-headed *M. adolphinae* 99

Scarlet *M. sanguinolenta* 106–109

Orange-breasted (Red-throated, Fiji) *M. jugularis* 110

Black-and-red *M. rosenbergii* 99

Honeyeater

Black *Certhionyx niger* 102, 104

Pied *C. variegatus* 102

Note: Most of the following *Meliphaga* are now included in *Lichenostomus*.

White-marked *Meliphaga albonotata* 100

Puff-backed *M. aruensis* 99

Diamond *M. auga* 99

Mimic *M. analoga* 100

Graceful (Slender-billed) *M. gracilis* 100, 108

Lewin's *M. lewinii* 106–108

Lesser Lewin's (Yellow-spotted) *M. notata* 108

Yellow *M. flava* 108

White-lined *M. albilineata* 101

Singing *M. virescens* 100, 102–104

Varied (Mangrove) *M. versicolor (fasciogularis)* 107, 108

Fuscous *M. fusca* 104, 106

Yellow-tinted *M. flavescens* 100, 101

Yellow-fronted *M. Plumula* 102

Yellow-faced *M. chrysops* 105–108

Purple-gaped *M. cratitia* 103, 104

Gray-headed *M. keartlandi* 102

White-plumed *M. penicillata* 102–106

Yellow-plumed *M. ornata* 103, 104

White-eared *M. leucotis* 103–106

Yellow-tufted *M. melanops* 106, 107

Helmeted *M. cassidix* 105

White-gaped *M. unicolor* 101, 108

Many-spotted *M. polygramma* 99

Macleay's *M. macleayana* 108

Bridled *M. frenata* 108

Black-throated (-fronted) *M. subfrenata* 99

Obscure (Lemon-cheeked) *M. obscura* 99

Wattled *Foulehaio carunculata* 110

Kadavu *F. provocator* 110

Brown-headed *Melithreptus brevirostris* 103, 104, 106

White-naped *M. lunatus* 103–108

White-throated *M. albogularis* 100, 101, 107, 108

Black-chinned *M. gularis* 101, 104, 106, 107

Blue-faced *Entomyzon cyanotis* 101, 104, 107, 108

Stitchbird *Notiomystis cincta* 111

Friarbird

Meyer's (Dwarf) *Philemon meyeri* 99

Little *P. citreogularis* 101, 104, 107

Sandstone (Melville Island) *P. buceroides (gordoni)* 101

Helmeted ("Leatherhead") *P. novaeguineae (yorki)* 100, 101, 108

Noisy (Bald) *P. corniculatus* 106–108

Silver-crowned *P. argenticeps* 101

New Caledonian *P. diemenensis* 109

Red-backed (Green-eyed) Honeyeater *Ptiloprora guisei* 99

Melidectes

Sooty ("Honeyeater") *Melidectes fuscus* 99

Cinnamon-bellied (Mid-mountain) *M. ochromelas* 99

Belford's *M. belfordi* 99

Cinnamon-breasted *M. torquatus* 99

Smoky (Common) Melipotes *Melipotes fumigatus* 99

Honeyeater

Giant Forest *Gymnomyza viridis* 110

Crow *G. aubryana* 109

Kauai Oo *Moho braccatus* 15

Honeyeater

Crescent *Phylidonyris pyrrhoptera* 105, 106

New Holland (Yellow-winged) *P. novaehollandiae* 103–106

White-cheeked *P. nigra* 103, 106, 107

White-fronted *P. albifrons* 102, 104

Tawny-crowned *P. melanops* 103, 104, 106

Barred *P. undulata* 109

Bar-breasted *Ramsayornis fasciatus* 101

Modest (Brown-backed) *R. modestus* 100

Striped *Plectorhyncha lanceolata* 104

Rufous-banded (-breasted) *Conopophila albogularis* 100

Painted *C. picta* 106

Regent *Xanthomyza phrygia* 106
Banded *Cissomela pectoralis* 101
Spinebill
    Eastern *Acanthorhynchus tenuirostris*
        104–108
    Western *A. superciliosus* 103
Miner
    Bell *Manorina melanophrys* 105–7
    Noisy *M. melanocephala* 104–108
    White-rumped (Yellow-throated) *M.
        flavigula* 101–104
    Black-eared (Dusky) *M. melanotis (ob-
        scura, flavigula)* 104
Honeyeater
    Bell ("Bellbird") *Anthornis melanura*
        111
    Spiny-cheeked *Anthochaera rufogularis*
        102–104
Wattlebird
    Little *A. chrysoptera* 103–106
    Red *A. carunculata* 103–107
Tui *Prosthemadera novaeseelandiae* 111
Cape Sugarbird *Promerops cafer* 71
    SUNBIRDS:*NECTARINIIDAE*
Sunbird
    Mouse-brown *Anthrepetes gabonicus*
        63
    Scarlet-tufted *A. fraseri (axillaris)* 63
    Blue-throated (Plain-backed) *A. rei-
        chenowi* 67
    Plain *A. simplex* 94
    Brown (Plain)-throated *A. malacensis*
        95–98
    Red-throated *A. rhodolaema* 94
    Ruby-cheeked *A. singalensis* 93, 94
    Western Violet-backed *A. longuemarei*
        62, 68
    Kenya Violet-backed *A. orientalis* 66
    Amani *A. pallidigaster* 67
    Gray-chinned (Green) *A. rectirostris*
        65
    Collared *A. collaris* 62–70, 72, 73
    Pygmy (Long-tailed) *A. platurus
        (metallicus)* 62
    Purple-naped *Hypogramma hypogram-
        micum (macularia)* 93–96
    Orange-breasted (Little Green) *Necta-
        rinia seimundi* 71
    Olive *N. olivacea* 63, 65, 67, 68, 72
    Mouse-colored *N. veroxii* 67, 72
    Green-headed *N. verticalis* 63, 65, 66
    Carmelite *N. fuliginosa* 63

Amethyst (Black) *N. amethystina* 66–
    70, 72
Scarlet-chested *N. senegalensis* 62, 64–
    70, 72
Hunter's *N. hunteri* 66
Buff-throated *N. adelberti* 63
Purple-rumped *N. zeylonica* 86
Purple-throated (Van Hasselt's) *N.
    sperata* 95, 97, 98
Black *N. sericea* 100
Copper-throated (Macklot's) *N. calco-
    stetha* 95, 97, 98
Seychelles *N. dussumieri* 76
Loten's *N. lotenia* 86
Olive-backed (Yellow-bellied) *N.
    jugularis* 93, 95–100, 108
Purple *N. asiatica* 78, 82, 83, 85, 86, 93
Souimanga *N. souimanga* 74
Variable *N. venusta* 62, 63, 65, 66, 68
White-bellied *N. talatala* 68–70, 72, 73
Lesser (Southern) Double-collared *N.
    chalybea (gertrudis)* 64, 68, 71
Eastern Double-collared *N. mediocris
    (moreaui)* 66, 68
Northern (Preuss's) Double-collared
    N. preussi 65, 66
Neergaard's *N. neergaardi* 72
Olive-bellied *N. chloropygia* 63, 65
Regal *N. regia* 64
Orange-tufted *N. bouvieri* 65
Copper *N. cuprea* 62–65, 68, 70
Tacazze *N. tacazze* 66
Shelley's *N. shelleyi* 68
Mariqua (Marico) *N. mariquensis* 66
Purple-banded *N. bifasciata (tsavoen-
    sis)* 64, 67, 68, 70, 72
Violet-breasted (Pemba) *N. chal-
    comelas (pembae)* 66, 67
Splendid *N. coccinigastra* 62, 63
Red-chested *N. erythrocerca* 64
Beautiful *N. pulchella* 62, 66
Little (Smaller) Black-bellied *N. nec-
    tarinioides* 66
Malachite *N. famosa* 66, 71
Scarlet-tufted Malachite *N. johnstoni*
    66
Madagascar Green *N. notata* 74
Superb *N. superba* 63
Bronzy *N. kilimensis* 64–66
Golden-winged *N. reichenowi* 66
Hachisuka's *Aethopyga primigenius* 97
Flaming *A. flagrans* 97

Mountain *A. pulcherrima* 97
Lovely *A. shelleyi* 97
Nepal *A. nipalensis* 83
Black-throated *A. saturata* 83, 93
Fork-tailed *A. christinae* 92
Crimson (Yellow-backed) *A. siparaja* 93, 95, 96
Scarlet *A. mystacalis* 83, 85, 94, 96
Fire-tailed *A. ignicauda* 83, 84
Spiderhunter
Little *Arachnothera longirostra* 93, 95–97
Long-billed *A. robusta* 94
Spectacled *A. flavigaster* 94
Naked-faced *A. clarae (philippensis)* 97
Gray-breasted *A. affinis* 94–96, 98
Streaked *A. magna* 85
Whitehead's *A. juliae* 96
Bowbill (Longbill) Note: usually placed in *MELIPHAGIDAE*
Yellow-bellied (Canary) *Toxorhamphus novaeguineae* 99, 100
Gray-winged (Slaty-chinned) *T. poliopterus* 100
Green Hylia *Hylia prasina* 62, 63, 65
FLOWERPECKERS:*DICAEIDAE*
Berrypecker
Black *Melanocharis nigra* 99, 100
Yellow-bellied (Mid-mountain) *M. longicauda* 99
Fan-tailed *M. versteri* 99
Spotted *Rhamphocharis crassirostris* 99
Flowerpecker
Olive-backed *Prionochilus olivaceus* 97
Yellow-breasted *P. maculatus* 95
Palawan *P. plateni* 97
Thick-billed *Dicaeum agile (modestum)* 82, 83, 86, 93
Striped *D. aeruginosum* 97
Gray-breasted *D. proprium* 97
Yellow-vented *D. chrysorrheum* 93, 95, 98
Yellow-bellied *D. melanoxanthum* 83
Legge's *D. vincens* 86
Olive-capped *D. nigrilore* 97
Yellow-crowned *D. anthonyi* 97
Bicolored *D. bicolor* 97
Philippine *D. australe* 97
Orange-bellied *D. trigonostigma* 95–98
White-bellied *D. hypoleucum* 97
Pale-billed (Tickell's) *D. erythrorhynchos* 83, 86

Plain *D. concolor (minullum)* 83, 96
Pygmy *D. pygmaeum* 97
"Mistletoebird" *D. hirundinaceum* 101–104, 107, 108
Black-sided *D. celebicum* 96
Fire-breasted (-throated, Buff-bellied) *D. ignipectus* 83, 92, 97, 98
Scarlet-backed *D. cruentatum* 98
Scarlet-headed *D. trochileum* 98
Red-capped *D. geelvinkianum* 99, 100
Berrypecker
Tit (Painted) *Oreocharis arfaki* 99
Crested *Paramythia montium* 99
Pardalote
Spotted *Pardalotus punctatus* 103, 104, 107, 108
Yellow-rumped (-tailed) *P. xanthopygus* 104
Red-browed *P. rubricatus* 102
Striated (Black-headed) *P. substriatus (melanocephalus)* 101–103, 107
WHITE-EYES:*ZOSTEROPIDAE*
White-eye
Japanese (Chinese) *Zosterops japonica (simplex)* 15, 87, 88, 91–2
Oriental *Z. palpebrosa* 79, 81–83, 85, 86, 93, 95
Ceylon (Hill) *Z. ceylonensis* 86
Black-capped *Z. atricapilla* 96
Everett's *Z. everetti* 96, 97
Philippine Yellow *Z. nigrorum* 97
Mountain *Z. montana* 97
Black-fronted *Z. atrifrons (minor)* 99, 100
New Guinea Mountain *Z. novaeguineae* 99
Mangrove (Yellow) *Z. lutea* 98, 101
Philippine *Z. meyeni* 97
Layard's *Z. explorator* 110
Green-backed *Z. xanthochroa* 109
"Silvereye" (Gray-backed) *Z. lateralis* 103–111
Broad-ringed *Z. abyssinica* 66
Cape (Pale) *Z. pallida* 71, 72
Yellow *Z. senegalensis* 62–66, 68, 70, 72
Green *Z. virens* 68
Mascarene Gray *Z. borbonica* 75
Madagascar *Z. maderaspatana* 74
Seychelles *Z. modesta* 76
Olive *Z. olivacea (chloronothus)* 76

Goodfellow's *Lophozosterops goodfellowi* 97
Javan Gray-throated *L. javanica* 98
Pygmy *Oculocincta squamifrons* 96
Mountain Blackeye *Chlorocharis emiliae* 96, 97
Cinnamon White-eye *Hypocryptadius cinnamomeus* 97
VIREOS:*VIREONIDAE*
Pepper-shrike (Note: usually separate family *CYCLARHIDAE*)
Rufous-browed *Cyclarhis gujanensis* 18, 19, 21–23, 27–30, 43–48
Black-billed *C. nigrirostris* 31
Shrike-Vireo (Note: usually separate family *VIREOLANIIDAE*)
Chestnut-sided *Vireolanius melitophrys* 17, 21
Green *Smaragdolanius pulchellus (eximius)* 18, 20, 22
Slaty-capped *S. leucotis* 31
Vireo
Hutton's *Vireo huttoni* 3, 12–14, 16, 17, 21
Black-capped *V. atricapillus* 16
White-eyed *V. griseus (perquisitor)* 7–9, 18–20, 25
Jamaican White-eyed *V. modestus* 25
Mangrove *V. pallens* 16, 18–20
Cozumel *V. bairdi* 18
Cuban *V. gundlachii* 25
Thick-billed *V. crassirostris* 25
Bell's *V. bellii* 9, 12, 13, 16
Gray *V. vicinior* 12, 13
Golden *V. hypochryseus* 16, 17
Flat-billed *V. nanus* 25
Puerto Rican *V. latimeri* 25
Blue Mountain *V. osburni* 25
Yellow-winged *V. carmioli* 22, 23
Solitary *V. solitarius* 3, 6–9, 12, 13, 16, 17, 21
Yellow-throated *V. flavifrons* 6–9, 19, 20, 22–25, 30
Philadelphia *V. philadelphicus* 6, 7, 9, 22, 23
Red-eyed (Yellow-green, Chivi) *V. olivaceus (flavoviridus, chivi)* 3, 6–9, 16, 18–20, 22, 24, 27, 28, 30, 31, 33, 36, 37, 43–48
Yucatan *V. magister* 18, 25
Black-whiskered *V. altiloquus* 8, 25–27

Warbling *V. gilvus* 3, 6, 7, 9, 10, 12–14, 16, 17
Brown-capped *V. leucophrys (gilvus)* 22, 23, 28, 30, 31, 36
Greenlet
Rufous-crowned *Hylophilus poicilotis* 44, 45
Lemon-chested *H. thoracicus* 37, 45–48
Gray-chested *H. semicinereus* 47
Ashy-headed *H. pectoralis* 48
Rufous-naped *H. semibrunneus* 31
Golden-fronted *H. aurantiifrons* 24, 27–30
Dusky-capped *H. hypoxanthus* 37
Scrub *H. flavipes* 24, 27–30
Tawny-crowned *H. ochraceiceps* 20, 31, 33, 37
Lesser (Gray-headed) *H. minor* 19, 20, 22, 24
AMERICAN WARBLERS (PARULAS):*PARULIDAE*
Warbler (Parula)
Black-and-white *Mniotilta varia* 6–9, 16–28, 30, 31
Bachman's *Vermivora bachmanii* 25
Golden-winged *V. chrysoptera* 6, 7, 9, 19, 22–25, 28, 30, 31
Blue-winged *V. pinus* 6, 7, 9, 19, 20, 25
Tennessee *V. peregrina* 5–9, 17–25, 28, 30, 31
Orange-crowned *V. celata* 2, 3, 5–9, 12–14, 16, 17, 21
Nashville *V. ruficapilla* 6, 7, 9, 11–13, 16, 17, 21
Virginia's *V. virginiae (ruficapilla)* 12, 17
Colima *V. crissalis (ruficapilla)* 17
Lucy's *V. luciae* 12, 16
Flame-throated *V. gutturalis* 22, 23
Crescent-chested *V. superciliosa* 16, 17, 21
Parula (Warbler)
Northern *Parula americana* 6–9, 18, 19, 25, 26
Tropical (Olive-backed) *P. pitiayumi* 9, 16, 22, 23, 27–31, 36, 42–46, 48
Warbler (Parula)
Yellow (Mangrove, Golden) *Dendroica petechia (erithachorides)* 2–14, 16–22, 24–31, 33, 34, 48
Chestnut-sided *D. pensylvanica* 6–9, 19, 20, 22–24, 28

Cerulean *D. cerulea* 6, 7, 9, 28, 30, 33
Black-throated Blue *D. caerulescens* 6–8, 25
Plumbeous *D. plumbea* 26
Arrow-headed *D. pharetra* 25
Elfin Woods *D. angelae* 25
Pine *D. pinus* 6–9, 25
Grace's *D. graciae* 12, 16, 17, 21
Adelaide's *D. adelaidae* 25, 26
Olive-capped *D. pityophila* 25
Yellow-throated *D. dominica* 7–9, 18–20, 25
Black-throated Gray *D. nigrescens* 8, 12–14, 16, 17
Townsend's *D. townsendi* 3, 10, 12–14, 16, 17, 21, 22
Hermit *D. occidentalis* 12–14, 16, 17, 21
Black-throated Green *D. virens* 6–9, 17–23, 25, 30
Prairie *D. discolor* 7, 8, 25, 26
Vitelline *D. vitellina* 25
Cape May *D. tigrina* 6–8, 21, 25–27
Blackburnian *D. fusca* 6–9, 22–24, 28, 30–32
Magnolia *D. magnolia* 6–9, 18–21, 24, 25
Yellow-rumped (Myrtle, Audubon's) *D. coronata (auduboni)* 2, 3, 5–14, 16–21, 23, 25
Palm *D. palmarum* 6–8, 18, 25
Kirtland's *D. kirtlandii* 25
Blackpoll *D. striata* 2, 4–9, 25–28, 33
Bay-breasted *D. castanea* 6, 7, 9, 18, 24, 25, 28, 30, 31
Whistling *Catharopeza bishopi* 26
American "Redstart" *Setophaga ruticilla* 6–9, 12, 16, 18–20, 23–28, 30–32, 36
Ovenbird (Oven Warbler) *Seiurus aurocapillus* 6–9, 16, 19, 20, 22, 23, 25, 26, 30
Waterthrush
    Northern *S. noveboracensis* 2, 5–9, 16, 18–20, 23–31, 33, 48
    Louisiana *S. motacilla* 7–9, 17, 19, 20, 25, 30
Warbler (Parula)
    Swainson's *Limnothylpis swainsonii* 9, 19, 25
    Worm-eating *Helmitheros vermivorus* 7, 8, 16, 19, 20, 25
    Prothonotary *Protonotaria citrea* 6–9, 18–20, 24–27, 30

Yellowthroat
    Northern *Geothlypis trichas* 3, 6–10, 12–14, 16, 18–21, 25
    Bahama *G. rostrata* 25
    Olive-crowned *G. semiflava* 31
    Chiriqui *G. chiriquensis* 23
    Masked *G. aequinoctialis* 27, 28, 30, 36, 37, 42–44, 46–48
    Gray-crowned (Ground-chat) *G. poliocephala* 16–19, 22
Warbler (Parula)
    Kentucky *Oporornis formosus* 7–9, 16, 18–20, 22–24
    Connecticut *O. agilis* 7, 8, 37
    Mourning *O. philadelphia* 6, 7, 23, 24, 30, 31
    MacGillivray's *O. tolmiei* 3, 10–14, 16, 17, 21
    Ground *Microligea palustris* 25
    White-rumped (Ground-) *Xenoligea (M.) montana* 25
    Yellow-headed *Teretistris fernandinae* 25
    Oriente *T. fornsi* 25
    Semper's *Leucopeza semperi* 26
    Hooded *Wilsonia citrina* 7–9, 16, 18–20, 25, 30
    Wilson's *W. pusilla* 1–3, 5–14, 16, 17, 19–24
    Canada *W. canadensis* 6, 7, 9, 22–24, 31, 33, 37
    Red-faced *Cardellina rubrifrons* 12, 16, 17, 21
    Red *Ergaticus ruber* 16, 17
    Pink-headed *E. versicolor* 21
Whitestart (Redstart)
    Painted *Myioborus pictus* 12, 16, 17, 21
    Slate-throated *M. miniatus* 16, 17, 21–23
    Collared *M. torquatus* 22, 23
    Spectacled *M. melanocephalus* 32, 36
    Yellow-crowned *M. flavivertex* 30
Warbler (Shade-Parula)
    Fan-tailed (Lacrimose) *Euthlypis lachrymosa* 16
    Pale-legged *Basileuterus signatus* 36
    Flavescent *B. flaveolus* 28
    Citrine *B. luteoviridis* 32, 36
    Black-crested *B. nigrocristatus* 32
    Santa Marta *B. basilicus* 30
    White-lored *B. conspicillatus* 30
    Russet-crowned *B. coronatus* 31, 36

Golden-crowned *B. culicivorus* 20, 22, 23, 27, 28, 30, 31, 43–46

Rufous (Chestnut)-capped *B. rufifrons (delatrii)* 16, 17, 21–24, 30

Golden-browed *B. belli* 16, 17, 21

Black-cheeked *B. melanogenys* 22, 23

Three-striped *B. tristriatus* 22, 28, 31

White-browed *B. leucoblepharus* 43–45

Wrenthrush *Zeledonia coronata* 22, 23 (usually separate family: *ZELEDONIIDAE*)

Warbler (Parula)

Buff-rumped *Phaeothlypis fulvicauda* 24, 31

River *P. rivularus* 33, 37, 44, 47

Olive *Peucedramus taeniatus* 12, 16, 17, 21

Chat (Skulker)

Red-breasted *Granatellus venustus* 16

Gray-throated *G. sallaei* 18

Rose-breasted *G. pelzelni* 48

Yellow-breasted *Icteria virens* 6–9, 12, 13, 16, 19, 20

Bananaquit *Coereba flaveola* 19, 20, 22, 24–31, 33, 44–48

Conebill (Note: *Coereba* and *Conirostrum* usually placed in *COEREBIDAE*)

Chestnut-vented *Conirostrum speciosum* 29, 43, 44, 46

White-eared *C. leucogenys* 28

Bicolored *C. bicolor* 27, 30, 46, 48

Cinereous *C. cinereum* 32, 35, 36

Tamarugo *C. tamarugensis* 38

White-browed *C. ferrugineiventre* 36

Blue-backed *C. sitticolor* 36

Capped *C. albifrons* 36

TROUPIALS:*ICTERIDAE*

Oropendola

Casqued *Psarocolius oseryi* 37

Crested *P. decumanus* 24, 27, 28, 30, 33, 37, 44, 48

Green *P. viridis* 47, 48

Dusky-green *P. atrovirens* 36

Russet-backed *P. angustifrons* 28, 31, 33, 37

Chestnut-headed *P. wagleri* 24, 31

Montezuma *Gymnostinops montezuma* 19, 20, 24

Para *G. bifasciatus* 47

Olive *G. yuracares* 33, 37

Cacique

Yellow-rumped *Cacicus cela* 24, 27–30, 33, 37, 47, 48

Red-rumped *C. haemorrhous* 37, 44, 45, 47, 48

Scarlet-rumped *C. uropygialis* 24, 31

Golden-winged *C. chrysopterus* 43, 45

Solitary Black *C. solitarius* 33, 37

Yellow-winged (Mexican) *C. melanicterus* 16

Yellow-billed *Amblycercus holosericeus* 19, 21–24, 31

Oriole (Troupial)

Epaulet *Icterus cayanensis* 37, 42–44, 48

Moriche *I. chrysocephalus* 27, 33, 48

Yellow-backed *I. chrysater* 19, 21, 24, 28, 30, 31

Yellow *I. nigrogularis* 27–30, 48

Jamaican *I. leucopteryx* 25

Orange *I. auratus* 18

Yellow-tailed *I. mesomelas* 19, 24, 30, 31

Orange-crowned *I. auricapillas* 28–30

Spotted (Spot-breasted) *I. pectoralis* 8

Altamira (Lichtenstein's) *I. gularis* 9, 18, 21

Streak-backed (Scarlet-headed, Pacific) *I. pustulatus (sclateri)* 16

Hooded *I. cucullatus* 9, 12–14, 16–19

"Troupial" (Orange-backed) *I. icterus* 25, 29, 30, 33, 37

Northern (Baltimore, Bullock's, Black-backed) *I. galbula (bullockii)* 6–9, 12–14, 16, 17, 19–24, 30

Orchard *I. spurius* 6–9, 16–21, 24, 30

Black-cowled *I. dominicensis (prosthemelas)* 19, 20, 25

Black-vented *I. wagleri* 16, 17, 21

St. Lucia *I. laudabilis* 26

Martinique *I. bonana* 26

Montserrat *I. oberi* 26

Green-backed (Black-headed) *I. graduacauda* 9

Scott's *I. parisorum* 12, 16, 17

Blackbird (Marshbird)

Jamaican *Nesopsar nigerrimus* 25

Oriole- *Gymnomystax mexicanus* 29, 33

Yellow-headed *Xanthocephalus xanthocephalus* 8–13, 16

Pale-eyed *Agelaius xanthophthalmus* 33, 37

Yellow-winged (-shouldered) *A. thilius* 36, 38, 39, 42

Red-winged *A. phoeniceus* 3, 5–14, 16, 17, 19, 25

Tricolored (California) *A. tricolor* 13, 14

Yellow-hooded *A. icterocephalus* 27, 29–31, 35, 48

Tawny-shouldered *A. humeralis* 25

Yellow-shouldered *A. xanthomus* 25

Unicolored *A. cyanopus* 43, 46

Chestnut-capped *A. ruficapillus* 43, 46

White-browed *Leistes (Sturnella) superciliaris* 42–44, 46

Red-breasted *L. (S.) militaris* 24, 27, 29–31, 33, 48

Meadowlark

Peruvian Red-breasted *Sturnella bellicosa* 32, 35

Lesser Red-breasted *S. defilippi* 42

Long-tailed *S. loyca* 39–41

Eastern *S. magna* 6–9, 12, 19, 22, 25, 29, 48

Western *S. neglecta* 3, 5, 9–15

Marshbird

Yellow-rumped *Pseudoleistes guirahuro* 43

Brown-and-yellow *P. virescens* 42

Blackbird

Scarlet-headed *Amblyramphus holosericeus* 42

Austral *Curaeus curaeus* 39, 41

Chopi *Gnorimopsar chopi* 43, 45

Cuban *Dives atroviolaceus* 25

Melodious *D. dives* 18–21

Scrub *D. warszewiczi* 35

Grackle

Great-tailed *Cassidix mexicanus* 12, 16–21, 24, 30, 31

Boat-tailed *C. major* 8, 9

Eastern (Common) *Quiscalus quiscula* 6–9

Greater Antillean *Q. niger* 25

Carib *Q. lugubris* 26–29, 48

Blackbird

Rusty *Euphagus carolinus* 1, 2, 5–7, 9

Brewer's *E. cyanocephalus* 3, 9–14

Cowbird

Bay-winged *Molothrus badius* 42, 43

Screaming *M. rufoaxillaris* 42, 44

Shiny *M. bonariensis* 25–31, 33, 35, 39, 41–46, 48

Bronzed *M. aeneus* 9, 12, 16–19, 21

Brown-headed *M. ater* 3, 6–14, 16, 17

Giant *Scaphidura oryzivora* 19, 20, 24, 27, 28, 30, 31, 33, 37, 44, 47, 48

Bobolink *Dolichonyx oryzivorus* 6–8, 10, 25, 29, 33–35, 43

Dickcissel *Spiza americana* 7, 9, 16, 25, 27, 29

TANAGERS: *THRAUPIDAE*

Swallow-Tanager *Tersina viridis* 27, 28, 30, 33, 37, 44, 46, 48

Tanager

Brown *Orchesticus abeillei* 45

Black-faced *Schistochlamys melanopis* 47, 48

Red-billed Pied *Lamprospiza melanoleuca* 37, 47, 48

Magpie *Cissopis leveriana* 33, 37, 44, 45, 48

Grass-green *Chlorornis riefferii* 31, 32

Puerto Rican *Nesospingus speculiferus* 25

Bush-Tanager (Cloud-Tanager)

Common (Variable) *Chlorospingus ophthalmicus* 21–23, 28

Dusky-bellied *C. semifuscus* 31

Sooty-capped *C. pileatus* 22, 23

Yellow-throated *C. flavigularis* 31

Ash-throated *C. canigularis* 31

Hemispingus

Black-capped *Hemispingus atropileus* 32, 36

Superciliared *H. superciliaris* 32, 36

Oleaginous *H. frontalis* 28

Three-striped *H. trifasciatus* 36

Tanager

Chestnut-headed *Pyrrhocoma ruficeps* 44

Fulvous-headed *Thlypopsis fulviceps* 28

Orange-headed *T. sordida* 45, 46

Rust-and-yellow *T. ruficeps* 36

Guira *Hemithraupis guira* 28, 33, 44, 47, 48

Rufous-headed *H. ruficapilla* 45, 46

Yellow-backed *H. flavicollis* 33, 37, 46, 48

Scarlet-and-white *Chrysothlypis salmoni* 31

Hooded (Savanna) *Nemosia pileata* 29, 43, 48

Tanager (Palm Tanager)
  Black-crowned *Phaenicophilus palmarum* 25
  Gray-crowned *P. poliocephalus* 25
Chat-Tanager *Calyptophilus frugivorus* 25
Rosy (Rose-breasted) Thrush-Tanager *Rhodinocichla rosea* 16, 24, 28
Tanager
  Dusky-faced *Mitrospingus cassinii* 24, 31
  Carmiol's *Chlorothraupis carmioli* 24
  Lemon-browed *C. olivacea* 31
  Ochre-breasted *C. stolzmanni* 31
  Olive-green *Orthogonys chloricterus* 45
  Gray-headed *Eucometis penicillata* 19, 20, 24, 28, 30, 33, 37
Shrike-Tanager
  Fulvous *Lanio fulvus* 33, 48
  Black-throated *L. aurantius* 18, 20
  White-throated *L. leucothorax* 37
Tanager
  Scarlet-browed *Heterospingus xanthopygius* 31
  Sulfur-rumped *H. rubrifrons* 24
  Flame-crested *Tachyphonus cristatus* 37, 46–48
  Fulvous-crested *T. surinamus* 33, 47, 48
  White-shouldered *T. luctuosus* 24, 27, 31, 33, 37
  Tawny-crested *T. delatrii* 24, 31
  Ruby-crowned *T. coronatus* 43–46
  White-lined (Roadside) *T. rufus* 24, 27, 28, 30, 31, 43, 44, 47, 48
  Red-shouldered *T. phoenicius* 48
  Black-goggled *Trichothraupis melanops* 44–46
Ant-Tanager
  Red-crowned *Habia rubica* 16, 18–20, 27, 33, 37, 44–46
  Red-throated *H. fuscicauda* 18–20, 24
  Crested *H. cristata* 31
Tanager
  Flame-colored (Stripe-backed) *Piranga bidentata* 16, 17, 21, 23
  Hepatic *P. flava* 12, 16, 17, 19, 21–23, 27, 28, 30, 31, 35, 48
  Summer *P. rubra* 7–9, 12, 16–25, 27, 28, 30, 31, 33
  Rose-throated *P. roseogularis* 18

Scarlet *P. olivacea* 6–9, 18, 22, 24, 25, 30, 33, 37
Western *P. ludoviciana* 3, 8, 10, 12–14, 16, 21
White-winged *P. leucoptera* 20, 22, 23, 28, 31
Red-headed *P. erythrocephala* 16, 17
Crimson-collared *Ramphocelus sanguinolentus* 19
Masked Crimson *R. nigrogularis* 33, 37
Crimson-backed *R. dimidiatus* 24, 30, 31
Silver-beaked *R. carbo* 27, 28, 33, 37, 47, 48
Brazilian *R. bresilius* 46
Scarlet-rumped *R. passerinii* 18, 19, 23
Bright (Yellow, Flame)-rumped *R. icteronotus (flammigerus)* 24, 31
Stripe-headed *Spindalis zena* 18, 25
Blue-gray *Thraupis episcopus (virens)* 18, 19, 21–24, 27–31, 33, 36, 37, 47, 48
Sayaca *T. sayaca* 43–46
Glaucous (Greenish) *T. glaucocolpa (sayaca)* 28–30
Golden-chevroned *T. ornata* 45, 46
Yellow-winged *T. abbas* 19–21
Palm *T. palmarum* 24, 27–31, 33, 37, 45–48
Blue-capped *T. cyanocephala* 27, 28, 30–32, 36
Blue-and-yellow *T. bonariensis* 32, 35, 36, 38, 42
Blue-backed *Cyanicterus cyanicterus* 48
Golden-chested *Bangsia (Buthraupis) rothschildi* 31
Moss-backed *B. (B.) edwardsi* 31
Mountain-Tanager
  Hooded *Buthraupis montana* 32
  Scarlet-bellied *Anisognathus igniventris* 32, 36
  Blue-winged *A. flavinuchus* 28, 31, 32
  Black-cheeked *A. melanogenys* 30
Tanager
  Diademed *Stephanophorus diadematus* 42, 45
  Purplish-mantled *Iridosornis porphyrocephala* 31
  Golden-crowned *I. rufivertex* 32
Mountain-Tanager
  Buff-breasted *Dubusia taeniata* 32
  Chestnut-bellied *D. castaneoventris* 36

Fawn-breasted Tanager *Pipraeidea melanonota* 28, 31, 32, 36, 44–46
Euphonia
Jamaican *Euphonia jamaica* 25
Scrub (Pale-vented) *E. affinis* 16, 18–20
Yellow-crowned *E. luteicapilla* 24
Purple-throated *E. chlorotica (trinitatis)* 43, 44, 46, 47
Trinidad *E. trinitatis* 27–30
Finsch's *E. finschi* 48
Violaceous *E. violacea* 27, 44, 46–48
Thick-billed *E. laniirostris* 24, 28–30, 33, 37
Yellow-throated *E. hirundinacea (lauta)* 18–20
Green-throated *E. chalybea* 44
Blue-hooded *E. musica (elegantissima)* 17, 21–23, 25–28, 31, 32
Fulvous-vented *E. fulvicrissa* 24, 31
Olive-backed *E. gouldi* 19, 20
Golden-bellied *E. chrysopasta* 33, 37, 48
White-vented *E. minuta* 24, 31, 37, 48
Tawny-capped *E. anneae* 22
Orange-bellied *E. xanthogaster* 28, 31, 33, 37
Rufous-bellied *E. rufiventris* 33, 37
Chestnut-bellied *E. pectoralis* 44–46
Golden-sided *E. cayennensis* 47, 48
Chlorophonia
Yellow-collared *Chlorophonia flavirostris* 31
Chestnut-breasted *C. pyrrhophrys* 31
Blue-naped *C. cyanea* 30, 31, 44, 45
Golden-browed *C. callophrys (cyanea)* 22, 23
Tanager
Glistening-green *Chlorochrysa phoenicotis* 31
Multicolored *C. nitidissima* 31
Plain-colored *Tangara inornata* 24
Gray-and-gold *T. palmeri* 31
Turquoise *T. mexicana* 27, 33, 37, 47, 48
Paradise *T. chilensis* 33, 37, 48
Green-headed *T. seledon* 44–46
Red-necked *T. cyanocephala* 46
Brassy-breasted *T. desmaresti* 45
Gilt-edged *T. cyanoventris* 45
Blue-whiskered *T. johannae* 31
Green-and-gold *T. schrankii* 33, 37
Emerald *T. florida* 31

Golden *T. arthus* 28, 31
Silver-throated *T. icterocephala* 22, 23, 31
Saffron-crowned *T. xanthocephala* 31, 36
Flame-faced *T. parzudakii* 31
Yellow-bellied *T. xanthogastra* 33, 37
Spotted *T. punctata* 47, 48
Speckled *T. guttata (chrysophrys)* 27, 28
Rufous-throated *T. rufigula* 31
Bay-headed *T. gyrola* 23, 24, 27, 28, 30, 31, 47, 48
Rufous-winged *T. lavinia* 31
Burnished-buff (Rufous-crowned) *T. cayana* 28, 29, 45, 48
Scrub *T. vitriolina (cayana)* 31, 32
Lesser Antillean (Hooded) *T. cucullata* 26
Chestnut-backed *T. preciosa* 44
Rufous-cheeked *T. rufigenis* 28
Metallic-green *T. labradorides* 31
Blue-necked *T. cyanicollis* 31
Golden-hooded (Masked) *T. larvata* 19, 20, 23, 24, 31
Masked *T. nigrocincta* 33, 37
Spangle-cheeked *T. dowii* 22
Beryl-spangled *T. nigroviridis* 28, 31, 36
Blue-and-black *T. vassorii* 31, 32, 36
Black-capped *T. heinei* 28, 30, 31
Silvery *T. viridicollis* 36
Black-headed *T. cyanoptera* 28, 30
Opal-rumped *T. velia* 33, 37, 47, 48
Opal-crowned *T. callophrys* 33, 37
Dacnis (Note: This and the 5 following genera usually placed in *COEREBIDAE*)
Black-faced *Dacnis lineata* 33, 48
Yellow-bellied *D. flaviventer* 33, 37
Scarlet-thighed *D. venusta* 22–24, 31
Blue *D. cayana* 24, 27, 28, 30, 31, 33, 37, 44–48
Honeycreeper
Green *Chlorophanes spiza* 19, 20, 24, 27, 28, 31, 33, 37, 47, 48
Shining *Cyanerpes lucidus* 24
Purple *C. caeruleus* 27, 28, 30, 31, 33, 37, 47, 48
Red-legged (Blue) *C. cyaneus* 19–21, 24, 25, 27, 28, 30, 31, 47, 48
Tit-like Dacnis *Xenodacnis parina* 36, 38
Giant Conebill *Oreomanes fraseri* 36, 38

Flower-piercer
Garden (Cinnamon (-bellied), Slaty, Rusty) *Diglossa baritula (plumbea, sittoides)* 17, 21–23, 30–32, 36
Glossy *D. lafresnayii* 32, 36
Carbonated *D. carbonaria (humeralis)* 30, 32, 36
White-sided *D. albilatera* 30–32
Indigo *D. indigotica* 31
Bluish *D. caerulescens* 28
Masked *D. cyanea* 32, 36
Orangequit *Euneornis campestris* 25
Plush-capped Tanager (Finch) *Catamblyrhynchus diadema* 30, 32
(Note: this species is usually placed in its own family: *CATAMBLYRHYNCHIDAE*)
      WEAVERS:*PLOCEIDAE*
Buffalo-Weaver
White-billed *Bubalornis albirostris* 62, 66
Red-billed (Black) *B. niger* 66, 69, 73
White-headed *Dinemellia dinemelli* 66
Sparrow-Weaver
White-browed *Plocepasser mahali* 66, 68–70
Donaldson-Smith's *P. donaldsoni* 66
Rufous-tailed Weaver *Histurgops ruficauda* 66
Social-Weaver
Gray-headed *Pseudonigrita arnaudi* 66
Black-capped *P. cabanisi* 66
Sparrow (Weaver)
House (English) *Passer domesticus* 3, 5–17, 21, 25, 31, 35, 38–44, 49–60, 71–73, 75, 77, 78, 81–83, 85, 86, 104–107, 109, 111
Spanish (Black-sided) *P. hispaniolensis* 55, 60, 61
Jungle *P. pyrrhonotus* 79
Cinnamon (Russet) *P. rutilans* 80, 81, 87, 88, 91
Great (Kenya Rufous) *P. iagoensis (motitensis)* 66
Gray-headed (Swahili, Parrot-billed) *P. griseus (suahelicus, diffusus, swainsonii, gongonensis)* 62–66, 68–70, 72, 73
Desert *P. simplex* 60
Tree *P. montanus* 51–53, 55–59, 83, 87–92, 95, 97, 98, 105
Golden *P. luteus (euchlorus)* 62

Chestnut *P. eminibey* 66
Petronia (Rock-Sparrow)
Pale *Petronia (Carpospiza) brachydactyla* 77
Chestnut-shouldered *P. xanthocollis* 79, 82
Rock *P. petronia* 55, 59–61
Yellow-throated *P. superciliaris* 62, 68–70, 72
Yellow-spotted *P. pyrigita* 66
Bush *P. dentata* 62
Eurasian Snow-Finch *Montifringilla nivalis* 57
Weaver
Speckle-fronted *Sporopipes frontalis* 62, 66
Thick-billed (Grosbeak) *Amblyospiza albifrons* 63, 65–68, 72
Reichenow's (Baglafecht) *Ploceus baglafecht (stuhlmanni, reichenowi, emini)* 65, 66
Bertram's (Bertrand's) *P. bertrandi* 68
Slender-billed *P. pelzelni* 64
Little *P. luteolus* 62, 64
Spectacled *P. ocularis* 64–67, 69, 72, 73
Black-necked *P. nigricollis* 62–65
Black-billed *P. melanogaster* 65
Cape *P. capensis* 71
Eastern (African) Golden *P. subaureus* 66–68, 72
Holub's (Great) Golden *P. xanthops* 63
Orange *P. aurantius* 63
Taveta Golden *P. castaneiceps* 66, 67
Southern Brown-throated (Golden) *P. xanthopterus* 72
Northern Brown-throated *P. castanops* 64
Northern Masked *P. taeniopterus (reichardi)* 66
Lesser (Cabinis's) Masked *P. intermedius* 64, 66, 68, 69, 72, 73
Vitelline (Greater) Masked *P. velatus (vitellinus)* 63, 66, 68, 70, 72, 73
Speke's *P. spekei* 66
Village (Black-headed, Spot-backed) *P. cucullatus (nigriceps)* 25, 62–69, 72, 73, 75
Vieillot's Black (Chestnut-and-black) *P. nigerrimus* 63–66
Clarke's *P. golandi* 67
Gambian Black-headed (Yellow-backed) *P. melanocephalus* 62, 65

Golden-backed (Jackson's) *P. jacksoni* 65
Yellow-mantled *P. tricolor* 63, 65
Nelicourvi *P. nelicourvi* 74
Compact *P. superciliosus* 63, 65
Bengal *P. benghalensis* 82
Streaked (Striated) *P. manyar* 79, 82, 86, 98
Baya *P. philippensis* 82, 83, 85, 86, 95
Dark-backed (Forest) *P. bicolor* 65, 67, 68, 72
Usambara (Olive-headed Golden) *P. olivaceiceps (nicolli)* 68
Brown-capped *P. insignus* 65, 66
Malimbe
Red-vented *Malimbus scutatus* 63
Ibadan *M. ibadanensis* 63
Blue-billed (Gray's) *M. nitens* 62
Red-headed *M. rubricollis* 62, 63, 65
Crested *M. malimbicus* 63
Red-headed "Weaver" *M. rubriceps (melanotis)* 66, 68, 73
Quelea
Cardinal *Quelea cardinalis* 65, 66, 69
Red-headed *Q. erythrops* 63, 68
Red-billed (Dioch) *Q. quelea* 62, 64–70, 72, 73
Fody
Red *Foudia madagascariensis* 74–76
Sakalava ("Fody") *P. sakalava* 74
Mauritius *F. rubra* 75
Seychelles *F. sechellarum* 76
Forest *F. omissa* 74
Bishop
Yellow-crowned (Golden) *Euplectes afer (afra)* 62, 63, 66
Black *E. gierowii* 65
Zanzibar Red (Black-vented) *E. nigroventris* 67
Fire-crowned (Black-winged) *E. hordeaceus* 62, 64, 68, 69
Red (Orange) *E. orix* 64, 66, 68–72
Yellow (Cape) *E. capensis* 64, 66, 68, 69, 71
Widowbird (Whydah)
Fan-tailed (Red-shouldered) *E. axillaris* 64, 66, 68, 72
Yellow-mantled *E. macrourus* 62, 63, 65
Marsh *E. hartlaubi* 65
White-winged *E. albonotatus* 65–70, 72, 73

Red-collared *E. ardens* 64–68, 72
Long-tailed *E. progne* 66
Jackson's *E. jacksoni* 66
Parasitic (Cuckoo) Weaver *Anomalospiza imberbis* 68
Indigobird *Vidua chalybeata (wilsoni, funerea, purpurascens)* 62, 66, 68, 69, 72
Whydah
Steel-blue *V. hypocherina* 66
Straw-tailed *V. fischeri* 66
Shaft-tailed *V. regia* 70
Pin-tailed *V. macroura* 62–69, 71, 72
Paradise *V. paradisaea* 66, 68–70, 72, 73
Northern Broad-tailed *V. orientalis* 62
Southern Broad-tailed *V. obtusa* 68, 69
WAXBILLS:*ESTRILDIDAE*
Negro-Finch
White-breasted *Nigrita fusconota* 65
Chestnut-breasted *N. bicolor* 62, 63
Gray-headed *N. canicapilla* 63–66
Pytilia
Orange-winged *Pytilia afra* 67–69
Green-winged (Melba "Finch") *P. melba* 62, 64, 66, 68, 69, 72
Crimsonwing
Red-faced *Cryptospiza reichenovii* 68
Dusky *C. jacksoni* 64
Seedcracker
Black-bellied *Pirenestes ostrinus* 63
Lesser *P. minor* 68
Twinspot
Green (-backed) *Mandingoa nitidula* 65–68, 72
Pink-throated *Hypargos margaritatus* 72
Peter's *H. niveoguttatus* 67, 68
Red-headed Bluebill *Spermophaga ruficapilla* 65
Fire-Finch (Waxbill)
Bar-breasted *Lagonosticta rufopicta* 63
Brown *L. nitidula* 70
Red-billed *L. senegala* 64, 66, 68, 69, 72, 73
Blue-billed (African) *L. rubricata* 65, 66, 68, 72
Jameson's *L. rhodopareia (jamesoni)* 68–70
Black-faced (Vinaceous) *L. larvata (vinacea)* 62

Cordon-bleu
Southern (Angola, The, Blue "Waxbill") *Uraeginthus angolensis* 68–70, 72, 73
Red-cheeked *U. bengalus* 62, 65–67
Blue-capped *U. cyanocephala* 66
Purple Grenadier *U. ianthinogaster* 66
Waxbill
Western Lavender *Estrilda caerulescens* 62
Southern Lavender *E. perreini* 68
Yellow-bellied (Swee) *E. melanotis* 65, 66, 68
Fawn-breasted *E. paludicola* 65
Orange-cheeked *E. melpoda* 15, 25, 62, 63
Crimson-rumped *E. rhodopygia* 66
Common *E. astrild* 46, 62, 64–73, 75, 76, 109
Black-crowned *E. nonnula* 64, 65
Black-headed *E. atricapilla* 64, 66
Black-cheeked *E. erythronotos (charmosyna)* 66
Strawberry Finch (Red Avadavat) *Amandava amandava* 15, 75, 79, 85, 98, 110
Orange-breasted (Zebra) Waxbill *A. subflava* 68, 69
Common Quail-Finch *Ortygospiza atricollis* 62, 63, 66
Firetail (Finch)
Red-crowned *Aegintha temporalis* 103, 105–109
Painted "Finch" *Emblema picta* 102
Beautiful *E. bella* 105
Red-eared *E. oculata* 103
Diamond *E. guttata* 104, 106
Finch
Crimson *Neochmia phaeton* 101, 108
Star *N. ruficauda* 108
Zebra *Poephila guttata* 102–104, 106, 107
Double-barred *P. bichenovii* 101, 106–108
Masked *P. personata* 101
Long-tailed *P. acuticauda* 101
Parrot-Finch
Tawny-breasted *Erythrura hyperythra* 96
Pin-tailed *E. prasina* 93
Blue-faced *E. trichroa* 99
Red-throated *E. psittacea* 109
Red-headed *E. cyanovirens* 110

Pink-billed *E. kleinschmidti* 110
Gouldian Finch *Chloebia gouldiae* 101
Munia (Mannikin)
White-throated (Warbling "Silverbill") *Lonchura malabarica* 62, 66, 82
Gray-headed ("Silverbill") *L. griseicapilla (caniceps)* 66
Madagascar *L. nana* 74
Bronze *L. cucullata* 25, 62–70, 72
Red-backed (Black-and-white) *L. bicolor (poensis)* 63, 65–68, 72
Pied (Magpie) *L. fringilloides* 68
White-rumped (White-backed, Sharp-tailed) *L. striata* 86, 90, 91, 95
Javan *L. leucogastroides* 95, 98
Dusky *L. fuscans* 96
Spotted (Nutmeg, Spice "Finch") *L. punctulata* 15, 83, 85, 86, 91–93, 95, 97, 98, 106–108
Black-throated *L. kelaarti* 86
White-bellied (-breasted) *L. leucogaster* 94, 97
Streak-headed *L. tristissima* 99, 100
Black-headed (Chestnut) *L. malacca (atricapilla)* 15, 86, 95–98
White-headed *L. maja* 95
Grand (Great-billed) *L. grandis* 99, 100
Gray-headed *L. caniceps* 100
New Britain *L. spectabilis* 99
Chestnut-breasted *L. castaneothorax* 99–101, 106–109
Pictorella ("Finch") *L. pectoralis* 99
Java Sparrow *Padda oryzivora* 15, 25, 86, 95, 97, 98, 110
Cut-throat Finch *Amadina fasciata* 62, 68, 70
FINCHES:*FRINGILLIDAE* (includes *EMBERIZIDAE*)
Chaffinch *Fringilla coelebs* 50–53, 55–61, 111
Blue Chaffinch *F. teydea* 61
Brambling *F. montifringilla* 1, 50–58, 87–90
Bunting
Crested *Melophus lathami* 82, 83, 92
Corn *Emberiza calandra* 50–53, 55–61
"Yellowhammer" *E. citrinella* 51–58, 111
Pine *E. leucocephala* 88, 89
Rock *E. cia* 55, 57–60, 79, 81, 89
Meadow *E. cioides* 87–89
White-capped *E. stewarti* 80, 82

Ortolan *E. hortulana* 53, 55–60, 77, 78
Cretzchmar's *E. caesia* 55, 77
Cirl *E. cirlus* 51, 55, 58–60, 111
House (Striped) *E. striolata* 60
Cinnamon-breasted (Rock) *E. tahapisi* 66, 68–70, 72
Cape *E. capensis* 68, 71
Marsh (Japanese Reed) *E. yessoensis* 87, 88, 90
Gray-hooded (-headed) *E. fucata* 85, 87, 88, 92
Little *E. pusilla* 54, 83, 84, 89, 90, 92
Yellow-browed *E. chrysophrys* 89
Rustic *E. rustica* 54, 87–90
Yellow-throated *E. elegans* 88–90
Yellow-breasted *E. aureola* 54, 83, 85, 87, 89, 90
Somali *E. poliopleura* 66
Golden-breasted *E. flaviventris* 64, 66, 68–70, 72, 73
Cabanis's *E. cabanisi (orientalis)* 68
Chestnut *E. rutila* 89, 90
Black-headed *E. melanocephala* 55, 77, 82
Red-headed *E. bruniceps* 79, 82
Japanese Yellow *E. sulphurata* 87, 88
Black-faced *E. spodocephala* 87–92
Japanese Gray *E. variabilis* 87, 88
Pallas's (Reed) *E. pallasi* 89, 90
Reed *E. schoeniclus* 50–60, 87, 88
Longspur (Bunting)
McCown's *Calcarius mccownii* 12
Lapland *C. lapponicus* 1, 2, 4, 5, 7, 10, 52–54, 87, 89
Smith's *C. pictus* 5
Chestnut-collared *C. ornatus* 12
Bunting
Snow (McKay's) *Plectrophenax nivalis (hyperboreus)* 1, 2, 4–7, 10, 49, 50, 52–54
Lark *Calamospiza melanocorys* 10, 12
Sparrow (Bunting)
Fox *Zonotrichia (Passerella) iliaca* 1–3, 5–7, 13, 14
Song *Z. (Melospiza) melodia* 3, 5–14
Lincoln's *Z. (M.) lincolnii* 2, 5–10, 12–14, 16, 17, 21
Swamp *Z. (M.) georgiana* 5–9
Rufous-collared (Garden) *Z. capensis* 21–23, 25, 30–32, 35, 36, 38, 39, 41–46
Harris's *Z. querula* 4, 5

White-crowned *Z. leucophrys* 1–7, 9–14, 16
White-throated *Z. albicollis* 5–9, 12
Golden-crowned *Z. atricapilla* 1–3, 13, 14
Junco
Northern (Dark-eyed, Slate-colored, Oregon) *Junco hyemalis (oreganus)* 2, 3, 5–7, 9–14
Gray-headed (Dark-eyed) *J. caniceps (hyemelis)* 12
Mexican (Yellow-eyed, Chiapas) *J. phaeonotus* 12, 16, 17, 21
Volcano *J. vulcani* 22
Sparrow (Bunting)
Savannah (Ipswich) *Ammodramus (Passerculus) sandwichensis (princeps)* 1–14, 16, 25
Seaside *A. (Ammospiza) maritimus* 7–9
Sharp-tailed *A. (A.) caudacutus* 7–9
Le Conte's *A. (A.) leconteii* 9
Baird's *A. bairdii* 12
Sierra Madre *A. baileyi* 17
Henslow's *A. henslowii* 6, 7
Grasshopper *A. savannarum* 6–9, 12, 14, 16, 19, 25
Grassland *A. humeralis* 29, 43, 48
Yellow-browed *A. aurifrons* 33, 37, 47
Winter (Tree) *Spizella arborea* 2, 4–7, 10
Chipping *S. passerina* 3, 6–10, 12–14, 16, 17
Field *S. pusilla* 6–9
Black-chinned *S. atrogularis* 12–14
Clay-colored *S. pallida* 6–9, 16, 17
Brewer's *S. breweri* 10, 12, 17
Vesper *Pooecetes gramineus* 6–12, 16, 17
Lark *Chondestes grammacus* 7–9, 11–13, 16, 17
Black-throated *Amphispiza bilineata* 9, 12
Sage *A. belli* 11
Stripe-headed (Pacific) *Aimophila ruficauda* 16, 17
Bachman's *A. aestivalis* 8, 9
Botteri's *A. botterii (petenica)* 9, 12, 16
Cassin's *A. cassinii* 9, 12
Five-striped *A. quinquestriata* 12
Rufous-winged *A. carpalis* 12
Rufous-crowned *A. ruficeps* 12–14, 17
Rusty *A. rufescens* 17, 21
Zapata *Torreornis inexpectata* 25

Striped *Oriturus superciliosus* 17
Sierra-Finch
  Black-hooded *Phrygilus atriceps* 38
  Gray-hooded *P. gayi* 36, 38, 39, 41
  Patagonian *P. patagonicus* 39, 41
  Mourning *P. fruticeti* 36, 38, 39, 41
  Plumbeous *P. unicolor* 32, 36, 38, 39, 41
  White-throated *P. erythronotus* 38
  Ash-breasted *P. plebejus* 32, 36, 38
  Band-tailed *P. alaudinus* 32, 36, 38, 39
Finch
  Black-throated *Melanodera melano-dera* 40
  Yellow-bridled *M. xanthogramma* 39
  Slaty *Haplospiza rustica* 22, 30
  Peg-billed *Acanthidops bairdii* 22
  Long-tailed Reed *Donacospiza albi-frons* 42, 45
Diuca-Finch
  White-winged *Diuca speculifera* 36, 38
  Common *D. diuca* 39, 41
Slender-billed Finch *Xenospingus con-color* 35
Warbling-Finch
  Bay-chested *Poospiza thoracica* 45
  Black-and-rufous *P. nigrorufa* 42
  Red-rumped *P. lateralis* 45
  Chestnut-breasted ("Mountain-Finch") *P. (Poospizopsis) caesar* 36
  Collared *P. hispaniolensis* 35
  Black-capped *P. melanoleuca* 43
Yellow-Finch
  Puna *Sicalis lutea* 38
  Bright-rumped *S. uropygialis* 38
  Greater *S. auriventris* 39
  Greenish *S. olivascens* 36, 38
  Saffron ("Finch") *S. flaveola* 24, 25, 27, 29–31, 42–44, 46
  Grassland *S. luteola* 26, 32, 35, 39, 41, 42, 44, 46
  Raimondi's *S. raimondii* 36
  Patagonian *S. lebruni* 41
Wedge-tailed Grass-Finch *Emberizoides herbicola* 43, 46, 48
Great Pampa-Finch *Embernagra platen-sis* 42, 43, 45
Blue-black Grassquit *Volantinia jacarina* 16, 18–20, 24, 26–31, 33, 35, 37, 43–46, 48
Seedeater
  Buffy-fronted *Sporophila frontalis* 45
  Temminck's *S. falcirostris* 44, 45

Slate-colored *S. schistacea* 27, 31
Gray *S. intermedia* 27–31
Plumbeous *S. plumbea* 44
Variable (Wing-barred) *S. americana (aurita)* 19, 24, 27, 31, 33, 47, 48
White-collared *S. torqueola* 9, 16–21
Rusty-collared *S. collaris* 43
Lined *S. lineola* 27, 33, 37, 47, 48
Black-and-white *S. luctuosa* 30, 33, 36
Yellow-bellied *S. nigricollis* 24, 26–31, 33, 37, 46, 47
Double-collared *S. caerulescens* 37, 44–46
White-bellied *S. leucoptera* 43
Parrot-billed *S. peruviana* 35
Drab *S. simplex* 35
Ruddy-breasted *S. minuta* 27–31, 47, 48
Tawny-bellied (Marsh) *S. palustris* 43
Chestnut-bellied *S. castaneiventris* 33, 37, 48
Chestnut-throated *S. telasco* 35
Seed-Finch
  Large-billed *Oryzoborus crassirostris* 27, 29, 47
  Great-billed *O. maximiliani* 33
  Lesser (Thick-billed) *O. angolensis (funereus)* 19, 24, 27, 30, 31, 33, 37, 43, 44, 47, 48
Seedeater
  Blue *Amaurospiza concolor (relicta)* 23
  Blackish-blue *A. moesta* 44
Cuban Bullfinch *Melopyrrha nigra* 25
Seedeater (Andean-Finch)
  Band-tailed *Catamenia analis* 32, 35, 36, 38
  Plain-colored *C. inornata* 32
  Paramo *C. homochroa* 32, 36
Grassquit
  Cuban (Melodious) *Tiaris canora* 25
  Dull-colored *T. (Sporophila) obscura* 37, 44–46
  Yellow-faced *T. olivacea* 18, 21–25, 31
  Black-faced *T. bicolor* 25, 27, 30
  Sooty *T. fuliginosa* 27
  Yellow-shouldered *Loxipasser anoxan-thus* 25
Bullfinch (Black-Finch)
  Puerto Rican *Loxigilla portoricensis* 25
  Greater Antillean *L. violacea* 25
  Lesser Antillean *L. noctis* 26

St. Lucia Black-Finch *Melanospiza richardsoni* 26

Ground-Finch
Large *Geospiza magnirostris* 34
Medium *G. fortis* 34
Small *G. fuliginosa* 34
Sharp-beaked *G. difficilis* 34
Cactus "Finch" *G. scandens* 34
Large Cactus "Finch" *G. conirostris* 34

Tree-Finch
Vegetarian ("Finch") *Camarhynchus crassirostris* 34
Large *C. psittacula* 34
Floreana (Medium) *C. pauper* 34
Small *C. parvulus* 34
Woodpecker "Finch" *C. pallidus* 34
Mangrove "Finch" *C. heliobates* 34

Warbler Finch *Certhidea olivacea* 34

Towhee
Green-tailed *Pipilo (Chlorura) chlorurus* 10, 12, 13, 16
Rufous-sided (Spotted) *P. erythrophthalmus* 3, 6–9, 12–14, 16, 17, 21
Olive-backed *P. macronyx (erythrophthalmus)* 17
Brown *P. fuscus* 12–14, 17
Abert's *P. aberti* 12

Ground-Sparrow (Bush-Sparrow)
Rusty-crowned *Melozone kieneri* 16
Prevost (Chiapas) *M. biarcuatum* 21
White-eared *M. leucotis* 22

Sparrow (Greenback)
Pectoral *Arremon taciturnus* 37, 47, 48
Orange-billed *A. aurantiirostris* 18–20, 24, 30, 31, 33
Golden-winged *A. schlegeli* 30
Olive *Arremonops rufivirgatus* 9, 18
Tocuyo *A. tocuyensis* 30
Black-striped (Green-backed) *A. conirostris (chloronotus)* 19, 20, 23, 24, 29, 30

Brush-Finch
Yellow-throated *Atlapetes gutturalis* 21–23, 31
Santa Marta *A. melanocephalus* 30
Pale-naped *A. pallidinucha* 32
Rufous-naped *A. rufinucha* 32
Tricolored *A. tricolor* 31, 32
Ochre-breasted *A. semirufus* 28
White-winged *A. leucopterus* 32
Slaty *A. schistaceus* 31, 36
Rusty-bellied *A. nationi* 38

Chestnut-capped *A. brunneinucha* 21–23, 31
Stripe-headed *A. torquatus* 28, 30, 32
Green-striped *A. virenticeps* 16, 17
Black-headed *A. atricapillus* 23, 31
Rufous-capped *A. pileatus* 16, 17

Finch
Large-footed *Pezopetes capitalis* 22, 23
Tanager- *Oreothraupis arremonops* 31
Yellow-thighed *Pselliophorus tibialis* 22, 23
Olive *Lysurus castaneiceps* 31
Sooty-faced *L. crassirostris* 22
Black-backed "Bush-Finch" ("Bush-Tanager") *Urothraupis stolzmanni* 32 (formerly in *THRAUPIDAE)*
Pileated (Black-capped) *Coryphospingus pileatus* 29, 30
Red-crested *C. cucullatus* 43, 44, 47

Cardinal
Red-crested *Paroaria coronata* 15, 42, 43
Red-capped (Riverside) *P. gularis* 27, 29, 33, 37
Yellow-billed *P. capitata* 43
Northern (Common, Red) *Cardinalis cardinalis* 7–9, 12, 15, 18, 19
Vermilion (Gray-beaked) *C. phoeniceus* 30
"Pyrrhuloxia" (Desert) *C. sinuatus* 9, 12, 16

Grosbeak
Yellow *Pheucticus chrysopeplus* 16, 22, 30, 32
Black-thighed *P. tibialis* 23
Black-backed *P. aureoventris* 32, 36
Rose-breasted *P. ludovicianus* 6–9, 12, 16, 19, 21–26, 30, 31
Black-headed *P. melanocephalus* 3, 12–14, 16, 17, 21
Yellow-green *Caryothraustes canadensis* 47, 48
Black-faced *C. poliogaster* 19, 20
Slate-colored *Pitylus grossus* 24, 31, 33, 37, 48
Black-throated *P. fuliginosus (grossus)* 45

Saltator
Black-headed *Saltator atriceps* 18–20, 24
Buff-throated *S. maximus* 19, 22–24, 28, 30, 31, 33, 37, 46–48

Black-winged *S. atripennis* 31

Green-winged *S. similis* 44–46

Grayish *S. coerulescens* 16, 18–21, 27–30, 33, 37, 43, 47, 48

Orinocan *S. orenocensis* 29, 30

Thick-billed *S. maxillosus* 45

Golden-billed *S. aurantiirostris (nigriceps)* 36, 38

Streaked *S. albicollis* 23, 24, 26–28, 30, 31, 35

Grosbeak (Bluefinch)

Blue-black *Passerina (Guiraca) cyanoides* 7–9, 12, 13, 16–20, 25

Ultramarine *P. (Cyanocompsa) brissonii* 28, 31, 44

Blue *P. (Guiraca) caerulea* 7–9, 12, 13, 16–20, 25

Bunting (Bluefinch)

Blue *P. parellina* 16, 18

Indigo *P. cyanea* 6–9, 16–21, 23, 25, 30

Lazuli *P. amoena* 11–14, 16

Varied *P. versicolor* 12, 16, 17

Painted *P. ciris* 8, 9, 16, 18, 20, 25

Serin

Red (Gold)-fronted *Serinus pusillus* 55

European (Common) *S. serinus* 52, 55, 57–60

Citril Finch (European Citril) *S. citrinella* 57

African Citril *S. citrinelloides* 64–66, 68

Canary (Seedeater)

Island (Common, The) *S. canaria* 61

Yellow-crowned *S. canicollis (alario)* 64, 66, 71

White-rumped *S. leucopygius* 62

Black-throated (Yellow-rumped) *S. atrogularis* 65–67

Yellow-fronted *S. mozambicus* 62, 64–70, 72, 73, 75

Yellow *S. flaviventris* 71

Brimstone *S. sulphuratus* 65, 66, 68, 71, 72

White-throated *S. albogularis* 71

White-bellied *S. dorsostriatus* 66

Streak-headed *S. gularis (reichardi)* 72

Black-eared *S. mennelli* 68

Streaky *S. striolatus* 64–66

Thick-billed *S. burtoni* 64–66

Protea (White-winged) *S. leucopterus* 71

Cape "Siskin" *S. totta* 71

Oriole-Finch *Linurgus olivaceus* 65, 66

Greenfinch

Eurasian (European) *Carduelis chloris* 51–53, 55–60, 105, 106, 111

Oriental (Gray-capped) *C. sinica* 87–89, 92

Himalayan (Yellow-breasted) *C. spinoides* 80, 81, 83, 84

Eurasian (European) Goldfinch *C. carduelis* 51–53, 55–61, 77, 81, 104–107, 111

Siskin

Eurasian *C. spinus* 50–55, 57–60, 87–91

Tibetan *C. thibetana* 83

Pine *C. (Spinus) pinus* 3, 6, 7, 9, 10, 12–14, 16, 17

Black-capped *C. (S.) atriceps* 21

Andean *C. (S.) spinescens* 30, 31

Thick-billed *C. (S.) crassirostris* 38, 39

Hooded *C. (S.) magellanica* 32, 35, 36, 38, 42, 43

Antillean *C. (S., Loximitris) dominicensis* 25

Black-headed *C. (S.) notata* 16, 17, 21

Yellow-bellied *C. (S.) xanthogaster* 22, 23, 28, 31

Black *C. (S.) atrata* 36, 38

Yellow-rumped *C. (S.) uropygialis* 38, 39

Black-chinned *C. (S.) barbata* 39–41

Goldfinch

American *C. (S.) tristis* 3, 6–14

Lesser *C. (S.) psaltria* 12–14, 16, 17, 21, 23, 25, 30, 31, 36

Lawrence's *C. (S.) lawrencei* 12–14

Redpoll

Common (Lesser) *C. (Acanthis) flammea* 1, 2, 4–7, 10, 49–54

Hoary (Arctic) *C. (A.) hornemanni* 1, 4, 5, 54

Twite *C. (A.) flavirostris* 50, 53

Linnet *C. (A.) cannabina* 51, 52, 55–61

Rosy-Finch (Mountain-Finch)

Hodgson's *Leucosticte nemoricola* 81, 84

Brandt's *L. brandti* 84

Arctic *L. arctoa* 87, 88

Gray-crowned *L. tephrocotis* 1, 2, 10

Black *L. atrata* 10

Finch

Himalayan Spectacled (Red-browed) *Callacanthis burtoni* 80

Crimson-winged *Rhodopechys sanguinea* 60

Trumpeter ("Bullfinch") *R. githaginea* 60, 61, 77

Long-tailed Rosy-Finch *Uragus sibiricus* 87, 88

Rosefinch (Finch)

Nepal (Dark-breasted) *Carpodacus nipalensis* 83, 84

Scarlet (Common, "Grosbeak") *C. erythrinus* 53, 83–85, 89

Purple "Finch" *C. purpureus* 3, 6, 7, 12–14

Cassin's "Finch" *C. cassinii* 10, 12, 13

House "Finch" *C. mexicanus* 3, 7, 12–17

Beautiful *C. pulcherrimus* 84

Pink-browed *C. rhodochrous* 80, 83, 84

Vinaceous *C. vinaceus* 91

Pallas's *C. roseus* 87–89

Spot-winged *C. rhodopeplus* 84

White-browed *C. thura* 84

Streaked (Eastern Great) *C. rubicilloides* 84

Pine Grosbeak *Pinicola enucleator* 2, 5, 10, 53, 54, 87

Scarlet Finch *Haematospiza sipahi* 83

Crossbill

Parrot *Loxia pytopsittacus* 53, 54

Red *L. curvirostra* 3, 7, 10, 12, 17, 21, 53–55, 57, 59, 60, 87–88, 97

White-winged *L. leucoptera* 2, 7, 10, 25, 87

Bullfinch

Brown *Pyrrhula nipalensis* 83, 91

Red-headed *P. erythrocephala* 83

Beavan's *P. erythaca* 91

Eurasian (Common, The) *P. pyrrhula* 51, 53–55, 57, 87

Hawfinch *Coccothraustes coccothraustes* 51, 53, 55–60, 87–90

Grosbeak (Hawfinch)

Yellow-billed *C. migratorius (melanura)* 87, 88, 90, 92

Black-and-yellow *C. icterioides* 80, 81

Spot-winged *C. melanozanthos* 84

White-winged *C. carnipes* 84

Evening *C. (Hesperiphona) vespertinus* 3, 6, 7, 10, 12, 17

Hooded *C. (H.) abeillei* 17, 21

Gold-crowned (-naped) Black Finch *Pyrrhoplectes epauletta* 83

HAWAIIAN HONEYCREEPERS: *DREPANIDIDAE*

Amakihi *Loxops virens* 15

Anianiau (Lesser Amakihi) *L. parva* 15

Hawaiian Creeper *L. maculata* 15

Akepa *L. coccinea* 15

Kauai Akialoa *Hemignathus procerus* 15

Nukupuu *H. lucidus* 15

Akiapolaau *H. wilsoni* 15

Maui Parrotbill *Pseudonestor xanthophrys* 15

Poo-uli (Black-faced Honeycreeper) *Melamprosops phaeosoma* 15

Ou *Psittirostra psittacea* 15

Palila *P. bailleui* 15

Apapane *Himatione sanguinea* 15

Crested Honeycreeper *Palmeria dolei* 15

Iiwi *Vestiaria coccinea* 15

Alphabetical Key to the Taxonomic Index

This is an alphabetical listing of "generic" names as featured in the taxonomic index. The numbers after each entry in this listing refer to the *pages in the index* wherein each species is listed by its given English and scientific names.

For the sake of brevity compound names of birds within a family are not listed. Thus one would look for Bush-Lark and Finch-Lark (being true larks) under Lark in the "L" section. A Meadowlark (not being a true lark) is listed in the "M" section.

Birds with a standard name not including the "generic" name are alphabetized by their first letter and reference is made to the page in the index where it is found. Thus, "Killdeer" is listed under "K," and one is referred to a page where plovers are listed. As it is a true *Charadrius* plover it will be found somewhere in the group of plovers.

Birds with a compound name, such as Fruit-Pigeon, Night-Heron, and Wood-Wren, where the latter name is capitalized and correctly indicates the family or group to which it belongs, are not listed in this key. Look directly under Pigeon, Heron, and Wren in these cases.

In the few cases where the same generic name is in use for birds of unrelated families, geographical symbols are used as follows (after the listing):

AF = Africa	MA = Madagascar	OW = Old World
AS = Asia	NA = North America	SA = South America
AUS = Australia	NG = New Guinea	SP = South Pacific
EU = Europe	NW = New World	
HA = Hawaii	NZ = New Zealand	

ccentor 655	Alethe 645	Antpipit 629
ccipiter 589	Amakihi 675	Antpitta 628
kalat 640, 645	Amazon 608	Antshrike 627
kepa 675	Anhinga 584	Ant-thrush 628
kialoa 675	Anianiau 675	Antvireo 627
kiapolaau 675	Ani 610	Antwren 627
lbatross 582	Antbird 627, 628	Apalis 650

Apapane 675
Apostlebird 638
Aracari 622
Asity 634
Astrapia 639
Attila 631
Auk 603, 604
Auklet 604
Avadavat 670
Avocet 598
Azurecrown 616

Babbler 640–642
Bananaquit 664
Barbet 621
Barbtail 626
Barbthroat 614
Bare-eye 627
Barkrunner 640
Barwing 641
Bateleur 588
Batis 654
Baza 587
Becard 632
Bee-eater 619
Bellbird (NW) 634
Bellbird (AUS) 655
Bellbird (NZ) 660
Bentbill 630
Berrypecker 661
Bird-of-Paradise 639
Bishop 669
Bittern 585
Blackbird (NW) 664, 665
Blackbird (OW) 647
Blackcap 649
Blackeye 662
Blossomcrown 616
Bluebill 669
Bluebird (AS) 643
Bluebird (NA) 646
Bluefinch 673
Bluetail 645
Bluethroat 645
Boatbill 654
Bobolink 665
Bobwhite 595

Bokmakierie 657
Booby 584
Boubou 657
Boulderwren 634
Bowbill 661
Bowerbird 638
Brambling 670
Brant 592
Brilliant 616
Bristlebill 643
Bristlebird 651
Bristlefront 628
Broadbill (AS, AF) 6
Broadbill (SP) 654
Bronzewing 605
Brownbul 643
Brubru 657
Brushturkey 594
Budgerygah 607
Bufflehead 593
Bulbul 642, 643
Bullfinch 672, 675
Bunting 670, 671, 674
Bushchat 645, 646
Bushcurlew 599
Bush-hen 597
Bushlark 634
Bushtit 639
Bushwren 634
Bustard 598
Bustardquail 596
Butcherbird 638
Buttonquail 596
Buzzard 587–590

Cachalote 626
Cacique 664
Caique 609
Calfbird 634
Camaroptera 651
Canary 674
Canastero 626
Canvasback 593
Capercaillie 594
Capuchinbird 634
Caracara 590
Cardinal 673
Carib 615

Casiornis 632
Cassowary 582
Catbird (AUS, NG) 638
Catbird (NA) 644
Chachalaca 594
Chaffinch 670
Chat (EU, AF, AS) 645, 646
Chat (AUS) 652
Chat (NA) 663, 664
Chatterer 641
Cheer-for-will 613
Chickadee 639
Chicken 594, 596
Chiffchaff 649
Chilia 625
Chloropeta 649
Chlorophonia 667
Chloropsis 643
Chough (EU, AF, AS) 638
Chough (AUS) 638
Chowchilla 642
Chuck-will's-widow 613
Chukar 595
Cinclodes 625
Cisticola 650
Citril 674
Cockatiel 606
Cockatoo 606
Cock-of-the-Rock 634
Coleto 658
Comet 617
Condor 587
Conebill 664, 667
Conure 609
Coot 597
Coquette 615
Cordon-bleu 670
Corella 606
Cormorant 584
Coronet 616
Cotinga 633
Coua 611
Coucal 611
Coural 619

Courser 599
Cowbird 665
Crabplover 598
Crake 596, 597
Crane 596
Creeper 640
Creeper (HA) 675
Creeper-Warbler 652
Crescentchest 628
Crimsonwing 669
Crocodilebird 599
Crombec 651
Crossbill 675
Crow 638, 657
Cuckoo 609–611
Cuckoo-falcon 587
Cuckoo-Roller 619
Cuckoo-shrike 636
Curassow 594
Curlew 600
Currawong 638
Curvebill 658
Cutia 641

Dabchick 584
Dacnis 667
Darter 584
Dayal 645
Dickcissel 665
Dikkop 599
Dipper 643
Diucon 631
Diver 583
Diving-Petrel 583
Doradito 629
Dotterel 599, 600
Dove 604–606
Dovekie 604
Dowitcher 601
Drongo 637
Duck 591–594
Dunlin 601
Dunnock 655

Eagle 588–590
Earthcreeper 625, 626
Egret 585
Eider 593

Elaenia 629
Elepaio 654
Emerald 615, 616
Emu 582
Emu-tail 650
Emu-wren 651
Eremomela 651
Eupetes 642
Euphonia 667

Fairy 617
Fairywren 651
Falcon 590, 591
Falconet 591
Fantail 655
Fernbird 651
Fernwren 652
Fieldfare 647
Fieldwren 652
Figbird 637
Finch 668–675
Finfoot 598
Firecrest 650
Firecrown 616
Fire-eye 627
Firetail 670
Firewood-gatherer 626
Flamingo 587
Flatbill (NG) 654
Flatbill (NW) 630
Flicker 623
Florican 598
Flowerpecker 661
Flower-piercer 668
Flufftail 596
Flycatcher (OW) 652–655
Flycatcher (NW) 629–632
Flycatcher-shrike 637
Flyrobin 654
Fody 669
Foliage-gleaner 626
Forktail 646
Francolin 595
Friarbird 659
Frigatebird 584
Frogmouth 612

Fruitcrow 633, 634
Fruiteater 633
Fulmar 582
Fulvetta 641

Gadwall 592
Galah 606
Gallinule 597
Gannet 584
Gardenerbird 638
Garganey 593
Gerygone 651
Glider 635
Gnatcatcher 648
Gnateater 628
Gnatwren 648
Go-away-bird 609
Godwit 600
Goldcrest 650
Goldeneye 593
Goldenthroat 615
Goldfinch 674
Gonolek 657
Goosander 594
Goose 591, 592
Goshawk 589
Grackle (NW) 665
Grackle (OW) 658
Grandala 642
Grassbird 650, 651
Grassquit 672
Grasswren 651
Grebe 583, 584
Greenback 673
Greenbul 642, 643
Greenfinch 674
Greenlet 662
Greenshank 600
Grenadier 670
Greybird 636
Grosbeak 673–675
Ground-Roller 619
Grouse 594
Guaiabero 607
Guan 594
Guillemot 603
Guineafowl 596
Gull 602

Gymnogene 588
Gyrfalcon 591

Hammerkop 586
Harrier 588
Hawfinch 675
Hawk 588–590
Hazelhen 594
Heathwren 652
Helmetbird 656
Helmet-Shrike 657
Hemipode 596
Hemispingus 665
Hen 583, 597
Hermit 614
Heron 585, 586
Hillstar 616
Hoatzin 611
Hobby 591
Honeychat 652
Honeycreeper (NW)
    667
Honeycreeper (HA)
    675
Honeyeater 658–660
Honeyguide 621
Hookbill 626
Hoopoe 619
Hornbill 620
Hornero 625
Huet-huet 628
Hummingbird 614–617
Hylacola 652
Hylia 661
Hyliota 651

Ibis 586
Ibisbill 598
Iiwi 675
Illadopsis 640
Inca 616
Indigobird 669
Iora 643

Jabiru 586
Jacamar 620
Jacana 598

Jackdaw 638
Jacky Winter 653
Jacobin 615
Jaeger 602
Jay 637
Jery 641
Jewel-Babbler 642
Jewelfront 616
Junco 671
Junglefowl 596

Kaka 607
Kakapo 607
Kagu 598
Kea 607
Kestrel 591
Kingbird 632
Kingfisher 618
Kinglet 650
Kiskadee 632
Kite 587
Kittiwake 602
Kiwi 582
Knot 601
Koel 609
Kokako 657
Kookaburra 618
Korhaan 598

Lammergeier 588
Lancebill 614
Lapwing 599
Lark 634, 635
Laughing-thrush 641
Leafbird 643
Leaf-love 643
Leafscraper 626
Leaftosser 626
Leiothrix 641
Lily-trotter 598
Limpkin 596
Linnet 674
Loerie 609
Logrunner 642
Longbill 658, 661
Longclaw 656
Longspur 671

Loon 583
Lorikeet 608
Lory 608
Lovebird 607
Lyrebird 634

Macaw 609
Magpie (AS, EU, NA)
    637, 638
Magpie (AUS) 638
Magpielark 638
Malimbe 669
Malkoha 610
Mallard 592
Malleefowl 594
Manakin 633
Mango 615
Mannikin 670
Manucode 639
Marshbird 664, 665
Martin 635, 636
Meadowlark 665
Megapode 594
Melidectes 659
Melipotes 659
Merganser 594
Merlin 591
Mesites 596
Metaltail 617
Micrastur 590
Miner (SA) 625
Miner (AUS) 660
Minivet 636
Minla 641
Mistletoebird 661
Mockingbird 644
Mockingthrush 645
Moho 651
Monarch 654
Monia 596
Monjita 631
Monklet 620
Moorhen 597
Motmot 619
Mountaineer 617
Mountaingem 616
Mourner 632

Mousebird 617
Mouse-babbler 652
Mudlark 638
Munia 670
Murre 603
Murrelet 603
Myna 658
Myzomela 658

Needletail 614
Negrito 631
Newtonia 653
Nicator 643
Nighthawk 613
Nightingale 645
Nightjar 613
Niltava 653
Noddy 603
Nothura 582
Nukupuu 675
Nunbird 620
Nunlet 620
Nutcracker 638
Nuthatch 640
Nuthatch (MA) 656

Oilbird 612
Oldsquaw 593
Oo 659
Orangequit 668
Oriole (OW) 637
Oriole (NW) 664
Oropendola 664
Osprey 587
Ostrich 582
Ou 675
Ouzel 643, 647
Ovenbird 663
Owl 611, 612
Owlet 611, 612
Owlet-Nightjar 612
Oxpecker 658
Oxylabes 642
Oystercatcher 598

Painted-snipe 598
Palila 675

Palmchat 656
Palmcreeper 626
Parakeet 607–609
Pardalote 661
Parotia 639
Parrot 607–609
Parrotbill (AS) 643
Parrotbill (HA) 675
Parrotlet 608
Partridge 594, 595
Parula 662–664
Pauraque 613
Peacock 596
Peafowl 596
Pelican 585
Peltops 653
Penguin 583
Pepper-shrike 662
Petrel 582
Petronia 668
Pewee 630
Phainopepla 656
Phainoptila 656
Phalarope 601
Pheasant 595, 596
Phoebe 631
Piapiac 638
Piculet 622
Pigeon 604–606
Piha 633
Pintail 593
Pilotbird 652
Pipit 656
Pitohui 655
Pitta 634
Plantain-eater 609
Plantcutter 634
Ploughbill 655
Plover 599, 600
Plovercrest 615
Plumeleteer 616
Plushcrown 626
Pochard 593
Poor-will 613
Poo-uli 675
Potoo 612
Prairie-chicken 594

Pratincole 599
Prinia 650
Prion 582
Ptarmigan 594
Puffback 654
Puffbird 620, 621
Puffin 604
Puffleg 617
Purpletuft 633
Pyrrhuloxia 673
Pytilia 669

Quelea 669
Quetzal 617
Quail 594–596
Quail-thrush 642

Racquet-tail 617
Rail 596, 597
Rail-Babbler 642
Raven 638
Rayadito 625
Razorbill 603
Recurvebill 626
Redhead 593
Redpoll 674
Redshank 600
Redstart (OW) 646
Redstart (NW) 663
Redthroat 652
Redwing 647
Reedhaunter 626
Reedling 643
Regentbird 638
Rhea 582
Riflebird 639
Rifleman 634
Roadrunner 611
Robin (AUS, NG, SP) 653, 654
Robin (OW) 645, 646
Robin (NW) 648
Rockjumper 645
Rockwren 634
Roller 619
Rook 638
Rosefinch 674

Rosella 607
Ruby 616
Rubythroat 645
Ruff 602
Rushbird 626

Sabrewing 615
Saddleback 657
Saltator 673
Sanderling 601
Sandgrouse 604
Sandpiper 600–602
Sapphire 615
Sapphirewing 616
Sapsucker 622
Saw-wing 636
Scaup 593
Scimitarbill 620
Scoter 593
Screamer 594
Scrub-bird 634
Scrubfowl 594
Scrubwren 652
Scythebill 625
Secretarybird 590
Seedcracker 669
Seedeater (NW) 672
Seedeater (AF) 674
Seedsnipe 602
Seriema 598
Serin 674
Shag 584
Shama 646
Sharpbill 634
Sharptail 658
Sheartail 617
Shearwater 583
Sheathbill 602
Shelduck 592
Shieldbill 653
Shoebill 586
Shortwing 645
Shoveler 593
Shrike 657
Shrikebill 654
Shrike-thrush 655
Shrike-tit 655

Shrike-Vireo 662
Sibia 642
Sicklebill 615
Silktail 652
Silky-flycatcher 656
Silverbill 670
Silverbird 652
Silvereye 661
Sirystes 632
Siskin 674
Sittella 640
Skimmer 603
Skua 602
Skulker 664
Skylark 635
Smew 594
Snipe 601
Snowcock 595
Solitaire 646
Songlark 651
Spadebill 630
Sparrow 668, 670–673
Sparrowhawk 589
Spiderhunter 661
Spinebill 660
Spinetail 625, 626
Spoonbill 587
Spurfowl 595
Stage-maker 638
Starfrontlet 616
Starling 657
Starthroat 617
Stilt 598
Stint 601
Stitchbird 659
Stonechat 646
Stonecurlew 599
Stork 586
Storm-Petrel 583
Streamcreeper 626
Streamertail 615
Sugarbird 660
Sunangel 616
Sunbeam 616
Sunbird 660
Sunbittern 598
Sungrebe 598

Surfbird 601
Swallow 635, 636
Swallow-wing 621
Swamphen 597
Swan 591
Swift 613, 614
Swiftlet 613
Sylph 617

Tachuri 629
Tailorbird 650
Takahe 597
Tanager 665–668, 673
Tapaculo 628
Tattler 601
Tchagra 657
Teal 592, 593
Tern 603
Tesia 648
Tetraka 643
Thick-knee 599
Thistletail 625
Thornbill (AUS) 652
Thornbill (SA) 617
Thornbird 626
Thorntail 615
Thrasher 645
Thrush 645–648
Tinamou 582
Tinkerbird 621
Tit 639, 643
Titmouse 639
Tityra 633
Tody 619
Tomtit 653
Topaz 616
Torrentlark 638
Toucan 622
Toucanet 621, 622
Touit 608
Towhee 673
Tragopan 595
Trainbearer 617
Treecreeper 640
Treehunter 626, 627
Treepie 638
Treerunner 626

Treeswift 614
Trembler 645
Triller 636
Trogon 617
Tropicbird 584
Troupial 664
Trumpetbird 639
Trumpeter 596
Tuftedcheek 626
Tui 660
Turaco 609
Turca 628
Turkey 594
Turnstone 601
Twinspot 669
Twite 674
Tyrant 629–631
Tyrannulet 628, 629

Umbrellabird 634

Vanga 656
Veery 647
Velvetbreast 616
Verdin 640
Violetear 615
Vireo 662
Vulture (OW) 588
Vulture (NW) 587

Wagtail 655

Warbler (EU, AF,
    AS) 645, 648–651
Warbler (NW)
    662–664
Warbler (AUS, NZ,
    NG) 651, 652
Waterthrush 663
Watercock 597
Waterhen 597
Wattlebird 657, 660
Wattle-eye 654
Waxbill 669, 670
Waxwing 656
Weaver 668, 669
Wedgebill 642
Weka 597
Weebill 652
Whalebird 582
Whip-poor-will 613
Wheatear 646
Whimbrel 600
Whinchat 646
Whipbird 642
Whistler 655
White-eye 661, 662
Whiteface 652
Whitehead 652
Whitestart 663
Whitethroat 649
Whitetip 616
Whydah 669
Widowbird 669

Wigeon 592
Willet 600
Wiretail 625
Woodcock 601
Woodcreeper 624
Woodhewer 624
Woodhaunter 626
Wood-Hoopoe 619
Woodnymph 615
Woodpecker 622–624
Woodshrike 637
Woodstar 617
Woodswallow 656
Wren (NW, EU, AS)
    644
Wren (AUS, NG) 651
Wrenthrush 664
Wrentit 643
Wrybill 600
Wryneck 622

Xenops 626
Xenopsaris 632

Yellowbill 610
Yellowhead 652
Yellowlegs 600
Yellowshank 600
Yellowthroat 663
Yuhina 642

Zenops 626